Past and Present Publications

*Landlords, Peasants
and Politics in
Medieval England*

Past and Present Publications

General Editor: PAUL SLACK, *Exeter College, Oxford*

Past and Present Publications comprise books similar in character to the articles in the journal *Past and Present*. Whether the volumes in the series are collections of essays – some previously published, others new studies – or monographs, they encompass a wide variety of scholarly and original works primarily concerned with social, economic and cultural changes, and their causes and consequences. They will appeal to both specialists and non-specialists and will endeavour to communicate the results of historical and allied research in readable and lively form.

For a list of titles in Past and Present Publications, see end of book.

Landlords, Peasants and Politics in Medieval England

Edited by

T. H. ASTON

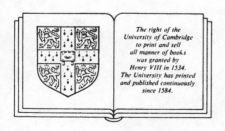

The right of the
University of Cambridge
to print and sell
all manner of books
was granted by
Henry VIII in 1534.
The University has printed
and published continuously
since 1584.

CAMBRIDGE UNIVERSITY PRESS

Cambridge
London   New York   New Rochelle
Melbourne   Sydney

CAMBRIDGE UNIVERSITY PRESS
Cambridge, New York, Melbourne, Madrid, Cape Town, Singapore, São Paulo

Cambridge University Press
The Edinburgh Building, Cambridge CB2 2RU, UK

Published in the United States of America by Cambridge University Press, New York

www.cambridge.org
Information on this title: www.cambridge.org/9780521324038

First published 1987
This digitally printed first paperback version 2006

A catalogue record for this publication is available from the British Library

Library of Congress Cataloguing in Publication data

Landlords, peasants, and politics in Medieval England.
(Past and present publications)
Includes index.
1. Great Britain—Politics and government—1066–1485.
2. Land tenure—England—History.   3. Peasantry—England
—History.   4. Landlords—England—History.   5. England
—Economic conditions—Medieval period, 1066–1485.
6. England—Social conditions—Medieval period, 1066–
1485.   I. Aston, T.H. (Trevor Henry)   II. Series.
DA175.L36   1987   942.03   86-30990

ISBN-13 978-0-521-32403-8 hardback
ISBN-10 0-521-32403-3 hardback

ISBN-13 978-0-521-03127-1 paperback
ISBN-10 0-521-03127-3 paperback

Contents

Preface

This volume of articles from *Past and Present* was planned by T. H. Aston shortly before his death, in October 1985. It was the last of his many services to the series of Past and Present Publications which he had founded, and of which he was General Editor. At the time of his death, twenty-six volumes were in print, published by the Cambridge University Press, and there had been three earlier volumes, published by Routledge and Kegan Paul. The list of titles speaks for itself. It includes original monographs and translations of notable works in other languages, as well as conference proceedings and collections of articles from *Past and Present*, which Trevor Aston also edited. It ranges far and wide, from Byzantine literature to modern medicine, from popular disturbances to crime and the family, and from the history of towns to the history of traditions.

Historical breadth in its coverage of major areas of social, economic and cultural change was one of Trevor Aston's guiding principles for the series. The other was an insistence on the need to communicate and stimulate. Original research should be published in readable and lively form, and it should not be the deadening, definitive last word but a spur to discussion and further investigation. Diversity and debate have been welcomed, and these have been the marks of the volumes with which Trevor Aston was most closely associated, from the first, *Crisis in Europe, 1560-1660* (1965), edited by him and published by Routledge, to the later collections co-edited by him and published by Cambridge University Press: *Social Relations and Ideas: Essays in Honour of R. H. Hilton* (1983), *The English Rising of 1381* (1984) and *The Brenner Debate* (1985). The present volume is a fitting successor. It reflects Trevor Aston's own scholarly interests in the English middle ages. It is also a reminder of his conviction that historical knowledge advances through controversy and of his success as an Editor in fostering that necessary lively debate.

PAUL SLACK

Editorial Note

The articles in this volume (1-3, 5-9, 11 and 12) first appeared in *Past and Present*, nos. 67, 102, 57, 47, 68, 62, 89, 90, 93 and 96, and the Debate on "Politics and Property in Early Medieval England" (4) in no. 65. J. R. Maddicott's "The English Peasantry and the Demands of the Crown, 1294-1341" was published as a *Past and Present* Supplement in 1975. They are now reprinted as originally published, except for some slight rephrasing and updating here and there, the correction of factual errors, and some amendment of the footnotes.

Particular thanks go to R. H. Hilton for writing the introduction. We are also grateful to all at the Cambridge University Press who have assisted in the preparation of the volume.

Introduction

R. H. HILTON

The articles in this collection were published in *Past and Present* between 1970 and 1984. They are concerned with various aspects of landed property in medieval England, with those who owned it and those who worked it. It continues (as in the case of the articles by R. A. Dodgshon and John Hatcher) some of the themes already reprinted in a previous Past and Present Publication, *Peasants, Knights and Heretics*. Here, however, there is a considerable emphasis on those owners – or feudal tenants – of landed estates who made up the ruling class, Anglo-Norman or English, between the Norman Conquest and the end of the thirteenth century. Vital problems are posed, some are left on one side, as is inevitable in a group of articles by different scholars, focused on issues of particular interest at particular moments. Among the contributions concerning those who worked the land, we are very pleased to be able to reprint J. R. Maddicott's now classic "The English Peasantry and the Demands of the Crown, 1294-1341", the first of the *Past and Present* Supplements, which appeared in 1975. And, most recent, John Langdon's innovative contribution to our understanding of agrarian technology in the middle ages, which appeared in 1984.

As can be concluded from J. C. Holt's study of "Politics and Property in Early Medieval England", one of the conditions for the stabilization of a landowning aristocracy was the preservation of the family patrimony by a system of inheritance by a single heir, so that, as on the European continent even earlier than in England, a family lineage could be established. Unfortunately, even if primogeniture was recognized (and, as will be seen, Holt's suggestion about the chronology of its establishment is challenged by Stephen D. White), the problem of what to do with younger sons, not to speak of daughters, was always present. It is clear that a neat division between a heritable patrimony and disposable acquisitions did not solve the problems. Demographic factors, such as the failure of male heirs, further complicated matters, as did the existence of collateral lines with possible claims. With these and other natural uncertainties, the intervention of political interests would inevitably contribute still further to the instabilities of a class whose position in many respects seemed so dominating.

Holt attributes an accentuation of the landed class's problems after the death of William the Conqueror to the complex issues of loyalty presented to the Anglo-Norman barons when the Norman ducal patrimony and the English royal acquisition were allotted to different heirs. Tenurial crises developed, accentuated by the conflict between Stephen and Mathilda. This provided an ample opportunity for the manipulation by rulers of an uncertain system of heritability, by supporting those whom they considered politically loyal, even though their family status might be weak. Edmund King considers that Holt overemphasizes this political manipulation and that the baronage managed to cope with problems arising from divided lordship and loyalties. Nevertheless, as Holt has noticed, manipulation in the interests of royal power did not cease when the particular political difficulties of the late eleventh and twelfth centuries were over. Edward I, as K. B. McFarlane pointed out, was quite capable of operating in a manner analogous to that described for the earlier period – showing "an unscrupulousness" in pursuing his dynastic aims.[1] No doubt the problems of the baronage in the twelfth century were very acute, but it would be a mistake to assume that, even under the control of a strong and unchallenged king, a landed feudal aristocracy could ever become a stable ruling class; still less if the king, as one should expect, was behaving with the self-interest of a landed magnate, which he undoubtedly was. Was stability ever achieved by the English aristocracy during the whole of the middle ages?

Other articles in this collection pose the problem not only of the stability, but of the homogeneity of the medieval ruling aristocracy. The barons, who are the concern of Holt and his commentators, by no means constituted the effective totality of the landed class. If the medieval peasantry was stratified (an issue obliquely posed in the Russian historiography described by Peter Gatrell), so was the class which ruled them. If it was the nature of a peasant economy that it should require "kulaks", middling peasantry and a group of smallholders providing wage labour, was it not also the case that an aristocracy of great barons must have depended for its effective power – whether military, political or social – in the counties, on a sub-class of tenants and retainers, some well-to-do knights, other lesser families of gentle status? But as Edmund King and P. R. Coss both show, this group too is by no means stable. King is mildly sceptical of the suggestion that there was a crisis of this "knightly/gentle" class in the thirteenth century, that some families fell in status because of the increasing costs of a "gentle" or "knightly"

<hr />

[1] K. B. McFarlane, "Had Edward I a Policy towards the Earls?", in his *The Nobility of Later Medieval England* (Oxford, 1973), p. 266.

style of life, so that they had to borrow on the security of their lands and in some cases lose them. Nevertheless both he and Coss produce actual evidence of the double process of promotion and of demotion. Instability, in an era of demographic, social and economic change, seems to have been as much a characteristic of the lesser as of the higher aristocracy.

A dimension that is sometimes lacking in studies of the problems of the landed class, is the economic. It is proper to concentrate on legal issues of inheritance and tenure in a political context. But what made an estate valuable enough to be disputed or even fought for? No doubt there were aesthetic and sporting pleasures to be found on their estates by barons, knights, gentry and their ladies. But what mattered most was the value of the estate, universally expressed at this period in cash terms. King, when considering rising and declining families in the Soke of Peterborough, raises the question as to where the money came from to invest in the land market. Coss, in fact, faces up to the question. Obviously much of Geoffrey de Langley's success comes from his career as a royal official, but it is suggested too that, like so many contemporary landowners, he was intensifying his pressures on his peasant tenants for rents. At the same time he was acquiring land from the losers on the property market and concentrating his estates for the purpose of better management.

Estates would have been valueless without peasant tenants to work the land. One has only to analyse the account rolls of the manors which were the basic units, however variable in structure, of these estates, to appreciate this fact. Rents, the sale of demesne produce and the profits of manorial jurisdiction – all ultimately derived from peasant labour – constituted the principal values which sustained the aristocracy, great and small. This will seem obvious to those who are well read in the long line of English manorial and estate histories. Unfortunately, while we know much about the economies of the great lay and ecclesiastical, especially monastic, estates, there is much less evidence for the working of the properties of the middling and lesser landowners. R. H. Britnell's study of some small Essex properties is therefore apposite in connection with the questions posed by King and Coss. Britnell's article is written in the context of E. A. Kosminsky's analysis of the Hundred Rolls of 1279-80. He supports Kosminsky's general conclusions about the structure of small manors as being dominated by the demesnes worked by wage labour, producing mainly for the market and with relatively low rent income. Unfortunately the accounts analysed are half a century later than those described in the Hundred Rolls. But this does not necessarily invalidate Britnell's conclusion, opposed to that of Kosminsky, that the smaller land-

owners, in spite of being market-oriented, were no more entrepreneurial than the owners of big estates, even though their level of
investment might be higher.

In a sense we return again to the political dimension when
considering landowner incomes from the estates. Was the level of
peasant rents and services determined largely by market and
demographic forces, the land/labour ratio, the supply of and the
demand for land, as Hatcher is inclined to argue? In the era covered
by most of the articles in this collection, there was a very heavy
population pressure on scarce resources. Probably, as suggested by
Guy Bois for Normandy at the same time, there was a fall, not
necessarily of the total rent revenue on particular estates, but of the
rate of extraction.[2] The demographic and economic context of rent,
whether paid by villeins, leaseholders or free tenants, must not be
minimized. But does this mean that there was no "political" as
distinct from "economic" element in the taking of rent? By
"political" is meant a relation between lords and peasants where the
balance of forces is by no means expressible solely in terms of supply
and demand on a land market. The private jurisdictional power of
the lords, their ability to manipulate at the regional level the
procedures of the royal courts, their influence on, if not control of,
royal officials, have to be balanced against the extraordinary tenacity
and potential rebelliousness of peasant communities, however
stratified (see Zvi Razi's vivid description of such a community in
this collection). And to this must be added peasant skills in
defending their perceived rights by calling on custom – as the lords
did for opposite reasons.[3] An unequal balance, no doubt, but
political as much as economic.

If surplus extraction at the level of manor and estate may be
debated in terms of the relative importance of the "economic" and
the "political", it hardly seems debatable that the demands of the
crown – the greatest power in English feudal society even when it
seemed weak and divided – constituted a purely political form of
extraction. As Maddicott shows, the operations of the royal
purveyors and tax-collectors must have added a terrible burden,
additional to seigneurial rents and services, on to the English
peasantry. In no sense was there an economic quid pro quo between
the taxed and the taxer. The peasants had no voice in tax bargaining;
the profits of the tax (in so far as they were not appropriated by the
tax-collectors) were mainly spent on aggressive wars and in no way

[2] Guy Bois, *The Crisis of Feudalism: Economy and Society in Eastern Normandy, c. 1300-1550* (Cambridge, 1984).
[3] These matters are discussed in J. R. Birrell, C. C. Dyer and R. H. Hilton, "La société paysanne et la loi en Angleterre au moyen âge", *Etudes rurales*, nos. 101-2 (1987).

for the protection of the people, as contemporary estate theory would have it. And in so far as there was any downward dissemination, through the networks of patronage, of crown income, derived quite considerably from tax, it would stop short at the landed aristocracy.

The tradition of purely political history, whether of medieval or of modern times, has quite rightly been eroded. But it would be foolish not to recognize the significance of the "political", in the sense of power relationships both lateral and horizontal, at all levels of medieval society.

1. *The landholding foundations of the open-field system*

ROBERT A. DODGSHON

THE DISPOSITION OF LANDHOLDING ON A SUB-DIVIDED[1] OR STRIP-FIELD basis represents a vital ingredient of any open- or common-field system. Without it, other ingredients, such as the communal regulation of cropping, the practice of common grazing across the arable after harvest or the open, unenclosed character of the system, lose much of their meaning. Indeed, at a time when so much doubt is being expressed as to whether all the various regional types of field system incorporated these other ingredients,[2] the fragmentation and intermixture of holdings stands out as the one indisputable characteristic which all open-field systems worthy of the name did possess. However, in spite of its importance, little agreement exists over how such an arrangement first developed. In fact, four quite separate interpretations can be recognized in the literature, each invoking a single factor or process — the techniques of early ploughing, the method of land colonization, the effects of partible inheritance or the nature of early land tenure — to explain the problem. This paper proposes to examine the merits of these four interpretations and, on the basis of the points so made, to formulate a view of the problem which relies on the integration of three of them.

I

Among historians, the most popular interpretation seems to be that developed by the Orwins.[3] The Orwins put forward the view that the first appearance of sub-divided fields dated from the introduction of the heavy mould-board plough. Early versions of this plough were equipped with a non-reversible mould-board, a facility which

---

[1] "Sub-divided fields" is a phrase coined by A. R. H. Baker in his "Some Terminological Problems in Studies of British Field Systems", *Agric. Hist. Rev.*, xvii (1969), p. 139. It refers to the organization of landholding in the form of intermixed strips or parcels without implying that such strips or parcels were unenclosed or that they were overlaid with rights of common grazing.

[2] See, for instance, the debate between J. Thirsk, "The Common Fields", *Past and Present*, no. 29 (Dec. 1964), pp. 3-25, and J. Z. Titow, "Medieval England and the Open-Field System", *ibid.*, no. 32 (Dec. 1966), pp. 86-102. Relevant comment can also be found in G. C. Homans, "The Explanation of English Regional Differences", *ibid.*, no. 42 (Feb. 1969), pp. 18-22.

[3] C. S. and C. S. Orwin, *The Open Fields* (Oxford, 1938), ch. iv.

restricted it to throwing the soil in one direction only, normally to the plough's right. Inevitably, this created problems as the ploughman worked his way back and forth across a field. The solution which early communities devised involved the division of the field into narrow strips called "lands". The ploughman then moved along either side of each "land" turning the furrow in towards the centre of the "land". As the Orwins made clear, the movement of soil in towards what became the crown of each "land" led to the formation of a "succession of ridges and furrows", a feature that many would regard as something of a *leit-motif* of sub-divided fields. However, the creation of a ridge-and-furrow system did not on its own lead automatically to a pattern of intermingled shares or selions based on such a system. To explain this aspect, the Orwins referred to the practice of collective ploughing which, they argued, was widespread among early communities and which carried with it an implicit need for a division of land between the members of each ploughing partnership. Having defined what they considered to be the essential issues — the use of a mould-board plough and collective ploughing — they then suggested that as each "land" was ploughed, it was only logical, not to say convenient, for it to be allocated to the various landholders in turn. Needless to say, the overall effect was the formation of sub-divided fields.

The reaction of many historians to their argument has been similar to that of Professor H. R. Loyn and Professor M. M. Postan, both of whom accepted it as a common-sense explanation, a practical antidote to the abstract notions of primitive equality with which an earlier generation of historians had explained the problem.[4] However, despite this impressive stamp of approval, the Orwins' interpretation is open to serious criticism. Quite apart from its dubious assumption that the logic and convenience of doling out strips as they were ploughed outweighed the considerable and permanent inconvenience of having intermixed property, its power as an explanation is greatly weakened by the fact that it receives little support from the available evidence. In fact, except for a questionable fragment of support culled from early Welsh laws,[5] the Orwins were unable to cite a single example in which the allocation of "lands" was combined with the

[4] H. R. Loyn, *Anglo-Saxon England and the Norman Conquest* (London, 1962), p. 152; M. M. Postan, *The Medieval Economy and Society* (London, 1972), p. 129.
[5] Orwin and Orwin, *op. cit.*, p. 41. For a critical discussion of this evidence, see G. R. J. Jones, "Field Systems of North Wales", in A. R. H. Baker and R. A. Butlin (eds.), *Studies of Field Systems in the British Isles* (Cambridge, 1973), p. 436.

process of ploughing. Their inability to do so cannot be attributed
to any basic lack of evidence regarding early land-division, since
evidence of this kind does exist. Their difficulty was that it
points towards the use of methods quite different from that which
they proposed.

In Scotland, for instance, an area which affords ample opportunity
for looking closely at methods of land-division, the ploughing and
allocation of strips invariably appear as two separate acts with the
latter being achieved by means of a lot division.[6] Where descriptions
are sufficiently explicit, they suggest that the procedure followed
involved the laying out of strips with the use of a measuring rod or
rope. The group of strips comprising each person's share was then
identified, both on the ground and in the lottery, by means of a mark
or token.[7] A mark system of particular interest was that based on
the use of a sun-division. If sixteenth- and seventeenth-century
charters for the north-east of Scotland are examined, one sometimes
finds landholders possessing the sunny or shadow portions of a
particular farm or township. Early legal texts, such as Sir Thomas
Craig's *Jus Feudale*, make it abundantly clear that shares so designated
were meant to be divided after the fashion of a sun-division, with the
person holding the sunny share being given the strips which lay in
the east or south of each furlong or sequence of allocation and the
person holding the shadow share being given those which lay to the
west or north.[8] In some cases, more elaborate systems of apportion-
ment were achieved by having a mid-share or by having the sunny and

[6] *The Commissioners of Inquiry into the Condition of the Crofters and Cottars
in the Highlands and Islands of Scotland*, Parliamentary Papers, 1884, i, app. xcix,
pp. 451-73; J. Robertson, *General View of the Agriculture of the County of
Inverness* (Edinburgh, 1813), p. 335; G. L. Gomme, *The Village Community*
(London, 1890), pp. 144-5 and 201; J. H. Romanes, "The Land System of a
Scottish Burgh", *Juridical Rev.*, xlvii (1935), pp. 117-18; *Dictionary of the
Older Scottish Tongue*, ed. W. Craigie (Chicago, 1962), p. 174; *The Records of
Elgin 1234-1800*, ed. W. Cramond (Aberdeen, 1869), p. 130; R. A. Dodgshon,
"Towards an Understanding and Definition of Runrig: the Evidence for
Roxburghshire and Berwickshire", *Trans. Inst. Brit. Geographers*, lxiv (1975), p. 19.
[7] See esp., *Commissioners of Inquiry into the Condition of the Crofters and
Cottars*, pp. 456-8; Robertson, *op. cit.*, p. 335.
[8] *Sir Thomas Craig's Jus Feudale 1655*, ed. J. Baillie (Edinburgh, 1732), p. 425.
Baillie's edited version is in the original latin. Interestingly, a more recent
translation by J. A. Clyde (Sir Thomas Craig, *Jus Feudale*, 2 vols. [Edinburgh,
1934]) loses much of the meaning in Craig's reference to sun-division. For a
more sympathetic translation of Craig's point, see the relevant sections of
J. Erskine, *The Principles of the Law of Scotland*, 2nd edn. (Edinburgh, 1757).
Erskine's text was, in fact, based on Craig's. A fuller discussion of this and
other evidence for sun-division in Scotland can be found in R. A. Dodgshon,
"Scandinaviar Solskifte and the Sun-Wise Division of Land in Eastern
Scotland", *Scottish Studies*, xix (1975), pp. 1-14.

shadow portions further sub-divided into sunny and shadow sub-portions so that a landholder might hold the sunny portion of the shadow half of a farm or township. Like those methods of land-division which employed less formal systems of laying out and identifying shares, the "kenning of a landowner to his share" in a sun-division was achieved by means of a lottery: "be cavillis drawine & in Judgement cassine".[9] Altogether, the use of a lot system for allocating shares can be extended back to at least the early fifteenth century. The *Liber Melros*, for example, provides a detailed description of a lot division at Hassington (Berwickshire) in 1428.[10] The fact that this and other early references involve divisions presided over by the local sheriff court[11] suggests that the use of a lot division was accepted legal procedure in Scotland and not just an archaic folk practice confined to areas like the Hebrides.

Conditions in England were, of course, different in the sense that the laying out of sub-divided fields had largely ceased by the end of the medieval period. Information on the precise method used, therefore, tends to be scarce. However, the scraps of evidence which can be gleaned indicate methods similar to those used in Scotland.

Thus, unequivocal evidence for the use of a lot-based division occurs in Bracton's thirteenth-century law text. Commenting on the division of land "equally" between co-heirs, Bracton declared that it should not be carried out in

> such a way that each may choose his share in order, but rather, so that fortune is made the judge of such distribution, that each may have the portion that falls to him by lot. Therefore let the names of the co-heirs and their parcels be written in separate schedules and the several schedules of parcels placed without warning in the hands of a layman unable to read, he is to give each parcener one of the schedules and each of them to remain content with the portion contained in the schedule, whether he likes it or not.[12]

Also productive of evidence are those townships which faced the continuing need to allocate land as part of a shifting system of outfield cultivation. Their approach is perhaps typified by the practice

---

[9] See, for instance, *Illustrations of the Topography and Antiquities of Aberdeen and Banff*, ed. J. Robertson (Aberdeen, 1861), iii, pp. 33 and 419.

[10] *Liber Sancte Marie de Melros*, ed. C. Innes, 2 vols. (Bannatyne Club, Edinburgh, 1837), ii, p. 521.

[11] This is particularly well illustrated by *The Sheriff Court Book of Fife 1515-1572*, ed. W. C. Dickinson (Scottish Hist. Soc., 3rd ser., xii, Edinburgh, 1928), pp. 237, 257 and 343.

[12] Bracton, *On the Laws and Customs of England (De Legibus et Consuetudinibus Angliae)*, translation by S. E. Thorne of the latin text edited by G. E. Woodbine, 2 vols. (Cambridge, Mass., 1968), ii, p. 220.

followed at Cowpen in Northumberland. A late sixteenth-century survey of Cowpen explains how

> at the layenge forth of any decayed or wasted corne feilde, and takinge in any new feildes of the common wastes in liewe thereof, everie tenaunte was and is to have so much lande in everie new feilde as everie of them layde forth in everie wasted or decayed corne fielde, or accordinge to the rents of everie tenaunte's tenement . . . as did befall everie of them by their lot.[13]

An entry in the Black Book of Hexham relating to the township of East Maften provides us with a fifteenth-century example. The entry records that:

> if the present lord of Fenwick and lord of Maften wish to bring under the plough the waste land in the said common, then the said prior and convent shall receive their share for their portion in such plough land by lot; as they did before in the other arable land; namely, by the old intakes, in each place a third.[14]

Elsewhere in England, references to the allocation of land by lot are more difficult to find but by no means non-existent. Mr. G. E. Elliot, for instance, has suggested that it was the method used to allocate outfield land in Cumberland.[15]   G. H. Tupling hinted at its use in Rossendale.[16]   In Lincolnshire, evidence is available showing that arable land on the Isle of Axholme was "cavelled out" by lot during the sixteenth century.[17]   Professor M. W. Beresford has described a system of lot acres which existed on the manor of Sutton Coldfield in Warwickshire.[18]   C. I. Elton reported in 1886 that at least one manor near London contained land called "terra lotabilis".[19]   Lastly, G. L. Gomme documented the use of a lot division by commoners at Malmesbury in Wiltshire. The example he provides is especially interesting for, like a number of townships in the west of Scotland and Ireland, it involved the use of twigs to identify shares both on the ground and in the lottery. The actual

[13] H. H. E. Craster, *A History of Northumberland*, ix (Newcastle, 1909), p. 324.

[14] M. Hope Dodds, *A History of Northumberland*, xii (Newcastle, 1926), p. 366. See also, *The Priory of Hexham*, ii, ed. J. Raine (Surtees Soc., xxxxvi, Durham, 1865), p. 50.

[15] G. E. Elliot, "The System of Cultivation and Evidence for Enclosure in Cumberland Open Fields in the Sixteenth Century", *Géographie et Histoire Agraires. Annales de l'Est*, xxi (1959), pp. 127-9.

[16] G. H. Tupling, *The Economic History of Rossendale* (Manchester, 1927), pp. 103-4.

[17] I. F. Grant, *The Social and Economic History of Scotland before 1603* (Edinburgh, 1930), p. 102.

[18] M. W. Beresford, "Lot Acres", *Econ. Hist. Rev.*, xiii (1943), pp. 74-9.

[19] C. I. Elton, "Early Forms of Landholding", *Eng. Hist. Rev.*, i (1886), p. 435.

handing over of each person's share, or the act of seisin, was accompanied by the jingle:

> This land and twig I give to thee,
> As free as Athelstan gave it to me,
> And I hope a loving brother thou wilt be.[20]

Whether this association between the tokens used to allot shares and those used in the ceremony of seisin has any wider significance is difficult to say. However, one cannot help noticing that extant descriptions of the ceremony of seisin elsewhere[21] display a striking similarity with the ceremonies built around the lotting of land.[22] Both occurred at the same point in the transfer of land and both involved identical tokens (that is turf cuttings, stones, twigs, and so on).

Explicit evidence for lot division is not the only way in which we can establish that the Orwins' suggested method of land division was not being used. In some instances it can be deduced from the simple fact that the strip shares into which land was divided were carefully measured out using the customary rod or rope rather than created as a by-product of ploughing. This can be illustrated by Professor H. E. Hallam's work on medieval reclamation in the Lincolnshire Fenland. Altogether Professor Hallam distinguished three stages in the process of reclamation. The first comprised the division of new land between hundreds. The second, its division between the villages within each hundred. And the third, its division between lord and villeins. In the case of the first two stages, Professor Hallam established that the division was carried out by "twelve law-worthy men" by means of "rod and cord".[23] The precise method used at the crucial third stage is more difficult to discern; a valuable clue, however, is provided by the description of reclaimed land in some townships as *offoldfal*. *Offoldfal*, it seems, was always measured in acres not bovates. Indeed, Professor Hallam suggests that an alternative name for it might be *terra mensurata* or "land measured out carefully with a rod and minutely surveyed".[24]

[20] Gomme, *The Village Community*, p. 191.

[21] See, for example, Sir Frederick Pollock and F. W. Maitland, *History of English Law*, 2nd edn. (Cambridge, 1968), ii, pp. 83-5; W. S. Holdsworth, *A History of English Law*, 2nd edn. (London, 1927), ii, pp. 76-7.

[22] See especially, *Commissioners of Inquiry into the Condition of the Crofters and Cottars*, p. 462; Robertson, *Inverness*, p. 335; J. Mill, "Tenants and Agriculture Near Dublin in the Fourteenth Century", *Proc. Roy. Soc. Antiq. Ireland*, xxi (1890-1), p. 57; Gomme, *op. cit.*, pp. 268-70; F. W. Maitland, "The Survival of Archaic Communities", in *The Collected Papers of Frederic William Maitland*, ed. H. A. L. Fisher (Cambridge, 1911), ii, pp. 344-5.

[23] H. E. Hallam, *Settlement and Society: a Study of the Early Agrarian History of South Lincolnshire* (Cambridge, 1965), p. 29.

[24] *Ibid.*, p. 160. For additional comment, see N. Neilson, *A Terrier of Fleet, Lincolnshire* (Brit. Acad. Records of Soc. and Econ. Hist., iv, Oxford, 1920), p. lxxv.

Outwardly this suggests that "twelve law-worthy men" were also set the task of dividing up the individual township portions between lord and villeins. Aware of how this would contradict the Orwins' hypothesis of a land division "which the plough directed", Professor Hallam attempted to reconcile the two by arguing that the surveyor's measurement must have been based on what, in the first place, had already been allocated as part of the process of ploughing. However, one need only look at the way in which strip shares were laid out by rod or rope elsewhere, to realize there are really no firm grounds for this reasoning. Might one suggest that, as happened at Dawpath in Northumberland where reclaimed land was cast into equal shares "by the conscience of XII men",[25] it was likewise the "twelve law-worthy men" rather than the Lincolnshire ploughman who first laid out the shares of *terra mensurata*?

Our understanding of early land division in England can also be furthered by looking at the evidence for the former practice of sun-division. Following the lead given by Professor D. C. Douglas and Professor G. C. Homans, a comprehensive review of this problem has been published by Professor S. Göransson.[26] Although one or two writers had previously been sceptical of the idea that sun-division had once been practised in England,[27] Professor Göransson's paper greatly strengthens the belief that it was. Significantly, recent work has refined the meaning of the term sun-division to the extent that it is now seen solely as a method of systematizing and ordering the laying out and allocation of strips.[28] It did not contain within itself any particular cause of division, nor was it necessarily related to a contemporaneous reorganization of the village site. Needless to say, this refinement of meaning makes it more amenable to the English situation. At the same time, the extra emphasis now given to it as strictly a method of dividing up land means that, once its former practice in England is accepted, it then provides at a single stroke a substantial body of evidence for the laying out of sub-divided fields by means other than the Orwins' method.

[25] H. H. E. Craster, *A History of Northumberland*, x (Newcastle, 1914), p. 270.

[26] D. C. Douglas, *The Social Structure of Medieval East Anglia* (Oxford Studies in Social and Legal History, ix, Oxford, 1927), p. 35; G. C. Homans, *English Villagers in the Thirteenth Century* (Cambridge, Mass., 1941), chap. vi; S. Göransson, "Regular Open-Field Pattern in England and Scandinavian Solskifte", *Geografiska Annaler*, xliii (B) (1961), pp. 80-101.

[27] See, for instance, R. H. Hilton, "Kibworth Harcourt", in W. G. Hoskins (ed.), *Studies in Leicestershire Agrarian History* (Leicester, 1949), pp. 30-1.

[28] S. Göransson, "Solskifte: A Misinterpreted Term", unpublished lecture given at The Queen's University of Belfast, July 1971.

II

As long ago as 1905 Sir Paul Vinogradoff considered but then discounted the possibility that the fragmentation and intermixture of holdings resulted from the piecemeal colonization of land and its equal apportionment between the landholding members of the community, so that in time their respective properties became slowly extended over an expanding arable area.[29] His rejection of this "gradualist" interpretation was premature. More recent work has confirmed the essential validity of its underlying assumptions, at least in certain areas.

In some cases, the link which it presupposes between new land and old was formal and specific, with each bovate or virgate having the right to an equal share of all colonized land. Professor Homans was especially concerned to stress this point. Among the evidence he presented was a charter granting an oxgang of arable to the nuns of Ormsby in Yorkshire. The charter contained the provision that if "it happens that the bounds of the tilled land be extended further than they are, their oxgang will be increased as much as other oxgangs are increased".[30] The same dependence of new land on old permeates Professor Hallam's work on medieval reclamation in the Fens, with numerous references being made to what he called "the land sharing function of the bovate". To cite an example, at Whaplode a certain Hubert Iuuenis was, like the nuns of Ormsby, to receive from any reclamation "as much land as fell to half a bovate".[31] Professor J. A. Raftis discovered a similar relationship between new land and old on the lands of Ramsey Abbey, with new land being "strictly apportioned according to the size of tenements in the village".[32] That tenements had a right to maintain an equality with one another during times of change is also the conclusion to be drawn from evidence from the manor of West Angmering in Sussex. Sixteenth-century evidence from the manor makes it clear that its customary tenants and copyholders

> vsed tyme owt of mynd to have to and for euery yard lond beyng Copyhold xx acres for the yard lond, and yff any suche Copyholders dyd lacke any part of the seyd nomber of xx acres to hys yard lond that then he shuld have so many acres of the wast ground as he shuld lacke of yt to make vpp hys nomber of xx acres for hys yard lond.[33]

[29] P. Vinogradoff, *The Growth of the Manor* (London, 1905), p. 177.
[30] Homans, *op. cit.*, p. 84.
[31] Hallam, *op. cit.*, p. 20.
[32] J. A. Raftis, *Tenure and Mobility* (Toronto, 1964), p. 29.
[33] *Tudor Economic Documents*, ed. R. H. Tawney and E. Power, 3 vols. (London, 1924), i, p. 23.

Dr. H. S. A. Fox has published the interesting example of the free tenants of Otterton in Devonshire who, despite the Statute of Merton, were acknowledged by the prior of Otterton to have the right "to cultivate the waste so long as it is thrown open to pasture after harvest".[34]   As the evidence quoted above for Cowpen and East Maften bears out, occupied waste in parts of the north-east was also divided strictly between the tenements of the township.[35]   Across the Border, a similar arrangement can often be found underpinning outfield cultivation.[36]

Viewing the problem in a broader perspective, it is an established fact that while in some townships colonization was carried out by the community, in others it was largely the work of individuals.   Given this dichotomy of approach, it would be convenient when trying to summarize the problem if we could assume that the strict apportionment of new land among old occurred only where land was colonized by the community and that, where land was colonized on the initiative of individuals, no such relationship existed.   However, this neat division of the problem soon meets with difficulties.   Professor Hallam, for instance, specifically noted "that individuals rather than townships acting in concert led the colonization movement.   Even so the enclosers divided the new enclosures proportionally according to the amount of land they defended, that is, according to the number of bovates they held".[37]   Clearly, the colonizing efforts of individuals acting independently of the community were not sufficient to sever the fundamental nexus of rights which, in these townships, bound new land to old.

Of course, such a strict relationship did not prevail everywhere. In what was possibly the majority of English townships, lords not peasants controlled the occupation of waste, a balance of control confirmed by the Statute of Merton in 1235.   Some lords exercised

[34] H. S. A. Fox, "Field Systems of East and South Devon", pt. 1, "East Devon", *The Devonshire Association*, ci (1972), p. 99.
[35] See also, J. C. Hodgson, *A History of Northumberland*, iv (2) (Newcastle, 1897), p. 328.   Pertinent comment also occurs in R. A. Butlin, "Field Systems of Northumberland and Durham", in Baker and Butlin (eds.), *Studies of Field Systems in the British Isles*, pp. 117-20.
[36] Typical of the evidence for south-east Scotland is the comment from the division proceedings of the runrig township of Eildon that "whatever outfield was going in Corn at a time Every Husband land had an equal proportion of the Same": Roxburghshire Sheriff Court MSS., Jedburgh, Decreet of Division of the Runrig Lands of Eildon, 13 Dec. 1748.
[37] Hallam, *Settlement and Society*, p. 110.   See also, J. Sheppard, "Pre-Enclosure Field and Settlement Patterns in an English Township. Wheldrake near York", *Geografiska Annaler*, xlviii (B) (1966), p. 68; F. M. Stenton, "Sokemen and the Village Waste", *Eng. Hist. Rev.*, xxxiii (1918), pp. 344-7.

their authority in this matter by creating a pattern of new, independent holdings unrelated to those already within the township. Professor E. Miller's work on the lands of Ely abbey yielded a good illustration of this with new land being used "to endow a rent paying tenancy" in marked contrast to the customary tenements which occupied the existing arable.[38]   However, it must not be thought that this exercise of authority by the lord over who should occupy the waste always led to a discontinuity between new land and old in terms of landholding.   Numerous medieval surveys are available to show that, even where communities had no standing right to occupy the surrounding waste, and where such colonization was only allowed by special grant from the lord or with his indulgence, some connection between the two could still emerge.   The point is well made by a comment of Professor M. M. Postan that "in many cases in which we find newly assarted holdings held as free land they were frequently no more than appendages to customary tenancies held by villein title by villeins".[39]   Strong lordship then did not necessarily militate against the gradual extension and consequent fragmentation of holdings in this manner.[40]

Whatever the merits of a gradualist interpretation, however, its ability to explain the growth of sub-divided fields is restricted to particular situations, situations in which such fields can be seen as the relatively undisturbed product of piecemeal colonization by the farming community.   What it cannot explain so readily is why intermixture occurred when entire farms or townships were divided or re-divided *en bloc*.   Farms and townships in Scotland, for instance, regularly faced the need to re-cast all or part of their sub-divided field systems.[41]   In England, a comparable situation arose when

[38] E. Miller, *The Abbey and Bishopric of Ely* (Cambridge, 1951), p. 120. Discussion of this point can be found elsewhere in: R. H. Hilton, *A Medieval Society: The West Midlands at the End of the Thirteenth Century* (London, 1966), pp. 22-3 and 114; and B. Dodwell, "Holdings and Inheritance in Medieval East Anglia", *Econ. Hist. Rev.*, 2nd ser., xx (1967), p. 55.

[39] M. M. Postan, "Legal Status and Economic Conditions in Medieval Villages", in his *Essays on Medieval Agriculture and General Problems of the Medieval Economy* (Cambridge, 1973), p. 286.   An examination of the wider significance of this emerging distinction between customary land and freehold can be found in R. A. Dodgshon, "Infield-Outfield and the Territorial Expansion of the English Township", *Jl. of Historical Geography*, 1 (1975), pp. 327-45.

[40] Instances of the gradualist interpretation at work are referred to in T. A. M. Bishop, "Assarting and the Growth of the Open Fields", *Econ. Hist. Rev.*, vi (1935-6), pp. 13-29; M. W. Beresford and J. K. S. St. Joseph, *Medieval England* (Cambridge, 1958), pp. 22-3; Baker and Butlin, "Conclusion: Problems and Perspectives", in *Studies of Field Systems in the British Isles*, pp. 637-41.

[41] An attempt to place these changes in the layout of Scottish sub-divided fields or runrig in some kind of perspective can be found in Dodgshon, "Towards an Understanding and Definition of Runrig", pp. 19, 26-7.

farms or holdings were cast into sub-divided fields as a result of division between co-heirs. Equally relevant is the possibility that many English villages experienced a wholesale reorganization of their sub-divided field system at the point when they first adopted a two- or three-field system of cultivation.[42] Lastly, one must not overlook the fact that a number of writers have suggested that individual furlongs within a sub-divided field system may have begun their life as newly assarted blocks of land held in severalty by a single landholder.[43] Under these circumstances we are clearly forced to seek out other reasons as to why sub-division, with all its attendant inconvenience, developed.

<h1 style="text-align:center">III</h1>

As the basis for an alternative explanation, partible inheritance, or the equal division of land between co-heirs, was used as early as 1915 when H. L. Gray argued that sub-divided fields in highland Britain and in parts of Kent and East Anglia were influenced in their development by its former practice.[44] Although neglected during the inter-war years, more recent work on sub-divided fields has revived it as a factor of some importance. Professor G. R. J. Jones and Dr. A. R. H. Baker, for example, working on Wales and Kent respectively, have both shown how successive partition between co-heirs could fragment and reduce to intermingled shares what had initially been a consolidated holding.[45] There are also grounds for believing that the custom aided the formation of sub-divided fields in parts of Scotland. Thus the bishop of Orkney, writing about both Shetland and Orkney in 1642, observed that:

> Thir lands be the law of Norroway, were equallie divyded among children, be ane inquest founded upon a warrand of the superior, and now be oft divisione of air to air, yt many hath not one rig or two, and in some places one rig is divyded in foure.[46]

[42] There is of course the possibility, outlined by Thirsk, *op. cit.*, pp. 20-2, that the adoption of a two- or three-field system may not have involved a sweeping reorganization of landholding. Instead, the even distribution of each person's holding between fields may have come about by private agreements between pairs or groups of landholders.

[43] See, for instance, the conclusions of Bishop, *op. cit.*, p. 27.

[44] H. L. Gray, *English Field Systems* (Cambridge, Mass., 1915), chaps. v, vii and viii.

[45] Jones, "Field Systems of North Wales", pp. 449-51; G. R. J. Jones, "The Pattern of Settlement along the Welsh Border", *Agric. Hist. Rev.*, viii (1960), pp. 66-81; A. R. H. Baker, "Open Fields and Partible Inheritance on a K⸢ Manor", *Econ. Hist. Rev.*, 2nd ser., xvii (1964-5), pp. 1-22.

[46] A. Peterkin, *Rentals of the Ancient Earldom and Bishoprick of Orkney* (Edinburgh, 1820), pt. 3, p. 20. See also, A. J. G. Mackay, "Notes and Queries on the Custom of Gavelkind in Kent, Ireland, Wales and Scotland", *Proc. Soc. Antiq. Scotland*, xxxii (1897-8), pp. 133-58.

Conscious of the growing amount of direct evidence for a link between partible inheritance and sub-divided fields, Dr. J. Thirsk has invested the relationship with a general significance. In a paper published in 1964, she emphasized that historians were then more prepared to accept coparcenage as having been widespread in the years before the Norman Conquest. The real novelty of her argument, however, was in the emphasis which she placed on its survival after the Conquest. It survived, she argued, wherever lordship was weak, a conclusion subsequently endorsed by Dr. R. J. Faith.[47]

The drawback of her view in so far as it relates to the origin of sub-divided fields was pointed out by Dr. J. Z. Titow and Professor G. C. Homans. They accepted that the custom was practised during the post-Conquest period in areas like the north and west of England, as well as in its traditional areas of Kent and East Anglia, but went on to assert that in the very part of England where sub-divided fields were most developed, the midland counties, little pre- or post-Conquest evidence for the custom has been uncovered.[48]

A less fundamental criticism of the partible inheritance interpretation as it now stands is that it fails to lay bare the precise logic by which partible inheritance led to intermixture. Writers like Professor Jones and Dr. Baker have demonstrated that partible inheritance could lead to intermixed property, but they have not answered the question of why this was so. This is far from being a pedantic point. If a farm was going to be divided, it could, one presumes, be divided just as easily into consolidated holdings as it could into sub-divided holdings. That this choice was real and not hypothetical is spelt out for us by the relevant sections of early Scottish law texts, for they lay down the procedure to be followed in both types of division.[49] However, given that a choice existed, it follows that to understand why some co-heirs opted for a division into intermingled shares requires the addition of something extra to the bald equation partible inheritance *plus* co-heirs *equals* sub-divided fields, if the exact process involved is to be made fully explicit.

IV

The final interpretation to be examined was originally put forward by Vinogradoff. Vinogradoff took the view that the tenurial basis of

[47] Thirsk, "The Common Fields", pp. 11-14; R. J. Faith, "Peasant Families and Inheritance Customs in Medieval England", *Agric. Hist. Rev.*, xiv (1966), pp. 77-95.
[48] Titow, "Medieval England and the Open-Field System", pp. 92-3; Homans, "English Regional Differences", pp. 22-6.
[49] Erskine, *The Principles of the Law of Scotland*, bk. II, tit. 9, para. 29; Craig, *Jus Feudale*, trans. Clyde, i, p. 43.

English sub-divided fields was of a distinctive type which he called shareholding.[50]   By such a tenure, each person's holding was seen as being in essence a *share* in the township or village rather than a holding that was fixed and defined in terms of its precise layout on the ground.   Its origin, he suggested, could be traced back to the tribal organization of society which had once prevailed throughout Britain. Furthermore, it was these tribal roots which endowed it with its overriding character as a form of communal tenure.[51]   Whether shareholding can be seen as a form of communal tenure, however, is open to serious doubt.   F. W. Maitland, who shared Vinogradoff's belief in the shareholding character of early tenure, disagreed sharply with him on this point, arguing that to classify it as communal was to confuse communal ownership with co-ownership.[52]

As regards its bearing on the development of sub-divided fields, the most important feature of shareholding was the basis on which the equality of each share unit or tenement was interpreted.   They were, argued Vinogradoff, equal in value as well as in acreage.   Such an interpretation, however, raised problems when it came actually to distributing shares on the ground.   Altogether, he saw two ways in which this "equalization of shares" could be achieved.   In his own words:

> ... the territory of the township is not an homogeneous sheet of paper out of which you may cut lots of every desirable shape and size: the tilth will present all kinds of accidental features, according to the elevation of the ground, the direction of the watercourses and ways, the quality of the soil, the situation of the dwellings, the disposition of wood and pasture-ground, etc.   ... Over the irregular squares of this rough chess-board a more or less entangled network of rights and interests must be extended.   There seem to be only two ways of doing it: if you want a holding to lie in one compact patch you will have to make a very complicated reckoning of all the many circumstances which influence husbandry, you will have to find some numerical expression for fertility, accessibility and the like; or else you may simply give every householder a share in every one of the component areas, and subject him in this way to all the advantages and drawbacks which may bear upon his neighbours.   If the ground cannot be made to fit the system of allotment, the system of allotment must conform itself to the ground.   There can be no question that the second way of escaping from the difficulty is much the easier one.

However, if chosen, it leads "necessarily to the scattering and inter-mixture of strips".[53]

[50] An extended discussion of his ideas can be found in *The Growth of the Manor*, chaps. iii and iv.
[51] His clearest treatment of the tribal origins of shareholding occurs in P. Vinogradoff, *Outline of Historical Jurisprudence* (Oxford, 1920), i, pp. 321-43.
[52] Maitland's strongest reply on this point can be found in his "The Survival of Archaic Communities", pp. 314-65.
[53] P. Vinogradoff, *Villeinage in England* (Oxford, 1892), pp. 235-6.

In spite of the care with which Vinogradoff laid out his ideas, they have, for the most part, been largely rejected. Neither Dr. Thirsk nor Dr. Titow, for instance, mentioned them during their notable debate of the problem. Nor were they given a mention in the wide-ranging collection of essays on field systems edited by Dr. Baker and Mr. Butlin.[54] The basis for this apparent rejection has never been made entirely clear. If anything, it appears to centre on the fact that Vinogradoff provided little in the way of tangible support for his ideas so that a great deal depended on the plausibility or otherwise of their underlying assumptions. This being the case, it is crucial to the understanding of their rejection that some writers have seized upon the fact that he was expounding an interpretation rooted in notions of primitive equality, an interpretation that cast early communities in the mould of little commonwealths practising a form of primitive communism, with each landholder having not only an equal share of the good and bad, but also an equal amount of land. Given this kind of emphasis, it was hardly surprising that his argument should founder when confronted with the seemingly more robust and practical inter-pretation of the Orwins.

However, his ideas can be substantiated with a wider and more specific range of evidence than is generally realized. My own work on early landholding in south-east Scotland, for example, has yielded quite strong support. A fuller statement of the conclusions reached by this work can be found elsewhere.[55] For the purpose of the present discussion, only a brief summary need be given. Altogether, it was found that where sub-divided fields existed, or on what are termed runrig farms and townships, each landholder's share was expressed in one of two ways. The commoner method of description, especially on those runrig farms which involved only tenants, was that of explicitly stated shares: thus a farm might be divided between four tenants with each holding a "quarter", or one tenant might hold a "half" and the remaining tenants a "sixth" each. The second method was largely, but not exclusively, confined to runrig farms and townships which involved the intermixture of land belonging to different landowners. It consisted of the apportion-ment of land on the basis of land unit shares such as husbandlands or merklands with each proprietor holding so many land units out of the total in the township.

[54] Thirsk, *op. cit.*, pp. 3-25; Titow, *op. cit.*, pp. 86-102; Baker and Butlin (eds.), *Studies of Field Systems in the British Isles.*
[55] Dodgshon, "Towards an Understanding and Definition of Runrig", pp. 15-33.

At first sight this dual system of land description might be taken as signifying real differences in the manner in which land was held. However, examination of the division proceedings for proprietary runrig townships leaves little doubt that their land unit holdings conveyed a share no less than the more explicitly stated shares of tenant runrig farms. In fact, their evidence not only confirms the equivalence of their tenure to that of explicitly stated shares, but it also helps tighten one of the basic assumptions of the shareholding interpretation. According to Vinogradoff, shares were meant to be equal in value, but, as a consequence of the way in which they were divided, they ended up by being equal in both extent and value.[56] The evidence for proprietary runrig townships, however, makes it clear that shares were interpreted from the outset as being of "of equal extent & value".[57] Some even make it clear that the runrig intermixture of holdings was a direct outcome of this broadly based definition of equality.[58]

To some extent the conditions prevailing in south-east Scotland were exceptional, in that the distinction between land held in the form of explicitly stated shares and that held in the form of land units coincided with the distinction between tenant and proprietary runrig. Elsewhere in Scotland no such coincidence occurred, with the two methods of land description being freely used at both the tenant and proprietary levels. In north-east Scotland, for instance, one can find many proprietary runrig townships divided into halves, quarters or thirds during the sixteenth and seventeenth centuries.[59] Conversely, many tenant runrig farms and townships in northern and western Scotland employed a land unit system of tenure until their disappearance in the late eighteenth century onwards.[60] Taking everything into consideration, it seems likely that the use of pure fractions by some townships developed out of an earlier system based on land units. Certainly there were factors at work which might have encouraged this development, even though it amounted to no

---

[56] Vinogradoff, *Villeinage*, pp. 240-1.
[57] Dodgshon, *op. cit.*, pp. 28-9; R. A. Dodgshon, "The Removal of Runrig in Roxburghshire and Berwickshire 1680-1766", *Scottish Studies*, xvi (1972), p. 130.
[58] Dodgshon, "Towards an Understanding and Definition of Runrig", pp. 28-9.
[59] Dodgshon, "Scandinavian Solskifte", pp. 9-10.
[60] M. Gray, *The Highland Economy 1750-1850* (Edinburgh, 1957), pp. 19-21; A. McKerral, "Ancient Denominations of Agricultural Land in Scotland", *Proc. Soc. Antiq. Scotland*, lxxviii (1943), pp. 55-7; A. Geddes, "Conjoint-Tenants and Tacksman on the Isle of Lewis 1715-26", *Econ. Hist. Rev.*, 2nd ser., i (1948-9), pp. 54-60.

more than a change in the denomination of shares rather than in their intrinsic meaning.[61]

Turning to the problem of shareholding in England, two areas — East Anglia and Northumberland — have so far produced what might be called substantive evidence. The East Anglian evidence was published by Professor D. C. Douglas. Although later writers would probably not agree with the extent to which he developed the argument, Professor Douglas suggested that the original tenure of East Anglian sub-divided fields, with its system of *manloths* (or *manneslots*) and references to *deleland*, was of a shareholding character. In keeping with Vinogradoff, he also argued that this "fundamental notion of shareland" underpinned in a formative way "the system of intermixed strips".[62]

Possibly less debatable is the evidence for Northumberland which was published in the late nineteenth century by C. Creighton and F. W. L. Dendy.[63] Working independently of each other, Creighton and Dendy uncovered an early nineteenth-century lawsuit in which evidence was presented to show that the word *farm* in Northumberland had traditionally denoted an aliquot part in the value of the township. In effect, the term *farm* had a meaning equivalent to land unit shares in Scotland, with townships in Northumberland consisting of a fixed number of *farm* shares, each *farm* or *farmhold* being treated as equal in value one with another. One of the examples given by Dendy, for instance, was the township of North Middleton: this comprised "14 ancient farms", ten of which were held by the duke of Portland, one and five-eighths *farms* by George and Robert Hepple, one *farm* by Lord Carlisle, seven eighths of a *farm* by William Hodgson and four eighths of a *farm* by John Arthur.[64] A township with a similar number of *farms* was Amble in Warkworth parish. According to a survey of 1663 its fourteen *farms* were held as follows:

---

[61] A key factor may have been the physical expansion of townships into their outfield during the fifteenth, sixteenth and seventeenth centuries. As shown elsewhere, this had the effect of reducing the value of their husbandland assessment (or its equivalent) as a measure of how much arable land the township contained since each now comprised their assessed land plus outfield. Faced with this situation, the response of some townships, perhaps those which involved only a few landholders, may have been to adopt a more explicit share system. See R. A. Dodgshon, "The Nature and Development of Infield-Outfield in Scotland", *Trans. Inst. Brit. Geographers*, lix (1973), pp. 1-23.

[62] Douglas, *The Social Structure of Medieval East Anglia*, pp. 20-1 and 29-30.

[63] C. Creighton, "The Northumbrian Border", *Arch. Jl.*, xlii (1885), pp. 41-89; F. W. L. Dendy, "The Ancient Farms of Northumberland", *Archaeologia Aeliana*, xxi (1894), pp. 121-56.

[64] *Ibid.*, p. 138.

Nicholas Lewin rated at £40 or four-fourteenth parts in value of the township
Rt. Widdrington rated at £30 or three-fourteenth parts in value of the township
Edward Cook rated at £30 or three-fourteenth parts in value of the township
Edward Browell rated at £10 or one-fourteenth part in value of the township
William Smith rated at £10 or one-fourteenth part in value of the township
William Reed rated at £10 or one-fourteenth part in value of the township
John Taylor rated at £10 or one-fourteenth part in value of the township.[65]

Like the use of explicit shares in Scotland, these *farm* shares probably
evolved out of an earlier system based on conventional land units.
In fact, both Creighton and Dendy noted that some townships
employed a "plough or ploughland" system, while Mr. Butlin has
recently postulated a direct link between *farms* and an earlier system
of husbandlands.[66]

Both Creighton and Dendy stressed the fact that *farms* were meant
to be equal in value within each township. Although this adds to the
empirical basis of Vinogradoff's argument, it does not, by itself,
strengthen his reasoning for the link between sub-divided fields and
the way in which communities approached the problem of equalizing
shares. However, as in Scotland, where the opportunity arises to
probe into the community's attitude on this matter, support for even
this aspect of his argument is forthcoming.

Taking a very general view of the problem, it is not without some
significance that communities in Northumberland were, in the first
place, concerned with equalizing their *farm* shares. One finds, for
instance, references to shares having to be "just and equal" or each
person having "justice and right". Identical phrases are used by
Scottish leases and charters when conveying shares.[67] What a "just
and equal" share constituted is perhaps a matter for debate, but
Maitland, speaking as the lawyer as well as the historian, once
described an "equitable quarter" of a hide as something that was
"equal in value as well as extent to every remaining quarter".[68] His
opinion can be buttressed by evidence from Cowpen. Following
a trend in Northumberland, the township of Cowpen was split into
two parts in 1619, each part forming a smaller but still sub-divided
unit. How the community of Cowpen approached this opportunity

[65] J. C. Hodgson, *A History of Northumberland*, v (Newcastle, 1899), p 285.
[66] Butlin, "Field Systems of Northumberland and Durham", pp. 138-9.
[67] Creighton, *op. cit.*, p. 87; Craster, *A History of Northumberland*, ix, p. 325;
J. C. Hodgson, *A History of Northumberland*, vii (Newcastle, 1904), p. 314;
Dodgshon, "Towards an Understanding and Definition of Runrig", p. 28; *Powis
Papers 1507-1594*, ed. J. G. Burnett (Aberdeen, 1951), pp. 147-9; Robertson,
Aberdeen and Banff, pp. 36-7; *Bammf Charters A.D. 1232-1703*, ed. J. H. Ramsay
(Oxford, 1915), pp. 210-11; *Old Lore Miscellany of Orkney, Shetland and Sutherland*,
ed. A. W. Johnston (London, 1921-33), ix, p. 125.
[68] F. W. Maitland, *Domesday Book and Beyond* (London, 1960 edn.), p. 446.

to lay out their sub-divided fields anew, therefore, allows some insight into the possible rationale which lay behind them. It required, they argued, a "cunning expert and trustie surveyor of landes" to measure out the lands and to ensure "that some have not all the best ground and the other the worst, but that each have justice and right, having good consideration to the quantitie and also the qualitie of the partes so allotted".[69] A hint that such an interpretation was general in the county is given by evidence for the township of Chatton. A seventeenth-century document concerning Chatton describes how tenants

> had their lands allotted rigg by rigg as is the custom in every husband towne, so that each should have land of like quality, but by reason of encroachments the value of the different holdings varied very much.... The majority of tenants therefore petitioned ... to have the land re-divided rigg by rigg according to the old order of division.[70]

Similar logic was expressed during the division of Auchencraw, a "husband towne" in Berwickshire. In reply to a plea for the consideration of possible differences in quantity between the township's husbandlands, it was rather cynically pointed out that "often ... heretors and unjust persons Steal and plow away by degrees pieces of their neighbours land and then pretend that theirs is larger than their neighbours" while, as regards possible differences in quality, it was simply stated that "differences in that respect cannot be considerable where lands ly run rige at least it ought not to be ... heretors haveing by their originall Charters and securities a lyke quantity of land Should have a lyke possession".[71]

Outside East Anglia and Northumberland, evidence for the use of explicit shares appears, at first sight, to be limited. Occasionally one finds townships or manors split into halves or thirds.[72] More occasionally still one finds land which, possibly because of its extreme morcellation, existed in the form of undivided shares.[73] Otherwise

[69] Craster, *A History of Northumberland*, ix, p. 325.
[70] M. Hope Dodds, *A History of Northumberland*, xiv (Newcastle, 1935), p. 212.
[71] Berwickshire Sheriff Court MSS., Duns, Register of Decreets, 24 Feb. 1715.
[72] For examples, see *Bolton Priory Rentals and Ministers' Accounts 1473-1579*, ed. I. Kershaw (Yorks. Arch. Soc., Record Ser., cxxxii, 1970), p 6; *Lancashire Inquests, Extents and Feudal Aids*, pt. 3, *A.D. 1315-A.D. 1355*, ed. W. Farrer (Rec. Soc. for Lancs. and Cheshire, lxx, 1915), pp. 19, 45 and 102-3; T. E. Scrutton, *Commons and Common Fields* (Cambridge, 1887), p. 16.
[73] H. P. R. Finberg cites the Devonshire example of "an undivided 4th part of SEVEN FIELDS, about 19 acres; and a 4th Part of a 3rd undivided PART of a FIELD" in his *West Country Historical Studies* (Newton Abbot, 1969), p. 144. See also, C. D. Drew, "Open Fields at Portland and Elsewhere", *Antiquity*, xii (1948), p. 80; Hope Dodds, *A History of Northumberland*, xii, p. 286. The latter gives the example of "Five undivided 24ths of three undivided fourths of lands in Rochester".

the evidence for the use of explicitly stated shares must be considered sparse.   Under these circumstances, establishing the wider relevance of shareholding in an English context must depend largely on how we interpret alternative forms of evidence.

One approach can be made by looking again at the ability of partible inheritance to produce sub-divided fields.   Built in to this process was the need to divide land into equal shares.[74]   It matters not whether such shares were couched in terms of so many land units out of a fixed total or as an aliquot share of the whole; the interpretation of either, it seems, could lead to sub-division.   As already indicated, for it to do so requires the addition of something extra to the summary equation partible inheritance *plus* co-heirs *equals* sub-divided fields.   This additional element is surely the reasoning provided by Vinogradoff's shareholding interpretation.

That shareholding may provide the missing logic is confirmed by Bracton.   In his section on the division of land between co-heirs, he stresses throughout the need for making "an extent and valuation" beforehand.   Among the situations he considered was one in which the first attempt at division had been carried out improperly. "Twelve lawful men" who knew the property concerned were brought before the sheriff, who was then

> to cause to be extended and valued by their oath each vill separately, in demesne, villeinages, etc. according to how they now are [*or* in the condition they now are] in all things that can and ought to be extended and valued. Having made an extent in that way, let each vill be divided into halves so that one half of each vill is equal to the other half of the same vill.   And this division having been made, let a lot be assigned to each half and by lot each party be assigned his half.[75]

Perhaps Bracton's most revealing passage is on the "duty of extenders":

> The office of extenders lies in the extending and valuing of things comprised in an inheritance; first that they see what and how much there is in demesne in each manor, that is, how many acres or virgates of arable land and the annual value of each acre or virgate.   Also how many acres there are in pasture and what each is worth per annum.   Also what and how much lies in waste.   Also how many acres of meadow and in what year they may be mowed and in what year not . . . in brief all the other things that belong to the *corpus* of the manor and from which profit could be derived.   Also what and how much there is in villeinage, how many virgates, and how much they are worth in rents, tallages and all other things.   Then let the services and rents of the free tenants be extended.   After the extent and valuation have been made as aforesaid they may be disputed and impugned in many ways, by saying that they were not properly made . . .   The assignment may be contested as well as the valuation . . .   When the extent and valuation has

---

[74] Maitland, *Domesday Book and Beyond*, pp. 182-3; *The Coucher Book of Selby Abbey*, ed. J. T. Fowler (Yorks. Arch. Soc., Record Ser., x, 1891), p. 237.
[75] Bracton, *On the Laws and Customs of England*, trans. Thorne, ii, pp. 211-12.

been properly made, let partition be made of the things comprising the inheritance into two or more parts, depending on the number of co-heir parceners, so that each part is equal in every respect to the other.[76]

Given that such divisions could lead to intermixed holdings, it is difficult to avoid the conclusion that they did so because they were founded on the strict interpretation of the rule "that each part is equal in every respect to the other" as regards both "extent and valuation".

An equally rewarding path to the problem lies in establishing the exact meaning of land units when used within the framework of English sub-divided fields. Generally speaking, there is no doubt that the majority of historians see tenemental units like virgates and bovates as denoting what Postan has called "standardized shares".[77] On the face of it, this appears to shift their meaning in the direction of a shareholding interpretation. But, with the notable exceptions of Maitland and Professor Douglas, few would accept Vinogradoff's views on the extent to which such shares were equalized. However, in so far as the evidence for areas like south-east Scotland and north-east England helps validate a link between the interpretation of land units as equal shares and their division into sub-divided fields, the association of "standardized shares" with sub-divided fields in an area like the midlands must surely admit of the real possibility that a functional link between the two existed there also.

On a slightly different approach, an idea which is central to Vino-gradoff's argument is that, being essentially shares, individual land units were not necessarily tied to any specific layout within the township.[78] This was certainly the case in Scotland for, as the widespread use of lots to apportion land demonstrates, only after shares had been allotted did each landholder know where his holding was going to be. Indeed, as I have argued elsewhere, this apportion-ment of shares into known or particular property may be the real

[76] *Ibid.*, pp. 219-20.
[77] Postan, *The Medieval Economy and Society*, p. 128.
[78] To use Vinogradoff's own words: "the possibility of re-divisions, starting from the idea that the actual holdings in the field ought to be commensurate to the shares which they represent in the village group, was not excluded . . . although the strips of arable land held and cultivated by the different households were usually handed over from generation to generation . . . they constituted at bottom the shares of the households as members of a community, and could be shifted bodily from one place to the other provided their proportionate value was maintained". Vinogradoff, *The Growth of the Manor*, p. 179. Without imply-ing that such re-divisions were common, Vinogradoff illustrates their *possibility* in terms of customary law by citing the twelfth-century re-division at Segeho. For an endorsement of his principle in so far as it can be extended to Scottish shareholding, see *Habakkuk-Bisset's Rolment of Courtis*, ed. P. J. Hamilton-Grierson (Edinburgh, 1920), i, pp. 297-8.

meaning behind the term runrig.[79]   Whether the tenure of English
land unit shares was equally permissive of their disposition in any
part of the township is less clear, but a *prima facie* case that it was
can be made out on the grounds that many early land charters defined
a person's holding as simply so many land units "in the township
of . . .".   A fine illustration of this is provided by F. Seebohm.
After citing a pair of tenth-century charters for land at Kingston in
Berkshire, Seebohm makes the point that, although the charters
referred to different holdings, each had appended to it the same set of
boundaries, boundaries which, according to him, were those of the
township as a whole and not those of the individual holdings being
conveyed.[80]   Sir Frank Stenton's work on the Danelaw provides us
with a general statement on this problem based on the systematic
analysis of a large number of early charters.   The earliest example
which he can cite of a charter detailing the selions or layout of a bovate
dates from just before 1200.   It would be difficult, he says, to find an
earlier mention of "the component parts of an open field bovate . . .
precision of this sort is rare . . . the earlier the charter the more
concise will be its notes of identification".[81]   Current opinion on this
lack of specificity in early land description attaches no tenurial
significance to it whatsoever.   Instead it tends to be seen as indicating
either a shorthand designed to avoid the tedious listing of selions[82] or
the crude state of the surveyor's art at this period.[83]   However, its
open-endedness is entirely consistent with a shareholding tenure.
Coupled with the early use of terms like *gedalland* or *deleland*, terms
which, like runrig, may denote shares of a township or farm which
have been divided into known or particular property, it offers strong
circumstantial evidence for a shareholding interpretation.

It has to be admitted, however, that attempts to extend Vinogradoff's argument to an area like the midlands comes up against a
difficulty centring on the fact that, while early charters do give the
impression of dealing with shares, later charters do not.   In fact,

[79] Dodgshon, "Towards an Understanding and Definition of Runrig", pp. 29-31.
For a reference to *farms* in Northumberland being laid out into "knowne grownd",
see M. Hope Dodds, *A History of Northumberland*, xv (Newcastle, 1940), pp. 158
and 489.
[80] F. Seebohm, *The English Village Community* (London, 1896), p. 112.
[81] F. M. Stenton, *Documents Illustrative of the Social and Economic History of
the Danelaw* (Oxford, 1920), p. xlvii.
[82] H. P. R. Finberg, "Anglo-Saxon England to 1042", in H. P. R. Finberg
(ed.), *The Agrarian History of England and Wales A.D. 43-1042* (*The Agrarian
History of England and Wales*, ed. H. P. R. Finberg, i, part ii, Cambridge, 1972),
p. 488.
[83] Stenton, *Danelaw*, pp. xlvii-xlviii.

from about 1200 onwards, to take Stenton's suggested point of change, one finds an increasing number of holdings within sub-divided field systems being described, and therefore fixed, down to the last selion or acre. This contrasts with the position in Scotland and north-east England where, in general, the share basis of holdings was maintained throughout their history as part of a sub-divided field system. Clearly, if sub-divided fields in the midlands were at some point bound up with the notion of holdings as shares, then the disappearance of this notion before the disappearance of the fields themselves cannot be passed over without comment.

Assuming there is a problem to be explained, the prime cause of this change in attitude towards land may well be the more permanent or fixed layout of English sub-divided fields when compared with those of Scotland, a point of difference that is widely acknowledged in the literature. Over time, this greater stability must have enabled English holdings to develop an association with particular strips and parcels, an association which possibly encouraged landholders to see their land not as a share in the township but as an amalgam of specific strips and parcels. However, long-term stability was not the only solvent at work on the shareholding ethos of English sub-divided fields. Helping to undermine the practicability of a share system was the fact that, during the twelfth and thirteenth centuries, rapid population growth, coparcenage and an active land market combined to bring about the general fragmentation of the land units around which the system was developed. The effect of this fragmentation is conveniently summarized by Stenton. Commenting on the practice in East Anglia of measuring land in terms of acres rather than bovates, he suggested that it "provided an excellent illustration of the way in which ancient terms of land measurement could be abandoned when the irregular division of tenements has deprived them of obvious meaning".[84] Writing of the equally volatile freehold conditions of Lincolnshire, Professor Hallam reached the same conclusion: there were, he wrote, "bovates so sub-divided that all pretence at fractioning them had ceased and parceners simply held two or three acres or even less individually".[85] Further north, in Yorkshire, Mr. T. A. M. Bishop felt that active land colonization also played a part. In his own words, if you add to the "free commerce in land and continual division of tenements a widespread reclamation

---

[84] F. M. Stenton, "The Danes in England" (*Raleigh Lecture*, 1927), *Preparatory to Anglo-Saxon England*, ed. D. M. Stenton (Oxford, 1970), p. 161.
[85] H. E. Hallam, "Some Thirteenth-Century Censuses", *Econ. Hist. Rev.*, 2nd ser., x (1957-8), p. 346.

of waste ... you have all the conditions which lead economic historians to look for the rapid disappearance of any such tenemental unit as the bovate".[86]

How reclamation could serve to destroy the meaning of a township's land unit framework is worth exploring further since it adds materially to our understanding. Its effect on the problem operated through the fact that, during the twelfth and thirteenth centuries, relatively few townships absorbed new land by creating extra bovates or virgates. Instead, it was simply measured in acres.[87] Now in one sense, the use which some townships made of their land unit or tenemental framework when apportioning new land endowed it with a vital self-preserving rôle which presumably outweighed its increasing discordance with the amount of arable in the township as a whole. However, in another sense, the growing amount of land now measured in acres, some of which may have been attached to bovate or virgate tenements as appendent property, could only serve to undermine its usefulness still further. The turning point was probably reached when such townships had colonized all their available land. To adapt Professor Hallam's phrase, their "land sharing function" gone, the meaningful use of bovate and virgate units, and with it the whole notion of shareholding, may have faded rapidly. Significantly, this turning point may have been reached as early as 1300 in central and southern England if we are to believe the Postan thesis on the growth of medieval population.

Putting aside the factors which may have brought it about, the discarding by a township of its land unit framework symbolizes the final abandonment of one interpretation of landholding for another, or that of holdings as shares in the township for one in which they are seen as fixed and defined on the ground in terms of their layout and acreage. Such a development is by no means alien to what has been written on the history of English land law. Maitland, for instance, once questioned whether the conclusion to be drawn from the history of field systems was not that landholding progressed from communalism to individualism, or from individualism to communalism, but "from the vague to the definite".[88] More recently his point has been echoed by Professor D. R. Denman. Discussing the problem in the context of the medieval period as a whole, Professor

[86] Bishop, "Assarting and the Growth of the Open Fields", p. 27.
[87] Hallam, *Settlement and Society*, pp. 13-14 and 159; Sheppard, "Pre-Enclosure Field and Settlement Patterns", p. 65; Hilton, *A Medieval Society*, pp. 113-14; Dodgshon, "Infield-Outfield and the Territorial Expansion of the English Township", p. 331.
[88] Maitland, "Archaic Communities", p. 363.

Denman summarized the broad trend of landownership as passing from "an empirical order of things to a realm of permanent definition".[89] More recently still, the idea that the nature of land tenure altered during the high middle ages has been used by Professor D. C. North and Professor R. P. Thomas as a corner-stone in their proposed model of the rise of the western world. They maintain that during this period (between 900 and 1500) property rights became less and less subject to what they call "common-property uses" and more and more exclusive in character, a change which they attribute to the rapid growth of population and increasing land scarcity.[90] In so far as it is premised on the broad assumption that property rights were being clarified (as one reviewer has put it[91]), then their argument in regard to this matter is clearly analogous to that which is being presented here. The only real difference between the two is that Professor North and Professor Thomas portray early tenure as communal not shareholding in character, as a case of communal ownership rather than co-ownership.

V

Perhaps as a consequence of their rather singular character, the origin of sub-divided fields has, in the past, been sought in the operation of a single process. However, the foregoing discussion has tried to show that evidence is available to support any one of three possible interpretations: the gradualist, partible inheritance and shareholding interpretations. Even accepting that the partible inheritance interpretation may only be a special instance of the more general shareholding interpretation, this still leaves us with two separate explanations. Significantly, Dr. Baker and Mr. Butlin appear to have reached a similar conclusion, for in their recent review of the problem they endorsed both the gradualist and partible inheritance interpretations as being viable.[92] Their discussion, however, does little to dispel the disquiet which must surely arise when one tries to argue that a very distinct pattern of agrarian organization was formed in at least two ways by the action of two unrelated processes. In my opinion, the merit in presenting the

---

[89] D. R. Denman, *The Origins of Ownership* (London, 1958), p. 107.

[90] D. C. North and R. P. Thomas, *The Rise of the Western World: A New Economic History* (Cambridge, 1973), pp. 19-24; D. C. North and R. P. Thomas, "The Rise and Fall of the Manorial System: a Theoretical Model", *Jl. Econ. Hist.*, xxxi (1971), pp. 777-803.

[91] Review by J. Hicks in *Econ. Hist. Rev.*, 2nd ser., xxvii (1974), pp. 692-4.

[92] Baker and Butlin (eds.), *Studies of Field Systems in the British Isles*, "Conclusion", pp. 635-41.

gradualist and shareholding interpretations as the operative processes is that although, outwardly, they appear independent of each other, at root they can be integrated to form a single, compound interpretation.

As a first step in laying the foundations of this compound interpretation, an assumption must be made as to whether the sub-divided fields which we see in the latter part of the medieval period developed out of a nucleus which, from the beginning, was sub-divided in character, or whether they form a pattern which somehow developed out of a nucleus of consolidated holdings. This, of course, is still very much an open question, yet selecting the one rather than the other makes quite different demands on the first stage of our interpretation.

If, for instance, we assume that from their very outset, perhaps at the point of the Anglo-Saxon conquest, the original nuclei of sub-divided fields were cast into the form of sub-divided fields, then undoubtedly we need an interpretation which specifies intermixture as part of the objectives of the original scheme of land division. Among the possibilities available, only Vinogradoff's shareholding interpretation provides a satisfactory solution. Whatever the cause of division, this alone could produce intermingled shares as the end-result. Furthermore, the suggestion that such an interpretation was rooted in notions of primitive equality would, if valid, be consistent with an explanation that supposedly operated from a very early date onwards. When the township came to expand beyond its early limits, the same principles which had served to create intermixed holdings in the first place would further ensure the equal allocation of new land as it was colonized. Even if we relax some of the demands for absolute equality on the assumption that communities must have become further and further removed from their tribal origins, the cruder notion of each landholder having only an equal amount of newly colonized land could still work to extend the area of intermixture.

Although this compound interpretation covers certain crucial aspects of the problem, it is not one which I put forward with conviction. This is because it is far from certain that sub-divided fields were always sub-divided.[93] If they were not, then the basis of our compound interpretation must account for their development out of an initial pattern or nucleus of consolidated holdings. The chief merit of the gradualist interpretation is that it covers precisely this kind of situation. However, since it operated through specific processes — the gradual colonization of land and its apportionment between landholders — it has only a limited application. As already

[93] See, for example, J. Thirsk, "Field Systems of the East Midlands", in Baker and Butlin (eds.), *op. cit.*, pp. 272-4.

made clear, in order to account for those instances where sub-division resulted from the division or re-division of entire farms or townships, we need an explanation which incorporates intermixture into the very objectives of the division. Almost inevitably we are forced to invoke shareholding again as the only convincing explanation. But, once holdings generally had already become fragmented through the piecemeal colonization of land and its equal apportionment, then we need not be dealing with a type of shareholding that had its roots in some primitive or tribal system of landholding. For an alternative explanation of how such a tenure developed, we need only consider more closely the situation produced by the gradualist interpretation. According to this interpretation, the natural growth of the township could extend and fragment the property rights of each holding or share unit over a variety of different types of land. Understandably, therefore, when the need arose to re-divide the township, or to divide what had previously been a consolidated unit, it was only to be expected that communities should seek to preserve what had become the accepted pattern of holding layout and composition. In this way holdings may have become established in a *de jure* as well as *de facto* sense as shares which could embrace equally a portion of all the different types of land within the township. A lawyer like Bracton probably played a vital rôle in this process since, by defining equal shares of a township as equal in both extent and value and by laying down the procedure by which their division could be executed, he was, as in other matters, trying to impose a uniformity of principle and practice with regard to this aspect of land law. It must be appreciated that this did not constitute a change in the type of land tenure. Rather should it be seen as an attempt, during a moment of reorganization in the layout of a township or farm, to remove the ambiguity or vagueness which had possibly surrounded the earlier definition of land unit shares. After all, as Professor North and Professor Thomas have so forcibly reasoned, it was only when land started to become scarce that early communities or their lords may have bothered themselves with tightening their definition of property rights.[94] However, once land unit shares had become established in a *de jure* sense as equal in both extent and value, then what began as a by-product of piecemeal colonization was able to become a force of its own, helping partible inheritance to create sub-divided fields in medieval Kent and Wales, or share-tenancy to produce runrig in eighteenth-century Scotland.

[94] North and Thomas, *op. cit.*, p. 19.

VI

If one has to distil an overall conclusion from the foregoing discussion, it is that, in so far as it relates to the development of sub-divided fields, land law may have altered in a direction which has not generally been recognized by previous writers on the problem. Stated briefly, the direction of change was towards greater and greater precision in the definition of what each land unit share or tenement actually comprised. Their definition in some townships as shares that were equal in both extent and value possibly depicts one stage in this move towards greater precision. The eventual total abandonment of a land unit system of assessment in favour of the detailed description of what each person's holding contained in terms of its strips and their acreages, a change-over which finally anchored holdings to a specific layout within the system, may mark another. If one is seeking a simple organizing principle beside which to place the differences that existed between sub-divided fields in the various parts of Britain, then perhaps it should be seen as this trend "from the vague to the definite", rather than some basic evolutionary scheme which distinguishes between fundamentally different *types* of tenure and then attaches the more primitive to the field systems of the Celtic fringe and the more advanced to the field systems of lowland England.

2. Horse hauling: A revolution in vehicle transport in twelfth- and thirteenth-century England

JOHN LANGDON

INTEREST IN TECHNOLOGICAL DEVELOPMENTS IN MEDIEVAL ENGLAND has quickened in recent years.[1] Part of this is undoubtedly in reaction to the frequently expressed view that significant improvements in medieval technology were virtually non-existent, especially after the first millennium A.D.[2] This has been stressed in the case of agricultural production, where it has been shown that grain yields in England at least had a tendency to decline over much of the period, in particular during the thirteenth and early fourteenth centuries.[3] As a result, a position was supposedly being reached of a society that was not able to feed itself adequately, a situation that technical developments apparently did little to alleviate. The reasons put forward for this critical stagnation in technological matters are varied, ranging from the view that medieval man simply lacked a sufficient fund of technical ideas to perhaps the most commonly held view that capital investment in medieval times was generally so low as to allow virtually no new technical input.[4]

What has given credence to these ideas for the English case is that it has been very difficult to find incontrovertible examples of technological advance that had any wide-ranging effects upon the

* I would like to thank Dr. Christopher Dyer for his helpful criticisms of an earlier draft of this paper and for all his encouragement over recent years. Professor R. H. C. Davis also kindly made several useful comments and recommendations.

[1] Particularly in the agricultural sphere: for example, B. M. S. Campbell, "Agricultural Progress in Medieval England: Some Evidence from Eastern Norfolk", *Econ. Hist. Rev.*, 2nd ser., xxxvi (1983); R. H. Britnell, "Agricultural Technology and the Margin of Cultivation in the Fourteenth Century", *Econ. Hist. Rev.*, 2nd ser., xxx (1977); C. Dyer, *Warwickshire Farming 1349–c.1520: Preparations for Agricultural Revolution* (Dugdale Soc. Occasional Papers, no. 27, Warwick, 1981).

[2] M. M. Postan in 1950, for instance, characterized technical development as being "remarkably static for the whole of the Middle Ages": M. M. Postan, "The Economic Foundations of Medieval Society", in his *Essays on Medieval Agriculture and General Problems of the Medieval Economy* (Cambridge, 1973), p. 17; see also his "Why was Science Backward in the Middle Ages?", *ibid.*, p. 84. For similar views concerning agricultural technology specifically, see M. M. Postan, *The Medieval Economy and Society* (Harmondsworth, 1975), p. 49; J. Z. Titow, *English Rural Society, 1200–1350* (London, 1969), pp. 37, 50; G. E. Fussell, "Social Change but Static Technology: Rural England in the Fourteenth Century", *Hist. Studies*, i (1968), pp. 23-32.

[3] See especially J. Z. Titow, *Winchester Yields* (Cambridge, 1972), pp. 12-29.

[4] Postan, *Medieval Economy and Society*, pp. 45-9; R. Brenner, "The Agrarian Roots of European Capitalism", *Past and Present*, no. 97 (Nov. 1982), pp. 34-6.

society of the time, particularly during the post-Conquest period.[5]
Recent work has qualified this pessimistic view somewhat by indicating that some regions in Europe and England did respond to population pressure during the period with a significant raising of
agricultural production through improved techniques.[6] But these
areas were few and far between, and their progressiveness seemingly
depended on very special sets of conditions that effectively excluded
most of medieval society.[7] As a result, technical progress at the time
can at best be seen as patchy or applicable only to certain sectors of
the medieval populace.[8]

This view of the general failure of medieval technology to make
much impact upon English society in the centuries following the
Conquest has also spread to the innovation considered in this article:
the introduction of horses as replacements for oxen in draught work.
Lynn White Jr. claimed that this was one of the cornerstones of an
agricultural revolution that supposedly swept through Europe during
the early middle ages.[9] Here the speed and stamina of the horse led
to quicker ploughing and hauling; indeed, it has been claimed that
the animal could do twice as much work in a day as an ox.[10] Despite
these theoretical advantages, however, horses were adopted less than
wholeheartedly by farmers in medieval England. Walter of Henley,
for example, writing towards the end of the thirteenth century,
clearly recommended oxen for most English farms at this time,[11] and
medieval demesne accounts for the country show oxen dominating as
draught animals over horses to the end of the fourteenth century and
beyond.[12] Although there is evidence that the English peasantry
used horses to a much greater degree than on demesnes, the adoption

[5] Even the wind- or water-powered mill, the best known of medieval innovations,
is often thought to have contributed relatively little in the way of material benefit to
medieval society: see, for example, S. Thrupp, "Medieval Industry", in C. M. Cipolla
(ed.), *The Middle Ages* (The Fontana Economic History of Europe, i, London, 1972),
esp. p. 234.
[6] Campbell, "Agricultural Progress in Medieval England", *passim*; B. H. Slicher
van Bath, *The Agrarian History of Western Europe, A.D. 500-1850* (London, 1963), pp.
175-80, 240-3; P. F. Brandon, "Demesne Arable Farming in Coastal Sussex during
the Middle Ages", *Agric. Hist. Rev.*, xix (1971), esp. pp. 123-9.
[7] Most of these areas displayed a high degree of personal freedom among the
peasant tenantry, flexible field systems and easy access to urban centres: see, for
example, Campbell, "Agricultural Progress in Medieval England", p. 43.
[8] See, for example, Postan, "Why was Science Backward in the Middle Ages?", p.
85.
[9] Lynn White Jr., *Medieval Technology and Social Change* (Oxford, 1962), pp. 57-
69.
[10] Lynn White Jr., "The Expansion of Technology, 500-1500", in Cipolla (ed.),
Middle Ages, p. 151.
[11] Mainly for economic reasons: *Walter of Henley*, ed. D. Oschinsky (Oxford,
1971), p. 319; see also J. Langdon, "The Economics of Horses and Oxen in Medieval
England", *Agric. Hist. Rev.*, xxx (1982), *passim*.
[12] J. Langdon, "Horses, Oxen and Technological Innovation: The Use of Draught
Animals in English Farming from 1066 to 1500" (Univ. of Birmingham Ph. D. thesis,
1983), esp. 49-59, 117-33.

of horses was not ovewhelming even here.[13] Ploughing in particular was slow to be affected by the use of horses, and, as it was in this task that the majority of draught animals was employed, it is not surprising that the proportion of horses found among medieval farmers' draught animals showed only a gradual change over the period.[14]

In one respect, however, the use of horses did have a much more profound and rapid effect. This was in relation to hauling — that is, the drawing of goods by vehicle. Until the medieval period the use of horses for everyday hauling took a distant second place to that performed by oxen. In the centuries following the millennium, however, the incidence of horse hauling increased dramatically. This distinct change in the mode of medieval haulage has been previously recognized,[15] but the timing of it and more particularly its magnitude have never been precisely determined. As transport is a key element of all but the most primitive of economies, it may be here that a significant technical contribution to medieval society may be found. Accordingly this article will examine the rise of horse hauling in England during the period of its most apparent increase, namely the twelfth and thirteenth centuries. In particular, we shall attempt to determine when most of the increase in horse hauling in England took place, its magnitude, the reasons for its adoption, and the likely effects that it had on contemporary English society. Because of the nature of the records, these enquiries will be approached mainly from the point of view of farming. Relevant documents relating to road transport do exist and will be referred to from time to time, but the rural records are the best for obtaining a comprehensive and consistent view of the problem, including comparisons over time.

I

The use of horses for hauling was not a medieval invention. Horses for drawing chariots were a feature of very early times,[16] and their use for the vehicle transportation of goods rather than people dates from at least the middle or late Roman period.[17] Horses for hauling,

---

[13] *Ibid.*, pp. 229-67.

[14] It was only in the sixteenth century that work-horses began to outnumber oxen significantly on English farms: *ibid.*, pp. 267-74.

[15] A. C. Leighton, "A Technological Consideration of Early Medieval Vehicles", *Fifth International Conference of Economic History, Leningrad 1970* (Paris, 1977), pp. 346-8; A. C. Leighton, "Eleventh Century Developments in Land Transport Technology", in *The Eleventh Century: Acta* i (New York, 1974), pp. 20-2.

[16] Probably as early as 2000-1500 B.C.: C. Singer *et al.* (eds.), *A History of Technology*, i, *From Early Times to Fall of Ancient Empires* (Oxford, 1954), pp. 720-1; A. Burford, "Heavy Transport in Classical Antiquity", *Econ. Hist. Rev.*, 2nd ser., xiii (1960), pp. 7-8.

[17] According to illustrations of the time: A. C. Leighton, *Transport and Communication in Early Medieval Europe, A.D. 500-1500* (Newton Abbot, 1972), pp. 77, 80-1.

however, always took second place at this time to haulage by oxen or other animals such as donkeys and mules,[18] and indeed such horse haulage as there was in western Europe seems to have declined in the very early middle ages.[19] Towards the end of the first millennium A.D., however, there was a marked resurgence in the use of horses for all facets of agricultural work. The reason for this appears to have been a radical improvement to horse traction, which included not only the development of the modern harness, but also the revival of horseshoeing, the arranging of teams in single or double file, changes in the design of vehicles and other farming equipment, and possible improvements in horse breeding.[20] The cumulative effect of these developments was to alter markedly the appearance and effectiveness of horse traction. (See Plate 1.) Compared to ancient times, when little more than half a ton was considered the maximum load that a pair of horses or other animals could reasonably haul,[21] it was alleged by the fourteenth century that a *single* horse could pull well over a ton on his own.[22] The ability of horses to compete with oxen as hauling beasts was thus greatly improved, although with some qualifications. Broadly speaking, horses were quicker than oxen and could work a longer day and in smaller teams. Against this, they were more costly to keep and were suspect in certain hauling situations, such as over heavy ground or up steep hills, where horses tended to break down while oxen were able to plod on. These opposing sets of attributes and disabilities — to be discussed in more detail later — meant that the use of horses for hauling was not a foregone conclusion, even with the substantial improvements to horse traction that were a feature of the medieval period. By the end of the eleventh century, nevertheless, the evidence suggests that the horse was already gaining considerable ground as a hauling animal in much of Europe.[23]

In England, however, this initial phase came later. All the signs point to the fact that haulage in the country was virtually only performed by oxen before the year 1100 and probably for a number

---

[18] Burford, "Heavy Transport in Classical Antiquity", esp. pp. 7-13; Leighton, *Transport and Communication in Early Medieval Europe*, pp. 65, 79-80.
[19] Leighton, "Technological Consideration of Early Medieval Vehicles", pp. 344-5.
[20] Each of these developments plus others, such as whippletrees, are discussed in Langdon, "Horses, Oxen and Technological Innovation", pp. 9-20.
[21] According to the Theodosian Code of 438 A.D.: R. Lefebvre des Noëttes, *L'attelage et le cheval de selle à travers les âges* (Paris, 1931), pp. 157-8; Leighton, *Transport and Communication in Early Medieval Europe*, p. 72. The degree of trust that should be attached to the code is in dispute, but at least two other sources from antiquity support it: Burford, "Heavy Transport in Classical Antiquity", pp. 4-5.
[22] As a Writtle in Essex: see p. 59 below.
[25] Leighton, "Eleventh Century Developments in Land Transport Technology", pp. 20-2; Leighton, "Technological Consideration of Early Medieval Vehicles", pp. 347-8.

1. Three-horse cart, *circa* 1340, showing modern elements of horse traction, including tandem harnessing, horse-collars, traces, cart-saddle, double-shafted vehicle and horseshoes: Luttrell Psalter, Brit. Lib., Add. MS. 42130, fo. 162.

By permission of the British Library

of years after that. An early eleventh-century Anglo-Saxon calendar shows a two-wheeled cart near which stand two oxen still in their yoke, resting before being hitched up to the cart again. (See Plate 2.) No other such definite indications are evident from the Anglo-Saxon period, but at Domesday more references to ox haulage are found. Thus, on the demesne at Offenham, Littleton and Bretforton in Worcestershire, it is stated that "there are oxen for one plough, but they draw stone to the church".[24] An even better set of references from the survey relates to the Cheshire salt towns of Nantwich, Middlewich and Northwich. Here hauling by oxen is mentioned several times, as at Northwich, where it was noted that "a man who brought a cart with two or more oxen from another shire paid four pence in toll".[25]

References to ox haulage continue into the twelfth century. Thus at Burton-on-Trent, circa 1114-18, the demesne there employed four oxen for hauling wood and four more for hauling lime. Later in the century it is recorded at Hampton Lucy (Warwickshire), circa 1170, that part of the services owed by the keepers of the oxen (bovarii) was to haul material for the demesne ploughs with the lord's plaustrum and oxen. The same predilection for ox haulage is evident at the peasant level. Thus a certain Godwin, holding half a hide at Nettleton (Wiltshire) in 1189, owed four oxen to carry a load (carriatam) of hay as part of his labour services. Similarly wine hauling services involving the use of oxen were owed by well-to-do tenants at several Durham villages in 1183.[26] All these references to ox hauling occur in the north and west of the country. We are less certain about the south and especially the east at this time, a crucial point because the use of horses was always to be greater here than elsewhere, perhaps because of contacts with the Continent. It may be that the employment of the animals for hauling in this area significantly pre-dated that for other parts of the country. Nevertheless, as we shall see, references to vehicles that we associate with ox hauling are also found in the east during the twelfth century, and the same is implied in the Domesday survey, where the level of horses on East Anglian demesnes is so low that the extensive use of

[24] Domesday Book, 4 vols. (Record Commission, London, 1783-1816), i, fo. 175b.
[25] Ibid., fo. 268; see also English Historical Documents, ii, 1042-1189, ed. D. C. Douglas, 2nd edn. (Oxford, 1961), p. 871.
[26] The Burton Abbey Twelfth Century Surveys, ed. C. G. O. Bridgeman (William Salt Archaeol. Soc., Historical Collections [for 1916], Stafford, 1918), p. 212; The Red Book of Worcester, ed. M. Hollings, 4 vols. (Worcs. Hist. Soc., Worcester, 1934-50), iii, p. 277; Liber Henrici de Soliaco abbatis Glastoniensis, ed. J. E. Jackson (Roxburghe Club, London, 1882), p. 103; Boldon Buke: A Survey of the Possessions of the See of Durham, 1183, ed. W. Greenwell (Surtees Soc., xxv, Durham, 1852), pp. 2 (bis), 6, 18, 20, 27 (bis), 31 (bis), 32, 36. Ploughing and hauling by oxen was also a regular event in twelfth-century Wales according to Giraldus Cambrensis, "Descriptio Kambriae", in his Opera (Rolls ser., London, 1861-91), vi, p. 259.

2. Cart and oxen for drawing wood, from an Anglo-Saxon calendar from the first half of the eleventh century: Brit. Lib., Cott. MS. Tib. B.V (pt. 1), fo. 6ʳ. The same scene is shown in a slightly different form in Cott. MS. Jul. A.VI, also from the early eleventh century.

By permission of the British Library

the animals for hauling in this part of England at the time seems very unlikely.[27]

Instead, when the Domesday material does indicate the employment of horses for carrying, it is solely in regard to their function as pack-animals. Thus, in the case of the Cheshire salt towns referred to above, in addition to the hauling by oxen, it was specified that men who loaded up their horses so much as to break their backs paid a fine of 2s. if caught within a league of the town. Similarly, in Bedfordshire, pack-horses (*sumarii*) are mentioned in relation to carrying services owed to the queen at Leighton Buzzard, Luton and Houghton Regis,[28] while in Worcestershire and Warwickshire the renders of several mills and salt-works are expressed in pack-loads (*summae*) of corn or salt.[29] The use of horses for carrying is also indicated in the earlier *Rectitudines singularum personarum*, where the *gebur*, beekeeper and swineherd were all supposed to supply a horse to perform carrying services, again almost certainly as a pack-animal.[30] If any hauling by horses was being performed at all before the end of the eleventh century, it was probably limited to light passenger transport.[31]

In any event, the first possible reference to horse hauling for more arduous duties in medieval England does not occur until the year 1100, when it is stated that the body of William Rufus was brought by peasants to Winchester in a horse-drawn conveyance (*rheda caballaria*), possibly owned by the peasants themselves.[32] Horses for general goods transportation are not definitely recorded until sometime later. Thus, in 1155, a *carectarius equus*, or cart-horse, is listed among the stock on the St. Paul's demesne at Sandon in Hertfordshire, and cart-loads (*caretate*) of barley and hay, presumably horse-hauled from the vehicle indicated (see below), are mentioned in 1141

[27] For example, well over a third of demesnes in Norfolk, Suffolk, Essex and Cambridgeshire had no working horses at all, while on the rest such horses as there were seem only to have been used for harrowing: Langdon, "Horses, Oxen and Technological Innovation", pp. 43-5.

[28] *Domesday Book*, i, fo. 268.

[29] *Ibid.*, fos. 173b, 174, 175, 176b (*quater*), 178, 238, 239, 243 (*ter*), 243b, 244. A few examples are found in other counties: for example, Herefordshire (fo. 179b) and Shropshire (fos. 255b, 260).

[30] In the beekeeper's case, for instance, the carrying service is specifically referred to as a *summagium*, the usual term for carrying by pack-animals: F. Liebermann, *Die Gesetze der Angelsachsen*, 3 vols. (Halle, 1903-16), i, pp. 446-9. The *gebur* was a form of landed peasant probably equivalent to the later villein.

[31] As in Ireland, where light, horse-hauled vehicles are in evidence from the sixth to the eight centuries: Leighton, "Technological Consideration of Early Medieval Vehicles", p. 345; Leighton, *Transport and Communication in Early Medieval Europe*, p. 111. One of these Irish vehicles — a two-horse chariot — was brought briefly to Cornwall in the early sixth century, when St. Samson of Dol crossed the Cornish peninsula with it on his way to Brittany: *The Life of St. Samson of Dol*, ed. T. Taylor (London, 1925), pp. 48-9.

[32] William of Malmesbury, *De gestis regum Anglorum*, 2 vols. (Rolls ser., London, 1887-9), ii, p. 379.

on the demesne at Ardeley in the same county.[33] Towards the end
of the twelfth century references to horse hauling are definitely on
the increase. Thus, a grant to the nuns at Yedingham in Yorkshire,
1185-95, gave them permission to take a horse and cart every year
to fetch timber for their ploughs from a wood in Staindale. Similarly
a mixed hauling team of two oxen and two horses was used to cart
turves or peat at "Fuelesholme" near Fraisthorpe, Yorkshire, also
circa 1185-95.[34] Alexander Neckam also mentions horses for hauling
and ploughing as a common occurrence in England at this time.[35]

This trickle of references to horses hauling in the twelfth century
becomes a flood in the thirteenth. It may be argued that a large part
of this was due to the steadily improving standards of record-keeping
in the latter century, but it is also evident that references to horse
hauling were multiplying out of all proportion to the increase in
documentation. A measure of this can be discerned in the growth in
the number of horses known as *equi carectarii*, or cart-horses. From
a sample of 4,294 demesne horses recorded during the period 1250-
1320, 591 (or 14 per cent) were listed as such, and this proportion
is probably a substantial underestimate since many demesne horses
not specifically given as "cart-horses" were nonetheless definitely
used for hauling.[36] A marked increase in the use of horses for hauling
is also indicated for the peasantry at this time, where horses for
hauling are frequently alluded to in the description of carrying
services recorded in surveys, extents or custumals. Thus, at Abbots
Ripton (Huntingdonshire), each virgate holder in 1252 was to find a
cart with one or two horses (*unam carrectam cum equo vel duobus*) for
carrying hay or corn, while at Crawley (Hampshire), *circa* 1280, half-
virgate and other tenants were each to carry hay "with horse and
cart" (*cum equo et carecta*), probably of a type similar to that shown
in Plate 3. Even peasants with very small holdings were thought
likely to have horses and carts at this time, as at Colne in Somersham
(Huntingdonshire) in 1251, where cottagers holding five acres apiece
were each expected to perform carrying services if they had a cart
and horse (*carectam et equum*). In a few instances we can see the actual
process of changing to horse haulage taking place. Thus, at Pilton
(Somerset) in 1260 Robert Hostarius, holding a half-virgate, was
charged with carrying the lord's hay and corn for six days with a cart
(*carecta*; invariably horse-hauled in the records, as we shall see). The
custumal, however, goes on to say that Simon, Robert's predecessor,

[33] *Domesday of St. Paul's of the Year 1222*, ed. W. H. Hale (Camden Soc., old ser.,
lxix, London, 1858), pp. 134, 136.
[34] *Early Yorkshire Charters*, ed. W. Farrar, 3 vols. (Edinburgh, 1914-16), i, p. 314,
and ii, p. 154.
[35] Alexander Neckam, *De naturis rerum*, ed. T. Wright (Rolls ser., London, 1863),
p. 259 (late twelfth century).
[36] Langdon, "Horses, Oxen and Technological Innovation", pp. 128-9.

had been accustomed to find three oxen and half a wain (*plaustrum*) for the same service. The indication is that Robert had changed his mode of hauling from ox-drawn wain to horse-hauled cart.[37]

It should not be thought that hauling by oxen was being eradicated completely at this time, however, since there are frequent signs that it still commanded a certain popularity, both on demesnes and among the peasantry, even to the end of the thirteenth century and beyond. Thus, at Awre (Gloucestershire) in 1328-9 the oxen of the lord were engaged in carrying provisions to Hereford, while at Huntington (Herefordshire) in 1372-3 the reeve recorded that more ploughing services than usual were required because the lord's oxen were occupied in carrying wood and stone to the castle. Similarly, a certain Sampson at Stoke sub Hamdon (Somerset) in 1251 was required to find a *carrus* and four oxen to haul the lord's hay, corn and wood, while Adam Attehulle of Brockthorpe (Gloucestershire), *circa* 1266-7, who held a virgate of 64 acres, had to perform carrying services at the harvest with a *plaustrum*, six oxen and two men.[38]

II

The overriding impression, then, is that horses were increasingly taking over hauling from oxen in medieval England, beginning sometime in the twelfth century and continuing strongly into the thirteenth, but that this transformation, although apparently sizeable, was not total. Given that there was a substantial change to horse hauling during the period, how do we measure it? One way might be to simply add up all the references found for horse hauling over the period and compare them to those for ox hauling. For instance, the presence of "cart-horses" (*equi carectarii*) could be used as an indicator of horse hauling, especially on demesnes. We also have direct references of the type given above, and often the fact of horse hauling can be inferred by the presence of horse gear, such as traces and halters, which is often recorded alongside the farm vehicles. But even here we are faced with problems of underassessment, since, despite these clues, we are often still left without any certain indication that horses were in fact used for hauling on a manor,

---

[37] *Cartularium monasterii de Rameseia*, ed. W. H. Hart and P. A. Lyons, 3 vols. (Rolls ser., London, 1884-93), i, p. 324; N. S. B. and E. C. Gras, *The Economic and Social History of an English Village* (Harvard, 1930), p. 232; Brit. Lib., Cott. MS. Claud. C.XI, fo. 100; *Rentalia et custumaria Michaelis de Ambresbury, 1235-1252, et Rogeri de Ford, 1252-1261, abbatum monasterii beatae Mariae Glastoniae*, ed. C. J. Elton (Somerset Rec. Soc., v, Taunton, 1891), p. 210.

[38] Gloucestershire Record Office, D421/M4; P.R.O., S.C. 6/861/1; *Two Registers Formerly Belonging to the Family of Beauchamp of Hatch*, ed. H. C. Maxwell-Lyte (Somerset Rec. Soc., xxxv, Taunton, 1920), p. 8; *Historia et cartularium monasterii Sancti Petri Gloucestriae*, ed. W. H. Hart, 3 vols. (Rolls ser., London, 1863-7), iii, p. 143. For other examples of oxen hauling in the thirteenth century and afterwards, see Langdon, "Horses, Oxen and Technological Innovation", pp. 146-7, 282-4.

3. One-horse (?) cart, *circa* 1300, from an English Apocryphal scene dealing with the infancy of Christ: Bodleian Lib., MS. Selden supra 38. This cart, with its one-animal team, was probably a fairly typical medieval peasant vehicle. The beast drawing the cart is in question, however, and may have been meant to represent a small pony or even a donkey, although the latter is in direct contradiction with the documentary evidence, which indicates no other equids than horses for peasant and demesne hauling: see, for example, p. 41 above.

By permission of the Bodleian Library

although it seems clear from the number of horses about that they must have been so employed. The situation is even worse for ox hauling. Although it is suspected that ox haulage was still a significant force in farm and road transport even to the end of the thirteenth century and beyond, the number of references to the practice after 1250 is relatively small compared to that for horse hauling. The reason for this seems to have been because hauling was a very secondary occupation for oxen compared to ploughing, and as a result the former task tended to be very underrecorded in the documents. For example, in accounts, equipment for the oxen, such as yokes and bows, was most often included in the plough costs section instead of in the section for vehicle costs, thus tending to hide the fact that these oxen often hauled. The same sort of thing may also have applied to the peasant case, where references to oxen ploughing in the description of labour services are generally more frequent than those where the animal was hauling. In short, as the amount of hauling that oxen did appears to be very much underrecorded, a simple comparison of references to ox hauling compared to those for horse hauling is likely to make the former seem much less frequent than it really was.

There is, however, a method of correcting for this source of bias so as to arrive at a reasonable estimate of the relative importance of horse versus ox hauling. This is by vehicle analysis. As an examination of the examples given above will indicate, the connection between horse hauling and the vehicle known as the *carecta* (or cart) is very strong, and the same applies to the association between ox hauling and the vehicles known as *plaustra* and *carri* (or *carrae*).[39] The *plaustrum*, especially, appears to have been the equivalent of the sixteenth-century ox-hauled two-wheeled wain, and the *carrus* was probably the same.[40] In short, it seems there was a very definite split in farm hauling at this time, one side linking oxen with *plaustra*, *carri* and similar wain-like vehicles, and the other linking horses with carts (*carectae*). The distinction is so consistent over hundreds of references in the accounts, surveys and other types of documents that it appears to have applied virtually without exception,[41] and

[39] The gender of the term *carrus* tends to fluctuate from the masculine to the feminine according to the document employed, although in most cases the same type of vehicle is meant (see n. 40 below). Unless otherwise in a direct quote, the masculine form will henceforward be used.

[40] The evidence for the equation *carrus* = *plaustrum* = wain is given in Langdon, "Horses, Oxen and Technological Innovation", pp. 175-8, 306. The parallel is somewhat complicated by the simultaneous existence of a four-wheeled, horse-drawn *carrus*, which seems to have been a sumptuous travelling coach or wagon. As these vehicles, however, were in no way involved in farm work, they are easy to distinguish from the two-wheeled, ox-hauled variety and so do not affect our study.

[41] Although it is blurred in the literature by faulty translation. There is, for instance, a tendency to translate *carrus* as "cart"; similarly the term *plaustrum* is often wrongly translated as "wagon". C. A. McNeil also notes this striking documentary distinction between ox-hauled and horse-hauled vehicles, although she indicates, too,

indeed continued into the sixteenth century with the appearance in the records of horse-hauled "carts" and ox-hauled "wains".[42] The practical basis for this distinction was between light and heavy hauling. Both the *plaustrum* and the *carrus* had double the capacity of the *carecta*, as indicated in several carrying service formulae.[43] Despite their greater stamina in other respects, it appears that horses were generally incapable of pulling the heavy loads in these larger two-wheeled vehicles, and so oxen were used because they were physically more suited to the slow-moving situations that hauling these larger vehicles often entailed, particularly in heavy soils or over rough, hilly terrain.[44]

In any case, this ability to distinguish between horse-hauled and ox-hauled vehicles according to terminology is very convenient for our purpose. We can now gain some impression of the extent of horse hauling versus ox hauling across medieval England by simply noting the distribution of the various vehicle types associated with each animal. Manorial accounts in particular are very useful in dealing with demesne vehicles, especially during the late thirteenth and early fourteenth centuries when a great many demesnes were being farmed directly by their lords. Thus accounts for this period generally have a section dealing with vehicle expenses, and here the various carts and wains on the demesne are recorded in relation to their repair or purchase costs, although the number of each type of vehicle is seldom given. Occasionally the demesne vehicles are listed elsewhere in the accounts, especially among the demesne equipment or "dead stock" (*staurum mortuum*) sometimes included at the end, but it is from the vehicle costs sections that the bulk of information for this study was obtained. Accordingly, a sample of 509 demesnes having accounts with vehicle costs detailed enough to determine the types of vehicles used was obtained for the period 1250-1320. The frequency with which each vehicle type occurred is shown in Table 1.

As can be seen, the most popular type of vehicle was the *carecta*

(*n. 41 cont.*)
that it may not have applied on the Continent, where horse-hauled, four-wheeled *plaustra* are occasionally found: C. A. McNeil, "Technological Developments in Wheeled Vehicles in Europe, from Prehistory to the Sixteenth Century" (Univ. of Edinburgh Ph.D. thesis, 1978), p. 57, also plate 23.

[42] For example, Langdon, "Horses, Oxen and Technological Innovation", p. 393, nn. 98-9.

[43] As at Tillingham (Essex) in 1222, where customary tenants had to haul "one *plaustrum* or two *carectae* of firewood" as part of their labour services: *Domesday of St. Paul's of the Year 1222*, p. 62. For other references equating one *plaustrum* or one *carrus* to two *carectae*, see *ibid.*, p. 94; *Rentalia et custumaria . . . Glastoniae*, pp. 65, 67, 68, 140, 210; *Red Book of Worcester*, i, p. 14, and ii, p. 194; *Historia et cartularium . . . Gloucestriae*, iii, p. 62.

[44] William Marshall, for instance, noted that oxen were still considered necessary for hauling in hilly parts of Yorkshire during the eighteenth century: William Marshall, *The Rural Economy of Yorkshire*, 2nd edn., 2 vols. (London, 1796), i, pp. 246-9.

or cart, being found on nearly 90 per cent of demesnes for which vehicle details are available. As we have already indicated, it was invariably horse-hauled. Next came the ox-hauled *plaustrum* and *carrus*, with the remaining vehicle types only accounting for a small proportion of the total number of references. Of these five remaining types, the *curtena* was ox-hauled, while the *biga* and *tumberellus* (tumbrel) were horse-hauled, both the latter being small vehicles of

TABLE 1

FREQUENCY OF VEHICLE TYPES ON ENGLISH DEMESNES 1250-1320*

Type of vehicle	Number of demesnes	Percentage of all 509 demesnes with vehicle references
Carecta	453	89·0
Plaustrum	102	20·0
Carrus	43	8·4
Curtena	8	1·6
Tumberellus	7	1·4
Biga	6	1·2
Quadriga	2	0·4
Curta	2	0·4

* Note and sources: As given in Langdon, "Horses, Oxen and Technological Innovation: The Use of Draught Animals in English Farming from 1066 to 1500" (Univ. of Birmingham Ph.D. thesis, 1983), appendix C pt. 1, pp. 421-38. As many demesnes had more than one type of vehicle, the total number of vehicle references exceeds the number of demesnes (and hence the percentages add up to more than 100).

TABLE 2

FREQUENCY OF HORSE-HAULED VERSUS OX-HAULED VEHICLES ON ENGLISH DEMESNES BY REGION 1250-1320*

	Number of demesnes	Percentage of demesnes with horse-hauled vehicles	Percentage of demesnes with ox-hauled vehicles
East Anglia	98	100·0	0·0
Home Counties	93	100·0	6·5
The South	111	90·1	25·2
The South-West	39	41·0	87·2
East Midlands	70	98·6	11·4
West Midlands	40	92·5	62·5
The North	54	79·6	77·8

* Notes and sources: Sources as in Table 1, with the exception that this table excludes three demesnes which could not be placed in any particular region, and one which had no vehicles that could be specifically classified as horse- or ox-hauled.

Each region is composed of the following counties: *East Anglia*: Norfolk, Suffolk, Essex, Cambridgeshire; *Home Counties*: Surrey, Middlesex, Hertfordshire, Bedford-shire, Buckinghamshire, Oxfordshire, Berkshire; *The South*: Kent, Sussex, Hampshire, Wiltshire; *The South-West*: Dorset, Somerset, Devon, Cornwall; *East Midlands*: Huntingdonshire, Northamptonshire, Rutland, Leicestershire, Nottinghamshire, Lincolnshire; *West Midlands*: Warwickshire, Worcestershire, Gloucestershire, Hereford-shire, Shropshire, Staffordshire, Cheshire, Derbyshire; *The North*: Lancashire, Westmorland, Cumberland, Northumberland, Durham, Yorkshire.

a size similar to the *carecta*. Evidence as to which animal, horse or ox, drew the *quadriga* and *curta* is ambiguous or lacking altogether.[45]

In short, we have six types of vehicles for which the draught animal employed can be ascertained, three horse-hauled and three ox-hauled. When only these types are considered, horse-hauled vehicles (*carecta, tumberellus* or *biga*) were found on 90·0 per cent of demesnes, and ox-hauled vehicles (*plaustrum, carrus* or *curtena*) on 28·5 per cent of demesnes with 18·5 per cent of demesnes having both types. The distribution of these horse-hauled and ox-hauled vehicles is shown in Maps 1 and 2. The former were found virtually countrywide, but their main concentration was in the south and especially the east. In contrast, demesnes with ox-hauled vehicles were situated much more to the north and west, with only a scattering of demesnes in Kent, Surrey and Sussex breaking this rule. The geographical domination of horse-hauled vehicles, in fact, is even more marked than Map 1 indicates, since the tailing off of horse-hauled vehicles towards the north and west is exaggerated by the relative scarcity of manorial accounts in these areas. When the data are arranged by region, as in Table 2, the widespread domination of horse- over ox-hauled vehicles becomes even clearer. Thus, as a region, only the south-west had a greater incidence of ox-hauled vehicles over those drawn by horses, although the north had at least a rough parity between both types. All the other regions showed horse hauling as the pre-dominating mode of vehicle transport, especially in East Anglia, the Home Counties and the east midlands.

What does all this tell us about demesne hauling across the country as a whole? First of all, from this sample, 71·5 per cent of demesnes (100 − 28·5) seemingly employed only horses for hauling. If we assume that the average amount of hauling per demesne in terms of weight of goods transported varied little from region to region,[46] then at least 71·5 per cent of demesne farm hauling across the country was carried out by horses. We have as well a further 18·5 per cent of demesnes that used both horses and oxen for hauling, particularly in the north and the west midlands. If we assume that horses did at least half of the hauling on these demesnes (a reasonable assumption, since the hauling oxen were almost always expected to plough as well, while many of the horses did carting full-time), then the proportion of demesne haulage performed by horses overall would rise to a minimum of $71·5 + (18·5 \div 2) = 80·8$ per cent.

From these figures it would appear that horses performed some-

---

[45] For the evidence relating to these five minority vehicles, see Langdon, "Horses, Oxen and Technological Innovation", pp. 93-4, 178-9, 308-9.

[46] This may be a questionable assumption, especially given that demesnes tended to vary in average size from region to region. To a large extent, however, these variations are evened out by the 1377 poll tax correction procedure below.

MAP 1
DEMESNE HORSE-HAULED VEHICLES 1250-1320

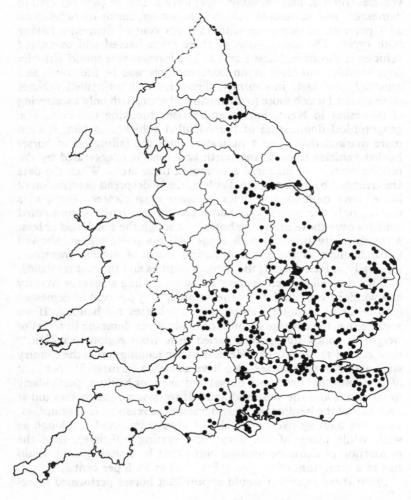

• location of demesnes with horse-hauled vehicles

MAP 2

DEMESNE OX-HAULED VEHICLES 1250-1320

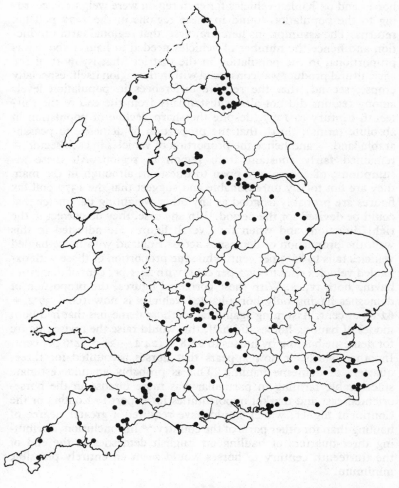

• location of demesnes with ox-hauled vehicles

thing like four-fifths of all demesne hauling in England by the end
of the thirteenth century. However, because ox hauling was most
prevalent in the least documented areas, there is a distinct possibility
that we are seriously underestimating the proportion of hauling
carried out by these animals. To attempt to determine how much
effect this geographical distortion would have, the proportions of
horse- and ox-hauled vehicles for each region were weighted according to the population found in these regions in the 1377 poll tax
returns. The assumptions here are, first, that regional farm production and hence the number of vehicles needed to haul it about was
proportional to the population in the district (that is, most of the
agricultural product was consumed within the region itself, especially
crops); second, that the relative differences in population levels
among regions did not alter substantially from the end of the thirteenth century to 1377 (despite the sharp decline of population in
absolute terms); third, that the proportion of demesne to peasant
arable land — and hence the proportion of vehicles in each sector —
remained fairly constant from region to region. All these assumptions, of course, are open to question, although in the main
they are not totally unreasonable and suggest that the 1377 poll tax
figures are probably as good as any other weighting parameter that
could be devised for the period.[47] In any case, they do correct in the
right direction, and when the overall figures are adjusted in this
way, the proportion of demesnes across England with horse-hauled
vehicles falls to 86·9 per cent, while the proportion of those with ox-
hauled vehicles rises to 37·2 per cent, with 24·1 per cent of demesnes
having both types. With these corrected figures, the proportion of
demesnes having only horse-hauled vehicles is now 100 − 37·2 =
62·8 per cent. Assuming again that on those demesnes that had both
modes of hauling horses did half, this would raise the revised figure
for demesne hauling by horses to 62·8 + (24·1 ÷ 2) = 74·9 per cent.
In other words, it now appears that horses accounted for three-
quarters of demesne hauling. This is probably an underestimate
since arable farming in particular was more intense in the horse-
oriented east and market opportunities for export to London or the
Continent higher, which would have required a greater degree of
hauling than for other parts of the country.[48] In conclusion, attribut-
ing three-quarters of hauling on English demesnes at the end of
the thirteenth century to horses would seem an entirely plausible
minimum.

[47] As discussed in Langdon, "Horses, Oxen and Technological Innovation", pp.
122-3. The same passage also outlines the method of calculation.
[48] To some extent this is balanced by the somewhat greater access to sea and river
transport that these eastern regions enjoyed, in particular counties such as Norfolk;
but even so hauling seems to have been more developed here.

III

To assess the relative levels of horse and ox hauling in the peasant sector, we must turn to other documentary sources. Records such as court rolls and detailed lay subsidy returns occasionally itemize peasant vehicles, but the most useful documents for comparative purposes are surveys, extents and custumals. Here references to peasant vehicles often occur in regard to carrying services, for which a number of examples have already been given. These surveys, extents and custumals are not as numerous as the accounts, but they do cover most of the two centuries which we are concerned with in this article. Thus the progression of the peasantry towards horse hauling is easily observable in these documents, as vehicle terms we associate with ox hauling are replaced by those relating to horse haulage. Table 3 shows the frequency which these horse and ox vehicle terms appeared by region in surveys, extents and custumals over the two centuries. As in the case of Table 2, only the vehicles *carecta*, *plaustrum*, *carrus*, *curtena*, *biga* and *tumberellus* were considered.[49].

The table shows a marked overall trend from ox to horse hauling over the two centuries. This tendency is also reflected in each of the individual regions, although there are some anomalies, only to be expected given the small number of manors making up each regional sample. In particular, the 100 per cent figure for horse-hauled vehicles in the north during the 1251-1300 period is based on only one manor and is almost certainly unrepresentative in view of the high proportion of ox-hauled vehicles on demesnes in the north at this time. (See Table 2.) The south-west too had a rather higher percentage of manors with horse-hauled peasant vehicles in the 1251-1300 period than might have been expected from demesne experience at this time.[50]

Nonetheless, the progression towards horse hauling in the country as a whole is very clear in Table 3. By the second half of the thirteenth century, horse hauling had apparently become the exclusive mode of peasant vehicle transportation in at least three regions — East Anglia, the Home Counties and the east midlands — an almost identical situation to that encountered for the demesne. In no region was there a greater incidence of ox over horse hauling for the peasantry, although the situation in the north and possibly the south-west must remain uncertain. In summary, the proportion of horse-

[49] The only other vehicle listed in the surveys, extents and custumals consulted in this study was the *quadriga*. Again, because of uncertainties as to which animal hauled it, references to this particular vehicle have been excluded from the analysis, although it figures prominently in the *Burton Abbey Twelfth Century Surveys* and *Boldon Buke* (where, in the latter case at least, it was ox-hauled).

[50] This is probably due to the complete exclusion from the sample of manors from Devon and Cornwall, the more ox-oriented area in the south-west region.

TABLE 3

FREQUENCY OF PEASANT HORSE-HAULED AND OX-HAULED VEHICLES IN ENGLAND BY REGION 1101-1300*

	1101-1150			1151-1200			1201-1250			1251-1300		
	a	b	c	a	b	c	a	b	c	a	b	c
East Anglia	—	—	—	5	40·0	80·0	9	55·6	66·7	31	100·0	0·0
Home Counties	—	—	—	—	—	—	8	87·5	37·5	6	100·0	0·0
The South	—	—	—	3	33·3	100·0	12	91·7	33·3	14	64·3	42·9
The South-West	—	—	—	6	0·0	100·0	15	35·7	100·0	7	71·4	57·1
East Midlands	10	0·0	100·0	5	60·0	40·0	12	100·0	8·3	8	100·0	0·0
West Midlands	—	—	—	10	10·0	90·0	—	—	—	19	78·9	42·1
The North	—	—	—	—	—	—	—	—	—	1	100·0	0·0
Totals	10	0·0	100·0	29	24·1	82·8	56	73·2	51·8	86	87·2	20·9

Key to Column Headings

a Number of manors
b percentage of manors with recorded peasant horse-hauled vehicles (*carecta, biga, tumberellus*)
c percentage of manors with recorded peasant ox-hauled vehicles (*plaustrum, carrus, curtena*)

* Notes and sources:
1101-1150
"Liber niger monasterii S. Petri de Burgo", in *Chronicon Petroburgense*, ed. T. Stapleton (Camden Soc., old ser., xlvii, London, 1849), pp. 159, 160 (*bis*), 161 (*bis*), 162, 162-3, 163, 164, 165.

1151-1200
Records of the Templars in England in the Twelfth Century, ed. B. A. Lees (Brit. Acad. Records of Social and Econ. Hist., ix, London, 1935), pp. 7-8, 9; *Cartularium monasterii de Rameseia*, ed. W. H. Hart and P. A. Lyons, 3 vols. (Rolls ser., London, 1884-93), iii, pp. 243, 245, 249-50, 259, 280, 300, 306, 309, 312; *Liber Henrici de Soliaco abbatis Glastoniensis*, ed. J. E. Jackson (Roxburghe Club, London, 1882), pp. 34, 77, 81, 95, 103, 107, 123, 134-5, 138, 141; *The Red Book of Worcester*, ed. M. Hollings, 4 vols. (Worcs. Hist. Soc., Worcester, 1934-50), i, p. 35; ii, pp. 148, 167-70, 233; iii, pp. 277-8, 293-4; iv, pp. 352, 367, 408.

1201-1250
Select Documents of the English Lands of the Abbey of Bec, ed. M. Chibnall (Camden Soc., 3rd ser., lxxiii, London, 1951), pp. 29, 37, 54, 70-3, 74, 85, 106; *Domesday of St. Paul's of the Year 1222*, ed. W. H. Hale (Camden Soc., old ser., lxix, London, 1858), pp. 16, 42, 47, 61-4, 72, 82, 94, 105; *Cartularium monasterii de Rameseia*, i, pp. 371-2, 385-6, 394, 416, 442-53, 476-8, 488, 493; ii, pp. 6-12, 24-5, 28-33, 43-5; *Rentalia et custumaria Michaelis de Ambresbury, 1235-1252, et Rogeri de Ford, 1252-1261, abbatum monasterii beatae Mariae Glastoniae*, ed. C. J. Elton (Somerset Rec. Soc., v, Taunton, 1891), pp. 7, 12-13, 53, 58, 61-4, 65-7, 68, 72, 82-6, 96-7, 103-6, 108, 115, 123, 125-6, 129-33, 135-40, 148-50, 153, 156-7, 165; *The Medieval Customs of the Manors of Taunton and Bradford on Tone*, ed. T. J. Hunt (Somerset Rec. Soc., lxvi, Taunton, 1962), pp. 4, 13; *Documents Relating to the Manor and Soke of Newark-on-Trent*, ed. M. W. Barley (Thoroton Soc., Rec. Ser., xvi, Nottingham, 1956), pp. 17-19, 21, 22, 23, 24, 26.

1251-1300
Brit. Lib., Cott. MS. Claud. c.xi, fos. 25-32, 36ᵛ, 39ᵛ-40, 45ᵛ-7ᵛ, 56-7ᵛ, 66ᵛ, 82ᵛ-3, 96-106, 112ʳ⁻ᵛ, 116ᵛ, 122-3, 146ʳ⁻ᵛ, 152ᵛ-3, 160, 165ᵛ, 169ᵛ, 172-3ᵛ, 177-8, 184ʳ⁻ᵛ, 193ᵛ-5ᵛ, 200-1ᵛ, 211-15ᵛ, 224-31ᵛ, 244ᵛ-5, 250, 256, 261ᵛ, 266ᵛ-7, 272ᵛ, 279ᵛ, 287ʳ⁻ᵛ, 296, 304-5ᵛ; Norfolk Record Office, Norwich, 21187 (I am indebted to Dr. J. Williamson

for supplying me with a transcript of this document); *Custumals of Battle Abbey in the Reigns of Edward I and Edward II, 1282-1312*, ed. S. R. Scargill-Bird (Camden Soc., new ser., xli, London, 1887), pp. 4-14, 28-39, 73-8, 90, 98; *Cartularium monasterii de Rameseia*, i, pp. 289-90, 298, 309-17, 324, 335-7, 346-7, 358, 467; *Custumals of the Sussex Manors of the Archbishop of Canterbury*, ed. B. C. Redwood and A. E. Wilson (Sussex Rec. Soc., lvii, Lewes, 1958), pp. 48, 108; *Thirteen Custumals of the Sussex Manors of the Bishop of Chichester and Other Documents*, ed. W. D. Peckham (Sussex Rec. Soc., xxxi, Lewes, 1925), pp. 9, 14; N. S. B. and E. C. Gras, *The Economic and Social History of an English Village* (Harvard, 1930), p. 232; *A Collection of Records and Documents Relating to the Hundred and Manor of Crondal*, ed. F. J. Baigent (Hampshire Rec. Soc., Winchester, 1891), pp. 85, 87, 91, 95, 99, 102; *Two Registers Formerly Belonging to the Family of Beauchamp of Hatch*, ed. H. C. Maxwell-Lyte (Somerset Rec. Soc., xxxv, Taunton, 1920), pp. 4-23, 36, 48; *Medieval Customs . . . of Taunton and Bradford on Tone*, p. 87; *Rentalia et custumaria . . . Glastoniae*, pp. 183-9, 210-16, 220-5; *Historia et cartularium monasterii sancti Petri Gloucestriae*, ed. W. H. Hart, 3 vols. (Rolls ser., London, 1863-7), iii, pp. 62, 116, 124, 129, 138, 143, 159-62, 167, 172, 182, 185; *Red Book of Worcester*, i, pp. 14, 45-50; ii, pp. 177, 194; iii, pp. 268, 282; iv, pp. 357, 386; *Extents of the Prebends of York*, ed. T. A. M. Bishop (Yorks. Archaeol. Soc., Rec. Ser., xciv [Miscellanea, iv], Leeds, 1937), p. 7.

In many instances the vehicles were indicated by their vehicle-load equivalents (*carectata, plaustratum, carriatus*, etc.). Where printed sources were used, only Latin terms were taken (that is, not English translations). Manors with two or more references to either horse- or ox-hauled vehicles were only counted once for that category of vehicle, while one instance of a mixed team (*Thirteen Custumals . . . of the Bishopric of Chichester*, p. 101) was not included. The villages making up the large composite manors of Newark-on-Trent and Crondal were counted as one "manor" each. The counties comprising each region are as in Table 2.

---

hauled vehicles among peasants by the end of the thirteenth century seems to have been very similar to that on the demesnes, with 87·2 per cent of manors (where peasant vehicles were indicated) having horse-hauled vehicles, 20·9 per cent having ox-hauled vehicles, and 8·1 per cent having both types. From this it would appear that horse hauling accounted for a minimum of 100 − 20·9 = 79·1 per cent of peasant hauling.[51] Assuming, as in the case of the demesne, that on manors with both modes of hauling horses did half, then this proportion would rise to 79·1 + (8·1 ÷ 2) = 83·2 per cent.

Again we are faced with the problem that the data from the surveys, extents and custumals are not evenly spread over the country. The poor showing of the northern counties is one symptom of this. We can, however, as in the demesne case, weight the data according to the 1377 poll tax returns in order to damp out as much as possible these variations in geographical representation, although it is only really worth doing for the 1251-1300 sample. Accordingly, using the same procedure and assumptions as outlined in the demesne case,[52] the overall percentage of manors with peasant horse-hauled vehicles,

[51] Assuming, in a fashion analogous to the demesne case, that the average amount of peasant hauling per manor in terms of the weight of goods carried was the same from region to region.

[52] The main difference being that, in the absence of suitable peasant figures for the north, the demesne figures from Table 2 for the region were used as a substitute.

as weighted by the 1377 poll tax population figures, drops to 85·7, while the percentage of manors with peasant ox-hauled vehicles in the same period rises to 30·2, with 15·9 per cent of manors having both types of vehicles. In this instance, horses would account for a minimum of 69·8 per cent of peasant hauling (100 − 30·2). Assuming as before that half of the peasant hauling on manors with both types of vehicles was done by horses, this proportion would rise to 69·8 + (15·9 ÷ 2) = 77·8 per cent. In other words, as in the demesne case, it appears that at least three-quarters of peasant hauling was performed by horses. Again, this may well be an underestimate. The hauling service formulae mainly applied to more substantial tenants, usually half-virgaters or better. Smallholders, who were more likely to use horses, not only for hauling but also for ploughing,[53] were called on less often for carrying services. Had they been so to the degree of their larger landholding neighbours, then the proportion of peasant horse-hauled vehicles indicated in the records may have been even greater.

IV

It is clear from all this that, for both the demesne and peasant sector, horse hauling was a very important feature of farm transport by the end of the thirteenth century. Countrywide it accounted for a good three-quarters of hauling, and in several regions — notably East Anglia, the Home Counties and the east midlands — it had replaced haulage by oxen almost completely. As indicated by Table 3, the main period of this rise in horse hauling was from the second half of the twelfth century to the first half of the thirteenth, where the proportion of manors with peasant horse-hauled vehicles rose from a quarter to nearly three-quarters. Ox hauling was a little slower to die away, and it appears that the first half of the thirteenth century was a period of transition, where more manors (25·0 per cent) had both horse- and ox-hauled peasant vehicles than in any other half-century interval. By the end of the thirteenth century, the transformation was virtually complete, with horse hauling effectively replacing ox hauling as the premier mode of vehicle transport. There are signs that the end of the thirteenth century was a peak period for horse hauling and that vehicle transport by oxen made something of a recovery in the later middle ages, but this recovery never seriously challenged the horse's new position as the country's main hauling beast.[54]

[53] For this bias shown towards horses by smallholders, see Langdon, "Horses, Oxen and Technological Innovation", ch. 4, *passim*.

[54] Another sample of accounts involving 399 demesnes from the 1350-1420 period indicates that the horse's share of vehicle transportation fell back from 75 to 65-70 per cent over the fourteenth century (as analysed from data, *ibid.*, pp. 442-53).

Indeed, horse hauling may also have displaced much of the moving of goods by pack-horse, since the trend in England over the middle ages seems to have been away from the latter mode of transportation. Sixteenth- and seventeenth-century evidence indicates that vehicle hauling was by far the most dominant form of farm transport at this time,[55] and the same was probably true of road transport.[56] In contrast, transport by pack-horse at Domesday seems to have been of considerable importance, judging by the Cheshire salt town references above, the various references to pack-loads of salt and corn, and the numbers of donkeys and mules — the archetypal pack-animals — evident in the survey.[57] A few centuries later, however, it is notable that the level of pack-animal carrying on demesnes had largely dwindled to that performed by peasants as part of their labour services.[58] Nor should this decline in pack-animal carrying be especially surprising, since it was patently less efficient than vehicle transport. Loads carried on the backs of horses, mules or donkeys could not have been much more than 200-300 lbs. per animal on average,[59] and although a somewhat greater speed may have been achieved by these pack-animals it was a poor substitute for vehicle transport in terms of the weight of goods transported. In the end, the transportation of goods by pack-animal was thought, at best, to be only half as effective as hauling by vehicle.[60] Clearly the development of a new mode of hauling that substantially cut into the speed advantage formerly held by pack-animals would have seriously detracted from the latter, and the general inference is that transportation by pack-animal continued to be known in medieval England — it was, after

(n. 54 cont.)
Because of the scarcity of relevant survey material after 1300, it is difficult to tell if the same applied to peasant hauling, but haulage by oxen was certainly a notable feature in many parts of sixteenth-century England.

[55] A preliminary survey of sixteenth- and early seventeenth-century probate inventories carried out by the author indicates that the main concentration of pack-horses and pack-horse equipment was found in the south-west with occasional references in the north and East Anglia; elsewhere, vehicle hauling dominated almost totally.

[56] The Southampton brokage books in the fifteenth century, for instance, show a very clear dominance of vehicle over pack-horse travel: see n. 72 below.

[57] Although mules and donkeys comprise only about 2 per cent of the working equids recorded at Domesday, this proportion is much in excess of that found later in the medieval period: Langdon, "Horses, Oxen and Technological Innovation", pp. 38, 97 (n. 22), 118, 200 (n. 21), 247.

[58] There are, for instance, virtually no pack-animals among the demesne stock listed in accounts: *ibid.*, pp. 148-9, 285-7.

[59] This is the sort of range most usually given by historians, although loads in excess of 400 lbs. may have been possible in exceptional circumstances: D. Hey, *Packmen, Carriers and Packhorse Roads* (Leicester, 1980), pp. 90-1; Leighton, "Eleventh Century Developments in Land Transport Technology", p. 30; Leighton, *Transport and Communication in Early Medieval Europe*, p. 104; M. E. Seebohm, *The Evolution of the English Farm* (London, 1927), p. 220.

[60] As indicated by the surveys: Langdon, "Horses, Oxen and Technological Innovation", pp. 148, 286. See also Hey, *Packmen, Carriers and Packhorse Roads*, p. 98, for the same conclusion in the eighteenth century.

all, very useful for difficult terrain or in times of inclement weather —
but that it was tending to decline in overall importance.[61]

V

The rise of horse hauling at the expense of haulage by oxen and
probably carrying by pack-animal is in many ways curious. Why did
it become so popular? It certainly was a more expensive exercise. On
demesnes, for instance, it cost on average nearly 24s. per year to
keep a cart-horse compared to 7s. per year for an ox.[62] Strictly
speaking, this is not comparing like with like, since the oxen in this
instance were primarily used for ploughing rather than hauling.
There was also a tendency for ox-hauling teams to be larger than
horse-hauling teams, and thus the ability to use fewer animals in the
latter case may have somewhat reduced the economic inequality
between the two animals. Nonetheless the use of horses still seems
to have cost considerably more, as was the perennial complaint of
Walter of Henley and others, and thus the advantages of using horses
rather than oxen for hauling must have been very substantial to
support such a rise in costs.

What these advantages were is not always easy to discern. The
most obvious benefit of course was speed, and it has been conjectured
that the introduction of horse traction may have increased the speed
of hauling as much as tenfold — that is, from two miles per hour
for heavy ox-hauled transport to twenty miles per hour for light
horse-hauled chariots.[63] But these figures are hardly comparable,
since the loads and circumstances of carrying patently differed. The
best medieval evidence that allows a relevant comparison to be made
comes from a Florentine manual giving instructions on the route to
China in the first half of the fourteenth century. Here it is recorded
that the time needed to transport goods from Azov to Astrakhan by
ox wagon required twenty-five days, but only ten to twelve days by
horse wagon. Significantly the normal loads for these wagons are
also indicated, the ox wagon containing 2,500 Genoese pounds and
the horse wagon 1,625 Genoese pounds; in both cases the wagons
were to be hauled by one animal apiece.[64] Although horse hauling
was patently quicker in this case, its superiority in terms of hauling
efficiency over the equivalent ox transport was only about 50 per

---

[61] Although it was always to be associated with the transportation of certain types
of goods, particularly perishables, such as fish: J. F. Willard, "Inland Transportation
in England during the Fourteenth Century", *Speculum*, i (1926), pp. 368-9.

[62] Langdon, "Economics of Horses and Oxen in Medieval England", p. 37.

[63] S. Piggott, " 'The First Wagons and Carts': Twenty-Five Years Later", *Bull.
Inst. Archaeol.*, xvi (1979), p. 11.

[64] R. S. Lopez and I. W. Raymond, *Medieval Trade in the Mediterranean World:
Illustrative Documents* (London, 1955), pp. 355-8.

cent or so,[65] since the ox was able to make up for much of its slower speed through its ability to pull a heavier load. This was a phenomenon that also held true in medieval England. We have already noted that the ox-hauled *plaustrum* or *carrus* had double the capacity of the horse-hauled *carecta*, a distinction that was always made in the description of carrying services when a set number of vehicle loads was to be carried. However, when the survey, extent or custumal is concerned with the amount of time spent on hauling rather than the number of trips, the distinction is no longer made. Thus at Gorton (Lancashire) in 1320 it is stated that Henry le Reve, villein, was required to carry grain at the lord's harvest with either a *carrus* or *carecta*. Similarly at Elsworth (Cambridgeshire), *circa* 1195, each virgate holder was to supply carrying services three times at the harvest (that is, three separate days) with his *carra* or *carecta*.[66] In both these cases the carrying efficiency of the two types of vehicle over a set period of time appears to have been considered more or less the same, the speed of the horse-hauled cart or *carecta* being more or less balanced by the larger load of the ox-hauled *carrus*. Given that the *carrus* normally had twice the carrying capacity of the *carecta*, then this again implies that horses hauled at about twice the speed of oxen, similar to the Azov-to-Astrakhan case already mentioned.

In such circumstances it may be difficult to see what the attraction was for horse hauling, in England or elsewhere. For small loads, however, horse hauling must have been a boon, halving the time needed to get these relatively modest amounts of crops or other goods from place to place. This was particularly important during the harvest, when time was apt to be short. Even in this case, however, it is difficult to know whether horse hauling was much of an improvement over hauling by oxen. Substantial farmers, clearing large numbers of sheaves from relatively consolidated holdings, might find the two modes of transport roughly comparable, since the speed of one would be balanced by the fewer trips the other would have to make. On the other hand, if, as was the case for much of the peasantry, a farmer's lands were highly fragmented, requiring a lot of travelling from one strip to another with relatively light loads,

[65] That is, for the ox wagon the hauling efficiency would be $2,500 \div 25 = 100$ Genoese lbs. per day over the distance travelled. For a horse wagon taking twelve days, it would be $1,625 \div 12 = 135\cdot4$ Genoese lbs. per day over the same distance (or a $35\cdot4$ per cent improvement in hauling efficiency over the ox wagon), while for the same horse wagon taking only ten days it would be $1,625 \div 10 = 162\cdot5$ Genoese lbs. per day equivalent (or a $62\cdot5$ per cent improvement). Improvements of this order (that is, about 50 per cent or so) are also borne out by modern experience when comparing the advantages of horse over ox traction: A. P. Usher, *A History of Mechanical Inventions*, 2nd edn. (Harvard, 1954), p. 156.

[66] *Mamacestre*, ed. J. Harland, 2 vols. (Chetham Soc., old ser., liii, lvi, Manchester, 1861), ii, p. 280; *Cartularium monasterii de Rameseia*, iii, p. 249.

then the smaller, faster vehicle was patently better. At the very least we can say that horse hauling was always competitive with ox haulage for general farm work and was very often a considerable improvement. Nonetheless, in many cases the savings in time may only have been marginal, unless the fields were extremely distant.

If hauling with horses about the manor often provided only relatively minor advantages over ox hauling, why was it adopted so freely? Horses were admittedly more versatile and could be used not only for hauling, but also harrowing, ploughing, riding and pack-carrying. This versatility was particularly useful for peasant small holders, when one or two animals may have had to satisfy the entire draught requirements for a holding and where the cost difference between horses and oxen could be minimized because of their relatively infrequent use.[67] Nevertheless the introduction of the horse to hauling was so rapid, far outstripping its application to ploughing, that the advantage of its versatility was manifestly a secondary one. In fact the main reason for the popularity of horse hauling would seem to lie in extra-manorial interests, especially in the much closer relationships that both peasant and demesne farmers were beginning to forge with the market. Horse hauling in particular made peasant and demesne goods much more available to the outside world. It did this in two ways. First, if we assume, as seems to have been the case, that horse hauling was normally carried out at twice the speed of ox hauling, then the time in which it took a farmer to get his goods to market and back would have been halved. Second, and more important, a peasant or demesne farmer could now travel twice as far to get to a market than he could before, with the result that his range of operations would quadruple (in proportion to the increase in area which was now accessible in, say, a day's travel). Demesne and peasant farmers thus had a much greater leeway in seeking out better prices for their produce and for the goods they had to buy than they had formerly. Conversely, urban specialization was made much more possible by increasing the intake of potential customers, and the addition of the horse-hauled cart to the range of urban vehicles also meant that manufactured goods reached peasants that much more easily.

In short, the efficiency of getting goods in bulk to where they were most needed and could fetch the highest price must have improved considerably. Again it is true that horses were limited to hauling relatively light loads and that this may have been inconvenient at times, but this liability should not be exaggerated. Horse-hauled vehicles, despite being of a lesser capacity than their ox-hauled counterparts, were still capable of carrying substantial loads. An

---

[67] Langdon, "Economics of Horses and Oxen in Medieval England", pp. 37-40.

illuminating example of this is provided by a late fourteenth-century court roll from Writtle in Essex, in which one tenant of the manor sued another over the sale of a horse which the vendor had allegedly claimed could pull a cart (*carecta*) and five quarters of wheat. At the modern conversion of 63 lbs. per bushel, this works out to a load of 2,520 lbs., excluding the cart.[68] As the entry goes on to record, the claim was almost certainly an incorrect one, but it does indicate that horse-hauled vehicles in medieval England were probably capable of hauling up to, say, a ton.[69] Such a capacity, far from severely restricting a farmer's ability to haul his goods to market efficiently, would likely be as much as he would ever need. A fairly well-off peasant, having for example 20 acres of sown crops (that is, equivalent to a thirty-acre virgate farmed by a three-course rotation), would, in an average harvest and subtracting seed and tithes, be lucky to have twenty to twenty-five quarters left over. Assuming that a ton of grain (about four quarters) was in fact a reasonable load for a horse-hauled cart, then no more than seven trips would be needed to take all of this net crop to market. In reality, of course, it is highly unlikely that a peasant's entire crop would be sold in this way. Much of it — perhaps a half or more — would be held back for his own consumption. Furthermore, since the most sensible selling policy was usually to hold on to his surplus grain for as long as possible, in order to take advantage of higher prices late in the farming year, he would at any one time probably only sell that amount of grain required for immediate cash needs. It is unlikely that this would take up even a full cart-load. In other words, a horse-drawn cart, even though its capacity was only half that of an ox-hauled wain, was more than adequate for all but the most exceptional trips to market, a trifling disadvantage when considering that trips could now be made so very much more quickly.

What seems surprising is that demesne managers also showed such a preference for horse hauling. The volume of grains and other goods generated on demesnes should have meant that there was little difference in hauling efficiency between horse- and ox-powered vehicles when it came to carrying these goods to market, where again the speed of one mode of hauling would be balanced by the greater capacity of the other. Nevertheless, from the number of demesne "cart-horses" about, the former mode of hauling was obviously the more preferred, despite the sizeable extra cost involved in keeping horses. Presumably they chose horses and carts simply because they

[68] Essex Record Office, Chelmsford, D/DP M189. I am much indebted to Dr. Christopher Dyer for providing me with this reference; the 63 lb. conversion rate for a bushel of wheat has been kindly supplied to me by Mr. A. M. A. Woods, agricultural correspondent for the *Stratford-upon-Avon Herald*.

[69] A ton load was perfectly feasible for a two-horse cart in early modern times: Hey, *Packmen, Carriers and Packhorse Roads*, p. 90.

were the most versatile form of carrying, generally suitable for all but the largest of loads. In particular, for both peasant and demesne farming, horse hauling filled in the light hauling gap between the heavier ox transport and the lighter carrying by pack-animals. It was quicker and more convenient than the former and more efficient than the latter, and not surprisingly it expanded at the expense of both, especially ox hauling, which was virtually wiped out in many areas.

Although we have been largely concerned with farm transport in this article, it is clear that similar trends were occurring in road transport. Thus we read of *carectae* (or *carretae*), presumably horse-hauled, being used to carry goods for the king to all parts of England as early as 1171-2.[70] By the fourteenth century, horse-hauled vehicles were an extremely common sight on English roads, where they were used to haul a great variety of goods, ranging from farm stuffs to military equipment.[71] A detailed search of other types of records than those examined in this study will be required to obtain a definite figure as to what proportion of road haulage was performed by horses at this time, but the evidence from the Southampton brokage books in the fifteenth century suggests that the ratio of horse-hauled to ox-hauled vehicles on the road was four to one or more.[72]

VI

In response to the question posed in the title of this article, then, did horse hauling revolutionize vehicle transport in twelfth- and thirteenth-century England? The answer would appear to be yes. The imposing magnitude of the change from ox to horse hauling over the relatively short period of little more than a century was certainly revolutionary by medieval standards. And it is likely that this change in the mode of vehicle transport had important consequences for the economy as a whole. From the magnitude of the change and the amounts of money that demesne farmers in particular were willing to expend on this new mode of transportation, it does appear that vehicle transport by oxen had previously been a bottleneck restricting the flow of goods at the time. Thus it is

---

[70] *Pipe Roll 18 Henry II*, p. 53; *Pipe Roll 24 Henry II*, p. 97; *Pipe Roll 30 Henry II*, pp. 80, 85, 92; *Pipe Roll 31 Henry II*, pp. 78, 127; *Pipe Roll 34 Henry II*, p. 13; *Pipe Roll 6 Richard I*, pp. 113, 211; etc. (References are to the volumes published by the Pipe Roll Society.)

[71] Willard, "Inland Transportation in England during the Fourteenth Century", esp. pp. 363-4, 366-7; J. F. Willard, "The Use of Carts in the Fourteenth Century", *History*, xvii (1932-3), pp. 246-8.

[72] In the 1443-4 brokage book, for instance, 218 *carectae* entered or left the city gates compared to only 49 (presumably ox-hauled) wains; similarly the weight of goods transported by pack-horse through these same gates was only one-tenth of that carried by vehicle (as calculated by the author, taking into account the various carrying capacities): *The Brokage Book of Southampton, 1443-1444*, ed. O. Coleman, 2 vols. (Southampton Rec. Ser., iv, vi, Southampton, 1960-1).

interesting to note that the rise in horse hauling coincided with the well-known expansion of the English economy in the twelfth and thirteenth centuries. Explanations for this agricultural and commercial upsurge and the price inflation that accompanied it have generally centred round the amount of money in circulation, especially in silver, or on the demands of a growing population.[73] Little attention has been paid to the velocity of circulation, either of money or commodities.[74] Yet, as we have indicated, there are strong reasons for thinking that the rise of horse hauling increased the velocity of goods transportation and, hence, the opposite flow of money to pay for them. An increase in the amount of buying and selling would seem to be inevitable, the only real restriction on this increase in exchanges being production. But, at the beginning of the twelfth century at least, there was plenty of elasticity in the system for expanding production, not only in agriculture through the agency of land clearance and reclamation, but also in the expansion of urban industry and commerce. By markedly improving the opportunities for buying and selling in bulk, horse hauling provided a stronger incentive for mobilizing this extra production. Indeed, the rise of horse hauling and the renewed growth of market activity in England occur so closely together as to be almost simultaneous, although uncertainties over the exact timing of each make it difficult to attribute cause and effect.[75] In any case, it appears that they were mutually reinforcing, particularly as horse hauling was geared to a more active and fast-paced economy. It is significant too that as the economy showed signs of contraction in the later middle ages, so did the incidence of horse hauling. Finally, the rise of horse hauling accords well with the pattern of population growth over the period. It has been suggested that the proliferation of markets occurring up to the middle of the fourteenth century was largely due to "an increase in local purchases by small households".[76] With its emphasis on light, small-scale hauling, it was just for these lesser, mainly peasant households that the benefits of horse hauling were most relevant.

[73] P. D. A. Harvey, "The English Inflation of 1180-1220", in R. H. Hilton (ed.), *Peasants, Knights and Heretics: Studies in Medieval English Social History* (Past and Present Pubns., Cambridge, 1976), esp. pp. 79-84; Postan, "Economic Foundations of Medieval Society", esp. pp. 7-16; M. M. Postan, "The Rise of a Money Economy", in his *Essays on Medieval Agriculture and General Problems of the Medieval Economy* (Cambridge, 1973), pp. 28-40.

[74] Although Postan does mention the development of new credit and payment arrangements, which also quickened commercial transactions: Postan, "Economic Foundations of Medieval Society", p. 10; see also Postan, "Rise of a Money Economy", p. 34.

[75] As discussed in Langdon, "Horses, Oxen and Technological Innovation", pp. 379-80.

[76] R. H. Britnell, "The Proliferation of Markets in England, 1200-1349", *Econ. Hist. Rev.*, 2nd ser., xxxiv (1981), p. 218.

The correlation between the rise of horse hauling and the expansion of the English economy in the twelfth and thirteenth centuries would thus seem to be more than coincidental. This is not to argue that population growth and possible increases in the money supply were unimportant factors in this expansion, but simply that horse hauling provided an important technical element that must also be considered, especially as it was pre-eminently directed at the then fastest growing sector of society, namely small peasant farmers. In short, it would appear that here we have a good example of technical innovation in the middle ages that was far from negligible in its effects upon the society of the time. In particular, horse hauling, by markedly increasing the speed and range of marketing journeys, contributed to a more active interchange between town and country, from which the renewed vitality of urban culture and commerce was one direct result. As a development, this was both significant and lasting. The view that medieval society was largely incapable of important technical change, particularly during the twelfth and thirteenth centuries, thus needs to be modified substantially. Part of this misconception over the efficacy of medieval technology lies in the tendency to think that only innovations directly improving agricultural production are worth considering. But even here, medieval farmers were well capable of significantly improving their agricultural production, given the right circumstances.[77] It is more in the ordering of these circumstances and less in medieval man's technical inadequacies that the solutions to the problems concerning the material well-being of medieval society — or lack of it — should be sought.

[77] See especially Campbell, "Agricultural Progress in Medieval England", pp. 41-4.

Note, 1987

I would like to add two comments to my article. First, further evidence has come to my attention regarding the possible use of horses for light passenger carrying in Anglo-Saxon England. One of the versions of Aelfric's translation of the Heptateuch contains a series of illustrations which show a number of four-wheeled coaches being hauled by what look to be mules (which may also help to explain the relatively high percentage of these animals in the Domesday survey compared to later times; see above, p. 55, n. 57). They might, however, have been meant to represent horses, since the rudimentary harnessing arrangements shown on the illustrations resemble those evident on horse-hauled chariots and the like from continental manuscripts of about the same time or before. The same document also shows two (peasant?) carts being pulled in one case by a team of four oxen and in the other by a mixed team of two oxen and what again look to be two mules. The interesting thing to note about this mixed team is that both the oxen and mules/horses are *yoked* to the vehicle, indicating again that modern improvements to equid harnessing shown in Plate 1 (above, p. 37) had not yet penetrated to England by the time of the document (early eleventh century) (Brit. Lib., Cott. MS. Claud. B. IV; also shown in Lynn White Jr., "The Origins of the Coach", in his *Medieval Religion and Technology* (Berkeley, 1978), esp. figs. 12-14).

Second, it appears likely that my estimate (above, p. 59) as to the load that could be carried in a horse-hauled cart is too high. This figure was based on a modern weight conversion of 63 lbs. for a bushel of wheat. It has been suggested to me, however, that the weight of the medieval bushel of grain may have been considerably lighter, due to, if nothing else, the fact that medieval grains were almost certainly less full in the ear than modern ones. For instance, one fourteenth-century treatise puts the weight of a bushel of wheat at 48 lbs. and the quarter at 384 lbs. (*Select Tracts and Table Books Relating to English Weights and Measures, 1100-1742*, ed. H. Hall and F. J. Nicholson (Camden Miscellany, xv, 1929), p. 8). It is not clear from the passage which pound – avoirdupois, Troy or Tower – is meant here, but avoirdupois is probably the most likely (e.g., M. Prestwich, "Victualling Estimates for English Garrisons in Scotland during the Early Fourteenth Century", *English Historical Review*, lxxxii (1967), p. 357). Assuming again that a cart could in fact haul the five quarters indicated in the Writtle (Essex) case on p. 59 above, this would result in a cart-load of only 1,920 lbs. (avoirdupois).

However, if Troy or even Tower lbs. were intended then this would drop to as little as 1,480 lbs. avoirdupois. (The conversion here has been made using tables from R. E. Zupko, *British Weights and Measures* (Madison, 1977), pp. 155-6). It might be safer in the circumstances to put the upper limit of a cart-load of grain – or at least wheat – at three-quarters of a ton rather than the full ton originally given, although this would still leave the average peasant farmer with plenty of hauling capacity. In all this, I am indebted to Miss Barbara Harvey for pointing out the problem and for providing me with a number of useful references.

3. Politics and property in early medieval England*

J. C. HOLT

BETWEEN 1066 AND THE CLOSE OF THE THIRTEENTH CENTURY ENGLISH kings, landowners and lawyers established a sophisticated law of property. This was concerned, among other things, with title, inheritance and succession. The law came to define the relationship between patronage and inheritance, between the power of kings and lords to exercise favour to political or financial advantage, and the desire of their vassals to ensure heritable title to land, privilege and office. How far was patronage, ruthless or beneficent, limited by law? How far was law beaten into shape by political necessity?

These questions have lain at the source of a curiously diffuse collection of views expressed by English and American scholars in the last decade or so. Professor S. E. Thorne (1959), in an important paper concerned with the concepts of heritability and alienability rather than the practice of inheritance, argued for a gradual process continuing to *c.* 1200, whereby, through the accumulation of judgements and legal notions about homage and warranty, life interests in fees, which may in practice have passed from father to son, developed into incontrovertible heritable tenures.[1] Sydney Painter (1960) suggested that there was a more sudden and decisive move towards the establishment of inheritance *c.* 1150.[2] Sir Richard Southern (1962) put the critical point earlier, in the reign of Henry I.[3] Professor R. H. C. Davis (1964) argued emphatically that the succession of

* This paper was first composed in 1966. Since then it has been read at many British universities. I am grateful to all those who in discussion have have enabled me to see a little clearer. I am particularly indebted to my colleagues Miss Barbara Dodwell, Dr. B. R. Kemp, Miss Patricia McNulty and Dr. C. F. Slade for help on particular points. The final stages of the work coincided with parallel investigations by Dr. Paul Hyams, and I have benefited from an interchange of views with him. I am also grateful to Professor John Le Patourel for his helpful comments on the final draft.

[1] "English Feudalism and Estates in Land", *Cambridge Law Jl.*, new ser., vi (1959), pp. 193-209.
[2] S. Painter, "The Family and the feudal system in twelfth-century England", *Speculum*, xxxv (1960), pp. 1-16, reprinted in his collected essays *Feudalism and Liberty*, ed. Fred. A. Cazel, Jr. (Baltimore, 1961), pp. 195-219: see especially p. 198.
[3] "The place of Henry I's reign in English history", *Proc. British Acad.*, xlviii (1962), pp. 127-69, especially p. 145. This view is also followed by Mrs. Marjorie Chibnall, *The Ecclesiastical History of Orderic Vitalis* (Oxford, 1969), ii, pp. xxxvi-xxxvii.

Henry II was the decisive point — "The barons . . . demanded that the King [Stephen] should recognize their hereditary right in specific and unambiguous terms . . . .   That was what the barons fought for in Stephen's reign, and that is what they won".[4]

These views should be compared with other assessments of periods bounding these alleged developments. At the latter end Jolliffe (1955) saw the Crown's capacity to interfere with right, title and lawful process becoming rapidly more powerful and inimical to aristocratic interests under the Angevin kings until the culmination under John;[5] his argument would scarcely substantiate any major surrender by the Crown in 1154 or at any time in the twelfth century. McFarlane (1965), in his turn, seemed to doubt whether any significant change had occurred even by the end of the thirteenth century, for he maintained that both Henry III and Edward I readily ignored the accepted provisions of the law in discontinuing earldoms or disposing of them in the interests of the Crown.[6]   In this matter, McFarlane's argument implies, not much had been achieved by 1215, let alone 1100 or 1154. At the earlier bound stands Maitland:

> We are thus led to question whether the followers of the Conqueror who received great gifts of English land held these lands heritably. *It is certain that they did;*[7] but this answer may require qualifications and the difficulty of the question should be seen.[8]

Some of Maitland's qualifications and difficulties foreshadowed recent discussion.[9] Nevertheless his opinion was firm and convinced. Further comments were added by Sir Frank Stenton,[10] Professor David Douglas[11] and Professor V. H. Galbraith,[12] but otherwise the argument remained very much as Maitland left it until the appearance of Professor Thorne's work in 1959.

There is another more serious difficulty. Painter made a single reference to the studies of Marc Bloch.[13] Otherwise all this recent

[4] "What happened in Stephen's reign?" *History*, xliv (1964), pp. 1-12, especially pp. 11-12. Professor Davis restated and developed his views in *King Stephen* (London, 1967); see especially pp. 123-5.
[5] J. E. A. Jolliffe, *Angevin Kingship* (London, 1955), pp. 50-86, 131-6.
[6] K. B. McFarlane, "Had Edward I a 'policy' towards the earls?" *History*, l (1965), pp. 145-59.
[7] The italics are mine.
[8] F. Pollock and F. W. Maitland, *History of English Law* (Cambridge, 1911), i, p. 314.
[9] *Ibid.*, i, p. 314-6; ii, p. 260-313.
[10] F. M. Stenton, *The First Century of English Feudalism*, 2nd edn. (Oxford, 1961), pp. 33-41, 154-6.
[11] D. C. Douglas, "A Charter of Enfeoffment under William the Conqueror", *Eng. Hist. Rev.*, xlii (1927), pp. 245-7.
[12] V. H. Galbraith, "An episcopal land-grant of 1085", *Eng. Hist. Rev.*, xliv (1929), pp. 353-72.
[13] *Feudalism and Liberty*, p. 196.

work has by-passed continental scholarship, formidable both in bulk and learning, extending from Guilhiermoz,[14] through Bloch,[15] to Professor Georges Duby,[16] and, with particular reference to Normandy, from Génestal, Lagouëlle and others to Lucien Musset, Professor Carabie and Professor Jean Yver.[17] These studies have developed a single consistent argument, best summarized by Professor Duby: namely that *lignage*, with all its concomitants including inheritance, was established for "the territorial princes and comital families by the middle of the tenth century ... among the castellan families about the year 1000, and among the ordinary knights some fifty years later".[18] Whether such a timetable is universally applicable may be doubted; Picardie, for example, does not quite conform to it,[19] and it is likely that Brittany also may prove exceptional. But for Normandy roughly such a pattern of development was traced independently by Professor Douglas in 1947. He showed that one of the aspects of the rise of the duchy in the eleventh century was the emergence of those aristocratic families, which, subject to the accidents of descent and political fortune, were still in possession of estate and office in 1204.[20] It seems inescapable that the Norman aristocracy which settled in England after 1066 was already accustomed to inheritance. The higher the rank the more certain and secure the enjoyment of heritable family property. It might be expected in 1066 that knights were likely to be insecure in their possessions, such

---

[14] A. Guilhiermoz, *Essai sur les origines de la noblesse en France au moyen âge* (Paris, 1902), especially pp. 195-207.

[15] *La Société Féodale. La formation des liens de dépendance* (Paris, 1939), especially pp. 299-304; English edition, trans. G. A. Manyon (London, 1961), pp. 194-7.

[16] G. Duby, *Le Société aux XIe et XIIe siècles dans la région mâconnaise*, 2nd edn. (Paris, 1971), pp. 149-65, 174-201, 235-45, 317-58. See also, by the same author, "La Noblesse dans la France médiévale", *Revue Historique*, ccxxvi (1961), pp. 1-22; "Au XIIe siècle: les "Jeunes" dans le société aristocratique", *Annales, E.S.C.*, xix (1964), pp. 835-46, especially p. 841; "Structures de parenté et noblesse. France du nord. IXe-XIIe siècles" in *Miscellanea Mediaevalia in memoriam Jan Frederik Niermeyer* (Groningen, 1967), pp. 149-65; "The diffusion of cultural patterns in feudal society", *Past and Present*, no. 39 (Apr. 1968), pp. 1-10; "Structures familiales aristocratiques en France du XIe siècle en rapport avec les structures de l'Etat", *L'Europe aux IXe-XIe siècles, aux origines des Etats nationaux*, ed. T. Manteuffel and A. Gieysztor (Warsaw, 1968), pp. 57-62.

[17] This work is noted in detail below.

[18] "The diffusion of cultural patterns in feudal society", *Past and Present*, no. 39 (Apr. 1968), p. 6.

[19] R. Fossier, *La terre et les hommes en Picardie* (Louvain, 1968), ii, pp. 511-46.

[20] "The Rise of Normandy", *Proc. British Acad.*, xxxiii (1947), pp. 115-20; *William the Conqueror* (London, 1964), pp. 83-104.

as they were, but not the great baronial families of the Anglo-Norman dominion.[21]

There are strong reasons for thinking that the Conqueror, however he magnified his new-found royalty and right of conquest, did not, perhaps could not, interfere to any significant degree in these general trends.[22] The feudal nomenclature of Normandy and England suggests an early development of hereditary tenure in the duchy, which was transferred without apparent hesitation to the kingdom. In Normandy the word *alodium*, whatever its sense in other parts of the continent, meant, not land held free of seigneurial services, but land held by hereditary right.[23] *Alodium*, used in this sense, was a commonly recurrent word in Norman charters of the eleventh century; it was casually accepted by Dudo of St. Quentin, in the second decade of the century, when he stated that Rollo had received Normandy *in alodo et in fundo*.[24] Now *alodium* had the same sense in the eleventh century as *feodum* in the twelfth; the one term was succeeded by the other. Hence the word *feodum* from its first appearance in Normandy implied a hereditary tenure.[25] Both *alodium* and *feodum* stood in contrast to the more precarious *beneficium;* indeed the emergence of the term *feodum* is probably to be explained by the varied, even contradictory senses which had come to be attached to *beneficium*.[26] It follows that *alodium* and *feodum* should be given the same meaning in England.

[21] The social variation of tenurial security is discussed further below, pp. 94-9.

[22] The argument that William had the power to impose unusually severe terms on his vassals is balanced by the opposite case, that he could not muster adequate support through offering unattractive terms of settlement. Some "French" settlers, notably Gherbod the Fleming and Aubrey de Coucy, apparently withdrew voluntarily from their English estates.

[23] This is fully developed with extensive annotation by R. Carabie, *La Propriété Foncière dans le très Ancien Droit Normand (xie-xiiie siècles)* : i, *La Propriété Domaniale* (Bibliothèque d'Histoire du Droit Normand, 2nd ser., Études, vol. 5, Caen, 1943), pp. 230-9. See also H. Lagouëlle, *Essai sur la conception féodale de la propriété foncière dans le très ancien droit normand* (Caen, 1902), pp. 118-20, 125-6, 247-9, and L. Musset, "Reflexions sur *alodium* et sa signification dans les textes normands", *Revue historique de droit français et étranger*, 4th ser., xlvii (1969), p. 606.

[24] *De Moribus et Actis primorum Normanniae Ducum*, ed. J. Lair (Caen, 1865), p. 169. For the interpretation of this much discussed passage see Lagouëlle, *op. cit.*, pp. 85-8 and H. Prentout, *Étude Critique sur Dudon de Saint-Quentin* (Caen, 1915), pp. 207-49.

[25] Carabie, *op. cit.*, pp. 242-3, 248-50.

[26] *Ibid.*, pp. 245-54. Carabie insisted on the precarious sense of *beneficium*. This is strongly marked in a series of charters of Richard II of Normandy confirming the privileges of Fécamp, Jumièges and St. Ouen in 1025: *Recueil des Actes des Ducs de Normandie (911-1066)*, ed. Marie Fauroux, Mémoires de la Société des Antiquaires de Normandie, xxxvi (1961), nos. 34, 36, 53.   The

Maitland found that the *alodarius* of Domesday was a tenant owing seigneurial service and holding by hereditary right.[27] He demonstrated that the word *feodum* had the same hereditary connotation[28] and noted that "we can hardly say for certain that D.B. does not use *alodium* and *feodum* as equivalents, both representing a heritable estate, as absolute an ownership of land as is conceivable".[29] He drew a sharp distinction between the hereditary *feodum* and the non-hereditary *beneficium* which the fee was supplanting.[30] Maitland was cautious. He presented the emergence of the fee as a process which had already "gone far" by the time of Domesday and noted that "a trait of precariousness clings to the fee: it is easily forfeitable, and the lord's rights in the land appear in the shape of reliefs and wardships".[31] But essentially he reached the same conclusion for England as Lagouëlle, Carabie and Musset for Normandy. The very language of feudalism, from its inception in Norman England, implied inheritance. A non-hereditary fief was a contradiction in terms; it might occur in practice, but it was not what men normally intended when they gave or accepted fiefs.[32]

The family nomenclature of England and Normandy tells a similar story. One of the more obvious features of the new notion of *lignage* emerging in the tenth and eleventh centuries was the use of family names, frequently toponymic in form.[33] The toponym

(*note 26 cont.*)
significant words in the first of these are: "we wish . . . to confirm those gifts which our faithful men, with our agreement, have made of *precaria* or benefices which belonged to us, or of the inheritances which belonged to their fathers" ("placuit . . . firmare ea que fideles nostri, nostro consensu, aut precario vel beneficiis quae nostri juris erant, vel de hereditatibus quas paterno jure possidebant, concesserunt . . .") (no. 34). The other two charters contain closely similar passages. Certainly two and possibly all three were issued at Fécamp. None survive as originals. There are other instances where *beneficium* is applied to apparently less precarious tenures (*ibid.*, nos. 21, 43, 48, 131, 145). It was also used to describe a tenancy held of a church or property belonging to a church, or simply an act of endowment. In some instances the word is capable of more than one interpretation. See the charter of Albert abbot of St. Mesmin de Micy to Jumièges of 1023-6: "I held a certain alod through maternal inheritance, not as a benefice held of anyone [? not through anyone's gift]" ("erat michi quidam alodus ex materna hereditate, non ex alicujus beneficio . . .") (*ibid.*, no. 51).

[27] *Domesday Book and Beyond* (Cambridge, 1897), pp. 153-4.
[28] *Ibid.*, p. 152, especially n. 3. Cp. Pollock and Maitland, *History of English Law*, i, p. 68.
[29] *Domesday Book and Beyond*, p. 154, n. 1.
[30] *Ibid.*, p. 152; Pollock and Maitland, *History of English Law*, i, pp. 67-8.
[31] *Ibid.*, p. 68.
[32] The argument is not defeated by examples of fees which did not ultimately descend to heirs. Southern, however, has taken a different view on this basis (*op. cit.*, pp. 161-2n.). For non-hereditary tenancies in the generation following the Conquest see below, pp. 95-8.
[33] Duby, "Structures de parenté et noblesse", pp. 150-9.

identified the family with the chief seat of its property. Hence such toponyms provide a very rough and ready minimal measure of the development of inherited estate; indeed the Norman evidence suggests that the two emerged side by side.[34]   Now the majority of the great Norman families which settled in England used French toponymic names: Aubigny, Beaumont, Bully, Grandmesnil, Mandeville, Montfort, Montgomery, Montbrai, Tosny, Warenne. Patronymics were still common, some of which, like fitzWalter, developed into family names.   There were also a few family surnames: Bigod, Malet, Martel, Giffard, Maudit; and a few tenants-in-chief took English toponyms: Tonbridge, Salisbury, Gloucester, Totnes, Stafford, Berkeley, Lincoln, Essex.   But French toponyms were overwhelmingly preponderant among the upper ranks of the new aristocracy.   How far the English adventure, by placing the Normans in foreign context, encouraged this usage is at present a matter for conjecture.   It is possible that families began to adopt French toponyms after rather than before the Conquest of England. But the most likely explanation of the evidence is that hereditary family property, which underlay such toponyms, had been securely established in Normandy among the great tenants of the duke by the third quarter of the eleventh century.[35]

There is also direct evidence.   Inheritance was the received legal doctrine of Norman England.   The Conqueror can scarcely have done other than reinforce a generally accepted convention when he instructed the Londoners that "every child be his father's heir after his father's day".[36]   None of the law-books question it; on the contrary they accept it without comment as an established principle.[37]

[34] The following toponyms are attested in the *acta* of the Norman dukes before 1066: among the greater families, Montgomery, Bellême, Tosny, Beaumont, Ferrières, Grandmesnil, l'Aigle, Warenne, Montfort, Mandeville, Gournay, Bully, Port, Mowbray, Tracy, Sai, St. John; and among the lesser, Drincurt, Planches, Granville, Le Mesnil, Vernon, Aunou, Limesy and Luvetot (*Recueil*, ed. Fauroux, *passim*).   For references to hereditary tenements in Normandy before 1066 see *ibid.*, nos. 12, 34, 42, 53, 61, 93, 119, 120, 122, 125, 129, 130, 167, 173, 220.   No. 200, witnessed by Duke William 1051-66, demonstrates that Roger de Bully held Bully *iure hereditario*.   Nos. 34, 73, 74, 146 refer to the hereditary possessions of the duke.   Nos. 147 and 233 refer to claims based on hereditary title.

[35] J. C. Holt, *What's in a Name? Family Nomenclature and the Norman Conquest* (Stenton Lecture, Reading, 1982).

[36] W. Stubbs, *Select Charters*, 9th edn., ed. H. W. C. Davis (Oxford, 1921), p. 97; *English Historical Documents, 1042-1189*, ed. D. C. Douglas and G. W. Greenaway (London, 1953), p. 945.   For comment see *Facsimiles of English Royal Writs to A.D. 1100 presented to Vivian Hunter Galbraith*, ed. T. A. M. Bishop and P. Chaplais (Oxford, 1957), no. 15.

[37] "Leges Henrici Primi", cap. 70, sections 18, 20, 20a, 20b, 21: ed. F. Liebermann, *Die Gesetze der Angelsachsen* (Halle, 1903), i, p. 589; ed. and trans. L. J. Downer (Oxford, 1972), p. 225.

Furthermore, the charter of liberties of Henry I clearly assumes the whole structure of inheritance as it is later revealed in the records of the twelfth century.[38] It assumes that earls and barons are succeeded by their heirs on the payment of a relief; it assumes that heiresses inherit just as certainly as heirs; it accepts the institutions of dower, marriage portion, and wardship both of heirs and their land; it emphasizes that these relationships are to apply between barons and their men as between barons and the king.[39] The subsequent history of the charter is as significant as its content. It lay in diocesan and monastic repositories throughout the land. It came to hand readily enough in the years before 1215 when it provided a model for Magna Carta.[40] Yet apparently no-one thought it worth reviving earlier in the twelfth century, even in the circumstances of the "Anarchy". Inheritance was not in question. The one other formal enactment which is known from the Norman period, a *statutum decretum* providing for partition among heiresses, was concerned, like the charter of 1100, with the definition of the hereditary principle.[41]

These are emphatic indications that the inheritance of feudal property was part of the natural order of things in Norman England. There is equally certain evidence that even the greatest in the land might suffer dispossession, and his family disinheritance. The problem is to reconcile this apparent contradiction. The first difficulty, as so often, is one of language. The term "law" is scarcely to be applied to this period except to denote an assemblage of customs and conventional practices which were still malleable and only slowly setting into hard and fast rules, some moulded by ancient texts or new regulations, others deriving their strength simply from inherent social needs. But if "law" must remain vague, "inheritance" cries out for definition. Inheritance by whom? and of what? Were all heirs, direct, collateral, immediate or distant, on the same footing? Was all property, land held in fee or otherwise, castles, office, title, equally heritable? All these questions can be answered. This itself argues for the existence of a complex system of inheritance.

The critical question is inheritance by whom? Was there any law

---

[38] *Select Charters* (9th edn.), pp. 116-9; *English Historical Documents, 1042-1189*, pp. 400-2.
[39] Caps. 2, 3, 4.
[40] For the distribution of the charter of Henry I see F. Liebermann, "The text of Henry I's Coronation Charter", *Trans. Royal Hist. Soc.*, new ser., viii (1894), pp. 21-48. For its political importance in the late twelfth century see J. C. Holt, *Magna Carta* (Cambridge, 1965), pp. 135-41, 150-1.
[41] Stenton, *op. cit.*, pp. 38-41, 260-1. The "decree" is mentioned in a charter of Roger de Valognes of *c.* 1145.

of descent and, if so, what?   For Normandy the outline of an answer is clear enough.   The Pays de Caux adopted absolute primogeniture; the rest of Normandy, partition among sons, who succeeded to their portion in order of seniority.[42]   Génestal maintained that primogeniture was the older of the two systems, but it is more likely that they developed in parallel, each subject to different external influences from neighbouring provinces.[43]   Each system came to be qualified, the primogeniture of the Pays de Caux by the slow acceptance of a provision for younger sons, partition in the rest of Normandy by *parage* which helped to maintain the unity of the family property.[44] Practice was also determined by a *constitutio*, usually attributed to Henry II, which forbad partition when it led to the division of a fief; henceforth feudal property was divided among male heirs only when there was more than one fief.[45]   There was an even more important restriction, namely that there could be no partition of baronies, fiefs and sergeanties held of the duke.   In the *Très Ancien Coutumier* of *c.* 1199, this appears not as part of the *constitutio* but as a separate, and almost certainly older, regulation.[46]   In Normandy the division of a tenancy-in-chief among sons was rare by the end of the eleventh century so that younger sons could only participate in the inheritance

---

[42] R. Génestal, "La formation du droit d'Aînesse dans le Coutume de Normandie", *Normannia*, i (1928), pp. 157-79; J. Yver, "Les caractères originaux du groupe de coutumes de l'Ouest de la France", *Revue historique de droit français et étranger*, 4th ser., xxx (1952), pp. 18-79, especially pp. 41-7.

[43] Génestal argued that primogeniture was earlier on two main counts: first, that it determined the early descent of the Duchy, and secondly that the Normans introduced primogeniture into England. The first point fails to give due weight to the principle of the indivisibility of the fief which might have the same effect as primogeniture. Génestal himself noted that the custom of Caux was related to that of neighbouring provinces of northern France whereas that of the rest of Normandy marched with the customs of western provinces. Yver, who further developed this line of approach to the problem, was cautious about Génestal's argument (*op. cit.*, p. 46, n. 2). The second point, of course, begs a question which is part of the present argument.

[44] On the provision for younger sons in the Pays de Caux see Génestal, *op. cit.*, pp. 174-7. On *parage* see Appendix I, below, pp. 106-7.

[45] *Très Ancien Coutumier*, cap. viii, *Coutumiers de Normandie*, i, E. J. Tardif (Société de l'histoire de Normandie [1881]), pp. 8-9. The attribution to Henry II has not been substantiated; it depends largely on analogy with the assize of 1185 whereby Geoffrey, duke of Brittany, introduced primogeniture into Brittany and likewise forbad the division of fiefs: R. Génestal, *Le parage normand* (Bibliothèque d'histoire du droit normand, 2nd ser., études i, fasc. 2, Caen, 1911), pp. 1-2; Yver, *op. cit.*, p. 46, n. 2.

[46] *Très Ancien Coutumier*, cap. viii, 5, ed. Tardif, p. 9. The *Summa de Legibus* also includes comtes: cap. xxiv, 1, *Coutumiers de Normandie*, iii, ed. E. J. Tardif (Société de l'histoire de Normandie [1896]), p. 79.

if there was more than one tenement.[47] In England Glanville did not even consider multiple tenements; for him all properties held by military service were a single estate subject to primogeniture.[48] Here also the subdivision of a barony among sons was unusual even in the generation immediately following the Conquest and later examples are exceptional.[49]

[47] The succession to Tancred de Hauteville provides the most famous early example of the maintenance of the unity of a tenancy-in-chief. However, the circumstances are far from certain. According to Ordericus Vitalis the decision was Tancred's own and he implies that Tancred had a choice in the matter (ed. Chibnall, ii, pp. 98-100). Malaterra in contrast states that Tancred's elder sons decided to emigrate since the family estate was clearly insufficient for their father's numerous progeny (Geoffrey Malaterra, *De Rebus Gestis Rogerii Calabriae et Siciliae Comitis*, ed. E. Pontieri, *Rerum Italicarum Scriptores*, v, pt. i [Bologna, 1924], p. 9), and certainly the first Hautevilles to arrive in Italy in 1037-8 were the two eldest, William and Drogo. Geoffrey, Tancred's fourth son by his first marriage, succeeded to the Norman patrimony. (Ordericus Vitalis, ed. Chibnall, ii, p. 98). Robert I de Grandmesnil is said by Orderic to have divided his lands among his sons at his death in *c.* 1040 (ed. Chibnall, ii, p. 40). It may be that such option was still possible at this early stage, as Génestal suggested ("Droit d'Aînesse", pp. 173-4). Some examples should be used warily. The descent of the estates of Giroie also illustrates division, but these came to Giroie in right of his betrothed through confirmation by the Duke. They were therefore strictly an acquisition, not an inheritance (Orderic Vitalis, ed. Chibnall, ii, pp. 22, 28; cp. below, pp. 74-5). The division of the estates of the first house of Bellême between Yves and William Talvas involved two distinct French and Norman tenements: G. H. White, "The first house of Bellême", *Trans. Royal Hist. Soc.*, 4th ser., xxii (1940), pp. 67-99; cp. Chibnall, *op. cit.*, pp. 362-5. The division of the estates of the Paynel family (1151-3) also involved two separate tenements, Les Moutiers-Hubert and Hambye: *Early Yorkshire Charters*, vi, ed. C. T. Clay (Yorkshire Archaeological Society, Record Ser., extra ser., iii, 1939), pp. 1-2, 97-8.

[48] Glanville, vii, 3, ed. Hall, p. 75.

[49] William de Rames divided his barony of Rayne between his two sons *c.* 1130 (J. H. Round, *Geoffrey de Mandeville* [London, 1892], pp. 399-404) and Hardwin de Scales made a similar division of his barony of Caxton after 1086 (*Curia Regis Rolls*, v, pp. 139-40). The division of the English estates of William Paynel between his sons Fulk and Hugh *c.* 1151-3 provides a late example, but it was complicated by the intrusion of Robert de Gant, husband of their half-sister (*Early Yorkshire Charters*, vi, pp. 7, 32-3; 97-8); on their Norman estates see above n. 47). Painter's example of the "division" of the barony of Weldon between Geoffrey Ridel and Ralph Basset was not a division but the creation of a large mesne tenure for a younger son: *op. cit.*, p. 201; *The Red Book of the Exchequer*, ed. Hubert Hall (Rolls Series, 1896), i, pp. 329-31; *Documents illustrative of the social and economic history of the Danelaw*, ed. F. M. Stenton (British Academy, 1921), no. 458. For a similar example see the agreement between Geldwin son of Savaric and Savaric, his brother, of 1156-8: *Sir Christopher Hatton's Book of Seals*, ed. Lewis C. Loyd and Doris M. Stenton (Oxford, 1950), no. 434.

Whether any of the above partitions arose from twinning it is impossible to say. Primogeniture was applicable to twins and took effect in the one well substantiated case of the succession to Robert, count of Meulan (see Appendix II, note C, below, pp. 111-13). Approximately 0·5 per cent of male adults would have surviving male twins. This calculation is based on the figures given in L. Penrose, *Outline of Human Genetics* (London, 1959), pp. 87-8, and H. H. Newman, *Twins and Super-Twins* (London, 1942), pp. 33-7. It may simply be coincidental that this matches the known cases of partition.

This rule was softened by another. Both in England and Normandy the law drew an apparently sharp distinction between inheritance and acquisition. The law of descent, whatever it might be, applied to inherited feudal property; acquisitions, in the form of conquests or purchases, were at their owner's disposal. In fact they were often used to endow younger sons, and very soon legal thinking hardened into the assumption that this was proper custom. Glanville drew on this distinction,[50] but on the whole in England it represents a passing phase. In Normandy it appears in a developed form in the *Très Ancien Coutumier* and it became axiomatic in Norman law.[51] Its first official appearance is much earlier, in the "Leges Henrici Primi", where it retains its more primitive form of free parental disposition.

> The ancestral fee of the father is to go the first-born son; but he may give his purchases or later acquisitions to whomsoever he prefers.[52]

In the generation after 1066 there was no shortage of acquisitions. Few younger sons had to go a-begging.

The distinction was not as sharply cut as seems at first sight. There were marginal situations where inheritance and acquisition were confused or only indistinctly separated. Land acquired by marriage, whether as the wife's portion or inheritance, could be used to endow younger sons as if it were an acquisition.[53] Land obtained

---

[50] See his discussion of inheritance and alienability. Glanville does not place an absolute restriction on the alienation of the inheritance or allow absolute freedom to dispose of the acquisition, but he allows a free hand over the latter to those who hold both inheritance and acquisitions (cap. vii, i, ed. and trans. G. D. G. Hall [London, 1965], pp. 70-1). For further discussion of this see below, pp. 104-5.

[51] "The first-born knight shall have the knight's fee complete, and it shall not be divided. The rest shall share the acquisitions equally" ("Miles primogenitus feodum lorice integrum habebit, et non partietur, ceteri vero escaetas habebunt equaliter") (cap. viii, 2, ed. Tardif, p. 8). The sense of "escaeta" has been debated. In the thirteenth century and earlier it generally denoted acquisitions, including those held by military service, but it could also mean non-military tenures: the two categories frequently overlapped: Génestal, *Le parage normand*, pp. 7-8; cp. H. Navel, "Recherches sur les institutions féodales en Normandie", *Bulletin de la Société des Antiquaires de Normandie*, li (1948-51), p. 20.

[52] "Primum patris feodum primogenitus filius habeat: emptiones vero vel deinceps acquisiciones suas det cui magis velit" ("Leges Henrici Primi", cap. 70, 21; ed. Liebermann, *Gezetze*, i, p. 589; ed. Downer, p. 224). This important passage was discussed by Pollock and Maitland (*History of English Law*, ii, p. 268) but has been overlooked by many subsequent scholars.

[53] The allocation of Eleanor of Aquitaine's inheritance to Richard the Lion-Heart is the most obvious example. Geoffrey of Anjou is said to have made a similar distinction between his own and his wife's inheritance (see below, p. 80). Godfrey de Bouillon, second son of Count Eustace II of Boulogne and Ida, heiress of Godfrey, duke of Lower Lorraine, was heir to his mother's inheritance: S. Runciman, *History of the Crusades* (Cambridge, 1951), i,

by collateral succession came to be regarded as acquisition in mature Norman custom.[54]   It is probable that these and similar problems were settled *ad hoc* in the late eleventh and early twelfth centuries. By the time of Glanville the divergence of English and Norman law in such matters as indivisibility, points to the emergence of hard and fast rules which determined actions in the courts.[55]   But this was not necessarily so earlier.   Moreover, when the distinction first appears it was permissive, not compulsory.   It allowed, but did not oblige, the father to divert acquisitions away from the eldest son, and then not necessarily to his younger children.   Hence it permitted a wide variety of *post obitum* and testamentary dispositions.[56]   Most important of all, it was limited in its application, for, whatever the precise variant, it was effective only if acquisitions and younger sons or other suitable recipients coincided.   A single heir united inheritance and acquisition and once that was done the result was irreversible.   The father's acquisition became the son's patrimony. Of its nature the rule could be applied only to one succession and one generation.

(note 53 cont.)
pp. 145-6; J. H. Round, *Studies in Peerage and Family History* (London, 1907), p. 152.   The honour of Belvoir, which came to Roger Bigod (d. 1107) either as the inheritance or marriage-portion of his wife, Adelicia de Tosny, did not descend to his son, but was used in turn as a marriage-portion for his daughter, Cecily, who married William I de Albini Brito: *Early Yorkshire Charters*, i, ed. W. Farrer (Edinburgh, 1914), pp. 461, 466.   When William de Warenne died in 1088 his English and Norman lands went to his elder, and his Flemish lands to his younger son.   Practically all his property was acquired, but the Flemish estates probably came through his marriage to Gundreda, sister of Gherbod the Fleming: *Early Yorkshire Charters*, viii, ed. C. T. Clay (Yorkshire Archaeological Society, Record Ser., extra ser., vi, 1949), pp. 1-7, 44.
[54] The ordinary rules of succession applied to collaterals: *Summa de Legibus*, caps. xxiii, xxiv, ed. Tardif, pp. 72-9.   For an English example in which land acquired by collateral succession was alleged to count as an acquisition see the succession to Hugh Bigod, Appendix II, note B, below, pp. 110-11.   Compare the descent of the estates of Stephen, lord of the honour of Richmond, d. 1135-6. Stephen was heir to his eldest brother Geoffrey Boterel I, d. 1093, or Geoffrey's son Conan, d. 1098, in his Breton property, and to less senior brothers, Alan Rufus and Alan Niger, in Richmond.   The Breton property had belonged to his father, Eudo d. *c.* 1079, but the English lands had been acquired by Alan Rufus. Stephen inherited both properties, but was heir to his father in the Breton property and to his brother in the English.   The Breton lands descended to his eldest son, the English to a younger: *Early Yorkshire Charters*, iv, ed. C. T. Clay (Yorkshire Archaeological Society, Record Ser., extra ser., i, 1935), pp. 84-8.
[55] For an example see Appendix II, note B, below, pp. 110-11.
[56] M. M. Sheehan, *The Will in Medieval England* (Pontifical Institute of Medieval Studies, Studies and Texts, vi, Toronto, 1963), pp. 110-9.   This work does not place the Anglo-Norman *post obitum* gift or bequest of land in the context of the pertaining rules of succession.   However, it presents no obstacle to the present analysis; indeed it largely dovetails into it.   See also below, pp. 104-5.

So much for theory. The principles involved were certainly current in northern and western France at the time of the conquest of England.[57] Some Anglo-Norman descents conformed strictly to the letter. Where there was more than one son in the generation after the Conquest, the inheritance went to the elder and the acquisition to the younger. This holds good for fitz Osbern,[58] Montgomery,[59] Grandmesnil,[60] Clare,[61] the senior branch of Beaumont,[62] and Montfort.[63] In these cases it followed that the Norman property remained with the senior branch and the English went to the junior. Usually the division extended only to the two elder sons; any others seem to have been expected to provide for themselves or find a career in the church.[64] But not all families

[57] See the agreement made by Tescelinus, priest of Verri, with the monks of St. Florent-lès-Saumur, arranging for his entry into the monastery. This provided for an annual payment of 10s. during life plus a *post obitum* gift of all his property "without share of anyone, because I have acquired all I hold through my own labours and initiative and therefore do not recognize therein any share either of relative or friend, but leave it all complete to St. Florent and to my lord, Abbot Sigo, and the monks of that house to be held for ever" ("sine parte alicujus, quia omnia quae habeo laboravi et ex ingenio meo acquisivi, idcirco amici aut parentis in hoc partem non recognosco, sed omnia ex integro beato Florentio ac domino meo abbati Sigoni et monachis istius cenobii relinquo habenda in perpetuo") (Liber Niger of St. Florent-lès-Saumur, Bib. Nat., Nouv. Acq. Lat., 1930, fo. 113v). The date limits are 1055-70.
[58] *Complete Peerage*, vi, p. 449; vii, p. 530, n. (b).
[59] J. F. A. Mason, "Roger de Montgomery and his sons (1067-1102)", *Trans. Royal Hist. Soc.*, 5th ser., xiii (1963), pp. 13-18.
[60] Ordericus Vitalis, ed. Chibnall, iv, pp. 336-40.
[61] *Complete Peerage*, iii, pp. 242-3; Ordericus Vitalis, ed. Chibnall, iv, pp. 210-12.
[62] See Appendix II, note C, below, pp. 111-13.
[63] *The Domesday Monachorum of Christ Church, Canterbury*, ed. D. C. Douglas (Royal Hist. Soc., 1944), pp. 67-70.
[64] Eustace of Boulogne made no provision for his third surviving son, Baldwin, subsequently count of Edessa and king of Jerusalem. On the death of Roger of Montgomery in 1095, Robert of Bellême got his Norman possessions and Hugh of Montgomery the English. Roger and Arnulf already enjoyed wide possessions in north-west England and Pembroke respectively, but, as Orderic noted, no provision was made for Philip and Everard (ed. Chibnall, iv, p. 302) and Robert succeeded to Hugh's English holdings when he died without heirs (Mason, *op. cit.*, p. 20). The Grandmesnil division was also limited to two sons and excluded two other survivors, one of whom had acquired estate by marriage in southern Italy (Ordericus Vitalis, ed. Chibnall, iv, p. 338). For a similar limitation in the Beaumont descent see the settlement of 1107 discussed below, Appendix II, note C, below, pp. 111-13.
William the Conqueror made no territorial provision for Henry, according to Ordericus simply leaving him 5000 lbs. of silver (ed. Chibnall, iv, p. 94). Geoffrey of Anjou apparently made a division between Henry and his second son, Geoffrey (see below, p. 80), but nothing was done for his third surviving son, William. Henry II made no initial provision for John Lackland. In all this the notion that tenements should not be subdivided was probably a decisive factor.

reacted so. In a significant number of instances the Norman patrimony and the English acquisition descended as a single inheritance. In a few of these, Giffard and Chester for example, it seems that this was because there was only one son at the critical succession, but this is difficult to establish with certainty.[65] In others, Malet,[66] Mandeville,[67] Vere,[68] Boulogne[69] and Bigod,[70] there was more than one son at the death of the first of the Anglo-Norman line, and yet in these families the eldest succeeded to the English acquisition and in some to the lordship of the whole estate. In the case of Boulogne this in all probability represented a deliberate bid to unite cross-channel holdings. Some families, most strikingly the Beaumonts, are *sui generis,* since their estates seem to have descended by special settlement.[71] Hence there is no doubt that families exercised some control. The matter was not simply settled for them accidentally by the number of surviving legitimate sons at the critical succession.

This creates a difficulty. In default of a full survey of the pattern of succession in the first generation after the settlement of England it is not easy to determine whether the differences illustrated above should be explained as variants within or breaches of the rule stated in the "Leges Henrici Primi". If the latter, there was clearly no rule at all. However, the former is much the more likely. There are convincing reasons for thinking that most of the apparently divergent successions arose from the parental disposition which the primitive form of the rule and the *post obitum* gift allowed. There is independent evidence that the father might determine the pattern of

[65] *Complete Peerage,* ii, pp. 386-7; *ibid.,* iii, pp. 164-6. In both these cases the heirs were minors. The matter is debatable because in the last resort there is no way of proving that there were no other legitimate children except where the heir was born after the father's death.

[66] *Dict. Nat. Biog., sub. nom.* William Malet.

[67] *Complete Peerage,* v, pp. 113-4.

[68] *Ibid.,* x, pp. 193-6.

[69] Eustace II of Boulogne was succeeded both in Boulogne and in his English acquisitions by his eldest son Eustace III. However, by the time of Eustace II's death in *c.* 1093-6, his second son, Godfrey, was already established in Lower Lorraine. See above, p. 74, n. 53.

[70] Roger Bigod was succeeded in his English acquisitions by William, who died in the White Ship in 1120. William in turn was succeeded by Hugh, first earl of Norfolk. The evidence is not perhaps wholly conclusive but it is generally accepted that William and Hugh were half-brothers, William being the elder. *Complete Peerage,* ix, pp. 578-9; W. Dugdale, *Monasticon Anglicanum,* new edn. J. Caley *et al.* (London, 1817-30), v, p. 148. The genealogy given in *Early Yorkshire Charters,* i, p. 461 is inaccurate at this point; cp. *ibid.,* p. 466.

[71] See Appendix II, note C, below, pp. 111-13.

succession. Some of this depends on Ordericus Vitalis,[72] but Ordericus is not alone. Geoffrey de Mandeville's foundation charter of Hurley Priory stated:

> I have given this to God and St. Peter with the consent of my wife Lethselina and by the concession of my son William, whom I have designated as my heir.[73]

William succeeded to the English acquisitions of the Mandevilles; Geoffrey's charters make it clear that there was at least one other son.[74] It also seems probable that families did not act at random. Where acquisition and inheritance were separated, the inheritance was often large so that the Norman patrimony still constituted a fair share for the eldest son as against the English acquisition. This was so, for example, for fitz Osbern, Montgomery, Grandmesnil and Montfort. In contrast, where the eldest son succeeded to the acquisition with or without the patrimony, the acquisition might exceed many times the old Norman patrimony. This was true, for example, of Bigod, Vere and Lacy.[75] By the end of the twelfth century Norman custom allowed the eldest son to choose the acquisition rather than the inheritance if he wished. This rule is first recorded in the "Très Ancien Coutumier" but not as a new provision;[76] it is likely that it arose from the circumstances of the Conquest in which the acquisition frequently exceeded the inheritance. It was apparently applied in the succession to Henry, earl of Warwick in 1119.[77] It seems probable therefore that the Conquest, far from leading to a rejection of these notions, contributed to their later formulation. Furthermore, even where the descent of property was determined by a series of complicated settlements, the original patrimony tended to descend by primogeniture. It was still Waleran, count of Meulan, the eldest son of the eldest son of Roger de Beaumont, who held the ancestral estates of Beaumont-le-Roger and Pont-Audemer in the twelfth century.[78] Finally, direct contraven-

---

[72] For Hauteville see Orderic Vitalis, ed. Chibnall, ii, p. 98; for Beaumont and Grandmesnil, ibid., ed. Chibnall, iv, pp. 302-4, 338.

[73] "Et hoc donum Deo et sancto Petro cum uxore mea Lethselina concessione filii mei Willelmi quem michi heredem facere disposui, quos eciam hujus elemosine participes fieri per omnia volo ... presentavi": Complete Peerage, v, p. 114, n. (c).

[74] Ibid., v, pp. 113-14.

[75] The Bigods and Lacys were tenants of Odo of Bayeux, the Veres of the bishops of Coutances and probably the count of Brittany. See L. C. Loyd, The Origins of some Anglo-Norman Families (Harleian Society, ciii, 1951) sub. nom., and for Vere, Complete Peerage, x, p. 193.

[76] Cap. viii, 2, 3, ed. Tardif, p. 8.

[77] See Appendix II, note C, below, pp. 111-13.

[78] Ibid.

tions of this slowly hardening system of descent seem to have been rare. Henry I intervened in the descent of the barony of Marshwood to enfeoff the son of a second marriage on the ground that "he was a better knight", but this was done *per voluntatem regis;* in 1206 the decision was reversed and the descendant of the elder line was recognized as the lawful heir.[79] When in 1162-6 Henry and Sewall, grandsons of Saswalo, tenant of the Ferrers fee, decided to reverse their order of seniority, they did so by record of final concord in their lord's court; Sewall and Fulcher son of Henry confirmed the arrangement in like manner thirty years later.[80]

The ruling house was equally subject to these rules. A proper distinction between public and private law was still in the distant future. Even after 1199, when Roman concepts of *iura coronae* were taking shape, John's succession, the *casus regis,* determined the competing claims of uncle and nephew in private actions for two generations.[81] Earlier the options available within the distinction between inheritance and acquisition as it appears in the "Leges Henrici Primi", could easily accommodate other ideas. The king/duke could designate his eldest son as his successor in the Carolingian style and direct to him both the inheritance and acquisition, but none of this infringed convention.[82] What he could not do was to prevent his eldest son from succeeding to the patrimony. The Conqueror, or later Henry II, might threaten this, even pronounce sentence of disinheritance on a rebellious eldest son, but it never came to much. The eldest son's claim on the patrimony, and the resulting potential patronage which he could wield, were always too strong. The "Leges Henrici Primi" allowed that a father, if abandoned by his son in mortal need, illness or poverty, might adopt any who aided him, relative or stranger, as his heir, but the matter was not automatic for the competing claims of the immediate heir and the newcomer had to be settled by the judgement of wise men.[83] In 1087, as the Conqueror lay on his deathbed at Caen, the wise men advised in favour of Robert.[84] The two successions where there was more than one surviving son, to the

---

[79] *Hist. MSS. Com.,* Wells, i, pp. 527-8; *Pipe Roll 10 John* (Pipe Roll Soc., new ser., xxiii, 1945), p. 113; Stenton, *op. cit.,* pp. 37-8.

[80] Stenton, *op. cit.,* pp. 52-4, 263-4.

[81] T. F. T. Plucknett, *A Concise History of the Common Law,* 4th edn. (London, 1948), pp. 678-80.

[82] John Le Patourel, "The Norman succession 996-1135", *Eng. Hist. Rev.,* lxxxvi (1971), pp. 225-30; *Normandy and England 1066-1144* (Stenton Lecture, University of Reading, 1971), pp. 4-9.

[83] Cap. 88, 15 (ed. Liebermann, *Gesetze,* i, p. 604; ed. Downer, pp. 274-6).

[84] The monk of Caen, in William of Jumièges, *Gesta Normannorum Ducum,* ed. J. Marx (Rouen, 1914), pp. 145-7.

Conqueror and Henry II, reveal the rules operating in conventional form: the patrimony to the eldest, the acquisition to the younger.[85] Normandy and England, separable as inheritance and acquisition in 1087, became a single patrimony after 1135; England/Normandy and Maine/Anjou separable under Geoffrey of Anjou, became a single inheritance under Henry II.[86] The Norman/Angevin dominions and the lands of Eleanor of Aquitaine, separable under Henry II, were treated as a single inheritance after 1189. Henry II refused to acknowledge the division which his father Geoffrey of Anjou apparently made on his death-bed,[87] and after the death of the Young King in 1183 Richard the Lion Heart refused to "move up one" and make way for John Lackland in the maternal succession,[88] but otherwise the settlements of the ruling house executed the accepted division between inheritance and acquisition. The idea still survived in the thirteenth century. Gerald of Wales exhorted King John to pay due attention to Ireland so that it might provide a kingdom for a younger son.[89] It was largely from acquisitions, conquests and escheats that the appanages of both the English and French royal houses were formed under Henry III and Louis VIII.

The distinction between inheritance and acquisition was remarkably

[85] Professor Le Patourel has taken a different view. See Appendix II, note A, below, pp. 107-10.

[86] The pattern may have been broken in 1187, when, according to Gerald of Wales, Henry planned to give all his French possessions except Normandy to John, leaving Richard with the old Anglo-Norman dominion: Opera, viii, ed. G. F. Warner (Rolls Series, 1891), p. 232. The story may simply derive from a tactical manoeuvre by Henry or Philip Augustus. It is not supported in the Gesta Henrici. In 1183, after the young King's death, Henry had intended Aquitaine alone for John: Gesta Henrici, i, pp. 308, 311.

[87] According to William of Newburgh, Geoffrey of Anjou provided on his death-bed (1151) that Henry should hold Normandy, Maine and Anjou until England was conquered; once that was achieved the maternal inheritance of England and Normandy was to go to Henry and the paternal inheritance of Maine and Anjou to his younger brother, Geoffrey. Meanwhile Geoffrey was to have the three castles of Chinon, Loudun and Mirebeau. This reversal of the usual order, giving the marital acquisition to the elder brother, recognized the fact that Henry was already involved in the conquest of England and in 1150 had succeeded his father as duke of Normandy. Henry did not execute the settlement and apparently obtained papal dispensation from his oath to it in 1156. Chronicles of the reigns of Stephen, Henry II and Richard I, ed. R. Howlett (Rolls Series, 1884-90), i, pp. 112-14; J. Boussard, Le Comté d'Anjou sous Henri Plantagenêt et ses fils (1151-1204) (Paris, 1938), pp. 68 ff.; Le Gouvernement d'Henri II Plantagenêt (Paris, 1956), pp. 8-11, 408-10. A fragmentary Angevin chronicle lends some support to Newburgh's account: Chroniques des Comtes d'Anjou, ed. L. Halphen and R. Poupardin (Paris, 1913), pp. 251-2. It should be noted that Maine was an anomaly in this respect since it was part of both the Angevin and the Norman inheritance.

[88] Gesta Henrici, i, pp. 308, 311.

[89] Opera, ed. J. F. Dimock (Rolls Series, 1858), v, p. 407.

convenient for an aggressive and burgeoning aristocracy. At one and the same time it resolved the problems created by the accumulation of both estates and sons. For it to work effectively there had to be a steady flow of acquisitions; enough to provide for the family; not so much as to upset the balance between acquisition and ancestral lands. The conquest of England upset this balance. In 1087 the eldest son succeeded to the Duchy while the younger acquired a kingdom. In the quarrel among the Conqueror's heirs families found themselves in one of three situations. Either the feoffee of the Conqueror was still alive; or he had been succeeded by a single heir, thus establishing a united Anglo-Norman patrimony; or he was dead and his land divided, the Norman patrimony usually going to the eldest son, the English acquisition to the younger. The first two circumstances encouraged rebellion. Men could not serve two conflicting lords; lay barons and great ecclesiastical lords alike had perforce to choose sides, if only because they had an obvious interest in re-establishing the single lordship which William's death had divided.[90] The third circumstance was even more dangerous to the ruling house because it was more complicated and more enduring. To deprive a tenant for treason often did no more than drive him into the protection of a brother, uncle or cousin across the Channel. If he were replaced in his estates, he still nursed a claim to them, a claim which was carefully tended by his heirs, direct or indirect, and strengthened by the political weight of the collateral branch of the family still undisturbed in its possessions. This was the substance of the tenurial and political crisis of the Anglo-Norman period. Rules of succession were applied in political circumstances quite unsuited to them.

The division between England and Normandy compelled the ruling house to intervene in title and succession. But such intervention could also be acceptable, even essential, in other circumstances. Title to an acquisition was not so strong as title to ancestral possessions. The Conqueror was able to readjust the initial acquisitions of the Normans in England without any apparent difficulty or friction; exchanges were made and compensation provided when a new tenant-in-chief was accommodated on land

[90] See the speech which Ordericus puts in the mouth of Odo of Bayeux — "How can we give proper service to two mutually hostile and distant lords. If we serve Duke Robert of Normandy properly we shall offend his brother William, and he will deprive us of our revenues and honours in England. On the other hand if we obey King William, Duke Robert will deprive us of our patrimonies in Normandy": Orderic Vitalis, ed. Chibnall, iv, pp. 120-4.

already occupied;[91] and it was still possible under Henry I for Ranulf le Meschin to exchange one acquisition, the lordship of Carlisle, for another, the earldom of Chester.[92] Moreover, succession was not always simple. There were many circumstances involving twins, or claims through heiresses, or collateral title, or claims in the half blood, in which there was no consistent practice, let alone established custom. The more distant or divided the succession the more likely it was to be settled by an *ad hoc* arrangement. Such arrangements required the approval of the king/duke; many he no doubt instigated.[93] There were therefore many situations in which the ruling house might intrude. Intrusion for political reasons was all the easier.

Such intervention had to contend with a fundamental principle of title and succession: property law was family law.[94] The distinction between inheritance and acquisition was one of several means whereby the family sought both to maintain the unity of its property and to make some provision for cadet branches. Hence the family retained an interest until the relationship between collateral branches became so tenuous that it ceased to have any relevance, and this only

[91] The best example is provided by the Sussex baronies. See J. F. A. Mason, *William the First and the Sussex Rapes* (The Hastings and Bexhill Branch of the Historical Association, 1966), especially pp. 13-17.

[92] See Appendix II, note D, below, pp. 113-14.

[93] See: Henry I's confirmation *c.* 1107 of the division between the Beaumont twins (*Regesta Regum Anglo-Normannorum*, ii, ed. C. Johnson and H. A. Cronne [Oxford, 1956], no. 843) — the agreement took effect in 1118; Henry I's grant (1121) of Sibilia, daughter of Bernard of Neufmarché, to Miles of Gloucester, along with Bernard's acquisitions — "I give and concede this to him as Bernard's purchase which Bernard has restored to me, and this at the request of Bernard, his wife and his barons" ("Et hoc ei dono et concedo sicut emptionem Beornardi quam mihi reddidit et hoc requisitione ipsius Beornardi et uxoris suae et baronum suorum") (J. H. Round, *Ancient Charters prior to A.D. 1200* [Pipe Roll Society, x, 1888], no. 6); Henry's confirmation (1123) of the arrangements for the succession to the lands of Geoffrey Ridel, which passed by marriage to the Bassets (F. M. Stenton, *op. cit.*, pp. 34-6, 259-60; *Regesta*, ii, no. 1389), subsequently confirmed by Matilda and Henry of Anjou (*Regesta Regum Anglo-Normannorum*, iii, ed. H. A. Cronne and R. H. C. Davis [Oxford, 1968], nos. 43, 44); Stephen's confirmation (*c.* 1137) of the marriage arrangements between Roger, son of Miles of Gloucester, and Cecily, daughter of Pain fitz John, which is remarkable for its careful distinction between inheritance, acquisition and *maritagium* and its enumeration of the last two (*Regesta*, iii, no. 312); Henry of Anjou's confirmation of the division of the Paynel estates (1151-3) (*Early Yorkshire Charters*, vi, pp. 96-7); letters of Robert de Caux to Henry II sent when on the point of departing for the Crusade (1188), attorning his nephew to take charge of his land and making him heir to his estate (J. H. Round, *Calendar of Documents preserved in France* [London, 1899], no. 277).

[94] "The family . . . is at the same time a group of persons and a group of possessions": Génestal, *Le Parage normand*, p. 40 and *ibid.*, pp. 38-40.

occurred after the lapse of several generations.[95]   The family always sought to ensure reversion.   Possession always left a residual family claim, strong or weak, depending on the length and terms of tenure and the distance of the relationship.

The consequences of the Norman Conquest must be understood within this emerging system of family law.   It led to an enormous increase in the number and value of acquisitions.   This in turn created a large number of collateral titles to property which became more distant and more complex as each generation passed.   But one family settlement, that of the ruling house, cut across all the rest. The structure of inheritance assumed dependence on a single feudal lord.   In 1087 this ceased to hold good.   Title and succession were now at odds with the demands of political allegiance.   The great noble families tried to resolve this dilemma by rebellion, the king/duke by using disseisin and disinheritance as penalties for disloyalty. This only made matters worse, for the regrant of sequestered estates created rival family claims.

This tenurial crisis had serious and permanent effects on the development of English law.   First, it focussed attention on the use of disseisin and disinheritance as penalties for political misbehaviour, on all those questions of process and punishment which came to a head in Magna Carta.   Secondly, it probably contributed to and may explain a unique feature of Anglo-Norman custom: the wardship of heirs belonged not to the family as in other parts of western France, but to the feudal lord; in the case of tenants-in-chief, to the king/ duke.[96]   In 1100 Henry I promised in his charter of liberties to accept the more general system of family wardship,[97] but seigneurial ward-ship remained the rule.   In the circumstances which followed the separation of England and Normandy in 1087 it was the only practicable system for all concerned, for the nobility as well as the ruling house.   Thirdly, it imposed essential limitations on the law of succession.   Direct succession of son to father was not in question. This might be denied in practice to the sons of traitors, but that arose from the development of felony and treason, not from any attempt to

---

[95] Pollock and Maitland, *History of English Law*, ii, pp. 295-308; Plucknett, *op. cit.*, pp. 680-1.   Germanic law fixed surprisingly wide limits, i.e. the fifth, sixth or seventh *parentela*.   Bracton allowed six, but in England in the thirteenth century the point was determined procedurally by the dates of limitation of legal memory.

[96] J. Yver, "Groupe de Coutumes", pp. 40-1.

[97] Cap. 4 (*Select Charters*, 9th edn., p. 118).

deny the normal rule of inheritance.[98]   However, collateral succession, succession through married heiresses, indeed distant succession of any kind, were a different matter.   They were likely to lead under Rufus or Henry I to a vassal of Duke Robert or an ally of William Clito, and under Henry II, his sons and grandson, to a vassal of the Capetian house.   There was genuine doubt whether such an heir could lawfully perform homage and fealty to a king of England. Hence the answer to the question — "inheritance by whom?" — was for a son or an unmarried daughter in the king/duke's custody, "yes"; but for a married daughter, brother, uncle, cousin or relation of the half blood, "maybe".   This was the critical point where politics and patronage intruded into custom and law.   Intervention was not limited to those situations where the claimant's loyalty was immediately suspect.   Indirect succession was less certain *in toto* and in principle.   The more distant or debatable the claim, the more substantial would be the overlord's consent and the more likely that he would be concerned with the political import of the settlement.

Such claims and the resulting conflicts were an important element in the tenurial crisis of the early twelfth century.[99]   The quarrel for

---

[98] The punishment of such felony, like the law of succession, developed under political pressures.   It seems likely that Henry I was much less lenient than Rufus and enforced confiscation more rigorously and permanently.   It may be that he deliberately set out to endow his immediate supporters with landed estate.   He was also for a time in a more precarious situation than his brother. Rufus was the lawful successor to the English crown; Henry was a usurper who had overridden the claims of his elder brother and feudal lord.

[99] The point may be illustrated by many well-known examples.   For the pursuit of a distant claim *iure uxoris* see the interest of Robert de Beaumont in the lands and titles of Roger, earl of Hereford, his wife's great-uncle, deprived in 1075, which brought him into conflict with Miles of Gloucester, earl of Hereford: *Complete Peerage*, vii, pp. 529-30; *Regesta*, iii, nos. 437, 438, 439. For a conflict lying between claims of a daughter and her husband against a nephew see the dispute between Hugh de Beaumont and Miles de Beauchamp over the custody of Bedford castle: Round, *Geoffrey de Mandeville*, p. 171 n.; Stenton, *op. cit.*, pp. 237-8.   For a dispute between collaterals where the matter was complicated by confiscation see the quarrel between Gilbert de Lacy and Roger, earl of Hereford, the one the grandson and the other the husband of the great-grand-daughter of Walter de Lacy; Cronne, *The Reign of Stephen*, pp. 156-63, which gives the best summary of the plentiful literature on this problem. For a claim arising in the half-blood through the successive marriages of an heiress see the conflict between Simon II de Senliz, son of the first marriage, and King David of Scotland, husband of the second marriage of Maud, daughter of Waltheof: *Regesta Regum Scottorum*, i, ed. G. W. S. Barrow (Edinburgh, 1960), pp. 102-3.   For a conflict arising from the claims of co-heiresses see the quarrel between the Marmions and William de Beauchamp over Tamworth, pursuing claims based on marriage to daughters of Urse d'Abetot, brother of Robert the Dispenser: Cronne, *op. cit.*, p. 173.   All these disputes played an important part in the politics of the Anarchy.   Finally for a conflict between cousins, the one female and the other disadvantaged by title through a female and the existence of an elder brother, see the quarrel between the Empress Matilda and Stephen of Blois for the realm of England.

the Crown itself was simply one of many, but one which exacerbated all the rest since it provided rival sources of patronage and encouraged rival claimants in their mutually inconsistent ambitions. Henry II's accession did not put an end to this. The loyalty of the expectant heir, the "foreign" connections of the family, clearly weighed in the recognition of William II de Forz, titular count of Aumâle, as claimant to the honours of Holderness and Skipton in 1214,[100] in the differing treatment of the two halves of the honour of Leicester between 1204 and 1231 when Simon III de Montfort's claim was finally recognized,[101] and in the wavering and occasional acknowledgement of the succession of the counts of Eu in the honour of Tickhill.[102] The royal line itself was affected; in 1199 John's succession was assisted by the fact that the Bretons had placed Arthur in the custody of Philip Augustus of France.[103]

Intervention was not based solely on the need to arbitrate or ensure a loyal successor. Loyalty was relative. There was no obvious borderline between royal rejection of a claimant as an actual or potential enemy, and royal preference on personal or political grounds for one claimant over another. The Crown exercised its patronage with confidence in cases where there was no danger of treason, where it was simply a matter of preferring one claimant over another because he could pay more, or because he was a favoured royal agent, or perhaps on both counts for the two not infrequently went together. On the death of William de Mandeville, earl of Essex, in 1189, the nearest heir was his aunt, Beatrice, widow of William de Say (d. 1144). Richard I first accepted a proffer of 7,000 m. for the Mandeville estates and the earldom from Geoffrey de Say, Beatrice's younger son, but Geoffrey failed to meet the terms of payment and the land was taken into the Crown's hand. The King then accepted a proffer

---

[100] William de Forz was instated in October 1214: *Rot. Chartarum,* p. 201b; *Rot. Litt. Pat.,* p. 122b. He had been invited to England at the request of Robert de Ros in October 1213 (*ibid,* p. 104b); it seems likely that he proved his loyalty by service on the Poitevin expedition in 1214 (*Rot. Litt. Claus,* i, p. 200b).

[101] On the death of Robert, earl of Leicester in 1204, his property was divided between his sisters, Amice, wife of Simon I de Montfort, vassal of King Philip of France, and Margaret, who married Saer de Quenci, cr. earl of Winchester 1207. In 1207 Simon II de Montfort firmly committed himself to the French cause; as a result this half of the honour of Leicester was taken into the Crown's hands and was only restored, with the earldom of Leicester, to Simon III in 1231-9. Simon III was the younger son of Simon II and had abandoned any interest in the French patrimony of his house. He was therefore free of the political ties which had led to the forfeiture. *Complete Peerage,* vii, pp. 537-45.

[102] See Appendix II, note E, below, p. 114.

[103] This was in 1196. Richard began to treat John as his successor almost immediately.

of 3,000 m. from Geoffrey fitz Peter, husband of Beatrice de Say, daughter of William de Say (d. 1177), Geoffrey de Say's elder brother, and grand-daughter of Beatrice in the senior line. Richard I confirmed this at Messina in January 1190 in a charter which referred to fitz Peter "as the right and nearest heir". The claims of Beatrice de Say's sister, Maud, wife of William de Bocland, were totally ignored, despite the fact that the two sisters had divided the lands of their father, William. The bid of William's brother, Geoffrey, was also shelved. It was only revived in 1213-14 when in different political circumstances, King John encouraged Geoffrey and his son to renew it; they then proffered 15,000 m. The succession raised an uncertain point of law, namely representation, complicated in this case by the fact that the senior line was represented by two daughters. But there can be little doubt that Geoffrey fitz Peter won in 1190 because he was a trusted supporter of the Crown. His winnings were put in jeopardy in 1213-14 because this was not true of his son, Geoffrey de Mandeville, son-in-law of Robert fitz Walter and one of the leaders of the rebellion of 1215.[104]

The relative insecurity of indirect succession had a cash value. The more distant the succession the more likely it was that the claimant would have to pay a heavy *finis terrae* or offer a high price for the good will or arbitration of the king in order to defeat his rivals.[105] Distant and collateral succession remained relatively weak. Here as elsewhere Edward I had a shrewd eye for the exercise of royal influence. His arrangements with Aveline, countess of Aumâle, were to the detriment of distant heirs going back to Stephen, count of Aumâle, d. 1127. His settlement with Isabella, dowager countess of Aumâle, excluded the Courtenays, her cousins, from the greater part of her inheritance. The marriage of Edward's daughter, Elizabeth, to Humphrey de Bohun was to the detriment of Humphrey's brother. Edward's settlement with Roger Bigod damaged the interests of Roger's brother and cousin. The marriage of Thomas of Lancaster to Alice de Lacy excluded Lacy collateral claims, and the marriage of Joan of Acre to Gilbert of Clare excluded Gilbert's daughters by his first wife.[106] Edward was no tyrant denying right, title and inheri-

[104] *Complete Peerage*, v, pp. 120-4; xi, pp. 465-6. See also S. Painter, *The Reign of King John* (Baltimore, 1949), pp. 262-3; J. C. Holt, *Magna Carta* (Cambridge, 1965), pp. 121-3.

[105] It should be noted that the history of relief in the twelfth century requires reassessment in the light of the type of succession involved. There is no doubt that direct succession involved much lower reliefs than indirect. The point is difficult to express statistically since reliefs for indirect succession cannot always be distinguished from proffers for royal arbitration in legal actions or simple fines for land.

[106] McFarlane, "Had Edward I a 'policy' towards the earls?".

tance: in the true line of the Norman and Angevin kings he was simply exploiting the relative weakness of indirect and collateral succession.

Hence the certainty of title depended on the directness of the claim: on the answer to the question — "inheritance by whom?" But this was not the only variable. At any succession, whatever the precise claim of the heir, and at any time, whatever the exact title of the possessor, certainty of tenure also turned on the nature of the property, on the answer to the question — "inheritance of what?" Property was not homogeneous. In the main it lay in land, but it also included castles, office and title. Each of these categories was subject to its own rules; each followed its own peculiar line of development within the whole. The strength of hereditary title might wax in one setting while it waned in another.

Title to castles was markedly less secure than title to land. The distinction between royal and private castles was blurred by the need to license private castle-building, by the creation of hereditary castellanships and by a prerogative right of seizure. The Norman "Consuetudines et Justicie" of 1091 state that castles could only be built by ducal licence and that the duke might seize them into his hand if he wished.[107] This last prerogative was openly admitted in 1090 in the dispute over the castle of Brionne between Robert fitz Baldwin and the Beaumonts. According to Ordericus neither would admit the claim of the other, but Robert fitz Baldwin accepted the overriding right of Duke Robert even though he regarded Brionne as his hereditary property: "If you desire to have Brionne as your father had it as his own property, I will make no difficulty in delivering it to you; but otherwise I will keep my inheritance and will not transfer it to anyone while I live".[108] The right of seizure was not abandoned. In 1154, Henry II, far from bowing to title and inheritance in this type of property, proceeded to undermine them with persistent intent. Already before his accession he had taken over Wallingford from Brian fitz Count. He probably regarded this as the resumption of a custody, but his actions were not restricted to this. In 1153 he concluded an agreement with Bishop Jocelyn of Salisbury providing for the temporary retention of Devizes which Stephen had seized

---

[107] "Consuetudines et Justicie", cap. 4; C. H. Haskins, *Norman Institutions* (Cambridge, Mass., 1918), p. 282. For comment see J. Yver, "Les châteaux forts en Normandie jusqu'au milieu du XIIe siècle", *Bulletin de la Société des Antiquaires de Normandie*, liii (1955), pp. 60-3.

[108] Ordericus Vitalis, ed. Chibnall, iv, pp. 204-8. The situation was confused by the fact that both parties had a hereditary claim to the castle. It had belonged to Gilbert de Brionne, Robert fitz Baldwin's grandfather; it had also been granted to Roger de Beaumont, Robert of Meulan's father, in exchange for the custody of Ivry (*ibid.*). See also Yver, *op. cit.*, pp. 66-9.

from Bishop Roger in 1139.[109] He did not return it; instead in 1157 he bought off Jocelyn's claims by the grant of 30 librates of land from the royal demesne and various churches along with a promise of royal support in recovering the lost rights of the see of Salisbury.[110] After the death of Ranulf de Gernons, earl of Chester, he retained Nottingham, Stafford, Newcastle-under-Lyme, Tickhill, Bolsover and the Peak. In 1154 he recovered Northampton during the minority of Simon de Senliz and between 1155 and 1157 he took Scarborough from the fee of Aumâle, Hereford from the fee of Roger, earl of Hereford, Norwich, Pevensey, Eye, Lancaster, Lewes, Conisborough and Sandal from William, count of Boulogne, Stephen's son, and Framlingham, for a time, from Hugh Bigod, earl of Norfolk. In 1158 the Mandeville castles of Pleshey and Saffron Walden were destroyed. Similar action was taken by Henry again in 1174 and by Richard I in 1194.[111] Just as Henry seized Devizes from Bishop Jocelyn of Salisbury, so Richard seized Les Andelys from the see of Rouen for the construction of Château Gaillard.[112] John was equally demanding; when in 1213 he had to restore the traitors, Eustace de Vesci and Robert fitz Walter, he first destroyed their castles.[113] In 1215 the security of tenure of castles was raised in principle. The restoration of castles was included in chapter 52 of Magna Carta,[114] and John had to restore fortifications which he had seized during the recent crisis.[115] Furthermore, he was now faced by a number of claims to hereditary title: Robert fitz Walter to Hertford, William de Lanvallei to Colchester, William de Mowbray to York, Henry de Bohun, earl of Hereford, to Trowbridge, and Geoffrey de Mandeville to the Tower of London. The first two were

[109] *Regesta*, iii, no. 796.

[110] *Charters and Documents illustrating the history of the cathedral city and diocese of Salisbury*, ed. W. D. Macray (Rolls Series, 1891), pp. 29-30.

[111] R. Allen Brown, "A list of Castles, 1154-1216", *Eng. Hist. Rev.*, lxxiv (1959), pp. 250-5. The evidence for the seizure of the castle of William, count of Boulogne, in 1157, two years before his death, is provided by Robert of Torigny (*Chronicles of the reigns of Stephen, Henry II and Richard I*, iv, pp. 192-3); if correct Henry must have overridden the terms of the Treaty of Westminster of 1153.

[112] F. M. Powicke, *The Loss of Normandy* (Manchester, 1961), pp. 115-16. Like Jocelyn of Salisbury, Archbishop Walter of Rouen received compensation, in Dieppe, Louviers and elsewhere.

[113] R. Allen Brown, *op. cit.*, pp. 254-5; J. C. Holt, *The Northerners* (Oxford, 1961), pp. 94-5; *Histoire des ducs de Normandie et des rois d'Angleterre*, ed. F. Michel (Société de l'histoire de France, 1840), pp. 118-19.

[114] It did not, however, figure in cap. 25 of the *Articuli*.

[115] Richmond to Ruald fitz Alan, Fotheringhay to Earl David of Huntingdon (*Rot. Litt. Pat.*, pp. 143b, 144, 148b).

admitted,[116] but John contested the rest. A local enquiry was held into William de Mowbray's right to the hereditary custody of York.[117] When the honour of Trowbridge was restored to Henry de Bohun on 19 June 1215 a distinction was made between the *planae terrae* and the castle, for the restoration of which the King was allowed respite until 28 June; there is no evidence that it was restored.[118] The Mandeville claim to the Tower was never accepted.[119] Moreover, John clearly believed that he had rights similar to those outlined in the "Consuetudines et Justicie" of 1091. The confusion which arose over the arrangements he had made with Stephen Langton for the custody of the archbishop's castle of Rochester was the immediate cause of the renewed civil war in the autumn of 1215. In the King's eyes Langton was a "notorious and barefaced traitor" because "he did not surrender our castle of Rochester to us in our great need".[120]

Property in office was more of a problem. The rule stated in the "Dialogus de Scaccario", that officials were liable in their bodies for the proper performance of their duties, applied to hereditary as well as temporary officials.[121] That tenure should be justified by good behaviour was an unchallengeable and enduring doctrine. But the strength of hereditary title also varied with the nature of the office. Foresterships-in-fee exemplified hereditary office at its most precarious. From Henry I onwards foresters were deprived of office or compelled to fine heavily for restoration when it was discovered that they had transgressed the somewhat lax standards set

[116] Hertford was restored to Robert fitz Walter "as his right" (*ibid.*, p. 144b). The terms of the transfer of Colchester to William de Lanvallei are not recorded (*ibid.*, p. 151), but the Barnwell chronicle states that he had claimed the castle as of right (*Memoriale Fratris Walteri de Coventria*, ed. W. Stubbs [Rolls Series, 1872-3], i, p. 221). The Lanvallei barony was formed from land held earlier by Eudo Dapifer. Henry I granted the tower and castle of Colchester to Eudo in 1101 (*Regesta*, ii, no. 552).

[117] For the basis of Mowbray's claim see *Complete Peerage*, ix, p. 370, n.a. For the enquiry see *Rot. Litt. Pat.*, p. 143b, *Rot. Litt. Claus*, i, p. 215, reprinted in Holt, *Magna Carta*, p. 346. The case is discussed by J. C. Holt in "The Making of Magna Carta", *Eng. Hist. Rev.*, lxxii (1957), pp. 408-9; *The Northerners*, p. 120; *Magna Carta*, pp. 158, 254, 306.

[118] *Rot. Litt. Claus.*, i, p. 215, reprinted in Holt, *Magna Carta*, p. 346 and discussed *ibid.*, pp. 254, 259.

[119] Geoffrey de Mandeville's claim must have been based on the grants of Stephen and Matilda to Geoffrey II de Mandeville (*Regesta*, iii, nos. 274-6) or on the fact that his father, Geoffrey fitz Peter, had custody of the Tower until his death in 1213, probably as Justiciar. Geoffrey de Mandeville was required to surrender it on succeeding to his father's lands and rights in November 1213 (*Rot. Litt. Pat.*, p. 105b; Holt, *Magna Carta*, pp. 122-3).

[120] V. H. Galbraith, *Studies in the Public Records* (London, 1948), pp. 136, 161-2; Holt, *Magna Carta*, pp. 255-6.

[121] *Dialogus de Scaccario*, ed. and trans. Charles Johnson (London, 1950), pp. 78-81.

to their honesty and efficiency.[122]   Some of the offices of state, in contrast, the stewardships, constableships, marshalcy and chamberlainships, represented hereditary office at its most ancient and secure; some of these enjoyed a continuous history from the Conquest onwards despite the accidents of family history.[123]

Between these two extremes lay the major offices of local government.   In Normandy the *vicomté* was already heritable by the end of the eleventh century.   In England the equivalent office, the shrievalty, sometimes associated with one or more castellanships, was held by two or more generations of the same family in Gloucestershire, Worcestershire, Herefordshire, Wiltshire, Devon, Kent, Norfolk, probably in Leicestershire and possibly Warwickshire and Essex.[124] Whether the office was properly hereditary may be doubted.   In some counties the family lost control at an early date;[125] in others its tenure of the office was discontinuous.[126]   Formal confirmation of hereditary title to the office was unusual, except under Stephen. The shrievalty of Worcester passed from Urse d'Abetot to his son and then to his son-in-law, Walter de Beauchamp and to Walter's son, William.   But in 1131 Henry I confirmed William de Beauchamp in his father's lands and in his father's office of Dispenser, without mentioning any title to the shrievalty; this was not confirmed *in feodo et hereditarie* until Matilda's grant to William of 1141.[127]   Similarly there is no direct evidence of a Mandeville claim to the hereditary constableship of the Tower and the shrievalties of London and Middlesex, Essex and Hertfordshire until the charters of Stephen and Matilda of 1141.[128]   By Stephen's time tenure of local office had become the object of aristocratic ambition.   Here the issue of hereditary title may have been one of principle between the Crown and its vassals.   But if so, the accession of Henry II brought defeat

[122] *Regesta*, ii, no. 1518; Holt, *The Northerners*, p. 161.

[123] J. H. Round, *The King's Sergeants and Officers of State* (London, 1911), especially pp. 35-51; G. H. White, "The Constables under the Norman Kings", *The Genealogist*, new ser., xxxviii (1921), pp. 113-27; "The household of the Norman Kings", *Trans. Royal Hist. Soc.*, 4th ser., xxx (1947), pp. 127-55; *Regesta*, ii, pp. xi-xvii.

[124] W. A. Morris, *The Medieval English Sheriff to 1300* (Manchester, 1927), pp. 50-2.   For Gloucestershire and Herefordshire see also D. Walker, "Miles of Gloucester, earl of Hereford", *Trans. of the Bristol and Gloucestershire Arch. Soc.*, lxxvii (1958), pp. 66-70.

[125] Morris, *op. cit.*, p. 51.

[126] For example the successive tenure of Wiltshire by Edward, Walter, William and Patrick of Salisbury was interrupted by William de Pont de l'Arche in 1110 and by Warin the sheriff in 1128-30: Morris, *op. cit.*, p. 78; Pipe Roll 31 Henry I, *Magnum Rotulum 31 Henry I*, ed. J. Hunter (London, 1833), p. 12.

[127] *Regesta*, ii, no. 1710, appendix, no. cclvi; *Regesta*, iii, no. 68.

[128] *Regesta*, iii, nos. 275-6; Round, *Geoffrey de Mandeville*, pp. 151-4.

not victory for the hereditary principle. The sheriffs were investigated, many were removed, and the office ceased to be hereditary. Another local office to which heritable title had been claimed, the county justiciarship, was abolished. Title to local office became more precarious as title to land became more secure. By 1215 it was beyond revival.[129]

It may be that this also affected the earldoms. The idea that an earldom was an office was still represented vestigially by the receipt of the third penny. Under Stephen the earls had exercised real power.[130] In the late twelfth century succession to the title and the associated estates did not always go together. William de Albini was styled earl of Arundel in 1189; he did not receive the honour and castle of Arundel until June 1190.[131] William de Ferrers succeeded to the honour of Tutbury in 1190-1. He was styled earl of Ferrers on the Pipe Roll of 1194, but was not girded with the sword of the county of Derby until 1199.[132] Geoffrey fitz Peter acquired the lands of William de Mandeville, earl of Essex, in 1190 and received the third penny from that day. He styled himself earl of Essex in a charter of 1191 but was not granted the sword of his county until 1199.[133] Ranulf of Chester obtained the lands of his Roumare cousins in 1198, but was not recognized as earl of Lincoln until 1217. In this case there was an alternative claim from Gilbert de Gant, but this probably did little to deter King John after 1205 when his relations with Ranulf became settled for the rest of the reign. It is more likely that recognition of the claim was delayed because the title had lapsed after the death of William I de Roumare in 1159-61.[134]

These were not the only varieties of property. Mrs. Wood has illustrated another in her discussion of monastic patronage. This was attached to estate in land, yet here also there was room for argument and royal intrusion. The rights of the founding family

[129] William de Mowbray's claim to the castle of York, the forest of Yorkshire and the manor of Pocklington is a possible example of such a claim, but by implication only; the shrievalty was not mentioned specifically: *Rot. Litt. Claus.*, i, p. 215; Holt, *Magna Carta*, pp. 346-7.

[130] Davis, *King Stephen*, pp. 129-44.

[131] *Complete Peerage*, i, pp. 235-6.

[132] *Pipe Roll 6 Richard* (Pipe Roll Soc., new ser., v, 1928), *passim*; *Complete Peerage*, iv, p. 194.

[133] *Complete Peerage*, v, pp. 122-4. The title appears in Geoffrey's charter to William Pointel, concerning the custody of one of the undertenancies of the Mandeville fee, witnessed by Reginald, bishop of Bath, d. 26 Dec. 1191 (William Salt Library, MS, S.D. [Pearson], no. 248). I am obliged to Mr. F. B. Stitt for bringing this charter to my notice.

[134] Holt, *The Northerners*, pp. 26-7; *Complete Peerage*, vii, pp. 667-75.

were re-asserted both in 1215 and 1258.[135] Nor was the Crown always the aggressor. The movement towards the mediatization of boroughs under Stephen illustrates yet another area of confused property rights; here the nobility was on the attack.[136] Property varied in nature just as claims to it varied in immediacy. Security of tenure and strength of title varied with both.

These conditions established both opportunities for and constraints on the actions of the Norman and Angevin kings. The gap between the political interest of the Crown and the extremes of baronial expectations, between one baronial claim and another, created a running argument which took place within a context of conventional practices and legal notions, some settled as hard and fast rules, others slowly crystallizing through the accumulation of precedent and recurrent political pressures. It remains to ask how serious was the argument, how deep the crisis, and in what ways the context altered in the course of the twelfth century.

Crises are not readily susceptible to measurement. One estimate is that up to 1135 53 per cent of the Anglo-Norman baronies descended undisturbed in the male line and 10 per cent through heiresses.[137] This leaves 37 per cent in which the succession was broken for one reason or another. This probably overestimates the disturbance since it seems to include discontinuity arising from the extinction of lines, voluntary abandonment or sale. Approaching the problem from the opposite logical pole it seems that deprivation and disinheritance affected the descent of twenty-four major baronies, that is 13 per cent of the total. It is arguable that even this is an over-estimate. It refers to baronies, not barons, still less families. Hence it ignores, for example, the fact that Pevensey, Berkhamstead and Launceston were all held by the count of Mortain and that Arundel, Shrewsbury, Lancaster and Pembroke were all in the hands of the sons of Roger of Montgomery. Stated in terms not of baronies, but of families the proportion would be much less. Conversely it would be very much more if it were stated in terms of Domesday *valets*, for it would include the lands of some of the most powerful men of the realm: Odo of Bayeux, the count of Mortain, and the families of fitz

---

[135] Susan Wood, *English Monasteries and their Patrons in the thirteenth century* (Oxford, 1955), pp. 8-28, 96-100.

[136] Stenton, *op. cit.*, pp. 234-5, 239-41.

[137] Davis, "What happened in Stephen's reign?", p. 9. Professor Davis's figures like my own are based on I. J. Sanders, *English Baronies* (Oxford, 1960). This does not trace all descents in sufficient detail for such analysis and hence sometimes presents discontinuity where in fact there was continuity, e.g. the barony of Staunton le Vale, which was the Domesday holding of Rainer de Brimou.

Osbern, Montgomery, Mowbray and Malet. Whether such a calculation would be worthwhile may be doubted. Whatever numerical expression it might yield to indicate disturbance in descent, there is at present no norm. Is 10 per cent per century about right as a general expression of the natural intransigence of barons and the wilfulness of kings? or 20 per cent or 30 per cent? And how would this compare with disturbance produced by natural causes: death, division and marriage? Until such figures are established the extent of one particular crisis cannnot be assessed arithmetically.

There are other more important difficulties. Forfeiture was not always complete. Sometimes baronies were transferred in marriage with an heiress of the deprived family to some reliable supporter of the Crown.[138] Sometimes a forfeiture was wholly or partly reversed.[139] Sometimes the succession was simply transferred within the owning family.[140] No doubt some of these arrangements arose from immediate political convenience, but there was also a powerful stream of thought running in favour of heritable title. The agreement of September 1146 between Robert, earl of Gloucester and Philip, bishop of Bayeux arranged that Robert should hold the lands which Ranulf of Chester held of the see of Bayeux "until there is an heir whom the Duke of Normandy recognizes as Ranulf's lawful heir". This was despite the fact that the charter marked the point at which Ranulf's lands were seized by the Angevins for his adherence

[138] The barony of Robert de Mowbray, confiscated in 1095, was transferred to Nigel de Albini who married Robert's widow: *Complete Peerage*, ix, pp. 368, 705-6. The barony of Robert de Montfort, banished in 1107, was transferred to Robert de Vere, second husband of Robert de Montfort's sister: *Domesday Monachorum*, pp. 68, 70; *Complete Peerage*, x, appendix (j), pp. 111-12. The estates of Roger d'Abetot, exiled in 1114, were transferred to Walter de Beauchamp who married Roger's sister: *Regesta*, ii, p. xvi, no. 1062, appendix no. lxxxiv. The lands of Ernulf de Hesding, hanged at Shrewsbury in 1138, went with his sister to Alan fitz Flaad: Sanders, *op. cit.*, p. 124.

[139] See the recurrent interest in Pevensey of the l'Aigle family which recovered seisin thrice — c. 1118, 1163-5 and 1212-6: Sanders, *op. cit.*, pp. 136-7. Stephen count of Aumâle was restored to Holderness c. 1102 after forfeiture in 1095 and interim possession by Arnulf de Montgomery, lord of Pembroke: Round, *Cal. Docs. France*, pp. xl-xli. Robert de Stuteville lost Cottingham in 1106; his grandson was reinstated under Stephen: *Early Yorkshire Charters*, ix, ed. C. T. Clay (Yorkshire Archaeological Society, Record Series, extra series, vii, 1952), pp. 1-5. The Lacys lost Pontefract c. 1114 but were restored in or after 1135: W. E. Wightman, *The Lacy Family in England and Normandy 1066-1194* (Oxford, 1966), pp. 66-73.

[140] When Roger de Lacy was banished in 1096 he was succeeded by his brother Hugh: Wightman, *op. cit.*, p. 169. Geoffrey de Mandeville, d. 1144, was not succeeded by his eldest son Arnulf, who was associated with his rebellion in East Anglia, but by his younger son Geoffrey: Round, *Geoffrey de Mandeville*, pp. 227-42.

to the cause of Stephen.[141]   The Crown also was affected; its
exercise of patronage could be expressed in terms which acknowledged the principles into which it was intruding.   Henry I's charter
granting Sybil of Neufmarché to Miles of Gloucester emphasized
that Bernard her father had surrendered his lands into the King's
hands so that they might be regranted.[142]   When Henry gave William
Mauduit the lands of Michael of Hanslope with his daughter Matilda
in marriage, the charter stated that Michael had made the king his
heir.[143]

One further limitation is striking and very important.   The
forfeiture of many of the leading families of the Conquest often had
very little effect on their immediate tenants.   It is likely that one of
the consequences of the Salisbury Oath of 1086 was that under-
tenants could expect security of tenure from the Crown in return for
loyalty.   That they got it is demonstrated by surviving acts which
converted undertenancies of rebellious lords into tenancies-in-chief
of the Crown,[144] or excepted the estates of loyal undertenants from
the grant of a rebel's estates to a new tenant-in-chief.[145]   This left
a permanent mark on the tenurial structure of the realm.   Many of
the established baronies of the late twelfth century originated in
enfeoffments made by the first great Norman lords: Aldington,
Chilham, Folkestone, Port and Ros by Odo of Bayeux; Castle Holgate,
Cause, Pulverbatch, Wem and Wigmore by Roger of Montgomery;
Chiselborough, Hatch Beauchamp, Fossard and Trematon by
Robert, count of Mortain;[146] some of the Lancaster baronies by
Roger of Poitou,[147] some of the Northumbrian baronies by Robert de
Mowbray.[148]   The forfeiture of these men made a splash in the
chronicles, but where tenants remained loyal, it was only a surface

[141] *Regesta*, iii, no. 58.
[142] Round, *Ancient Charters*, no. 6.
[143] *Regesta*, ii, no. 1719.
[144] See Henry I's confirmation to Roger de Lacy of Bowland, which Roger
formerly held of Roger of Poitou: *Regesta*, ii, no. 611.
[145] Hence Stephen's grant of Hereford to Robert earl of Leicester excluded
the fees of Hugh de Mortimer, Osbert fitz Hugh, William de Briouze and Gotso
de Dinant, with the proviso that the earl could enjoy a mesne tenancy in Gotso's
case by his agreement: *Regesta*, iii, no. 437.
[146] Details of the above may be drawn from Sanders, *English Baronies, sub.
nom.*
[147] Clitheroe, Hornby, and probably Manchester and Penwortham; the fee
of the Constable of Chester was also an early creation but not certainly of
Roger: *V.C.H., Lancashire,* i, pp. 297-336; James Tait, *Medieval Manchester,
and the beginnings of Lancashire* (Manchester, 1904), pp. 120-30.
[148] Callerton (De la Val) certainly and possibly Redesdale and Mitford:
W. P. Hedley, *Northumberland Families* (The Soc. of Antiquaries of Newcastle
upon Tyne, 1968), i, pp. 18 ff.

disturbance which did not seriously affect the immediate management of much of the realm of England. The one obvious exception to the security of the undertenant itself proves the rule: if he owed his estate to an interloper in the tenancy-in-chief, then it might be vulnerable if the original owner was reinstated, especially after a short interval.[149] Otherwise the tenant was relatively secure if he remained loyal to the Crown. Liege lordship was a reality.

This leads to an awkward and important problem. In most countries in western Europe security of title and succession spread downwards from the upper to the lower social strata.[150] Much of the English evidence is consistent with this. Some is not.

In England life-tenures survived for a time after the Conquest. There are three clear and certain examples of the grant of estates for life or a term of lives in return for military service: by Robert Losinga, bishop of Hereford, Gilbert Crispin, abbot of Westminster, and Reginald, abbot of Abingdon.[151] Possibly similar tenancies, not certainly held by military service, can also be traced on the estates of the sees of Worcester and Winchester and the abbeys of Ely and Shrewsbury,[152] and it may be that all undertenancies recorded as held *de victu monachorum* or simply *de dominio* were regarded as temporary by monastic houses and cathedral chapters.[153] However, practice varied. At Abingdon, tenants recorded in Domesday were succeeded by their sons; the early evidence has been claimed to reveal "the extreme stability of the feudal arrangements on the Abingdon lands".[154] At Canterbury also, the families enfeoffed by Lanfranc were often still in possession of their estates in 1171; here inheritance

---

[149] Hence the grants which Arnulf of Pembroke made in free alms to the monastery of La Sauve and the cell of St. Martin of Sées at Pembroke from the lands of the honour of Holderness lapsed when Stephen of Aumâle was restored: Round, *Cal. Docs. France*, pp. xl-xli.

[150] See, for example, the views of Professor Duby, who established this for the Mâconnais, above, p. 67, n. 16. For Normandy see Carabie, *op. cit.*, pp. 276-7.

[151] V. H. Galbraith, "An episcopal land grant of 1085", *Eng. Hist. Rev.*, xliv (1929), pp. 353-72; J. Armitage Robinson, *Gilbert Crispin, Abbot of Westminster* (Cambridge, 1911), p. 38; *Chronicon monasterii de Abingdon*, ed. J. Stevenson (Rolls Series, 1858), ii, pp. 34-5. In the last instance life-tenure was emphasized deliberately in the teeth of the tenants' claim to inherit. However, this case was complicated by the grant of marriage portions to the three daughters and sole heirs of the tenant and a *post obitum* gift involving coparceny for which the Abbot claimed his approval had not been sought.

[152] Galbraith, *op. cit.*, pp. 363-8. For Winchester, see V. H. Galbraith, "Royal Charters to Winchester", *Eng. Hist. Rev.*, xxxv (1920), p. 387; for Shrewsbury see H. M. Colvin, "Holme Lacy: an episcopal manor and its tenants in the twelfth and thirteenth centuries", *Medieval Studies presented to Rose Graham*, ed. Veronica Ruffer and A. J. Taylor (Oxford, 1950), p. 17, n.

[153] V. H. Galbraith, "An episcopal land grant of 1085", pp. 363-8.

[154] D. C. Douglas, "Some early surveys from the abbey of Abingdon", *Eng. Hist. Rev.*, xliv (1929), pp. 620-2.

was a "matter of course".[155] Moreover, even the most striking examples of life-grants were only unavailing attempts to stay the establishment of hereditary tenure. Robert Losinga's grant of Holme, albeit a life-tenancy, confirmed Roger de Lacy in a holding of his father. Abbot Reginald's grant of Garsington was to the heirs of the previous tenant, Geoffrey Marshal. Both the Lacys and Geoffrey Marshal's heirs soon established hereditary control of all or part of these estates. Gilbert Crispin's grant of "Totenhall" to William Baynard also descended to his successors, the fitz Walters.[156] And this was typical; at Hereford grants in fee are recorded by c. 1110.[157] It is hazardous therefore to argue solely on the basis of this evidence that "heritability of fiefs was far from being generally established in the period immediately following the Norman Conquest".[158] None of the early life-tenures were described as fiefs unless or until they became hereditary.[159] As Professor Galbraith

[155] H. M. Colvin, "A list of the Archbishop of Canterbury's tenants by knight-service in the reign of Henry II", *Kent Records*, xviii (1964), pp. 1-40, especially pp. 3-4; F. R. H. Du Boulay, *The Lordship of Canterbury* (London, 1966), pp. 60-1. Compare also the peculiarly full statement of the arrangements made for a succession to an estate held of the abbey of Burton 1094-1113 — "he is to come into our chapter to give for his relief such a sum as a noble man ought to give for such land, swearing an oath as his father swore, giving as his father gave, holding as his father held" ("in capitulum nostrum veniet daturus pro relevatione ipsius terrae tantum pecuniae quantum nobilis homo dare debet pro tali terra, jurando similiter sicut pater ejus juravit, donando sicut pater ejus donavit, tenendo sicut pater ejus tenuit"): *The Burton Chartulary*, ed. G. Wrottesley (William Salt Society, v. pt. 1, 1884), p. 30.

[156] For Holme Lacy, see Colvin, *op. cit.*, pp. 15-40. The descendants of Gilbert Marshal were less successful at Garsington. William, son of Abbot Reginald of Abingdon, acquired an interest in land there for a time, and half the fee was subsequently granted by Abbot Vincent (1117-30) to Simon Dispenser (*Chron. Abingdon*, ii, pp. 166-7); the Marshals retained the other half (*V.C.H., Oxfordshire*, v, p. 139). For the descent of "Totenhall" see Armitage Robinson, *op. cit.*, p. 38-9.

[157] Galbraith, *op. cit.*, p. 368.

[158] E. L. Ganshof, *Feudalism*, 3rd English edn. (London, 1964), p. 135, a view followed by R. Allen Brown — "In the beginning the fief was not hereditary, and was scarcely to become so of right in England before 1154": *The Normans and the Norman Conquest* (London, 1969), pp. 241-2. Ganshof, however, thought that heritability was a characteristic feature of the English fief in the twelfth century (*loc. cit.*). Professor Galbraith emphasized that the evidence should not be pressed beyond the ecclesiastical estates from which it is drawn. Likewise, in considering the evidence concerning Bury, Peterborough, Abingdon and Canterbury, Professor Douglas attributed the reluctance of ecclesiastical lords to enfeoff beyond their service-quotas to the desire to avoid "hereditary military tenures which might entail a permanent alienation of ecclesiastical land": *Domesday Monachorum*, p. 71.

[159] For the Holme Lacy charter see Galbraith, *op. cit.*, p. 372; Holme Lacy was first described as a fief in the bishop's *carta* of 1166 (*ibid.*, p. 368; *Liber Niger Scaccarii*, ed. T. Hearne, Oxford, 1728, i, p. 150). For Garsington see *Chron. Abingdon*, ii, pp. 34-5. For Shrewsbury, see *Collectanea Topographica et Genealogica*, i (London, 1833), p. 25. For "Totenhall" see Armitage Robinson, *op. cit.*, p. 38.

suggested, it is likely that some conservative churchmen tried to stave off aristocratic importunity by resorting to an older form of tenure,[160] and it may be no accident that much of the evidence for life-tenancy comes from the west Midlands and the Marches where Wulfstan survived in the see of Worcester until 1095. But an English origin, although probable, is not certain; similar grants are also recorded in France and elsewhere on the continent.[161]

There are other weighty reasons for believing that tenure and succession were less secure in the lower ranks of the feudal hierarchy. The toponymic names of English knightly families are preponderantly English; only a minority attached their lineage to French estates. At this social level the French conquerors were much less conscious of family traditions of hereditary property and perhaps much readier to accept landed endowment on less certain terms. That there was a large contingent of adventurers and mercenaries in the armies which conquered and settled England is certain,[162] and it is equally certain that on some estates there were petty military tenements which were very different from the estate of several fees with which one tenant-in-chief might enfeoff another.[163] It also seems very probable that the term applied to this class in the mid-twelfth century — *miles* — had a more general meaning a century earlier, that it only acquired a restricted social sense as the men so described established their titles to heritable landed property or stemmed from families which enjoyed such title.[164] Finally the establishment of the action of *mort d'ancestor* and the assumption that it would normally be used by men

---

[160] *Op. cit.*, p. 369; cp. Wightman, *op. cit.*, pp. 128-9.

[161] See M. Prou, *Manuel de Paléographie* (Paris, 1904), ii, pl. 14 for examples of 1100 and 1138; these do not specify military service, but nor do the pre-Conquest equivalents or many of the Anglo-Norman examples. The existence of precarious military tenures on the continent has long been recognized. The work of Flach and Luchaire on this point is conveniently summarized in *Feudal Documents from the Abbey of Bury St. Edmunds*, ed. D. C. Douglas (London, 1932), pp. ciii-civ, nn. 5, 1. See also Guilhiermoz, *op. cit.*, pp. 195-201. Bloch gave considerably less weight than these earlier authorities to the late examples of a precarious tenure: *op. cit.*, Paris, 1939, pp. 303-4; London, 1961, pp. 196-7.

[162] See especially J. O. Prestwich, "War and Finance in the Anglo-Norman state", *Trans. Royal Hist. Soc.*, 5th ser., iv (1954), pp. 19-43.

[163] See especially Sally Harvey, "The Knight and the Knight's fee in England", *Past and Present*, no. 49 (Nov. 1970), pp. 3-43.

[164] H. G. Richardson and G. O. Sayles, *The Governance of Medieval England* (Edinburgh, 1963), pp. 55-61; Duby, *La Société . . . dans le région mâconnaise*, pp. 191-6; "La noblesse dans la France médiévale", pp. 1-22; "Les origines de la chevalerie", *Ordinamenti Militari in Occidente Nell'alto Medioevo* (Settimane di studio del Centro Italiano di Studi sull'alto Medioevo, xv, Spoleto, 1968), ii, pp. 739-61, and the contribution by L. Musset, *ibid.*, pp. 845-7.

of small estate against the denial of succession by a feudal lord suggests that as late as the reign of Henry II undertenants were especially vulnerable.[165]   In these circumstances it may well be that development was uneven and depended on the vigour and effectiveness of the feudal courts of the great Anglo-Norman baronies.[166]

All this is consistent with the continental evidence. However, it is not the whole story. If the chief cause of insecurity was the division between England and Normandy, and if the greater part of the lesser nobility in England had comparatively insignificant possessions in France or none at all, then men of this class must have been relatively immune from the main source of tenurial disturbance. This presumably is why many of the tenants of Robert of Mortain, Odo of Bayeux and the rest of the great rebel lords in England remained loyal to the Crown. The same argument applies all the way down the social scale to the holder of a fraction of a fee. Indeed the central stark reality of English politics from 1087 to 1154 was that title and inheritance were really weak right at the top, with the Crown itself. The next weakest were those most closely affected by the royal dispute, the tenants-in-chief. Others might avoid the conflict and backwash of insecurity which it produced. Indeed insecurity at the top encouraged security lower down. Actual or potential rebels could be undermined by securing the loyalty of their tenants.[167]

England may also have been peculiar in the opportunities it provided for the exercise of patronage. It is only too easy to think of the great lords, lay and ecclesiastical, as if they were hard-bitten puritans, nursing their resources, concerned above all to avoid the permanent alienation of their newly acquired or recently confirmed property. In reality their world was one where resources included expectant followings and settled tenants, only to be retained if expectancy was satisfied and tenure confirmed. The *tabula rasa* of the Conquest provided room enough to satisfy all without exhausting demesne resources. On any of the accepted interpretations of Anglo-Norman history the "ready-witted, outrageous, rumbustious" Ranulf Flambard would figure as one of the chief agents of royal

[165] See the very important comments of Professor S. F. C. Milsom in Pollock and Maitland, *History of English Law* (Cambridge, 1968 edn.), i, pp. xxvii-xlix, especially pp. xxxvi-xxxviii. He points out that Glanville's example for the writ is a claim for one virgate.

[166] *Ibid.*, pp. xxxiv-v.

[167] This technique of government is implied by the Salisbury Oath and was exploited very explicitly by King John. See, for example, his agreement with John de Lacy of 1213: Holt, *The Northerners*, p. 182.

autocracy and predatory administration.[168] Yet among his *acta* as bishop of Durham none of the six surviving charters of enfeoffment create life tenures; none leave the issue of inheritance in any doubt; all convey hereditary title, emphasizing it with the characteristic formulae, *iure hereditario, per hereditariam successionem,* or *in feodo sibi et heredibus suis.*[169] Some of these grants were in favour of members of Flambard's family, but he was not unique in having relatives or being able to endow them.[170] Coming from one so closely involved in the government of William Rufus, these enfeoffments stand in sharp contrast to the evidence from Hereford, Worcester and elsewhere.

Special English circumstances also determined the general development of security of tenure and succession. It is normally assumed that on the continent, especially in France, it was gradual and progressive. In England this was not so. It has already been suggested that in the Salisbury Oath of 1086 the Crown implicitly accepted that undertenant-families enjoyed security of tenure.[171] By the same token the Domesday Survey and the pattern in which its information was recorded county by county and fief by fief, reveal that tenancies-in-chief were now firmly established as tenurial units. Domesday Book implies permanence and the corollaries of permanence are secure tenure and settled succession. To have envisaged the destruction and reconstruction of the great honours it records would have been contradictory both to its form and purpose. Yet this is what happened in many cases. If this reasoning is correct, it follows that the separation of England and Normandy in 1087, with all its consequences, marks a set-back to a straightforward, even precocious development, a set-back which undermined the security of tenancies-in-chief more than undertenancies. By the same reasoning the reunification of England and Normandy, first by Henry I 1106-35, then by Henry II from 1154 removed the major source of instability.

[168] R. W. Southern, "Ranulf Flambard and early Anglo-Norman administration", *Trans. Royal Hist. Soc.,* 4th ser., xvi (1933), pp. 95-128. The quotation is taken from "The Place of Henry I's reign in English History", p. 153. The earlier views of Stubbs and Freeman that Flambard inspired the system of military tenures in England were castigated by Round: *Feudal England,* London, 1909, pp. 226-8.

[169] *Durham Episcopal Charters, 1071-1152,* ed. H. S. Offler (Surtees Society, clxxix, 1968), nos. 11, 12, 13, 19, 22, 23. I am grateful to Professor Offler for drawing my attention to this evidence and for making the documents available to me in proof. No. 23 which uses the formula *in feudo et in hereditate* is possibly suspect in detail but not in substance; it was confirmed by Henry I in no. 23a. See *ibid.,* pp. 101-7.

[170] Round, *Feudal England,* pp. 301-3.

[171] See above, p. 94.

There remained the after-effects: the prolonged legal actions among the successors of the disputants of an earlier age,[172] the continuing relative weakness of collateral or distant succession, and the opportunities which this presented to the Crown in the exercise of its patronage.[173] The Angevins may also have recognized the problems which the Normans had created. Within the more developed legal structure of the late twelfth century the Crown devised subtler means of dealing with rebellion. The destruction of castles and the payment of ransom replaced the blunt instrument of confiscation and disinheritance: "non fiat exhaeredatio sed redemptio".[174] Moreover, when Normandy and England were separated once more in 1204 great care was taken to avoid a new crisis.[175]

The surviving charters of the Norman kings tell yet another story. Indeed, they provide little warranty at all for believing that the barons of the Conqueror, in Maitland's phrase, "held their lands heritably". Charters of enfeoffment of the eleventh century are very rare. Some, no doubt, have been lost. But it is also very likely that men gave and received tenancies without any kind of title deed. Among the earliest surviving charters, whether royal, ecclesiastical or baronial, a high proportion is concerned with the enfeoffment of the grantors' relatives and household-officers. Written record seems to have been sought and obtained first by those who had immediate access to a writing office, and it is no accident that the charters given to such men are among the first to resort to the formulae of the heritable grant. But this development was scarcely under way in England before the reign of Henry I. From the reigns of William I and William II there are only five surviving documents recording royal grants of land to laymen.[176] None survives in the original. None implies life-

[172] Among the more obvious examples are Stuteville v. Mowbray, Lacy v. De la Val, Bully v. the Counts of Eu, Bohun v. the earls of Salisbury.

[173] See above, pp. 85-7.

[174] Dictum de Kenilworth, cap. 12 (Select Charters, 9th edn., p. 409). A punitive ransom was effectively the same as disinheritance. See the deed of surrender of the estates of Robert de Ferrers, earl of Derby, in 1269: Sir Christopher Hatton's Book of Seals, no. 411. For earlier examples of ransoming see the rebellion of 1215-17 (Holt, The Northerners, pp. 246-8) and for the destruction of castles see Henry II's treatment of the rebels of 1173 and John's treatment of the traitors of 1212.

[175] See the arrangements for the terra Normannorum which were placed in a tenurial limbo until the Treaty of Paris of 1259: Pollock and Maitland, History of English Law, i, p. 461. Some of those who suffered loss in Normandy were given temporary compensation in England. It is worth emphasizing that it is only hindsight which allows the historian to interpret the rift of 1087 as temporary and the loss of Normandy as permanent.

[176] Regesta Regum Anglo-Normannorum, i, ed. H. W. C. Davis (Oxford, 1913), nos. 226, 346, 435, 442, 456. No. 432 duplicates no. 226.

tenancy. One, which is a writ of seisin rather than a charter, confirms a tenant in the land of his father at the services his father used to render.[177] One is a grant *in feodo* of a house in Hertford and the manor of Bayford to Peter de Valognes. This was subsequently confirmed to Peter by Henry I in the same terms and by Matilda *in feodo et hereditate* to Peter's son, Roger. Roger, or his son, lost the manor by 1154-5 when it was once more in the hands of the crown.[178] Henry I's charters, as Southern has observed,[179] resorted increasingly to the formulae of inheritance. But the total evidence is still slight, amounting in all to thirty or so such acts.[180] Nearly two thirds of these come from the last fifteen years of the reign. Even so, it was still possible for the King to confirm lands and rights to direct heirs without using the formulae which were coming to be considered appropriate.[181] Equally he might notify his confirmation of a grant in inheritance by a vassal without repeating the formulae of the original deed.[182] The next reign presents clearer evidence. The surviving records of grants to laymen by Stephen, Matilda, Count Geoffrey and Henry of Anjou number nearly one hundred. Over sixty of them are grants in inheritance. Most of these resort to the language characteristic of the late twelfth century; they record grants from the donor and his heirs to the recipient and his heirs *in feodo et hereditate*. Whether the grantor was Stephen, Matilda, Geoffrey or Henry makes no difference; all equally made grants in inheritance. The date of the grant is immaterial; they are as characteristic of the

[177] *Ibid.*, no. 456.

[178] *Regesta*, i, no. 346; *Regesta*, ii, no. 1121; *Cartae Antiquae Rolls 1-10*, ed. L. Landon (Pipe Roll Soc., new ser., xvii, 1939), nos. 305, 306; Southern, "The Place of Henry I in English History", p. 161 n.

[179] *Op. cit.*, p. 145.

[180] It should be noted that the calendared versions in *Regesta*, vol. ii are inadequate for the present purpose, since the terms of the grant are not accurately noted. Among grants in inheritance not so calendared are nos. 609, 793, 1087, 1121, 1256, 1395, 1524, 1723, 1730, 1760 and 1930. The same applies to *Regesta*, i, no. 346.

[181] See the grant to Miles of Gloucester, 1128, of the lands and constableship of his father, Walter (*Regesta*, ii, no. 1552; C. Johnson, "The constableship of Walter of Gloucester", *Eng. Hist. Rev.*, xlix, 1934, p. 34) and the grant, 1128, to William son of Robert son of Walter of Windsor of the lands of his father (*Regesta*, ii, no. 1556; *Cal. Charter Rolls*, ii, p. 137). With no. 1552 compare no. 1723 a grant in inheritance to Miles of Gloucester of the land of Bicknor (*Trans. of the Bristol and Gloucestershire Archaeological Society*, iv [1879-80], p. 319).

[182] In 1121-2 William Peverel of Dover granted to Thurstan his steward Gedding and Daywell "to be held of me and my heirs in fee and inheritance": Stenton, *op. cit.*, p. 274. Henry I's confirmation of this grant does not repeat the formula: *Regesta*, ii, no. 1295; *Cartae Antiquae Rolls 11-20*, ed. J. Conway Davies (Pipe Roll Soc., new ser., xxxiii, 1957), no. 476.

earlier as of the later years of the reign. By 1135 practice had hardened. At one and the same time there was a sharp rise in the number of grants and in the use of the relevant formulae.

This arose both from the renewed conflict over the Anglo-Norman dominion and from slower, less dramatic changes. The origin of these formulae lay far back in the development of western Francia and the emergent duchy of Normandy. From the onset of the great revival of the Norman church under Duke Richard II grants were made to cathedral churches and abbeys of land or rights to be held *iure hereditario,* or *in perpetuam hereditatem.*[183] These phrases were intended to emphasize that the church held such benefactions in perpetuity. The language chosen is at first sight strange for the church did not die and had no heirs. One source of the usage was Roman civil law.[184] Another is probably to be found in the church's concern to express its everlasting title in terms which lay benefactors could readily comprehend; if so, it assumed that they already had a securely embedded concept of what inheritance was. The church was using the idea in its own context. A grant to a monastery *iure hereditario* or *in perpetuam hereditatem* expresses an intention: the gift *is to be* passed on by the monks from generation to generation, in lay terms inherited. But the words can also be used in another fashion: to express not an intention but a fact, to describe property which *has been* or *is now being* inherited. Wherever the phrase is applied to laymen in the surviving acts issued or attested by the dukes of Normandy before 1066 it is used in this second sense.[185] This explains why there were no enfeoffments in inheritance in the first generation after the settlement of England. No land had been inherited. Every man's title was *a conquestu.* If Duke William only used these phrases in referring to estates which had passed down from ancestor to heir in Normandy, then King William could scarcely use them at all in England. The formulae of the heritable grant could not take root until inheritance itself had taken place; the documentary expression of the idea had to follow the fact.

The use of the formulae to express intent only came in gradually. William Rufus's grant to Peter de Valognes *in feodo* 1087-93 seems to be the first.[186] Only a dozen or so of the grants of Henry I seem to

---

[183] *Recueil,* ed. Fauroux, nos. 7, 9, 24, 34, 43, 71, 84, 101, 103, 134, 143, 147, 201, 202, 233. Compare no. 95 in which property is described as the *legitima hereditas* of the abbey of St. Wandrille.

[184] "Inheritance has no other sense than succession to every right which the decedent held" ("Nihil est aliud 'hereditas' quam hereditas est successio in universum jus, quod defunctus habuit"): *Digest,* L, 16, 24 (ed. T. Mommsen, p. 910).

[185] For instances see above, p. 70, n. 34.

[186] *Regesta,* i, no. 346.

create hereditary title *de novo*,[187] and of these nearly half are grants to officers or servants of the King.[188]   The rest are confirmations of undertenancies in which the hereditary arrangements certainly or probably originated in the private grants which they confirmed,[189] or confirmations of hereditary succession which had already taken place or was taking place at the time of the grant.[190]   The formulae came to be used not just because men wanted to hold land heritably, but because they already held inheritances or land to which private title deeds attached hereditary right.   If this is correct there is an obvious enough explanation of the change after 1135: it was simply that the disputed succession allowed men to press claims based on tenure by ancestors and compelled Stephen and his rivals to acknowledge them.   This explanation is not new.   It was emphasized by Round and Stenton[191] and has recently been confirmed by Professor Davis and Professor Cronne.   It rests securely on the documentary evidence in which ancient and often distant title form the basis of the concessions of both Stephen and Matilda.

By the second half of the twelfth century the formulae of inheritance had become conventional, and by Bracton's day they were essential to a heritable grant.[192]   The words now expressed intent; laymen had come to enjoy the formal security devised by and for the church. Since this was already envisaged in the solitary surviving enfeoffment of Rufus, in the charters of Ranulf Flambard and some of the enfeoffments of Henry I, it may seem a natural enough development.[193] In reality it was one of several interrelated changes.

In the eleventh and early twelfth centuries secular property which had not yet been inherited was not yet an inheritance but an acquisition.   To describe an initial grant as an inheritance overrode

---

[187] *Regesta*, ii, nos. 793, 911, 987, 992, 1134, 1256, 1395, 1723, 1777, 1946. No. 1121, to Peter de Valognes is a confirmation *in feodo* of property already in the grantor's hands.   Nos. 793 and 992 are grants of a fee farm.   No. 1777 is a grant of the master-chamberlainship.

[188] *Ibid.*, nos. 911 (William de Albini, butler), 1134 (Robert Achard, the King's master), 1395 (Walter of Gloucester, constable), 1723 (Miles of Gloucester, constable), 1777 (Aubrey de Vere, chamberlain), 1946 (two *loricarii*).

[189] *Ibid.*, nos. 783, 1268, 1603, 1722, 1730, 1758, 1778, 1872.   Express dependence on the original private grant is clear in nos. 783, 1268, 1603, 1778, and 1872.   In the case of no. 1603 the original grant of Ranulf Flambard still survives.   See above, p. 99, n. 169, *Durham Episcopal Charters*, nos. 23, 23a.

[190] *Regesta*, ii, nos. 609, 1087, 1524, 1668, 1719, 1749, 1760, 1835, 1930. Of these nos. 1719 and 1930 are concerned with the transmission of property with an heiress.

[191] Round, *Geoffrey de Mandeville*, pp. 53, 109, 149; Stenton, *op. cit.*, pp. 224-6.

[192] Pollock and Maitland, *History of English Law*, i, pp. 307-8.

[193] See above, pp. 98-101.

this distinction, and the point was material since the acquisition was distinguished from the inheritance not only by origin, but also by the lord's capacity to alienate.[194]   This was likely to last as long as acquisitions proved an effective means of providing for younger sons. But every acquisition which passed from ancestor to heir became an inheritance.   The distinctive quality of the acquisition was ineluctably eroded by the years for no amount of forfeiture and re-grant could stay the consequences of death and succession.   Hence other means were needed to provide for junior members of the family. Part of the answer in Normandy was to refine and extend the practice of *parage*.   In England a solution was found through the enfeoffment of younger sons during the father's life.

This change was under way in Glanville's day.   Glanville assumed that all land held by military service descended by primogeniture; he had abandoned any distinction between inheritance and acquisition at death.   He allowed a military tenant to distribute his acquisitions during his life if he also held an inheritance; but denied that he could distribute them all, thereby disinheriting his heir, if he held nothing but acquisitions.   Hence the alienability of the acquisition was restricted on two counts.   As if in compensation, Glanville accepted that the lord, with his heir's consent, could endow younger sons with a reasonable portion of his estates, including his inheritance, during his lifetime.[195]   Hence the distinction between inheritance and acquisition was being replaced by alienability applied to the whole property.   In practice the division of the property as separate units among collateral branches was replaced by the sub-enfeoffment of junior branches, in short by the appanage, ultimately by the conditional feoffment and the fee-tail.   It now became possible to make new grants *in feodo et hereditate,* for inheritance and acquisition were no longer potentially subject to different rules of succession.[196] Indeed it was now essential to use these formulae to express intention for the object of such enfeoffment was to make a permanent provision both for the younger son and his descendants.

The tenant's control of his acquisitions was not the only casualty. At exactly the same point in time land came to be excluded from

---

[194] See above, pp. 74-5.

[195] Glanville, cap. vii, i (ed. Hall, pp. 69-71).

[196] It also follows that land could be sold to be held *in feodo et hereditate.* For instances see the sale of Langham by Hugh Tirel to Gervase of Cornhill 1146-8 (*Sir Christopher Hatton's Book of Seals,* no. 84) and, from the reign of Henry II, *Recueil des actes de Henri II,* ed. L. Delisle and E. Berger [Chartes et Diplômes relatifs à l'histoire de France, 4 vols., Paris, 1909-27], nos. dxlvii, dlxiv, dcvi, and Stenton, *Danelaw Documents,* nos. 542, 551.

testamentary bequests and *post obitum* gifts. With a few exceptions, of which the most important was burgage tenure, land ceased to be devisable.[197]

The change was not sudden. The distinction between inheritance and acquisition can still be traced under Henry II.[198] Likewise Glanville presents the two related notions of heritability and alienability still only incompletely formed.[199] However, the origin of the change went much further back. Many of the essentials of Glanville's position were already implied in the provision which William de Anesye, tenant of the honour of Port, made for his younger son, Richard, *c.* 1120-40. He gave him a knight's fee in Sherfield, Hants, "which is of my acquisition", but did so with the consent both of his lord and his elder son; the acquisition was still the suitable endowment for the cadet, but the elder son already had a voice in its disposal.[200] The change was not difficult to achieve for the endowment of younger sons within the family inheritance was practised by the Norman ducal house from the time of Richard I onwards. It was an older tradition into which the distinction between inheritance and acquisition may simply have been an intrusion resulting from a period of expansion. By the reign of Henry I the enfeoffment of younger sons in this way was unexceptional. The *cartae* of 1166 suggest that such provision was common by 1135 and it developed rapidly in the next thirty

[197] Pollock and Maitland, *History of English Law*, ii, pp. 325-9; Sheehan, *op. cit.*, pp. 269-80.

[198] See above, p. 80, and especially the arguments on the succession to Hugh Bigod, Appendix II, note B, below, pp. 110-11. For a late example of the disposition of an acquisition see the grant of Henry II 1166-1172/3 to Hugh of Hanslope of 100 acres of assarts in Perry "which may be inherited as he decides" (*Recueil*, ed. Delisle, no. ccccxxx). Compare the purchase of two tofts in Cadwell (Lincs.) by Maud, wife of Matthew of Hamby "to sell or give to whomsoever she wishes" (Stenton, *Danelaw Documents*, no. 478). For another grant *de escaeta* see *Recueil*, ed. Delisle, no. ccccxcii and for the continued distinction between inheritance and acquisition *ibid.*, nos. cccxxv, ccccviii. The notion that it was more suitable to create enfeoffments from acquisitions than from demesne was expressed in charters of Robert, earl of Leicester, 1170-5 (Stenton, *Danelaw Documents*, no. 495) and Simon de Senliz, earl of Northampton, 1176-84 (*Sir Christopher Hatton's Book of Seals*, no. 439).

[199] On the subsequent parallel development of heritability and alienability see Thorne, *op. cit.* (cited note 1); Glanville, ed. G. D. G. Hall, pp. 184-5, and A. W. B. Simpson, *An Introduction to the History of the Land Law* (Oxford, 1961), pp. 44-9. I intend to discuss elsewhere the implications of my argument for Professor Thorne's examination of charters of enfeoffment.

[200] *Sir Christopher Hatton's Book of Seals*, no. 301. This is of further interest since the fee was surrendered to the chief lord, Henry de Port, who enfeoffed the younger son as his immediate vassal. However, the elder line of Anesye ultimately defeated what was presumably an attempt to avoid a mesne tenancy (*ibid.*, pp. 307-8).

years.[201] Wherever it occurred it was likely to produce a grant in inheritance and where such deeds survive, even for the reign of Henry I, they are likely to use the formulae of the heritable grant as an expression of intention. This was the change in practice on which Glanville built his theory.

The arguments which have been advanced above are necessarily schematic. Some are by intention conjectural. Some of the problems may prove susceptible to statistical analysis. Others require a thorough survey of feudal succession and the formulae of title deeds. There is great temptation both in the call of "new methods" and in the quieter lure to act as family solicitor to the aristocracy of Norman England. This paper has been intended to provide a context for discussion, a scheme of things, dare it be said a "model". That "model" is not simple. The tenurial crisis of the Anglo-Norman period arose not because there was no law governing title and inheritance, or because kings flouted it, but because of the difficulties they encountered and created in applying it.

APPENDIX I

Parage

Parage was a refinement of partition whereby the younger sons were represented by the eldest, who was treated as the sole heir. This lasted as long as the relationship lasted, according to the "Très Ancien Coutumier" of c. 1199 until the fourth degree,[202] and according to the "Summa de Legibus" of 1235 until the seventh.[203] It was not until this point that the junior line performed homage; until then also the senior branch recovered on the extinction of the junior.[204]

Génestal, following Guilhiermoz, associated the establishment of parage in its classic form with the ordinance on the indivisibility of fiefs and he attributed both to the reign of Henry II.[205] However, Dr. Wightman has pointed out that the Lacy fee held of the bishopric

[201] The only analysis of this, regrettably brief, is by Painter, Feudalism and Liberty, pp. 207-11.
[202] Très Ancien Coutumier, cap. xlv, Coutumiers de Normandie, i, ed. Tardif, p. 38.
[203] Summa de Legibus, cap. xxiii, 7, Coutumiers de Normandie, iii, ed. Tardif, p. 77.
[204] Génestal, Le parage normand, pp. 16-30.
[205] Ibid., pp. 3-4; Guilhiermoz, op. cit., p. 214.

of Bayeux provides a possible example of *parage* in the early twelfth and perhaps the late eleventh century.[206] Another example of the early use of the term in Normandy, 1070-81, was found by H. Navel.[207]

Maitland discussed the considerable number of examples of tenure *in paragio* in the Domesday of Dorset and Somerset.[208] See also the many instances in Hampshire.[209] Many of these examples do not coincide with later Norman tenure *in paragio*. However the D.B. clerks clearly used the word in a technical sense. Guilhiermoz's criticism of Maitland, that the term was not always applied strictly in English circumstances, is beside the point.[210] It was not generally current in England, if indeed it was known at all, before the Conquest; like *villanus* it was used to cover a variety of circumstances.

It is also worth noting that the Norman system of *parage* underlay the feudal arrangements between co-heiresses described by Glanville.[211]

APPENDIX II

A. The succession to Normandy and England 1087

I have been indebted at many points to Professor John Le Patourel's recent paper on "The Norman succession 996-1135"[212], not least for his informed and considered views on the general relationships between England and Normandy in the eleventh and twelfth centuries. Nevertheless there are some matters, mostly of detail, where I have followed a different line.

I have not been convinced by Professor Le Patourel's argument that there was "no distinction in William's mind between *propres* and *acquêts*".[213] There must have been, for he allowed it to determine the pattern of descent of the lands of some of his barons. How far the distinction influenced him in settling his own succession is

---

[206] Wightman, *The Lacy Family in England and Normandy 1066-1194*, pp. 218-20.

[207] Navel, "Recherches sur les institutions féodales en Normandie", p. 36.

[208] Maitland, *Domesday Book and Beyond*, p. 145; Pollock and Maitland, *History of English Law*, ii, p. 264.

[209] D.B., i, fols. 38-51b, *passim*.

[210] *Op. cit.*, p. 215 n.

[211] Glanville, vii, 3, ed. and trans. Hall, p. 76; Pollock and Maitland, *op. cit.*, ii, p. 276.

[212] *Eng. Hist. Rev.*, lxxxvi (1971), pp. 225-50.

[213] *Op. cit.*, p. 234.

a different matter.   If, as Professor Le Patourel contends, he planned
to leave a single dominion, first to Robert and then to William, this was
not inconsistent with the parental disposition which the distinction
allowed at this time, or with the policy followed by some of his
tenants, so long as it was accepted that Robert might be deprived on
grounds of filial infidelity.   However, there are serious objections to
thinking that these were William's intentions either on his deathbed
or at any other time:

1.   Robert was recognized as heir to Normandy but there is no
evidence that he was ever recognized as heir to England.   No mention
was made of England when his succession to Normandy, first
recognized in 1063, was confirmed as a *post obitum* gift in 1079.[214]
Moreover, at no point in the subsequent disputes between him and
William Rufus or Henry did Robert ever argue that he had been
recognized as heir to the kingdom; the case stated in his favour is that
he was the eldest son to whom homage had been sworn as successor
to Normandy, and in 1100, that he was Henry's feudal lord.[215]
Neither the agreement with William Rufus in 1091 nor that with
Henry in 1101 suggest that Robert had any stronger claim. Indeed the
1091 terms clearly indicate that the Conqueror had divided his
possessions — "And the king promised him [Robert] in return to
reduce to obedience Maine, which his father had conquered, which
had then revolted from the count [Robert] and all that his father had
over there, except that which he had granted to the king".[216]
Robert's rights in England in contrast were determined by his present
agreement with Rufus.[217]   The evidence on the agreement of 1101
adds little to the argument except in Ordericus's account, which
indicates that Robert's claim to England was associated with the fact
that Henry had performed homage to him; he now abandoned both
together — "Duke Robert resigned to his brother the claim which he
had brought to the realm of England and because of his royal dignity
released him from the homage which he had once done to him".[218]
Robert's readiness to compromise with Henry is all the more striking
because Henry was the third surviving son of the Conqueror who had
been excluded from any territorial share in the succession in 1087.
The evidence on the treaties was fully examined by Freeman.[219]

[214] Ordericus Vitalis, ed. Chibnall, iii, p. 112.
[215] Ordericus Vitalis, ed. Chibnall, iv, p. 122; v, p. 290.
[216] A. S. Chronicle, MS(E): *Two Saxon Chronicles,* ed. C. Plummer and
J. Earle (Oxford, 1892), i, p. 226; trans. Dorothy Whitelock (London, 1961),
p. 169.
[217] *Ibid.*
[218] Ordericus Vitalis, ed. Chibnall, v, p. 318.
[219] E. A. Freeman, *The Reign of William Rufus* (Oxford, 1882), ii, appendices
N and XX, pp. 522-8, 688-91.

Professor Le Patourel has kindly pointed out to me that Orderic's account of Robert's part in the negotiations between Rufus and King Malcolm of Scotland in 1091 implies that Malcolm had performed homage to Robert.[220] However, the apparently inevitable conclusion that Robert must have been recognized as heir to England does not follow. Orderic's story, which is highly coloured and cast in the rhetoric of direct speech, states that the Conqueror "commended" Malcolm to Robert as his eldest son. But there is no evidence that Robert was a party to the settlement at Abernethy in 1072, the only occasion when the two kings met. Robert and Malcolm met in 1080 when Robert commanded an expedition against the Scots. In submitting on this occasion Malcolm must have performed homage to Robert, but simply as the Conqueror's representative.[221] It seems that in recalling it, Orderic recast this incident in terms which fitted the quarrel among the Conqueror's sons for the crown of England.

2. The impression that the Conqueror divided his lands on his deathbed was stronger than Professor Le Patourel allows. Ordericus not only laid emphasis on Robert's title to the patrimony in his famous set piece on the Conqueror's deathbed in book vii,[222] but also earlier in book v in a much more circumstantial and convincing note — "So [Robert] left his father, never to return, until his father on his deathbed sent Earl Aubrey to him in France that he might take possession of the duchy of Normandy".[223] That Rufus was designated heir of England at the same time is, as Professor Le Patourel argues, clearly implied by the grant of the regalia to him recorded by the monk of Caen.[224] Further evidence is provided by the Latin account of the acts of Lanfranc added to the "A" version by the scribe of the "F" version of the Anglo-Saxon Chronicle. "On the death of King William overseas, Lanfranc chose his son William as king as his father had arranged".[225] This was composed at Christ Church, Canterbury. This necessarily detracts from Eadmer's statement that Lanfranc was loath to recognize Rufus's claim.[226] The two accounts are roughly contemporaneous. Eadmer was biased in his attitude to Rufus by his devotion to Anselm.

---

[220] Ordericus Vitalis, ed. Chibnall, iv, pp. 268-70.
[221] *Chron. Abingdon,* ii, pp. 9-10; C. W. David, *Robert Curthose* (Cambridge, Mass., 1920), pp. 13-15, 67-8.
[222] Ordericus Vitalis, ed. Chibnall, iv, pp. 80-94.
[223] Ordericus Vitalis, ed. Chibnall, iii, p. 112.
[224] *Op. cit.,* p. 232.
[225] *Two Saxon Chronicles,* i, p. 290.
[226] *Historia Novorum,* ed. M. Rule (Rolls Series, 1884), p. 25.

3.   It is true that Robert was recognized as heir of Maine, but it does
not follow that this constitutes a breach of conventional practice on
the ground that Maine was as much an acquisition as England.   The
succession to Maine was determined by agreement between Duke
William and Herbert, count of Maine in 1063, when it was settled on
Robert and Margaret, Herbert's sister.   Margaret died before the
marriage took place.   Nevertheless William maintained the Norman
claim and Robert performed homage for Maine to Fulk, count of
Anjou in 1073.   The succession to Maine within the Conqueror's
family was predetermined by these arrangements and there is no
evidence that it was in doubt in 1087 or indeed at any other point in
the Conqueror's reign.[227]   Both this and Professor Le Patourel's
arguments assume that Maine had never been part of the Norman
lands.   Flodard's statement that it was ceded to the Normans in
924[228] is now generally dismissed, but for no very compelling reasons.

B. The succession to Hugh Bigod 1177

On the death of Hugh Bigod, cr. earl of Norfolk 1141, his second
wife and widow, Gundreda, step-mother of Hugh's eldest son,
Roger, claimed all the dead earl's acquisitions, including his earldom,
for her son, Hugh — "she said that Earl Hugh Bigod devised all his
purchases and acquisitions to her son whom he begat of her"
("dicebat enim quod comes Hugo Bigot divisit filio suo quem de ea
genuit omnes emptiones et perquisitiones suas").   The word
"divisit" implies a *post obitum* gift.   Roger Bigod in contrast "offered
the King great sums to have his inheritance complete as his father
held it".[229]   He later obtained a charter from Richard I confirming his
succession to the whole estate and title, but the matter was only
settled by final concord in 1199.[230]   Most of the properties at issue
fell into two groups: the four manors of Earsham, Halvergate, Acle and
Walsham, confirmed to Earl Hugh by Henry II in 1155[231] and
probably acquired with the earldom in 1141; and Holbrook,
Setterington, Hollesley and Staunton which descended to him from
his aunt, Albreda, relict of Berengar de Tosny, on the death of her
husband and survivor, Robert de Lisle, *c.* 1130.[232]   Despite the fact
that the lands in dispute were acquisitions, Roger Bigod was able to

[227] Ordericus Vitalis, ed. Chibnall, ii, pp. 305-11.
[228] *Annales*, ed. P. Lauer (Paris, 1905), p. 24.
[229] *Gesta Henrici*, ed. W. Stubbs (Rolls Ser., 1867), i, p. 144.
[230] *Cartae Antiquae Rolls 11-20*, ed. J. Conway Davies (Pipe Roll Soc., new ser., xxxiii, 1957), no. 554; *Curia Regis Rolls*, i, p. 93.
[231] *Cartae Antiquae Rolls 11-20*, no. 553.
[232] *Early Yorkshire Charters*, i, pp. 466-7.

establish his right to them and Hugh finally settled for 30 librates of land held of Roger by the service of two knights.[233] The case demonstrates the application of Glanville's doctrine that all land held by knight-service should descend by primogeniture. Nevertheless, the matter was in dispute for twenty years, despite the fact that the arguments of Gundreda and Hugh were by then outmoded. Under Henry II Roger was not recognized as earl and held some of the disputed estates *per regem*.[234]

C. The descent of the lands of the Beaumont family

Roger de Beaumont did not take part in the conquest of England in 1066, but was one of those left in charge of Normandy. His two sons, Robert, count of Meulan, and Henry, subsequently earl of Warwick, did. Each of these sons had more than one son. The descent of the family's possessions is complicated and at some points difficult.

Roger de Beaumont entered the monastery of Préaux *c.* 1090 and died some years later. His inherited lands, Beaumont-le-Roger and Pont-Audemer, descended to his eldest son, Robert, count of Meulan. Robert also succeeded to Brionne which Roger had acquired in return for the castellanship of Ivry.[235] There were other Norman lands which did not descend in the senior line. These comprised: fees held of the bishopric of Bayeux in St. Vaast and Boulon, which appear in the possession of Roger's younger son, Henry; the barony of Annebecq, which was held by Roger, subsequently by Henry's son, Robert de Neubourg, and presumably also by Henry; and Neubourg, which was a member of the honour of Beaumont and descended to Robert de Neubourg.[236] This can only be brought within the current distinctions by assuming, first, that although Brionne was an acquisition it was regarded as part of the family property because Ivry had been surrendered in exchange, and, secondly, that all the Norman lands which descended to Henry were Roger's acquisitions. Neubourg is a special case. *The Complete Peerage* states that it was granted to Robert de Neubourg by his uncle, Robert, count of Meulan, on the ground that it was in his possession in 1118, a year before his father, Henry, died.[237] Le Prévost in contrast indicated that it was not originally part of the honour of Beaumont,

[233] *Curia Regis Rolls*, i, p. 93.
[234] For further discussion see S. J. Bailey, "The Countess Gundred's lands", *Cambridge Law Jl.*, x (1950), pp. 84-103.
[235] *Complete Peerage*, vii, pp. 522-4.
[236] *Ibid.*, xii, pt. ii, Appendix A, pp. 4-5.
[237] *Loc. cit.*

but was seized from the property of the abbey of Bernay; it might thus have fallen to Henry as an acquisition.[238] All this is not impossible, but it would be easier to accept if these were the only peculiarities in the Beaumont succession. They are not, and the possibility that these arrangements were part of a general settlement also involving the descent of the English estates of the family cannot be excluded.

Roger and his two sons all acquired property in England. Roger's lay in Dorset (Sturminster), Gloucestershire and Warwickshire (Arlscott). The land in the first two counties descended in the senior line to Robert, count of Meulan and his eldest son, Waleran.[239] Robert was also in possession of Arlscott by 1086 before his father retired to the monastery of Préaux.[240] However, this passed with the rest of Robert's extensive holdings in Warwickshire to Henry on or after his creation as earl of Warwick in 1088.[241]

Hence Robert, the elder son, succeeded to the patrimony and also to Brionne and some of his father's acquisitions in England; Henry succeeded to some Norman estates, which may have been acquisitions, and also acquired the Warwickshire estates of his brother. The possibility that Robert and Henry were twins cannot be excluded, but it is likely that if this had been so it would have led to some comment, especially since Robert's elder sons were twins.

In the senior line in the next generation the succession was more straightforward. Robert, count of Meulan and possibly earl of Leicester, d. 1118, was succeeded by his sons Waleran and Robert. They were twins, and this probably accounts for the fact that the proposed division was confirmed by Henry I c. 1107;[242] the arrangement was not changed to make any provision for a third son, Hugh "the poor", born subsequently. As a result Waleran, the first born, succeeded to Beaumont-le-Roger, the *comté* of Meulan, Sturminster and other English estates which had belonged to his grandfather, Roger de Beaumont in 1086. Robert succeeded to the Leicestershire lands, most of which Robert of Meulan had acquired from Ivo de Grandmesnil, and became earl of Leicester.[243]

In the junior line the normal relationship of inheritance and

[238] Ordericus Vitalis, ed. Le Prévost, iv, pp. 327-8 n.
[239] *Complete Peerage*, vii, p. 522, n.f.
[240] Round, *Cal. of Docs. France*, pp. xlix-l, no. 318.
[241] *Complete Peerage*, xii, pt. 2, p. 358; *V.C.H., Warwickshire*, i, pp. 276-7.
[242] *Regesta*, ii, no. 843.
[243] Ordericus Vitalis, ed. Chibnall, vi, pp. 18-20, 44-6, 328-30; G.H. White, "The career of Waleran, Count of Meulan and Earl of Worcester 1104-66", *Trans. Royal Hist. Soc.*, 4th ser., xvii (1934), pp. 20-1; *Complete Peerage*, vii, pp. 522-7, 737-40; *V.C.H., Leicestershire*, i, pp. 289-91.

acquisition was reversed. The title and English acquisitions of Henry, earl of Warwick, descended to his eldest son, Roger; his younger son, Robert de Neubourg, succeeded to the Norman possessions which Henry had inherited or received by gift from his father.[244]

D. *The succession to the earldom of Chester 1120-1*

It is normally assumed that Ranulf le Meschin had to surrender the lordship of Carlisle as the price of his succession to the earldom of Chester after the death of his cousin, Earl Richard, in the White Ship, but there is in fact no evidence which establishes that the loss of Carlisle coincided with the succession to Chester.[245] It is certain that he had to pay a large fine or relief for the earldom, for £1,000 was still outstanding against his son in 1130.[246]

The usual account of Ranulf de Gernon's interest in Carlisle requires revision in the light of the distinction between inheritance and acquisition and the relative weakness of title in the latter. The following points merit consideration:

1. Carlisle was never the patrimony of either Ranulf le Meschin or Ranulf de Gernons.[247] Ranulf de Gernons could maintain that his father had held the land, but it had not been inherited; Ranulf le Meschin was established as lord of Carlisle by Henry I;[248] he surrendered it before he died and hence it did not descend to his son.

2. Ranulf le Meschin was required to surrender his rights in the inheritance of his wife, Lucy, at the time of his accession to Chester.[249] Ranulf de Gernons could claim the most direct interest in these lands which descended to his half-brother, William de Roumare. On the analogy of Carlisle, this might have brought Ranulf and William into conflict. In fact the two worked in close co-operation throughout Stephen's reign.[250] The Chester interest in Lucy's lands was recognized after the extinction of the Roumare line in 1198.

3. Ranulf le Meschin was not required to surrender his patrimony in Normandy on succeeding to Chester, viz. the *vicomté* of the

---

[244] *Complete Peerage*, xii, pt. 2, pp. 358-61, appendix A, pp. 4-5.

[245] H. A. Cronne, "Ranulf de Gernons, earl of Chester, 1129-53", *Trans. Royal Hist. Soc.*, 4th ser., xx (1937), p. 105; *The Reign of Stephen* (London, 1970), p. 175; R. H. C. Davis, "King Stephen and the Earl of Chester revised", *Eng. Hist. Rev.*, lxxv (1960), pp. 658-9.

[246] *Pipe Roll 31 Henry I* (ed. Hunter, p. 110).

[247] Cp. Cronne, *op. cit.* (1937), p. 112; Davis, *King Stephen*, pp. 49-50.

[248] *The Place Names of Cumberland*, pt. iii, ed. A. M. Armstrong *et al.* (English Place-Name Society, xxii, 1952), pp. xxiv-v.

[249] Ordericus Vitalis, ed. Chibnall, vi, p. 332.

[250] Cronne, "Ranulf de Gernons", pp. 108-9.

Bessin. Nor was he denied the Chester inheritance in Normandy, viz. the *vicomté* of the Avranchin. The "strategic" consequence was to unite the Bessin and the Avranchin in the hands of a single family.

4. There is no hint of any unease between Henry I and le Meschin following the settlement of 1120. Ranulf continued to act until his death as a royal agent in the affairs of Lincolnshire.[251]

5. Ranulf de Gernons naturally objected to the intrusion of David of Scotland into Carlisle. If he nursed a grievance it had no stronger base than that his father had surrendered an acquisition in order to gain recognition of a collateral and relatively distant succession to Chester. If so, it illustrates both a wide interpretation of collateral succession and a strict view of title to acquisition. In the previous generation practice was less hard and fast.

E. The descent of the honour of Tickhill

The death of Roger II de Bully, lord of Tickhill, after 1114, left two claimant lines descended respectively from Roger's sister, Beatrice, wife of William, count of Eu, and from Ernald de Bully said to be Roger's uncle, ancestor of Idonea de Bully, who married Robert de Vipont d. 1228. Both Beatrice and Ernald predeceased Roger II de Bully. Robert of Bellême, described as Roger I de Bully's kinsman,[252] intruded into Tickhill prior to 1102. After the death of Roger II the honour remained in the hands of the Crown. The claims of the counts of Eu were acknowledged at two points: King Stephen granted it to John, count of Eu, who lost it sometime after his capture at Lincoln in 1141 to Ranulf of Chester;[253] and King John granted it to Ralph de Lusignan in May 1214 in right of his wife, Alice, countess of Eu.[254] Both Stephen's and John's concessions seem to have been bids for political support. The descendants of Ernald held six fees of the honour. They were never apparently able to press their claim in court until Idonea's marriage to Robert de Vipont. Robert, an important agent of King John, obtained the Bully undertenancy in 1213,[255] and claimed the honour against Alice, countess of Eu, in 1219-20.[256]

[251] *Regesta*, ii, *passim*.

[252] Marjorie Chibnall, "Robert of Belleme and the Castle of Tickhill", in *Droit privé et institutions régionales: Etudes historiques offertes à Jean Yver* (Rouen, 1976), pp. 151-6.

[253] *Regesta*, iii, no. 178.   [254] *Rot. Litt. Pat.*, p. 116.

[255] *Rot. Litt. Claus.*, i, p. 136 b.

[256] *Curia Regis Rolls*, ix, pp. 1, 153, 212-13; *Rolls of the Justices in Eyre for Yorkshire, 1218-19*, ed. Doris M. Stenton (Selden Soc., lvi, 1937), pp. xxiv-v; *Pleas before the King or his Justices, 1198-1202*, ed. Doris M. Stenton (Selden Soc., lxvii, 1948), p. 68; J. Hunter, *South Yorkshire* (London, 1828), i, pp. 225-8, 261-3.

4. Debate: Politics and property in early medieval England

(a) The tenurial crisis of the early twelfth century

EDMUND KING

PROFESSOR J. C. HOLT'S "POLITICS AND PROPERTY" WILL HAVE BEEN a notable event for all those concerned with the Anglo-Norman and early Angevin periods, forcing them to re-examine many of the presuppositions of their research and their teaching. It shows the existence of a complex and continually developing law of inheritance. Asking his two questions, "inheritance by whom" and "inheritance of what", Professor Holt helps to clarify many of the most difficult topics in twelfth-century tenurial and institutional history. His general concern, as his title indicates, is to examine the inter-relationship between political change (*Politics*) and changes in the law of inheritance (*Property*). He examines the political history of the Anglo-Norman period, and the way that the changing lordship of Normandy in particular influenced the development of the law of inheritance. At several points there came to be a tension between the application of inheritance laws, involving what men thought of as their rights in land, and the realities of political power. "This was the substance of the tenurial and political crisis of the Anglo-Norman period. Rules of succession were applied in political circumstances quite unsuited to them".[1] Professor Holt is an authority on a later political crisis; when he claims to have discovered an earlier tenurial one, he will be listened to with respect.

Professor Holt first refers to a "tenurial and political crisis", but his is primarily a paper on inheritance, and it concentrates on the tenurial side: there is subsequent reference to the "tenurial crisis", the "tenurial crisis of the early twelfth century", and the "tenurial crisis of the Anglo-Norman period".[2] It is the purpose of this short note to examine Professor Holt's argument for a *tenurial* crisis,

---

[1] J. C. Holt, "Politics and Property in Early Medieval England", *Past and Present*, no. 57 (Nov. 1972), pp. 3-52; repr. above, pp. 65-114; reference to p. 81.
[2] *Ibid.*, above, pp. 81, 83, 84, 106.

and to question whether this is the right phrase to use. The key section of the argument, where the politics and the property come together and where the references to crisis cluster, is on pp. 80-87. I shall be concentrating in this note on the arguments and the examples of this section of Professor Holt's paper. While there is a discussion of the meaning of crisis in general terms,[3] the tenurial crisis is not specifically defined, but the argument as I see it is as follows.

Up to the passage that I am concerned to scrutinize in detail, Professor Holt has been answering his "inheritance by whom" question, and arguing for "the existence of a complex system of inheritance".[4] He shows how the Norman Conquest brought to prominence the distinction between a man's inheritance and his acquisitions, and how the use of this distinction allowed a younger son to inherit either the family's Norman or English estate. With the actuality or threat of a division between England and Normandy between 1087 and 1154, application of the customary rules of inheritance was often complicated by political factors. Most obviously was this true when a man rebelled, that is to say made the wrong prognostication of political developments: his land did not descend to his heirs, but was forfeit to the king or duke. The men thus replaced, and their successors, nursed claims to their ancestral property. This was one area where the king "intervene[d] in title and succession".[5] There were other cases, for which Professor Holt also uses the word intervene, where the descent was complicated, and the issue primarily a legal one. In all such cases, of course, there would be political considerations; we are no longer in any danger of forgetting the political implications of Henry I's patronage. Judgement here created complication also: "Possession always left a residual family claim".[6]

The key point, and where I think that Professor Holt and myself part company, is how all this is to be interpreted in general terms. Professor Holt seems to me to be setting up a tension between the necessity of politics and the law of inheritance. Each form of political intervention sets up tenurial claims; from one form you have the disinherited, from another the disappointed, and in any age you have the disenchanted. After a number of generations there are so many of these that effective government in some situations becomes

[3] Ibid., above, pp. 92-3.
[4] Ibid., above, p. 71.
[5] Ibid., above, p. 81.
[6] Ibid., above, p. 83.

extremely difficult. There was, says Professor Holt, a "critical point where politics and patronage intruded into custom and law".[7] In using the word intrusion here, he might seem to be suggesting that law and politics were opposed.

The law existed within, and not outside, the framework of lordship. The exercise of lordship was a necessary part of the development of the law of inheritance; it does not represent "intervention" or "intrusion" in that development. Yet royal judgement, in cases before the *curia regis*, appears to be one factor in the tenurial crisis. Professor Holt's evidence on this point would seem to be listed in a long note, which gives six examples of royal involvement in particular landed settlements.[8] The particular examples prompt specific reflections. There is the Ridel-Basset inheritance. Stenton instanced this as a rare and interesting record of the kind of business that must have come before the royal court very frequently, and he commented that this settlement, which involved among others the earl of Chester, "shows the care with which the king moved in matters interesting his greater barons".[9] Then there is the division of the Beaumont inheritance between Waleran of Meulan and Robert of Leicester, which gave the elder twin the Norman patrimony and a foothold in England, and the younger the English lands. This is a fascinating charter, not least in its final provision, which states that "if it should happen that they lose their inheritance on one side of the channel or the other, then I grant and command that as brothers together they should together share what remains".[10] This settlement determined the actions of the twins for as long as they lived; for one of the greatest Anglo-Norman houses it created no crisis and resolved many, not least that caused by Stephen's capture in 1141. In general, obviously, such royal involvement resolved tensions rather than created them. In none of the cases mentioned here were there "residual family claims" left that can be held to have contributed to any tenurial crisis.

Even were this accepted, however, it would not dispose of the disinherited and the disappointed. In a further long note Professor

---

[7] *Ibid.*, above, p. 84.

[8] *Ibid.*, above, p. 82, n. 93. I hope this is a fair interpretation. There are no cases cited in the paragraph in which the phrase "possession always left a residual family claim" occurs; note 93 is the chief documentation of the previous paragraph, which is discussing the same point.

[9] Sir Frank Stenton, *The First Century of English Feudalism*, 2nd edn. (Oxford, 1961), p. 36.

[10] *Regesta Regum Anglo-Normannorum*, ii, ed. C. Johnson and H. A. Cronne (Oxford, 1956), no. 843, text on p. 319.

Holt lists five examples of disputed inheritances arising through forfeiture or the uncertainty of indirect succession: "All these disputes played an important part in the politics of the Anarchy".[11]   Now when he is most precise about the date of his tenurial crisis he refers to the early twelfth century, and I think it would be fair to presume that what he says about the Anarchy is central to his argument. What part then, in the Anarchy, did these disputed inheritances play? Did they in any way create the Anarchy; did they assist in keeping it in being once it had started; or were they the result of it?   If Professor Holt is saying the first or the second I would disagree with him; if the third then the crisis is in no way tenurial   The first example given is the "conflict" between Robert of Leicester and Miles of Gloucester, the result of "a distant claim *iure uxoris*" going back to 1075.   It was in effect created by the empress's arrival in the west of England and her formation of a party there.   It turned on the possible forfeiture of Miles of Gloucester's lands, and it was indeed distant; it is difficult to believe that members of the house of Beaumont had lost much sleep over the matter between 1075 and 1139. As to its effects on the politics of the Anarchy, we know of no conflict and only that Robert and Miles's son Roger concluded an agreement between 1143 and 1149.[12]   Then there is the Lacy case, one of a "dispute between collaterals", which has been fully examined by Professor Cronne.   He concluded:

> This complicated history of family and feudal relationships and territorial claims suggests that hostilities in Gloucestershire, Herefordshire and Worcestershire in Stephen's reign were as much an outcome of conflicting claims to the inheritance of the late Hugh de Lacy and of the far-reaching ambitions of Miles of Gloucester and his son and of the earl of Leicester as they were the outcome of the dynastic struggle between the daughter and the nephew of Henry I.[13]

Here it is indeed being suggested that conflicting claims to land assisted in keeping the Anarchy in being, when combined with "the far-reaching ambitions" of men like the earls of Hereford and Leicester.   The combination is a necessary one: the baronage have to have been far-reachingly ambitious if this argument is to hold good.   The tenurial crisis seems to me here to be resting upon an analysis of baronial behaviour that is far too deterministic.

[11] Holt, "Politics and Property", above, p. 84, n. 99.

[12] R. H. C. Davis, "Treaty between William Earl of Gloucester and Roger Earl of Hereford", in Patricia M. Barnes and C. F. Slade (eds.), *A Medieval Miscellany for D. M. Stenton* (Pipe Roll Soc., new ser., xxxvi, 1962), pp. 141, 144.   There is a possible temptation to presume that every such agreement resolved an armed conflict.   It should be resisted.

[13] H. A. Cronne, *The Reign of Stephen 1135-54* (London, 1970), p. 160.

"Wherever we turn", according to Professor Davis, "the politics of Stephen's reign seem to dissolve into family history".[14] The word dissolve is well chosen: the mind boggles at the analysis of human motivation that can result from a long, hard evening spent in front of a well-developed family tree. A good example of the logic which lies behind any theory of an aggressive and ambitious baronage is found in another case instanced by Professor Holt in note 99, "the quarrel between the Marmions and William de Beauchamp over Tamworth". Tamworth was held by Robert Marmion, and was "given" to William de Beauchamp by the empress in the summer of 1141. The two men, we are told, "were on opposite sides in the wars of Stephen's reign because of their rival claims to the inheritance of Robert the dispenser".[15] Before we accept this simple "because" we need to be satisfied on at least two questions: how central was this relationship to the concerns of either party, and what part did any dispute play in the politics of the Anarchy? William de Beauchamp seems the more active party; how is his behaviour to be explained? The first point, according to Professor Cronne, is that William was bitterly resentful of "the extension of Beaumont power into Worcestershire",[16] represented by the earldom granted to Waleran of Meulan *c.* 1138. This would incline him against Stephen. The evidence here is the empress's charter for William in the summer of 1141, in which "William became my liege man against all men and especially against Waleran of Meulan".[17] There is a point at issue between the two men here, but it does not prove their personal enmity, or make any dispute between them a force in the Anarchy.[18]

[14] R. H. C. Davis, "What happened in Stephen's reign", *History*, xlix (1964), p. 10.

[15] Cronne, *The Reign of Stephen*, p. 173.

[16] *Ibid.*, p. 172.

[17] *Regesta Regum Anglo-Normannorum*, iii, ed. H. A. Cronne and R. H. C. Davis (Oxford, 1968), no. 68.

[18] The point at issue was whether the earldom granted to Waleran meant that William held his lands as Waleran's man and his offices as Waleran's subordinate. The empress's charter dealt first with the offices, the castellanship and shrievalty of Worcester: "with regard to these the said William became my liege man against all men and especially against Waleran count of Meulan, so that neither Count Waleran nor any other man may make an agreement with me concerning them [the offices] which shall involve William ceasing to hold of me in chief, unless of his own free will and consent he agrees to hold of the said count": *ibid.* Cf. Cronne, *The Reign of Stephen*, p. 173. William had been exercising his offices, but Waleran had been sending him orders: see R. H. C. Davis, *King Stephen* (London, 1967), p. 131. The empress was saying that when Waleran changed allegiance (for this was foreseen) William should no longer be his subordinate. We see from other charters that William had close contacts

William might also have been moved to allegiance, we are told, because of his claim to the constableship held by Brian fitz Count: "since Brian was a staunch supporter of the empress this might have been expected to make William de Beauchamp an adherent of Stephen".[19] Then there was the claim to Tamworth, which seems to have been a comparatively minor concern. Professor Cronne has three shots at explaining William's allegiance in terms of tenurial claims: they produce a hit (Tamworth), a miss (the constableship) and a doubtful (the Beaumont earldom). In terms of motive, this hardly gives us a law of universal application. As to the effect of the Tamworth claim, there seems no evidence that Robert Marmion lost control over Tamworth, or suffered a serious military attempt at its capture. In short, there is no evidence for any tenurial crisis to be gleaned from this episode either.

I would suggest then that Professor Holt's thesis that a tenurial crisis contributed to the political uncertainty of the Anarchy is open to serious objection, because of the interpretation of baronial behaviour on which it rests.[20] In some cases, his detailed work helps to defuse particular tenurial conflicts. There is, for instance, the valuable discussion of the nature of the claims of the earls of Chester to Carlisle, which by implication makes its possession less of a driving force governing the attitude of Ranulf of Chester in Stephen's reign. This makes it easier to explain Ranulf's undoubted neutrality for the greater part of the reign, and the comparatively limited tenurial implications of his major victory at the battle of Lincoln in February 1141.[21] We have a valuable analysis of the effects

---

(note 18 cont.)

with the Beaumonts in the period 1139-41. He witnessed Robert's charter for Alcester abbey: W. Dugdale, *Monasticon Anglicanum* (first published London, 1655-73; London, 1846 edn.), iv, pp. 175-6. He was an early benefactor of Waleran's foundation Bordesley abbey: *ibid.*, v, p. 410. In a charter of *c.* 1145 Waleran addresses William, who acts as his agent alongside Robert of Leicester: H. W. C. Davis, "Some Documents of the Anarchy", in H. W. C. Davis (ed.), *Essays in History presented to R. L. Poole* (Oxford, 1927), pp. 168-72; and by this time William had married Waleran's daughter. William de Beauchamp's support for the empress in 1141 is not to be explained in terms of any opposition to Waleran of Meulan.

[19] Cronne, *The Reign of Stephen*, p. 172.

[20] See my article, "King Stephen and the Anglo-Norman Aristocracy", *History*, lix (1974), pp. 180-94.

[21] Holt, "Politics and Property", above, pp. 113-14. William Malmesbury, who chose his words with care, wrote that by 1141 Ranulf of Chester had offended his father-in-law Robert of Gloucester, "maxime quia in neutro latere fidus videretur esse" (translated as "chiefly because he seemed faithful to neither side"): *Historia Novella*, ed. K. R. Potter (London, 1955), p. 47. The phrase seems to mean that he was neutral, not that he was disloyal to both sides.

upon the Mowbray honour: Dr. Greenway discusses, *inter alia*, two marriages into the Chester connection, and what seems to have been a beneficial enfeoffment of a Mowbray estate to Eustace fitz John.[22] And this is not the only example of one of Ranulf's lieutenants being intruded within the tenurial structure of an honour.[23] Patronage, however, did not extend to disseisin. Ranulf's career is not one of unbridled opportunism. It shows rather the baronial search for effective lordship; his support, if accepted, might have given Stephen the victory in 1146, and certainly was the crucial factor in Henry's advance in 1153.[24] It is difficult to believe that Ranulf of Chester's peers, any more than he, were moved by mindless atavism to pursue incompatible family claims; if their past taught them anything, it taught them the tactics of survival.

In this context, I would like to make one comment on the valuable section in which Professor Holt answers his second question, "inheritance of what". With regard to shrievalties, he makes the excellent point: "Here the issue of hereditary title may have been one of principle between the Crown and its vassals".[25] The same point might be made with regard to the inheritance of castles. The crown retained the right of seizure, and Henry II used this right "with persistent intent", as Professor Holt shows.[26] It might be argued that the first king systematically to assert the right of seizure was Stephen. The royalist chronicle, the *Gesta Stephani*, is too diffuse to have a theme, but time and again it refers to Stephen's claims to control castles in time of war.[27] The question of the tenure of castles might have something to contribute to this argument insofar as it focuses attention on the *strategic* importance of the major forfeitures of the reign: the arrest of the bishops early in 1139, and

---

[22] *Charters of the Honour of Mowbray 1107-1191*, ed. D. E. Greenway (London, 1972), pp. xxvii-xxviii, 253-4. The evidence for the enfeoffment is *ibid.*, no. 397, a charter of 1157-69. It is not clear whether this confirmed a previous enfeoffment or an effective intrusion.

[23] Hugh Wake was intruded into a number of small Peterborough abbey tenancies in Lincolnshire: Edmund King, *Peterborough Abbey 1086-1310* (Cambridge, 1973), pp. 21-2; "The Origins of the Wake Family", *Northamptonshire Past and Present*, v no. 3 (1975), pp. 166-76.

[24] For 1146, see *Gesta Stephani*, ed. K. R. Potter (London, 1955), pp. 128-32; and note the attitude of J. E. Lloyd, *A History of Wales* (London, 1911), ii, pp. 479-80. For 1153 note the charters issued by Henry [II] to Ranulf of Chester (at Devizes) and Robert of Leicester (at Bristol): *Regesta*, iii, nos. 180, 438.

[25] Holt, "Politics and Property", above, p. 90.

[26] *Ibid.*, above, pp. 87-8.

[27] *Gesta Stephani*, ed. Potter, pp. 18, 21, 31, 49-50, 108, 116-17, 131, 133; and see Stenton, *The First Century of English Feudalism*, pp. 237-40.

the arrest of Geoffrey de Mandeville late in 1143.[28]   Historians need their family trees, but they also need their maps; before speculating what men stood to gain by the pursuit of distant claims, they should reflect on how much the same men stood to lose by supporting one party in an area which the other controlled.

I feel, in conclusion, that Professor Holt's excellent and clear analysis of the law of inheritance as applied to land and office, in some ways argues against the general remarks that he makes when he relates this development to the political history of the Anglo-Norman period. We are given a system of inheritance that is both sophisticated and flexible; if it seems to break down, it is not because it cannot cope with collaterals, but because lordship breaks down.   As he says, "the structure of inheritance assumed dependence on a single feudal lord".[29]   Divided lordship between England and Normandy was being coped with.[30]   Divided lordship within England caused fresh problems, though the baronage coped here again, by recognizing effective lordship where it existed, by the various private agreements on the frontiers of lordship, and by a general policy of watchful inertia.   The history of their coping can reasonably be called a crisis, but there can be little doubt that in terms of Professor Holt's categories this crisis was political and not tenurial.

[28] Several of the bishops' castles, especially Devizes and Sherborne, were of the highest importance strategically: see the map in Davis, *King Stephen*, p. 74, and note the remarks of Henry of Huntingdon, *Henrici Archidiaconi Huntendunensis Historia Anglorum*, ed. T. Arnold (Rolls Series, 1879), p. 265. The arrest of Geoffrey de Mandeville should similarly be seen in the context of the imminent loss of Normandy, and the expectation of a further invasion.

[29] Holt, "Politics and Property", above, p. 83.

[30] Note the remarks of J. Le Patourel, "What did not happen in Stephen's Reign", *History*, lviii (1973), pp. 10-17.

(b) *Succession to fiefs in early medieval england*

STEPHEN D. WHITE

PROFESSOR HOLT'S ARTICLE ON "POLITICS AND PROPERTY IN EARLY
Medieval England" raises many important questions about the
history of English feudalism during the century following the Norman
Conquest and throws light on all of them; but his attempt to explain
the Anglo-Norman "tenurial crisis" mainly in political terms is not
entirely convincing.   He has not proved that Anglo-Norman fiefs
were heritable, or that Anglo-Norman law provided the holders of
fiefs with adequate security of title.   He has also made what may be
a somewhat anachronistic distinction between judgements made in
accordance with "law" and judgements based upon "political"
considerations.   His article may therefore underestimate the extent to
which intrinsic features of the law contributed to the Anglo-Norman
tenurial crisis.

I

Professor Holt maintains that "the inheritance of feudal property
was part of the natural order of things in Norman England",[1] but his
arguments in support of this position are at best inconclusive.   He
has shown that phrases like "by hereditary right (*iure hereditario*)",
"by hereditary succession (*per hereditariam successionem*)", "in fee to
him and his heirs (*in feodo sibi et heredibus suis*)"[2] and "in fee and
inheritance (*in feodo et hereditate*)"[3] sometimes occur in Anglo-
Norman charters of enfeoffment.   But he has not explained precisely
what these phrases meant in this period, or proved that feoffments
made under these terms, like thirteenth-century gifts to a man and his
heirs, gave the feoffee the entire estate and nothing to his heirs.[4]   In

---

[1] J. C. Holt, "Politics and Property in Early Medieval England", *Past and Present*,
no. 57 (Nov. 1972), pp. 3-52; repr. above, pp. 65-114; reference to p. 71. Professor
Holt also suggests that a tenant's status may have determined the strength of his
hereditary title (above, pp. 67-8, 94-9); but this qualification is a bit unclear, since
he alludes sometimes to "social" status (above, p. 68, n. 21, and p. 95) and at other
times to "tenurial" status (above, pp. 68, 83, 95) without indicating how closely
"social" and "tenurial" status coincided in Anglo-Norman England.
[2] *Ibid.*, above p. 99.
[3] *Ibid.*, above p. 101.
[4] See below, pp. 127-30.

addition, his remarks about the feoffments made by the Anglo-Norman kings are not clearly supported by two of the charters that he cites. Henry I's gift to the butler, William de Albini, did not create "hereditary tenure *de novo*", as Professor Holt claims.[5] The charter that records it concludes with the phrase "as King William my brother gave and granted to him".[6] Professor Holt may also be mistaken in stating that Henry I's gift to Roger nephew of Hubert created hereditary tenure at all.[7] The charter recording this gift reads: "Know that I have given and granted to Roger nephew of Hubert the land of 'Chelca' . . . at farm to him and his heir in fee and inheritance (*in feodo et hereditate*) for his service".[8]

Grants to a man and his heir do not seem to have been uncommon in the earlier twelfth century. The Burton and Ramsey cartularies and the Register of St. Benet of Holme all contain a number of them.[9] The earliest grant in fee recorded in the Burton cartulary, for example, is one made to a man and his heir in fee and inheritance: "I G[eoffrey] abbot and the monks of Burton with me grant to this Orm and his heir in fee and inheritance (*in feudum et hereditatem*) 6 bovates in Stretton . . .".[10] The monks later granted (? the same) six bovates to Orm's son Ralph and Ralph's heir in fee farm in fee and inheritance:

---

[5] Holt, "Politics and Property", above, p. 103, and notes 187, 188.

[6] *Regesta Regum Anglo-Normannorum 1066-1154*, vol. ii, *Regesta Henrici Primi 1100-1135*, ed. Charles Johnson and H. A. Cronne (Oxford, 1966), no. 911 at p. 322.

[7] Holt, "Politics and Property", above, p. 103, and note 187.

[8] *Regesta*, vol. ii, no. 1256 at p. 340.

[9] *An Abstract of the Contents of the Burton Chartulary*, ed. G. Wrottesley, (Collections for a History of Staffordshire, Wm. Salt Arch. Soc., vol. v, part I, 1884), pp. 31-8 *passim*; *The Register of the Abbey of St. Benet of Holme*, ed. J. R. West, 2 vols. (Norfolk Rec. Soc., ii-iii, 1932), i, nos. 121, 124, 126, 132-4; *Chronicon Abbatiae Rameseiensis*, ed. W. Dunn Macray (Rolls Series, 1886), nos. 242, 248, 254-5, 306.

[10] *Burton Chartulary*, p. 31. For other grants to a man and his heir in fee and inheritance or in fee, see p. 33 ("the abbot granted to him, that is to Ralph himself and his heir in fee [*in feudum*] . . ."), p. 34 ("The abbot granted to Edda himself and his heir in fee and inheritance [*in feudum et hereditatem*] . . ."). See also *Chronicon . . . Rameseiensis*, no. 248 ("Know that I have granted . . . to this William . . . that land in fee [*in feodum*] to him and his heir . . ."), and nos. 255 and 306; and *Register . . . of St. Benet*, no. 126 (". . . to him and his heir in fee and inheritance [*in feudo et hereditate*] . . ."), no. 133 (". . . in fee and inheritance [*in feudo et hereditate*] to him and his heir . . ."). See also *Charters of the Earldom of Hereford, 1095-1201*, ed. David Walker (Camden Misc., xxii, Camden 4th ser., i, 1964), no. 7: "And I have granted to him the land in which he resides in fee and inheritance (*in feudo et hereditate*) to him and his heir and by that service . . .". It should be noted, however, that the grant to Roger de Girros and his heir by the monks of St. Benet was to have been held "by hereditary right in perpetuity (*hereditario iure in perpetua*)": *Register . . . of St. Benet*, no. 131.

"... we grant to this Ralph the son that land in Stretton, that is 6 bovates in fee farm (*in feufirmum*) .... We grant that is to say to him and his heir in fee and inheritance (*in feudum et hereditatem*) that land in Stretton that his father Orm held ...".[11] Reginald Lennard maintained that grants to a man and his heir may have created "fully hereditary tenure", particularly if they included phrases like *in feodo et hereditate*; but as he noted, Round regarded them as leases for two lives, even when they included such additional phrases.[12] If Round's interpretation is correct, then Professor Holt may be mistaken in suggesting that no charter which includes phrases like *in feodo et hereditate* leaves "the issue of inheritance in any doubt"[13] and in contending that "a non-hereditary fief was a contradiction in terms".[14]

Professor Holt claims that the feudal aristocracy of Normandy (and presumably of Norman England as well) had "a securely embedded concept of what inheritance was",[15] and that "inheritance was the received legal doctrine of Norman England".[16] He has not explained, however, what this Anglo-Norman concept of inheritance was, or elucidated the legal reasoning that lies behind the usage of words like *hereditas* and *heres* in Anglo-Norman texts. Although Henry I's charter of liberties may be consistent with "the whole structure of inheritance as it is later revealed in the records of the twelfth century", it does not necessarily assume it, as Professor Holt claims.[17] The author of the *Leges Henrici Primi* refers to "inheritances (*hereditates*)" and can thus be said to accept the heritability of real property as "an established principle";[18] but as Maitland pointed out,[19] his treatment of the law of inheritance is quite peculiar. It neither assumes, nor is consistent with, later inheritance law. He

---

[11] *Burton Chartulary*, p. 31. For grants to a man and his heir in fee farm (sometimes with additional phrases), see *ibid.*, p. 31 ("... The abbot granted him in fee farm [*in feofirma*], that is to William himself and his heir [*sic* editor] ..."), and pp. 33 (*bis*), 34 (*bis*), 36, 37, 38; and *Register ... of St. Benet*, no. 132.

[12] Reginald Lennard, *Rural England 1086–1135. A Study of Social and Agrarian Conditions* (Oxford, 1959), p. 173 and p. 174, n. 1; J. H. Round, "The Burton Abbey Surveys", *Eng. Hist. Rev.*, xx (1905), p. 279.

[13] Holt, "Politics and Property", above, p. 99.

[14] *Ibid.*, above, p. 69.

[15] *Ibid.*, above, p. 102.

[16] *Ibid.*, above, p. 70.

[17] *Ibid.*, above, p. 71.

[18] *Leges Henrici Primi*, ed. and trans. L. J. Downer (Oxford, 1972), *cap.* 70, sects. 18, 20, 20b (pp. 224–5), and *cap.* 88, sects. 13, 13a, 14a (pp. 274–7).

[19] Sir Frederick Pollock and Frederic William Maitland, *The History of English Law before the Time of Edward I*, 2nd edn., 2 vols. (Cambridge, 1923), reissued with a new introduction and select bibliography by S. F. C. Milsom (Cambridge, 1968), ii, p. 267.

states that a man can succeed to his deceased son's "inheritance"[20] and can make an heir,[21] whereas Glanvill later maintains that "only God, not man, can make an heir",[22] and that land "never normally ascends".[23] These passages from the *Leges* (and some charter evidence as well[24]) suggest that the Anglo-Norman concept of inheritance may have differed significantly from that of later periods.

Since Professor Holt wishes to show that Anglo-Norman fiefs were heritable, he naturally has to explain "why there were no enfeoffments in inheritance in the first generation after the settlement of England",[25] but his ingenious answer to this question has little documentary support. First, after examining "the surviving acts issued or attested by the dukes of Normandy before 1066", he argues that Norman scribes of this period never applied formulae of inheritance expressing intention to newly created lay tenancies;[26] in other words, that they never described new enfeoffments as having been made "in inheritance". He then argues that early Anglo-Norman scribes generally followed the same practice.[27] In support of his first argument, however, he does not cite a single eleventh-century Norman charter of enfeoffment. Nor does he refer to any passage from an eleventh-century charter in which it would have been necessary, appropriate or meaningful for formulae of inheritance expressing intention to have been applied to a lay tenancy, but in which no such formulae are actually used.

Professor Holt also claims that the use of toponyms by members of the Norman and Anglo-Norman aristocracy provides "a very rough and ready minimal measure of the development of inherited estate" in Normandy and England.[28] This claim is based upon his assumption that Professor Duby and other French historians have shown that members of *lignages* must have held their lands heritably.[29]

---

[20] *Leges Henrici Primi, cap.* 70, sect. 20 (pp. 224-5).
[21] *Ibid., cap.* 88, sect. 15 (pp. 274-7).
[22] *The Treatise on the Laws and Customs of the Realm of England commonly called Glanvill,* ed. and trans. G. D. G. Hall (London and Edinburgh, 1965), book VII, sect. 1 (p. 71).
[23] *Ibid.,* book VII, sect. 1 (p. 73).
[24] For cases of men appointing heirs, see Geoffrey de Mandeville's foundation charter to Hurley Priory (quoted by Holt in "Politics and Property", above, p. 78). p. 16). See also *Chronicon . . . Rameseiensis,* no. 245; and *Charters of the Honour of Mowbray 1107-1191,* ed. D. E. Greenway (Records of Social and Economic History, new ser., i, 1972), no. 3.
[25] Holt, "Politics and Property", above, p. 102.
[26] *Ibid.*
[27] *Ibid.,* above, pp. 102-4.
[28] *Ibid.,* above, p. 70.
[29] *Ibid.,* above, p. 67.

In his article on cultural diffusion, however, Professor Duby is not very precise about what system of property law accompanies family structure organized "on the basis of lineage". He only alludes to "everything connected with" this type of family structure, "such as matrimonial customs, primogeniture, patronymic surnames, and heraldic signs".[30] In two of his other articles which Professor Holt cites, Professor Duby argues that changes in aristocratic family structure, genealogical consciousness, and degree of political autonomy took place when counts, castellans or mere knights began to transmit to their sons their fiefs, which were henceforth held hereditarily.[31] Despite his references to the heritability of feudal property, however, Professor Duby is not at all concerned with the way in which fiefs passed from one member of a *lignage* to another, or with the nature or origin of the French heir's right to his ancestor's fief. His work only shows that by about 1050 the heir of a count, castellan or knight generally succeeded to his ancestor's fief and had some sort of right to do so.

II

Professor Holt has shown that Anglo-Norman tenants by military service, like their Northern French counterparts, often succeeded to their ancestor's fiefs, that they were generally thought of as having some sort of right to do so, and that this right was sometimes described as a "hereditary" one. He has not discovered exactly what sort of right they had, nor proved that the Anglo-Norman concept of inheritance closely resembled that of the early thirteenth century. He also fails to deal with one major objection to his thesis that Anglo-Norman fiefs were heritable. Maitland maintained that in order to prove this conclusively one had to show that in this period, as in the thirteenth century, a feoffment by X to "A and his heirs" gave A a heritable estate and gave nothing to A's heirs — that is, that the words "and his heirs" were not words of purchase but words of limitation.[32] Maitland also perceived one major difficulty with such

[30] G. Duby, "The Diffusion of Cultural Patterns in Feudal Society", *Past and Present*, no. 39 (April 1968), p. 6.

[31] G. Duby, "Structures de parenté et noblesse. France du nord. IXᵉ-XIIᵉ siècles", in *Miscellanea Medievalia in memoriam Jan Frederik Niermeyer* (Groningen, 1967), pp. 164-5; and "Structures familiales aristocratiques en France du XIᵉ siècle en rapport avec les structures de l'Etat", in T. Manteuffel and A. Gieysztor (eds.), *L'Europe aux IXᵉ-XIᵉ siècles, aux origines des Etats nationaux* (Warsaw, 1968), p. 60.

[32] See A. W. B. Simpson, *An Introduction to the History of the Land Law* (Oxford, 1961), p. 49.

an interpretation of Anglo-Norman charters of enfeoffment. In this periced, A was apparently unable to alienate part of his fee in perpetuity without the consent of his heirs;[33] and the existence of this restraint at least suggested that X's feoffment to A and his heirs gave something to A's heirs. This in turn implied that on A's death, his heir B succeeded to A's fief by the form of X's gift and did not inherit from A. Maitland claimed that only by the early thirteenth century, when restraints on the tenant's power of alienation had disappeared, did it become "plain" that

> the words "and his heirs" did not give the heir any rights, did not decree that the heir must have the land. They merely showed that the donee had "an estate" that would endure at least so long as any heir of his was living. If on his death his heir got the land, he got it by inheritance and not as a person appointed to take it by the form of the gift.[34]

Maitland, of course, ultimately took the position that fiefs were heritable from the time of the Conquest,[35] but in the passage quoted above he laid part of the foundation for Professor S. E. Thorne's later claim that "the military fief was not heritable until about the year 1200 and [previously] its tenant held merely an estate for life".[36]

Professor Holt devotes several pages of his article to the problem of the alienability of the fief, but he only discusses rules governing a tenant's alienations to his younger sons and the gradual disappearance of the distinction between his "inheritance" on the one hand, and his "acquisitions", "purchases" or "conquests" on the other.[37] Two of his remarks about this aspect of the problem of alienability seem questionable. First, it is hard to see how the passage that he cites from the *Leges Henrici Primi* can be regarded as an "*official*" statement of a distinction between inherited and acquired property.[38] This treatise had no "official" status; it contains only one truly "official" document (Henry I's charter of liberties); and it is the work of a man

---

[33] On these restraints, see Pollock and Maitland, *History of English Law*, ii, pp. 13-14 and 308-13. See also S. E. Thorne, "English Feudalism and Estates in Land", *Cambridge Law Jl.*, new ser., vi (1959), pp. 193-209. On family restraints on alienation in northern France, see Louis Falletti, *Le retrait lignager en droit coutumier français* (Paris, 1923), esp. chapter i; and J. de Laplanche, *La réserve coutumière dans l'ancien droit français* (Paris, 1925).

[34] Pollock and Maitland, *op. cit.*, ii, pp. 13-14.

[35] *Ibid.*, p. 314. For a discussion of Maitland's views on the problem of the heritability of the fief, see Thorne, "English Feudalism", pp. 193-5.

[36] *Ibid.*, p. 195. Professor Milsom's writings on twelfth-century property law tend to support Professor Thorne's position. See S. F. C. Milsom, *Historical Foundations of the Common Law* (London, 1969), pp. 88-93 and 103-19, and his "Introduction" to Pollock and Maitland, *op. cit.*, i, pp. xxvi-xlix.

[37] Holt, "Politics and Property", above, pp. 74-83, 103-6.

[38] *Ibid.*, above, p. 74 (italics mine).

whose official status and legal training are unknown.[39] Second, Professor Holt may be wrong in claiming that this distinction between a tenant's "inheritance" (which had to pass to his eldest son) and his "acquisitions" (which he could give to whomsoever he wished) was "certainly current in northern and western France at the time of the conquest of England".[40] Louis Falletti maintained that the principle that acquisitions were freely alienable was known but not well-established in eleventh-century northern France.[41]

More importantly, Professor Holt's discussion of alienability is open to criticism because it is incomplete. Since he says nothing directly about restraints on a tenant's power to alienate to people other than his sons, or about the disappearance of these restraints in the later twelfth century, he is unable to rebut Professor Thorne's contention that Anglo-Norman law recognized succession by hereditary right, but not inheritance.[42] As Professor Holt points out,[43] Professor Thorne's article on "English Feudalism and Estates in Land" is not concerned with the practice of inheritance, but the distinction that he makes between succession and inheritance may have some practical ramifications. If an heir (*B*) succeeds to the fief of his ancestor (*A*) and does not inherit it, then he takes it from *A*'s lord (*X*) free of any gifts that *A* had made.[44] If *B* is then legally bound to renew any feoffments made by *A*, the distinction between succession and inheritance may not be of major practical significance — at least with respect to feudal tenures.[45] But it seems quite possible that in the Anglo-Norman period *B* was not always automatically bound to recognize *A*'s feoffments (not to mention *A*'s gifts in free alms) and that as a result the position of *A*'s feoffees was not very secure in certain cases.

First, suppose that *A* alienates most of his fief to *P* in perpetuity without *B*'s consent and takes *P*'s homage. After *A*'s death, can *B* claim all or part of the land now held by *P*? By the early thirteenth century, he can make no such claim, or if he does he will fail; and in the later twelfth century, the homage that *A* had taken from *P* will bar *B* from entering on *P*.[46] It is not clear, however, that this so-called "homage-bar" existed in the Anglo-Norman period. Nor is it clear

[39] See Downer's "Introduction" to the *Leges Henrici Primi*, pp. 2-5 and 37-44.
[40] Holt, "Politics and Property", above, p. 76.
[41] Falletti, *Retrait lignager*, p. 22.
[42] Thorne, "English Feudalism", p. 198.
[43] Holt, "Politics and Property", above, p. 65.
[44] Thorne, "English Feudalism", p. 197.
[45] On gifts free of service, see *ibid.*, pp. 204-6.
[46] *Ibid.*, pp. 200-4.

that the homage-bar was always absolute — that is, that the homage that A had taken from P would bar B from reclaiming a gift to which he had not consented, which was unreasonable, and which could be thought of as disinheriting him.   It seems possible, therefore, that in the early twelfth century B might complain that he had not consented to A's gift to P and that the gift was unreasonable and/or disinherited him, and he might have been able to reclaim at least part of P's land.

Secondly, suppose that A alienates most of his fief to P in perpetuity with B's consent and takes P's homage.   Then, in the Anglo-Norman period and in later times, B can claim nothing from P after A's death.   If he is not barred from doing so by the homage that A took from P, he will almost certainly be barred by his own consent.   But suppose that B predeceases A and that A is succeeded either by his second son (B^1) or by B's son (C).   Can either B^1 or C claim anything from P?   In the early thirteenth century, neither can[47] but in the earlier twelfth century, B's consent may not bar B^1 or C from making a claim against P.[48]

In these cases, early thirteenth-century law probably gave tenants like P greater security than Anglo-Norman law and thus may have given them greater legal protection in periods of tenurial instability. This greater security can be seen as stemming, at least in part, from the fact that the thirteenth-century heir's rights differed from those of his Anglo-Norman counterpart.   Whereas the former clearly had a right to inherit from his ancestor, the latter may have had a right to succeed to his ancestor's fief under the form of the gift to his ancestor. In the early thirteenth century, therefore, a donee may have been better protected against the claims of his donor's heirs than he was in the Anglo-Norman period.[49]

III

Professor Holt proposes three ways of reconciling the "apparent contradiction" between the fact that "the inheritance of feudal property was part of the natural order of things in Norman England"

[47] See Pollock and Maitland, *History of English Law*, ii, p. 311.

[48] See *ibid.*, pp. 310 and 312-13.   In his discussion of the *laudatio parentum* in northern France, Falletti states that by giving his consent to a relative's gift, a man barred only himself: *Retrait lignager*, pp. 25 and 41.

[49] Professor Milsom adopts a similar view.   He maintains that a feoffment to a man "and his heirs" gave "a legal right of some sort to the heirs, and this was not the same as giving 'ownership' to the tenant.   The difference comes over an alienation; and it was only indirectly that the tenant for the time being at length acquired a power to alienate without regard to the claims of his heirs". *Historical Foundations of the Common Law*, p. 92.

and the fact that "even the greatest in the land might suffer dispossession, and his family disinheritance".[50]

1. "No law governing title and inheritance" existed in this period.
2. Such law existed but kings (and possibly other lords) "flouted
it".
3. Such law existed, but kings (and possibly other lords)
encountered and created "difficulties . . . in applying it".[51]

Professor Holt argues for the third position,[52] and claims that "the
separation of England and Normandy in 1087"[53] led to the
"intrusion" of political considerations into legal decisions.[54] He has
ignored, however, two other ways of accounting for his "apparent
contradiction": first, Anglo-Norman law may not have given adequate
security to tenants like *P* in the cases discussed above, or in other
cases like them; and secondly, Anglo-Norman courts may have taken
legal notice of facts whose consideration he regards as political
intrusions.

Confronted by the "important legal problem" posed in book VII of
Glanvill, for example, the members of an Anglo-Norman court might
not have decided the case as "those learned in the law of the realm" of
Henry II's court apparently did (or tried to) — by debating the
proper application of the "general rule . . . that no man can be both
heir and lord of the same tenement".[55] Instead, they might have
taken notice of the personal qualities of the disputants, their feudal
ties with other lords (such as the duke of Normandy), and their
relative abilities and willingness to pay a substantial relief — all issues
which Glanvill's discussion ignores and of which the possessory and
proprietary actions would have taken no notice. A decision by an
Anglo-Norman court based upon such considerations need not be
regarded as an illegal or extra-legal one which resulted from the
"intrusion" of political or personal considerations into a legal judgement. Rather, it may reflect the fact that Anglo-Norman law
generally recognized the legal rights of the heirs of a deceased tenant
by military service, as later law did, but that unlike later law, it
sometimes recognized the right of the deceased tenant's lord to decide,
in consultation with his barons, which of these rights, if any, to
recognize and upon what terms.

[50] Holt, "Politics and Property", above, p. 71.
[51] *Ibid.*, above, p. 106.
[52] *Ibid.*
[53] *Ibid.*, above, p. 99.
[54] *Ibid.*, above, p. 82; cf. pp. 83, 84.
[55] *Glanvill*, book VII, sect. 1 (pp. 72-3).

IV

If Anglo-Norman law gave military tenants less security of property in some cases than later English law and sometimes took legal notice of what would later seem to be extra-legal issues, then Professor Holt's conclusions about the causes of the Anglo-Norman tenurial crisis may require some slight modification, so as to allow for the possibility that inherent features of Anglo-Norman law may have heightened, if they did not create, that tenurial crisis.

(c) *A rejoinder*

J. C. HOLT

I USED THE WORD "CRISIS" QUITE PRECISELY AS A SHORTHAND description of a situation many of the features of which have been well known to historians from Ordericus Vitalis on to J. H. Round, his successors and critics. To summarize: succession to estates in the Anglo-Norman realm involved a distinction between inheritance and acquisition, the application of which depended on the number of male children and the policy of particular families; this distinction was applied to the royal/ducal house in 1087, so that political loyalty was at odds with the way in which tenancies-in-chief had descended, and influenced, sometimes determined, the way in which such estates were to descend; necessarily the conflict affected the law of property and had a prolonged aftermath. That, very baldly, was the crisis. It began in 1087 after some preliminary symptoms. It ended in 1106 with recurrent complications and minor outbreaks thereafter. It recurred under Stephen because of a genealogical accident consequent upon a shipwreck.

I am at a loss to understand how Dr. King can claim that what I say about the Anarchy is central to my argument. I happened to illustrate some of the disputes of the first half of the twelfth century by examples chosen from the time of Stephen.[1] My intention was to indicate the variety and complexity of family claims. I also stated that they played an important part in the politics of the Anarchy, which is correct. That some of them were resolved by agreement

---

[1] J. C. Holt, "Politics and Property in Early Medieval England", *Past and Present*, no. 57 (Nov. 1972), pp. 3-52; repr. above, pp. 65-114; reference to p. 84, n. 99.

rather than by war is obvious, and Dr. King is right to emphasize the fact. But it is he, not I, who is seeking to discuss them as though some global explanation of the Anarchy were at stake. I was concerned rather to suggest a general explanation of the many claims in inheritance which Stephen and Matilda encountered and admitted, separately or in turn.

I have no evidence that family trees were studied during long, hard evenings in front of the fire; but that they were studied and recalled over many generations, that family claims were long remembered and that they were one of the springs of aristocratic action, seems to be one of the more certain features of medieval politics. This does not stand or fall on a "law of universal application", to use Dr. King's unfortunate phrase, but on legal records, on chroniclers like Ordericus and Roger of Howden and on the literary themes which the nobility no doubt found more entertaining in the evening than the bare bones of a family tree. Examples abound. Under Stephen, Robert de Beaumont pursued claims which went back to the years before 1075.[2] In 1201 William de Mowbray and William de Stuteville finally resolved a dispute which had originated in the confiscations following the battle of Tinchebrai in 1106 and brought their ancestors into court under Henry II.[3] The descendants of Roger de Bully, dead before 1099, still disputed his lands in 1220.[4] It was not until 1284 that William de Say finally abandoned claims which his great-grandfather had advanced to the lands and earldom of William de Mandeville in 1189.[5]

It is not unreasonable to suppose that interests long nursed were deeply felt. They can be excluded as springs of human action at the cost of drawing sharp distinctions between litigation, politics and war. But these often differ only in their means. It would be easier to share Dr. King's concerns if Stephen's reign could be regarded as something altogether exceptional, perhaps as an anarchic upheaval of orderly policies and relationships. It is more realistic to suppose that the disputed succession created circumstances in which the ordinary motives of twelfth-century politics are revealed in greater detail and contrasting clarity, heightened and exaggerated by war and the threat of war, but not essentially different from the ambitions achieved through less obvious means in earlier and later periods.

[2] *Ibid.*
[3] *Early Yorkshire Charters*, ix, ed. C. T. Clay (Yorks. Arch. Soc., Rec. Ser., extra ser., vii, 1952), pp. 3-6.
[4] Holt, "Politics and Property", above, p. 114.
[5] *Feet of Fines for Essex*, ed. R. E. G. Kirk (Essex Archaeological Society, 1899-1928), ii, no. 136; *Complete Peerage*, vi, pp. 120-4; xi, pp. 465-6.

Both Dr. King and Dr. White are very properly concerned about the relationship between politics and law. My argument was cast very much in terms of the brusque questions which I put as preliminaries—"How far was patronage ruthless or beneficent, limited by law? How far was law beaten into shape by political necessity?" We are all agreed that the exercise of lordship could be lawful, that law was created by the interplay of political interests in a feudal context, and that men genuinely seeking to discover and apply the law might reasonably turn to a lord, who, with his barons, might reasonably seek to determine and execute it. We may differ on how far this is to imagine a real, as opposed to an idyllic situation; that could be a matter of endless debate. We certainly seem to disagree on the possibility of any tension between "law" and "politics" or of any conflict, potential or actual, between political interests and customary rules. I did, and do, indeed maintain that "law" and "politics" may be and were at times opposed, and nothing said by Dr. King or Dr. White has brought me to accept that such a distinction is anachronistic when applied to the first century of the Norman settlement. If the exercise of lordship created no such conflict, wherefore the charter of liberties of Henry I? And what was that charter but an attempt to state feudal custom in a manner which, in many of its provisions, sought to contain the exercise of lordship? What finally are my preliminary questions but extensions of the contemporary distinction between law and will, kingship and tyranny?

So much for generalities. In addition Dr. White raises a formidable number of arguments which require detailed discussion. It is impossible to do full justice to them within the space of a short Rejoinder. Hence I leave what he says about the *Leges Henrici Primi*, the charter of liberties of Henry I, toponymic family names and the distinction between inheritance and acquisition for discussion on some subsequent occasion. On these points the arguments of the original paper can be left to stand on their merits. It is more important to discuss the new issues raised by Dr. White which only figured in it incompletely or not at all.

First there is a problem of selecting evidence. The documents collected in Mlle. Fauroux's *Recueil* and the various volumes of *Regesta* provide an almost complete run of the surviving *acta* of the ducal and royal house between 968 and 1154.[6] Those which refer

⁶ *Recueil des Actes des Ducs de Normandie de 911 à 1066*, ed. M. Fauroux (Mémoires de la Société des Antiquaires de Normandie, xxxvi, 1961); *Regesta Regum Anglo-Normannorum 1066-1154*, 3 vols., ed. H. W. C. Davis, Charles Johnson and H. A. Cronne, and H. A. Cronne and R. H. C. Davis (Oxford, 1913-68).

to tenure by laymen record a change in the usage of the language of inheritance. It is used first to describe fact and then subsequently to declare intention. Now this is not an argument, ingenious or otherwise, designed to escape a logical predicament. It is an empirical observation which gains strength from the fact that it is based on all the evidence we are ever likely to have on the point. By comparison the evidence of private charters is bound to be selective, not only because of the number involved but also because it is likely that practice varied to some degree from fief to fief. Until this large mass is reduced to order it is not going to be very easy to distinguish the usual from the exceptional or to categorize and attempt to explain local or chronological variations.

Dr. White has made an important contribution to this problem in drawing attention to a number of grants made to a man and his heir. He tends to think that such grants, by restricting the heir to the singular, were limited to the two lives of the grantee and his immediate successor. However, Lennard found no provision for the reversion of the estate or stock in any of the grants made to a man and his heir in phrases which implied perpetuity.[7] Moreover, it would surely have been hazardous to allow the issue of perpetuity to depend on the use of the singular or plural. The pressure to convert life-tenancies into hereditary estates was strong enough for men to be aware of the problem.[8] Yet they varied the number of the noun quite inexplicably. William, abbot of Holme, granted Tibenham to Roger de Girros "and his heirs" (1127–34),[9] but his successor Anselm confirmed it to Roger "and his heir" "by hereditary right in perpetuity" (1134–40).[10] Abbot Richer of Holme granted Filby to Robert son of Walter "and his heir" "by hereditary right" (1101–11),[11] but Henry I confirmed it to Robert "in fee to him and his heirs" (1111).[12] Abbot Anselm granted land in South Erpingham and elsewhere to Wither Turnel "and his heir in fee and inheritance" and in the very same deed recorded that Wither "and his heirs after his death" would pay the rent.[13] To suggest that the singular was intended to indicate a term of lives is to ignore this casual inconsistency of usage. Stenton suggested that a grant to a man and his heir implied that the heir was

---

[7] R. Lennard, *Rural England 1086-1135* (Oxford, 1959), p. 173.
[8] *Ibid.*, p. 174, n. 3; Holt, "Politics and Property", above, p. 96.
[9] *The Register of the Abbey of St. Benet of Holme*, ed. J. R. West, 2 vols. (Norfolk Rec. Soc., ii-iii, 1932), i, no. 127.
[10] *Ibid.*, no. 131.
[11] *Ibid.*, no. 121.
[12] *Regesta*, ii, no. 987.
[13] *Register of the Abbey of St. Benet of Holme*, i, no. 137.

present at the occasion;[14] this is a possible explanation of these phrases. There are others. It may be that the men who drafted these documents sometimes described the heir in the singular because the next succession was the only one which might concern them; the rest was too far in the future, perhaps beyond their lifetime. It may have been that the grantee was known to have an heir but that the heir as yet had no direct successor. It may be that men were thinking within the developing sense of the word inheritance which seems to be indicated in ducal/royal *acta* and assumed that one lawful succession made an inheritance. It may simply be that by "heir" in the singular, they meant "any heir".[15]   At all events the words might be repeated from one generation to the next, so that the apparent limitation in one grant was extended in a second. Geoffrey, abbot of Burton, granted land in Stretton "to Orm and his heir in fee and inheritance". He subsequently granted the same land at the same rent to Ralph son of Orm "to him and his heir in fee and inheritance".[16]   This second charter specifies that the tenancy was a fee farm and it may be significant that many of the examples cited concern land held at rent. Many of the instances at Burton are stated to be fee farms;[17] some of those at Holme were made "in fee and at farm".[18]   It seems inescapable that the singular usage, appearing as it does in the acts of at least three monasteries, is connected with the creation of hereditary fee farms. For this, the language of leases drew on the language of enfeoffments. Not one of these grants provides an example of a non-hereditary fief. It would be no surprise to discover such examples for men use words in a contradictory manner to express intentions which themselves conflict. But in all these instances the

---

[14] Lennard, *op. cit.*, p. 174, n. 1, noting Stenton's suggestion. This is recorded in the case of Darlaston, one of the tenancies of the abbey of Burton, which Abbot Geoffrey (1114-50) granted to Orm and his son Robert. The agreement records that he took homage from both of them. It did not employ any of the conventional language of inheritance, but laid down that they were not to be deprived "by French or English, or by monks or other men, now or in the future". *The Burton Chartulary*, ed. G. Wrottesley (Collections for a History of Staffs., Wm. Salt Arch. Soc., v, pt. 1, 1884), p. 35.

[15] This was certainly the case in the charter of Miles, earl of Hereford, which Dr. White notes. This refers to succession by an heir or relative. It also permits sale. *Charters of the Earldom of Hereford, 1095-1201*, ed. David Walker (Camden Misc., xxii, Camden 4th ser., i, 1964), no. 7.

It is unnecessary to pursue one further possible implication of the use of the singular: that there was to be one heir and one only. However, those who believe that the singular created a term of lives are committed by the same logic to the exclusion of coparcenery.

[16] *Burton Chartulary*, p. 31.

[17] *Ibid.*, pp. 31-8.

[18] *Register of the Abbey of St. Benet of Holme*, i, nos. 124, 132.

word *feodum* is used to establish the hereditary element in the grant. There was no doubt about the sense of the word at Ramsey: a fief was land to which there was heritable title; a tenancy which was to revert to the church on the tenant's death was not a fief.[19]

The hereditary sense of the word "fief" seemed clear enough to contemporaries. How far they appreciated the complexity of the notion is not so easy to determine. Dr. White, following Professor Thorne and Maitland, maintains that such estates were not truly heritable since the tenant was encumbered by the interest of his lord and heirs. Hence for Dr. White "Anglo-Norman law recognized succession by hereditary right, but not inheritance".[20] That is a distinction which contemporaries did not admit. Their language made no provision for it. "Inheritance" and "hereditary right" were one. "Heritability", involving the definition of the tenant's right, especially of his power to alienate, is a lawyer's notion. Glanvill discussed some aspects of it, but it required a sophistication which was only becoming apparent in his day. Dr. White is correct in arguing that "early thirteenth-century law probably gave tenants like *P* greater security than Anglo-Norman law", but the plight of *P*, if such indeed it were, cannot be left as a series of contingencies founded on legal logic.

How typical was *P*? Who indeed was he? If *A* may be equated with the crown, *B* is the tenant-in-chief and *P* his under-tenant; that is to give him the highest possible feudal status. Now Dr. White has not established that the condition of *P*, whatever it may have been, had any serious effect on the relations between *A* and *B*. Indeed his account of the insecurity of *P* is irrelevant to the position of *B* since *P*'s insecurity is derived from the limits placed on *B*'s powers of alienation by the terms on which he was enfeoffed by *A*. It follows that *B* can never suffer from *P*'s insecurity unless he takes up a similar tenement. This is to treat the situation schematically. In real terms, of course, tenants-in-chief were themselves tenants of other tenants-in-chief; they were at once *B* and *P*. Even so there is no good reason to think that their relations with the crown or with each other were

[19] *Chronicon Abbatiae Rameseiensis*, ed. W. D. Macray (Rolls Series, 1886), no. 255: a deed of 1114-30 in which Abbot Reginald conveyed Leofric's land in London to Andrew "in fee to him and his heir". In return Andrew granted to the monastery tenements which he retained for life and which were to revert to the monastery on his death. These are not described as a fee but simply as "lands".

[20] A view which Dr. White attributes to Professor Thorne. Professor Thorne in fact wrote that "by the second quarter of the twelfth century tenants by military service had come to hold their lands heritably": S. E. Thorne, "English Feudalism and Estates in Land", *Cambridge Law Jl.*, new ser., vi (1959), p. 198.

seriously affected by the kind of insecurity which Dr. White attaches to *P*. Indeed it would be hazardous to assume that the apparent logic of the terms of enfeoffment at a particular feudal and social level may be used to define rights of inheritance in general. To be sure, one level infected another; the provisions about relief, marriage, widow-hood and wardship in the charter of liberties of Henry I were extended beyond the king to the conduct of his barons;[21] but the infection moved down rather than up the feudal hierarchy and tended towards inheritance rather than against it. Moreover, each level in the hierarchy carried its own particular problems. Tenants-in-chief were not seriously affected by the circumstances of under-tenant *P*. Their security depended more on the arrangements they made for the family control of cross-Channel holdings and the skill with which they manoeuvred politicially. These in turn were problems which under-tenant *P* was unlikely to have to face. To imply that *P*'s condition was of general significance only confuses these and similar issues. So also does Dr. White's addition to my summary concluding statement about the relations between the Norman kings and their tenants-in-chief. By inserting the parenthesis "and possibly other lords" he obscures distinctions, qualifications and implications which are essential to the argument.

Is the condition of *P* even typical of under-tenants? That they were less secure than the tenants-in-chief seems likely. That some held tenancies for a term of lives is certain.[22] But is their relative insecurity to be explained by the terms of tenure which Dr. White attaches to *P*? It may be that such terms contributed to insecurity; they may even explain it in particular cases. However, in England the relief which *P* paid is an important obstacle to the argument, for he paid it only on succeeding to his ancestor. He was not liable to relief when his lord was succeeded by *his* heir.[23] This important limitation was applied not only to *P* and his lord but to all their descendants as well. The consent of the heirs of *A* and *B* to the alienation by *B* to *P* may have been attenuated with the passage of generations if it were not

[21] The last sentence of *cap.* 4 — "And I enjoin that my barons shall exercise similar restrictions in their treatment of the sons, daughters and wives of their men" — applies to the whole of *caps.* 3 and 4. The paragraphing of the charter is modern. For the text of the charter see, for example, W. Stubbs, *Select Charters*, 9th edn., ed. H. W. C. Davis (Oxford, 1913), pp. 117-19.

[22] For a summary of the evidence, see Holt, "Politics and Property", above, pp. 95-7.

[23] William Rufus's assessment of a relief on the tenants of the see of Worcester after the death of Bishop Wulfstan in 1095 is an exception. However this was an ecclesiastical barony and the occasion seems unique. See Stubbs, *op. cit.*, p. 109; J. H. Round, *Feudal England* (London, 1895), pp. 308-14.

renewed, but this never led to the establishment of a feudal incident on the death of a lord. Indeed *P*'s heirs benefited as well as lost from the passage of generations. Nothing made an inheritance more secure than the fact that it had been inherited.

This is not to argue that the succession of one lord upon another had no effect upon his tenants. Lords confirmed the privileges granted by their predecessors and no doubt took steps to ensure that their men had to buy such confirmations.[24] But these concerned all kinds of privileges held by all kinds of beneficiaries, churches and towns as well as tenants by knight-service. Such payments arose from the exercise of the new lord's will rather than the terms on which his predecessors had enfeoffed their tenants. Where such payments were described as reliefs it was probably to give them the respectability of a customary feudal incident. Tallages were sometimes described as aids and aids as tallages for similar or converse reasons.

Finally there is the problem of evidence. Glanvill was the first to comment usefully on heritability and alienability as Dr. White and Professor Thorne have defined them. For the period before Glanvill the argument depends almost entirely on the interpretation of charters. It was usual for the grantee to obtain a charter of confirmation from the successor of a grantor on the grantor's death. A grantor usually stated that his heir or heirs, whom he might name, were parties to the grant. He also frequently mentioned that his lord had consented to the grant. The lord might himself confirm the grant by charter, and his heir in turn might later do the same. All this provides the strongest evidence of the interest of both the tenant's lord and heirs.[25] The tenant's right was limited. His heirs wanted as complete a succession as possible. His lord wished to preserve the unity of the fief and the services it provided.

This leads to problems both of logic and interpretation. The notions of heritability and alienability were becoming increasingly precise and complicated in the late twelfth century. Whether they were preceded in the early twelfth century by equally precise and sophisticated converse notions, or whether they emerged from a welter of practice which gradually settled into some consistency is a matter for debate. Some may hesitate to read so precise a legal logic into the earlier period. A similar doubt surrounds the notion which

[24] Compare King John's instructions to his justices of Michaelmas 1200 that they were not to accept any plea based on the charters or letters of his predecessors unless accompanied by his confirmation: *Curia Regis Rolls*, i, p. 331.

[25] I summarize here evidence sketched more fully by Professor Thorne: *op. cit.*, pp. 193-209.

led grantees to seek support and confirmation from the grantor's lord
and heir.   It may be that they might suffer a serious challenge from
these interests.   It could equally be that they were simply seeking the
convenience of a primitive form of warranty in a world in which
actions of right were determined in feudal courts.   The legal logic of
the two situations is identical but their social and political importance
is very different.

Limitation and insecurity are not the same.   They overlap
most obviously at the point where the power of the lord and the
tenant's heirs to concur in the tenant's alienations affects the security
of the tenant's feoffees.   There were other causes of insecurity, many
of them much more dramatic in their effects, especially on the
baronial class.   Even so estates passed from ancestors to heirs.   Such
descent can usually be traced in the case of baronies, and it is far from
difficult to demonstrate in the case of under-tenancies.[26]   Some
breaks in descent are apparent.   However, these were not scattered
or sporadic.   They arose not from widespread and occasional
refusal by lords to recognize the claims of their tenants' heirs, but
from the application of rules governing descent in the circumstances
created by the association of England and Normandy.   In many
cases it is obvious that politics, not terms of tenure, determined who
suffered confiscation and whose title was denied.   Despite this,
inheritance took root early.   Already in 1100 the charter of liberties
of Henry I was concerned not with the right of inheritance, but with
the assessment of payments for it and the feudal incidents surrounding
it.[27]   The case against William Rufus was not that he had denied this
right but that he had charged too much for it.   If Rufus was
denounced only on the minor count who is to be arraigned on the
major?

[26] For a recent collection of such pedigrees, rich in information, see Sir
Charles Clay, *Early Yorkshire Families* (Yorks. Arch. Soc., Rec. Ser., cxxxv, 1973).
[27] Cf. A. W. B. Simpson, *An Introduction to the History of the Land Law*
(Oxford, 1961), pp. 46-7.

5. *Large and small landowners in thirteenth-century England: The case of Peterborough abbey**

EDMUND KING

THE POOR AND NEEDY, ACCORDING TO THE AUTHOR OF THE *Life of Edward the Second*, were inevitably avaricious, for they lacked the necessities of life. Now, in his day, the rich were emulating them:

> Observe how the earls and other magnates of the land, who could live according to their station on their inheritance, regard all their time as wasted, unless they double or treble their patrimony; wherefore they pester their poorer neighbours to sell what they have inherited, and those who will not be persuaded they plague in many ways, until they are so straitened that they perhaps offer for a song what they could earlier have sold for a good price.

The only example given, however, is very far from precise. "There was a certain knight, a simple man of great innocence", who "left behind him flourishing sons whose way of life was pleasing to God and man. But there came a certain great and powerful son of the devil, a minister of Satan, and expelled the children from their paternal inheritance."[1] No names, no pack-drill; but significantly it is a member of the knightly class who is singled out as a typical object of magnate greed. There is much to suggest that behind such examples lies a movement of considerable importance and much wider scope. Professor Postan, in his survey in volume one of the *Cambridge Economic History of Europe*, had a section on "magnates and gentry in the thirteenth century".[2] "The surviving records of land transactions", he points out, "bear witness to the accretions to the estates of lay magnates and of nearly all the great abbeys at the expense of smaller landowners". One of the examples cited is Peterborough abbey; in the Soke of Peterborough especially, those selling land to the abbot and his villeins "comprise a large proportion of local gentry and yeomanry".[3]
The Postan thirteenth century, as is well known, is a long hundred

* Mrs. Marjorie Chibnall and Professor Edward Miller read a draft of this paper, and I am grateful to them for many helpful suggestions. My research has been aided by a grant from the University of Sheffield Research Fund.

[1] *Vita Edwardi Secundi*, ed. N. Denholm-Young (London, 1957), pp. 99-100.
[2] M. M. Postan, *The Cambridge Economic History of Europe*, i, 2nd edn. (Cambridge, 1966), pp. 592-5.
[3] *Ibid.*, p. 594.

and something more; the scope of his remarks covers the period between the mid-twelfth century and the Black Death. What is at issue, as he suggests, is whether during this period the position of a "class" of gentry altered vis-à-vis that of the aristocracy. Were the smaller landowners at any time in particular economic difficulties? If so, then why? This article is intended as a contribution to a discussion on these matters. Its main material comes from the Peterborough records, to whose interest in this connexion Professor Postan kindly drew my attention. The purpose of the first section is to note some of the difficulties involved in taking either "the surviving records of land transactions" or the chronicles at their face value. It is then suggested that a possible approach to this problem can be found in the detailed study of individual family histories. The history of seven families, each of them in some way connected with Peterborough abbey, is examined in the second section. The concluding section discusses whether there is any common pattern in these histories, and whether it is possible to form a balanced view of the trends in the land market in the thirteenth century, as they affect the smaller members of the landholding class.

At the beginning of this period such men occur in feudal groupings; they hold knight's fees, and they are listed as knights. But to study knightly families through from the Conquest immediately raises a difficulty: the term "knight" in 1300 means something very different from what it had meant in 1100. The knight's function changes, and with it his status and his whole outlook. There are then problems of interpretation connected with each set of records. The private records which survive are necessarily the reflection of an active lordship. Among them those of religious corporations predominate; in Davis's list of cartularies the ecclesiastical outnumber the lay by more than seven to one, and the discrepancy in their bulk is much greater still.[4] Only a limited number of knightly families are reached by such sources. By contrast the central, governmental records are more comprehensive but also more inadequate. The *Book of Fees* and other feodaries are not lists of "knights"; they are lists of military tenancies, made largely for fiscal purposes. The lordship they show is static, "little more than a servitude over the land of another, and its content is fixed and economic".[5] There are problems of defining the group, therefore, and there are problems connected with the records. The earliest feudal records have no high standards of knighthood:

[4] G. R. C. Davis, *Medieval Cartularies of Great Britain* (London, 1958).
[5] S. F. C. Milsom, intro. to F. Pollock and F. W. Maitland, *The History of English Law*, 2nd edn. (Cambridge, 1968 edn.), i, p. xlvii.

"under the name *milites* are . . . described many different types of men who unite only in a common function".[6] Indeed, "the record of the knights of Peterborough abbey" made *c.* 1105 includes sokemen; not all the individuals listed served as knights.[7] And in charters of the first half of the twelfth century their descendants are never listed as "knights". The only men thus described are the household knights of the honorial barons — "Ansfrid the knight of Benceline" (1112), "Herbert the knight of Ascelin" (1116).[8] There are clues in all this as to the knight's status in early Norman society. The chief servants of the abbey had knight's corrodies in the household list of 1125-8.[9] In 1147 an agreement with Roger of Torpel when he retired to the abbey gave him a monk's corrody, and the four servants who came with him were to have knight's corrodies.[10] The usage of this period is consistent. In no sense of the word were these knights "gentry".[11]

Pick up Glanville, from the end of Henry II's reign, and you are in a different world. Knights are required for the grand assize, and for a multitude of other purposes within the local government.[12] These knights were to be "good and lawful" landowners; Henry would probably have looked unkindly on Roger of Torpel's valet, or Peterborough's assistant cook. Alongside this development, and serving further to differentiate the knight, changes in warfare combined with inflation called forth a new warrior. In the early Norman period "it cannot have been difficult to fit out a man as a knight. Horse, sword and hauberk were almost all that he needed".[13] In the thirteenth century a knight's horse alone cost £40 to £80.[14] Under these conditions the number of military tenants qualified for knighthood fell rapidly, and not all those qualified became knights. In the mid-thirteenth century around 6,500 fees were liable for scutage. For the same period Mr. Denholm-Young has estimated

---

[6] D. C. Douglas (ed.), *Feudal Documents from the Abbey of Bury St. Edmunds* (London, 1932), p. ci note 1.

[7] Edmund King, "The Peterborough 'Descriptio Militum' (Henry I)", *Eng. Hist. Rev.*, lxxxiv (1969), pp. 84-101; the document, hereafter cited as *Descriptio*, is there edited pp. 97-101.

[8] Peterborough Dean and Chapter, MS. 5 ("Henry of Pytchley's Book of Charters"; hereafter cited as P.B.C.), fos. 27r, 30v.

[9] *Chronicon Petroburgense* (hereafter cited as *Chr.P.*), ed. T. Stapleton (Camden Soc., xlvii, 1849), pp. 167-8.

[10] P.B.C., fo. 27r-v.

[11] There are parallels with Norman usage here: see L. Musset, commenting on G. Duby, "Les Origines de la Chevalerie" (Settimane di Studio, 15, *Ordinamenti militari in occidente nell'alto medioevo*, Spoleto, 1968), ii, pp. 845-7.

[12] See the Index to *Glanvill*, ed. G. D. G. Hall (London, 1965).

[13] N. Denholm-Young, "Feudal Society in the Thirteenth Century: the Knights", *Collected Papers* (Oxford, 1946), p. 57.

[14] F. M. Powicke, *The Thirteenth Century* (Oxford, 1953), p. 549.

that there were 3,000 men qualified for knighthood, of whom 1,250 actually were knights, and only 500 of these were "fighting" knights.[15] More recently Professor Hilton has calculated figures for three counties in the West Midlands: "we find that in the second half of the thirteenth century, and primarily during the three decades of Edward I's reign, there were at least two hundred families from which knights were dubbed". (The head of such a family would not invariably be a knight.) At least as important, for it gives a visual impression of the countryside, is his calculation that there were more than 1,100 villages and hamlets in this area; that is, there was perhaps one knightly family for every five villages.[16] And with 1,250 knights there was one knight for every five knight's fees. The knights have become an élite among the tenants by military service.[17]

It is important that these points should be borne in mind when considering the history of individual families. Now the majority of Peterborough tenants were on the margins of knightly tenure even in early Norman terms. Peterborough carried the service of sixty knights, which was a unique burden for a monastic house, and largely as a result the size of each fee was extremely small. Around 1100 the "average" Peterborough knight had a fee worth £2 10s. a year, amounting to two hides. In consequence, the "knights of Peterborough" in Henry I's day are a motley and singularly unimpressive crew.[18] Not all their descendants, obviously, are to be regarded as knights in the terms of the thirteenth century. In this period witness lists to charters, the best evidence of a man's status in his own community, and the feudal records may give two quite distinct impressions. Thus in 1100 Turold of Castor had two hides and a virgate, for which he owed the service of two knights. Service of half a knight was remitted when his son gave the advowson and some land to the abbey. His successors, whose holding seems not to have changed greatly, owed the service of one and a half knights throughout the thirteenth century.[19] But this ceases to be a knightly family. In 1242 "the lord William son of Thorold" was chief witness to a charter; in the 1280s his son was described as "Henry who is called

---

[15] Denholm-Young, *Collected Papers*, pp. 58-61.

[16] R. H. Hilton, *A Medieval Society* (London, 1966), pp. 54-5.

[17] E. Miller, "The State and Landed Interests in Thirteenth Century France and England", *Trans. Roy. Hist. Soc.*, 5th ser., ii (1952), p. 128.

[18] See King, "The Peterborough 'Descriptio Militum' (Henry I)".

[19] *Descriptio*, no. 21; P.B.C., fos. 25v-26r; *Henry of Pytchley's Book of Fees* (hereafter cited as *Pytchley*), ed. W. T. Mellows (Northamptonshire Rec. Soc., ii, 1927), p. 153.

the lord of Castor".[20]   This is a nickname, not a title of rank. Others may have been more fortunate in their friends, for instance the Peverel family.   They were descended from Walo of Paston, who in 1100 had a hide and a virgate in Paston and Warmington and owed the service of one knight.   The Peverels sold the Warmington portion to the abbey in the last quarter of the twelfth century, and in the thirteenth owed the service of two-thirds of a knight.   But it is as freeholders that a succession of Robert Peverels appear in the chronicle and in charters.[21]   Only the feudal records regard this as a knightly family, and their definition is no more than Bracton's definition of military tenure: anyone who pays even a halfpenny in scutage holds thus.[22]

The governmental records are unhelpful, therefore, and the surviving records of land transactions are biased towards landlord enterprise.   More than this, obviously, they show the land market through the landlord's eyes.   From the cartularies it is possible to list and date the major purchases of land, and such lists provide important indications of landlord policy.   But however many of them are taken together they will not provide a barometer to measure the economic position of any knightly class.   For individual transactions provide a very imperfect picture of the family, and may well produce a false perspective.   A family selling its chief manor in, say, 1285, may well change little in economic position between 1225 and 1350.   Their fall seems dramatic because then they vanish from the feudal records.   The current tenant will be granted a corrody, and "the family as a landowning group simply ceases to exist".[23]   But with most of the families selling to Peterborough all that can be said is that then they cease to exist as military tenants of this particular corporation, which is not quite the same thing.   A way to avoid at least some of these difficulties is to look at the land market from a different viewpoint.   "The proper unit of study is the individual family; it must be seen from the inside; and the most fruitful path in this field is the detailed study of particular cases, based upon the

---

[20] "Dominus Willelmus filius Thoraldi": Northamptonshire Rec. Off., Fitzwilliam (Milton) charter, no. 4; "Henricus dictus le Lord de Castre": *Pytchley*, p. 64.

[21] *Descriptio*, no. 16; *Pytchley*, p. 123; *Historiae Coenobii Burgensis Scriptores Varii*, ed. J. Sparke (London, 1723), p. 112; *Pytchley*, p. 69; *Carte Nativorum*, ed. C. N. L. Brooke and M. M. Postan (Northamptonshire Rec. Soc., xx, 1960), p. lxii.

[22] *Bracton. On the Laws and Customs of England*, ed. G. E. Woodbine, trans. etc. S. E. Thorne (Cambridge, Mass., 1968), ii, p. 117.

[23] Hilton, *A Medieval Society*, p. 52.

family documents, where these are available".[24]   The family, either growing or in decline, must be looked at not at a single point of time, but in the perspective of seven or eight generations.   The simple knight must speak for himself.

*   *   *   *

The history of seven families will be considered in this section. They are chosen because they can be studied in some detail, and they are a sample in this respect only.   There is no family here which stayed relatively still in the thirteenth century, for stable families leave few records.   The first two families, the Torpels and the Wondervilles, are related.   These are baronial families within the honour, and their history shows similar features.   The next three families are on a lower level.   The Northboroughs were sub-tenants of Torpel; the Miltons, with just over two hides, and Tot with just under one, held directly of the abbey.   Finally there are two families, the Hotots of Clapton and the Thorpes, which built up estates in the thirteenth century.   Each history will be presented in a similar way.   It will start with the knightly estate around 1100, the size of the properties which made it up and the pattern of their distribution.   It will then note any changes in this pattern during the twelfth century, in particular grants away from the fee either to members of the family or to the church.   The circumstances behind these grants will be considered; in this way we may perhaps turn to our profit "the piecemeal reconstructions of manorial descents and . . . the study of twelfth-century charters by the methods of Horace Round".[25]   In the thirteenth century the first five of these families decline, and the last two prosper.   The stages in either process will be worked out as fully as possible.

The devolution of property at the knightly level was for a long time controlled.   From one point of view this is surprising, for there was pressure on the knights to devolve land no less than on their lords. The claims of relatives, and the claims of piety, had each to be met according to the fashion of the group; this stress existed even if the family's economic position was assured.[26]   There was some natural pressure towards fragmentation, for the knight's holding was often no

---

[24] H. J. Habakkuk, intro. to M. E. Finch, *The Wealth of Five Northamptonshire Families, 1540-1640* (Northamptonshire Rec. Soc., xix, 1956), p. xix.

[25] Postan, *Cambridge Economic History*, i, p. 592.

[26] The best general discussion of these matters is in S. Painter, "The Family and the Feudal System in Twelfth-Century England", *Feudalism and Liberty* (Baltimore, 1961), pp. 195-219.

more an economic unit than was the great estate.[27]   In this it probably differed from a normal freehold. Thus, of the Peterborough fees, that at Milton included six bovates in Cleatham, a good sixty miles away in Lincolnshire. The small Tot fee in Paston was partly made up of land in Prestgrave, Leicestershire, nearly twenty-five miles away. The baronial fees within the honour show the same distribution. St. Medard, with six fees, had land in six villages in three counties; Torpel, with the same, had land in fourteen villages in Northamptonshire; Gunthorpe, with three fees, had land in thirteen.[28] Already in 1086 there are on most knightly estates properties clearly marked out for subinfeudation. When did this happen? At this point, with this question, each of the family histories starts.

Torpel was one of two families to owe the service of six knights, the other being St. Medard. The property of each of them was assessed at four fees within the Soke of Peterborough, and two outside. In each case the latter became separate tenancies in the mid-twelfth century. The Torpel manors in this category were Cotterstock and Glapthorne, in the Nene valley, twelve miles from the abbey and the same distance from the manor of Torpel. Around 1100 their occupation was disputed. Perhaps still in dispute, for such was the ideal portion, they were given to Roger of Torpel's daughter on her marriage with Richard of Reinbuedcurt. They were purchased back by Roger's heir, Robert, and sometime before 1135 given to Robert as a separate tenancy when infirmity forced him to hand on the honour to his younger brother.[29] This land was given him, we are told, "with the assent of King Henry and many of the barons of the land, to remain with Robert to hold and alienate as he please".[30] He then gave the two manors to the hospital of St. Leonard outside Peterborough when he entered it in Stephen's reign, and in this way details of a very interesting family settlement have been preserved. But the family regained control during the next reign, and these were demesne manors of Torpel in the thirteenth century. The Torpels were the chief of the honorial barons; it was a powerful family which could regain property from an abbey like Peterborough.

---

[27] F. M. Stenton, *The First Century of English Feudalism,* 2nd edn. (Oxford, 1961), pp. 158-9, 169.
[28] The Peterborough knights' holdings are usefully tabulated in *Pytchley,* pp. xviii-xxi, from where these figures are taken.
[29] *Descriptio,* no. 3; P.B.C., fo. 27r-v; *Pytchley,* pp. 28-34.
[30] P.B.C., fo. 27r-v. For similar clauses see *The Cartulary of Tutbury Priory,* ed. A. Saltman (Historical Manuscripts Commission, JP. 2, 1962), no. 103; *Durham Episcopal Charters, 1071-1152,* ed. H. S. Offler (Surtees Soc., clxxix, 1968), no. 11.

The next event materially affecting the family's position was the marriage of the second Roger of Torpel with Asceline de Waterville. This was an alliance with another Peterborough family of similar rank. Ascelin de Waterville around 1100 had held fourteen hides in Northamptonshire, as three fees.[31] This comprised two large manors in the Soke, Marholm and Upton, and an interest in several manors in the Nene valley. A charter of between 1133 and 1155 shows the family settlement of the next generation. The manors in the Soke, each rated at two hides and a virgate, went to Ascelin's two sons, Hugh and Geoffrey. His two daughters had each a virgate, one in Stanwick and one in Irthlingborough — his two most distant manors, and those where his lordship was least secure.[32] The younger son Geoffrey was a knight of Robert earl of Gloucester early in the civil war, and married Asceline, the youngest of the four sisters of Pain Peverel, who were his heirs to the barony of Bourne. He was lucky in his generation and lucky in his marriage; in such circumstances a younger brother might thrive. Their son died without heirs, and their two daughters, Asceline and Maud, inherited. It was the elder of these who married Roger of Torpel.[33]

The manors of Torpel and Upton, together thereafter and much transferred, are the tenurial product of this union. At the end of the century grants were made from them, by Asceline and Maud de Dive her sister, chiefly to the nuns of Stamford. Asceline's great-grandson, William of Torpel, died in 1242 and was succeeded by his sister, who naturally found a husband within the year.[34] This man, Ralph de Camoys, held Torpel and Upton, as did his son. But by this stage the family was heavily in debt both to Jew and Gentile.[35] The first step to relieve the pressure seems to have been taken early in 1280, when the manors of Torpel and Upton were leased to the crown for ten years in quittance of a debt of 500 marks. But the relief was short-lived, and by the end of the year the manors had been granted away permanently.[36] Early in 1281 the king granted the manors to Queen Eleanor, who seems to have been everywhere in the property

[31] Descriptio, no. 6; Pytchley, pp. 41-5.

[32] Peterborough Dean and Chapter, MS. 1 ("Swapham's Cartulary"; hereafter cited as Swa.), fos. 204v-205r.

[33] Sir Christopher Hatton's Book of Seals, ed. L. C. Loyd and D. M. Stenton (Oxford, 1950), nos. 212, 514; I. J. Sanders, English Baronies. A Study of their Origin and Descent 1086-1327 (Oxford, 1963), pp. 19-20.

[34] Francis Peck, Academia Tertia Anglicana; or, the Antiquarian Annals of Stamford (London, 1727), vi, pp. 16-21; Sanders, English Baronies, p. 19; Pub. Rec. Off., CP. 25(1), 173/32/469.

[35] Cal. Close Rolls, 1268-72, p. 392; ibid., 1272-9, p. 259.

[36] Ibid., 1279-88, p. 46; Cal. Pat. Rolls, 1272-81, pp. 366-7; Cal. Close Rolls, 1279-88, pp. 66, 81.

dealings of the day. She leased them in turn to Geoffrey of Southorpe, another Peterborough tenant whose family is the next considered, and to Gilbert Pecche as a life tenancy, after she had been granted the whole of his estate. When she died in 1290 the manors were granted to the abbey to farm for £100 a year.[37] The wheel had come full circle, but the lordship remained with the crown. The properties were granted successively to Piers Gaveston and Edmund of Woodstock. Their history becomes that of Edward II's patronage, yet that history to be understood must start with the family history of a couple of Peterborough tenants in the mid-twelfth century.

What were then transferred were the two manors which Torpel and then Camoys retained in demesne. Now this was not the whole property which earlier had owed the service of four knights. Lordship and land occupancy were two quite different things. The fragmentation of the original Torpel fee cannot be examined in detail, but several fractions of fees can be identified early in the thirteenth century. One of them, half a fee, was held by Geoffrey of Northborough.[38] There were many like him, and about most of them we know little. But this was purchased by Peterborough in the next quarter-century, and the central and local records give an unusually complete picture of a fee of this size. If looked at carefully they may show more than the simple fact of decline.

Geoffrey occurs as a juror in the early part of the century. Between 1214 and 1222 he sold twenty acres of meadow to the abbey, and was given forty marks, to acquit him of a debt to the Jews.[39] He died in 1225 and his wife brought claims for her dower; then one gets behind the feudal façade. There had been numerous alienations in Geoffrey's lifetime. His younger son, the priest of the church, had been given a third of the estate, which he had then sold. His three daughters had their portions, subsequently bought by the abbey for £20, £4 and £2, which may roughly indicate the scale of their respective endowments. There had been other alienations. And at the time of his death the whole of his tenancy was leased to his lord, Roger of Torpel.[40]

What was left of this estate when the claims of family and creditors had been met was purchased by Peterborough Abbey. The younger brother gave it the tithes from the estate, while he gave the advowson

---

[37] Peterborough Dean and Chapter, MS. 6, fo. 151r; *Cal. Pat. Rolls, 1281-92*, pp. 114, 421.
[38] *Pytchley*, p. 34 note.
[39] Swa., fo. 224v.
[40] *Curia Regis Rolls*, xii, nos. 230, 916, 967, 998, 2336; Swa., fos. 181v-182r, 219v, 250v.

to Fineshade Priory.[41]   Other entries in the cartulary clearly represent an attempt at consolidation.   The daughters' portions have already been mentioned; rather earlier a tenancy was purchased from Wiliam Blevet for seven marks; finally, in 1258, the abbey bought the advowson and the land which had been given to Fineshade.[42]   As well as the abbey, therefore, there were several parties with an interest in this property in 1225 — Roger of Torpel, Robert of Braybrooke,[43] and Fineshade Priory.   But the abbey saw its competitors off the field, and in the second quarter of the century largely rebuilt the estate which Geoffrey of Northborough had dissipated in the first.

From Northborough we now go up the scale, as it were, to the family of Southorpe.   In 1100 Geoffrey "the abbot's nephew" *(nepos abbatis)* had eight hides in Northamptonshire, for the service of three knights.[44]   As with Torpel and St. Medard the proportion was two fees in the Soke to one outside.   The chief manors in the Soke were Gunthorpe and Southorpe, while Stoke Doyle and Hemington were in the Nene valley ten miles away.   As above, it is the pattern of family settlement that is first considered; after this their thirteenth-century history is traced from the abbey records, for this was the most substantial of the families forced by indebtedness to sell to the abbey.

Geoffrey had four sons.   The eldest, Ives, had the whole of the estate for a good forty years, from *c.* 1135 to at least 1178.   The second son, Richard, had part of the third fee, in Hemington, by 1176. Of the third son nothing is known.   The fourth occurs around 1150 holding a virgate in Helpston "of the fee of Ives his brother".[45] Ives, the tenant of the main fee, was in debt to the abbey by the middle of Henry II's reign.   To redeem this, shortly after 1170, he mortgaged the smaller part of the third fee, Stoke Doyle, and the services, not the land, of his tenants in Etton, Gunthorpe and Paston.[46]   One should note here the tight hold kept throughout the twelfth century on the two main fees; it was the property ten miles away that was used to meet the various economic and dynastic pressures on the family in the second half of the twelfth century.

[41] Swa., fos. 219r-220r, 224r-v; Fineshade Cartulary (Lambeth Palace, Records of the Court of Arches, MS. Ff. 291), fo. 27r.

[42] Swa., fos. 231r, 246r, 290r.

[43] On Robert see H. G. Richardson, *The English Jewry under Angevin Kings* (London, 1960), pp. 100-2, 270-80; and for his dealings in Northborough see his cartulary, Brit. Mus., MS. Sloane 986, fo. 17r-v.

[44] *Descriptio,* no. 5.

[45] *Pytchley,* pp. 68-9; *Facsimiles of Early Charters from Northamptonshire Collections,* ed. F. M. Stenton (Northamptonshire Rec. Soc., iv, 1930), p. 66; P.B.C., fo. 24v.

[46] *The Peterborough Chronicle of Hugh Candidus,* ed. W. T. Mellows (Oxford, 1949), p. 129.

There were a number of alienations to the abbey in the period 1175-1225 — a good deal of woodland, and ten solidates of rent for the almonry.[47] Such transactions seem common to all the tenants of this rank in the Soke. Clearly such pressure did not improve the family's economic position, but these were major tenants and the alienations are not remarkable. Between 1275 and 1290, however, the patrimony, the two carefully guarded fees in the Soke, was bought by the abbey of Peterborough, and as a knightly family that of Southorpe disappeared. The story of its demise is told in great detail in the various Peterborough sources,[48] and in its barest outline it is as follows.

Geoffrey of Southorpe sold Gunthorpe to the abbey *c.* 1276, for 550 marks.[49] But this was not successful in getting the family out of debt and by 1280 the second manor, Southorpe, was in the hands of a London merchant, Stephen of Cornhill — foreclosing on his own debts, and perhaps providing capital for Geoffrey to settle his debts with other merchants.[50] Geoffrey retired to the small manor of Lolham in the north of the Soke, which was his wife's marriage portion, and there prepared to build anew. As already seen, he leased Torpel and Upton from Queen Eleanor in 1281, and he seems also to have borrowed money from her. Yet the profits which were thus to revive the family's fortunes proved illusory and brought only more debt. In 1285 a case came up concerning some of this property, and seemingly the whole area vouched him to warranty — that is to say he had alienated most of it in small portions for ready cash.[51] This was unwise. A year later the Queen took the manors back and took Geoffrey to the debtor's prison. While he was thus occupied the abbey purchased Southorpe from Stephen of Cornhill.[52]

Geoffrey secured his release in 1289 by creating a perpetual rent-charge of £10 a year on Lolham, which was all that was left to him.[53] Then, Pytchley says:

> He returned and was at Lolham on the vigil of St Nicholas the bishop, and forthwith broke out into malicious repudiation, saying that all the deeds which he had executed had been executed in prison under duress, and were therefore of no effect. But William of Woodford, then sacristan, having respect to his poverty and in order to avoid a scandal, gave him ten marks in ready money, and two horses to the value of ten marks.[54]

[47] Swa., fos. 205r-206r.
[48] In particular, *Pytchley*, pp. 61-72.
[49] Swa., fo. 36v; *Chr.P.*, p. 25.
[50] *Cal. Close Rolls, 1272-9*, pp. 233, 248; *ibid., 1279-88*, p. 53.
[51] *Cal. Inq. Post Mortem*, iii, no. 38; Peterborough Dean and Chapter, MS. 6, fo. 151r-v; P.R.O., CP. 25(1), 175/56/252, 174/54/184.
[52] *Pytchley*, pp. 62-4.
[53] Pub. Rec. Off., CP. 25(1), 175/56/252.
[54] *Pytchley*, p. 70.

And thus, with the last vestiges of gentility, he leaves the Peterborough record. Shortly afterwards Richard of Southorpe witnessed a homage as "Richard, brother of the lord Geoffrey who was once lord of Southorpe".[55] What seems to have been the end of the story is related by Francis Peck:

> At this time divers most excellent soldiers of the equestrian rank, stroke with admiration at the holy lives of several White Friars then living, became Carmelites, of which number Sir Geoffrey Southorpe, who entered himself into their monastery at Stamford, was one.[56]

Southorpe, Torpel and Waterville were substantial tenants of the abbey, and each of them had scope to alienate parts of their holding in the twelfth century. Torpel, the largest, did so by the second quarter of the century, then Waterville in the mid-century, and finally Southorpe in the third quarter. Alienation was possible because "there was a good deal of play in the joints of the average fee".[57] But in some fees, those of men at the bottom of the feudal ladder, there was no play at all. These will be called "basic" fees; all the families which follow had holdings of this sort.

Geoffrey of Tot had in 1100 a hide in Paston, a hamlet of Peterborough, and a virgate at Prestgrave in Leicestershire.[58] This tenancy descended as a single unit throughout the twelfth century. It was held as one fee until 1195, when the service was reduced by a half. Around the same time, in 1191, Elias of Tot owed nearly £15 among the debts of Aaron the Jew.[59] This of itself was in no way remarkable; he was in good company. But there is at least the suggestion here of a discrepancy between the family's economic position and its feudal position. And this was precisely the area of the abbey's most dynamic lordship in the next half-century. The family went under during this period, and an archive of twenty charters enables the story to be traced step by step.

Between 1200 and 1210, Robert of Tot was given six marks for a grant of woodland and arable, "to acquit him of his debts to the Jews". Other transactions in this period brought a further twenty acres to the abbey. In the next generation his son, another Robert,

[55] "Richardi fratris domini Galfridi quondam militis de Sutthorp": *Chr.P.* p. 147.

[56] *Antiquarian Annals of Stamford*, xi, p. 45. Geoffrey's son and grandson appear as freeholders, "of Lolham", in the next century: Boughton House near Kettering, Buccleuch Charters, B1. nos. 314, 327 (there are photostat copies of these in the Northants Rec. Off.); *Cal. Pat. Rolls, 1345-8*, p. 87.

[57] S. E. Thorne, "English Feudalism and Estates in Land", *Cambridge Law Jl.* (1959), p. 205.

[58] *Descriptio*, no. 18.

[59] *Pytchley*, pp. 107-10; *Feet of Fines 10 Richard I* (Pipe Roll Soc., xxiv, 1900), no. 245; *Pipe Roll 3 and 4 Richard I* (Pipe Roll Soc., xl, 1926), p. 159 (3 Richard I).

made three further alienations, the largest of them a grant of woodland for which he was given five marks.[60]   Finally, in 1222, he mortgaged the bulk of his estate to the abbey for twenty years.   He was given sixteen marks, to acquit him "against the Jews of Stamford and against others", and the abbey undertook to pay £10 "for the debts of Aaron the Jew".[61]   The treble pressure — from the Exchequer, from the Jews, and from other creditors — seems finally to have extinguished this small fee.   In charters of *c.* 1220 to *c.* 1240 Geoffrey of Tot appears in witness lists among freeholders of only modest size, and on his death his wife was granted a corrody sufficiently substantial to suggest that it was conclusive.   Geoffrey's daughter was similarly pensioned off; while in 1284 his grand-daughter brought a claim for some woodland clearly sold half a century before.   It must have been more a plea for alms than a proper law-suit; the abbot, we are told, "out of the kindness of his heart", gave her a mark.[62]   A century later the last vestige of the family lay in the name *Totisgore,* and when the Paston demesne was surveyed it was noted that this referred to a certain Robert of Tot, "who was once one of the lords of Paston".[63]

The Milton family was slightly more substantial than that of Tot, and lasted slightly longer.   Turold of Milton had in 1100 two hides in Milton, a hamlet of Castor, and six bovates in Cleatham in Lincoln-shire, for the service of two knights.[64]   The property descended in the male line throughout the twelfth century.   Then, around the turn of the century, it was subdivided to provide for a younger son.   His portion was bought by the abbey *c.* 1230.[65]   The main fee broke up in the next generation, the final but hardly the decisive blow being that Geoffrey of Milton backed the wrong side in the civil war.   By 1267 he was in debt to various Jews for about £180.   In December of that year these Jews sold their rights to William Charles, a knight of the household.   It remained only to make a decent settlement, and in 1268 Geoffrey made over the Milton estate to William Charles for a corrody of 24 marks a year.[66]   The Lincolnshire estate was seemingly alienated around the same time.   Shortly afterwards, in an exchange of land, he described himself as "Geoffrey son of Robert the knight, formerly lord of Milton".[67]

[60] Swa., fos. 218v-221r.
[61] Boughton House, Buccleuch MS., "Register of George Franceys, Sacrist" (photostat in the Peterborough Dean and Chapter Library), pp. 40-1.
[62] *Ibid.,* pp. 43, 45-7, 59-60, 95-6; *Chr.P.,* p. 71.
[63] Franceys Register, p. 427.   [64] *Descriptio,* no. 11.
[65] *Pytchley,* pp. 78-80; Swa., fos. 216r, 243r-v.
[66] *Cal. Pat. Rolls, 1266-72,* p. 172; *Cal. Plea Rolls of the Exchequer of the Jews,* i, p. 195; *Cal. Close Rolls, 1264-8,* pp. 531-2.
[67] *Pytchley,* p. 79; "Galfridi filii Roberti militis quondam domini de Melletona", Fitzwilliam charter, no. 1360.

Each of the above, the four main families, and the two considered along with Torpel, have this in common. Their main property was in the Soke of Peterborough. They are chiefly studied from sources compiled at the abbey, and it is not surprising that in them the abbey appears as the dominant agent. Yet the detail of the sources is valuable, for it illustrates the chronology of knightly indebtedness, and the various steps taken to meet it. The range of the sources is now extended and a new element introduced into the discussion by the history of two families that can be studied from their own records. These families are Hotot of Clapton and Thorpe of Longthorpe near Peterborough.

Recently there turned up in the Phillips collection a small family cartulary, Richard of Hotot's "estate book", seemingly one of the earliest lay cartularies to survive.[68] It is called an estate book, perhaps, after that of another Northamptonshire man of similar substance, Henry de Bray.[69] But this is from the first half of the thirteenth century; shorter, a lot less polished, and at least as interesting. There is no tradition behind this document. It is difficult to convey its atmosphere in print, but when handled it gives a vivid impression of the small landowner at the very beginning of literacy. It starts with a family chronicle; not that of Richard's family, but that into which his father had married. The size of the script here matches any monastic cartulary, though the spelling does not. The chronicle merges into a list of Richard's purchases of land; then there are details of the services he owed, and that were owed to him. In the middle of the document there is a complete quire comprising Magna Carta 1215, the Charter of the Forest, and a couple of ecclesiastical records from the reign of King John. Some smaller pieces of parchment are attached to the end, and contain memoranda of Richard's son. He had his own estate book, now lost, but seen in the eighteenth century by John Bridges, who transcribed from it an inquisition made in the 1250s,[70] extracts from which he used in his county history.[71]

The short history of the family in the earlier book begins as follows:

Turold abbot of Peterborough gave Roger of Lovetot baron of Southoe a fee of two knights in Clapton, Polebrook and Catworth, to hold of the said abbot and his successors. The same Roger of Lovetot gave the same Alfred de Grauntcourt his knight the whole fee which he had by gift of the said abbot

[68] Brit. Mus., Add. MS. 54228. The text is edited by E. J. King in "Estate Records of the Hotot Family", in E. J. King (ed.), *A Northamptonshire Miscellany* (Northamptonshire Rec. Soc., xxxii, 1983; hereafter "Hotot Records"), pp. 16-42.
[69] *The Estate Book of Henry de Bray*, ed. D. Willis (Camden Soc., 3rd ser., xxvii, 1916).
[70] "Hotot Records", pp. 43-58.
[71] J. Bridges, *The History and Antiquities of Northamptonshire* (Oxford, 1791), ii, pp. 367-72.

in Clapton, namely four hides as one knight's fee. And the same Roger gave the same Alfred in the same vill of Clapton one hide and one virgate for a quarter fee, and this was of Roger of Southoe's own barony, not pertaining to Peterborough in any way, save only that it was in the liberty of the said abbot.

That is the description of the Clapton holding. It goes on to say that he had land in Polebrook, which also was held partly of Peterborough and partly of Roger of Lovetot, and a hide and a virgate in Thurning.[72] This is the liberty of Peterborough seen from the outside, and a family history, which has its own dynamic and was quite independent of it.

This estate differs in several respects from those previously considered. Territorially it was compact, for these three villages were almost contiguous. Its obligations, further, were calculated at four to five hides the fee, not the Peterborough average of two hides. And in Domesday one finds that this Alfred had previously held of Eustace the sheriff, the tenant-in-chief before Roger of Lovetot.[73] Thus, as on many other estates around the turn of the century, there was continuity of occupancy through a change of lordship. The estate descended in its entirety to William son of Walter. This William de Grauntcourt, so the tradition went in the thirteenth century, became known as William de Clapton, "from the difficulty the lower people found in pronouncing his Norman name".[74]

Between 1175 and 1190, what had previously been maintained as a single tenancy was divided into numerous parcels. In this it resembles every family of "basic" knightly rank so far considered. Here the alienation was particularly extensive, and from the family's own records, combined with the normal feudal records, can be traced in particular detail. William, we are told, had four brothers and three sisters.[75] Robert, the eldest of the brothers, was given the Polebrook estate.[76] The next brother, Walter, had land unspecified in Kingsthorpe;[77] the next had two virgates in Clapton; the youngest was priest of the church. There is no obvious logic in the descent of

---

[72] "Hotot Records", p. 16.   [73] *Domesday Book,* i, fo. 228a.
[74] Bridges, *Northamptonshire,* ii, p. 367.
[75] The information in this paragraph is taken from the estate book, unless otherwise stated. The genealogy on the facing page may help explain these transactions. It is chiefly compiled from the two thirteenth-century family histories. The Peterborough cartulary and some central records provide more precise information on dates: Swa., fos. 1711-v, 249v-250v; *Curia Regis Rolls,* i, pp. 117, 119-20; viii, p. 69; x, pp. 18, 317; xi, no. 1818; *Rotuli Curie Regis,* ed. F. Palgrave (Rec. Com., 1835), i, p. 108; ii, p. 50; *Excerpta e Rotulis Finium,* ed. C. Roberts (Rec. Com., 1835), i, pp. 2, 20-1, 94. The above supplement the family's own history; at no point do they contradict it.
[76] *Curia Regis Rolls,* i, pp. 117, 119-20.
[77] *The Earliest Northamptonshire Assise Rolls, A.D. 1202 and 1203,* ed. D. M. Stenton (Northamptonshire Rec. Soc., v, 1930), pp. 46-7.

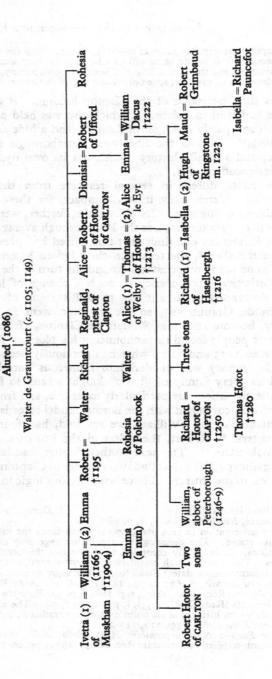

GENEALOGY OF THE FAMILY OF HOTOT OF CLAPTON

the rest of William's holding.   Some land went to the church; the bulk of it was divided between a nephew and a niece's husband. The nephew was Thomas of Hotot, the father of the man who compiled the estate book, who was given sixty acres of demesne and two virgates.   The niece's husband was William Dacus,[78] who was given a larger estate – 120 acres of demesne, the service of the freemen, seven virgates of villeinage, and the quarter fee in Thurning.   William of Clapton's gifts to the church are similar in scale to those of the other men of his rank considered.   He gave two virgates of land to the nuns of Stamford, with his daughter, and twenty-four acres of demesne to the nuns of Chicksands in Bedfordshire.   To Peterborough abbey he gave at least three virgates, professed himself a monk, and there died.[79]   To Richard Hotot, looking back from the vantage-point of the 1250s back over the alienations of the 1180s, this was a story difficult to understand. In the century after Domesday Book there had been only three lords of Clapton, "who succeeded by inheritance, the son following the father".   The last of these, William, "at first received the estate and held it in one piece, but afterwards it was dispersed, given away and sold".[80]

The dynamic of this story is now in the line of Thomas Hotot and Richard his son.   Put at its most brief, it sees the partial reconstitution and also the extension by Richard of the estate his great-uncle had dissipated.   Richard succeeded his father around 1213 and died around 1250.   He spent in all 413 marks in acquiring the portions of Isabella and Maud his cousins.   Isabella's first husband came from Somerset, and "was found in a wood barbarously murdered with his head cut off".   She moved north, married a man who held three fees of the bishop of Lincoln, and they sold the Clapton estate to Richard around 1240.   About this time also he purchased the other sister's portion.   The estate book records at least forty smaller purchases in Clapton, and several elsewhere, the largest of these being at Turvey in Bedfordshire, eighteen miles away, where he spent 182 marks.[81]   In

---

[78] This William has perhaps his securest fame as the plaintiff in a case from Somerset in 1204.   The defendant claimed kind treatment from the court "since he was native born and local gentry", and an interesting discussion ensued: *Curia Regis Rolls*, iii, pp. 129–30; cf. J. C. Holt, *Magna Carta* (Cambridge, 1965), pp. 56–7.

[79] Swa., fos. 249v–250r; Bridges, *Northamptonshire*, ii, p. 368; *Curia Regis Rolls*, i, p. 117.

[80] "Hotot Records", p. 44.

[81] Brit. Mus., Add. MS. 54228, fos. 2v, 3v–4r, 13v; Bridges, *Northamptonshire*, ii, p. 368.

all Richard spent at least a thousand marks on these purchases, the same amount seemingly as Peterborough abbey spent in acquiring Gunthorpe and Southorpe, and this half a century earlier. And this man is not in the *Book of Fees*, and not in any Peterborough cartulary — "in no way pertaining to Peterborough, save only that he was in the said abbot's liberty".

Whether this capital was generated entirely by good management it is impossible to say. There is a less creditable explanation. Though there is no hint of the relationship in the estate book, it must be very likely that Richard's elder brother was the William Hotot who was abbot of Peterborough from 1246 to 1249.[82] Now William was apparently a bad lot; he was deposed, says Matthew Paris, accused "of dilapidation and gifts to his kinsmen, of whom there were an inordinate number hanging around".[83] But most of Richard Hotot's major purchases were made before this abbacy. Clearly it did a family no harm when one of its members was the most powerful churchman in the area, but whether peculation contributed substantially to the Hotot fortune is open to doubt.

Richard Hotot must have died within about a year of his brother's deposition. His son Thomas inherited a viable estate, and he acquired little, save significantly a large tenancy which he bought from Robert Hotot of Carlton, which must be the holding of the elder branch of the family.[84] He conserved; and we know that he compiled a family chronicle a good deal more circumstantial than that of his father. The long and colourful generation of the late-twelfth century is shifted back to Stephen's reign, and becomes longer and more colourful still. Among many good stories a sober narrative can spare room only for one:

> Of Dionisia the second daughter of Walter de Grauntcourt it is recorded that when a maiden, clad in a tunic, with a hat upon her head and armed only with a hollow shield, about the seventeenth year of King Stephen she attacked a certain knight, with one blow of her spear bringing him to the ground, and carried off his horse.[85]

This may not be true, but in a sense it needed to be. There is in all this evidence of a landed family, secure in its position in the world, a position acquired by its industry, and defended by "the charters".

Of the last "knightly family" there are no twelfth-century records, for then they were freeholders. For the thirteenth century there are in the abbey's records, and then in their own, two rather different stories. The abbey had a manor two miles from Peterborough, at Longthorpe. Its records kept a note of the services,

[82] "Hotot Records", p. 8, note 46.
[83] *Matthaei Parisiensis Chronica Majora*, ed. H. R. Luard, v (Rolls ser., lvii, 1880), p. 84.   [84] Brit. Mus., Add. MS. 54228, fos. 23r, 22r.
[85] Bridges, *Northamptonshire*, ii, p. 368.

including ploughing and harvest work, owed by a number of freeholders. In 1230 William son of Thurstan of Thorpe held two of these tenancies, and a third was later acquired, probably by the William of Thorpe who appears in the Hundred Rolls also holding two virgates at Orton Waterville in Huntingdonshire. William's son Robert was in the abbey's service, and became steward in 1309.[86] It is as reasonably substantial freeholders, therefore, that members of this family appear in the thirteenth century. Then in the following century the family became strikingly more prosperous: Robert's son was a judge, his grandson a chief justice.[87] The latter in 1356 was allowed £40 a year from the Exchequer, to sustain him in the order of knighthood, which he had taken at the king's command.[88]

More tangible records of the family's substance survive to this day, and provide a rather different emphasis. Between 1263 and 1274 William of Thorpe received permission from the abbey to rebuild the chapel of St Botulph, described as being so far from the village that "the old and infirm often die without the sacraments, and the cure of souls is neglected to a dangerous extent".[89] This was done at William's own expense. The church survives practically unchanged. At the same time, alongside, William built a new manor house. William was not a knight; but there can have been no doubt who was lord of Longthorpe. Around 1300 his son Robert added to the manor house a tower three storeys high — perhaps this marks his appointment as steward in 1309. It is a remarkable building, reminiscent of the peel towers of the border counties, not of a manor house in the midlands. In the next generation Robert's son in turn commissioned in the great chamber a magnificent series of wall paintings, among the earliest and most impressive of those which survive.[90] This "seignorial skyscraper" serves as a reminder of how broad a class freeholder was in the thirteenth century, and how limited the concept of knighthood as an indication of economic position.

*　　*　　*　　*

It remains to be considered whether from this cumulative history of families any common pattern emerges. As a first point, it seems to

---

[86] Society of Antiquaries of London, MS. 60, fos. 183v, 184v; *Rotuli Hundredorum*, ii, p. 638a; *Pytchley*, p. 55 note; Brit. Mus., MS. Cott. Vesp. E. xxii, fo. 116r.
[87] *Pytchley*, p. 55 note.   [88] *Cal. Pat. Rolls, 1354-8*, p. 465.
[89] Brit. Mus., MS. Cott. Cleopatra C. i, fo. 102r-v.
[90] M. Wood, *The English Medieval House* (London, 1965), pp. 166-7, 399-401; E. C. Rouse and A. Baker, "The Wall Paintings at Longthorpe Tower, near Peterborough, Northants", *Archaeologia*, xcvi (1955), pp. 1-57.

show "the integrity of the knight's fee" as a feature of the "first century",[91] and up to *c.* 1175. This does not mean the integrity of every knightly holding, but rather that each knightly *family* should have *a* tenancy of this size to support its obligations. It is this that has been termed the "basic" fee. There was a limit to a family's alienations, and some families had no scope for alienation at all. In the last quarter of the century this basic fee was dissolved. The feudal unit broke up, and this made possible the construction — at times the reconstruction — of economic units. Hotot of Clapton provides the model here; in the next village but one a succession of Richards of Hemington are doing the same thing;[92] two miles from the abbey Thorpe of Longthorpe also.[93] The accidents of feudal geography may well have created a number of areas particularly suited to enterprise of this sort. Within the Peterborough "area of influence" there was perhaps most turnover in the Nene valley, for here lay the most dispensable units of several fees which had their "core" near the abbey. Again, the Norman settlement provides the key to later changes.

Any explanation of these changes, the stability of the fee up to the last quarter the century, and then its dissolution, must be largely hypothetical. There is no Stenton to guide us through the second century of English feudalism. But two recent contributions throw a good deal of light on the crucial period from *c.* 1175 to *c.* 1225. For Professor Miller this is the period of the "managerial revolution". Inflation, particularly marked from the 1180s,[94] eroded the largely fixed incomes of the major landowners. Not only did these men have a state to keep up, they were probably also driven on by new consumption standards. Under these pressures, the landowners changed their methods of exploiting the manors they held in demesne, and farmed directly for a market which population growth and the expansion of exchanges widened rapidly. "What may originally have been a defensive reaction on the part of landowners . . . was

[91] Stenton, *First Century*, p. 188.
[92] Boughton House, Buccleuch Charters, B1. nos. 136-251, *passim*.
[93] The records of a very interesting and perhaps comparable estate in Ewell (Surrey) have recently been printed. "Fitznells was a complex of property held from many lords . . . given unity by the members of one family who built it up by quasi-inheritance, marriage, purchase and perhaps a foreclosed mortgage or two in a thriving century between about 1220 and 1310": *Fitznells Cartulary*, ed. C. A. F. Meekings and P. Shearman (Surrey Rec. Soc., xxvi, 1968), p. xi.
[94] D. L. Farmer, "Some Price Fluctuations in Angevin England", *Econ. Hist. Rev.*, 2nd ser., ix (1956-7), pp. 34-43.

transformed into a more positive entrepreneurial attitude".[95]   Now
the managerial revolution began at just the time that the lords lost
the last vestiges of their control over the descent of feudal tenures.
The assise of novel disseisin, suggests Professor Milsom, was originally
part of "a policy of protecting tenants against their lords".[96]   The
protection of seisin meant the protection of the tenant.   It was the
tenant's right of unrestrained alienation which was the final blow to
the "integrity of the fee" — "the expectancies of heirs being lost with
the control of the lord, the law upon which they depended".[97]   This
change in the authority of lords over the lands held of them in feudal
tenure was therefore accompanied by (and may be another factor
accounting for) a change in their attitude to the property which they
held in demesne.

Free alienability, like heritability, was not something that emerged
at any single point of time.   This law was being moulded from
custom; custom varied from lordship to lordship, and at different
levels of society.[98]   The previous section, which refers to the
smaller knightly tenures of an ecclesiastical lord, may well turn
out to show control over alienation at its most tight.   Feudal
rules about descent would therefore be at their most inflexible with
regard to tenancies whose military value was dubious from the
beginning.   With the protection of seisin this control was finally lost.
It might be a possible extension of this theory that members of the
family obtained rights of ownership in those parts of the fee that they had
previously held as life tenancies; that is to say, that younger sons may
have occupied in 1120 the same estates which were occupied by other
younger sons in 1180.   All that may have changed was that in this
generation, for the first time, such properties could no longer be
recalled.   Around 1940 Peregrine Crouchback was explaining to his
niece why he had never married: "I was a younger son.   Younger
sons didn't marry in my day . . . It was thought rather *outré* among
landed people, unless of course they found heiresses.   There was no
establishment for them.   They had a small settlement which they
were expected to leave back to the family — to their nephews, other
younger sons".[99]   "Oh rot!" came the reply in 1940, as it may well

[95] Edward Miller, "England in the Twelfth and Thirteenth Centuries: an
Economic Contrast?", *Econ. Hist. Rev.*, 2nd ser., xxiv (1971), pp. 1-14.   I am grateful
to Professor Miller for allowing me to see a copy of this paper in advance of its
publication.   [96] Intro. to *History of English Law*, i, p. xliv.
[97] S. F. C. Milsom, *Historical Foundations of the Common Law* (London,
1969), p. 105.
[98] Milsom, intro. to *History of English Law*, i, pp. xxxiv-xxxviii.
[99] E. Waugh, *Unconditional Surrender* (Penguin edn., 1964), p. 135.

have come in 1180: it may have shocked several heads of knightly families, just as it shocked Uncle Peregrine.[100]

At a time when they were becoming more independent of their lords, the knights in local government were being placed in a direct relationship with the king. As a self-conscious class the knights were in part the creation of Angevin administration. The knight in 1175 had a position to keep up in the world, which had hardly been so in 1100. And it is not only Glanvill which suggests this; there is the same implication in their church patronage. For patronage is part of a broader process of family settlement. At each level of this society there is one generation — or at most two — where the family "opens out". Families make visible, independent provision for their daughters and younger sons. And they also, for the two things go together, make provision for their souls. Each phase of the religious patronage of the twelfth century is the work of a remarkably homogeneous social group. Henry I's aristocracy of service had largely founded their dynasties and their houses of Augustinian canons by 1135. Thus Geoffrey Ridel, the son of Richard Basset, had 86 per cent of his land enfeoffed in 1166, and the vast majority of this was of the "old enfeoffment".[101] The servants of Henry II and his sons more typically founded Premonstratensian houses, and they did so almost as a matter of course: Hubert Walter, in founding West Dereham in 1188, was "doing what his family and friends would expect of him now that he had achieved a certain age and status".[102] Then, if we look at the gifts to the monks of Peterborough and the nuns of Stamford in the latter part of the century, the knights are asking us to believe that they also have come up in the world. But are the knights perhaps going beyond their resources?

Professor Hilton suggests that they were: "this increase in social standing, as is so often the case, accompanied a severe social and economic crisis for the class as a whole".[103] Now some knightly families may well have been tempted to imitate the consumption standards of the aristocracy. They would hardly have been human if they had not. Even to maintain their standard of living, when the

---

[100] The classic discussion of the position of younger sons in this period is G. Duby, "Au XIIᵉ siècle: les 'Jeunes' dans la Société Aristocratique", *Annales E.S.C.*, xix (1964), pp. 835-46.

[101] R. W. Southern, "The Place of Henry I in English History", *Proc. Brit. Acad.*, xlviii (1962), pp. 137-9; *Red Book of the Exchequer*, ed. H. Hall (Rolls Ser., xcix, 1896), i, pp. 329-31. Painter noted that "a large proportion" of the "new enfeoffment" (1135-1166) consisted of grants to younger sons: *Feudalism and Liberty*, p. 209. It would be interesting to see if the families so doing exhibited any common features.

[102] C. R. Cheney, *Hubert Walter* (London, 1967), p. 29; H. M. Colvin, *The White Canons in England* (Oxford, 1951), pp. 35-6.

[103] Hilton, *A Medieval Society*, pp. 50-1.

tendency was towards the dispersion of the fee, would require some reorganization. Here the actual distribution of estates, the accidents of the Norman settlement, probably became very important. The scattered feudal units were reconstituted; those who were weak in the period of reconstruction may well have gone to the wall. Is there any more than this?

Certainly, from the end of the century onwards a number of knightly families appear in a position of weakness, and go into a steady decline. Donations reflecting family piety, at least in part, merge in the records with those which clearly reflect poverty. In any family archive it is difficult to draw the line between the two. But the large estates which Peterborough abbey acquired in the thirteenth century were clearly alienated because of economic necessity. The Southorpes, Tots and Northboroughs are reduced in substance to the point where they disappear from our records. The abbey in acquiring these estates regained some of the property it had lost to "the knights" just after the Conquest. Around fifty per cent of the abbey's Domesday property was enfeoffed; in the next two centuries — ten generations — it regained perhaps ten per cent of these alienations.[104] This land was in the area where the abbey was strongest, in the Soke and below Peterborough in the Nene valley.

The families which disappeared "were the ones whose incomes did not match their social pretensions".[105] But granted the world in which these families lived this judgement seems a bit harsh. It was a world, first of all, in which the rise and fall of landed families was a thing taken for granted.[106] The process was so frequent that it could hardly have been otherwise. In France, Professor Perroy has calculated, "the average duration of a noble line is hardly more than three or four generations; let us say, to be on the safe side . . . between three and six generations". And he calculates that in England the situation is roughly comparable: of the 210 baronies listed by Sanders[107] only 36 "remained more than two centuries in the hands of the same male line".[108] The knightly class is not likely to be any more stable. In this world social pretentiousness was only one, and that the least tangible, of many things which might put a family into difficulty. A prodigal father might leave his family in debt, but a careful man who left four daughters would effectively leave no family

[104] In 1346 the abbey held in demesne "de perquisito suo" just under five fees: Griffin Cartulary (Northamptonshire R.O., Box 1062), fo. 7r.
[105] Hilton, *A Medieval Society*, p. 51.
[106] There is a matter of factness in some contemporary references (see the items referred to in notes 55, 63 and 67 above), even of jocularity (note 20), which is in marked contrast to the tone of some modern historians.
[107] Sanders, *English Baronies*, passim.
[108] B. Perroy, "Social Mobility among the French *Noblesse* in the Later Middle Ages", *Past and Present*, no. 21 (Apr. 1962), p. 31.

at all. It is perhaps interesting to note that Professor Habakkuk, in his introduction to *The Wealth of Five Northamptonshire Families*, considers first individual competence, then family settlements, and only then "way of life".[109] Had we enough evidence this might prove to be the proper order in which to tackle thirteenth-century families also, for these families lived in a world in several respects similar, and they led no less complex lives.

If this is granted the question then becomes whether new families rose in the place of those which disappeared. Sometimes, it is true, the magnates stood in their stead. But how often? Any generalization from this will have to distinguish, in the first place, between areas where lordship was powerful and those where it was weak. Brockworth, a Cotswolds manor of Lanthony Priory, was built up from a couple of assarts in no less than 331 charters. The then lord of the manor, a descendant of the original donor, gave the last vestiges of the property to the priory in 1264.[110] How many knightly families were the objects of so close an interest, over so long a period of time? For clearly the strength of the religious lay in just this continuity.

A related question, on which also further work is needed, is whether the mobility of property was greater in some periods than in others. One of the difficulties here has already been noted: the major purchases come usually at the end of a long string of small alienations. More important, however, is not the chronology of the evidence but its bias. It is evidence for the landlords' operations: what the cartularies indicate is the availability of credit, and the attractiveness of land as an investment. The points made here must be largely hypothetical. But on this basis Peterborough abbey seems more active than Ramsey around 1200; it was less so in the mid-thirteenth century, when there was a lull in Peterborough's dealings, seemingly connected with a couple of weak abbacies, and then the civil disturbances of the 1260s. In neither case is there much activity after 1290.[111] The chronology of the acquisitions of lay magnates, on the surface at least, looks rather different. For the family of Clare the half century after *c.* 1275 was "the great age of economic activity and fluctuation", and the same is broadly true of the other families studied by Dr. Holmes. After 1330 purchases of land are much more rare, seemingly because "land was no longer a

---

[109] *Op. cit.*, pp. xi-xix.   [110] Hilton, *A Medieval Society*, pp. 39-40.
[111] These tentative points are based on a comparison of J. A. Raftis, *The Estates of Ramsey Abbey* (Toronto, 1957), ch. 4, and my own *Peterborough Abbey, 1086-1310. A Study in the Land Market* (Cambridge, 1973).

good object of deliberate investment".[112] The age of Edward II was not an age of particular avarice, therefore, but it may have been one in which the lay aristocracy was more active on the land market than for some time either before or after. But if afterwards they were less interested in buying land there were others to take their place. In the 1330s Archbishop Melton of York bought several manors, and set up his eldest nephew as head of a knightly line.[113] And, going downstream, the credit operations of William and Richard de la Pole of Hull brought them a huge landed estate, "the foundation of the great fortune of the house of Suffolk".[114] It seems likely that property was steadily available, and that what changed was the nature of the creditor class.

The acquisitions of large landowners remain one element — an important one, and much the best documented — in the thirteenth-century property market. But it is for the moment an open question whether this was the dominant one. Certainly it is doubtful whether this shows the decline of a "class". If there seems to be decay, is this not because the sources themselves are decayed? If the thirteenth-century feudal records preserve the assessment of 1166, clearly they cannot reflect economic enterprise. So younger sons like Thomas Hotot, or small knights like Geoffrey of Northborough, or the administrative class of stewards and the like, will not be found there. The limitations of the manorial surveys, to which Postan has drawn our attention, are precisely those of the *Book of Fees*. The life in the society is outside these records.

[112] G. A. Holmes, *The Estates of the Higher Nobility in Fourteenth-Century England* (Cambridge, 1957), ch. 4 (quotations from pp. 88, 114).
[113] L. H. Butler, "Archbishop Melton, his Neighbours, and his Kinsmen, 1317-1340", *Jl. Eccles. Hist.*, ii (1951), pp. 65-6.
[114] Eileen Power, *The Wool Trade in English Medieval History* (Oxford, 1941), p. 115.

6. Sir Geoffrey de Langley and the crisis of the knightly class in thirteenth-century England*

P. R. COSS

SOME YEARS AGO PROFESSOR HILTON AND PROFESSOR POSTAN suggested, independently of one another, that the thirteenth century in England was a time of great difficulty for the smaller landowner. This belief was prompted, in Professor Postan's case, by the acquisitions of Peterborough Abbey and, in Professor Hilton's, by those of west midland monastic houses, principally Worcester Cathedral Priory.[1] Their researches received support from earlier studies showing a decline in the number of knights during the course of the thirteenth century, and by Mr. H. G. Richardson's work which indicated the degree to which ecclesiastical landowners were involved in the redemption of land indebted to Jews.[2] For Professor Hilton this period of hardship is closely connected with the rise of chivalric knighthood from the mid-twelfth century. "This increase in social standing, as is so often the case, accompanied a severe social and economic crisis for the class as a whole".[3]

Since then, Dr. Edmund King has studied the Peterborough material more closely and, in a valuable article, has offered the subject for debate.[4] Rather surprisingly, given the numerical weight of his evidence — though perhaps less so given the smallness of his sample — he is reluctant to reach firm conclusions. "The acquisitions of large landowners remain one element — an important one, and much the best documented — in the thirteenth-century property market. But it is for the moment an open question whether this was the dominant one. Certainly it is doubtful whether this shows the

* I would like to thank Professor R. H. Hilton whose reading and commenting on a draft of this article is one of many kindnesses towards me since he agreed to supervise my research in 1967.

[1] M. M. Postan, *The Cambridge Economic History of Europe*, i, 2nd. edn. (Cambridge, 1966), pp. 590-5; R. H. Hilton, *A Medieval Society: The West Midlands at the End of the Thirteenth Century* (London, 1966), pp. 49-55.

[2] N. Denholm-Young, "Feudal Society in the Thirteenth Century: the Knights", *Collected Papers* (Cardiff, 1969), reprinted from *Collected Papers on Medieval Subjects* (Oxford, 1946); H. G. Richardson, *The English Jewry under Angevin Kings* (London, 1960), esp. ch. v.

[3] Hilton, *op. cit.*, pp. 50-1.

[4] E. King, "Large and Small Landowners in Thirteenth-Century England", *Past and Present*, no. 47, repr. above. For what follows, see above, pp. 159-65. This article was largely reprinted in his *Peterborough Abbey 1086-1310: A Study in the Land Market* (Cambridge, 1973), where it forms the basis of ch. ii.

decline of a 'class'". He would prefer to see no more than a degree of social mobility normal in feudal society. "It was a world . . . in which the rise and fall of landed families was a thing taken for granted". But if there was an extraordinary factor working at all in this period he sees it in the break-up in "the integrity of the knight's fee". The point that the bias of surviving evidence may distort the picture in favour of accretion by major landowners, also made by Dr. Titow,[5] has been partly countered, however, by a simple retort. "The fact that the records of large estates record a large number of purchases from smaller men and hardly any sales to them is sufficient to support the contention that land transactions were reducing the smaller man's share in England's land".[6]

The important questions now would seem to be: to what extent were persons other than religious corporations profiting on the land market? And, were the difficulties which beset the smaller landowners sufficient for us to speak of "a severe social and economic crisis for the class as a whole"? This article is intended as a contribution towards answering these two questions, and especially the latter. It is based upon evidence from a fifteenth-century cartulary which preserves details of the investment of Sir Geoffrey de Langley, a servant of Henry III.[7] It will be found useful, at the outset, to sketch his career: Born around 1200, the son of a modestly endowed Gloucestershire knight, Geoffrey became a characteristic product of the "familiar" administration fostered by the Angevins and sustained by Henry III.[8] First appearing as constable of St. Briavels and bailiff to Peter des Rivaux in 1233-4, he joined the royal *curia* where he rose to become knight-deputy to the earl marshal and marshal of the household. The Gascon campaign of 1242-3 proved a watershed in his career. On his return he was detached from the household, given custody of the honour of Arundel and then recruited to the forest eyre. His major posts were as chief justice of the forest, 1250-2, and steward to the Lord Edward, from 1254 to 1257.[9] His activities, therefore,

---

[5] J. Z. Titow, *English Rural Society, 1200-1350* (London, 1969), p. 47.

[6] M. M. Postan, *The Medieval Economy and Society* (London, 1972), appendix i, p. 247.

[7] "The Langley Cartulary": Brit. Lib., Harley MS. 7 (hereafter "Langley Cartulary"). References are to the numbered documents in my edition (Univ. of Birmingham Ph.D. thesis, 1971; Dugdale Soc., Main Ser., xxxii, 1980).

[8] J. E. A. Jolliffe, *Angevin Kingship* (London, 1955), esp. ch. xiii, "Familiar Administration".

[9] *Cal. Close Rolls, 1231-4*, pp. 331, 336; and *1254-6*, p. 14; *Cal. Patent Rolls, 1232-47*, pp. 95, 295, 408, 426, 442; and *1247-58*, p. 61; Matthew Paris, *Chronica Majora*, ed. H. R. Luard (Rolls Series, 1872-83), v, pp. 136-7; *Cal. Charter Rolls*, ii, p. 2.

spanned the period of Henry III's personal rule.   By 1258 he had
acquired estates whose value, based on the conservative estimates of
the inquisitions *post mortem* of himself and his son, was £200 a year.[10]
Less prominent during Henry's later years, he was dead by 22 September 1274.

Of Geoffrey's acquisitions, three in particular lend themselves to
detailed examination.   In each case the land was acquired through
the acquittance of debts to Jews.   The first part of this article will,
therefore, be devoted primarily to the history of these three estates,
concentrating on the following matters: the exact process by which
Geoffrey de Langley acquired them; the fortunes of the declining
families both before and after they parted with the land;
and the factors which led to the loss of their estates.   In the third case
the loss was closely related to the structure of the estate which will, in
consequence, be examined in some detail.   Some general features of
Geoffrey's investment will then be highlighted before returning to the
main question.   The second part of the article will review the
evidence for a crisis of the knightly class[11] and explore the links
between this and the political troubles of the reign of Henry III.

I

The first case illustrates the stages by which an estate might be
alienated through financial embarrassment.   Henry son of Henry
d'Aubigny of Great Wishford, Wiltshire, married Christine, daughter
of Nicholas fitz Nicholas of Coventry and Withybrook and heiress to
a complex of lands, mills and rents centred on Bisseley to the south of
Coventry and later known as the manor of Shortley.   However, all

---

[10] *Cal. Inquisitions Post Mortem*, ii, pp. 48, 353; Pub. Rec. Off., C138, File 4
(8), File 24 (18).   The Langley estates and their values are listed in my *The
Langley Family and its Cartulary: A Study in Late Medieval "Gentry"* (Dugdale
Society Occasional Papers, no. 22, Oxford, 1974), appendix A.   Geoffrey
inherited manors at Siddington near Cirencester and Pinley on the south side of
Coventry.   He was established at Pinley by 1222, but his Gloucestershire land
had been retained by relatives.   He finally recovered Siddington from Hasculf
de Harborough around 1230: "Langley Cartulary", no. 524; *Curia Regis Rolls*,
1227-30, pp. 660, 1,203, 1,384, 2,191, 2,198.   His father, Sir Walter de Langley,
seems to have acquired the Siddington estate with his wife, Emma de Lacy.
Between 1187 and 1213 he gave a church and three virgates of land at Siddington
to the knights of St. John of Jerusalem: calendar of the documents of the
"Nelthorpe Collection" in Gloucester Rec. Off., EL 37 V/7.
[11] The term "knightly" is used here to include all who held by military tenure
and were manorial landlords.   To limit the term to families who were producing
knights at any one time would tend to hinder examination of the fortunes of the
class over a long period.   Knighthood, by this time, denoted membership of
a prestigious social stratum, but not of a class.   Others may prefer to speak of
"the smaller landowners" or of "the gentry", but neither is wholly satisfactory.

was not well. On 5 March 1243 Henry and Christine sold Alderford Mill to Geoffrey de Langley for 30 marks which the latter promised to pay the London Jews, Deayus and Solmiahu, with the interest due by 1st August. The debt had been contracted by Henry d'Aubigny the elder "for the urgent business (*pro arduo negocio*)" of Henry and Christine. Twelve months later, the bulk of Christine's estate was leased to Geoffrey for a term of twelve years. The extent of their debts is now beginning to be revealed, for Geoffrey agreed to pay £120 to Slema, sister of Elias Bishop, and Diaie her son-in-law. Even this failed to solve the problem, partly perhaps because the exceptions they had made (the income from two of the mills) left insufficient margin on which to live, but mainly because there were other debts. On 20 January 1245 a final concord ratified the conclusive agreement between Geoffrey de Langley and Henry d'Aubigny junior. Geoffrey purchased the whole estate, comprising the chief messuage with two carucates of land and six acres of meadow, three mills, £5 annual rent in Coventry and neighbouring vills, and the dower of Christine's mother, there, and in Withybrook, Ryton, Stretton and Monks Kirby. So that Henry and Christine should not be left entirely without income, Geoffrey gave them part of his wife's inheritance, namely 70s. rent in Woodborough and Orcheston, Wiltshire, and 15s. rent in Bristol. In addition he delivered Henry d'Aubigny the elder from prison in Salisbury and paid his debt of 140 marks owed to Robert de Tottenhall for the marriage between Henry and Christine.[12] Although the agreement specifically cancelled the previous lease, the payment of £120 to the London Jews still stood.[13] He had spent a total of £233 6s. 8d. in cash and parted with 85s. annual rent but the gain was considerable: an estate whose centre was contiguous with his manor of Pinley, four profitable mills and an important foothold in urban realty in Coventry. The d'Aubignys had gained an heiress but lost her inheritance!

What, then, had brought the d'Aubignys to this pass? At first sight the answer seems obvious. Henry d'Aubigny wished to marry his son to an heiress; in order to purchase the marriage he had recourse to Jews; inability to repay led to his imprisonment for debt and the loss of Christine's inheritance. On closer inspection it is not quite so simple. Henry d'Aubigny was lord of Great Wishford in Wiltshire where he held one fee directly and half a fee indirectly of

[12] "Langley Cartulary", nos. 176-7, 216; *Warwickshire Feet of Fines*, i (Dugdale Soc., xi, 1932), no. 612.
[13] *Calendar of the Plea Rolls of the Exchequer of the Jews*, 3 vols. (Jewish Hist. Soc. of England, 1905-29), i-ii, ed. J. M. Rigg (hereafter *C.P.R.*, *Exchequer of the Jews*), i, p. 63.

Patrick de Chaworth in 1242-3.[14] He was not a rich man, and yet he was prepared to borrow large sums in order to marry his second son — for such Henry was — to an heiress as well endowed with land as himself. Why should he have risked so much to provide for his younger son when this could have been done more modestly? Another rather odd feature is that having repaid the Jews he should still owe a sizable sum to Robert de Tottenhall, since the debts had been incurred precisely to purchase the marriage from him.[15] Or had they? It is not inconceivable that the d'Aubignys were in financial trouble before the marriage. In which case they may have seized on an opportunity of acquiring additional property from which to pay off their debts; either out of the issues or, if necessary, by parting with part or even all of it. The very least that can be said is that Henry lacked both liquidity and the ability to meet his family commitments.

The d'Aubigny manor of Great Wishford is revealed in 1273 as a modest but well-balanced estate yielding a little under £27 per annum.[16] Such an income put Henry d'Aubigny above the minimum for distraint to knighthood, but while he seems to have evaded this obligation it still proved insufficient to meet his requirements. In one respect, however, the estate was yielding less in the reign of Henry III than it had in the recent past. In 1268 an inquiry was held into the liberties of the manor of Wishford, from which it appears that the first Henry d'Aubigny had been enfeoffed by Patrick de Chaworth in the reign of Henry I with full seigneurial rights. No suit was owed to hundred or county and the d'Aubignys enjoyed return of writs. This situation prevailed, we are told, until the death of William Longespee, earl of Salisbury, after which the sheriff (probably Simon de Hales, sheriff from March 1226 to January 1227[17]) entered the

---

[14] *Book of Fees*, pp. 716, 728.
[15] Robert de Tottenhall held two fees at Hanslope, Bucks., in 1242-3. He succeeded his brother Walter as sheriff of that county in October 1256: *ibid.*, pp. 873, 896; Pub. Rec. Off., Lists and Indexes, ix, p. i. How he came by the marriage is a mystery. Only the land in and around Withybrook was held in fee; the estate at Bisseley had been held of the earls of Chester in free burgage: *The Victoria History of the Counties of England* (hereafter *V.C.H.*), *Warwickshire*, vi, p. 265; "Langley Cartulary", no. 192; "Gregory Hood Collection", deposited with the Shakespeare Birthplace Trust, Stratford-upon-Avon (hereafter "Gregory Hood Coll."), no. 257.
[16] *Cal. Inq. Post Mortem*, ii, p. 24 (Pub. Rec. Off., C134, File 3 [4]); *Wiltshire Inquisitions Post Mortem, Henry II-Edward II* (Index Library, xxxvii, 1908), p. 85.
[17] The inquiry seems to be in error in calling him Robert de Hales. Simon was sheriff of Wiltshire from 23 March 1226 to 22 Jan. 1227: Pub. Rec. Off., Lists and Indexes, ix, p. 152.

manor and made two tithings where there had been only one, "both of the fee of Fancourt and the fee of d'Aubigny and doing suit only to the court of d'Aubigny"; he had distrained these to do suit at the hundred court of Branch and had taken fines including those for infringement of the assizes of bread and ale, for the hue and cry and for bloodshed. Since the intrusion the sheriff had been accustomed to take the above fines and, in addition, 6s. per annum from the tithing of Fancourt.[18]   In short, the d'Aubigny court seems to have taken a sizable fall in revenue. With a modest income, moreover, Henry had at least four children to provide for. Besides his sons, Walter and Henry, there were two daughters. In consequence he became indebted. An opportunity arose to marry his son into property and thereby prop up the family. Paradoxically, Henry did achieve a measure of success. Walter succeeded at Wishford, whilst Henry acquired rents in Bristol and in Wiltshire. Walter d'Aubigny later became a clerk to Queen Eleanor (of Provence). Towards the end of his life he was sufficiently wealthy to lend a modest sum himself on the security of land. He died in 1273 holding the manor of Great Wishford and a small manor at Rockborn, Hampshire, said to be worth £5 per annum.[19]   He was succeeded by his brother Henry who, in turn, died on or before 6 August 1278.[20]   Both died childless. Henry's heirs were his sister, Clarice, and Maurice de Bonham, his nephew by his sister Juliana. The lords of Wishford in 1316 were John de Bonham and Adam at Ford.[21]

The second case is, in outline at least, rather similar. The necessitous landowner, on this occasion, was Sir Robert de Willoughby of Willoughby in Kesteven, and the scene of his loss to Langley the manor of Ashover in Derbyshire. To understand the situation something must first be said of Robert's background. He was probably the son and certainly the heir of a Ralph de Willoughby who, in 1210-12, was said to hold a third of a fee at Willoughby of the honour of Gant, one fee of the archbishop of York at Sherburn and half a fee of the honour of Tickhill.[22]   This last was at Pleasley, Nottinghamshire, where Ralph and John de Aincourt had jointly acquired the land of Serlo de Pleasley before Michaelmas 1203.   It

---

[18] *Cal. Inquisitions Miscellaneous*, i, p. 356.
[19] See above, n. 16, and *C.P.R.*, *Exchequer of the Jews*, i, pp. 308-9.
[20] *Cal. Inq. Post Mortem*, ii, p. 271 (Pub. Rec. Off., C134, File 20 [1]).
[21] *Feudal Aids*, v, p. 202.
[22] *Red Book of the Exchequer*, ed. Hubert Hall (Rolls Series, 1896), pp. 491, 495, 593; *Book of Fees*, p. 179.

was augmented by the land of a Nottinghamshire heiress whose marriage Ralph purchased two years later.[23]   He was still living in 1222 when the sheriff of Derby was ordered to find another verderer as Ralph had shown that he held no land in the county.[24]   When and in what circumstances the family acquired its estate in Ashover is not revealed, but Sir John de Aincourt held one fee there in 1235-6 and the Willoughby manor would seem to have been held either of or in succession to him.[25]   In Lincolnshire the situation is made more complicated by the existence of a second, and possibly distantly related, Robert de Willoughby.   This Robert held one fee at Willoughby in the Marsh, in Lindsey, also of the honour of Gant, and most of the Lincolnshire property said to be held by a Robert de Willoughby in 1242-3 would seem to have been his.[26]   Robert, of Kesteven, held half a fee at Willoughby of Simon de Kyme, and he of Gilbert de Gant.[27]

By 1250, however, Sir Robert de Willoughby of Kesteven was in serious financial difficulties.   In attempting to free himself he was forced to a rather desperate measure.   This was to lease his manor of Ashover for a term of twenty-three years running from 11 November 1250.   If the annual value fell short of £22 the deficit (later found to be £4) was to be supplied from his land at Pleasley.   Robert bound himself to neither sell, pledge nor diminish his holding, except for land to the value of 100s. to his daughter, Amabel.   The lessee, a clerk named Walter de Bradley, acquitted him of a debt of £446 13s. 4d. towards the Jews.[28]   By the end of the term Walter would have recovered £506.   To make the lease more attractive, Robert included the marriage of his son and heir.   Bradley's tenure was, however, a short one for within a year he had passed the property on to Sir Geoffrey de Langley.   As the tenure of a lessee was liable to

[23] *Pipe Rolls*, 5 John, p. 17; and 7 John, p. 217 (page references here and subsequently are to the publications of the Pipe Roll Soc., new ser.).   His wife's land was at Holle, Moorhaigh and Radmanthwaite, Notts.: *Rotuli Litterarum Clausarum* (Record Commission, 1833) (hereafter *Rot. Litt. Claus.*), i, pp. 342, 403.
[24] *Ibid.*, p. 496b.
[25] *Book of Fees*, pp. 530-1.   The lord of Ashover in 1242-3 was Sir Ralph de Rerisby who later appears as Robert's overlord and who held, in the same year, one fee at Pleasley and elsewhere of the countess of Eu: *ibid.*, pp. 988, 998.
[26] *Ibid.*, pp. 1,011, 1,031, 1,039, 1,056, 1,058, 1,069-70.   This Robert was the son of William de Willoughby who held one fee in Willoughby in the Marsh and a quarter of a fee at West Ashby of the honour of Gant.   He had been succeeded by his own son, William, by October 1259: *ibid.*, pp. 161, 165; *Curia Regis Rolls, 1227-30*, p. 164; *Lincolnshire Final Concords*, ii (Lincs. Rec. Soc., xvii, 1920), p. 287.
[27] *Book of Fees*, pp. 1,031, 1,068.
[28] "Langley Cartulary", nos. 328-9, 442.

be precarious, especially vis-à-vis the rights of a feudal overlord, Geoffrey acquired confirmation from three interested parties. Sir Ralph de Rerisby relinquished any right to escheat or wardship and confirmed both the lease and the marriage of Robert's heir. The latter was also confirmed by the archbishop of York "as far as it pertained to him". Queen Eleanor acknowledged Walter de Bradley's gift and promised to defend Geoffrey, as far as she was able, should the chief lords attempt to disquiet or to deny him. She was herself lord of Tickhill since she held the lands of the countess of Eu, destined, as these were, to form part of the appanage of the Lord Edward.[29] There was no confirmation, however, from the lords of Willoughby to whom wardship of the heir, should it accrue within the term, would almost certainly have belonged as the lords of the oldest enfeoffment.[30]

Queen Eleanor was more closely involved in these transactions than would at first sight appear, for Walter de Bradley was, from May 1249 to December 1254, keeper of the Queen's Wardrobe. It seems unlikely that Walter was at any time acting on his own behalf. In November 1256 the Queen acknowledged receipt of £213 6s. 8d. which Geoffrey de Langley owed for the marriage of Robert de Willoughby and for twenty years' lease of the manor of Ashover.[31] As neither Geoffrey nor Ashover appear *per se* on Walter de Bradley's accounts it is not possible to discover the terms on which he acquired the lease.[32] By 1251 Geoffrey was chief justice of the forest and quite high in royal esteem. In the next few years he was to render the queen valuable service as "guardian" and as an escort to her daughter, Margaret of Scotland, as a member of the regents' council in 1253-4, and as steward to the Lord Edward.[33] It is not unlikely that he

[29] *Ibid.*, nos. 336, 367, 474; I. J. Sanders, *English Baronies: A Study in their Origins and Descent 1086-1327* (Oxford, 1963), p. 147.

[30] Robert's half-fee at Willoughby was said to be of old enfeoffment, i.e. before the death of Henry I: *Book of Fees*, p. 1,068. The rule that wardship of the heir and marriage should go to the lord of the oldest enfeoffment was established by the Statute of Westminster II, 1285, but seems to have had some validity earlier: T. F. T. Plucknett, *The Legislation of Edward I* (Oxford, 1949), pp. 113-14. For the lord's right to expel lessees, see J. M. W. Bean, *The Decline of English Feudalism* (Manchester, 1968), p. 9, and references given there.

[31] "Langley Cartulary", no. 522.

[32] The issues from the lands of the countess of Eu figure as plain sums in Walter de Bradley's accounts for 1253 and 1254, and dealings relating to Ashover may be subsumed there: Pub. Rec. Off., Pipe Rolls 33, 35, 36, 37 and 39 Henry III. Eleanor's household is discussed by Hilda Johnstone in T. F. Tout, *Chapters in the Administrative History of England* (Manchester, 1920), v, pp. 232-6, 267-70.

[33] *Cal. Patent Rolls, 1247-58*, p. 162; *Cal. Close Rolls, 1251-3*, pp. 43, 201, 371, 484; and *1253-4*, pp. 71, 86; *Chronica Majora*, v, p. 340; *Royal and other Historical Letters illustrative of the Reign of Henry III*, ed. W. W. Shirley (Rolls Series, 1862-6), ii, p. 99.

acquired Ashover on advantageous terms.   Whether this was the case
or not, Queen Eleanor of Provence was not quite as innocent of the
traffic in Jewish debts as her later actions might lead one to suppose![34]
Robert's burden seems to have stemmed from the debts of Ralph de
Willoughby.   As early as 1203 he and John de Aincourt owed the
crown 25 marks and a palfrey for their land at Pleasley, although this
was quickly paid.   He owed a further £27 for his heiress in 1205.
The turning point came, however, in 1207 when he owed 100 marks
and two palfreys for the hastening of judgement in an appeal against
him.   The bulk of this was still outstanding in 1212.[35]   Imprudence
during the civil war may have added to his difficulties for in September
1216 the sheriff of Lincoln was ordered to return those lands he had
held before the war.[36]   By this time Ralph was involved with the
Jews.   In 1220 he claimed that Aaron son of Josce was demanding
a debt he did not owe, perhaps justly for in the event Aaron
defaulted.[37]   Whether Robert's troubles were due to an accumulation
of earlier debts or whether he had borrowed extensively on his own
account, by 1250 his finances were in so parlous a state as to threaten
his family's very continuance.   The measure he took was a desperate
one, and was unlikely to succeed.   As in the case of the d'Aubignys,
a beneficial lease proved merely the preliminary to outright alienation.
Ashover passed to Sir Geoffrey de Langley for a further payment of
£40, probably before 9 August 1256 on which date he acquired a
charter of market, fair and warren.[38]   Even this did not put Robert's
house in order, for he was still (or again?) in debt, to Josce of York, as
late as 1270.   It is perhaps hardly surprising that when civil war
came again Robert de Willoughby should figure among the dissidents
in Lincolnshire associated with John de Eyvill.   He was finally
captured at the siege of Kenilworth.[39]   After 1270 he disappears from
view.   His land at Pleasley passed to the Willoughbys of Lindsey.
When Sir Robert de Willoughby, the grandson of Robert of
Kesteven's contemporary, died in 1317 he was said to have held a

[34] She had four Jewries suppressed in 1275 and is said to have urged the
expulsion of the Jews in 1290: Richardson, *The English Jewry*, pp. 227, 231;
Cecil Roth, *History of the Jews in England* (Oxford, 1941), p. 84.
[35] *Pipe Rolls*, 5 John, p. 17; 6 John, pp. 167-8; 7 John, p. 217; 9 John, p. 11;
14 John, p. 106.   In 1209 he fined 10 marks for having seisin of the lands he held
of the archbishop of York: *Pipe Roll*, 11 John, p. 117.
[36] *Rot. Litt. Claus.*, i, p. 322.
[37] *C.P.R., Exchequer of the Jews*, i, pp. 24, 39.
[38] "Langley Cartulary", nos. 325, 362.   For a third case, see King, "Large
and Small Landowners", above, p. 148.   The beneficial lease is discussed by
Richardson, *op. cit.*, pp. 84-5.
[39] *Cal. Patent Rolls, 1266-72*, pp. 143, 148, 490; *Cal. Close Rolls, 1264-8*,
pp. 148-9; and see below, n. 139.

moiety of Pleasley of the honour of Tickhill.⁴⁰   He had brought the
Lindsey family to new heights through his service as Lincolnshire
bailiff of the bishop of Durham.   His gains included the manors of
Lilford, Northamptonshire, and Eresby, Lincolnshire, whilst his
property at Willoughby in the Marsh with extensive appurtenances
was alone said to be worth over £114 per annum.⁴¹   The Willoughbys
of Kesteven could hardly provide a stronger contrast.   In 1303 one
Roger Morteyn was holding half a fee at Willoughby "which Robert
de Willoughby once held".⁴²

For the third case we return to the south side of Coventry where
Geoffrey de Langley purchased the Stivichall estate of Sir William de
Lucy by discharging his debt of 94 marks to the Jews Aaron son of
Abraham and Litoricia.   Around April 1240 he acquired Stivichall
Mill from the same grantor, one moiety in fee and the other for a term
of fourteen years, and the larger transaction was made either then or
soon after.⁴³   Sir William de Lucy was lord of Charlecote, Warwickshire.   Steward to Walter de Lacy of Weobley and constable of
Ludlow Castle, he became sheriff of Warwickshire in 1236-7.⁴⁴
According to Dugdale he had taken on Lacy's Jewish debts in return
for a lump sum, and agreed to discharge them at the rate of £80 per
annum.⁴⁵   It may be that William had overreached himself and was
out of funds by 1240, but this seems unlikely since in 1242-3 he took
on further debts of Lacy, and of his co-heir Margery, and her husband
John de Verdon.⁴⁶   William had, in fact, only recently acquired his
Stivichall estate from Master Simon de Walton, who had himself
received it from a lady, Margery de Nerbone.⁴⁷   Simon is in evidence
later as a purchaser of encumbered estates,⁴⁸ and the 94 marks

⁴⁰ *Cal. Inq. Post Mortem,* vi, p. 60.   The lords of Pleasley in 1316 were said
to be Robert de Willoughby and John de Harcourt: *Feudal Aids,* iii, p. 256.
⁴¹ *Cal. Inq. Post Mortem,* vi, p. 60 (Pub. Rec. Off., C134, File 57 [2]).
⁴² *Feudal Aids,* iii, p. 128.
⁴³ "Langley Cartulary", nos. 318-19.
⁴⁴ *Book of Fees,* pp. 508, 512, 956; *V.C.H., Warws.,* v, p. 35; Geoffrey
Templeman, *The Sheriffs of Warwickshire in the Thirteenth Century* (Dugdale
Soc. Occas. Papers, no. 7, Oxford, 1948), p. 45.
⁴⁵ Sir William Dugdale, *The Antiquities of Warwickshire,* ed. William Thomas
(London, 1730), pp. 502-3.
⁴⁶ *Ibid.*   Walter de Lacy, who succeeded his brother Gilbert in 1230, paid
3,100 marks to gain possession of his lands.
⁴⁷ "Gregory Hood Coll.", no. 586.
⁴⁸ Simon purchased the Warwickshire manor of Walton Deyville from the
heavily indebted Roger d'Eyville: *V.C.H., Warws.,* v, p. 195; *Cal. Ancient
Deeds,* iii, D 25, D 28; *Cal. Patent Rolls, 1258-66,* pp. 510, 614.   A clerk to
King John, he was presented to three livings in 1206-8; he became a chief
justice in 1251 and bishop of Norwich in March 1258: *Dict. Nat. Biog.,* xx,
p. 992.

which Geoffrey de Langley paid Lucy may represent part, or indeed the whole, of the debts of the lady of Stivichall. Within a short space of time the property had passed from an impecunious landowner to a royal clerk, from him to a member of a rising shrieval family, and thence to Sir Geoffrey de Langley.

The lord of Stivichall towards the end of the twelfth century, and probably earlier, was Stephen de Nerbone. He held in fee of the bishop of Chester.[49] Stephen himself may have lacked cash for he gave two virgates of his land at Stivichall to William de Fillongley for fighting a duel for him.[50] His heirs seem to have lost any effective lordship over the vill. His daughter, Margery, married Robert the Marshal of Stivichall but was widowed and left with several children by him. In widowhood her financial difficulties became acute and she proceeded to divest herself of her property. Her alienations were at first small: a croft to Geoffrey de Langley of Pinley for £1, half a mark rent from Park Mill to Nicholas fitz Nicholas for four and a half marks, and 4s. annual rent due from one of her tenants.[51] But she was soon obliged to adopt a more drastic measure, and a moiety of her land, in demesne, in villeinage and in free service, and of her mills, meadows and pastures passed to Simon de Walton. The only exceptions made were the chief messuage with its copse and garden and a parcel of land before the door. This was the estate which William de Lucy acquired and which passed swiftly into Langley hands. The fact that Lucy held only half the mill in fee and that Margery later quitclaimed her moiety of the fishpond suggest that the partition was carried out according to the letter.[52] Once again, the step taken was too drastic and too late. In 1249 Margery leased what remained of her demesne to the priory of St. Sepulchre, Warwick, for a term of thirty years and in return for a third of the annual produce. Her son, Ranulf, was hardly better off. In March 1242 he leased his hall with three furlongs in the territory of Stivichall to William of Pinley for a term of nine years. This was no ordinary lease but a share-cropping agreement. Each was to find half the corn for sowing, provide half the required labour and to take half the produce.[53] The rents from the remaining Nerbone tenant land were held, at least by 1279, by Ranulf's brother (perhaps paternal half-brother) Henry de Stivichall, although Henry had farmed them out

[49] "Gregory Hood Coll.", no. 576.
[50] "Langley Cartulary", no. 387.
[51] *Ibid.*, no. 191; "Gregory Hood Coll.", nos. 587-8.
[52] *Ibid.*, no. 593.
[53] *Ibid.*, nos. 579, 583.

to one of the tenants (see Appendix).   Margery, moreover, had not
found her association with Geoffrey de Langley a rewarding one; for
at Easter 1272 she brought a suit of novel disseisin against him
claiming a house and garden, two cottages, one and three-quarter
virgates, Heath Mill and a field called Oldland.   The arable probably
represents that leased to St. Sepulchre, with which house Geoffrey
may have had other financial dealings.[54]   The issue was settled out of
court; Margery withdrawing her plea, for 50 marks, and reserving
only the house and garden to her daughter Margery.   In her quitclaim
she calls herself Margery de Nerbone "formerly lady of Stivichall".
At court she was in mercy for failing to prosecute, but was pardoned
on grounds of poverty (*quia pauper est*).[55]   According to a survey made
for the bishop of Chester in 1299 the Langleys were then said to hold
half the vill of Stivichall directly of him.   The rents of Henry de
Stivichall had escheated and the family was represented by Ranulf's
son, Jolynus, who, bereft of lordship, held only the erstwhile manor-
house, the *Overhallstede*, and appurtenant land.[56]

What, then, had destroyed the Nerbone lordship over Stivichall?
The question can best be approached by looking at the structure of
the Nerbone estate, and for this the Hundred Rolls survey of 1279
provides both the basis and the starting-point (see below, Appendix).[57]
Admittedly, this survey was made forty years after Margery had
parted with half of her property, but an indication of the size and
structure of her manor can still be gained by adding the "Nerbone"
and Langley estates.   It had evidently been a small manor: the
demesne is revealed as a little less than a carucate, with tenant land of
twice that figure.   As there is nothing in the evidence to suggest
a recent disintegration of demesne, the Nerbones must have been
dependent on their income from tenant land.   The indications are
that this was not great.   The eight remaining Nerbone tenants pay
a total of 27s. rent for parcels adding up to three and a quarter virgates,
that is at a rate of 9s. per virgate.   Moreover, if Richard de
Montbray's holding is excepted, we are left with seven tenants paying
17s. for two and three-quarter virgates or at a rate of 6s. per virgate.
The contrast with the Langley estate is striking: nine tenants hold

[54] See below, n. 75.
[55] "Langley Cartulary", no. 419; Pub. Rec. Off., JI/1, no. 955, m. 12d.
[56] "The Gregory Leger Book" (deposited with the Shakespeare Birthplace
Trust, Stratford-upon-Avon), pp. 80-2.
[57] A transcript of the 1279 Hundred Rolls for Stoneleigh Hundred is to be
found in Stoneleigh MSS., the Shakespeare Birthplace Trust; and another in
Pub. Rec. Off., E 164/15.   Neither is printed in the *Rotuli Hundredorum*, ed.
W. Illingworth, 2 vols. (Record Commission, 1812-18).

three virgates in villeinage for a rent of 60s. 4d. — a rate of £1 per virgate — and four freeholders one and a half virgates, three acres, for 18s. 7d., or 11-12s. per virgate. The last figure is depressed by Ranulf son of Hugh who holds a virgate for 6d. per annum. The situation had clearly been revolutionized by the vigour of Langley lordship, a theme to which we shall return shortly. Of those eight Nerbone tenants, Richard de Montbray was a tenant at will, one owed an autumn boon work and another suit of court; the others paid a money rent only "for all service". In short, the Nerbone manor had comprised a small demesne and a group of *censarii* paying a low customary rent. The demesne was no larger in the time of Stephen de Nerbone. The two virgates which he gave William de Fillongley had been of tenant land.[58] There had almost certainly never been a sizable demesne cultivated by customary labour.

The Nerbone estate was in a number of respects untypical of the small manor, or at least of the small manor as revealed in the Hundred Rolls of 1279.[59] Not only was the demesne somewhat small — approximately 33 per cent of the arable — and the manor virtually coincident with the vill, but a large number of the tenants were half-yardlanders. Of the eight Nerbone tenants in 1279, four held a half and one a full virgate, whilst the farmer of their rents, William de Liston, seems himself to have held three quarters of a virgate. On the Langley holding two tenants held a half and one held three eighths of a virgate, with a freeholder holding a full virgate; the complexion here had been altered, however, by Geoffrey's purchases from tenants, for the virgate he acquired from John de Warwick and the two virgates from Martin Colebrand would seem to have been split into smaller tenancies.[60] At least 50 per cent of Nerbone tenants, perhaps as many as 75 per cent, had held a half-yardland or more.[61] This together with low customary rents and the absence of another manor in the vill will have tended to make communal organization strong and the Nerbone lordship comparatively weak. And this is true despite the fact that some held in villeinage and that the

[58] "Langley Cartulary", no. 387. These two virgates passed to William's daughter Margery and are probably those which Geoffrey purchased from William and Margery de Bishopbyre in 1251. They may account for the freeholdings held of the Langleys in 1279, including Ranulf son of Hugh's virgate for 6d. per annum: *ibid.*, nos. 297, 512.

[59] See E. A. Kosminsky, *Studies in the Agrarian History of England in the Thirteenth Century*, ed. R. H. Hilton (Oxford, 1956), esp. pp. 273-7.

[60] "Langley Cartulary", nos. 401, 516.

[61] Some of them, moreover, had sub-tenancies. When Ranulf le Prestis, for example, gave his rents to Sir John de Langley they came from Richard de Esseby for half a virgate of meadow, and from three other tenants for small parcels of arable. He may be identical with the Ranulf son of Hugh of 1279: "Langley Cartulary", no. 465.

Nerbones possessed at least two bondmen (*nativi*).[62]   To make matters worse the existence of the bishop's biannual leet will have tended to restrict the profit of any Nerbone court.   Unable to gain much from marketing produce and gathering what became uneconomical money rents, the Nerbones lived on a small and barely expandable income. Only in a period of stable prices could such a lordship have been profitable.

The explanation of the decline of the Nerbones is partly an economic and partly a social one; for what they lacked was the power to increase customary rents and hence to pass rising prices on to their tenants.   What was at issue was the quality of lordship.   The manorial situation was rarely, if ever, a static one, for it rested on the coercive power of the lord.   Kosminsky warned us that of the manors revealed in 1279, some were declining whilst others were in process of being formed.[63]   Perhaps Margery de Nerbone intended that the influx of power and capital from outside should bring pressure to bear on her peasants.   And this is precisely what the Langley lordship did do, although it was too late in the day to strengthen her position.   In 1279 most of the Langley tenants were paying three times the rent paid by the Nerbone tenants.   This had been achieved in part, at least, by repurchasing existing tenancies, in some cases splitting them, and granting them out on more lucrative terms.[64]   The manor court had probably been revitalized by the imposition of suit as a condition of tenure.   Nine of the fourteen Langley tenants held in villeinage, and could now be removed from their tenure at the will of the lord.[65]   Moreover, the phrase "for all service" does not follow the specification of their money rents as it does with the Nerbone tenants. As a result of their tenure at will, these nine were open to the arbitrary raising of their money rents and were vulnerable in the face of any demands which Geoffrey de Langley and his successors might choose to lay on them.[66]

[62] One of these Margery granted to the priory of St. Sepulchre, Warwick, and the other to the hospital of St. John, Coventry: "Gregory Hood Coll.", nos. 584-5.   [63] Kosminsky, *op. cit.*, p. 145.

[64] "Langley Cartulary", nos. 401, 506. A quarter of a virgate had been acquired from William de Morton for 2s. per annum, whilst David de Whitley had quitclaimed half a virgate "to his lord" for a cash payment of 8s.: *ibid.*, no. 439; "Gregory Hood Coll.", no. 581.

[65] "Et omni predicti possunt amoveri de tenura sua ad voluntatem domini".

[66] North Warwickshire, as a whole, bore the characteristic features of late colonization: enclosures, a high proportion of money rents, and a preponderance of freeholders. R. H. Hilton, *The Social Structure of Rural Warwickshire in the Middle Ages* (Dugdale Soc. Occas. Papers, no. 9, Oxford, 1950). By the thirteenth century seigneurial pressure was probably intensifying in this area. It is significant that almost all those described as serfs (*servi*) in the Coventry area in 1279 occur either on the estates of the priory of Coventry, or on the Langley manors of Wyken and Pinley where they form a majority of the tenants.

Some years ago Professor Hilton argued that villeinage in the classical sense was largely the product of the late twelfth and early thirteenth centuries as landlords responded to the rigours of inflation. "What could be more natural than that in a feudal agrarian society rising costs should be passed on to the basic producer, what more natural in the conditions of the time than that this must involve a worsening of his legal and social status?"[67]   Some eighty cases are reported on the Curia Regis Rolls during the first four decades of the thirteenth century as customary tenants sought to resist seigneurial pressure.   Professor Hilton believes it likely that many more cases did not reach the public courts.   Into this category falls Stivichall where, by 1279, the Langleys had gone a long way towards reducing their estate to "feudal order".[68]   They had done this by altering the size and yield of some of the tenancies and by imposing new conditions of tenure; by a combination, that is, of capital and coercion.   The contrast is not only between economic power and insolvency, but between vigorous and decadent lordship.   In 1280 the Langley manor including the mill was said to be worth £8 5s. 3d.[69]   It is a conservative figure for it is based on the inquisition *post mortem* of Sir Walter de Langley; but it is a good deal more than Stephen de Nerbone could have garnered.

At this point it will be profitable to look briefly at some of the characteristics of Geoffrey's investment.   First, his major acquisitions were virtually all made in what we might call middle age, that is forty plus, and for the most part in the dozen years following his return from Gascony and release from the royal household.   We have no reason to suppose that Geoffrey was untypical of Henry III's ministers — there is after all nothing very outstanding in his career — and it is probable that a study of his colleagues would reveal the same investment pattern.   One clear parallel is that of the royal clerk Walter de Merton.   Born between 1200 and 1205, Walter is in evidence in the Chancery in 1236-8.   He was released in 1241-2 to join

[67] R. H. Hilton, "Freedom and Villeinage in England", *Past and Present*, no. 31 (July 1965), p. 14.
[68] A similar case occurred at Meers Ashby, Northants., where a new lord, soon after he acquired his estate, attempted to reverse the freedom of his tenants and impose, *inter alia*, arbitrary tallage upon them.   He was strongly resisted and the case finally resulted in an inquisition at Northampton in 1261. R. H. Hilton, "Peasant Movements in England before 1381", in E. M. Carus-Wilson (ed.), *Essays in Economic History* (London, 1962), ii, p. 81; repr. from *Econ. Hist. Rev.*, 2nd ser., ii (1949-50).
[69] *Cal. Inq. Post Mortem*, ii, p. 353 (Pub. Rec. Off., C133, File 24 [18]).

the service of Bishop Farnham of Durham. His series of acquisitions, again chiefly through buying up encumbered estates, began in 1240. He was later to become chancellor of England and founder of the college which bears his name.[70]

Geoffrey's earliest gains were made through marriage. With Matilda de Brightwell, his second wife, he acquired a small manor at Turkdean, Gloucestershire, and scattered parcels of land and rents, some of which were to prove useful when he reached his final agreement with Henry d'Aubigny the younger.[71] Some estates came as rewards for service, including the Warwickshire manor of Stareton from his patron, Walter Marshal, earl of Pembroke.[72] One, Harborough Magna, was, in part at least, the result of a family settlement.[73] But for the most part they were the product of direct investment.

How was this financed? Partly, of course, by his wages and expenses in royal service. Between 1243 and 1254 payments amounting to £737 8s. were made to him, ranging from his 2s. a day as keeper of the honour of Arundel to his 200 marks a year as chief justice of the forest.[74] In the case of Ashover he was given credit. £213 6s. 8d. was paid to the queen in November 1256, five years after Geoffrey had acquired the lease. On another occasion he may never have paid the Jewish creditor. On behalf of William de Burley he agreed to redeem a £5 annual rent-charge in return for 20s. per annum from his estate at Bearley, Warwickshire. William seems to have been parting with his land in parcels over a period of years. In 1272, three Jews sued William's widow, Geoffrey de Langley, Thomas de Charlecote and the abbot of Bordesley for their quota of his debts. When the case continued in the following year, Geoffrey's place was taken by Margery de Cantilupe. She was found to owe £60.[75]

---

[70] Walter's career is traced by J. R. L. Highfield in his introduction to *The Early Rolls of Merton College, Oxford* (Oxford Hist. Soc., new ser., xviii, 1964). The parallel with Geoffrey de Langley was suggested to me by Professor R. H. C. Davis.

[71] "Langley Cartulary", nos. 38-9; and see above, n. 12.

[72] "Langley Cartulary", no. 395. Geoffrey de Langley was the Marshal's deputy in the household: *Chronica Majora*, v, pp. 36-7. He held land from the Marshal family at Long Compton, Warws., as early as 1234: *Cal. Charter Rolls*, i, pp. 188-9.

[73] Geoffrey had recovered Siddington from his relative Hasculf de Harborough around 1230: see above, n. 10. Before 1252 he acquired the manor of Harborough Magna from him and had given Hasculf a life-tenancy of Little Dorsington, Gloucs.: "Langley Cartulary", nos. 416, 514.

[74] *Cal. Liberate Rolls, 1240-5, 1245-51, 1251-60, passim; Cal. Patent Rolls, 1247-58*, p. 162.

[75] "Langley Cartulary", no. 374; *C.P.R., Exchequer of the Jews*, i, pp. 188, 281, 298-9, ii, pp. 6, 285. The prior of St. Sepulchre, Warwick, was also sued, but his case continued separately.

This is, however, a minor case as far as Geoffrey is concerned. The payments made on behalf of the d'Aubignys were paid, and paid promptly.[76] They amounted to £233 6s. 8d. When the 94 marks for the Stivichall estate is added he will be seen to have spent £296 between 1240 and 1245. During the same period moreover, he acquired an heiress for his son Walter, with manors at Wyken and Wolfhamcote, Warwickshire, and Bignell, Oxfordshire.[77] All this was expended before Geoffrey was drawing an appreciable sum in wages! His patrimony would have been insufficient, alone, to finance it. Pinley and Siddington were together valued at less than £27 per annum in 1280.[78] Even when his land at Long Compton and, after 1236, the Brightwell lands are added, his income from that source can hardly have been £50 per annum. Whilst he was maintained partly or wholly in the royal household, however, much of this could have been saved. His early life is obscure and it is impossible to know what opportunities he may have had for gain or, indeed, for peculation. He was not, perhaps, one for conspicuous waste. According to Matthew Paris he had a reputation for parsimony, for as marshal of the household "he lessened as far as possible the bounty and accustomed generosity of the royal table".[79] Geoffrey would seem to have stored his cash for a time and to have invested in earnest only after he left the royal household.

A close look at the geographical location of Langley estates reveals two interesting features. First, it becomes clear that Geoffrey's investment was concentrated in areas where wealthy religious houses did not dominate the land market.[80] This is particularly true of Warwickshire, which had an unusual preponderance of landowners of modest status.[81] Its largest monastery, the Benedictine priory of Coventry, was only beginning to emerge from a time of severe economic strain in 1250 and lacked the capital for large-scale investment for at least another generation.[82] Secondly, he had succeeded in building concentrations of estates in three areas: south

---

[76] C.P.R., Exchequer of the Jews, i, p. 63; "Langley Cartulary", no. 176.
[77] Cal. Close Rolls, 1242–7, pp. 116, 250–1; Cal. Charter Rolls, i, p. 461.
[78] £9 8s. 10d. and £17 7s. 10½d. respectively: Pub. Rec. Off., C133, File 24 (18).
[79] Chronica Majora, v, pp. 136–7.
[80] See below, n. 98.
[81] Hilton, The Social Structure of Rural Warwickshire, pp. 6–10.
[82] V.C.H., Warws., ii, p. 55. For the recovery of the priory economy, see my remarks in "Coventry before Incorporation: A Reinterpretation", Midland History, ii, no. 3 (Spring 1974), pp. 140–1, and references given there. Many other houses had gone through a similar period of difficulty: D. Knowles, The Monastic Order in England (Cambridge, 1949), pp. 302–3.

of Coventry; around Cirencester; and in south-west Warwickshire. These "concentrations" will have contributed both to ease of consumption and to efficient marketing; and must have helped generally to ease supervision and reduce administrative costs, making net profits the greater. Entire manors can have come onto the market only sporadically and Geoffrey was fortunate in being able to purchase Shortley and Stivichall, both contiguous with his manor of Pinley. These, together with intensive investment in urban realty and in water-mills on the south side of Coventry, gave him a complex of estates and rents valued in inquisitions *post mortem* at over £36 per annum, and probably worth much more.[83]

The core of the Langley concentration in the south-west of the county was the land given by Henry III for Geoffrey's maintenance in royal service. He acquired the reversion of the manors of Milcote and Dorsington in April 1245 and their outright grant a year later. In the meantime he had received Stamfordham, in Northumberland "of the lands of the Normans", initially until the reversion took effect, and later "until England and Normandy be united". This was retained only until the spring of 1248 when it was exchanged for Atherstone-upon-Stour, a manor in close proximity to Milcote and vacant by the death of the royal steward, Geoffrey de Crowcombe.[84] Milcote-Dorsington, operated as a single manor, was said to be worth £20 per annum in 1280, and Atherstone half that amount. The complex was completed with the acquisition of Weston Mauduit from the earl of Warwick some time before 1268.[85] The three estates together were valued at upwards of £45.

To complete the picture, Geoffrey acquired a manor adjacent to his ancestral home at Siddington. This was Chesterton, and was acquired from the baronial family of Monmouth at a date before July 1252. The property was conveyed in odd circumstances; it had been held in fee by Ralph Wysham, who quitclaimed so that Geoffrey de Langley might be enfeoffed. Moreover, Ralph's grandmother

---

[83] Pub. Rec. Off., C138, File 4 (8), File 24 (18). The actual figure is £36 13s. 1d., although four of the seven mills seem to have been omitted. Geoffrey's investment in Coventry realty figures prominently in the Langley Cartulary.

[84] *Cal. Close Rolls, 1242-7*, p. 411; *Cal. Charter Rolls*, i, pp. 296, 330, 394.

[85] Rather oddly, there is no charter of enfeoffment in the Langley Cartulary, and no final concord records the grant. The fine which the *V.C.H.* notices refers not to the manor but to three acres only, which William Mauduit parted with in 1248 as they lay near Milcote: *V.C.H., Warws.*, v, p. 199; Pub. Rec. Off., CP 25(1), 74/350. The inquisition in 1268 on the death of William's son, earl of Warwick since 1263, records his alienation of land worth £15 per annum in Weston: *Cal. Inq. Post Mortem*, i, p. 679.

held the manor in dower, so that Geoffrey could not have immediate possession.[86]   It is difficult to discover the terms on which the manor was granted.   Geoffrey had clearly had some association with the Monmouths in previous years, for in 1236 Sir John de Monmouth junior and Walter, his brother, had been the principal witnesses to a property transaction between Geoffrey and his brother-in-law; Chesterton may perhaps have been given for services which Geoffrey had rendered them.[87]   What is interesting, however, is that the family had debts to Jews.   In 1244 John de Monmouth acknowledged debts of 5 marks, £9 and £24, all of which had been due in 1232-3.   In 1253 Aaron, son of Abraham, acquitted a John de Monmouth of all debts owed by him, his ancestors and heirs.[88]   It is hard to see how the family could have been in serious difficulties; the sums mentioned are small, and the Monmouths had estates enough to pay off such debts and to enfeoff Geoffrey should they wish.   Perhaps the debts were incurred by John de Monmouth junior before his succession in 1248.   He and Geoffrey made an agreement of mutual benefit; John had his debts discharged for him, whilst Geoffrey acquired Chesterton.   The manor was in any case a small one, though a useful addition to Siddington.[89]

As a corollary of concentration one might expect that properties removed from these centres would be rented out.   This is precisely what did happen.   The manor of Turkdean, for example, the largest element in the property acquired with Matilda de Brightwell, and a dozen miles to the north-east of Cirencester, was leased to the abbey of Oseney for a term of ten years in 1246.[90]   His monastic benefactions must be seen against this background.   The outlying Warwickshire manors of Harborough Magna and Stareton passed to the Cistercian houses of Combe and Stoneleigh at annual rents of £10 6s. and £20 respectively.[91]   His only other "gift" was of his small estate at Long Compton in the southern tip of Warwickshire, and was made to the Augustinian priory of Wroxton "after the battle of Evesham".[92]

[86] "Langley Cartulary", nos. 45, 65-7, 82-3, 85.
[87] *Ibid.*, no. 38.
[88] *C.P.R., Exchequer of the Jews*, i, pp. 24, 39, 66-8, 116.
[89] The annual value given in 1274 was a derisory one of £3 8s. 4d.; see above, n. 10, and below, n. 127.   Siddington was said to be worth £17 7s. 10½d. in 1280.
[90] "Langley Cartulary", no. 10.   He excepted wardship and escheat from the tenement of William de Thorenny should either accrue.
[91] These gifts were made in May 1255 and at Easter 1247: *Warwickshire Feet of Fines*, i, no. 666; "Langley Cartulary", no. 434.   Geoffrey later remitted half of the £20 due from Stoneleigh and his son the remainder, though in each case "for a certain sum of money": *The Stoneleigh Leger Book*, ed. R. H. Hilton (Dugdale Soc., xxiv, 1960), p. 238.
[92] *Rotuli Hundredorum*, i, p. 228.

This policy of concentrating estates corresponds with a feature that has been noted recently on the lands of several of the more enterprising monastic houses. At Peterborough and Ramsey, particularly, capital was being expended in consolidating those manors which lay at the centre of the seigneury.[93] Similarly, on lay estates it was by abandoning outlying properties that families like the Willoughbys were attempting to cope with the consequences of debt. "Lordship", as Dr. King says, "was becoming more concentrated".[94]

II

But was lordship becoming concentrated in fewer hands? And was the thirteenth century a time of crisis for the knightly class as a whole? The evidence for the accumulation of estates by religious houses at the expense of the smaller landowners is fairly extensive. Mr. H. G. Richardson cited twenty-five houses which were involved in the redemption of indebted lands between the reigns of Henry II and Henry III.[95] The majority of his cases come from Yorkshire and Lincolnshire, but ten other counties and London are represented. He was quite clear where his evidence was leading, although he was not prepared to be dogmatic: "Since the evidence is fragmentary and fortuitous, it cannot be without significance that the examples cover so wide a geographical range and so many religious orders. It is obviously impossible to say how much land was acquired by religious houses by means of transactions in encumbered estates, but it is safe to infer that the practice was widespread and general".[96] To this list we must add the three west midland houses which Professor

---

[93] King, *Peterborough Abbey*, p. 69; J. A. Raftis, *The Estates of Ramsey Abbey* (Toronto, 1957), p. 112, n. 60. The consolidation of a newly acquired manor by buying up freeholds, either to augment the demesne or to increase the rent-roll, is a well-known feature of thirteenth-century investment in land. See also M. Chibnall (née Morgan), *The English Lands of the Abbey of Bec* (Oxford, 1946; 2nd impr. 1968), pp. 84-6; S. Raban, "Mortmain in Medieval England", *Past and Present*, no. 62, repr. below, p. 204; M. Altschul, *A Baronial Family in Medieval England: The Clares 1217-1314* (Baltimore, 1965), pp. 210-13; G. A. Holmes, *The Estates of the Higher Nobility in Fourteenth-Century England* (Cambridge, 1957), pp. 88-9, 113-14; Kosminsky, *Studies*, p. 251. It is evidenced on a number of Langley estates, viz at Ashcott in Somerset, at Ashover, at Pinley and Stivichall, and on Walter de Langley's manors of Wyken and Wolfhamcote: "Langley Cartulary", *passim*.
[94] King, *Peterborough Abbey*, p. 69.
[95] Richardson, *The English Jewry*, ch. v, esp. pp. 91 and 98-9.
[96] *Ibid.*, p. 99.

Hilton has noted as being engaged in the same activity;[97] whilst not forgetting the domination of the land market in the east midlands by the abbeys of Ramsey, Peterborough and Thorney, and in Somerset by the great abbey of Glastonbury.[98] Many purchases and redemptions are couched as pious donations and it seems comparatively rare for cartularies to contain bonds and acquittances. Moreover, charters of gift in such cases do not always contain telling phrases such as "for my urgent business (*ad urgens negocium meum*)" or "for my great necessity (*pro magna necessitate mea*)" which indicate debts.[99] Dr. King tells us that "the large estates which Peterborough abbey acquired in the thirteenth century were clearly alienated because of economic necessity",[100] and it can hardly be doubted that, for some areas of the country at least, the quantity of land passing from smaller landowners to the church was considerable.

As far as the magnates are concerned few are known, as yet, to have played any significant part in the thirteenth-century land market. One who did so was Richard de Clare, earl of Gloucester and Hertford, who, besides purchasing two thirds of the Huntingdonshire barony of Southoe-Lovetot in 1259, bought manors and rents from smaller landowners in at least five counties.[101] Humphrey de Bohun, earl of Hereford and Essex, was similarly active in the early decades of the fourteenth century.[102] William de Valence, lord of Pembroke, was among those who took annual rent-charges out of the hands of the Jews, especially towards the end of the reign of Henry III.[103] On the present state of evidence, however, the main rivals to the religious corporations would appear to be laymen in the service of the crown, such as the Braybrookes and Geoffrey de Langley, and royal clerks

---

[97] Hilton, *A Medieval Society*, pp. 51-2. The three are the abbeys of Winchcombe and Pershore, and Worcester Cathedral Priory. Two houses which were investing in Warwickshire, in a minor way at least, were St. Sepulchre, Warwick, and the Worcestershire abbey of Bordesley: see above, n. 72.

[98] Raftis, *op. cit.*, ch. iv; King, *Peterborough Abbey*, chaps. ii-iii; Raban, *loc. cit.*; *The Great Chartulary of Glastonbury*, ed. Dom A. Watkins, 3 vols. (Somerset Rec. Soc., 1947-64).

[99] *The Cartulary of Old Wardon*, ed. G. H. Fowler (Bedfordshire Rec. Soc., xiii, 1930), appendix iii.

[100] King, "Large and Small Landowners", above, p. 163.

[101] *Cal. Inq. Post Mortem*, i, pp. 530-1; Postan, *Cambridge Economic History of Europe*, i, p. 594; Sanders, *English Baronies*, pp. 80-1; Altschul, *op. cit.*, p. 77.

[102] Holmes, *op. cit.*, p. 113.

[103] Richardson, *op. cit.*, p. 73; *C.P.R., Exchequer of the Jews*, i, p. 228; *Select Pleas, Starrs and other Records from the Rolls of the Exchequer of the Jews*, ed. J. M. Rigg (Selden Soc., xv, 1901), pp. 56-60; *Cal. Patent Rolls, 1247-58*, pp. 543-4.

like Walter de Merton, Simon de Walton and Adam de Stratton.[104] It was precisely in those areas where the religious did not dominate the market that these men are most in evidence. Langley was most active in Warwickshire and Derbyshire, Merton in Leicestershire and Surrey. The Braybrookes had interests in a number of counties, some appearing in Mr. Richardson's list and some not, but their greatest gains were made in Leicestershire and Bedfordshire. In Buckinghamshire they, and later Walter de Merton, competed with the Cistercian abbey of Biddlesden.

The acquisition of encumbered estates was, for some at least, the result of a deliberate and determined policy. It was the principal means by which Walter de Merton endowed his college, for example. The strong links which some monastic communities had with particular Jewish concerns suggest well-organized marketing arrangements.[105] The histories of the Langley estates are equally indicative. The Nerbone estate at Stivichall passed speedily through the hands of two men who were profiting in their different ways through Jewish bonds, and became the property of a third for whom it was more profitable by virtue of its position close to his patrimony. The twenty-year lease of Ashover was acquired by a royal clerk on behalf of his employer and granted to a third party either for profit or as a favour and guarantee of future service. The d'Aubignys may have purchased Shortley knowing full well that they could dispose of it without loss and without difficulty should events take an unwelcome turn. And indeed, as Mr. Richardson says, the readiness of Jewish creditors to advance money on the security of land seems in itself to imply "the ultimate transfer of the debt to a religious house or other purchaser".[106] For the market to have been so buoyant and its participants so confident there can have been no dearth of desperate debtors!

Who were the debtors? They came in fact from the whole range of knightly or once-knightly families. Dr. King's sample is a useful cross-section ranging as it does from the Torpels who held six fees of the abbey of Peterborough and were "the chief of the honorial barons"

---

[104] The Braybrookes are dealt with by Fowler, *op. cit.*, appendix iii, and by Richardson, *op. cit.*, pp. 100-2, 270-80. For Walter de Merton, see *The Early Rolls of Merton College, Oxford*, ed. Highfield, esp. pp. 12-13, 17, 34-6. For Adam de Stratton, see *Starrs and Jewish Charters preserved in the British Museum*, ii, ed. H. Loewe (Jewish Hist. Soc. of England, 1932), Excursus by W. Page; and N. Denholm-Young, *Seignorial Administration in England* (London, 1937), pp. 77-85. Cf. also Richardson, *op. cit.*, pp. 71-2.

[105] *Ibid.*, pp. 95-7.

[106] *Ibid.*, p. 93.

to the Northboroughs who held half a fee of them.   The others held one, two and three fees respectively.[107]   The Langley acquisitions came from the single-manor families of Burley and Nerbone, the somewhat better endowed one-and-a-half-fee family of d'Aubigny, from the Willoughbys with several estates and from the baronial family of Monmouth.   Many of Walter de Merton's "victims" were lords of several manors — the Watevills, for example, the Amunde-villes and the Harcourts — whilst in 1268 he acquired no less than four manors from one debtor, Stephen Chenduit.   By contrast, most of those who sold out to the Braybrookes earlier in the century had been of the lesser sort.   The exception here was Wischard Ledet and his wife from whom they acquired two fees at East and West Langton, Leicestershire, and substantial land at Sutton, Bedfordshire.   In Dr. King's sample the least endowed, the Northboroughs and the Tots (one fee), were seriously embarrassed by the early years of Henry III, whilst the Miltons (two fees) managed to survive until a generation later.   The Southorpes, though in debt from the time of Henry II, survived until 1275-80, as did the Torpels.   In most cases which have received detailed study, the major sale came either after a period of leasing or following a string of minor alienations.   In most, again, the difficulties appear to range and in fact to deepen over several generations.   The better-endowed families survived for a time because they enjoyed some scope to alienate property without dire consequences and not necessarily because their debts were contracted later.   The impression which the monastic records give is of a traffic beginning in the middle years of Henry II and expanding steadily well into the thirteenth century.   Although some well-endowed families were disappearing earlier (one of Mr. Richardson's examples, the Fossards, were parting with land as early as 1176[108]) it does seem that by the reign of Henry III the net was spreading increasingly wide. The conclusion is hardly escapable: the knightly class was passing through a period of economic crisis, a crisis that was both extensive and prolonged.

Given that there was such a crisis, how could it have arisen? Pertinent here is Dr. Sally Harvey's refreshingly independent study of the size and evolution of the knight's fee in England.[109]   Her results may be swiftly summarized.   The evidence suggests two types of enfeoffment: that of the influential sub-tenant or honorial baron who

---

[107] King, "Large and Small Landowners", above, pp. 146-54.
[108] Richardson, *The English Jewry*, pp. 89-90.
[109] Sally Harvey, "The Knight and the Knight's Fee in England", *Past and Present*, no. 49 (Nov. 1970).

undertook to provide knights and received land, often on a five hide per knight basis; and that of the professional knight, or "vavassor", who received much less than five hides, the excess remaining as profit to the feudal middleman.[110] Domesday Book and early feudal documents reveal "the normal landed basis of the eleventh-century knight to be about 1½ hides".[111] On Domesday values of £1 per hide the serving knight had an income of between 30s. and £2 per annum, enough to sustain him but not nobly. On the ground his fee comprised a unit appurtenant to a manor, an outlying holding or berewick, land or charges from the demesne, or villein land. As a result many were, from the beginning, living largely off money rents. In time, given assarting and the tendency to hereditability, many of these units and berewicks became small manors and "offered the opportunity of a profitable and independent base for the descendants of many eleventh-century professional knights".

By the second half of the twelfth century, however, the increased range of military activity combined with the elaboration and consequent cost of knightly equipment to cause grave difficulties for the professional knight. Some knights would seem to have been insufficiently endowed from the beginning. Some joined the baronial middlemen in demanding a reduction in their commitment. This helps to explain the early appearance of fractional fees, although some fractions seem to have existed from the inception. The end-result was a thinning of knightly ranks and the victims were largely, of course, the "vavassors". But the cost of knighthood continued to rise and the number of actual knights to decline well into the thirteenth century. "The changeover to the knight of local importance had taken place by the mid-twelfth century, but by the close of the century, as costs mounted, many of these lesser 'gentry' types faced the same dilemma that had meant the opting out of the early knight".[112]

A decline in the number of knights does not in itself, however, constitute the decline of a class. Many professional knights did, no doubt, fade to become rent- and scutage-paying freeholders, but

---

[110] The term *vavassor* is used here in the sense of "the lowest grade among the holders of military fiefs": Marc Bloch, *Feudal Society*, trans. L. Manyon (London, 1961), p. 177. Technically it meant "the 'vassal of vassals' (*vassus vassorum*), who was not himself the lord of any other warrior" (p. 332). But now see also below, pp. 201-2.

[111] Standing between honorial baron and vavassor, in terms of endowment, were a few "middling knights", often the result of nepotic and preferential enfeoffments, holding one or two manors: Harvey, *op. cit.*, pp. 10-11.

[112] For the preceding two paragraphs, see Harvey, *op. cit.*, *passim*; the quotations are to be found on pp. 15, 31, 40-1. On the cost of knighthood see, in particular, Denholm-Young, "Feudal Society in the Thirteenth Century: the Knights".

what of those who had become manorial landlords? Though they ceased to be knight-producing families,their economic and something of their social position remained intact for they continued to live off their peasant tenants. Of the better-endowed families who survived as knight-bearing into the thirteenth century, many, in time, relinquished the burden and the prestige of knighthood. In the face of their reluctance the crown was forced, for military and administrative reasons, to the expedient of distraint of knighthood, and attempted to impose this at what proved to be unrealistic levels.[113] By 1285 the true knightly level may have been as high as the £100 freeholder.[114] However strong the lure of knighthood may or may not have been, few families were prepared to jeopardize their material position in an attempt to retain its benefits. The emergence of fractional and rotational fees in the twelfth century was almost certainly the result of the same feeling and of the same pressure. Hence, it is putting the case a little too strongly to speak of a "polarization of the class of military tenants and freeholders";[115] and the cost of knighthood alone cannot explain the large numbers who from the late twelfth century onwards became indebted, primarily to the Jews, and were ultimately forced to sell out. For this we have to invoke other factors, by far the most important being the general level of inflation.

That the turn of the twelfth and thirteenth centuries was a time of inflation has long been known, and the question was reviewed some years ago by Dr. P. D. A. Harvey.[116] The weight of evidence suggests that we are dealing not with a rise in prices of agricultural produce alone, but with a sudden and heavy monetary inflation lasting from *c.* 1180 - *c.* 1220 and affecting the general price and wage levels. This was followed by a fairly continuous but slower rate of inflation from *c.* 1220 to *c.* 1260. The gainers were the rent-payers — in particular the better-endowed peasants — and the sufferers all who were dependent on customary charges. Both the crown and the major landowners attempted to redress the balance; hence the social and political consequences: "the increasing legal disabilities of the peasantry, the change from leasing manors to demesne farming on large estates, and the political troubles of the reign of John".[117] Now,

---

[113] M. R. Powicke, "Distraint of Knighthood and Military Obligation under Henry III", *Speculum*, xxv (1950), pp. 457-70; Denholm-Young, *op. cit.*, pp. 90-1; F. M. Powicke, *The Thirteenth Century*, 2nd edn. (Oxford, 1962), pp. 546-8, 552-3.

[114] Denholm-Young, *op. cit.*, p. 91.

[115] Harvey, *op. cit.*, p. 41.

[116] P. D. A. Harvey, "The English Inflation of 1180-1220", *Past and Present*, no. 61 (Nov. 1973), where full references will be found.

[117] *Ibid.*, p. 4.

inflation must have worked equally to the disadvantage of the smaller landowners — the more so, in some cases, as they lived substantially, or even wholly, off rents and lacked the resources in land to shift to demesne farming. Once inflation is established as the crucial issue, other factors fit into place. The division of estates in pursuit of family settlements is an important, though secondary, factor for it depleted resources already strained in the face of rising costs. Indeed the rate of inflation may help to explain the break-up in the integrity of the knight's fee as it became increasingly difficult to provide for brothers, sisters and younger children. Of great importance is the structure of estates. To live off fixed rents was entirely acceptable, and even desirable, in mid-twelfth-century conditions,[118] but by the early thirteenth century the consequences for families like the Nerbones of Stivichall could be disastrous. This helps to explain why such a cross-section of the knightly class was affected. Standards of consumption, too, played their part, for "in face of the tendency for prices to rise, a more or less static income encouraged borrowing in order to sustain a customary level of consumption".[119] It was not just that their "incomes did not match their social pretensions",[120] but that those incomes were, in real terms, declining. The crucial issue for the smaller landowners was whether they could extract from their estates the increased profits necessary to maintain their position. Their difficulties tended to be cumulative, and some indebted families, as we have seen, had sufficient resources, for a time at least, to cope. Paradoxically, therefore, the height of the crisis was not the period of heaviest inflation but the reign of Henry III.

Such a protracted economic and social crisis cannot have been without repercussions, ultimately, in the political sphere. Professor Treharne saw the period of reform and rebellion from 1258 to 1267 as manifesting the emergence of a new knightly class, from whose ranks came the most sustained pressure for reform.[121] More recently, Professor Postan has suggested that the wide nature of the reform programme reflects not so much official recognition of a rising or a

[118] M. M. Postan, "The Chronology of Labour Services", *Trans. Roy. Hist. Soc.*, 4th ser., xx (1937), pp. 169-93, reprinted with revisions in his *Essays on Medieval Agriculture and General Problems of the Medieval Economy* (Cambridge, 1973), pp. 90-106; E. Miller, "England in the Twelfth and Thirteenth Centuries: An Economic Contrast?", *Econ. Hist. Rev.*, 2nd ser., xxiv (1971), pp. 1-14.
[119] *Ibid.*, p. 11. His remarks were intended to refer to the greater landowners but they are equally applicable to the class under discussion.
[120] Hilton, *A Medieval Society*, p. 51.
[121] R. F. Treharne, "The Knights in the Period of Reform and Rebellion, 1258-67", *Bull. Inst. Hist. Research*, xxi (1946), pp. 1-12.

risen class as the necessity of appealing to their grievances in the effort to achieve widespread support.[122] "In other words, if what Simon de Montfort and Edward I tried to do was to win the support of the knightly class, they did so not by bowing to its new strength but by coming to its relief".[123] This hypothesis will prove the more attractive the more the crisis is seen to have affected not just the lower but the middling and upper ranks of the knightly class. Those debtors who survived, at least for a time, with depleted resources but with social status intact, are likely to have been among the most vigorous and intransigent opposition in the counties.

Once the political crisis broke, moreover, both the exploiters of the land market and the moneylenders themselves came under fire. Clause twenty-five of the Petition of the Barons (May 1258) complains that "Jews sometimes transfer their debts and lands pledged to them to magnates and other powerful persons in the kingdom, who thus enter the lands of lesser men".[124] These "powerful persons" were, no doubt, men like Geoffrey de Langley and Walter de Merton. Both were, in fact, among the first to suffer pillaging of their lands and property at the hands of baronial partisans after their regrouping in the spring of 1263.[125] Simon de Walton, meanwhile, is reported to have fled for safety to the abbey of Bury St. Edmunds.[126] The attack upon Langley lands is recorded in the Annals of Dunstable and celebrated in the *Song of the Barons*.[127] "Accursed be he who complains of it",

---

[122] *Cambridge Economic History of Europe*, i, pp. 594-5; and Postan, *The Medieval Economy and Society*, pp. 164-5.   [123] *Ibid.*, p. 165.

[124] "Judaei aliquando debita sua et terras eis invadiatas [tradunt] magnatibus et potentioribus regni, qui terras minorum ingrediuntur ea occasione": *Documents of the Baronial Reform and Rebellion 1258-67*, selected by R. F. Treharne and edited by I. J. Sanders (Oxford, 1973), pp. 86-7. The translation of *terras minorum* as the lands of minors, favoured by Treharne and Sanders, by Roth (*History of the Jews in England*, p. 60) and by Richardson (*The English Jewry*, p. 103) seems to me unlikely. The use of *potentiores* would suggest that the *minores*, by contrast, were lesser men or smaller landowners, and this is the translation Professor Postan favours (*The Medieval Economy and Society*, p. 164). Otherwise, the passage would imply approval of the general process and seek remedy for a rather extreme abuse only, which is in fact the way Mr. Richardson interprets it.

[125] The damage to Merton's property at Malden and Farleigh, Surrey, was later said to have totalled £102: Highfield, *The Early Rolls of Merton College*, p. 22.   [126] *Dict. Nat. Biog.*, xx, p. 992.

[127] *Annales Monastici*, ed. H. R. Luard (Rolls Series, 1864-9), iii, p. 201; Thomas Wright, *The Political Songs of England* (Camden Soc., old ser., vi, 1839), p. 62. The seizure of his Oxfordshire lands is proven by a writ to the sheriff: *Cal. Close Rolls, 1261-4*, p. 333; and the pillaging may explain why, in the case of many of his manors, the inquisition *post mortem* of Geoffrey's son Walter gives higher values than his own. A month or so after Lewes he was obliged to submit his title deeds to Milcote, Dorsington and Stareton for confirmation: "Langley Cartulary", nos. 395, 529. At this stage at least, the baronial leaders wished to minimize the degree of spoliation.

sang the poet.[128] It can hardly be suggested, though, that resentment at their activities on the land market provided the prime motive for attack. Merton and Walton were royal ministers of the highest rank, whilst Langley had not only achieved notoriety as a particularly odious forest justice but had more recently received the lion's share of blame for the rising which destroyed English authority in north Wales in the autumn of 1256.[129] According to the Dunstable annalist only those were attacked who had refused to abide by the Provisions of Oxford, although this may have provided a blanket excuse for settling old scores.[130] Langley was later the victim of a second attack, this time by lesser men, in London in April 1267.[131]

It is possible, however, that the spectacle of crown servants investing in land may have weighed with men who were beginning to reflect on the character and calibre of royal government, especially when they were themselves suffering financial stringency. Warwickshire's final concords for this period show Langley pre-eminent in land transactions in the county,[132] and it may be that his intensive investment in one area, no less than his rapacity in the service of the king, helped to poison the political climate there. And he was undoubtedly only one of a group of men attached to the central government but operating in the localities.

As to the Jews, the reformist provisions were more concerned with

[128] Et Sire Jon [sic] de Langele
    Soun chose fu gainé
    Deheiz eit que l'en pleine!
    Tot le soen en fist porter
    De Cliffort mi Sire Roger
    Ne vout que rien remeine.
[129] According to Matthew Paris, "there were those who said that as it was he who had extended Edward's power so this same Geoffrey should willy-nilly restore his losses": *Chronica Majora*, v, pp. 592-3. Geoffrey de Langley was a member of the regents' council with particular responsibility for Prince Edward's English and Welsh lands from the spring of 1254. He is first described as Edward's steward on 13th December. Under the direction of the king he directed the attempted shiring of Perfeddwlad which led to the rising of November 1256. He seems to have been the scapegoat for this failure and was finally pardoned on 14 February 1258 "so that the king or his heirs will not be able to bring any charges against him on account of the war in Wales or any other cause": *Annales Monastici*, iii, p. 200; T. F. Tout, *Edward I* (London, 1932), pp. 20-1; *Cal. Close Rolls, 1253-4*, pp. 58, 63, 71, 86, 102, 281, and *1254-6*, p. 14; *Cal. Patent Rolls, 1247-58*, p. 616. For his reputation as chief justice of the forest, see *Chronica Majora*, iv, pp. 136-7.
[130] *Annales Monastici*, iii, p. 201.
[131] On 1 July 1272 John de Ludeham, Geoffrey Bigot and Robert de Putton were pardoned of robberies and trespasses committed by them against Geoffrey de Langley before Gilbert de Clare and his adherents entered London in April 1267: *Cal. Patent Rolls, 1266-72*, p. 657.
[132] *Warwickshire Feet of Fines*, i.

the abuse of debt by powerful Christians and with the running of the Exchequer of the Jews than with the Jewry itself.[133]   It is only with the outbreak of civil strife in 1263 that we see the full force of anti-semitic feeling within the Montfortian party.   This prejudice was, of course, deep and widespread in medieval society, but what is significant is the extent to which Jewish records were sought.   "In every city that the barons entered, the Jewry formed their first objective, and its business records were at once destroyed".[134]   Fresh disorders occurred after the battle of Lewes, whilst in the last flickering of the rebellion the "Disinherited" removed the Cambridge *archa* (the chest containing Jewish bonds) to the Isle of Ely and sacked the synagogue at Lincoln.   The Provisions of the Jewry of January 1269 reflect royal recognition of the extent of this feeling, and must be seen as part of the general pacification.   No debts were to be contracted with Jews in future on the security of land held in fee; all obligations of the sort already registered were to be cancelled; the transference to a Christian of a debt thus secured was to be treated as a capital offence; and debts of any other nature could henceforth be disposed of to a third party only by special licence, and on condition that the principal only, without any interest, was exacted.   Predictably, the legislation seems to have affected only the most overt forms of usury, and the traffic in encumbered estates continued as before.[135]   There can be little doubt, though, that the bitterness of feeling expressed during these years did much to worsen the condition of the Jews and to secure their ultimate expulsion.

That a considerable number of Montfortians were heavily indebted is beyond question.   The Fine Rolls for the period from October 1264 to June 1265 contain no less than forty-nine cases in which supporters were granted relief regarding their debts to the Jews.[136] Six were outright pardons; four were assignments of reasonable terms for repayment, whilst in another the debt was respited pending

---

[133] Petition of the Barons, cl. 25; Provisions of Oxford, cl. 17; Provisions of Westminster, Administrative cl. 23: Treharne and Sanders, *op. cit.*, pp. 25, 109, 155.

[134] Roth, *op. cit.*, p. 61; and, for what follows, *ibid.*, pp. 61-5.

[135] Richardson, *op. cit.*, pp. 106-7.

[136] Pub. Rec. Off., C60/61 and 62.   The roll for 49 Henry III has been analysed by C. H. Knowles in " 'The Disinherited' 1265-80" (Univ. of Wales Ph.D. thesis, 1959).   Of the twenty-nine debtors figuring there, he was able to identify seventeen from other sources as supporters of Simon de Montfort between Lewes and Evesham.   Of the twenty names on the previous roll a number, including Ralph de Camoys, Roger Bertram and David de Ashby, are cited as debtors by him from other sources: *ibid.*, part ii, pp. 36, 54.   There can be no doubt that the relief of Jewish debts by the Montfortian government was a partisan affair.

valuation. In the remaining thirty-eight cases the interest and sundry payments were remitted leaving the principal debt only, to be paid — at reasonable terms — either to the Jewish creditors or, if these had been killed or fled during the disturbances, to the Exchequer. Of the full pardons one was granted to Ralph de Camoys "for praiseworthy service" and two to men who had fought at Lewes.[137] Two other cases are less savoury and reflect the power of the earl of Gloucester. These were granted not to the original debtors but to men who had acquired their land: Henry de Sutley was pardoned a debt of £70 owed by Nicholas Poyner, at the instance of Gilbert de Clare, whilst Thomas de Clare was acquitted of the debts owed through his purchase of the land of William de Wryesdale. The first of the remissions of interest occurred on 26 October 1264, and was granted to nine men "so that they may be made more devoted and more resolute in our service".[138] Eight others received remission during the next few days; four of them at the instance of the leading Montfortian, Henry de Hastings. The remainder occur between late November and mid-March. One recipient was the later leader of the "Disinherited", John de Eyvill. There were other indebted Montfortians, moreover, who do not appear on the Fine Rolls; among them are Richard de Colesworth, Ralph Harengod, Robert de Willoughby and Saer de Harcourt.[139]

For these men the battle of Evesham was a double tragedy; for not only were their lands forfeit and had to be redeemed under the Dictum of Kenilworth, but the remission of their Jewish debts, or of the interest on those debts, was speedily revoked.[140] The redemption of forfeited land has been closely studied by Dr. C. H. Knowles. The methods of repayment devised — by instalments, by lease and by *vif-gage* — meant that despite some recourse to borrowing the great majority of rebels survived with their estates more or less intact. Most of those who ultimately did lose land were men who had been indebted before the outbreak of hostilities. Ralph de Camoys and

---

[137] "pro laudabili servicio quod dilectus et fidelis noster Ralph de Cameys nobis impendit perdonavimus . . ." (Pub. Rec. Off., Fine Roll 48 Henry III, m. 2); ". . . Gernasio de Bestenour qui fuit in conflictu nuper habito apud Lewes" (Fine Roll 49 Henry III, m. 6); ". . . Waltero Maureward qui fuit cum dilecto et fideli nostro Rogero de Huntingfeld in conflictu nuper habito apud Lewes" (*ibid.*, m. 7).

[138] "ut nobis devotiores et ad obsequia nostra promptiores efficiantur": Pub. Rec. Off., Fine Roll 48 Henry III, m. 1.

[139] Richard de Colesworth was captured at Evesham and Ralph Harengod was killed at Lewes: Knowles, " 'The Disinherited' 1265-80", part ii, p. 52. Robert de Willoughby was captured at Kenilworth: *ibid.*, appendix i, p. 9.

[140] Roth, *History of the Jews in England*, p. 64.

Henry de Crammarvill, for example, who both appear on the Fine
Rolls, lost land to the royal minister Robert Walerand.[141] The
greatest gainer, however, was Walter de Merton who in the years
immediately following the Dictum of Kenilworth reached the apogee
of his investment. A fairly typical case is that of Saer de Harcourt.
Saer was the younger son of Richard de Harcourt, from whom he
acquired the manors of Kibworth Harcourt and Newton in Leicestershire in 1258. He had become indebted, however, to the Jew Cresse,
son of Geuth. As a member of Simon de Montfort's own entourage
he was able to acquire a pardon of his debt when Simon was at the
height of his power. This the king revoked in 1266. Meanwhile
his lands had been seized and although he was given permission to
redeem them, in July 1267, the attempt to do so served only to
aggravate his financial difficulties. He made an effort to raise the
necessary money on the security of his manor of Kibworth Harcourt,
but to no avail. In 1270 he sold the manor to Walter de Merton for
£400. To safeguard his title, Walter then acquired a quitclaim from
Saer's creditor, Cok Hagin, son of Cresse.[142] Walter's greatest
coup, however, was the acquisition of the land of Stephen Chenduit.
Stephen, again, was indebted before the outbreak of war. He
suffered forfeiture as a Montfortian but successfully pleaded his
innocence and in consequence had his lands restored to him. However, he remained heavily in debt. In 1268 Walter de Merton paid
his debts to Manser, son of Aaron, Isaac, and Hagin of Lincoln, and
acquired four manors from him, one at Cuxham, Oxfordshire, and
three in Buckinghamshire.[143]

And, finally, the case of John fitz Saer brings together many of the
characteristics of the landed debtor in the reign of Henry III. Saer
had died about 1250 owing 50 marks to the Exchequer and £80 to
Benedict Crispin on the security of his land. Within a few years
Benedict had advanced further sums to Saer's son in return for an
annual rent-charge of £20. Consequently, between 1256 and 1260,
John fitz Saer was forced to sell his estate at Shenley, Hertfordshire,
and his land in Rotherhithe and London to Adam de Stratton.
Later he joined the Montfortian party and reoccupied Shenley from
which he was ejected after Evesham. He was allowed to redeem part,

[141] Knowles, *op. cit.*, part iii, ch. iv.
[142] The case is dealt with in some detail by R. H. Hilton in "Kibworth
Harcourt", in W. G. Hoskins (ed.), *Studies in Leicestershire Agrarian History*
(Leicester, 1949).
[143] Pub. Rec. Off., Fine Roll 49 Henry III, m. 9; Knowles, *op. cit.*, part iii,
p. 38; Highfield, *The Early Rolls of Merton College*, pp. 34-6; P. D. A. Harvey,
A Medieval Oxfordshire Village: Cuxham 1240 to 1400 (Oxford, 1965), pp. 5-8.

at least, of his land at Shenley, but Stratton, now Keeper of the King's Works at Westminster, acquired grants not only of 46 marks which John owed for the recovery of his land but of the 50 marks which John's father owed the Exchequer. As a result the manor of Shenley was made over to Stratton in its entirety in January 1268.[144]

Moneylending helped to facilitate the transfer of land; it also created a reservoir of bitter resentment. Sooner or later this was bound to be translated into political action. Mr. Richardson believes that in many cases the borrower may have had little idea of what would happen if he failed to pay his capital debt promptly, and even if he did "no matter what was written in the bond, the outcome was unexpected and dangerous".[145] Financial strain and the horrors of debt take us a long way towards explaining why the reformist earls received such widespread support from the knightly class in thirteenth-century England. "Our working hypothesis", writes Professor Postan, "must be not one of rising power and prosperity of smaller landowners but one of a gathering threat to their position".[146] Is it possible to escape this conclusion?

---

[144] *Excursus* by Page in *Starrs and Jewish Charters preserved in the British Museum*, ii, pp. lxxvi-vii; *V.C.H.*, *Hertfordshire*, ii, p. 265; *Ancient Deeds*, iii, A. 5121.
[145] Richardson, *The English Jewry*, pp. 81-2.
[146] *Cambridge Economic History of Europe*, i, p. 595.

APPENDIX

THE SURVEY OF STIVICHALL IN 1279*

The heirs of Margery de Neirburn hold the vill of Styvechale of the bishop of Chester by the service of one third of a knight's fee and the bishop holds of the king in chief.

These heirs hold in demesne 1 messuage [mess.] and ½ virgate [v.].

John Langl[ey] holds a moiety of the vill of the heirs for a rose and homage.

Henry de Styvechal holds 22s. rent of the heirs for 1d. for all service.

William de Liston holds 4 v. of the aforesaid Henry for 22s. 1d. and a rose for all service.

Richard de Montbray holds ½ v. of William for 10s. at his will *(ad voluntatem suam)*.

William Wynter holds 1 cottage [cott.] of William for 3s., 2 hens and 1 day in autumn.

John de Langl[ey] holds ¼ v. of William for 2s. for all service.

John de Barwe holds 1 mess., ½ v. of William for 4s. for all service.

Richard de Barow holds ½ v. of William for 1lb. cumin for all service.

John de Canele holds 1 mess., ½ v. of William for 4s. for all service.

Ranulf Want' holds 1 mess., 1 v. of William for 2s. and suit to his court every three weeks.

Stephen de Liston holds 1 cott. of William for 2s. for all service.

(Total: 8 tenants holding 3¼ virgates and paying 27s.)

John de Langley holds of the aforesaid heirs 3½ v. and 3 acres by service unknown.   The same John has in the same vill 3 v. of villeinage whereof:

Roger Russell holds 1 mess., ½ v. [of him] for 9s. and suit as above.

William le Westerne holds ¼ v. and ⅛ v. of him for 8s. and suit as above.

Richard le Pottere holds 1 mess., ¼ v., 3 acres of him for 7s. 6d. and suit as above.

Henry le Norreys holds 1 tenement of him for 7s. and suit as above.

* See above, n. 57.

Adam le Westerne holds 1 mess., ¼ v. of him for 8s. and suit as above.

John le Parlour holds 1 tenement [of him] for 3s. 10d.

William le Pestour holds 1 mess., 3 acres [of him] for 4s.

Jordan le Provost holds 1 mess., ½ v. [of him] for 9s.

John de Canele holds ¼ v. of him for 4s.

All the aforesaid may be removed from their tenure at the will of the lord.

(Total: 9 tenants in villeinage holding 2⅛ v., 6 acres and 2 tenements, and paying 60s. 4d.)

The same John Langley has these free tenants namely:

Alice la White holds 1 mess., ¼ v. of him for 8s. for all service.

Ranulf son of Hugh holds 1 mess., 1 v. of him for 6d., 1 lb. cumin and suit as above.

Roger le Coupere holds 1 mess., ¼ v. of him for 7s. and suit.

John de Canele holds 1 mess., 3 acres of him for 13d. for all service.

John de Canele holds 1 cott. freely of him for 2s. for all service.

(Total: 4 free tenants holding 4 mess., 1 cott., 1½ v., 3 acres for 18s. 7d.)

Ralph de Stratton holds 1 mess., 1 v. of the bishop of Chester for 6s. for all service. The same bishop has appropriated view of frankpledge of the vill by what warrant it is not known.

Robert le Forester holds 1 mess., 1 v. of Robert de Stoke for 9s. and suit of court for all service.

(The survey concludes with 2 sub-tenancies of John de Barowe and 2 of Robert le Forester.)

GENEALOGY I

THE D'AUBIGNYS OF GREAT WISHFORD

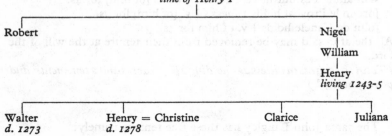

Henry d'Aubigny
time of Henry I

Robert   Nigel

William

Henry
living 1243-5

Walter   Henry = Christine   Clarice   Juliana
d. 1273   *d. 1278*

GENEALOGY II

THE WILLOUGHBYS OF KESTEVEN

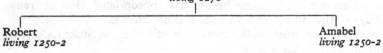

Sir Ralph de Willoughby
living 1222

(relationship uncertain)

Sir Robert de Willoughby
living 1270

Robert   Amabel
living 1250-2   *living 1250-2*

GENEALOGY III

THE NERBONES OF STIVICHALL

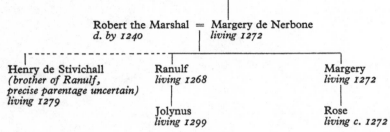

Stephen de Nerbone

Robert the Marshal = Margery de Nerbone
d. by 1240   *living 1272*

Henry de Stivichall   Ranulf   Margery
(brother of Ranulf,   *living 1268*   *living 1272*
precise parentage uncertain)
living 1279

Jolynus   Rose
living 1299   *living c. 1272*

Note, 1987

This essay is reprinted essentially as it was published in 1975. The author is aware, however, that the crisis hypothesis has not received universal accord; in particular it has been the subject of a substantial critique by Dr. D. A. Carpenter, in his article "Was there a Crisis of the Knightly Class in the Thirteenth Century? The Oxfordshire Evidence", *English Historical Review*, xcv (1980), pp. 721-52. There are clearly major issues, both of a conceptual and of a methodological nature, to be resolved, and these I intend to explore in a forthcoming book. There is, however, one essential point which is in need of clarification. The central hypothesis has sometimes been interpreted as "the decline of the knightly class" or even "the decline of the gentry". This was not my intention. I was suggesting, rather, that the knightly class, interpreted in a broad sense, was passing through a period of crisis in the early to mid-thirteenth century, and indicating some of the pressures and resource problems which lesser landowners were having to face and their possible consequences.

Crisis and decline are by no means synonymous, and as hypotheses they need to be more clearly distinguished. That the resources of members of the knightly class were extremely varied, in both nature and extent, is beyond doubt. Just as there were many families which succumbed under social and economic pressures, there must have been many more which faced, but ultimately overcame, those pressures. True enough, where a major resource is lacking or inadequate an individual or family may be cushioned by the existence of alternative resources; but it must not be forgotten that this will put those alternative resources into sharper relief. The ability to shift pressures, and especially on to others, is also a form of resource. All of this may be regarded as part and parcel of a crisis. Moreover, neither the existence of wealthier knights who were able to maintain or indeed improve their material position, nor the rise of new families through service and professional (or semi-professional) expertise, is necessarily any counter to the crisis hypothesis, and many of the charges laid against me have validity only in terms of a rival hypothesis of decline.

Closer definition of terms, however, will not dispose of all the points at issue, and there are many areas which require further exploration, development and revision.

On a technical point, I now consider the use of the word "vavassor" to describe the professional knight misleading and, despite some resemblance to the distinctive Norman usage, not justified in terms either of its usage in England or of its general development. For an exploration of the various meanings attached to the term and its evolution, see my "Literature and Social Terminology: The Vavasour in England", in T. H. Aston *et al.* (eds.), *Social Relations and Ideas: Essays in Honour of R. H. Hilton* (Cambridge, 1983), especially pp. 112-21.

7. Mortmain in medieval England*

SANDRA RABAN

IN NOVEMBER 1279 AN UNCOMPROMISING STATUTE WAS PROMULGATED
which, if strictly enforced, would have marked the end of the
church's territorial ambitions:

> no-one at all, whether religious or otherwise, may buy or sell any lands or
> tenements, or receive them from anyone else under the cover of gift or lease
> or any other title whatsoever, or presume to appropriate them to himself by
> any other device or subterfuge, so that they pass into mortmain in any way,
> under pain of forfeiture.[1]

In practice an arrangement which permitted alienations to the church
under royal licence in spite of the statute soon emerged. The first
of these licences appeared on the patent rolls in May 1280.[2] However,
such mitigation of the law still resulted in an extra and permanent
burden on the church whenever gifts were offered to it or purchases
negotiated. An attempt is made here, largely on a limited regional
basis, to assess how heavy this burden was and to what extent royal
control distorted the pattern of the land market.

The legislation, known familiarly as the Statute of Mortmain,
was echoed in various forms throughout Europe and reflected a
widespread concern about ecclesiastical property.[3] Over the
centuries the church had amassed great landed wealth. In England,
the possessory assizes developed in the twelfth century effectively
protected title, so that there was little incentive for the laity to invade
land once it had been acquired by the church. Consequently there
were few losses to balance the gains and the church was in a position
to expand its property indefinitely. Whether this was happening at
a significant rate by the later thirteenth century is debatable.
Contemporary lay landlords believed so, but their views were coloured
by the pressures of inflation. Fixed feudal dues no longer yielded
a realistic return, so occasional feudal incidents, chiefly wardship and

---

* My special thanks are due to Dr. M. M. Chibnall who read this article in draft
form and who supervised much of the work upon which it is based, and also to the
Calouste Gulbenkian Foundation which has financed it. See also now my *Mortmain
Legislation and the English Church, 1279-1500* (Cambridge, 1982).

[1] Translated from *Select Charters*, ed. W. Stubbs, 9th edn. (Oxford, 1913),
p. 451.
[2] *Cal. Pat. Rolls, 1272-81*, p. 372.
[3] E. Miller, "The State and Landed Interests in Thirteenth Century France
and England", *Trans. Roy. Hist. Soc.*, 5th ser., ii (1952), pp. 124-6; C. Gross,
"Mortmain in Medieval Boroughs", *Am. Hist. Rev.*, xii (1907), p. 736; A. Pertile,
Storia del Diritto Italiano, 2nd edn., 6 vols. (Torino, 1892-1903), iv, pp. 388 ff.;
G. Espinas, *Les Finances de la Commune de Douai* (Paris, 1902), pp. 348 ff.

escheat, which could be exploited at the market rate, assumed greater importance.[4] Neither incident could arise where land had been given to a church, which could not die or leave minors as heirs. Mortmain was thus an appropriate term for ecclesiastical tenure; the land was as good as dead to its overlord. How far lay resentment of this, vocal for half a century before the statute, was well founded is hard to establish.

In some regions secular concern appears justified. Glastonbury in the south-west was buying up land around its own manors.[5] In the east midlands too, several monasteries were making major additions to their endowments. Already strong in this area, the church provided a ready market when knightly families were forced to sell. Within the narrow confines of north-east Northamptonshire the result was specially marked. Thorney Abbey purchased a manor in Kingsthorpe in 1272 and another in Clapton about the mid-thirteenth century.[6] Ramsey Abbey spent the vast sum of £1,666 13s. 4d. on several properties including manors at Barnwell, Hemington and Crowethorpe c. 1275, while Peterborough Abbey recovered Gunthorpe from its own tenant c. 1276.[7] Both Thorney and Peterborough were also pursuing a systematic policy of recovering freeholds on existing manors at this time.[8] Small wonder that alarm was felt. On the other hand, neighbouring Bedfordshire presented a far less serious picture of encroachment. Lacking the entrenched influence of major foundations to use as a base, the pattern of ecclesiastical buying was not so clearly defined. Religious houses faced more vigorous competition from local laymen, notably the Salfords. Both the published assize rolls and the feet of fines show a flourishing lay land market in the county.[9] It is well to remember also that even in ecclesiastically dominated north-east

---

[4] J. M. W. Bean, *The Decline of English Feudalism* (Manchester, 1968), p. 15.

[5] M. M. Postan, *The Medieval Economy and Society* (London, 1972), p. 162.

[6] Camb. Univ. Lib., Add. MSS. 3020-1, "The Red Book of Thorney" (hereafter cited as "The Red Book"), fos. 379v, xviii, 214v-15, 228v; Northants. Rec. Off., B1, 145 and 436; Pub. Rec. Off., CP25(1)/174/50/902. There is some doubt as to the exact date of the latter transaction; it was probably between 1238 and 1254, but may have been later.

[7] J. A. Raftis, *The Estates of Ramsey Abbey* (Toronto, 1957), pp. 109-10; E. King, *Peterborough Abbey 1086-1310* (Cambridge, 1973), p. 43.

[8] This was most noticeable on the nearby Thorney manors of Woodston, Water Newton and Stibbington in north Huntingdonshire: *Rotuli Hundredorum*, 2 vols. (Rec. Comm., 1812-18), ii, pp. 643 ff. Many of the individual transactions can be found in "The Red Book". Peterborough's activities were mainly concentrated in the Soke: King, *Peterborough Abbey*, p. 67.

[9] I am indebted for this information to Miss K. Naughton of Lucy Cavendish College, Cambridge.

Northamptonshire, families like the Hotots of Clapton and the Thorpes of Longthorpe were able to buy themselves into local prominence.[10] Any comprehensive view must hinge on further regional studies. Conditions clearly varied, but the situation in the east midlands suggests that contemporary opinion will be vindicated in districts where the church was already powerful, if not elsewhere. In some areas at least, there can be little doubt that the church was aggressively engaged in the land market on the eve of the mortmain legislation, at least in terms of recoveries from its own tenants.

At first the 1279 statute almost certainly spelt ecclesiastical frustration. With eight hundred to a thousand institutions[11] and countless secular clergy also eligible, the paucity of licences in the two decades after 1279 implies some curtailment of activity, either voluntary or enforced. The Graph analysing the number of licences issued shows that it was not until the turn of the century that they appeared in appreciable numbers on a more regular basis.[12] Glastonbury achieved its first licence as early as 1284,[13] but the experience of the fenland houses was perhaps more typical. Ramsey and Thorney received their initial licences in 1304, and at nearby Crowland and Ely they were obtained in 1299 and 1303 respectively. Peterborough alone remained undeterred with three licences between 1279 and the end of the century.[14] The pressures which had dictated expansion in this area were not likely to disappear overnight, yet, with the exception of Peterborough, a moratorium of more than two decades supervened. Whether it was because licences were difficult to obtain, or whether churchmen hesitated, hoping for amelioration of the law, the immediate effect of the statute was to curb ecclesiastical gains.

In the longer term, the outlook was less gloomy. Neither in the early years after the statute, nor subsequently, should the impact of mortmain legislation be judged on the evidence of licences alone. Less formal means of satisfying a continuing interest in land existed and methods of manipulating the licensing system were devised which restored in practice much of the freedom theoretically denied by the crown. In particular, ecclesiastical sources reveal a flexibility of

---

[10] King, *Peterborough Abbey*, pp. 46-52.
[11] D. Knowles and R. N. Hadcock, *Medieval Religious Houses: England and Wales*, 2nd edn. (London, 1971), p. 45.
[12] See below, p. 206.
[13] *Cal. Pat. Rolls, 1281-92*, p. 114.
[14] *Ibid.*, pp. 214, 414; *Cal. Pat. Rolls, 1292-1301*, pp. 208, 481; *Cal. Pat. Rolls, 1301-7*, pp. 125, 221-2, 236, 291, 292.

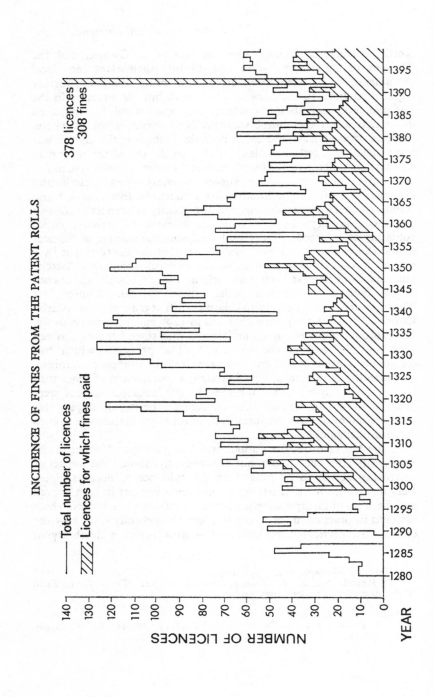

INCIDENCE OF FINES FROM THE PATENT ROLLS

378 licences
308 fines

— Total number of licences

▨▨▨ Licences for which fines paid

NUMBER OF LICENCES

140 130 120 110 100 90 80 70 60 50 40 30 20 10 0

YEAR

1280 1285 1290 1295 1300 1305 1310 1315 1320 1325 1330 1335 1340 1345 1350 1355 1360 1365 1370 1375 1380 1385 1390 1395

approach behind the formal procedures of alienation which must modify any harsh view of the law.

One alternative to permanent acquisition of property under licence was its limited enjoyment through leasehold. The terms of the statute could be interpreted as a prohibition of this too. Such a claim was brought in 1306, but dismissed.[15] Apparently no attack was intended upon leases made in good faith. Thus, in theory, there was nothing to prevent the church from exploiting leasehold opportunities. Of all transactions, however, leases are the most elusive. Once the term had been completed, there was no reason to preserve the agreement. Accordingly few leases have survived and those which have often owe their preservation to special circumstances such as enrolment in the royal chancery. For this reason, the evidence that certain houses became interested in leasing property after 1279 is suggestive rather than conclusive.

Several of the fenland monasteries were recipients of major crown leases in this period and for most of them it was a novel enterprise. Abbot William de Clapton (d. 1323) secured the lease of Glatton (Hunts.) for Thorney for his lifetime from the crown in 1314. This manor, for which he was to pay £100 per annum, was coterminous with the vill and consisted of eleven hides. The appurtenant hamlet of Holme numbered eight burgesses among its tenants.[16] In urban terms it was a poor gain, since the burgage tenure was more the product of seigneurial optimism than economic reality. Nevertheless it represented, for a time at least, control of a large estate immediately to the south of the abbey's existing manors and a further extension of influence within its private hundred of Normancross. Similarly in 1291, Peterborough had been granted custody of the manors of Torpel and Upton (Northants.) during the king's pleasure. The annual render was again £100.[17] These manors had formerly been held of the abbey in knights' fee, but were alienated to the crown by their tenant because of debt.[18] In other circumstances the monks might well have wished to buy back this part of their ancient endowment. It is likely that Crowland Abbey too was involved in leases of this type. Two estates, Holywell (Lincs.) and Stretton (Rutland), figure briefly in the account rolls between 1303 and 1307. Both these manors were assigned to Queen Margaret's dower at this time, so it is likely that they were on the leasehold market. The idea

[15] *Year Books XXXIV–XXXV Edward I*, ed. A. J. Horwood (Rolls Series, 1879), pp. 148–50.
[16] *Cal. Pat. Rolls, 1313–17*, p. 199; *Rotuli Hundredorum*, ii, pp. 650, 652.
[17] *Cal. Pat. Rolls, 1281–92*, p. 421; *Cal. Fine Rolls, 1272–1307*, p. 289.
[18] King, *Peterborough Abbey*, pp. 39–40.

that they were not a normal part of the abbey's demesne is reinforced by an atypical note about profits at the end of the first account. In this case the attraction of the properties would have been their proximity to Crowland's own manors of Langtoft and Baston (Lincs.).[19]

Leasehold might be expected to gain in attraction once more permanent forms of tenure were circumscribed. It was unlikely that royal estates would ever be available on other than restricted terms, so the barriers to purchase may well have opened up avenues hitherto unexplored. In each case, these three houses achieved the use of desirable properties, but the benefits were not unalloyed. Renders of £100 per annum seem hardly economic. Crowland's payment for Holywell and Stretton is unknown, but the profits for both manors, on the monks' own calculation, amounted to no more than £53 12s. 11d.[20] The Peterborough manors of Torpel and Upton were valued at £80 per annum in 1281 and the abbey account rolls suggest that even this may have been an over-estimate.[21] There were also other hazards of leasehold tenure as Crowland had found in the previous century when the dowager countess of Aumale had harassed the monks into converting a lease into purchase in self-protection.[22]

As an end in themselves leases could have drawbacks, but they had corresponding advantages when used as an interim measure before full ownership. They presented a chance to evaluate property before taking the more extreme step of acquiring it in mortmain. They could also be used to lure someone further into debt until a timely offer of purchase should prove irresistible. Their greatest merit, however, was to offer a safe and convenient way of holding land until the formalities of gaining a licence had been completed. Thorney preceded its purchase of a holding on the abbey manor of Woodston

[19] Camb. Univ. Lib., MSS. QC 32/2, Fd 1, Cd 8, Ad 1; *Victoria County History of Rutland*, ed. W. Page, 2 vols. (1908–35), ii, p. 147. Ely also took advantage of a royal lease. The prior and convent were granted the manor of Soham (Cambs.) for a thirteen-year term at £100 p.a. in 1369, but this was not the first such arrangement. In 1358 Queen Isabella had conceded a twelve-year lease on the same terms. Her acquittance of all arrears on the farm given at the same time suggests that the origin of the priory's interest can be still further antedated. Again the main appeal would have been proximity to existing estates: *Cal. Fine Rolls, 1369–77*, p. 30; Brit. Mus., MS. Egerton 3047, fos. 253v–4.

[20] Camb. Univ. Lib., MS. QC32/2, Fd 1.

[21] *Cal. Close Rolls, 1279–88*, p. 81; Northants. Rec. Off., Fitzwilliam Accs., 233, mm. 17–18; 2388, mm. 21r–v. The latter references were kindly supplied by Dr. E. King of Sheffield University.

[22] Gentlemen's Society, Spalding, "The Wrest Park Cartulary" (hereafter cited as "The Wrest Park Cartulary"), fos. 116v–18.

(Hunts.) from William de Waldeschef in 1304 by a lease for thirty years taken out in 1296. The terms of the lease provided for a flat payment of forty marks for the first ten years and forty shillings per annum for the following twenty. The purchase price in 1304 was a further one hundred marks.[23] The reasons behind this course of events are not stated. Most probably the abbey was squeezing out a tenant who was only prepared to sell as a last resort. Free holdings in the vill had already been eroded by abbey purchases before 1279, and Waldeschef was one of the few surviving free tenants of any consequence.[24] At Peterborough, a lease of 1288 had convenience rather than encroachment as its motive. Elias of Beckingham granted the abbey the manor of Southorpe:

> to have and to hold to the same abbot and convent at my will until I and the aforesaid abbot and convent have obtained permission from the lord king for them to retain the aforesaid tenement in perpetual alms.[25]

Many arrangements of this sort are likely to have perished, leaving the survivors as little more than the tip of an iceberg.

The 1279 statute had shown concern over fraudulent leases, and with reason. Very long leases could give the church something akin to perpetual tenure. Mullicourt Priory, for example, secured three acres of arable in Outwell (Norf./Cambs.) on a two thousand-year lease in 1306.[26] Even more of a problem and difficult to detect were illegal alienations to the church masked by leasehold agreements. In 1369 Barnwell Priory paid out a twenty pound fine in order to recover possession of a tenement in London, forfeit to the crown because of alienation without licence. John Noket of Barnwell had leased it to the priory for fifteen years and then surrendered all his rights, leaving the convent in control.[27] Much the same happened at Ely in 1461. Thomas Martyn of Ely expressed a wish in his last will and testament drawn up on 6th August that his tenement in Cambridge should be granted to the cathedral priory, if a licence could be procured. No trace of such a licence is to be found, but the priory received the property at farm from Martyn's feoffees for thirty-three years on 14 September 1461 and on 20th October

---

[23] "The Red Book", fos. 26v-7, iii-iiii, 123v-4, xxx; *Cal. Pat. Rolls, 1301-7*, pp. 236, 292; Northants. Rec. Off., Westmorland Coll., Box 2, Parcel ii, no. 1, C.
[24] *Rotuli Hundredorum*, ii, p. 643; "The Red Book", fos. 114v-15v, iiii-v, 128v, xlvii; Northants. Rec. Off., Westmorland Coll., Box 2, Parcel ii, no. 1, B. A note on the dorse of this last deed reveals it as a sale.
[25] *Henry of Pytchley's Book of Fees*, ed. W. T. Mellows (Northants. Rec. Soc., ii, 1927), pp. 68-9.
[26] Camb. Univ. Lib., E.D.C., 1B/15, no. 856.
[27] *Cal. Pat. Rolls, 1367-70*, p. 281.

following they too quitclaimed their rights.[28] Ely was more fortunate than Barnwell and the ruse passed unnoticed. An analogous, but in the event less fraudulent, instance of leasehold can be found at Thorney. Three parallel deeds drawn up on the same date (18 March 1325), with the same witnesses given in the same order, grant property in Bolnhurst (Beds.) and Yaxley (Hunts.), respectively for twenty years, two hundred years and in perpetuity. A licence to acquire followed in 1327, so if evasion had been mooted, the monks finally lost their nerve.[29]

Leasehold was not the only device which could confer freedom of action once formal alienation to the church had been decided upon. Another practice, which was sometimes used in conjunction with leasehold, was the employment of nominees. This had several advantages. They could work swiftly without having to wait on a licence whose delay might prejudice the purchase. They were also free to buy piecemeal over a long period, only resorting to a licence when the accumulation of property justified its expense. A Peterborough source explains why Elias de Beckingham, who had leased the manor of Southorpe to the monks pending a licence, was in possession in the first place:

> because the said abbot [of Peterborough] could not enter [Southorpe], on account of the king's statute against the religious, the said abbot arranged that dominus Elias de Beckingham, rector of the church of Warmington, in whom the abbot and convent had great confidence, should buy the aforesaid tenement.[30]

Similarly, when Holyrood Abbey suggested the sale of a twenty mark pension from Great Paxton church (Hunts.) to the dean and chapter of Lincoln, it was arranged that the latter should conduct the transaction through friends.[31] As with leases, the terms of the statute, if strictly interpreted, might seem to rule out such activities, but in practice there was little objection unless fraud was suspected.

The mechanics of acquisition at second hand can be observed at Thorney Abbey. A number of holdings at Bolnhurst (Beds.), Yaxley and Stanground (Hunts.), including those for which the leases have survived, were alienated under licence to the abbey by Thomas de Deeping in 1327. The grant represented the fruits of at

[28] Bodleian Lib., Oxford, MS. Ashmole 801, fos. 92v-5; Thomas Martyn died on 1 Sep. 1461.
[29] *Cal. Pat. Rolls, 1327-30*, p. 159; "The Red Book", fos. 332r-v.
[30] *Henry of Pytchley's Book of Fees*, ed. Mellows, p. 62.
[31] *The Registrum Antiquissimum of the Cathedral Church of Lincoln*, ed. C. W. Foster and K. Major, 9 vols. (Lincoln Rec. Soc., xxix, 1935), iii, pp. 178-81, nos. 837-8.

least four years of careful preparation. In 1323 he had received the entire holding of Thomas de Myvile in Bolnhurst. In the following year Walter de Upton, Richard de Haunes and Henry de Malverne granted further tenements there, and a year later still Thomas gained another from Robert Grym. Shortly before the licence was taken out, he also secured two acres of meadow from Peter de Paston and his wife Emma. Meanwhile, in Yaxley, he had negotiated the reversion of a messuage from Richard de Clapton. Thorney's position as *eminence grise* is emphasized by the way in which some of the deeds were executed at the abbey. Thomas de Myvile drew up his conveyance and appointed his attorney there in 1323. Thomas de Deeping himself appointed an attorney there in December 1323 and again in February 1324. The interest of the monks can be the only reason for conducting such business at Thorney, which was far from convenient for Bolnhurst. Furthermore, it all occurred three years before the abbey acquired any official standing in the matter. It is also revealing that the rubric to the grant of Peter de Paston and his wife attributes the gain to Abbot Reginald although the nominal recipient was Thomas.[32]

A more sophisticated version of the same procedure can be seen at the same house before 1343. In that year John de Yaxley granted the monks holdings at Yaxley, Stanground (Hunts.), Whittlesey (Cambs.), Bolnhurst and Husborne Crawley (Beds.) under licence. He was merely the final link in a chain of nominees. Much of the groundwork had been done by John de Newton. He, in turn, had made over his gains to Roger de Stanground, who then granted them to Robert de Thorney. Robert added further to this nucleus of property before surrendering to John de Yaxley in 1336. John continued in possession for the remaining seven years until the licence was obtained. As in the earlier transactions of Thomas de Deeping, some of the business was conducted at Thorney itself.[33] By no stretch of the imagination could this series of conveyances have been fortuitous. Thorney was clearly gathering land for a decade before the royal licence was granted, and employing chosen nominees to that end.

Who were these men? Their selection was of crucial importance since, in the event of duplicity, the principal was in no position to seek redress. In Elias de Beckingham, Peterborough had found a royal justice, bound in loyalty by the grant of its living of Warmington.[34] Many other houses also found secular clergy the

[32] *Cal. Pat. Rolls, 1327-30*, p. 159; "The Red Book", fos. 330v-2, 109v, 73.
[33] *Cal. Pat. Rolls, 1343-5*, p. 136; "The Red Book", fos. 36, 334v-5v, 110-12v, 201-2.
[34] King, *Peterborough Abbey*, p. 133.

most suitable choice, although they were usually of less exalted standing. All those involve in the dealings preceding Thorney's licences of 1327 and 1343 were in orders and several of them held abbey livings. Thomas, who featured in the first licence, was parson of East Deeping, John de Yaxley, Robert de Thorney and Roger de Stanground were all described as chaplains, while John de Newton was rector of Bolnhurst. The most distinguished of Thorney's nominees was William de Spanneby, who acted on behalf of the abbey early in the fourteenth century. He was then rector of Stanground, an abbey living. He also figured as a royal clerk in 1303, when the then vacant abbey of Crowland was committed to his keeping. In later years he was appointed guardian of the Templars' lands in Lincolnshire and served on several commissions of oyer and terminer.[35] There were many advantages in the employment of such men. Patronage was the time-honoured and inexpensive way of paying for their services. Preferment was an added incentive to loyalty. It was also relevant that, should the nominee die in possession, there was less likelihood of heirs disputing ownership. Such arguments were telling, but did not always weigh. Crowland favoured secular administrators in these duties. Reginald de Celario who granted property in Crowland, Langtoft and Baston (Lincs.) to the abbey under licence in 1300, presented the grange and stock account at Crowland itself between 1265-7 and it is likely that Walter de Somerby, an abbey steward, was also employed in the same way in the 1330s.[36] Ties of blood or origin might be an equally strong recommendation. It is probably more than coincidence that during the rule of Prior John de Fressingfield (1303-21) several men bearing the same name were involved in grants to Ely Priory.[37] Whatever the particular link, the major criterion for selection was trustworthiness. All these men had one thing in common. Their interests bound them to the churches which they represented.

A later extension of indirect acquisition, and one which offered greater safeguards for the church, was the use of groups of feoffees. These could be employed in exactly the same way as single nominees but with reduced risks from sudden death or dishonesty. An Ely cartulary shows this approach at work. The prior and convent

[35] See below, p. 215; Cal. Fine Rolls, 1272-1307, p. 484; e.g. Cal. Pat. Rolls, 1307-13, p. 438; ibid., 1313-17, pp. 313, 594.
[36] Cal. Pat. Rolls, 1292-1301, p. 492; Camb. Univ. Lib. MS. QC 32/1, Ad 2; Lincs. Archives Off., 6 Anc. 1/32-8; "The Wrest Park Cartulary", fos. 191r-v, xii-xiii. No final conveyance to the abbey is recorded.
[37] Brit. Mus., MS. Egerton 3047, fos. 50, 51; Camb. Univ. Lib., E.D.C., 1B/3, nos. 447, 663.

wished to buy a holding in Ely known as *Lilesplace,* which at that time
was already held by feoffees to the use of John Pelet. These were to
be replaced by other feoffees selected jointly by Pelet and the prior,
then:

> these nominees, after they have been enfeoffed, shall enfeoff the afore-
> mentioned prior and his successors when the prior has obtained a licence from
> the king and from any mesne lords that there may be.

Licences were duly obtained from the king on 21 May 1398 and from
the bishop of Ely early in the following November. Within a few
days, on 16th November, the feoffees conveyed the tenement to the
priory.[38]

Even this method was not entirely foolproof, as the drama at Louth
Park showed. Henry le Vavasour, knight, enfeoffed a group
consisting of the abbot and two monks of Louth, several laymen,
perhaps his wife and maidservant with the manor of Cockerington
(Lincs.) so that they could grant it to the abbey to provide for a further
ten monks to pray for his soul. Four of these feoffees were made to
swear on the Gospels that they would assign the manor to the abbey
as soon as the appropriate licences had been procured. Provision
was made for the heirs' patrimony to bear the cost of the abbot's
defence in a court of law should the family attempt to recover
possession. All reasonable precautions had therefore been taken to
bring the matter to a successful conclusion. In the event, however,
Henry's widow Constance was reluctant to part with the manor and
the fact that the conveyance was arranged on Henry's deathbed gave
her a lever against the abbey. Accusations of forgery were levelled
at the abbot, suggesting that he had set the hand of Henry's corpse to
a posthumous deed. The issue erupted into violence. The abbot
claimed that Constance and her henchmen had burgled the abbey
close, assaulted him and carried away some muniments, while
Constance later counter-claimed that the monks had seized her and
imprisoned her at Louth and made free of her goods. The
examination of those involved by royal justices in February 1345
provides a vivid picture of the negotiations leading to Henry's grant
and his subsequent demise.[39] There seems little doubt that the

[38] *Cal. Pat. Rolls, 1396-9,* p. 347; Brit. Mus., MS. Egerton 3047, fos. 113v,
243r-v, 117-18v.

[39] Since Henry died at the abbey, the question of undue pressure by the
church at a vulnerable moment arises. The blunt tone of his dealings as
reported by the abbot belies such a suggestion with its authentic ring.
Feeling himself inadequately welcomed on arrival, Henry summoned the
abbot remarking pointedly that "perhaps never would he take such a fish in his
net". All the witnesses except Constance agreed that Henry retained his
faculties until death: *Cal. Pat. Rolls, 1343-5,* pp. 490, 573; *ibid., 1345-8,*
pp. 1-7.

grant was a genuine one, challenged by the vested interest of the family. This would probably have occurred whatever the means of effecting the conveyance. Yet according to one witness Constance was a feoffee and feoffees had to be chosen for their integrity if the device was to work.

Louth Park was particularly unlucky. Some houses found that enfeoffment to their use was so satisfactory that there was no need to proceed to formal alienation. The implications of this for the enforcement of mortmain legislation were devastating. Accordingly, a statute was enacted in 1391 ordering that all lands held to the use of the church should either be disposed of or be amortized by the following Michaelmas under pain of forfeiture.[40] The upsurge in the licence figures to an all-time peak of 378 in 1392 which can be seen in the Graph is a sufficient comment on the extent of the practice, although the total inevitably included licences granted to those with tender consciences from other causes and some alert opportunists.[41]

Evasion of the 1279 statute through feoffees and through leases raises the question of how far evasion in general was prevalent. A scheme in use in the nineteenth century was for religious to acquire property in their secular names. Mark Pattison in his *Memoirs* recorded how some Rosminian nuns "evade the Mortmain Act by vesting property legally in the name of a member, while really it is at the disposal of the general". The same procedure was followed by the community at Llanthony in Wales. There is very little evidence that the medieval church found this approach useful.[42] A legal fiction which did find favour for a short time was for the church to sue for the recovery of property which had never been in its possession. Until 1285 it was possible, with the collusion of the grantor, who would fail to answer the case, for holdings to be awarded legally to the church by default. In that year, the second Statute of Westminster ordered that in such instances inquiry should be made as to the initial title, with forfeiture as the penalty for fraudulence.[43]

With the option of collusive actions removed, most illegal activities

---

[40] *The Statutes of the Realm*, 9 vols. (Rec. Comm., 1810-22), ii, pp. 79-80.

[41] See above, p. 206; only six licences out of the entire 378 were granted after Michaelmas (29 Sept.).

[42] Mark Pattison, *Memoirs* (London, 1885), p. 192; A. Calder-Marshall, *The Enthusiast* (London, 1962), p. 192. The canon law ruling on private property was probably an effective bar to this device in the medieval period.

[43] *Statutes of the Realm*, i, p. 87, ch. 32. Examples of this being carried out can be seen in *Year Books XII-XIII Edward III*, ed. L. O. Pike (Rolls Series, 1885), pp. 124, 334.

seem to have taken much the same form as legal acquisitions under licence, with the omission of the final seal of royal approval. Examples can easily be found. Thorney Abbey was unofficially active in the land market under Abbot William de Clapton (1305-23). He employed his nephew, helped by William de Spanneby, to consolidate the abbey's earlier gains at the expense of free tenants on its demesne manors. The rubric to one of the charters copied into the abbey cartulary is informative. The property was:

> granted to Robert de Clapton nephew of lord William II abbot of Thorney, which land and meadow with the land and tenements recorded below the abbot bought with the goods of the monastery. And he arranged that the aforesaid Robert should enter those lands and tenements in the name of the monastery and that at an opportune moment the tenements should be converted to the use of the monastery.

It is unlikely that Abbot William ever intended to act legally, since Robert surrendered everything at intervals between 1307 and 1312. To make the transfer less obvious, and perhaps as a reward, Robert received the tenements back on a life lease. Monastic control was thus postponed, but the complicated web of tenure was an added protection.[44]

The only licence concerning land taken out by Thorney during this period was a general licence, obtained in 1314, authorizing acquisitions to an annual value of twenty pounds.[45] No action was taken on this until some years after the abbot's death. It may have been designed as an insurance against discovery, since in 1312 for the first time, the crown had permitted religious houses to offset illegal acquisitions against such licences. This leniency was the result of Edward II's financial difficulties at the time of his defence of Piers Gaveston. The general licence granted to Selby Abbey for this purpose had been paid for in part by the cancellation of royal debts for the provisioning of the household. Other general licences of a more orthodox type were also financed in the same way.[46]

The prior and convent of Ely showed almost recidivist tendencies with a stream of illegal gains, most of which were exposed. The acquisition of part of a messuage in Sutton (Cambs.) bought by Stephen Prepositus "for the use of the prior on the prior's order" in 1303 apparently escaped detection, but in 1298 they had paid the swingeing fine of five hundred marks for the attempted appropriation of Wisbech and Foxton churches. In 1311 they again fined for the

---

[44] "The Red Book", fos. 126, xxxviii, 127v-8v, xlv-xlvi, 66v, ci, 67-8, ciiii-cvi, 106-7, lxxviii-lxxxi.
[45] *Cal. Pat. Rolls, 1313-17*, p. 183.
[46] *Cal. Pat. Rolls, 1307-13*, pp. 432, 435, 442.

unlicensed acquisition of one messuage and one hundred and sixty acres of arable in Eriswell (Suff.) and two further pardons were required in the early 1320s.[47] The fate of Ely illustrates the determination with which the crown pursued those acting in defiance of the statute. No offence was too ancient for punishment and the property could not always be recovered upon payment of a fine.

After 1391, when the major loop-hole in the law, concerning feoffees, was closed and many of the more dubious transactions regularized, the risks attaching to the unlicensed pursuit on any scale of land belonging to lay fees were even greater. Few such gains are likely to have escaped detection permanently, so extant proceedings probably give a fair guide as to their incidence. Exposure was much less certain where the church already figured at some point in the tenurial hierarchy. Thorney's experience showed that it was possible to buy back land on demesne manors with impunity. Discovery could be avoided where purchases were moderate and some precautions were taken. Yet precisely because caution was the key to success, overall gains of this nature should not be sufficiently numerous to impair the picture of accessions to the church provided by the patent rolls.

A disquieting feature attending royal enforcement of the law from the point of view of the church, and one which balances the picture of illicit gains, was the danger of wrongful accusation and the consequent confiscation of property. On several occasions Crowland Abbey was unjustly accused of contravening the statute. In 1315, the escheator was ordered to allow the monks peaceful possession of the manor of Dowdyke and the advowson of Sutterton (Lincs.) since an inquisition had shown that monastic tenure long antedated 1279. The matter did not end there. As late as 1321, the escheator was still threatening sequestration on the same grounds and the earlier writ was invoked against him. A further challenge to the same property was settled in 1329 after 5s. 8d. rent had been seized on the pretext that the earl of Richmond had granted it to the abbey without a licence. The details given in the Wrest Park cartulary suggest that the escheator had been maliciously misinformed. A similar case, at about the same date, occurred at Wigtoft (Lincs.). In 1299 the abbey had obtained a licence to receive three roods of land and the advowson there from Richard son of Peter de Hoddil. In spite of this, an inquisition accused the monks of illegal acquisition and the property was in the escheator's hands before the end of Edward II's reign, where it remained until at least July 1329. Another entry on the

---

[47] Camb. Univ. Lib., E.D.C., 1B/5, no. 299 dorse; *Cal. Pat. Rolls, 1292-1301,* p. 365; *ibid., 1307-13,* p. 387; *ibid., 1317-21,* p. 555; *ibid., 1321-4,* p. 108.

close rolls shows that a messuage and one bovate of land in Kirkby la Thorpe (Lincs.) had been taken into royal hands following an inquisition which had given incorrect information. The tenement had been surrendered by a tenant holding at will and not in fee. A final instance when Crowland land was impounded also appears to have been a mistake. A messuage in Oakington (Cambs.) had escheated through the death of its tenant without heirs and the abbey was accused of alienation without licence. A second inquisition upheld the abbey and in 1361 restoration was ordered.[48]

Crowland's experience adds a new dimension to any interpretation of the effects of the statute. Although the abbey's behaviour had been impeccably law-abiding on each of the occasions when it was challenged, seisin was lost for quite long periods. The ultimate restoration of income was hardly adequate compensation. This house was particularly unfortunate. Others escaped more lightly, but instances of unjustified accusation were by no means rare. Alvingham Priory, for example, also encountered problems of this sort, chiefly due to the date at which some of its holdings had been gained. The 1279 statute caught the canons in the process of acquiring the advowson of Yarburgh and other property in Yarburgh, Grainthorpe and Alvingham (Lincs.). Confusion as to the exact date of transfer emerged at inquisitions in 1289-90, 1291 and 1309. The escheator was almost certainly correct in suspecting that some unlicensed alienations to the priory had taken place, but the advowson of Yarburgh, queried in 1309, had been granted as early as 1275. A final compromise was achieved in 1327 when most of the disputed grants were confirmed in return for a twenty shilling fine.[49] The extent of the problem can be judged by a royal ordinance offering protection to those who could show that they had made their gains lawfully and permitting those who could not to make "a convenient fine".[50] The mortmain legislation and the lengthy processes by which it was enforced left the church exposed both to harassment and genuine mistake.

Although both illicit alienations to the church and false accusations of it occurred, there can be little doubt that the majority of ecclesiastical gains after 1279 were eventually brought under royal supervision

---

[48] *Cal. Close Rolls, 1313-18*, p. 143; *ibid., 1318-23*, p. 306; *ibid., 1327-30*, pp. 173-4, 480-1, 482; *ibid., 1360-4*, pp. 218-19; "The Wrest Park Cartulary", fos. 125r-v, ix, 126r-v, xi, 135v, v, 136v-7; *Cal. Pat. Rolls, 1292-1301*, p. 481.
[49] Bodleian Lib., MS. Laud 642, fos. 114v (parchment sewn in), 118v, 119v-20, 121r-v; Pub. Rec. Off., C143/16/12; *Cal. Close Rolls, 1307-13*, p. 113; *Cal. Pat. Rolls, 1327-30*, p. 167.
[50] *Statutes of the Realm*, i, pp. 302-3.

and that this need not have been unduly restrictive. The necessity for a licence in the event of permanent acquisition was an administrative inconvenience, but there is little reason to believe that such licences were stinted after the first two decades, nor that they necessarily curtailed freedom of action. In practical terms therefore, the church had considerable room for manoeuvre. A more serious aspect of governmental control was the additional expense that it entailed. This could place the church at a disadvantage *vis-à-vis* the laity when buying on the open market and also affect the profitability of purchases, particularly in the more difficult economic conditions of the later middle ages.

The Statute of Mortmain inevitably placed the church under some financial handicap, but the extent and importance of this varied. The cost of procuring a licence can be divided into two main constituents. First there were the routine expenses covering the cost of fees, the necessary inquisition *ad quod damnum* and other incidentals. A detailed account of such expenditure has survived for 1361 when the prior and convent of Ely acquired the manor and advowson of Mepal (Cambs.). Altogether £12 6s. 2½d. was disbursed. The most expensive part of the proceeding was the inquisition, when payments totalling £6 7s. 11d. were made to both officials and jurors, with the escheator receiving a pipe of Ely wine as well as forty shillings cash. Since the purchase price of the property was £241 13s. 4d. and a twenty mark pension for one lifetime, these expenses amounted to a surcharge of five per cent at the most.[51] Such a figure was by no means standard. Both the cost of the property to be alienated, supposing it were not a gift, and the cost of acquiring a licence varied considerably. The possible permutations make generalization difficult, but where licence costs formed only a small proportion of the overall expenditure, they were a tiresome but unimportant extra. Where, however, they were likely to be high, or the value of the projected alienation was slight, their incidence might be sufficient to discourage acquisition.

The second constituent in the cost of a licence was the fine which the crown might demand for its concession. At first sight the imposition of such fines appears haphazard, with the amount charged dependent upon royal vagary and the price each recipient was prepared to pay. In fact, a limited rationale can be observed behind their incidence. Royal policy can be seen as a progression. It appears from the patent rolls that the practice of licensing alienations

[51] S. J. A. Evans, "The Purchase and Mortification of Mepal by the Prior and Convent of Ely, 1361", *Eng. Hist. Rev.*, li (1936), pp. 119-20; Camb. Univ. Lib., E.D.C., 1B/23, unnumbered.

was not initially envisaged as a source of profit. As the Graph shows, no fines at all feature there until April 1299.[52] Absence from the patent rolls does not guarantee that they were not charged. The abbey of Shap received a licence permitting the alienation of the advowson of Warcop (Westm.) which was enrolled without mention of a fine in 1290, but the pipe rolls show a twenty pound fine and, owing to the death of the grantor before the transfer could be effected, two subsequent entries on the close rolls show the abbey petitioning for its pardon.[53] The pipe roll for 1298-9 shows St. John's Hospital, Northampton, liable for a forty mark fine for a licence to enter a lay fee in the previous year.[54] Such cases seem to be the exceptions rather than the rule, however, so that although the patent rolls cannot be taken as wholly reliable on this point, they seem to offer an accurate enough general picture.

In the century after 1299, fines appear on the patent rolls, but were far from universal.[55] It is this period which is the most exacting of interpretation. Attempts to correlate the sums charged with the value of the property to be acquired have proved abortive.[56] Values were not necessarily ignored, rather they formed one aspect only of an assessment. Others might include support from an influential sponsor, whether or not the property was held directly of the king, or even political conditions. Times of crisis or economic difficulty such as the last years of Edward I's reign or 1311-12 undoubtedly saw more rigorous exactions.[57] Discrimination was exercised both in relation to the recipient of the licence and its nature. General licences, such as that granted to Thorney in 1314, which allowed their beneficiaries to acquire property to a given annual value, were rarely burdened with fines. Only thirty-three out of the 781 granted between 1309, when they first appeared regularly, and 1377 were so charged. Once the general licence had been secured, accessions were made at the licensee's discretion, with a specific licence to cover each

---

[52] See above, p. 206.

[53] *Cal. Pat. Rolls, 1281-92*, p. 388; Pub. Rec. Off., E372/136, m. 7d and subsequent rolls; *Cal. Close Rolls, 1288-96*, p. 289; *ibid., 1296-1302*, p. 367.

[54] Pub. Rec. Off., E372/144, m. 4d. It is not immediately obvious to which transaction this applies. Property was alienated to St. John's in 1284, 1290 and 1299, and in the latter year an illegal acquisition was also discovered: *Cal. Pat. Rolls, 1281-92*, p. 353; *ibid., 1292-1301*, p. 403; *Cal. Close Rolls, 1279-88*, p. 289; *ibid., 1296-1302*, p. 267.

[55] See above, p. 206.

[56] K. L. Wood-Legh, *Studies in Church Life in England under Edward III* (Cambridge, 1934), p. 62.

[57] See above, p. 206; M. Prestwich, *War, Politics and Finance under Edward I* (London, 1972), p. 270; J. R. Maddicott, *Thomas of Lancaster 1307-22* (Oxford, 1970), chaps. iii-iv, pp. 114 ff.

individual gain. It was rare for fines to be charged at this stage either. When they occurred, they usually marked the last transaction before the general licence was exhausted and indicate that the final acquisition was deemed to exceed the permitted limit. Such was the case in 1361, when St. Osyth's paid a £2 fine for its last alienation under a general licence of 1333. Only £7 6s. 8d. of income was still outstanding, while the projected gain was assessed at £7 14s. 2d.[58] Until 1350 the mendicant orders, whose modest gains were usually for the enlargement of their premises, were normally exempt from fines. By contrast, licences for the foundation or augmentation of chantries show a high incidence of charges. The plague year of 1349 saw twenty-nine such licences incurring fines, as opposed to fifteen which did not. The comparison is even more telling if the eleven licences subject to general licences are discounted.[59] The diversity of practice regarding fines reflected the diversity of considerations applied in their imposition. This flexibility made it possible for the crown to combine a genuine concern for the needs and resources of the church with that of its own financial requirements.

Although many ecclesiastics were charged only a nominal sum or escaped payment altogether when acquiring property under licence, the element of uncertainty until a late stage in the procedure must have created its own problems. The development of general licences modified these by enabling planned expansion to a fixed target, usually free of charge. The benefit was short-lived however. After 1323 the crown began to draw a distinction between the valuation recorded in the inquisition *ad quod damnum* and that for which the property was to count against the general licence. The gulf between the two figures could mean that as little as a third of the face value of the licence was ultimately achieved. This is illustrated by alienations under a general licence granted to Crowland Abbey in 1327. According to its terms, the monks were allowed to acquire land and rent worth £20 per annum.[60] The Table below shows how this worked out in practice. Butley Priory was more fortunate in securing property worth £5 18s. 9¼d. under a 1321 licence for alienations to the value of £10 per annum and a further £13 15s. 5¾d. worth under a 1365 licence permitting alienations to the value of £20 per annum. In both cases the ultimate gains were nearer two thirds of the face value

---

[58] *Cal. Pat. Rolls, 1330-4*, p. 490; *ibid., 1340-3*, p. 565; *ibid., 1343-5*, p. 139; *ibid., 1361-4*, p. 48.
[59] Only five straightforward licences were free of fines in comparison with twenty-eight paying them.
[60] *Cal. Pat. Rolls, 1327-30*, p. 181.

TABLE

ALIENATIONS UNDER GENERAL LICENCE BY CROWLAND ABBEY

Date	Valuation of Inquisition *ad quod damnum*	Valuation against General Licence
1334	£2 8s. 5d.	£2 10s. 5d.
1336	14s. 0d.	£1 0s. 0d.
1377	13s. 4d.	£3 6s. 8d.
1398	£3 13s. 4d.	£13 2s. 11d.
Total	£7 9s. 1d.	£20 0s. 0d.

of the general licence.[61] Possibly the higher royal valuations were designed to combat habitual underestimates found when dealing with the government. Equally, they can be seen as the crown's growing awareness of the financial implications of mortmain procedure. Since the evidence implies that it was customary to permit alienations to the church under general licence free of charge, as long as the large number of such licences granted during the fourteenth century remained unfulfilled, they formed a barrier to the introduction of a more stringent policy towards fines. In effect, the crown's future freedom of action was mortgaged unless outstanding licences could be exhausted with artificial speed. From the middle of the century there was a slow but steady increase in the proportion of mortmain licences of all sorts for which fines were charged. This suggests that the crown was interested in extending liability and might therefore wish to see general licences more quickly satisfied. There are signs that general licences were receiving more cautious treatment in other respects. As a percentage of all licences granted, they showed a tendency to decline in the latter half of the century, and those granted by Richard II were more often the subject of fines.[62] It is instructive to see what happened in 1392 when the church, compelled to take out licences under pain of forfeiture, was at the royal mercy. Eighty-one per cent of the 378 mortmain licences of all types granted incurred fines. Sixty-nine general licences were judged fully satisfied, often with a fine charged on the last alienation. This compares with thirteen new general licences issued, all but one of which necessitated a fine.[63] Exploitation of the financial possibilities of

[61] J. N. L. Myres, "Notes on the History of Butley Priory, Suffolk", *Oxford Essays in Medieval History Presented to H. E. Salter* (Oxford, 1934), pp. 195-7.

[62] 20% of all the licences granted between 1310 and 1319 were general licences, 18% between 1320 and 1329, 16% between 1330 and 1339, 13% between 1340 and 1349, 15% between 1350 and 1359, 9% between 1360 and 1369, 8% between 1370 and 1379, 11% between 1380 and 1389, and 8% between 1390 and 1399.

[63] Six of these licences for which fines were paid also included the foundation of guilds and are not therefore truly representative.

mortmain was becoming more intensive, although it was still far from invariable.

By the end of the middle ages there are hints that practice concerning fines had hardened yet further into an established scale of charges based on the value of the property to be alienated. Henry Fillongley writing to his uncle Sir John Fastolf about the foundation of a college at Caister c. 1456 informed him that he would have to pay five hundred marks fine for every hundred marks that he wished to alienate for its endowment. This may have been an individual bargain since he sourly adds that there was no hope of the royal officials giving the licence more cheaply, but the sum charged was not random.[64] By the sixteenth century, it was accepted legal theory that a fine should amount to three years' income from the land alienated.[65] Theory and practice can be very different however. There is no indication that Peterborough Abbey, for example, paid fines on any of its fifteenth- or sixteenth-century gains. Yet although exceptions were made and individual negotiation remained, some systematization of charges had taken place. If Edward I had not had money at the forefront of his mind when the mortmain legislation was framed, it quickly came to assume a more dominant place both in his own and in those of his successors.

Fines levied at three times the annual income from the property to be alienated represented a considerable surcharge. It has been calculated that the market price of land or rent in the fifteenth century was approximately twenty times its annual value.[66] At this rate a fine amounted to an additional 15 per cent on the purchase price. For most of the period after 1279 acquisitions could be made more cheaply, but it should also be remembered that the workings of the Statute of Mortmain made it necessary to obtain licences not only from the king, but from any intermediate lord affected by the alienation. This too involved outlay. Dr. Wood-Legh cited several examples of monetary compensation for lords whose interests were to be harmed by the foundation of chantries.[67] In 1358 Crowland Abbey extracted 20s. rent from John de Kirketon in return for allowing him to alienate some abbey land to Holbeach Hospital.[68] Some lords, like Hugh Despenser and his wife giving their assent to an

---

[64] *The Paston Letters,* ed. J. Gairdner, library edn., 6 vols. (London, 1904), iii, p. 98, no. 340.
[65] Bean, *The Decline of English Feudalism,* p. 66, note 1.
[66] K. B. McFarlane, *The Nobility of Later Medieval England* (Oxford, 1973), p. 57.
[67] K. L. Wood-Legh, *Perpetual Chantries in Britain* (Cambridge, 1965), p. 47.
[68] *Cal. Pat. Rolls, 1358-61,* p. 93.

alienation to Tewkesbury Abbey in 1326, were prepared to settle for spiritual benefits alone, but even so the cost and inconvenience of securing the licence was an added imposition.[69] Taken together, a fine and the cost of obtaining all the necessary licences could inflict a burden on the church varying from the petty to the punitive, with little advance assurance as to which it was to be. The only crumb of comfort was that anyone, including laymen, who wanted to acquire land held directly of the king was subject to very similar limitations.[70]

Mortmain legislation involved the church in expense and effort. It did not greatly inhibit its freedom of action. There was little to prevent acquisition if the extra cost was judged worthwhile. The initiative therefore lay with the church. It only remains to consider how far this was taken. A simple computation of licences is in itself a poor guide to the amount of property passing into ecclesiastical hands because of the variation in the size of individual alienations. It does, however, indicate the number of churchmen who wished to receive property. Allowing for annual fluctuations, numbers built up over the first two decades of the fourteenth century and were sustained at a fairly high level until the year of the Black Death. After 1349, with the exception of the abnormal year 1392, numbers slowly declined.[71] Such a pattern tallies with what is known about movements in the lay land market. There too buying continued until the middle of the century, after which the relaxing pressure on land made it less rewarding either to cultivate or rent estates.[72]

A similar pattern, if not the exact chronology, was also to be expected from the long-term trends in ecclesiastical acquisition. The great era of endowment was long past. The ancient black monk houses had received the bulk of their property in the pre-conquest period. The twelfth century saw further foundations with new orders and further generous patronage, but already the scale was reduced.[73] Succeeding centuries found few patrons like Mary countess of Pembroke (d. 1377) prepared to set up and endow new houses.[74]

[69] *Ibid.*, *1324-7*, pp. 318-19.
[70] Bean, *The Decline of English Feudalism*, pp. 67 ff.
[71] See above, p. 206. This is so even allowing for evasion.
[72] G. A. Holmes, *The Estates of the Higher Nobility in Fourteenth-Century England* (Cambridge, 1957), pp. 113-14.
[73] R. W. Southern, "The Place of Henry I in English History", *Proc. Brit. Acad.*, xlviii (1962), pp. 138-9.
[74] She founded the abbey for Franciscan nuns at Denney, and Pembroke College, Cambridge. She also planned but never achieved a Carthusian house at Horne (Surrey) and another from estates in Hertfordshire: H. Jenkinson, "Mary de Sancto Paulo, Foundress of Pembroke College, Cambridge", *Archaeologia*, lxvi (1915), pp. 418 ff.

For those already established, the size of gifts dwindled with the status of their donors.[75] Landed families had registered their spiritual credit and society was no longer in sympathy with the ideals of the regular clergy. Increasingly new property was purchased rather than given. It was this phase of expansion which the 1279 statute interrupted in north-east Northamptonshire. Our interpretation of the effects of the mortmain legislation on the land market largely depends on whether the religious would have wished to continue such purchasing policies. The concept of husbanding wealth to the glory of God was deep-rooted and land was one of the few forms of investment open to those with surplus capital. Yet there are signs that thirteenth-century purchases were as much a defensive measure as an outlet for high farming profits. Both Ramsey and Peterborough Abbeys found it necessary to augment the income of obedientiaries. At Ramsey this was not just a response to higher numbers and a higher standard of living. It was also an attempt to make good deficiencies in the food farms which appeared in the third quarter of the century.[76] There are signs too that buyers found it difficult to raise ready cash. Thorney Abbey bought the manor of Clapton by means of leasing the demesne manor of Twywell (Northants.) to the vendor for his lifetime.[77] Crowland Abbey paid for a manor in Gedney (Lincs.) by installments in the 1260s and Peterborough borrowed part of the purchase price of Southorpe from Elias of Beckingham.[78] Liquidity should not be confused with solvency, but there is no suggestion of a superabundance of capital in search of an outlet. By the mid-fourteenth century it is even doubtful whether some monastic finances could inspire sufficient confidence to raise a loan.[79] Thus the 1279 statute erupted on to a thriving land market, but one likely to contract in the not too distant future. However much its immediate impact was restrictive and its subsequent economic pressure inhibited acquisition, it only reinforced trends which had already come into being of their own accord.

A special restriction on land passing into mortmain which was not considered earlier must be set in this historical context. Occasionally

---

[75] King, *Peterborough Abbey*, pp. 53-4; S. G. Raban, *The Estates of Thorney and Crowland* (Univ. of Cambridge, Dept. of Land Economy, Occasional Paper, vii, Cambridge, 1977), chaps. iii, iv.
[76] Raftis, *The Estates of Ramsey Abbey*, pp. 112-13, 217, 237; King, *Peterborough Abbey*, pp. 91-3.
[77] "The Red Book", fo. 228v.
[78] "The Wrest Park Cartulary", fos. 116v-17, xlii, 119v, xlviii; *Henry of Pytchley's Book of Fees*, ed. Mellows, p. 62.
[79] Wood-Legh, *Studies in Church Life under Edward III*, chap. i.

under Edward II and in the early years of Edward III houses making gains under general licence were confined to recoveries from their own tenants. Thorney was limited in this way in its general licence of 1314, as was Peterborough in 1327.[80] In practice such limitations are unlikely to have been onerous, since horizons were already narrowing. Peterborough in particular had concentrated on buying back its own fee before any restraints were introduced, while Crowland Abbey, which was not obliged to recover its own holdings, did so in three out of its four series of acquisitions under another general licence of 1327.[81] A more widespread embargo from the beginning of Edward III's reign prevented the alienation under general licence of land held directly of the king. Although more licences were affected, this was not such a strait jacket: there were plenty of alternatives to land held in chief, many of which might be more readily available. The restriction is interesting, therefore, more as a demonstration of the crown's concern for its own welfare than as a hindrance to the church.

Licences to alienate in mortmain fell to a lower level after 1349; they did not disappear. Whatever the economic situation, there were always some, both inside the church and out, who needed to acquire. Laymen might wish to provide for daughters or younger sons. John of Gaunt paid five thousand marks for an estate to settle on his bastard son in the last decade of the century.[82] The successful, whether soldiers, merchants or officials might thirst for landed eminence or to save their souls by means of one of the currently fashionable chantries. Sir John Fastolf in mid-century had sought both.[83] University expansion had its own dynamic. One of Crowland Abbey's few late acquisitions was two houses in Cambridge to accommodate its monk students.[84] At the humblest level, a parish priest might finally secure land for a much needed rectory. To all of these, financial considerations were largely irrelevant. High costs and low profitability were a disadvantage but not a disincentive to purchase.

Much of the evidence for these views about the effect of mortmain

[80] "The Red Book", fo. 33, iiii; *Cal. Pat. Rolls, 1327-30*, p. 131; the MS. patent roll for 1314 records Thorney's limitation although it has not been noted in the calendar: Pub. Rec. Off., C66/142, m. 18.

[81] Acquisitions took place in 1334, 1336, 1377 and 1398. Only the last of these — a messuage and two shops in London — was not an abbey fee: *Cal. Pat. Rolls, 1334-8*, pp. 42-3, 301-2; ibid., *1377-81*, p. 36; ibid., *1396-9*, p. 358.

[82] McFarlane, *The Nobility of Later Medieval England*, pp. 55, 84.

[83] K. B. McFarlane, "The Investment of Sir John Fastolf's Profits of War", *Trans. Roy. Hist. Soc.*, 5th ser., vii (1957), pp. 104 ff.; see above, p. 222.

[84] *Cal. Pat. Rolls, 1422-9*, p. 475; Brit. Mus., Add. MS. 5845, fos. 93v-4.

legislation has been drawn from eastern England, but licence figures for the country at large suggest a wider validity. Differences between types of ecclesiastical institution were more significant than geographical location. As an extreme example, alien priories were in no position to extend their possessions, wherever they were situated. Secular cathedrals, on the other hand, had a function and a body of officials whose importance made voluminous mortmain dealings a matter of course. If institutions might vary, so could the nature of their accessions. Land was not the only form of medieval wealth. One result of the statute may have been to divert pious expression into cash or luxury gifts. The Percy family in the fifteenth century financed its chantries out of income instead of endowments.[85] Mary de Sancto Paulo's landed benefactions were matched by other grants of money and plate. She gave two hundred pounds towards the foundation of the London Charterhouse during her lifetime and at her death an assortment of houses received cash bequests, relics, jewels and plate.[86] A building project might satisfy a patron where formerly land would have been the obvious choice.[87] It was not only donors who might find their objectives transformed. For the monks of Christchurch Cathedral Priory at least, plate and ornaments proved a more attractive investment than property in the later middle ages.[88] In spite of this, land remained the foundation of the church's wealth and much of its power. It was land which concerned contemporaries. The 1279 Statute of Mortmain was an expression of this concern, but it was issued long after the damage had been done. Its implementation may have had a limited success in diverting patronage into less alarming channels and in taxing such territorial gains as were made, but there is no convincing evidence that it had anything other than superficial effect on ecclesiastical participation in the land market.

[85] McFarlane, *The Nobility of Later Medieval England*, p. 54.
[86] Jenkinson, *Archaeologia*, lxvi (1915), pp. 417-18.
[87] McFarlane, *The Nobility of Later Medieval England*, p. 95.
[88] R. A. L. Smith, *Canterbury Cathedral Priory* (Cambridge, 1943), p. 13.

8. *Minor landlords in England and medieval agrarian capitalism*

R. H. BRITNELL

MANORIAL ACCOUNTS OF THE THIRTEENTH AND FOURTEENTH CENTURIES are so remarkably informative about the management of large estates that the comparatively inadequate representation of small estates affords poor grounds for complaint. Variations between the manors of large estates illustrate prevailing diversities of practice quite well enough for most purposes. Yet it is unfortunately true that the unrepresentative character of extant accounts hampers inquiry into one interesting aspect of social change. Kosminsky's studies in the Hundred Rolls showed structural differences between large and small manors which affected the extent to which their incomes depended on trade. Since small manors were characteristic of minor landlords, he argued that the response of such landlords to economic opportunity would tend to be qualitatively different from that of large landlords. "The small manor . . .", he says, "as is shown by its structure and the nature of its rents, evidently never attained full development as a feudal manor, and adapted itself to the requirements of the market by other methods which were a definite step towards 'more capitalistic forms of economic life' . . .".[1] This implies that surviving account rolls are unlikely to portray accurately the qualities of entrepreneurship to be found among medieval landlords.

Kosminsky questioned whether or not small estates kept detailed records at all,[2] and it is indeed unlikely that many did so at the time the Hundred Rolls were compiled. These were still early days in the development of estate records. By the second quarter of the fourteenth century, however, surviving archives are more varied and consequently more encouraging for the history of small estates. From this period account rolls survive from four small estates in north-eastern Essex, and they yield information of much the same quality as that to be extracted from those of larger estates, except that they are too few to provide anything but "still pictures". The accounts conform to the standardized accounting procedures in general use in the first half of the fourteenth century.[3] On the face of each account appear money receipts

* The research for this article was supported by Durham University Research Fund.

[1] E. A. Kosminsky, *Studies in the Agrarian History of England in the Thirteenth Century*, ed. R. H. Hilton, trans. R. Kisch (Studies in Mediaeval History, viii, Oxford, 1956), p. x.

[2] *Ibid.*, p. 269.

[3] Except in the case of the earliest Langenhoe account, which is continuous from the face to the dorse and has no record of livestock: Essex Record Office (hereafter E.R.O.), D/DC/2/11.

and money expenditures: on the dorse are produce receipts and produce expenditures. In the case of three of the estates, at least, the surviving accounts appear to have belonged to a year-by-year series,
though only at one of these was the drawing up of accounts explicitly a
charge on the manor.[4] The fact that so exacting a form of record-keeping was common to both large and small estates by the decade before
the Black Death is striking testimony to the development of clerical
professionalism during the preceding seventy or eighty years.[5]

The first section of the following study examines the estates from
which these four sets of accounts originate, describing briefly their
size, their ownership and their administration. The second section
shows that the structures of the manors documented were similar to
those of Kosminsky's small landowners. The third section uses the evidence of the accounts to investigate Kosminsky's hypotheses about the
importance of trade on such estates.

I

From the northern edge of Essex there are accounts of 1341/2 and
1342/3 from the manor of "Punt' in Bolemere",[6] which is the manor
known to Morant as Pontes in Bulmer.[7] The manor was part of the
scattered inheritance of the Fitz Ralph family, whose head at this time
was a knight,[8] Ralph son of William Fitz Ralph. In the late 1340s
the family held seven properties in Essex and Suffolk assessed at $2\frac{7}{24}$
knights' fees, and three more properties totalling approximately a
knight's fee were subinfeudated.[9] The home manor was at Pebmarsh:[10] wool from Pontes was sent there in 1342 and 1343, and deliveries of poultry may be interpreted as provisions for the household
there. Ralph was also engaged in direct demesne farming at Great
Henny. Pontes was in liaison with Pebmarsh and Great Henny for exchanges of livestock and seed-corn.

    [4] In both surviving Pontes accounts the clerk composing the account is paid 2s. 6d.
by prior agreement (de conuencione): Public Record Office (hereafter P.R.O.), S.C.6/
845/29ʳ, 30ʳ. At Langenhoe in 1347/8 the serjeant accounted for 2½d. spent on parchment for court rolls and accounts: E.R.O., D/DEl/M222ʳ, 223ʳ.
    [5] Manorial Records of Cuxham, Oxfordshire, circa 1200-1359, ed. P. D. A. Harvey
(Hist. MSS. Comm., JP 23, Oxfordshire Rec. Soc., l, London, 1976), pp. 20-1, 36-42.
    [6] P.R.O., S.C.6/845/29 (1341/2), S.C.6/845/30 (1342/3). Dates given in this form
refer, throughout this study, to the financial year from Michaelmas to Michaelmas.
    [7] P. Morant, The History and Antiquities of the County of Essex, 2 vols. (London,
1768), ii, p. 314. Morant calls it the manor of "Bonets and Poultes, otherwise Pontes",
and it is marked as "Bonets" on the map of Essex by Chapman and André published in
1777.
    [8] Parliamentary Writs, ed. F. Palgrave, 2 vols. in 4 (Rec. Comm., London,
1827-34), ii pt. 2, p. 589; The Feet of Fines for Essex, ed. R. E. G. Kirk et al., 4 vols.
(Essex Archaeol. Soc., Colchester, 1899-1964), iii, p. 90.
    [9] Feudal Aids, ii, pp. 163, 165, 166, 179, and v, pp. 49, 50, 69, 77.
    [10] Parliamentary Writs, i, p. 354b; Calendar of Patent Rolls, 1313-17, p. 109;
Calendar of Charter Rolls, iv, p. 455. In 1327 William Fitz Ralph was the biggest
taxpayer in Pebmarsh: P.R.O., E.179/107/13, m.14ʳ.

The second manor is that of "Braxstede", later called Kelvedon Hall in Braxted.[11] A view of account from Easter to Michaelmas 1330 was presented by John Her, serjeant of John de Kelleuedon.[12] John de Kelvedon had gained possession of the family estates in July 1322 shortly after the death of his father,[13] and in 1325 he and his wife secured their title to three messuages, a mill, 700 acres of land, 20 acres of meadow, 60 acres of pasture, 40 acres of wood and 10 marks of rent in Braxted and neighbouring villages.[14] Kelvedon Hall with $289\frac{1}{2}$ acres under crops in 1334/5 and $19\frac{1}{2}$ acres of meadow in 1330 must account for the greater part of the possessions so described. The manor was still in the hands of the Kelvedon family later in the fourteenth century.[15] But the second surviving account of the manor, from 1334/5, describes it as belonging to John de Schympplyngford,[16] whose relationship to the Kelvedon family is unknown. His estates were more scattered than those of John de Kelvedon had been. Their core lay in Suffolk, the main properties being the manor of Kirton in Shotley[17] and the manor of Shimplingford in Assington.[18] Both of these manors occur in the account of Kelvedon Hall in 1334/5: the serjeant received livestock from Assington, sent one plough-horse to Assington and sent grain and livestock to Kirton. The Shimplingford family also had smaller properties in Cockfield, Alpheton and Shimpling, later described as comprising 100 acres of arable, 6 acres of meadow, 10 acres of pasture, 16 acres of wood and 10s. 0d. of rent.[19]

The third manor is called "Wykes" or "Wykys" on the three surviving accounts. William de Atherby was its lord at the time of the first and second of these accounts, those for 1343/4 and for the eight months from Michaelmas 1346 to 31 May 1347. Thomas le Boteler had taken his place at the time of the third, from 31 May to Michaelmas 1347.[20] The manor constituted part of the later manor of Carbonels, having indeed formerly belonged to the Carbonel family,[21] but

---

[11] Morant, *History and Antiquities of the County of Essex*, ii, p. 153.
[12] E.R.O., D/DU/19/26A.
[13] *Calendar of Close Rolls, 1318-23*, p. 475.
[14] *Feet of Fines for Essex*, ii, p. 217.
[15] Morant, *History and Antiquities of the County of Essex*, ii, p. 153; W. A. Copinger, *The Manors of Suffolk*, 7 vols. (London and Manchester, 1905-11), iii, p. 108.
[16] E.R.O., D/DU/19/27.
[17] *Feudal Aids*, v, pp. 24, 48; *Suffolk in 1327, Being a Subsidy Return*, ed. S. H. A. Hervey (Woodbridge, 1906), p. 1; S. H. A. Hervey, *Shotley Parish Records* (Bury St. Edmunds, 1912), pp. 253-4.
[18] *Feudal Aids*, v, p. 69; Copinger, *Manors of Suffolk*, i, p. 20.
[19] Hervey, *Shotley Parish Records*, p. 12.
[20] E.R.O., D/DU/40/75 (1343/4), D/DU/40/76 (Michaelmas 1346-31 May 1347), D/DU/40/77 (31 May-Michaelmas 1347).
[21] There are four indications. 1, The records derive from the archive of the Mannock family, which held Carbonels in the fifteenth century: Morant, *History and Antiquities of the County of Essex*, i, p. 467. 2, The Boteler family acquired Carbonels in the fourteenth century: *ibid.* 3, Newton, held with Wix in 1343/4 by William de Atherby, was a former Carbonel manor: *Calendar of Charter Rolls*, iii, p. 22; *Calen-*

it did not contain all the property which that family had possessed in Wix.[22] From the accounts it is evident that William de Atherby had possession of another former Carbonel manor, the manor of Newton by Sudbury in Suffolk, for cheese, an ox and a plough-horse were sent there in 1343/4 and an ox and plough-horse were received from there during the same year. Little is known of William de Atherby, and nothing at all is known of his title to these properties, which he had probably acquired by 1339.[23] It is clear from the accounts that he was not normally resident in Wix. Deliveries of rushes, wild fowl, rabbits and red herrings to Sudbury in 1346/7, together with most of the cash surplus from the manor, imply that he was living there for at least part of the year. In the same year he was also on at least one occasion in the house of Nicholas Benorth (probably an inn) in Ipswich, and cash was sent to him there. His successor as lord of the manor at Carbonels, Thomas le Boteler, was heir by marriage to the Carbonel estates.[24] He may already have held the manor of Great Waldingfield, to which sheep and cows were sent from Wix in the summer of 1347.

The last set of accounts to be considered is a sequence from "Langenhoo" or "Langenho" (that is, Langenhoe) dating from 1324/5, 1338/9, 1342/3, 1344/5 and 1347/8.[25] At the time of the earliest account the manor was being managed for a woman, probably because Lionel de Bradenham was a minor.[26] He held three-quarters of a knight's fee in Langenhoe in 1328, but he does not appear in the subsidy lists either for the twentieth of 1327 or for the fifteenth of 1334.[27] Lionel had come of age and married by 1338,[28] however, and his name appears in the heading of the accounts for 1338/9 and 1344/5. He held the manor by inheritance.[29] There is no evidence of his holding more land in demesne than this manor and an outlying holding at Abberton. In 1342/3, for example, grain was received from Abberton and cows

(note 21 cont.)
dar of Inquisitions Post Mortem, vii, no. 502, p. 354. 4, Great Waldingfield, held with Wix in 1347 by Thomas le Boteler, was another former Carbonel manor: Feudal Aids, v, pp. 29, 69; Calendar of Inquisitions Post Mortem, vii, no. 502, p. 353.

[22] The accounts record an annual rent of 2s. 10d. paid at "le Parkhalle". The Parkhall had belonged to John Carbonel at his death in 1333: Calendar of Inquisitions Post Mortem, vii, no. 502, p. 353.

[23] In 1339 a man of Newton was pardoned for having robbed William de Atherby: Calendar of Patent Rolls, 1338-40, p. 339.

[24] Copinger, Manors of Suffolk, i, pp. 71, 238-9.

[25] E.R.O., D/DC/2/11 (1324/5), D/DC/2/12 (1338/9), D/DEl/M220 (1342/3), D/DEl/M221 (1344/5), D/DEl/M222 (Michaelmas 1347-Easter 1348), D/DEl/M223 (Easter-Michaelmas 1348).

[26] The farmer of cows "had an allowance by [permission of] the lady" and oats were given "for flour for the lady's famuli": E.R.O., D/DC/2/11 r-d.

[27] Calendar of Inquisitions Post Mortem, vii, no. 160, p. 127; P.R.O., E.179/107/13, m.6d, E.179/107/17, m.8r.

[28] Feet of Fines for Essex, iii, p. 46.

[29] There had been an earlier settlement of the manor on Simon de Bradenham and his wife: ibid., ii, p. 61.

were sent there. The only record of subinfeudated property is of a later date than the period of the accounts.[30]

Inevitably much responsibility for agricultural work and for commercial transactions on these manors devolved upon manorial officers, as in the case of larger estates. On the Fitz Ralph estates, for example, Edmund atte Noke at Pebmarsh is described as serjeant (*serviens*), Robert Dous at Great Henny as reeve (*prepositus*) and Thomas Weynild at Pontes by both terms.[31] Lionel de Bradenham had one serjeant at Langenhoe and another at Abberton.[32] A serjeant's duties depended upon the size and character of the manor where he served. At Kelvedon Hall in 1334/5 the serjeant had under him a substantial staff — a hayward (*messor*), six ploughmen, a carter and a housemaid, all employed for the whole year, a swineherd for thirty-five weeks, an employee with various unskilled tasks for twenty-seven weeks and a gardener for ten weeks. In such circumstances most of his time could be devoted to supervision and commercial operations. On the small manor of Pontes, by contrast, Thomas Weynild served as cowman and shepherd in addition to his duties as serjeant, and at harvest time he was reap-reeve.[33] The only subordinate demesne staff (*famuli*) were two ploughmen employed the whole year and a man employed for six weeks in each year at the winter sowing to water the furrows.[34] On small estates this low level of specialization was presumably common.

One would expect minor landlords to be more personally concerned with the details of manorial administration than the lords of large estates. The best examples of landlord supervision are from the two most compact estates — Langenhoe and Kelvedon Hall under John de Kelvedon. Lionel de Bradenham's household resided in Langenhoe,[35] and he was able to exercise a close control over the running of the manor. He made contracts with purchasers of grain and made gifts of produce.[36] Sometimes he directly paid manorial expenses from his own funds,[37] and sometimes he made cash available without tally to the ser-

[30] *Calendar of Inquisitions Post Mortem*, xii, no. 225, p. 200.

[31] The officers of Pebmarsh and Great Henny are named, for example, in the livestock accounts for 1341/2: P.R.O., S.C.6/845/29ᵈ.

[32] E.R.O., D/DEl/M223ʳ.

[33] He is described in the cash and grain accounts as "acting in turn as reeve [or serjeant], cowman and shepherd": P.R.O., S.C.6/845/29ʳ⁻ᵈ, 30ʳ⁻ᵈ.

[34] This temporary *famulus*, who appears in the grain accounts, is described as *spargen[s] sulcos*: see Walter of Henley, *Husbandry*, c.50, in *Walter of Henley and Other Treatises on Estate Management and Accounting*, ed. D. Oschinsky (Oxford, 1971), p. 322; and cf. p. 166.

[35] *Calendar of Patent Rolls, 1364-7*, p. 55.

[36] For example, "Item, sold by way of gifts from the lord and the lady, as also for a quarter of salt for the lord's household, 1 quarter 2 bushels 1 peck . . . Item, sold to William Buk, 10 quarters 4 bushels, by prior agreement with the lord (*per conuencionem domini*)": E.R.O., D/DC/2/12ᵈ, wheat account.

[37] For example, "Nothing [is entered] here for threshing because [it was paid for] by the lord": E.R.O., D/DEl/M222ʳ.

jeant.[38] Similarly, though John de Kelvedon lived in Cambridge for part of the period of the surviving account of 1330, he is on record as having personally supervised and directed a sale of timber. Even on estates such as those of Ralph son of William, John de Shimplingford and William de Atherby, where a scattered distribution of property reduced the lord's immediate powers of supervision, the evidence of direct personal contact between lord and manor is good. In each case the lord visited the manor from time to time, and in some cases frequently. Ralph son of William was at Pontes for hunting in 1341/2.[39] John de Shimplingford visited Kelvedon Hall more than once during 1334/5.[40] William de Atherby visited Wix more than once in 1343/4[41] and in 1346/7 he went there five times in the course of eight months.

Fragmented estates such as these could hardly avoid the need for supplementary supervision. Local clergy were of assistance at Pontes, where John the rector of Bulmer frequently supervised the manorial serjeant — in witnessing commercial transactions, counting new-born lambs, making small payments to demesne staff or paying fines at neighbouring manors[42] — and at Kelvedon Hall in 1330, where Sir John de Tendring witnessed purchases of livestock made in the lord's absence. Manorial officers from one manor might be sent to supervise those on another, as when in 1342/3 the serjeant of Pebmarsh went to supervise sales of timber from Pontes.[43] On one estate, moreover, there was a salaried intermediate official between lord and demesne staff: William de Atherby employed a bailiff for the general supervision of his estates, for in 1343/4 the Wix accounts note that he had been paid at Newton;[44] Thomas le Boteler subsequently employed a relative in the same capacity.[45] These examples provide an interesting insight into the problems of administering even small estates but they do not dispose of the contention that minor landlords were likely to busy themselves with minor matters. It can also be shown that the relatives

---

[38] For example, "[Received] from the lord for costs of harvesting, £3. 3s. 0d. without tally": E.R.O., D/DEl/M220ʳ.

[39] In 1341/2, 8d. was allowed for the expenses incurred on account of the lord's hunting: P.R.O., S.C.6/845/29ʳ.

[40] "Item, for the lord's expenses at his visits, £1. 12s. 6d. by tallies": E.R.O., D/DU/19/27ʳ.

[41] "For the lord's expenses on one occasion, 4d. And the lord paid the rest of his expenses at his departures": E.R.O., D/DU/40/75ʳ.

[42] For example, "For 2 quarters 2 bushels of wheat sold to Philip Bogays in October by view of Sir John the rector (per visum domini Johannis rectoris), 7s. 6d."; "Given to famuli carrying grain, 1d. by view of Sir John". Only 9 lambs were received, "because 33 ewes [were] sterile, by view of Sir John, rector of Bol'": P.R.O., S.C.6/845/30ʳ⁻ᵈ.

[43] "For 4 bent oaks sold by view of Sir John and Edmund ate Nok', 6s. 0d. the lot (ingrosso)": P.R.O., S.C.6/845/30ʳ.

[44] "Paid to the bailiff nothing, because [he was paid] at Newton": E.R.O., D/DU/40/75ᵈ.

[45] "Seneschal's expenses. For the expenses of Sir John le Boteler and John Thurgor by one sealed tally (per j talliam sigillatam), 1s. 8½d.": E.R.O., D/DU/40/77ʳ.

of minor landlords were potential recruits for manorial duties. The serjeant at Kelvedon Hall in 1334/5 was Constantine de Shimplingford. If John de Shimplingford had only just taken possession of the manor, as its extensive restocking with grain and livestock in that year would imply, it can easily be explained why he wanted a member of the family to superintend operations there.[46]

II

The records of these estates can be used to illustrate an aspect of the economy not capable of illustration from the Hundred Rolls — the small estate's relation to the market. But the appropriateness of this evidence for a commentary on Kosminsky's conclusions must depend on the structural characteristics of the manors concerned. If the four estates were uncharacteristic of small estates generally, no evidence from them could be held to affect his deductions concerning the entrepreneurial qualities of small landlords.

Kosminsky found that the majority of manors belonging to small landowners were small — mostly having fewer than 500 acres of arable — and that the major component of such manors was demesne land. For an illustration of this type of estate he chose that of James Grim, whose manor of Sibthorp and Brampton in Huntingdonshire had in 1279 a demesne of 542 acres (or 347 acres) and rents amounting to £3. 13s. 10½d.[47] A comparison of the four manors under consideration with this example shows that three of them are easily compatible with Kosminsky's expectations. If two-thirds of the demesne were sown annually the arable area was about 450 acres at Kelvedon Hall and about 150 acres each at both Pontes and Carbonels.[48] Rents of assize at Kelvedon Hall were £2. 12s. 8d. in 1329/30 and £2. 0s. 2d. in 1334/5. At Pontes rents of assize were £1. 4s. 4½d. (of which 4½d. was no longer collected) and at Carbonels they amounted to £1. 8s. 10d. in 1343/4 and £1. 13s. 6d. in 1346/7. These manors continue to look small if demesne pasture farming is taken into account. The Kelvedon Hall account of 1330 records £3. 1s. 3d. received for wool sold, representing the value of about 120 fleeces.[49] The manor had a small herd of pigs but no dairy. Carbonels produced 123 fleeces for sale in 1344 and

[46] The serjeant's full name appears at the foot of the account: E.R.O., D/DU/19/27ʳ.

[47] Kosminsky, *Studies in the Agrarian History of England in the Thirteenth Century*, pp. 260-1, 265-6; cf. p. 96.

[48] At Pontes, where 84 acres were sown in 1341/2 and 91 acres 37 perches in 1342/3, a three-year rotation may be inferred from the recorded sequence of cropping in the "Pourtemerefeld" shift: P.R.O., S.C.6/845/29ᵈ, 30ᵈ. At Carbonels, where 99¼ acres 8 perches were sown in 1343/4 and 99¼ acres in 1346/7, the pattern of cropping was the same in both years: E.R.O., D/DU/40/75ᵈ, 76ᵈ.

[49] Fleeces from the nearby manor of Feering were sold at 6d. each in 1333: P.R.O., S.C.6/841/6ʳ⁻ᵈ.

116 in 1347, and there were also 20 cows leased to a farmer.[50] At Pontes pasture farming was even less significant: 71 fleeces were produced for sale in 1342 and 72 in 1343. Five cows were leased out in the former year and 6 in the latter. Langenhoe conforms less well to Kosminsky's type of small manor, for though its arable area was only about 250 acres[51] its rents of assize were £5. 8s. 1d. in 1324/5 and increased slightly over the next twenty years. Langenhoe was a marshland manor and pasture was a major source of income there. Judging from the sheep on the demesne in 1343, 1344 and 1345 wool production would have been about 504 fleeces. These divergences from Kosminsky's typical example are not great enough to imply that Langenhoe should be excluded from further consideration.

Kosminsky also found that small manors characteristically had few labour services so that small landowners depended even more heavily than large ones upon wage labour.[52] At Langenhoe in 1338/9 and 1342/3 the labour services account records only 100 winter services owed by two customary tenants. In 1338/9 these labour services were used mostly for manuring the fields, weeding and collecting thatch. The two tenants also owed the harvesting of 18 acres between them. There is no labour services account after 1342/3, but the harvest services were being sold in 1344/5 and 1347/8. At Pontes in 1341/2 and 1342/3 the labour services account includes only a single harvest boon from a tenement called Spelman's which owed four men for one day taking the lord's food. These harvested only 2 acres between them, the rest of the harvesting being paid for at day-rates. All the threshing here was paid for at piece-rates. There are no labour services accounts from Kelvedon Hall, but the 253½ acres harvested at piece-rates in 1330 comes close to the acreage under crops in 1334/5 and it also seems that all threshing on the manor was at piece-rates. At Carbonels both harvesting and threshing were entirely dependent upon wage labour. The ploughing services on these manors were insignificant.[53] All in all these accounts can be said to illustrate very effectively Kosminsky's conclusion that customary labour was of small importance in the economy of small estates.

Another of Kosminsky's generalizations is that the manors of small estates were seldom equivalent to whole villages.[54] Langenhoe Hall appears as an exception, for Lionel de Bradenham was the principal

[50] There were only 16 cows in 1346/7: E.R.O., D/DU/40/76ʳ, 77ʳ.

[51] R. H. Britnell, "Production for the Market on a Small Fourteenth-Century Estate", *Econ. Hist. Rev.*, 2nd ser., xix (1966), pp. 381, 383-4.

[52] Kosminsky, *Studies in the Agrarian History of England in the Thirteenth Century*, pp. 269, 275-6.

[53] At Kelvedon Hall in 1329/30 the boons at fallowing and *rebinatio* together added up to the equivalent of eleven days' ploughing. In 1334/5 a boon at the time of wheat sowing mustered 4 ploughs: E.R.O., D/DU/19/26Aʳ, 27ʳ.

[54] Kosminsky, *Studies in the Agrarian History of England in the Thirteenth Century*, pp. 273-4.

landlord in Langenhoe and held courts there.[55] But the other three manors were by no means the most important manors in their respective villages, and though Carbonels received 1s. 3d. in court dues in 1343/4, perhaps no more than a single entry fine, it appears from the accounts that neither it nor Pontes nor Kelvedon Hall had any jurisdiction. In Wix the chief manor was a knight's fee held of the honour of Hastings, but another manor belonged to the de Sutton family, and Wix Priory had enough land to be sowing 368½ acres in 1381/2.[56] Pontes was a tiny manor, one of eight estates held in Bulmer and Pebmarsh by military tenure in 1346.[57] In the eighteenth century there were seven reputed manors in Bulmer alone, and so far from corresponding to a village, Pontes had most of its land in Pebmarsh.[58] In 1327 Ralph de Pebenmerssh was the third largest taxpayer in Bulmer, the largest being John de Goldingham of Goldingham Hall.[59] Kelvedon Hall had a larger demesne, but it too spread itself in two parishes, and there were several manors in both of them.[60] In 1327 John de Kelvedon was the second largest taxpayer in Great Braxted, the largest being the countess of Pembroke.[61] Kelvedon Hall had a complicated tenurial structure. The serjeant paid rents in 1330 to the prior of St. Botulph in Colchester, to Braxted Hall, to the abbot of Westminster, to John Filliol and to Prested Hall in Feering, and the manor thus illustrates Kosminsky's finding that the "small manor, like land in free tenure, brought further entanglements into the cobweb of feudal connections, as its separate parts belonged to various fees".[62]

If these account rolls had diverged from the evidence of the Hundred Rolls about the structure of small estates then their information could quickly be dismissed as irrelevant to the problems Kosminsky was tackling. As it happens, they conform to it, so far as the information they give is parallel. They reveal that the manors in question were small and that the demesne was their major component. This was "a special type of demesne economy", since the four manors were without the reserves of customary labour commonly available to large manors. With one exception the manors had little authority over the villages in which their lands were situated and derived next to nothing from seigneurial jurisdiction. These characteristics, according to Kosminsky's

---

[55] The highest recorded receipt from court perquisites is £1. 15s. 7½d. in 1344/5: E.R.O., D/DEl/M221ʳ.

[56] Morant, *History and Antiquities of the County of Essex*, i, pp. 466, 468; P.R.O., S.C.6/849/15ᵈ.

[57] *Feudal Aids*, ii, pp. 165-6.

[58] Morant, *History and Antiquities of the County of Essex*, ii, pp. 263, 310.

[59] P.R.O., E.179/107/13, m. 14ᵈ. Goldingham Hall had an arable area of 427½ acres in 1314: E.R.O., D/DEx/M25, fo. 16ʳ⁻ᵛ.

[60] Morant, *History and Antiquities of the County of Essex*, ii, p. 153.

[61] P.R.O., E.179/107/13, m. 7ʳ.

[62] Kosminsky, *Studies in the Agrarian History of England in the Thirteenth Century*, p. 274.

hypothesis, made such small landlords uncommonly dependent upon manorial trade. The commodity nature of production was developed on manors such as theirs earlier and more strongly than on large manors. This was reflected in the structure of a small landlord's expenditure as well as in the sources of his income. Whereas a large estate could meet most of its investment requirements out of its own resources, the small estate could not. "Although it had less revenue at its disposal in absolute terms, the demesne economy of a small manor needed to lay out a greater percentage of that revenue on reproduction expenses". Kosminsky further argues that, having less produce to sell, the smaller estate was likely to be more commercially managed than a large one. The "small estate-owner, who had a comparatively insignificant amount of produce to sell, was much more concerned with questions of price".[63] It is with these propositions that the remainder of my discussion will be occupied.

III

Turning now to examine the manor as a source of income to its lord, the receipts and expenses of each manor may be analysed for each complete year. (See Table 1.) Kosminsky's emphasis on the importance of production for the market in the incomes of small estates is here shown to have considerable support. At Kelvedon Hall in 1334/5 rents and dues — that is, income of a seigneurial character — formed 20 per cent of the money income (excluding foreign receipts, arrears and sales *super compotum*), but this, it will be suggested, was exceptionally high. The comparable average proportion of rents and dues at Langenhoe was 17 per cent and at both Pontes and Carbonels it was 8 per cent. Other sources of money income have been divided between *exitus manerii* (that is, sales of pasture, hay, straw and wood), incomes from the sales of cereals and income from sales and leases of livestock together with the sales of wool and hides. These divisions are implicit in the accounts. At Kelvedon Hall, despite sales of timber, the total receipt from sales of manorial produce was low in relation to the size of the manor. This was because in 1334/5 the manor had less than its normal complement of grain and livestock at the beginning of the office year. The account records the purchase of 6 oxen, 5 plough-horses, 8 quarters of wheat and 56 quarters $7\frac{1}{2}$ bushels of oats. The outlay on purchases must have been exceptional, and at the same time receipts from the sale of produce were very small: only $3\frac{1}{2}$ bushels of beans were sold from the barns. On the other three manors, meanwhile, the dependence on demesne agriculture as a source of cash is unmistakable. The importance of livestock, even on a predominantly arable manor like Pontes, stands out from Table 1. Cows, poultry and, at Langenhoe,

63 *Ibid.*, pp. 276-7.

TABLE 1

CASH RECEIPTS ON THE MANORS OF FOUR SMALL ESTATES*

	Rents and court receipts†	*Exitus manerii* (sales of pasture, hay, straw and wood)	Grain sales	Livestock sales and leases	Foreign receipts, arrears and sales *super compotum*	Total
(i) *Amounts in s. d.*						
Pontes						
1341/2	24 0	59 2	112 2¼	78 1½(*a*)	3 6	276 11¾
1342/3	24 0	31 0½	165 3½	85 0 (*b*)	1 1	306 5
Kelvedon Hall						
1334/5	49 8	198 6	1 3¾	– –	535 6¾	785 0½
Carbonels						
1343/4	30 1	32 8	116 7	198 6½(*c*)	30 2¼	408 0¾
1346/7	33 6	10 11	162 0¼	198 3½	46 10½	451 7¼
Langenhoe						
1324/5	169 11	11 7	308 2	545 6	106 8	1141 10
1338/9	167 8½	142 7	172 8¼	467 4	– –	950 3¾
1342/3(*d*)	161 5¾	30 0	98 2	558 0	66 0	913 7¾
1344/5(*d*)	182 3	104 0	396 6	560 0	110 11	1353 8
1347/8(*e*)	207 5½	55 2	125 0	704 4	91 11½	1183 11
(ii) *Amounts expressed as a percentage*						
Pontes						
1341/2	8·7	21·4	40·5	28·2	1·3	(100)
1342/3	7·8	10·1	53·9	27·7	0·4	(100)
Kelvedon Hall						
1334/5	6·3	25·3	0·2	0·0	68·2	100
Carbonels						
1343/4	7·4	8·0	28·6	48·7	7·4	(100)
1346/7	7·4	2·4	35·9	43·9	10·4	100
Langenhoe						
1324/5	14·9	1·0	27·0	47·8	9·3	100
1338/9	17·6	15·0	18·2	49·2	0·0	100
1342/3	17·7	3·3	10·7	61·1	7·2	100
1344/5	13·5	7·7	29·3	41·4	8·2	(100)
1347/8	17·5	4·7	10·6	59·5	7·8	(100)

* Notes and sources: The figures for Table 1 are calculated from Public Record Office, S.C.6/845/29, 30; Essex Record Office, D/DU/19/27, D/DU/40/74-7, D/DC/2/11-12, D/DEl/M220-3.

† Excluding decayed rents.

(*a*) Adding 38s. 5½d. for 71 fleeces at 6½d. each.

(*b*) Adding 39s. for 72 fleeces at 6½d. each.

(*c*) Including 66s. 7½d. for 123 fleeces at 6½d. each.

(*d*) Allowing 13s. 4d. for the rent of Tylenheyestenement and 86s. 8d. for John Ward's farm of 80 ewes, the combined rent being 100s.

(*e*) Allowing 13s. 4d. for the rent of Tylenheyestenement and 91s. for the farm of ewes, the combined rent being 104s. 4d.

sheep as well were leased out at so much a head. Wool from Carbonels was delivered to William de Atherby in 1344, and the wool from Pontes was similarly sent to be sold centrally, but in each of these cases it has been priced in Table 1 at 6½d. a fleece and included in the receipts of the manor: this was the price obtained for wool from Carbonels in 1347. Meanwhile Langenhoe, Pontes and Carbonels all sold grain. The evidence of the grange accounts relates the amount of grain sold to the amounts used for other purposes. Only Langenhoe was self-evidently a home manor, supplying grain, poultry, meat and fuel to the lord's household. But the de Bradenham household consumed only between 18¾ and 25½ quarters of wheat and a varying amount of other grains each year,[64] which regularly left a large surplus of marketable cereals in the barns. None of the other manors contributed grain to its lord's household, which shows that small estates might have distinct home manors and cash manors just as large estates did. It is impossible to say what normally happened to the surplus from Kelvedon Hall, but at Pontes and Carbonels it was sold.

The second of Kosminsky's arguments to be investigated is that small landlords were more dependent on trade than large ones for investment activity. The proportion of money income devoted to investment expenditure has been studied, chiefly from the records of some large estates, in a well-known paper by R. H. Hilton which establishes that "an investment of not more than 5 per cent of total income in buildings, stock and equipment seems to have been common in the thirteenth century".[65] There are good reasons for expecting cash investment ratios on small estates to be higher than this. Small landlords had to pay cash for repairs and maintenance which could be trusted to serf labour on larger estates. Smaller landlords were also less able than large ones to make up deficits of stock on one manor by transfer from another. For these reasons investment activity on small estates would raise the cash outlay in circumstances where large estates had the option of forgoing cash income instead. It can easily be shown that this would raise the cash investment ratios on small estates relative to those on large ones. And, in addition, the fact that income from demesne agriculture constituted a larger proportion of the income of small manors than of large ones would further raise the proportion of total income needed for maintaining demesne equipment, buildings and livestock.

Unfortunately the level of investment expenditures on small estates is unlikely to be adequately indicated by their account rolls on manors where abnormal expenditures were paid directly by the lord. This pro-

[64] Britnell, "Production for the Market on a Small Fourteenth-Century Estate", p. 381.
[65] R. H. Hilton, "Rent and Capital Formation in Feudal Society", in his *The English Peasantry in the Later Middle Ages* (Oxford, 1975), p. 196.

blem is illustrated by the Langenhoe account of 1342/3 when the live-stock accounts record 80 ewes received from the lord (*de domino*), a choice of phrase clearly implying that the animals were not simply transferred from some other property. The expenditures entered in the account rolls are likely to include most routine replacement expenditure, but to under-represent other types of cash outlay for investment. The investment ratios recorded are therefore to be considered as erring on the low side. The evidence of the accounts is marshalled in Table 2. In addition to expenditure on equipment (almost exclusively ploughs and carts), buildings and livestock, are included costs of ditching, making watercourses and planting trees. In order to present a standardized set of figures, the costs of shoeing oxen and horses — which in the Pontes accounts cannot be separated from other payments to smiths — are included in investment costs in Table 2. In calculating cash investment ratios in Table 3, however, a separate set of figures has been compiled to exclude the costs of shoeing animals. Both sets of calculations unambiguously illustrate the generally high level of the ratios by comparison with large manors. Admittedly they vary considerably from manor to manor and from year to year. At one extreme, Kelvedon Hall in the process of restocking spent most of its income for the year in investment, even when considerable expenditures on grain are left out of account, as in Tables 2 and 3.[66] At the other extreme, Langenhoe Hall in the 1340s showed hardly any investment expenditure in its accounts. But, as already suggested, these Langenhoe figures are demonstrably misleading. The sheep flocks were augmented by 40 wethers and 200 hoggets between Michaelmas 1339 and Michaelmas 1342, probably for pasturing on Houtmers which had previously been leased.[67] The 80 ewes added in 1344/5 were leased along with Tylenheyestenement.[68] This increased responsibility for stocking pastures which had previously been stocked by tenants, perhaps a consequence of agricultural depression,[69] had involved Lionel de Bradenham in cash outlays which do not appear in the manorial accounts. This explains the cash shortages on the manor[70] and the inability of the serjeant to undertake further investment activity, just as it explains Lionel's efforts to raise cash quickly by the expedient of ploughing up pastures to sow oats.[71] Averaged over the years, the true cash invest-

[66] In 1334/5 the serjeant spent £11. 0s. 8¼d. on purchases of grain, mostly oats, for use on the demesne: E.R.O., D/DU/19/27ʳ.

[67] Houtmers was leased for £2. 0s. 0d. in 1338/9: E.R.O., D/DC/2/12ʳ.

[68] This may be deduced from the livestock accounts of 1344/5: E.R.O., D/DEl/M221ᵈ.

[69] R. H. Britnell, "Finchingfield Park under the Plough, 1341-2", *Essex Archaeol. and Hist.*, ix (1977), p. 110.

[70] A note at the foot of the account for 1344/5 shows that at the time the account was drawn up Lionel owed arrears of wages to his *famuli*: E.R.O., D/DEl/M221ʳ.

[71] Britnell, "Production for the Market on a Small Fourteenth-Century Estate", pp. 384-5. The land ploughed was probably the cow pasture, since the 20 cows on the manor were sent to Abberton during 1342/3: E.R.O., D/DEl/M220ᵈ.

ment ratio at Langenhoe would be much higher than the figures in Table 3 imply.

TABLE 2

CASH EXPENDITURE ON THE MANORS OF FOUR SMALL ESTATES*

	Rent	Investment costs	Current costs	Foreign expenses and cash transfers	Total
(i) *Amounts in s. d.*					
Pontes					
1341/2	20 0	25 6½	83 0¾	148 4½	276 11¾
1342/3	20 0	40 1	81 1¾	165 2¼	306 5
Kelvedon Hall					
1334/5	25·0	217 10¼	415 8¾	126 5½	785 0½
Carbonels					
1343/4	2 10	74 3½	114 5½(*a*)	216 5¾	408 0¾
1346/7	2 10	98 8½	150 3¼	199 9½	451 7¼
Langenhoe					
1324/5	– –	169 2¾	261 10¾	710 8½	1141 10
1338/9	– 1½	105 3½	191 7¼	653 3½	950 3¾
1342/3	-- 1½	26 4¼	227 1½	660 0½	913 7¾
1344/5	– –	42 8¼	207 0	1103 11¾	1353 8
1347/8	– –	60 0½	327 2¾(*b*)	796 7¾	1183 11
(ii) *Amounts expressed as a percentage*					
Pontes					
1341/2	7·2	9·2	30·0	53·6	100
1342/3	6·5	13·1	26·5	53·9	100
Kelvedon Hall					
1334/5	3·2	27·8	53·0	16·1	(100)
Carbonels					
1343/4	0·7	18·2	28·0	53·1	100
1346/7	0·6	21·9	33·3	44·2	100
Langenhoe					
1324/5	0·0	14·8	22·9	62·2	(100)
1338/9	0·0	11·1	20·2	68·7	100
1342/3	0·0	2·9	24·9	72·2	100
1344/5	0·0	3·2	15·3	81·6	(100)
1347/8	0·0	5·1	27·6	67·3	100

* Notes and sources: The figures for Table 2 are calculated from the same sources as those for Table 1. Investment costs are estimated in accordance with the definition in R. H. Hilton, "Rent and Capital Formation in Feudal Society", repr. in his *The English Peasantry in the Later Middle Ages* (Oxford, 1975), p. 187. Costs of shoeing horses and oxen are included. Foreign expenses and cash transfers (that is, transfers of cash back to the lord or to his assigns) are estimated as the difference between total cash receipts (from Table 1) and expenditure on rent, investment costs and current costs (from the first three columns of Table 2).

(*a*) Adding 10s. 6d. for threshing and winnowing, which was paid for by the lord.
(*b*) Adding 20s. od. for threshing and winnowing.

TABLE 3

INVESTMENT EXPENDITURE AS A PROPORTION OF CASH RECEIPTS ON THE MANORS OF FOUR SMALL ESTATES*

	Investment expenditure as a percentage of rent and produce income	Investment expenditure as a percentage of total income
Pontes		
1341/2	9·3	9·2
1342/3	13·1	13·1
Kelvedon Hall		
1334/5	87·3 (84·0)	27·8 (26·7)
Carbonels		
1343/4	19·7 (18·8)	18·2 (17·4)
1346/7	24·4 (21·9)	21·9 (19·6)
Langenhoe		
1324/5	16·3 (15·2)	14·8 (13·8)
1338/9	11·1 (10·0)	11·1 (10·0)
1342/3	3·1 (1·9)	2·9 (1·8)
1344/5	3·4 (2·2)	3·2 (2·0)
1347/8	5·5 (4·8)	5·1 (4·4)

* Notes and sources: The figures in Table 3 are calculated from the same sources as Tables 1-2. Rent and produce income, in the first column, includes rent and court receipts, *exitus manerii* (sales of pasture, hay, straw and wood), grain sales, and livestock sales and leases (that is, as Table 1, cols. 1-4). Total income includes the aforementioned, together with foreign receipts, arrears and sales *super compotum*, and is equivalent to the figure in the final column of Table 1. Figures in brackets show the effect of excluding the costs of shoeing horses and oxen from investment costs.

It should perhaps be stressed that higher cash investment ratios do not imply that small landowners were in some sense more enterprising than large ones. The investment expenditures shown in Table 2 represent that part of total investment which involved cash payments. Expenditure on equipment represents almost exclusively the regular remaking and maintaining of ploughs and carts. At Kelvedon Hall in 1334/5 perhaps stocks of iron and steel were laid up for succeeding years,[72] but normally expenditure on equipment involved no expansion of manorial capital. At Pontes 90 per cent of the equipment costs comprised annual payments of a mark to a smith for providing, making and sharpening all the irons for a plough and shoeing the plough-team.[73] Building costs are easy enough to interpret when simply thatching or plastering is involved. In other cases there is more ambiguity, as in the construction of a sheep-cote at Wix in 1343/4. But even

---

[72] The manor bought and worked 275 lbs. of iron and six sheaves (*garbe*) and 20 bars (*gadda*) of steel: E.R.O., D/DU/19/27ʳ.

[73] "To the smith's wages for providing, working and sharpening all the ironwork for one plough and for shoeing 4 plough-horses and 3 oxen as piece-work, 13s. 4d. in all (*ad taxam ingrosso xiijs. iiijd.*)": P.R.O., S.C.6/845/29ʳ, similarly S.C.6/845/30ʳ.

here an older structure was probably being replaced, for the livestock accounts show a slight decline in the number of sheep during the course of the year 1343/4 and no significant change in the size of flocks over the following three years. The numbers of livestock fluctuated sufficiently markedly from year to year on these manors for the occasional purchases of animals to be of no significance as evidence of the direction of change. The most substantial annual expenditure on livestock in the accounts arose from the restocking of Kelvedon Hall in 1334/5. Other investment expenditures — the 18s. 11¾d. spent on ditching at Carbonels in 1343/4, and the 8s. 10½d. spent on ditching and hedging there in 1346/7, to cite the major examples — are slight and ambiguous. In short it is impossible in Table 2 to identify with certainty any element of net investment, and it can be confidently assumed that the overwhelming bulk of these payments were for dilapidations and replacements of stock. High cash investment ratios on these manors can accordingly not be taken as evidence of greater commercial acumen. Kosminsky's point was that such expenses helped to induce a more commercial attitude, not that they reflected one.

The case of Langenhoe seems to illustrate Kosminsky's hypothesis remarkably well. Here indeed there had been net investment on the manor which had necessitated considerable cash expenditure. The pressure on Lionel de Bradenham's finances had induced him to take exceptional measures to raise his cash income. It takes little imagination to suppose that in the mid-1340s he was personally interested in the prices fetched by his demesne produce. But it is not self-evident that such concern was more likely to be induced by high investment ratios than by other sources of expenditure. Even large landowners had expenses which might encourage them to keep a tight rein upon the management of their estates. Some drains on their cash — building programmes, purchases of land, ostentatious living — were self-imposed. Others, such as royal demands for military service, taxes and judicial fines, were imposed upon them. Either way, landowners were likely to be concerned with the size of grain surpluses and the prices at which they were sold. Kosminsky's a priori argument linking investment ratios to different qualities of entrepreneurship is accordingly a weak one.

The records permit a cursory examination of marketing policies on large and small estates, despite some obvious difficulties. Even during the course of a year prices varied considerably, tending to rise during the winter and spring and then to fall during the summer if a good harvest was expected.[74] This suggests that there are two ways in which a comparison between large and small estates might be attempted. One could ask whether large estates sold grain at any given time in the year

[74] R. H. Hilton, A Medieval Society: The West Midlands at the End of the Thirteenth Century (London, 1966), pp. 80-1.

at a lower price than small estates would tolerate; alternatively one could ask whether large estates sold grain earlier in the year, and at a lower price, than small estates. The first of these approaches is impossible because it would depend upon a detailed record in each account of the exact time when grain was sold and the quantity sold at each price. This is information sometimes to be found, but there is no single moment when, in north-eastern Essex, the prices obtained by a large estate can be compared with those obtained by a small one. The second approach may be hazarded, since it depends less upon accidents of documentary survival. It is not even necessary to compare the prices which different estates obtained in the same year if it is possible to gauge their general propensities to take advantage of price movements. There is every reason to suppose that these small estates played the market. The reeve at Pontes sold 4 quarters 2 bushels of wheat in October 1342 at 3s. 4d. and 3s. 6d. a quarter, 18 quarters 2 bushels in November at 3s. 8d. and 3s. 10d. a quarter, and 8 quarters 4 bushels in December at 4s. 0d. and 4s. 8d. a quarter. In the same winter some wheat from Langenhoe was sold at 4s. 8d. a quarter, but most of the wheat surplus was sold for 5s. 0d. a quarter, which suggests that grain was held in store until prices had risen well above the harvest price. At Carbonels the surplus from the harvest of 1346 was kept until January 1347 when it was sold for 6s. 0d. and 6s. 8d. a quarter. At Pontes in 1342, however, it will be observed that the heaviest sales came well before prices reached their peak. At Carbonels similarly in 1343/4, 2 quarters 7 bushels were sold at 6s. 8d. a quarter, 2 quarters 1 bushel at 7s. 4d. a quarter and only 3 bushels at 8s. 0d. a quarter. It may be that the grain had to be sold because it was showing deterioration, but smaller landlords may have been compelled to sell their grain fairly early in the year precisely because, as with peasant farmers, sales of produce accounted for so important a part of their money income. Sooner or later the grain would have to be sold because cash was needed for wages or purchases on the manor, if not for the lord's domestic needs. At Pontes in 1341/2, 4 quarters of wheat were sold straight after Michaelmas expressly for the payment of taxes, and subsequently 2½ bushels of rye and 1 quarter 6 bushels of peas were sold to pay the threshers. At Langenhoe in 1338/9 three separate consignments of wheat were sold at differing prices to raise money for the lord (*pro denariis leuandis ad opus domini*), suggesting that the timing of the sales had been governed by Lionel de Bradenham's need for cash.

On this reasoning, large estates might be better able to hold out for the best price, and there is good evidence that they did so. On the Essex manors of Westminster Abbey it was common for no grain to be sold before the spring. In the famine year of 1316/17 the surplus of peas from Feering was sold about Christmas time, but the 34½ quarters of wheat were sold in Lent and about the feast of St. Mark (25th April) for prices of 18s. od. to 18s. 8d. a quarter.[75] In 1332/3 the reeve had 100 quarters of wheat for sale, but held on to it all through the winter. He sold 60 quarters in March and April at 5s. 4d. a quarter and the rest in June and July at 5s. 8d. and 6s. od. a quarter. At least 40 out of the 100 quarters were carted to Colchester for sale at a distance of eight miles away.[76] In 1347/8 most of the oats and all the barley were sold in February and all the peas in March, but no wheat was sold until the price reached 9s. od. a quarter in April, and 82 per cent of the surplus was sold then before prices began to fall again.[77] Waiting for a good price was policy on the Clare estates as well. In 1346/7 and 1347/8 the small amounts of surplus winter grain from Claret Hall were sold in the autumn, but larger surpluses of spring crops were kept until the spring and early summer. In 1348/9, when the surplus of winter crops was larger, no wheat was sold before February 1349 and the spring crops were held back until at least March. The tenor of the accounts of Claret Hall is inconsistent with the idea that large estates were less particular than small estates about the selling price of their produce merely because it was not proportionately so large a source of income. In 1347 the 21 quarters of wheat sold to the lady's household, by accounting convention, was priced at 7s. od. a quarter, whereas the 2 quarters of wheat actually sold at All Saints time had then fetched only 5s. 4d. a quarter.[78] The price recorded for this fictitious sale must represent the way in which prices had moved in the course of the year. The Claret Hall accounts also include instances of the prices obtained by the serjeant being disallowed by the auditors on the grounds that a better price could have been obtained.[79] At the earl of Norfolk's manor of Dovercourt there is no record of the times of year when grain was sold, but an insertion by the auditors among the grain sales of 1294/5 shows that the reeve was charged with having lost money by sales of grain negotiated after Midsummer Day.[80]

These arguments cast doubt on Kosminsky's conclusion that small estates, because of their proportionately smaller income from rents, were liable to be more concerned with the prices obtained for demesne produce. It may even be that, in the absence of large periodic cash incomes from rents, small landowners were less likely than large ones to secure the best prices for their products. The accounts which have been examined can hardly be said to prove this point. But such an interpre-

[75] P.R.O., S.C.6/841/5, m. 2ʳ.
[76] P.R.O., S.C.6/841/6ʳ⁻ᵈ.
[77] P.R.O., S.C.6/841/9ʳ.
[78] P.R.O., S.C.6/838/21ʳ, 22ʳ, 23ʳ.
[79] For example, P.R.O., S.C.6/838/15, m. 1ʳ (1339/40), S.C.6/838/22ʳ (1347/8).
[80] P.R.O., S.C.6/840/8ʳ. For evidence of serjeants on other estates exploiting locational differences in grain prices, see M. Morgan, *The English Lands of the Abbey of Bec* (Oxford, 1946), p. 49; P. D. A. Harvey, *A Medieval Oxfordshire Village: Cuxham, 1240 to 1400* (Oxford, 1965), p. 103.

tation of the evidence has the merit of being more in accordance than Kosminsky's with recent research into the history of small landowners in the period of direct demesne farming. The concept of smaller landowners as a class rising through commercial endeavour[81] can no longer be accepted as a useful one if it is true that most examples of families increasing in wealth and power represent those who derived their income from services to large landowners or the crown.[82] It is not surprising that, of the three inferences of Kosminsky's concerning the trade of minor landlords which we have examined, this one should be the least convincingly supported. The idea that smaller landlords were more dependent on trade than larger ones both for their incomes and for investment expenditure is a logical inference from the large and authoritative body of evidence which Kosminsky assembled in the course of his remarkable studies in the Hundred Rolls. The view that smaller landlords were more enterprising than larger ones because of their greater dependence on trade is not a logical deduction from that evidence, but more in the nature of a guess. It depends upon assumptions concerning the economic motivation of medieval landlords which probably ought not to be made.[83]

Concern for high prices was a general preoccupation of medieval landlords, great as well as small. In so far as there were variations in attentiveness to market opportunities, there is no reason to suppose that differences in the structure of manors had much to do with them. Nor is there any necessary relationship between social status and concern with prices. Knights, who formed the upper crust of small estate owners, were liable to be hard pushed for cash to maintain their standard of living, however disparaging their attitude to trade.[84] Again, in the important matter of their investments and improvements, the distinction between small estates and larger ones seems to be of no great moment. A thorough examination of this problem is perhaps out of the question, since it would depend upon evidence from the mid-thirteenth century rather than from the second quarter of the fourteenth, when investment opportunities in the medieval countryside were few and far between. There seems, however, to be no very good reason for supposing that small landowners were generally pioneers of new technological or social systems of production. Any interest that there was in

[81] Kosminsky, *Studies in the Agrarian History of England in the Thirteenth Century*, pp. 258, 267, 278.

[82] A. C. Chibnall, *Sherington: Fiefs and Fields of a Buckinghamshire Village* (Cambridge, 1965), pp. 77-85; P. R. Coss, "Sir Geoffrey de Langley and the Crisis of the Knightly Class in Thirteenth-Century England", *Past and Present*, no. 68, repr. above, pp. 166-202; M. M. Postan, "Medieval Agrarian Society in its Prime: England", in *The Cambridge Economic History of Europe*, i, *The Agrarian Life of the Middle Ages*, 2nd edn., ed. M. M. Postan (Cambridge, 1966), pp. 593-5.

[83] This is not a new line of criticism: see, in particular, T. H. Aston, "The English Manor", *Past and Present*, no. 10 (Nov. 1956), p. 12.

[84] Hilton, *Medieval Society*, pp. 50-1, 84-7.

improved farming methods in the thirteenth century certainly did not bypass the greater estates, which were able to employ professional estate stewards to administer their properties.[85] Meanwhile it is chiefly the low level of interest in developing new systems of production and organization and the strikingly low level of capital formation in demesne agriculture which have impressed historians who have examined the matter.[86] This traditionalism in methods of production, which more than anything else stamps medieval landed society as pre-capitalist, was a general one, or there would be more evidence of improvements in cropping, manuring, breeding and animal care than is actually to be found. The differences between the structures of large and small estates are accordingly of no apparent significance for the dynamics of medieval economy. Neither the importance of trade for small landlords nor their greater dependence on wage labour can be shown to have made them more capitalist than large ones in any sense likely to be useful for the interpretation of long-term social change.

[85] *Walter of Henley and Other Treatises on Estate Management and Accounting*, ed. Oschinsky, pp. 56-67.

[86] Hilton, "Rent and Capital Formation in Feudal Society", p. 188; M. M. Postan, "Investment in Medieval Agriculture", *Jl. Econ. Hist.*, xxvii (1967), pp. 579, 581-4.

9. English serfdom and villeinage: Towards a reassessment

JOHN HATCHER

I

THERE CAN BE FEW HISTORICAL ISSUES WHICH COMMAND SO WIDE A measure of agreement as the wholly odious and reprehensible character of serfdom.[1] Time and again serfdom has been held to be an archetypal system of oppression and exploitation, combining harsh deprivation of freedom with ruthless depression of economic status. It would seem contrary to fact and reason, as well as to morality, to suggest that it could have had any redeeming features whatsoever. Were the unfree not at the mercy of their lords' wills, and subject to their justice alone? Were they not tied to land that they could never own, and forced to pay dearly for it? Were they not obliged to work long hours on their lords' lands, and burdened with an extensive range of onerous charges and degrading restrictions? Was their ability to be educated, to marry, to migrate, to buy and sell property, not dependent upon their lords' favour? Could they not be bought and sold as chattels?

Scarcely any more controversial can be the realization that the majority of thirteenth-century Englishmen were extremely poor. It is well enough appreciated that the prevalence of small holdings yielding exiguous quantities of food combined with high rents, low wages and high prices to drive substantial numbers to the very threshold of subsistence, over which many were forced by the harvest failures of the early fourteenth century. Running parallel with these morbid trends, it has been recently argued, there occurred a severe depression in the legal and social status of the mass of the peasantry; in short many were downgraded from freedom to servitude, and servitude itself became more oppressive.[2] The wretchedness of the conditions of life of so many

---

* I am grateful for helpful comments on an earlier draft of this paper by Edward Miller and Sir Michael Postan, and members of seminars in various universities. While preparing the final version I benefited from the comments of Paul Hyams, and from reading the manuscript of his then unpublished book, *King, Lords and Peasants in Medieval England: The Common Law of Villeinage in the Twelfth and Thirteenth Centuries* (Oxford, 1980).

[1] In this paper the words "serfdom" and "villeinage" have sometimes been used in a loose manner. The excuse is that contemporaries from the late twelfth century onwards did likewise, by often using *villanus* and *servus* as synonyms. Certain distinctions, however, should be maintained. Serfdom had a far longer history than villeinage, and the latter term should perhaps be avoided when writing of the era before the evolution of common law villeinage. "Villeinage", therefore, is the narrower and more specifically legal term, while "serfdom" may be taken to encompass the broad economic, social and legal system of unfreedom and dependence.

[2] R. H. Hilton, "Freedom and Villeinage in England", *Past and Present*, no. 31 (July 1965), pp. 3-19.

unfree peasants at this time would seem, therefore, to have derived from both the oppressiveness of their legal and social status and the adversity of prevailing economic and demographic trends. What could be more plausible than that the power of landlords increased sequentially with the growing scarcity of land, and that this power should manifest itself in a deterioration of the economic, legal and social status of their dependants?

If this brief summary does not do injustice to widely accepted views of thirteenth-century serfdom, it would be found by some to be unacceptably liberal. The conception of serfdom as unmitigated thraldom, of seemingly limitless exploitation of men by their lords, has recently been resurrected. In his article, "Agrarian Class Structure and Economic Development in Pre-Industrial Europe", Robert Brenner invited us to seek the causes of the widespread agrarian distress almost exclusively in the excessive exploitation of the unfree by their lords. He wrote: "the lord's surplus extraction (rent) tended to confiscate not merely the peasant's income above subsistence (and potentially even beyond) but at the same time to threaten the funds necessary to refurbish the peasant's holding and to prevent the long-term decline of its productivity". Moreover he told us that the pickings which seigneurial power bestowed were so easy they not only drove the masses to starvation; they also deprived lords of any incentive to invest or even to manage their affairs efficiently.[3] The boundless exploitation of the unfree is in this way made the prime mover of the crisis, and consequent decline, of serfdom and manorialism.

Yet even after the scholarly attention of generations of historians, as well as innumerable sociologists, anthropologists, economists, philosophers and lawyers, we cannot be certain that we have achieved a perfect understanding of serfdom. It will be suggested in this article that there are powerful reasons for such uncertainty. Studies of serfdom have been dominated by two distinct approaches: one which seeks to establish the position of the serf under the law, especially common law, and one which seeks to trace the nature and weight of seigneurial dues and obligations. With regard to English serfdom the former approach emphasizes the pronouncements of lawyers and legal theorists such as Bracton and Britton, and stresses the judgements of royal courts; while the latter approach observes a deterioration in conditions of tenure and an increase in the weight and number of obligations as the late twelfth and the thirteenth centuries progressed. By themselves, and even when combined, such approaches are inadequate and at times positively misleading: the former because the day-to-day relations of lords and tenants bore scant resemblance to the extremes of lordship and subjection asserted by lawyers and the royal courts; and the latter

---

[3] R. Brenner, "Agrarian Class Structure and Economic Development in Pre-Industrial Europe", *Past and Present*, no. 70 (Feb. 1976), pp. 30-75, at p. 48.

because it concentrates exclusively upon only one facet of unfree status and tenure, and thereby fails to take any account of changes in the value of the land which the unfree held and of their willingness to hold it.

To make progress, a reassessment of serfdom must take account of all elements in the relationship between the unfree and their lords. It must also view the institution of serfdom laterally as well as lineally, that is, both in the context of its own times and as part of a historical process. If this is attempted then, it will be suggested in this article, doubts may well arise as to the validity of many current opinions, primarily because they are too narrowly conceived. In particular a balance must be struck between the weight of seigneurial exactions and the restrictions and obligations of unfreedom on the one hand, and the benefits of landholding on the other. Serfdom was made more, or less, oppressive not by changes in seigneurial exactions alone, but also by fluctuations in the scarcity and value of land. As a consequence of rising and falling exactions and rising and falling land values the net balance shifted dramatically over time.

This balance of advantages and disadvantages is what must have mattered most to the unfree, and it must have played the dominant part in determining how they viewed their own condition. It should do likewise for the historian. In terms of causality we must make a clear distinction between those forces emanating from seigneurial power and those emanating from the economic and demographic context. In other words we must distinguish between oppressions caused by the institution itself and those caused by the environment in which the institution existed. As we shall see, the forces generated by status did not always go hand in hand with the forces generated by economic and demographic change. Indeed they often pulled in opposite directions.

In the century before the Black Death, for example, the fact that total payments by the unfree reached a peak, and that poverty was severe and widespread, does not prove that serfdom was then at its most oppressive. On the contrary there are good reasons for believing that in this adverse economic and demographic climate unfree status, through the restraint exercised by custom, afforded a considerable measure of protection from the full force of the market. In direct contrast status in the ostensibly more favourable conditions of relative labour shortage and land abundance of earlier centuries, although at that time not specified as unfree, appears often to have operated against the interests of tenants. Status was at its most oppressive when it facilitated the extraction from tenants of rents and services in excess of the value of the lands which they held, and attempted to bind men to their lords when they wished to seek more attractive opportunities elsewhere. These oppressions appear to have characterized much of the era before the establishment of common law villeinage in the late twelfth century, and it is well known that an attempt was made to resurrect them after 1350.

II

Our investigations will concentrate first upon the later thirteenth century. Since the character of serfdom and the absolute and relative weight of servile burdens changed over time, concentration upon a restricted period will help to avoid at least some complexities and confusions. The period chosen has other advantages. It is rich in manorial as well as legal documentation, which enables a comparison of the two classes of evidence to be made. It is also a time when, so it is widely accepted, the mass of the population was extremely poor, and becoming poorer. The role of serfdom in the creation of this poverty is a matter of prime importance.

Our first task must be to estimate the proportion of the population which was unfree. This is no easy matter, but it can be best attempted for our chosen period when the Hundred Rolls of 1279 provide what for medievalists is a veritable mountain of statistics. What is more, E. A. Kosminsky's detailed analysis of the Hundred Rolls gives us a firm foothold on this mountain.[4] Taking a sample of some ten thousand tenants drawn from the Cambridgeshire, Huntingdonshire, Bedfordshire, Buckinghamshire and Oxfordshire returns, Kosminsky found a ratio of not more than three unfree tenants to every two free tenants; and he saw no reason for not extending this ratio to the whole area covered by the Hundred Rolls, namely "more than 700 centres of habitation [stretching] in an almost unbroken band from Suffolk to Oxfordshire".[5] It needs no stressing that even if this ratio is felt to be applicable to the area covered by the Hundred Rolls it cannot be applied to England as a whole without further detailed investigation. For within the range of counties covered by the 1279 surveys the ratio of freemen to villeins fluctuated sharply from village to village,[6] and if we move outside these counties the fluctuations become still more pronounced.

Nonetheless a perusal of the evidence does suggest that nation-wide the proportion of unfree tenants is unlikely to have exceeded that in Kosminsky's Hundred Rolls sample. In the northern Danelaw (Yorkshire, Derbyshire, Nottinghamshire, Leicestershire, Lincolnshire and Rutland) the free often comprised more than 60 per cent of village ten-

---

[4] E. A. Kosminsky, *Studies in the Agrarian History of England in the Thirteenth Century*, ed. R. H. Hilton, trans. R. Kisch (Oxford, 1956). Although this work was first published (in Russian) more than thirty years ago the implications of a number of Kosminsky's more important findings have still not been completely assimilated.

[5] *Ibid.*, pp. 205-6. It must also be noted that some tenants listed among the unfree were freemen holding in villeinage.

[6] For example, R. H. Hilton, *The English Peasantry in the Later Middle Ages* (Oxford, 1975), pp. 126-7.

antry; surveys of manors in north-western counties suggest that there the proportion of landholders designated unfree may well have been less than 20 per cent; in the west midland and marcher counties of Gloucestershire, Staffordshire, Shropshire and Herefordshire free tenures frequently predominated; and although in east Sussex *nativi* were prominent and villeinage well developed, over the border in Kent villeinage was virtually non-existent. Furthermore throughout England, even in the most servile counties, there were pockets of freedom which had been nourished by the great colonizing movements of the central middle ages.[7] All in all probably not more than three-fifths of the English tenantry were unfree.[8]

If this were so then the proportion of the total population which was of servile status and, *a fortiori*, subject to servile obligations must have been substantially lower still. Though in law serfdom attached to the person and did not necessarily depend upon tenure, in the nature of things the servile status of landholders was more easily established and retained than was that of the landless. A migrant villein, and we should not underestimate the scale of mobility, might in practice acquire a "seisin" of liberty, both through the difficulty or lack of necessity of proving him otherwise outside his native village, and the presumption of the law which could favour *de facto* freedom. At all events the *de facto* and *de jure* free probably predominated among the landless and subtenants. We must also take account of those who lived in towns or engaged full-time in trade or industry, and of the clergy, gentry and nobility. In attempting to arrive at over-all estimates it is perhaps best to deal in households. Accordingly it seems most unlikely that households renting farm land directly from landlords constituted more than 75 per cent of total households, and probable that they constituted little more than half. Finally, if these parameters are correct, then households holding by unfree tenure may well have constituted little more than a third of total households.

If the numbers of unfree tenants in the later thirteenth century are frequently overestimated, so is the severity of the disabilities of their status. The source of much confusion is the conflict between the testimony of legal treatises and proceedings in the crown courts, and that of innumerable manorial and estate documents. It is a commonplace that under the common law the unfree had no rights against their lords,

---

[7] F. Stenton, "The Free Peasantry of the Northern Danelaw", *Bulletin de la Société royale des lettres de Lund* (1925-6); Hilton, *English Peasantry in the Later Middle Ages*, pp. 140-1, 226-8; N. Neilson, "Custom and Common Law in Kent", *Harvard Law Rev.*, xxxviii (1924-5). For a review of the distribution of free tenures, see R. H. Hilton, *The Decline of Serfdom in Medieval England* (London, 1969), pp. 18-24.

[8] Edmund King has recently suggested that a ratio of "two villein households for every three free peasant households, over the whole of England in the late thirteenth century, is unlikely to be underestimating the number of villeins": E. King, *England, 1175-1425* (London, 1979), p. 50.

saving only life and limb; for the unfree could not plead against their lords in royal courts. The inevitable corollary of this prohibition was that, in the eyes of the common law, the unfree were almost completely at their lords' mercy and subject to their justice alone. It could not be otherwise. Thus Bracton baldly states that all men are either free or serf (*omnes homines aut liberi sunt aut servi*) and, in the words of Maitland, "he will have no mere unfreedom, no semi-servile class, no merely praedial serfage, nothing equivalent to the Roman *colonatus*".[9] In the words of the eccentric author of the *Mirror of Justices*, therefore, serfs:

> cannot acquire anything save to the use of their lord; they do not know in the evening what service they will do in the morning, and there is nothing certain in their services. The lords may put them in fetters and in the stocks, may imprison, beat and chastise them at will, saving their life and limbs. They cannot escape, flee or withdraw themselves from their lords, so long as their lords find them wherewithal they may live, and no one may receive them without the will of their lords. They can have no manner of action without their lord against any man, save for felony. And if such serfs hold fees of their lords, it must be understood that they hold only from day to day at the will of their lords and by no certain services.[10]

All this and more is undoubtedly correct if one views from the perspective of the common law alone, but it tells us little of the actual status and conditions of the unfree. Lords had under the common law almost limitless rights over their serfs and villeins, but in practice they almost invariably recognized the restraints which custom imposed upon them. Precisely because the unfree were excluded from the cognizance of the common law they fell within the purview of private seigneurial tribunals and these tribunals operated according to customary rules. Herein lies the key to the reconciliation of law and practice. This being so, further apparent contradictions can also be reconciled. Most notable among these is the law's inability to recognize degrees of unfreedom but the existence everywhere of people whose unfreedom was manifestly relative rather than absolute. Wherever we look we find a

---

[9] Sir F. Pollock and F. W. Maitland, *The History of English Law before the Time of Edward I*, 2 vols. (Cambridge, 1968 edn.), i, pp. 412-14.

[10] *The Mirror of Justices*, ed. W. J. Whittaker (Selden Soc., vii, London, 1895), p. 79. It should also be noted that there was a marked lack of consensus among the legal commentators themselves. The author of *Fleta* concurs with Bracton: *Fleta*, ed. H. G. Richardson and G. O. Sayles, ii (Selden Soc., lxxii, London, 1955), p. 14; but Britton and the author of the *Mirror of Justices* are only in partial agreement with Bracton and with each other. For although Britton maintains that "one [cannot] be more a villein than another, for they are all of equal condition — whosoever is a bondman is as absolutely a bondman as any other", he also draws clear, though seemingly fallacious, distinctions between villeins, serfs and neifs: *Britton*, ed. F. M. Nichols, 2 vols. (Oxford, 1865), i, pp. 195 ff. To add greater confusion the author of the *Mirror of Justices*, who has admittedly been seen by Maitland as at turns "lawyer, antiquary, preacher, agitator, pedant, faddist, lunatic, romancer, liar", asserts on the one hand that "a neif is nothing else than a serf", but on the other that "villein and serf are not at all one in sound or meaning" and that "it is an abuse to count villeins as serfs": *Mirror of Justices*, ed. Whittaker, pp. 77, 165.

veritable multitude of degrees of unfreedom, each one dependent upon the type and weight of servile dues or upon the privileges of freedom from them. We know that from time out of mind local custom had displayed kaleidoscopic variety — the author of the early eleventh-century *Rectitudines singularum personarum* tells us so[11] — but even if there ever had once been uniformity the exigencies of landlords' policies and peasants' demands, acting and reacting upon fluctuations in economic activity, political stability and innumerable other factors would have been bound to produce a luxuriant diversity. This diversity is ample confirmation in itself of the efficacy of custom and the respect which lords showed to it.

It is possible to go much further than this. If in the eyes of the common law all the property of the unfree was the property of their lords, village and manorial records tell us that lords habitually treated their villeins and serfs as owners of chattels. On the death of unfree tenants, thirteenth-century lords, unlike the lord of the *geburs* in the *Rectitudines*, generally contented themselves with a specified heriot. And where, as in some remoter parts like Lancashire and Cornwall, lords retained a general claim upon the chattels of a dead serf, in practice it was very often reduced to some specified proportion of them such as a third.[12] Even tallage, one of the hallmarks of serfdom, frequently became a fixed, often annual, payment. Moreover for a fine villeins were permitted to buy and sell land, often including their unfree holdings, and perhaps most striking of all, lords frequently recognized their right to make wills. That the unfree held their land for uncertain and indeterminate services was a platitude of the common law, but everywhere as the thirteenth century progressed the obligations of tenants were defined in ever greater detail in rentals and custumals drawn up by seigneurial officials. In the definition of services the force of custom left its mark, for very commonly services were established by the verdict of manorial jurors who declared what had been owed in the past as a basis for determining what would be owed in the future. Some uncertainty might well remain as to the precise tasks which would be required when labour was performed (a heavy storm might render ploughing impossible and ditching desirable) but there was rarely much uncertainty about the frequency or duration of the work.[13] If the letter of the

[11] For the original text of the *Rectitudines*, see F. Liebermann, *Die Gesetze der Angelsachsen*, 3 vols. (Halle, 1903-16), i, pp. 445-53. For an English translation, see *English Historical Documents, 1042-1189*, ed. D. C. Douglas and G. W. Greenaway (London, 1953), pp. 813-16.

[12] *Lancashire Inquests, Extents and Feudal Aids*, ed. W. Farrer, 3 vols. (Lancs. and Cheshire Rec. Soc., xlviii, liv, lxx, Liverpool, 1903-15), ii, p. 51, and iii, pp. 87, 142; J. Hatcher, *Rural Economy and Society in the Duchy of Cornwall, 1300-1500* (Cambridge, 1970), p. 63.

[13] Maitland's suggestion that the uncertainty stressed by lawyers referred to uncertainty about the type of work seems rather strained: Pollock and Maitland, *History of English Law before the Time of Edward I*, i, p. 371.

law decreed that the unfree could be evicted at will, and could have no heirs but their lords, there can be no doubt whatsoever after studying manorial records that the unfree who paid their rent and performed their services almost invariably enjoyed an absolute hereditary security of tenure which rivalled that enjoyed by the free.[14] An exception in some places related to the rights of widows who might divert all or some part of a tenement to a second husband. But these, too, were customary rights.[15] Eviction was rare and arbitrary eviction scarcely known. A villein who defaulted on his rent or services, or allowed his holding to fall into disrepair, was commonly warned, then fined small sums, and finally if he refused to pay the fines or mend his ways much time usually elapsed before the ultimate sanction was reluctantly applied. What is more, if at all possible the holding was even then passed to the next of kin. Almost everywhere custom triumphed over caprice.

Thus custom protected. It could also oppress, for we must not forget that the customary conditions of tenure of the unfree were in essence a catalogue of obligations and restrictions. Prominent among these was the liability to labour on the demesne and serve in a variety of manorial offices. In addition a villein family's ability to marry, migrate, be educated, buy and sell property, and brew, mill and bake were all commonly dependent upon its lord's favour. Yet in the thirteenth century even these obligations and restrictions were in an important respect far less oppressive than they might at first appear. This was primarily because, with very few exceptions, they were ultimately financial burdens rather than direct and inescapable limitations upon freedom of action. Lords were concerned far less with controlling the lives of their villeins than with profiting from their right to do so. Thus permission to marry, to send sons to be educated or to enter the church, to emigrate from the manor, to sell animals, to alienate unfree land or acquire free land could almost invariably be purchased, and the size of the payment demanded was itself often determined by custom. The unfree could also fine to avoid serving as reeves or other manorial officers, and labour services were often commuted and if exacted could be performed by a substitute workman hired by the tenant.[16]

The role of labour services in particular has often been exaggerated and sometimes misunderstood. Forced labour has been viewed by both contemporaries and historians as constituting the core of serfdom, and yet on closer scrutiny it can be seen to have played a relatively minor part in the relationships between landlords and their unfree tenants, at

[14] The hereditary rights of villeins are expressed in forcible terms in a marginal entry made in the early fourteenth century on a Bracton MS., quoted *ibid.*, p. 416 n. 2.

[15] E. Miller and J. Hatcher, *Medieval England: Rural Society and Economic Change, 1086-1348* (London, 1978), pp. 135-6.

[16] This is not to deny, of course, that financial burdens could in themselves constitute grave limitations of freedom; see p. 258 below.

least from the second half of the thirteenth century. As long ago as 1886 Thorold Rogers asserted that only slight traces of the forced labour system remained by the eve of the Black Death.[17] The data collected subsequently by T. W. Page, H. L. Gray and E. A. Kosminsky, and the analyses made of them, have significant limitations, but handled with discrimination and supplemented and amplified by data derived from the many detailed studies of regions, estates and manors which are now available they provide an adequate base for generalization.[18] We now know, of course, that Thorold Rogers underestimated the extent to which labour services persisted into the fourteenth century, but it would appear that services of two or more days weekly were performed at that time by a relatively small minority of English villein tenants. In but a few counties (Norfolk, Suffolk, Cambridgeshire, Essex, Huntingdonshire, and parts of Lincolnshire, Hertfordshire, Sussex and Northamptonshire) was regular week-work rendered by a substantial proportion of the unfree, while in a large minority of counties (including Northumberland, Cumberland, Westmorland, Herefordshire, Cheshire, Lancashire, Yorkshire, Derbyshire, Nottinghamshire, Leicestershire, Kent and Cornwall) services were, with some exceptions, very light.[19] Even in the counties which lay between these two extremes services seem very often to have been slight. In 1279, for example, in the ninety-three villages and hamlets of the contrasting Warwickshire hundreds of Stoneleigh and Kineton the obligation to perform services lay heavily upon only a small minority of tenants: in more than a quarter of settlements no services at all were due from the inhabitants, and in scarcely more than 10 per cent were any inhabitants liable to week-works.[20]

Moreover the documents to which we have so far referred, the Hundred Rolls of 1279, *inquisitions post mortem* and manorial extents, surveys and custumals, record obligations not performance. If we turn to the annual reeves' and bailiffs' accounts we find that only a portion, and often a small portion, of the services which the lord could exact were actually performed. In the century after 1250 estate managers increasingly displayed a preference for hired rather than customary labour, no doubt encouraged by the abundance of labourers seeking work and the relative inefficiency of forced labour. Whatever the surveys might record, by the early fourteenth century commutation was proceeding apace even on the estates of ancient ecclesiastical

---

[17] J. E. T. Rogers, *A History of Agriculture and Prices in England, 1259-1793*, 7 vols. (Oxford, 1866-1902), i, p. 91.

[18] T. W. Page, *The End of Villainage in England* (New York, 1900); H. L. Gray, "The Commutation of Labour Services", *Eng. Hist. Rev.*, xxix (1915); Kosminsky, *Studies in the Agrarian History of England in the Thirteenth Century*, ch. 3.

[19] For a recent discussion, see Miller and Hatcher, *Medieval England: Rural Society and Economic Change*, pp. 121-8.

[20] Hilton, *English Peasantry in the Later Middle Ages*, p. 129.

foundations in the heartland of traditional manorialism.[21] It would appear likely, indeed, that at this time week-works were regularly performed by members of substantially less than a third of villein households, and consequently by no more than one in six of English households.

Thus in an era which has frequently been interpreted as one of increasing manorialization and seigneurial exploitation a central constituent of villeinage was relatively insignificant and declining. Yet this decline was not necessarily beneficial for the unfree. The changes which had occurred in the relative value of land and labour meant that work could be a cheap form of rent. For the poor and underemployed tenant and his family, commutation, even at a low customary rate, was not always welcome and was sometimes resisted.[22]

If we turn to other aspects of villeinage which have frequently been seen as constituting the gravest limitations of freedom, we find that here too there is room for misunderstanding. It needs no stressing that the dependance of man upon man was a central feature of the middle ages, and that there was no freehold in the sense in which we know it today. The possession of land at all levels of society carried obligations to a landlord and constraints upon the freedom of the landholder. We would be in error, therefore, if we saw all these constraints as deriving from unfreedom, or unique to it; indeed some of these constraints bore heaviest upon the nobility and gentry. This is not the place to elaborate upon the incidents of tenure in chivalry, the so-called "seven fruits" of aid, relief, primer seisin, wardship, marriage, fines for alienation, and escheat, but they should not be put out of mind when considering the powers exercised by lords over their unfree tenants in comparable circumstances.[23]

Considerable opportunities both for legitimate profit and for theft presented themselves to a lord when his vassal died. It was the lord's right and duty to determine the true heir to an inheritance, and if the heir were absent or not of age (twenty-one years) the lord had wardship of the land until he returned or came of age. During such time the lord

---

[21] In East Anglia, for example; see E. Miller, *The Abbey and Bishopric of Ely: The Social History of an Ecclesiastical Estate from the Tenth Century to the Early Fourteenth Century* (Cambridge, 1951), pp. 103-4; J. A. Raftis, *The Estates of Ramsey Abbey: A Study in Economic Growth and Organization* (Toronto, 1957), pp. 222-3, 242-4.

[22] See the interesting case at Elton in 1278, in which the reeve was accused "of taking gifts from the richer tenants as a consideration for not turning them into tenants at money rents, and with obliging the poorer tenants to become payers of money rents": *Select Pleas in Manorial and Other Seignorial Courts*, i, *Reigns of Henry III and Edward I*, ed. F. W. Maitland (Selden Soc., ii, London, 1889), p. 95.

[23] For discussions of tenure in chivalry, see Pollock and Maitland, *History of English Law before the Time of Edward I*, i, pp. 307-56; S. Painter, *Studies in the History of the English Feudal Barony* (Baltimore, 1943), pp. 56-72; A. L. Poole, *Obligations of Society in the XII and XIII Centuries* (Oxford, 1946), pp. 92-107.

could lawfully appropriate to his own use the rents and other proceeds of the estate, although he was expected to leave the capital intact. Upon taking his inheritance the vassal paid a relief to his lord. A lord also had the right to arrange the marriages of heirs, male or female, and widows; these rights were regarded as property and were saleable and assignable. Bracton maintained that the prerogatives of lords extended still further, and that no woman holding by military service could lawfully marry without consent, and a father could not lawfully give any of his daughters in marriage without similar consent. Such prerogatives Painter has termed "a magnificent source of revenue and patronage"; they were certainly open to immense abuse and were an almost continual cause of friction between lords and vassals, kings and barons.[24]

In comparison with such sweeping powers, not only over the inheritances but also the persons of heirs, those normally exercised by lords over their villeins might appear relatively mild. Upon the death of an unfree tenant the lord took a heriot of the best beast or chattel, sometimes more and sometimes less according to local custom, and the heir or other incoming tenant paid an entry fine. If the heir were not of age, in direct contrast to feudal law, the lord did not take possession of the holding or exercise wardship over him. Instead a guardian was normally appointed from within the family, commonly the mother or a close relative on the maternal side if she were also dead, and the profits of farming the holding remained within the family.[25] A marriage fine, merchet, was sometimes exacted upon the marriage of daughters of unfree tenants, but lords seem rarely to have pressed them to marry and their main concern appears to have been whether the spouse resided within or without their lordship. Female villein heirs and widows were, however, often encouraged to marry, and were sometimes fined if they delayed or refused, presumably because lords and village communities were anxious to ensure that family holdings were efficiently run and able to meet their obligations. A fine was also sometimes exacted if an unmarried female villein was discovered to have fornicated.

The emphasis which was increasingly placed upon extraordinary charges relating to the marriages, deaths and successions of vassals and their families was to a large extent an inevitable consequence of the inflexibility of ordinary sources of revenue in the face of the rising value of land and the falling value of money. The control of lords over their vassals steadily weakened as fees came to be regarded as patrimonies, and as the services rendered for them ceased to be "fully and in

[24] Painter, *Studies in the History of the English Feudal Barony*, pp. 67-8; Pollock and Maitland, *History of English Law before the Time of Edward I*, i, p. 320. See also E. Searle, "Freedom and Marriage in Medieval England: An Alternative Hypothesis", *Econ. Hist. Rev.*, 2nd ser., xxix (1976), p. 485.

[25] For an outline of common practices, see G. C. Homans, *English Villagers of the Thirteenth Century* (Cambridge, Mass., 1942), pp. 191 ff.

everything" and came to be fixed and certain. As we have seen, there were strong parallels in the villeinage. The extensive seigneurial powers confirmed by royal courts and legal commentators were everywhere limited by custom, which usually assumed the force of law within the manor and village. The consequence was often declining real incomes from the villeinage, and most enterprising landlords came to realize that the best and most acceptable opportunities for profit lay in the exploitation of favourable market forces rather than the exploitation of their villeins.

III

Since most of the disabilities of unfreedom in the later thirteenth century ultimately constituted financial burdens rather than direct and inflexible restrictions upon freedom of action, we are encouraged to view villeinage in predominantly economic terms. To do so is not, of course, to deny that freedom could be prized for its own sake, or that the weight of monetary exactions could in itself constitute a grave restriction of freedom. Such an approach does, however, centre upon a consideration of the balance of what the unfree rendered to their lords and what they received from them. If the renders were overwhelmingly pecuniary, the returns were also almost exclusively economic, for by the later thirteenth century the protection of one's lord had declined in significance. Our assessment of this central feature of villeinage, therefore, will depend largely upon what the unfree paid for their lands and what those lands were worth.

By any measure unfree landholders were at a substantial disadvantage when compared with the owners of ancient freeholdings. Acre for acre the unfree almost invariably paid far more. For the rents of such freeholders were usually extremely low and bore little relation to the value of the lands which they held; moreover their dues were not only lower, they were absolutely immutable. This is the comparison which is frequently made in order to stress the handicap of unfreedom. But it is not the only comparison which can be made, and it is doubtful whether these extremely privileged tenants provide the most relevant yardstick with which to measure the impact of unfree status.

More relevant would appear to be a comparison of total charges upon villein land with charges upon land which was not governed by custom; in other words, what a villein might have to pay for land if he were not a villein or what he did pay if he acquired additional land.[26] A comparison of villein payments with those borne by leaseholders, life tenants, cottagers and the tenants of recently created freeholdings

---

[26] This proposition does not depend upon the existence of a perfect free market for land outside the freehold and customary sectors, but simply upon the existence of a *freer* market.

is by no means unfavourable to the unfree holding in villeinage. Indeed there are very many indications that by the later thirteenth century the unfree, far from suffering from an excess of seigneurial exploitation, were normally paying less for their lands than they would have had to pay if their rents had been freely negotiated. It is indisputable that many, perhaps most, lords succeeded in burdening their unfree tenants with increased and additional payments and obligations of one sort or another in the course of the later twelfth and the thirteenth centuries, but it is also indisputable that land values rose sharply over the same period, along with the price of foodstuffs and other agrarian produce.[27]

Precise statistics are certainly no easier to come by in this area than in most other areas of medieval history, but it is not a difficult task to gather a formidable body of evidence which indicates that during the thirteenth century substantial economic benefits could be derived from holding land in villeinage. One consequence of those benefits which we can clearly observe is that landlords increasingly sought to augment their incomes by expanding the non-customary constituents of their rent-rolls. It was not simply that lords rarely created new villein holdings when they devolved portions of their demesnes, it was that they frequently took positive action on the failure of heirs to villein holdings and transferred them from the villeinage into more lucrative leaseholds or competitive tenancies at will.

The extensive archives of the abbey and bishopric of Ely contain many examples of these developments and are therefore a suitable place to begin.[28] In the great survey of the estates made in 1251 we find that customary penny, two-penny and four-penny acres were common in the villeinage, but also in evidence were tenants at will holding on precarious terms, *de anno in annum ad voluntatem domini*, at rents as high as 1s. 5d. per acre. There were also newly enfeoffed men (*novi feoffati*) who paid rents in excess of the general level: at Pulham (Norfolk) such men paid around 6d. per acre while the main body of *censuarii* paid on average 4d.; and further west in the same county at Bridgeham newly enfeoffed men paid 1s. or even 2s. (with tallage and other servile charges) for half-acre tofts. Leaseholds were carved out of the villeinage as well as the demesnes and assarts of Ely manors, and by the early fourteenth century there were many tenements which had been held in villeinage in 1251 but which were now held on leases at

---

[27] These dates provide, of course, only the broadest guide to the limits of the period when in general the advantages of holding in villeinage outweighed the disadvantages. We can be certain that there were exceptions, even at the height of land hunger, and we can discern from at least as early as the second decade of the fourteenth century an occasional indication of the first tentative slackening of the land market, which began to render some unfree holdings unattractive at their customary rent levels. See n. 89 below.

[28] This paragraph is based upon Miller, *Abbey and Bishopric of Ely*, chs. 5-6.

rents which were two, three or even more times greater. As Edward Miller has concluded: "Customary rents there might still be upon the bishop's rent-roll, but it was hardly to be expected that they would develop much when these far more lucrative forms of rent were at the bishop's disposal".

Some of the most dramatic revelations of relatively low rents in the villeinage occurred when a landlord seeking greater profits converted villein holdings into leaseholdings. Certainly such action provides much of our most direct evidence, and it seems to become ever more common as the thirteenth century progressed. The custumal of the Cotswold manor of Minchinhampton, dated by its editor as late thirteenth century, reveals an abundance of holdings which were once fully in the villeinage but at the time of the survey were held for life, often on servile terms.[29] In a number of instances the entry in the custumal is full enough to reveal that the life tenant is paying a substantially enhanced rent. A particularly informative entry in the court roll of 1316-17 shows that the initiative could come from the tenant, for we learn that William de Brechcumbe surrendered a holding into the hands of the abbess of Caen and gave his best sheep as a heriot. Then Robert, son of Richard de Nailesworth, and Benedict Howelot were granted William's holding by the abbess for life. The terms of the new life lease were that Richard and Benedict should render the same services and customs as William de Brechcumbe had formerly rendered, but pay 12s. 7¼d. annually in place of the former rent of 2s. 7¼d., and in addition a relief of 10s. each. No doubt they had also to pay William a substantial recompense for surrendering his land.[30]

It seems probable that the privileged ancient demesne status of Minchinhampton manor and the presence of industrial activity in the neighbourhood played a part in encouraging so substantial a margin between the customary rent and what outsiders were prepared to pay, but many comparable examples can readily be found elsewhere. Close by on the manors of St. Peter's Abbey, Gloucester, R. H. Hilton has discerned the beginnings of "the erosion of the old system by non-customary tenures" at an even earlier date.[31] He found, scattered among the customary tenements listed in extents made between 1265 and 1267, a number of tenements held for fixed terms; some for money alone, others for money and servile obligations. It appears that some of these tenures had their origins in old freeholdings, others in more recently acquired assarts, but some at least seem to have originated in

[29] "The Minchinhampton Custumal and its Place in the Story of the Manor", ed. C. W. Watson, *Trans. Bristol and Gloucs. Archaeol. Soc.*, liv (1932).

[30] *Ibid.*, pp. 223, 297. Watson mistranscribed the original rent as 1s. 7¼d. I am grateful to Dr. M. Chibnall for the correct figure.

[31] R. H. Hilton, "Gloucester Abbey Leases of the Late Thirteenth Century", repr. in his *English Peasantry in the Later Middle Ages*, pp. 139-60.

"ordinary customary holdings lapsed into the lord's hand, and released in such a way that the rent could be increased without the tenant or his heir being able to appeal to custom". What makes the St. Peter's Abbey archive so informative is the survival of a sizeable number of the actual agreements the abbey made with its tenants, usually in the form of chirographs. The majority of these agreements make it clear that they related to land previously held in villeinage, and many made provision for the continuing servile status of the life lessees, despite the new terms of tenure. Of still greater significance are the high premiums which were paid for these leases, premiums sometimes as great or greater than the price of freehold land and certainly far in excess of the entry fines charged upon comparable customary holdings. The majority of peasants who came forward to bid for these leases seem to have been villeins, but they must have been wealthy villeins anxious to profit from the possession of additional lands.

These Gloucestershire estates provide particularly full examples of the conversion of villein tenures into more precarious leaseholds. But there is no shortage of detailed evidence that landlords elsewhere were aware of the financial attractions of contractual tenure. For example, to the east of the main body of Ely estates at Bocking (Essex) we find that the monks of Christ Church, Canterbury, were "steadily converting customary holdings into small parcels of land to be relet as several holdings", and a few miles south-east of Bocking at Langenhoe Lionel de Bradenham, the lord of the manor, increased his seigneurial income from 169s. 11d. to 298s. 5½d. between 1325 and 1348 by substituting leasehold rents for customary rents.[32] In the far south-west of England, in the second half of the thirteenth century, we can trace leaseholds making considerable headway at the expense of bond-land on Tavistock Abbey estates, while in Cornwall leaseholds were even more prominent.[33] Conventionary tenure on the earldom, later the duchy, of Cornwall estates was in many respects a special case, but its history in the first half of the fourteenth century has relevance for us. On the accession of Queen Isabella to the estates in 1317, after a lengthy period in which conventionary rents and fines seem to have changed little, her officials began to take advantage of the active demand for land. The result was an increase in charges which sometimes exceeded 100 per cent over the next twenty years. But even before this steep rise in conventionary rents and fines took place the customary unfree (*nativi de stipite*) held on average 10 per cent more land than the conventionaries but paid around 40 per cent less for it. Small wonder that here too it

---

[32] R. A. L. Smith, *Canterbury Cathedral Priory: A Study in Monastic Administration* (Cambridge, 1943), p. 118 n.; R. H. Britnell, "Production for the Market on a Small Fourteenth-Century Estate", *Econ. Hist. Rev.*, 2nd ser., xix (1966), p. 386.

[33] H. P. R. Finberg, *Tavistock Abbey: A Study in the Social and Economic History of Devon* (Cambridge, 1951), pp. 249-51.

became the policy to transfer villein holdings to leaseholds when lines of succession failed.[34]

As in so many areas of medieval life, however, custom and tradition acted as restraints upon innovation and enterprise, and although the conversion of villein tenures into competitive tenures became ever more frequent it is unlikely that it became the normal method of dealing with escheated holdings before the Black Death. Nonetheless the relative benefits of villein tenure are revealed in many other ways. Even if lords refrained from taking the opportunity of a failure of heirs to change the status of land, they frequently used this circumstance to impose higher rents, services and entry fines upon prospective tenants from outside the family. The breaking of a line of inheritance was seen as releasing the grip of custom, and enabling payments more in line with the true market value to be exacted. Upon Chertsey Abbey manors, for example, in addition to higher fines, "it would appear that a fairly general practice was made of raising rent whenever a new tenant was admitted to a holding, except where he took it by inheritance: transference seems to have been regarded as decontrolling the rent".[35]

Landlords, supported by village communities, seem invariably to have displayed a strong bias in favour of customary heirs, and on very many estates this meant that those without family claims were charged higher entry fines. Although fines rose, sometimes sharply, as the thirteenth century wore on, there are clear indications from many estates that those imposed upon villein heirs were frequently substantially lower than outsiders were prepared to pay. At Halesowen (Worcestershire), for example, a low customary fine of 13s. 4d. per virgate was charged upon inheritance, but when a villager acquired a holding without a right of inheritance he was likely to be charged at a rate much closer to the true market value. Thus in 1294 Henry Osbern was fined £6. 13s. 4d. rather than 6s. 8d. for entry into a half virgate previously held by Thomas Robin, and when William Lee in 1310 acquired a vacant quarter-virgate holding from the lord he paid a fine of £2. 7s. 0d. rather than 3s. 4d. While at Launton (Oxfordshire) those with no family claims were likely to be asked double the sum for which a family heir would have been liable.[36]

---

[34] Hatcher, *Rural Economy and Society in the Duchy of Cornwall*, pp. 72, 85-92, 134-5.

[35] *Chertsey Abbey Court Rolls Abstract*, ed. E. Toms, 3 vols. in 2 (Surrey Rec. Soc., xxxviii, lii-liii, London, 1937-63), i; see also *ibid.*, pp. xxx, xxxiv. The increases in rent were often small, but higher entry fines were often also charged; see esp. nos. 146, 213, 668, 1015.

[36] Z. Razi, *Life, Marriage and Death in a Medieval Parish: Economy, Society and Demography in Halesowen, 1270-1400* (Past and Present Pubns., Cambridge, 1980), pp. 29-30; B. Harvey, *Westminster Abbey and its Estates in the Middle Ages* (Oxford, 1977), pp. 224-5. See also, *inter alia*, B. Harvey, "The Population Trend in England between 1300 and 1348", *Trans. Roy. Hist. Soc.*, 5th ser., xvi (1966), p. 27; E. King, *Peterborough Abbey, 1086-1310: A Study in the Land Market* (Cambridge, 1973), pp. 166-7, 182-8; J. Z. Titow, *English Rural Society, 1200-1350* (London, 1969), p. 77.

The examples which we have so far furnished are typical of the more detailed and specific sources at our disposal; they are also the most direct since they provide incontrovertible evidence of differing exactions from the same holdings. A multitude of further but briefer and less precise indications of the differential which normally existed between competitive and customary rents are contained in rentals, surveys and extents. Ideally for such a comparison we would wish to calculate the total burdens upon holdings of comparable size and quality. This is no simple task for to do so we require not just the rents and money equivalents of services due from villein holdings, but also the level of entry fines and the frequency with which they were paid, the incidence of merchet, *leyrwite* and heriot, and the financial cost of all the other *consuetudines non taxatas* which were the consequence of unfree status. On the other hand we would also need to discover the monetary value of the pasture and pannage which normally went with villein acres but not with leasehold. One such set of calculations has been attempted by R. H. Hilton for the Berkeley manor of Cam. He found there that the total rent burden on villein yardlands of sixty acres was 8·7d. per acre, including labour services and aid (tallage), but not including the other incidents of unfreedom which perhaps amounted to an additional penny or three halfpence per acre. By contrast competitive freehold rents at Cam ranged upwards from 9d. per acre to almost 3s.[37]

On very many manors in addition to the central body of freeholders and villeins there were tenants holding land on what appears to have been competitive terms.[38] In some records such tenants are clearly designated as holding for terms of years or for life, while in others they are grouped among the freeholders or cottagers, their sole distinguishing feature being the greatly enhanced rents which they paid. A brief perusal of the Hundred Rolls is sufficient to demonstrate that there were many free tenants who paid large sums for small holdings. On the prior of Ely's manor at Hauxton (Cambridgeshire), for example, there were four free life tenants whose holdings ranged from six acres for 6s. down to three rods for 16d. grouped among traditional free tenants paying far less for larger holdings.[39]

[37] R. H. Hilton, *A Medieval Society: The West Midlands at the End of the Thirteenth Century* (London, 1966), pp. 144-8 (assuming 8s. 7d. per acre to be a misprint for 8·7d. per acre). A very rough estimate, indeed inevitably an overestimate, of the absolute maximum monetary burden of the *consuetudines non taxatas* can be obtained by dividing total court receipts by the numbers of unfree tenants. Manorial court receipts included, of course, a wide range of payments which might properly be described as jurisdictional rather than seigneurial in character, such as payments and fines for transgressions and breaches of village by-laws, trespass, debt, and the like, in addition to seigneurial exactions from the free as well as the unfree.
[38] For a discussion of the legal characteristics of such holdings, see P. Vinogradoff, *Villainage in England: Essays in English Medieval History* (Oxford, 1892), pp. 330-2.
[39] *Rotuli hundredorum temp. Hen. III et Edw. I in turr' Lond' et in curia receptae*

Some competitive tenancies originated, as we have seen, from escheated holdings, others from the demising of portions of demesne or recently assarted lands. It is impossible to draw general conclusions regarding the rents of demised demesne or assart, since such lands varied so greatly in fertility and location, and therefore in value. Acres also varied in size, being frequently dependent upon local customary measures. As for former demesne, we must assume that it was often the poorest and least productive acres which were shed, while those which remained profitable were retained. Consequently some demesne acres were demised at low rents, while some seem to have slipped completely out of cultivation.[40] Other portions of demesne, by contrast, realized rents which were substantially in excess of those ruling in the villeinage. Even in the north of England, where pressure upon the land was generally less acute than elsewhere, rents for demesne leaseholds sometimes reached prodigious heights, even allowing for large customary acres: 2s. 9d. an acre at Tanshelf (Yorkshire) and 2s. 6d. to 3s. an acre at Bamburgh (Northumberland), for example.[41] Over all, however, the impression is that there was great diversity in rents and that this diversity reflected variations in fertility and managerial policy as well as in local demand.

Analysis of assart rents poses both similar and additional problems. Assarts were frequently marginal in location as well as in fertility, and the later the assart the more marginal it was likely to have been. Additionally the rent an assart commanded was likely to reflect the means by which it was brought into cultivation; peasant assarters were frequently rewarded for their effort and initiative with low rents as well as free status.[42] Nonetheless it seems indisputable that rents for fertile and infertile, peasant as well as seigneurial, assarts rose steeply as the thirteenth century progressed. Moreover the more recent assarts frequently commanded rents which were higher than those of older assarts, despite the probability that older assarts were intrinsically more desirable lands. Once again a major factor in this apparent inversion of values would appear to have been custom, which tended to freeze rents at the levels determined when the land was first brought into cultivation. By contrast the rents of later assarts, being free of customary restraints at the time when they were fixed, were likely to reflect increas-

(note 39 cont.)

scaccarii West. asservati, ed. W. Illingworth, 2 vols. (Rec. Comm., London, 1812-18), ii, p. 547. See also Kosminsky, Studies in the Agrarian History of England in the Thirteenth Century, pp. 242-8.

[40] A number of low contractual rents, many for demesne acres, are contained in Harvey, Westminster Abbey and its Estates in the Middle Ages, pp. 443-7.

[41] E. Miller, in The Agrarian History of England and Wales, ii (forthcoming), ch. 7.

[42] See the brief discussion in Miller and Hatcher, Medieval England: Rural Society and Economic Change, pp. 39-40.

ed competition for land.[43] Consequently, as we have noted at Pulham and Bridgeham (Norfolk), rents for assarts frequently exceeded those on villein holdings despite their relative infertility. The marshlands which the monks of Christ Church Priory, Canterbury, had reclaimed and embanked were let out at competitive leasehold rents which rose as high as 2s. 7d. per acre; and although in 1308-9 at Langdon (Staffordshire) sixty-six acres of waste were demised by the bishop of Coventry and Lichfield for the relatively low annual rent of 6d. an acre, they commanded entry fines which rose as high as an astronomical 10s. an acre.[44]

The final source of competitive tenures reflects seigneurial enterprise even more directly, for some landlords purchased lands with vacant possession with the express intention of leasing them at high rents. Once again the monks of Christ Church Priory were in the vanguard, and they invested considerable sums in such ventures. The leases they negotiated brought them up to 1s. an acre annually, which compared very favourably with the average *gafol* of 1d. an acre and *mala* of 3d. an acre received from their customary tenants.[45]

If landlords increasingly sought ways of circumventing the sluggishness of customary payments, the unfree themselves were not unaware of the opportunities of profiting from it, not simply by staying put but by selling and subletting. One prime prerequisite of the active market in unfree land during the century before the Black Death, hitherto somewhat neglected, is that the land so conveyed had a value over and above the seigneurial burdens which went with it. How large this gap between customary payments and value could be is evidenced by the costly procedures which usually had to be followed to effect a sale: the seller commonly paid to his lord a fine and a heriot, and the buyer paid an entry fine and commonly also an increased annual rent, in addition to the purchase "price" to the seller.[46]

IV

The emphasis which we have placed upon the inelasticity of customary payments, and the emphasis which landlords themselves placed

[43] For an alternative explanation based upon the hypothesis of the declining productivity of cultivated land, see *The Cambridge Economic History of Europe*, i, *The Agrarian Life of the Middle Ages*, 2nd edn., ed. M. M. Postan (Cambridge, 1966), pp. 557-8; M. M. Postan, *The Medieval Economy and Society: An Economic History of Britain in the Middle Ages* (London, 1972), p. 70.

[44] Smith, *Canterbury Cathedral Priory*, pp. 116-18; C. Dyer, in *Agrarian History of England and Wales*, ii, ch. 3.

[45] Smith, *Canterbury Cathedral Priory*, pp. 118-19.

[46] M. M. Postan, *Essays on Medieval Agriculture and General Problems of the Medieval Economy* (Cambridge, 1973), pp. 107-49; P. Hyams, "The Origins of a Peasant Land Market in England", *Econ. Hist. Rev.*, 2nd ser., xxiii (1970). See also the example from Minchinhampton manor, p. 260 above.

upon the exploitation of the non-customary elements in their rent-rolls, should not lead us to understate the attempts which many land-lords made to increase revenues from their villeinage. As we have seen, even lords who fully obeyed custom could raise entry fines. We have also seen that lords could take advantage of failures of heirs to increase charges upon unfree holdings or remove them from the villeinage, and in this way the numbers of villein tenants enjoying absolute protection of conditions of tenure must have contracted. But there can be no doubt that some landlords attempted to increase charges and alter con-ditions of tenure even on holdings that remained in the possession of the same family, and did so in a manner which involved breaches of custom. Indeed Hilton has found many disputes between landlords and tenants which centred upon alleged breaches of custom. Nor can there be any doubt that farmers and temporary guardians of manors some-times acted ruthlessly in search of short-term profits at the expense both of the true owners and their tenants.[47] Bailiffs and reeves could also oppress, sometimes, as the response to the Bocking petition tells us, against the express wishes of their lords.[48]

Nonetheless although large numbers of villeins may well have paid significantly more for their lands around 1310 than their predecessors had in the later twelfth century, once again it must be emphasized that placed in the context of a more than fourfold increase in the price of agricultural produce and of probably an even greater increase in land values it is not the breaching of custom which is most striking but the observing of it.[49] How each group of villeins fared depended upon an extensive range of particular factors as well as the more general ones we have been discussing, but the testimony of historians who have studied in great detail the relations of landlords and tenants on indi-vidual estates may well have a broad relevance. Of Westminster Abbey manors Barbara Harvey has written: "Remarkably, in view of the in-flationary character of the period, the annual dues for villein holdings . . . changed little in the century that separated the making of the cus-tumal of *c.* 1225 from the Black Death".[50] J. Z. Titow has written of the Winchester bishopric estates: "I have never come across any indi-cation of any attempt to increase services on any of the Bishop's many manors", and has concluded that "there were also no attempts, in so

---

[47] For struggles between landlords and tenants, see Kosminsky, *Studies in the Agra-rian History of England in the Thirteenth Century*, pp. 338-50; R. H. Hilton, "Peas-ant Movements in England before 1381", in E. M. Carus-Wilson (ed.), *Essays in Eco-nomic History*, 3 vols. (London, 1954-62), i, pp. 73-90.

[48] J. F. Nichols, "An Early Fourteenth Century Petition of the Tenants of Bocking to their Manorial Lord", *Econ. Hist. Rev.*, ii (1930).

[49] Breaches of custom involving increases of labour services, for example, may well have been less common and less severe than was once thought. See Raftis, *Estates of Ramsey Abbey*, p. 115 n. 68; T. H. Aston, "The English Manor", *Past and Present*, no. 10 (Nov. 1956), pp. 6-14.

[50] Harvey, *Westminster Abbey and its Estates in the Middle Ages*, p. 219.

far as one can see, to violate custom to introduce uniform practices even on the manors of the same administrative group".[51] J. A. Raftis has written of the Ramsey Abbey estates: "The student is liable to miss the vital problems facing abbey administration in the thirteenth century if he does not realize the powerful force of custom at that time. A close acquaintance with the extents and manorial court rolls of Ramsey estates does not leave one surprised with the evidence that purchase of property, rather than arbitrary seigneurial authority, was the most effective means of 'reaction'. While theoretically the lord might have a jurisdiction 'at will' over his villeins, in the practical order custom was upheld as law".[52] As Maitland put it: "A good proof that the lords in general felt themselves bound more or less conclusively by the terms of the customary tenures is to be found in the care they took that these terms should be recorded".[53] Oral custom was inevitably inconstant over the longer term, but the veritable explosion of written estate records as the thirteenth century progressed enhanced its stability; and the ever increasing precision with which obligations and rights were spelt out by estate officials greatly reduced the scope of arbitrary seigneurial action.

It is far simpler to establish that lords were bound by customs which could not be enforced against them than to explain why this should have been so. Even Maitland was somewhat perplexed, and he asked rhetorically whether a lord did so out of "provident self-interest, a desire for a quiet life, [or] humane fellow-feeling for his dependants".[54] One might also add the possibility that some lords sometimes followed traditional paths because they lacked awareness of or were indifferent to economic trends. Yet we must not fail to emphasize that if lords commonly respected custom, village and manorial communities nurtured and fostered it. To a great extent custom was community custom, and the support which it received from below was no less powerful than that which it received from above. This cannot be the place for a detailed discussion, but it must be noted that almost everywhere one looks in the middle ages one is likely to find men seeking to justify and perpetuate the present in terms of the past. Even Bracton's ruthless denigration of the status of customary law *vis-à-vis* common law was tempered by a recognition that "the authority of custom and long use is not slight".[55] How could he argue otherwise when so much constitutional law, canon law, even medicine and science, was governed by precedent and practice? In feudal courts custom regulated the relations of

[51] J. Z. Titow, "Land and Population on the Bishop of Winchester's Estates, 1209-1350" (Univ. of Cambridge Ph.D. thesis, 1962), p. 38.
[52] Raftis, *Estates of Ramsey Abbey*, p. 118 n. 74.
[53] Pollock and Maitland, *History of English Law before the Time of Edward I*, i, p. 362.
[54] *Ibid.*, p. 376.
[55] Bracton, *De legibus et consuetudinibus Angliae*, ed. G. E. Woodbine, rev. S. E. Thorne, 2 vols. (Cambridge, Mass., 1968), ii, p. 22.

lords and vassals no less strictly than it regulated the relations of lords and peasants in manorial courts.[56] We find that contracts once entered into or arrangements once made quickly became inflexible, and frequently assumed a hereditary immutability, whether they related to the knight's fee, or the shire, borough or manorial farm. The limited-term or negotiable contract, especially if it concerned land, was something which emerged only slowly and painfully in the context of sharply falling money values. Thus what we find in the humble world of the manor and village is but an expression of a force felt throughout the whole of medieval society.[57]

What we have so far attempted is an examination of the level and the form of rent payments by the unfree in the later thirteenth century. While it may be considered legitimate to view all rent as surplus transfer, such an indiscriminate approach will not advance us far towards an understanding of the special characteristics of serfdom. For such surplus transfer is inherent in all societies in which property is unequally distributed and in which owners receive recompense for allowing others the use of it.[58] What concerns us here is the mode of transfer and whether such transfer depended upon coercion. More precise reference points for our purpose are provided by an assessment of whether rents upon unfree holdings exceeded the levels dictated by the relative scarcity of land and, alternatively, whether the conditions of unfreedom were so restrictive and degrading that economic considerations became of secondary importance to the unfree. If either of these situations existed it would demonstrate the presence of coercion and exploitation, stemming from the political and class power of landlords.

The evidence and argument which we have put forward above run directly counter to the hypothesis that serfdom over much of the thirteenth century was an effective system of exploitation. Indeed we have suggested that in these economically unpropitious times, far from being the prime cause of poverty, the customary conditions of tenure of the unfree made them a protected, even privileged, tenurial group. More than this, just as there were some lords who burdened their dependants beyond the limits of custom, there were others, perhaps more numerous, who sometimes took less than their customary rights from indigent tenants, by granting them remissions of fines, heriots and other dues.[59]

[56] For a discussion of the role of custom in the relations between lords and vassals, kings and barons, see J. C. Holt, *Magna Carta* (Cambridge, 1967), esp. ch. 4.

[57] The persistence of some customary rents, especially on crown estates, through the great inflation of the sixteenth century is, perhaps, even more remarkable.

[58] It would not seem relevant to the present discussion to speculate on whether the ancestors of the medieval peasantry had in some distant era been the true owners of the land.

[59] For statements attesting the frequency of concessions to poor tenants, see A. N. May, "An Index of Thirteenth-Century Peasant Impoverishment?: Manor Court Fines", *Econ. Hist. Rev.*, 2nd ser., xxvi (1973), p. 398; Titow, *English Rural Society, 1200-1350*, pp. 95-6.

That land shortage rather than unfreedom was the root cause of poverty before the mid-fourteenth century is demonstrated by much additional evidence. For example, we can turn to the doleful experience of certain free communities which were only lightly touched by the hand of lordship and only lightly burdened by rent, but which practised partible inheritance. In these communities the effects of population increase were all too evident, for swollen with heirs the proliferation of exiguous holdings was inevitable.[60] Of course unfree tenants would have been better off if they had paid lower rents, but it is plausible to speculate that given the persistence of population increase and the absence of seigneurial restraints on the devolution of land, even the total abolition of all payments would not in the longer term have secured immunity from poverty for tenants but simply delayed its onset.

Indeed this approach highlights the artificiality of limiting the analysis of poverty to those fortunate enough to be tenants. Villeins holding in villeinage were probably only rarely among the poorest and most deprived members of village communities. Those villagers generally thought of as typical villeins seem to have comprised a middling rank, even if they held only a quarter virgate. The poorest and in some senses the most exploited were the landless and near-landless. The bulk of such folk lay outside the manorial system or only partly within it, and any benefits which we might be tempted to think their personal independence bestowed on them were in practice likely to be massively outweighed by their economic insecurity. Investigations of exploitation and deprivation must take full account of the large and increasing proportion of the thirteenth-century population which was completely unprotected because it did not hold customary land. Moreover the security of tenure enjoyed by unfree landholders and the uncompetitive nature of their rents were ultimately prejudicial to the interests of those who were outside the system, and who were thereby denied virtually any possibility of gaining access to a large part of the land of England.

The final proof of the balance of advantages and disadvantages of unfreedom in the later thirteenth century does not lie merely in the speculations of historians or even in the calculations of landlords; it lies in the behaviour of the peasants themselves. The purchase of freedom, manumission, appears to have lain well down the list of priorities of even the wealthiest villeins, and to have been overshadowed by the attractions of the acquisition of more land. For, as we have seen, money could invariably secure exemptions from servile restrictions, as and when they were applied. Examples before the agrarian crises of

---

[60] See, for example, the brief discussion in M. M. Postan and J. Hatcher, "Population and Class Relations in Feudal Society", *Past and Present*, no. 78 (Feb. 1978), pp. 24-37, at pp. 30-2.

1315-22 of villeins voluntarily relinquishing unfree holdings, except to their next of kin or to purchasers, are extremely rare, as are examples of villeins being forced to hold land. In direct contrast, examples of freemen willing, even anxious, to accept land on unfree terms are common. More than this, many freemen were willing to accept personal as well as tenurial servility in their quest for subsistence.[61] The oft-recalled tenant of the earl of Gloucester who drowned himself in the Severn in 1293 rather than submit to taking land on servile terms demands our admiration for his devotion to liberty,[62] but his striking sacrifice is overwhelmed by those who eagerly traded personal freedom for a greater measure of economic security. When land and work were scarce, and food expensive, abstractions were readily sacrificed to the practicalities of survival.

V

The proposition that in a time of extremely unfavourable land/labour ratios unfree tenants could derive benefit from their status should not be misinterpreted as a defence of serfdom, still less as intimating that serfdom was inherently beneficial to the unfree. Such conclusions would be patently absurd, and moreover would run directly counter to one of the central tenets of this article: namely that the balance of advantages and disadvantages of unfreedom altered dramatically over time. Some of the very incidents of servitude which became redundant in the overcrowded villages of the thirteenth century, or were even transformed into benefits, had been effective instruments of seigneurial oppression in earlier centuries and were to be applied once more, although with only temporary and limited success, when population fell in the fourteenth century. For much of the recorded history of rural society before the thirteenth century it would appear that lords strove to thwart the consequences, favourable for tenants but unfavourable for themselves, which would otherwise have flowed from a relative abundance of land and shortage of people. Manorialism and serfdom appear to have evolved in response to a scarcity of people, as well as to a need for protection and self-sufficiency. Many of the central features of serfdom seem well designed to cope with labour shortage, as does the prevalence of slavery in Anglo-Saxon times.

[61] For freemen holding in villeinage, including examples of men who had apparently voluntarily become villeins, see Poole, *Obligations of Society in the XII and XIII Centuries*, pp. 18-20. For further examples of freemen swearing away their freedom, see *Court Rolls of the Manor of Wakefield, 1274-1331*, ed. W. P. Baildon, J. Lister and J. W. Walker, 5 vols. (Yorks. Archaeol. Soc. Rec. Ser., xxix, xxxvi, lvii, lxxviii, cix, Huddersfield, 1901-45), i, ed. Baildon, p. 224; A. E. Levett, *Studies in Manorial History*, ed. H. M. Cam, M. Coate and L. S. Sutherland (Oxford, 1938), pp. 191-2.

[62] *The Inquisitiones post mortem for the County of Worcester*, ed. J. W. Willis Bund, 2 vols. (Worcs. Hist. Soc., Worcester, 1894-1909), i, p. 48; Hilton, "Peasant Movements in England before 1381", p. 90.

Labour services and the binding of men to the land and their lords are redolent of the scarcity of labourers and tenants and of the need to secure adequate supplies of them. Land without labourers to cultivate it or tenants to occupy it is worthless. It should come as no surprise, therefore, to discover in the sources of Saxon and early medieval centuries many indications of the struggles of lords to keep men on their estates by force while more attractive prospects elsewhere encouraged them to flee.

More studies of the early history of peasant status and conditions of life are sorely needed. Until they are written these remote centuries will remain a most treacherous epoch to venture into, not least because of the difficulties of determining what was typical and what untypical from the scanty evidence that survives. But it would be remiss not to comment, albeit briefly and superficially, on some of the possible ramifications of the concept of villeinage propounded in this article for our understanding of peasant status and conditions in centuries other than the thirteenth. While doing so, the proposition that the 1180s and 1190s constituted a crucial period for the depression of the rural population, and that freedom of personal status was for many at this time something that was only just being lost, must come under critical review.

However great the obstacles might be to a precise and detailed knowledge of pre-Conquest times, there can be scant grounds for optimism about the status and conditions of life of the majority of Saxon countrymen.[63] If we commence no earlier than the surviving late Saxon surveys, we find a pronounced emphasis on dependence and labour services.[64] The *geburs* of the early eleventh-century *Rectitudines singularum personarum*, who seem to have constituted the most numerous tenants on the estate which the anonymous author surveyed, owed two or three days weekly according to the season, boonworks, rent in money and in kind, and on their death all their property was ceded to their lord as heriot. There can scarcely be doubt that they were also tied to their lord and their lands. These *geburs* were unquestionably more sorely oppressed by their status than were most thirteenth-century villeins, but we cannot be absolutely certain that they were typical of late Saxon peasants. We can, however, see strong similarities with the status of the *ceorls* of early tenth-century Hurstbourne Priors (Hampshire) and the *geburs* of Tidenham (Gloucestershire) at the turn of the tenth and eleventh centuries, the only manors for which

[63] Some cogent arguments are put forward in T. H. Aston, "The Origins of the Manor in England", *Trans. Roy. Hist. Soc.*, 5th ser., vii (1958). See also *The Agrarian History of England and Wales*, i, pt. 2, ed. H. P. R. Finberg (Cambridge, 1972), pp. 430-82, 507-25; C. Stephenson, *Medieval Institutions: Selected Essays*, ed. B. D. Lyon (Ithaca, N.Y., 1967), pp. 234-60.

[64] The most important surveys are contained in *English Historical Documents, 1042-1189*, ed. Douglas and Greenaway, pp. 813-18.

pre-Conquest custumals have survived. We can also have few doubts that life for most lowly folk became still more burdensome with the arrival of the Normans. The substantial rise in the values of very many manors in the twenty years after the Conquest offers ample support for the Anglo-Saxon Chronicler's indictment of the behaviour of William, namely that he "gave his land for rent as dearly as he possibly could ... And he paid no heed how very sinfully the reeves got it from poor men, nor how many illegalities they did". William's example is likely to have been followed by lay and ecclesiastical tenants-in-chief, by knights, and by the farmers of manors, and inevitably a large share of the burden of these increased exactions ultimately rested on the shoulders of the peasantry.[65]

There is a widely-held belief that the great majority of the English peasantry were free or possessed a considerable measure of freedom in the century from the making of Domesday Book to the development of common law villeinage.[66] Yet it is a belief which seems at times to confuse two concepts of freedom which to contemporaries were quite distinct. The *villani*, who together with *bordarii* and *cottarii* comprised almost three-quarters of the persons listed in Domesday, were certainly free in the sense that they were not slaves; for they are clearly distinguished from the *servi*, who comprised a further 9 per cent of those listed. But the *villani* are also distinguished from the *liberi homines* and sokemen, who comprised a further 14 per cent, and the freedom of the latter is often directly contrasted with the relative unfreedom of the former.[67] We know, of course, that these names provide only the vaguest of guides to the status and conditions of tenure of the individuals to which they were appended, and we must assume that among those called *villani* were some who were virtually *liberi homines* as well as some who were almost *servi*. Those who were not *servi* were by this measure not unfree, yet there are grounds for believing that a substantial proportion of the countrymen of eleventh- and early twelfth-century England, perhaps even a large majority, would have been deemed unfree if subjected to the tests of villeinage applied by later Angevin lawyers. Within a century of Domesday nomenclature and definitions changed radically, and the most important status distinction made be-

[65] R. Lennard, *Rural England, 1086-1135: A Study of Social and Agrarian Conditions* (Oxford, 1959), pp. 155-7; F. W. Maitland, *Domesday Book and Beyond: Three Essays* (London, 1960 edn.), pp. 88-94; R. W. Finn, *The Norman Conquest and its Effects on the Economy, 1066-86* (London, 1971), *passim*; Miller and Hatcher, *Medieval England: Rural Society and Economic Change*, p. 23.

[66] See the discussion of this matter in Maitland, *Domesday Book and Beyond*, pp. 67-73; Vinogradoff, *Villainage in England*, pp. 218-20; Hilton, *Decline of Serfdom in Medieval England*, pp. 12-17.

[67] This contrast is emphasized by the formula that some freemen and sokemen could "depart", with the implication that freedom of movement did not apply to other dependent groups: Miller and Hatcher, *Medieval England: Rural Society and Economic Change*, pp. 22-3.

tween peasants ceased to be whether they were slaves or not and came to be whether they were villeins or not. As a consequence the meaning of "free" and "unfree" also changed. But there is little reason to believe that the powers and rights of lords over their dependents, or the status and conditions of the dependents themselves, underwent a parallel transformation.

Liability to perform week-works was probably the test of villeinage most frequently applied by royal courts in the early thirteenth century. In the available surveys of Henry I's reign heavy labour services feature prominently and, although a significant number of tenants were holding *ad malam* or *ad censum* rather than *ad opus*, liability to work two or three days weekly was the common lot of the recorded English peasantry.[68] The testimony of these surveys is very much in accordance with the admittedly even more scanty evidence dating from the tenth and eleventh centuries. The *ceorls* of Hurstbourne Priors had to "work as they are bidden every week but three"; from the *geburs* of Tidenham "much labour is due"; and the *geburs* of the *Rectitudines* were required to work "from two to three days a week according to the season".[69] The very vagueness of these obligations is perhaps sinister; for undefined obligations were potentially extensible up to the limit of coercive powers. Certainly it would not appear that labour services before the mid-twelfth century were any lighter or less widespread than they were in the later thirteenth century.

We are on much less secure ground when we come to most of the other incidents of villeinage commonly found in the thirteenth century, such as merchet, tallage, toll, heriot and *leyrwite*, for the early surveys are laconic and frequently make little or no reference to ancillary customary obligations or exactions. These are matters of current controversy and it is possible for us to do little more than draw attention to the proven early existence of some of these incidents on some estates, and to the dangers of arguing from the silence of records dating from an era when relatively little was committed to writing. In particular it seems that heriot, tallage and *leyrwite* long antedate common law villeinage, and it is possible that the former two exactions were heavier and more arbitrary in earlier times.[70]

Yet however taxing or downright debilitating labour services, merchet, *leyrwite* tallage, toll and other base services and payments might

---

[68] Lennard, *Rural England, 1086-1135*, pp. 375-87; M. M. Postan, "The Chronology of Labour Services", in his *Essays on Medieval Agriculture and General Problems of the Medieval Economy*, pp. 89-106.

[69] *English Historical Documents, 1042-1189*, ed. Douglas and Greenaway, pp. 812-14, 816-18.

[70] J. Scammell, "Freedom and Marriage in Medieval England", *Econ. Hist. Rev.*, 2nd ser., xxvii (1974); Searle, "Freedom and Marriage in Medieval England: An Alternative Hypothesis"; J. Scammell, "Wife-Rents and Merchets", *Econ. Hist. Rev.*, 2nd ser., xxix (1976). For comments on the misleading brevity of twelfth-century records, see Raftis, *Estates of Ramsey Abbey*, pp. 193-6.

prove to be, they were all of less significance than freedom of movement. Of all the limitations upon freedom the denial of the right to move, to seek new farms, new employment, new lords, was the most fundamental.[71] All other incidents of unfreedom can be interpreted as stemming from, or accessory to, the binding of men to the soil and to their lords and the denial of free will. As we have seen, the right of lords to restrict movement was of scant consequence in most parts of thirteenth-century England, since in the economic, demographic and tenurial conditions then prevailing scarcely any unfree tenants desired to leave their farms. There are very good reasons for believing, however, that this limitation of freedom bore heavily upon the greater part of the peasantry in the contrasting conditions of the eleventh and much of the twelfth centuries, and that it had done likewise upon their ancestors.

If we commence in the relatively well-documented era of Norman rule we find that the flight, enticement and stealing of men posed grave problems for lords. For the loss of tenants could prove almost as disastrous as the loss of the land itself. Thus in the early years of William I's reign we find the king ordering Richard, son of Earl Gilbert, and the sheriff of Suffolk to "reseise" Frodo of the men "of whom the said Frodo has been disseised by the men of Count Eustace in Buxhall". From the early years of William Rufus's reign we have a royal writ ordering the king's chaplain and his sheriffs and ministers that, "wherever the abbot of Ramsey or his men can find fugitives who fled from the land of the abbey without licence and unjustly" they should cause them to return "and see that nobody retains them unjustly in any way", and another ordering royal officials to make the men who had left the manor of Dereman after the death of a previous holder "return with all their chattels".[72] Writs relating to fugitive dependants were among the very earliest royal writs, and they show the crown giving the benefit of its authority to support the rights of landlords in this crucial area of jurisdiction. Although such writs, later to have the title *de nativo habendo*, became ever more common in succeeding reigns and were very numerous by Henry II's early years, we can be certain that they record only a tiny proportion of the peasants who sought to escape from the clutches of their lords. For the crown granted, or sold, assistance to only a small number of favoured lords; the vast majority

---

[71] The standard discussion of the legal context is *Royal Writs in England from the Conquest to Glanvill: Studies in the Early History of the Common Law*, ed. R. C. Van Caenegem (Selden Soc., lxxvii, London, 1959), pp. 336-44. It would appear that the full significance of this aspect of the relations between lords and men has not been appreciated. The discussion in Hyams, *King, Lords and Peasants in Medieval England*, ch. 13, adds to our understanding.

[72] *Royal Writs in England from the Conquest to Glanvill*, ed. Van Caenegem, pp. 445-6, 467-8; see also *Leges Wilelmi*, c. 30, in Liebermann, *Gesetze der Angelsachsen*, i, p. 153.

had to rely upon their own resources, and many must have preferred to do so.

So great was the likelihood of flight that when Robert de Sifrewast sold Wuluric the miller to the canons of Missenden (Buckinghamshire) for 5s. in the late twelfth century he promised that if Wuluric should "desert at any time the demesne of the canons, as my own man I shall take him and seize him wherever I shall find him".[73] Moreover the fact that Wuluric was bought and sold, that he commanded a price when separated from the land, is yet another indication of the relative scarcity of people and of the dire powers which lords exercised, or attempted to exercise, over them. The sale of land with tenants upon it was, of course, an everyday occurrence in the middle ages, but the sale of men and women without land occurred only when tenants and labourers were in short supply and lords were confident of their ability to coerce them. Such sales were by no means uncommon in twelfth-century England, and they continued into the early years of the next century in those parts of the country where the expansion of cultivation continued at a pace which exceeded the ability of the local population fully to occupy the land.[74] The brutal practice of sharing the children of the marriages of spouses of different lords between those lords also powerfully reflects the value placed upon people and the inability of those people to benefit from it. This practice, too, became archaic in the more populous thirteenth century.[75] Over a similar time span writs *de nativo habendo* came to be prosecuted primarily to introduce pleas of status rather than to secure the return of fugitives.

The relative values placed by many twelfth-century peasants on land and on freedom suggested by the frequency of flight is dramatically demonstrated by the thirty-eight *rustici* faced with eviction when William de Roumara, earl of Lincoln, founded Revesby Abbey in Lincolnshire in 1142. The *rustici* were offered by William the alternative of holdings elsewhere on terms which seem to have been identical with those to which they had previously been subject, with the bonus of a year's rent-free tenure, or "the liberty of going with all their goods where they wish without any claim". Despite the fact that Revesby was in a prosperous fen-edge region settled by Danes where we might well expect the hand of lordship to have been relatively light, only seven

[73] D. M. Stenton, *English Society in the Early Middle Ages, 1066-1307* (Harmondsworth, 1951), p. 142; *Royal Writs in England from the Conquest to Glanvill*, ed. Van Caenegem, p. 337 n. 2.

[74] Miller and Hatcher, *Medieval England: Rural Society and Economic Change*, pp. 114-15.

[75] *The Treatise on the Laws and Customs of the Realm of England Commonly called Glanvill*, ed. G. D. G. Hall (Edinburgh and London, 1965), p. 58. When Glanvill's treatise was revised about thirty years later this custom was described as *ius antiquum*: Hyams, *King, Lords and Peasants in Medieval England*, pp. 15-16.

chose to remain; thirty-one departed landless but lordless, confident that they could make better lives for themselves elsewhere.[76]

We cannot be certain what proportion of the later eleventh- and twelfth-century peasantry was bound to the land and its lords, but there are good reasons for believing that it was very substantial. Before *circa* 1155 writs directed against fugitives refer in the most general terms to the *homines* or *fugitivi* of this or that lord, and it seems plausible to assume that the terms were cast so broad because the writs were intended to apply to a broad spectrum, perhaps the substantial majority, of the peasantry.[77] We have seen that *rustici* rather than *nativi* or *servi* was the name given to the Revesby tenants who were likewise bound to the land. After *circa* 1155 the writs refer to *fugitivi* and *nativi*, perhaps thereby acknowledging the exemption which some peasants then enjoyed from such action. Some peasants could perhaps now plead that they were not revocable at their lords' will, and it is in Glanvill's legal treatise (*circa* 1187-9) that we first hear of the right of a fugitive to assert his freedom to leave the lands of the claimant by obtaining the writ *de libertate probanda*.[78]

Thus a very large, but unfortunately not precisely quantifiable, proportion of the population of England between the eleventh and the later twelfth centuries existed in a state of dependence and subjection, with many severe limitations on their freedom and many oppressive burdens on their shoulders. They were not free but nor were they specifically deemed unfree. Society at this early stage had no need of such specifications, and their conditions of tenure were rarely if ever elaborated in writing. In the sparse and brief manorial records of the early and mid-twelfth century we find that, in addition to *villani, rustici* and *homines*, tenants were given titles which derived from the size of their holdings, such as *virgarii, cotmanni* and *minimi homines*, or from the form which their rent took, such as *operarii, acremen, censarii* and *malmen*. In royal records they were dismissed as *homines, rustici, ascripticii, Anglici* or *Anglicani*, and only occasionally as *villani* or *nativi*.[79]

We must not be misled by such seemingly neutral titles into overestimating the status of such lowly folk, for we may search in vain in

[76] *Facsimiles of Early Charters from Northamptonshire Collections*, ed. F. M. Stenton (Northants. Rec. Soc., iv, Lincoln, 1930), pp. 1-7. For a similar episode consequent upon the building of Witham monastery in 1175, when some tenants chose freedom and others chose substitute holdings on other royal manors, see *Magna vita Sancti Hugonis*, ed. D. L. Douie and H. Farmer, 2 vols. (Oxford, 1961-2), i, pp. 61-2.

[77] See, for example, *Royal Writs in England from the Conquest to Glanvill*, ed. Van Caenegem, pp. 467-77 (writs nos. 103-24).

[78] *Glanvill*, ed. Hall, pp. 53-6. See also the discussion in Hyams, *King, Lords and Peasants in Medieval England*, ch. 13.

[79] A number of such examples are given in Hilton, "Freedom and Villeinage in England", pp. 7-9; R. C. Van Caenegem, *The Birth of the English Common Law* (Cambridge, 1973), pp. 96-7.

these times, well before the establishment of common law villeinage, for an effective source of protection against a ruthless lord. Numbered among the vulnerable were the *homines* of Billinghay (Lincolnshire) who were "ruined" when the archbishop of York took over the manor and increased its yield by almost half, and the *homines* who were forced to flee from their farms sometime around 1114-18 when Rannulf Flambard, bishop of Durham, attempted to extract from them money which he in turn was forced to pay to the king.[80] Flight, with the risk of recapture and punishment, was often their only means of defence. When Richard Fitzneal in the 1170s mentioned the common peasantry he left his audience in no doubt of their rightlessness, their vulnerability and their servility. He called them *ascripticii*, thereby stressing their bondage, and maintained that "by the law of the land, [they] may not only be transferred by their lords from the lands which they actually till to other spots, but may even themselves be sold or otherwise disposed of"; he also added that they "cannot alter their condition without leave of their masters".[81]

VI

We have so far concentrated on a broad comparison between the late eleventh century and the late twelfth century, but we must not ignore the changes which occurred in the middle decades of this latter century. These changes, stemming from methods of management rather than the law, were to have a major impact on the subsequent history of serfdom, and more particularly on the way in which tenants viewed their condition. It is well enough known that the greater landlords made a decisive move into the direct management and cultivation of their estates at the turn of the twelfth and thirteenth centuries, but less well appreciated is the significance for the peasantry of the era which preceded it. Although the scale of the seigneurial retrenchment of the middle decades of the twelfth century is frequently disputed, there can be no doubt of its existence. From many estates comes evidence of contracting demesnes. As demesnes shrank, so did demand for labour services, and we find that many tenancies were converted from labour rents to money. Moreover the hand of lordship seems often to have become lighter as supervision became intermittent and control remote; indeed it was virtually lifted when on occasion the villagers themselves leased manors *en bloc* from their lords, and were apparently thence-

---

[80] *Rotuli de dominabus et pueris et puellis de xii comitatibus*, ed. J. H. Round (Pipe Roll Soc., xxxv, London, 1913), p. 3; *Royal Writs in England from the Conquest to Glanvill*, ed. Van Caenegem, p. 336 n. 1 (writ no. 111).

[81] *Dialogus de scaccario: The Course of the Exchequer*, ed. C. Johnson (London, 1950), pp. 53, 56, 101.

forth free to manage their own affairs.[82] These gains and the payment of money instead of service seem everywhere to have been regarded by tenants as enfranchisements to be fiercely defended, and even within a relatively short space of time as ancient customs. For lords who in later years found themselves under assault from galloping inflation and sought to resume control of their manors, produce for the market and increase supplies of demesne labour, they were regarded as irksome temporary concessions to be revoked at the earliest opportunity.

This move into direct management and cultivation, which gained momentum in the decade after 1180, inevitably posed grave threats to the recently won improvements in status. The consequences of this reversal of managerial practice are exemplified in estate surveys and inquiries into how or why this holding or that ceased to render work or was made free, and on whose authority and with what justification; into whether the demesne is in cultivation or held in free or villein tenure, and whether it would be more profitable for the lord to take it in hand. Also exemplified in a variety of records is the resentment and at times resistance which such reversals provoked among the peasantry. For tenants not possessed of the long memories of lawyers and estate officials, or the remote perspectives of historians, these developments posed the threat of unjust losses of freedom. Men who had not rendered labour, nor perhaps even their fathers before them, were bound to resist the efforts of their lords to extract it, some even to the extent of seeking the protection of newly available royal justice. Their struggles undoubtedly lay behind many of the villeinage cases appearing in crown courts.[83]

It was at this point that the parallel but probably separate evolution of estate management and the common law came together. The reform and extension of royal justice necessitated the formulation of rules to determine who had the right of access to it. It was never for a moment intended that crown courts should be open to all lowly folk and to the petty disputes they had with their lords; such an intention would not only have been completely unworkable in practice, it would have appeared absurd to contemporaries. Yet seigneurial encroachments did encourage some of the more enterprising, and perhaps also more wealthy, tenants to plead their cases in the royal courts, and it seems plausible that the first concern of these courts should not have been the

---

[82] Postan, "Chronology of Labour Services", pp. 92-100; Miller and Hatcher, *Medieval England: Rural Society and Economic Change*, pp. 125, 209-10. The scale of the contraction of demesne cultivation has recently been challenged: see A. R. Bridbury, "The Farming Out of Manors", *Econ. Hist. Rev.*, 2nd ser., xxxi (1978); M. M. Postan, "A Note on the Farming Out of Manors", *Econ. Hist. Rev.*, 2nd ser., xxxi (1978).

[83] Hilton, "Freedom and Villeinage in England", pp. 11-13; Poole, *Obligations of Society in the XII and XIII Centuries*, pp. 27-8; Vinogradoff, *Villainage in England*, pp. 167-9; S. F. C. Milsom, *The Legal Framework of English Feudalism* (Cambridge, 1976), p. 24.

substance of their claims, but whether they had the right to plead. A dispute between a tenant and his lord over a particular obligation thus frequently turned into a dispute over status. If the tenant were deemed not to have the right to plead, he was cast back upon his lord's justice; which, it would seem, is where he and his fellows were before royal law was extended. If labour services for many were strictly not new impositions but reimpositions, so the denial of royal justice was usually not a depression of status but a confirmation of status.

If the deterioration in the conditions of tenure of many, but by no means all,[84] villagers around 1200 was severe, it must be considered not only in the context of the era of improvement which preceded it but in the context of the rampant inflation which accompanied it. Rent frequently altered in character, and in many cases it may well have increased, but at present there is no evidence to suggest that the rate of increase exceeded that of agricultural prices, which more than doubled in less than twenty years. Indeed rent as a proportion of the total product of unfree holdings seems to have declined substantially as the thirteenth century wore on. In the present state of knowledge there would thus seem to be no reason to believe that the majority of tenants after *circa* 1180 were more greatly oppressed by their lords than their predecessors had been before the temporary improvements of the midtwelfth century.

More than this, it would appear that in some important respects legal status was actually improving. If those deemed free henceforth enjoyed greater protection from the common law, those deemed unfree were at least protected to the extent that their lords could not lawfully kill or mutilate them.[85] A new and powerful protection can also be discerned in the presumption of the law that status had to be proved: thus by the later twelfth century we find that the writ *de nativo habendo* could be countered by the writ *de libertate probanda*, and we find in the Pipe Roll of 1175 that Osbertus de Torp' was fined no less than fifteen marks for imprisoning a man whom he wished to prove a *rusticus* but was unable to do so.[86] As for the unfree in the thirteenth century, we can discern them being increasingly viewed as royal subjects and expected to play a part in public life. Some of these developments admittedly resulted in new obligations, such as the liability to bear arms and pay royal taxes, but others, such as the widespread ac-

[84] Many holdings which had once rendered labour services were never reconverted and persisted as rent-paying tenancies; for example, Miller, *Abbey and Bishopric of Ely*, pp. 123 ff.

[85] Bracton, *De legibus et consuetudinibus Angliae*, ed. Woodbine, rev. Thorne, ii, p. 34; *Britton*, ed. Nichols, i, p. 195.

[86] *Royal Writs in England from the Conquest to Glanvill*, ed. Van Caenegem, p. 339 n. 1. See also Bracton, *De legibus et consuetudinibus Angliae*, ed. Woodbine, rev. Thorne, ii, p. 37; *Britton*, ed. Nichols, pp. 202 ff.; Pollock and Maitland, *History of English Law before the Time of Edward I*, i, pp. 417-18.

ceptance of a *de facto* right to possess charters, brought tangible benefits.[87]

In looking for favourable developments in England's social structure we must not fall into the trap of studying only the conditions of
villeins. The demise of slavery, which was fully accomplished before
the thirteenth century, effectively raised a sizeable proportion of the
population from the depths of subservience into the markedly more
beneficial state of villeinage. Likewise higher up the social hierarchy
we find abundant evidence that many escaped from dependence into
freedom. While part of the explanation of the substantial increase in
the numbers of Englishmen positively deemed free between 1086 and
1300 undoubtedly lies in the recognition that some Domesday *villani*
were closer to freedom than to villeinage, part also lies in real enfranchisements of the formerly servile.[88] The importance of these developments should not be underestimated.

VII

As this article amply demonstrates, any attempt to chart the changes
which took place in the quality of life and tenurial conditions of the
mass of English men and women over the half-millennium and more
before 1500 is a complex and at times overtly speculative task. Attempting to discuss why the changes we have charted occurred inevitably introduces many further dimensions of doubt, confusion and possible error. Our understanding of causality can be advanced by distinguishing, however crudely, those forces which stemmed primarily from
the economic and demographic context from those which stemmed primarily from the political, legal and social context. But such a distinction, although essential, is only a preliminary step. For closer investigation of these forces reveals that there was no predictable or enduring
pattern of relationships between them. There is one certainty: we must
search in vain for a constant "prime mover". We can also state with
assurance that the outcome was rarely, if ever, dictated solely by market forces.

How could it have been otherwise when most of the institutions,

[87] For ingenious, if not consistently convincing, arguments in favour of improve-
ments in the legal and public status of the unfree, see H. G. Richardson and G. O.
Sayles, *Law and Legislation from Aethelberht to Magna Carta* (Edinburgh, 1966), pp.
138-49. See also V. H. Galbraith, "Thoughts on the Peasants' Revolt", in F. R. H. Du
Boulay and C. M. Barron (eds.), *The Reign of Richard II: Essays in Honour of May
McKisack* (London, 1971).

[88] For details of the processes and scale of enfranchisement on a variety of estates,
see Harvey, *Westminster Abbey and its Estates in the Middle Ages*, pp. 106-15; Miller,
Abbey and Bishopric of Ely, pp. 119-26; Hilton, *Decline of Serfdom in Medieval
England*, pp. 18-24.

mores, and administrative and legal precepts by which medieval society was structured and governed were inimical to the free play of the market? For unfree medieval peasants the strength of custom was ranged against the rights and powers of their lords. Thus although economic and demographic trends and fluctuations invariably generated powerful forces for change, a miscellany of social, political and legal influences acted and reacted upon them, sometimes compounding their impact, sometimes inhibiting, and sometimes reversing. Changes in the level of population or the supply of land could make labour or land more scarce or more abundant, but for tenants both in the power of their lords and protected by custom these changes alone did not determine the amount and type of rent they paid.

More than this, we have seen that in practice the correlation between the status of dependent tenants and the state of the labour market was often inverse. That is, over much of the broad sweep of history that we have surveyed the scarcity of labour did not lead to an alleviation of seigneurial oppressions nor its abundance to an intensification. Thus in the early middle ages it was the very scarcity of labour and the threat this posed to the prosperity of lords which, as in eastern Europe from the later fifteenth century onwards, lay behind endeavours to impose the most stringent restraints upon the peasantry. Quite contrary, but no less paradoxical from the perspective of market forces, was the experience of the central middle ages reviewed in this article. Despite the growing surplus of labour in the thirteenth century the level of rents paid by the unfree failed to keep pace with the rising value of the lands which they held; or to put it another way, during this century the proportion of the product of unfree holdings extracted by landlords declined significantly. Indeed although market forces manifestly favoured landlords many aspects of manorialism and serfdom weakened. Perhaps well under half of the population at the end of the thirteenth century were unfree, and labour services were not of great consequence and were declining. And if the strength of custom amply protected ancient freeholders and customary tenants, in this inflationary era it drove lords to seek profits outside the traditional framework, most notably from the sale of produce and from competitive tenancies.

Yet if the balance between economic and demographic forces and social, legal and political forces altered radically over these long centuries, in an important sense the consequences for the mass of the peasantry were depressingly consistent. The majority of the population rarely prospered: when land was abundant they were oppressed by their lords; when land was scarce they were oppressed by the poverty which inevitably stemmed from the excess of people. Perhaps the later fourteenth and the fifteenth centuries constituted the sole "golden age" of the English peasantry. For in this era the increasing scarcity of people led to both rising real incomes and the loosening and eventual dissolution of the bonds of serfdom.[89]

The long decline in the value of land in the course of the fourteenth and fifteenth centuries inevitably set the scene for confrontation between landlords and customary tenants. Customs which in a time of land shortage had been protective, in a time of land surplus became exploitative. There was no doubt about the legal right of lords to insist upon their villeins holding land, and holding it for rents and services which were now in excess of its value; what was contested was their ability to enforce that right in the teeth of peasant resistance. Coercion or compromise were the alternatives, and it was the latter which progressively became the norm.[90] Yet tenants were relentless in their demands. It was of little concern to the villeins of the 1370s and early 1380s that concessions granted since the Black Death usually meant that they were enjoying a greater measure of freedom and rendering less for their land than their predecessors had a generation and more before. What really mattered was whether they were being asked to render more than they thought the lands they occupied were worth, or whether they were being forced to occupy land when they preferred otherwise. In the end, as is well known, landlords lacked the ability, and possibly even the will, to struggle successfully against the combined assault of demographic collapse and peasant assertiveness. The relaxation of customary dues and obligations was eagerly sought and eventually readily enough conceded, and flexible tenancies and leaseholds developed rapidly at the expense of villein tenure.

Even this "golden age" was, however, tarnished. Not only were these advances at root purchased by the inability of the population to reproduce itself in the face of high death rates and low expectations of life, in the long run they were to be turned decisively against the des-

[89] The first incontrovertible indication that desperate land hunger was abating occurs well before the Black Death, when we find instances of villeins appreciating that some poor holdings were no longer attractive propositions at their customary rent levels. At this early stage the unwillingness to hold land, although not widespread, was likely to be countered by landlords seeking to enforce their rights to compel villeins to take up vacant holdings. Thus on Chertsey Abbey manors and at Chalgrave villeins refusing to hold land might be fined or even put in the stocks: *Chertsey Abbey Court Rolls Abstracts*, ed. Toms, nos. 240-1; *Court Roll of Chalgrave Manor, 1278-1313*, ed. M. K. Dale (Beds. Hist. Rec. Soc., xxviii, Streatley, 1950), pp. 42, 46. While, on the other side, some reluctant tenants imaginatively resorted to the expedient of claiming illegitimate birth, for bastards were of free status and thus could not be compelled to hold land. Instances occur in the Cottenham (Cambridgeshire) manor court rolls in the 1320s (I am grateful to Richard Smith for this reference).

[90] The implication must be that lords in the fourteenth and fifteenth centuries were less able to coerce their dependent tenantry than their predecessors had been in the previous era of low population before the twelfth century. The reasons for their comparative weakness are many and complex and must lie outside the scope of this article, but would seem to owe something to the growth of centralized government and the rule of law within England.

cendants of many of those who had won them. When in the sixteenth century population and prices rose, when land became ever more scarce and expensive, and real wages fell, those tenants unprotected by ancient custom were acutely vulnerable to eviction and rack-renting. The demise of custom gave a freer rein to market forces: in the fifteenth century this was beneficial, but the adversity of market forces in the following century ensured that, viewed in the broad perspective, the decline of serfdom produced for a sizeable proportion of the peasantry only short-term benefit but long-term harm.

Note, 1987

I would like to take this opportunity to correct a misunderstanding of my views on the role of custom in the relations between landlords and tenants. I had hoped that my position had been made clear in this article, but Richard M. Smith, in his "Some Thoughts on 'Hereditary' and 'Proprietary' Rights in Land under Customary Law in Thirteenth and Early Fourteenth Century England", *Law and History Review*, i (1983), p. 97, has claimed that I view custom as "the stationary component ... in the social system", and that for me "custom is hermetically sealed from the influences of exogenous forces". This is not so, as I believe I have made explicit on pages 252-3, 259, 265-6, 268, 272, 277-8 and 282 above. Some customs were, of course, more durable than others, but if Richard Smith believes that in general custom could not act as "a frictional drag", or that it changed as rapidly as "the exogenous forces" themselves, then there is indeed a major point of difference between us.

10. *The English peasantry and the demands of the crown 1294-1341*

J.R. MADDICOTT

When Edward I committed his country to military intervention in France and Scotland in the mid-1290s, he inaugurated a period of warfare which was to last intermittently until 1453. During that period the pressures brought by war, particularly the pressure of taxation, shaped the economy and political development of England as they had not done in any previous century. Long and expensive wars were in themselves nothing new: there is an obvious parallel between the stresses produced by the maintenance of the Angevin Empire between 1154 and 1215 and those created by the attempts of the three Edwards to defend their cause in Scotland, France and Gascony. Reaction to the innovations forced on the crown by its involvement in large-scale warfare came, *mutatis mutandis,* in broadly similar ways — with Magna Carta in 1215, *Confirmatio Cartarum* in 1297, the Ordinances in 1311, and the constitutional crisis of 1340-1. And yet, despite these resemblances, much had changed between the late twelfth and the late thirteenth centuries. War had become much more expensive. Edward I's armies were almost certainly larger than those of his predecessors and, although feudal service might sometimes be called for, they were for the most part paid. The price of effective fortifications had also risen. Castle-building in England had cost the Angevin kings some £46,000 in the sixty years between 1155 and 1215, while from 1277 to 1304, a period of only twenty-seven years, Edward I spent just over £78,000 on his Welsh castles alone.[1] Still more costly was the purchase of political and military support. It is doubtful if even during the mid-1190s, when the demands on Angevin government were at their peak, the crown had spent sums comparable with the £166,000 given

---

* Mr. James Campbell, Dr. Ian Kershaw and Dr. Michael Prestwich were all kind enough to read an earlier draft of this paper and I have learnt a great deal from their valuable comments. My particular debt to Dr. Prestwich's published work will be obvious throughout what follows. The responsibility for the opinions expressed remains my own.

[1] R. A. Brown, H. M. Colvin and A. J. Taylor, *The History of the King's Works,* 2 vols. (London, 1963), i, p. 64; ii, p. 1,027.

by Edward I to his allies in the Low Countries between 1294 and 1298, or with the £130,000 expended in the same way by his grandson between 1337 and 1341.[2]

If warfare had become more expensive, the fiscal burdens which it entailed were coming to bear on a wider circle of the king's subjects. The original landed revenues of the Angevin kings had never been sufficient to do more than supplement their income from taxation, but taxation which (at least after the demise of Danegeld in 1162) weighed most heavily upon particular groups, like the Jews and those living within boroughs or on ancient demesne. Tallage, scutage, the profits of justice, and feudal aids and incidents (to name the most valuable of the crown's revenues) had affected only sections of the population, though we cannot of course tell what proportion of these exactions was passed on to the tenantry in the form of increased dues and rents.[3] General levies, like the carucages of the 1190s or the thirteenth on movables of 1207, had been rarely used. From Edward I's reign, however, the crown's taxative resources broadened considerably in their variety and social impact. The customs system instituted in 1275 provided a revenue which was valuable not only for its regularity and its function as a security for loans, but also because it could be profitably manipulated at the expense of the crown's subjects, most notably by the maltolts of 1294-7 and of the late 1330s. From the 1290s the levy on movables, merely an occasional measure during the previous hundred years, became a much more frequent expedient, and this was a tax which was paid by all except the very poorest. The main types of indirect taxation, especially purveyance and the provision of unpaid military service or of service which had to be partly paid for by the local communities, fell hardly at all upon the rich and moderately wealthy, but principally upon the peasantry. By contrast with the late twelfth century, the costs of warfare were being borne more immediately by the lower classes.

More was implied here than just the surrender to the king of cash or provisions or service, for one important consequence of the extension in the scope, variety and frequency of taxation was the

[2] M. Prestwich, *War, Politics and Finance under Edward I* (London, 1972), p. 173; E. B. Fryde, "Financial Resources of Edward I in the Netherlands, 1294-8; Main Problems and some Comparisons with Edward III in 1337-40", *Revue Belge*, xl (1962), p. 1,170.

[3] For an instance of villeins being forced to pay scutage in 1196, see A. L. Poole, *Obligations of Society in the XII and XIII Centuries* (Oxford, 1946), p. 47. For the way in which landlords may have compensated for the crown's fiscal pressure upon them by depressing the legal status of their tenants, see R. H. Hilton, "Freedom and Villeinage in England", *Past and Present*, no. 31 (July 1965), esp. pp. 13-14.

opportunities which it brought for increased interference in men's lives. More taxes meant more local officials. A commission of 1341 to inquire into their misdeeds speaks of:

> Escheators; sub-escheators; coroners; sheriffs; under-sheriffs; taxers;. . .keepers and constables of the peace and of castles and land on the coast; takers and receivers of wool; assessors and receivers of the ninth and other subsidies;. . . keepers of forests, verderers, clerks and other ministers of forests, chases and parks; collectors and controllers of customs; troners, butlers and their substitutes; keepers of the king's horses and their grooms;. . . purveyors of victuals; purveyors for the king's household and its subsidiary households; keepers of gaols; electors, triers and arrayers of men-at-arms, hobelars and archers; bailiffs itinerant and other bailiffs and ministers. [4]

A hundred years earlier this impressive list would have been much shorter. There would, for instance, have been no keepers of the peace, no collectors of customs or other men associated with levies on wool, and no military officials; while purveyors and taxers would have been very rare visitors. The multiplication of officials, together with an increase in the powers delegated to those already existing, vastly enlarged the opportunities for the peculation and graft which had always characterized local government. It would be going too far to say that the popular grievances of the period were directed against the administration of war-time burdens rather than against the burdens themselves, [5] but undoubtedly the oppressiveness of taxation was much aggravated by the corruption and extortion which accompanied its levying.

Royal taxation was superimposed on to an economic situation which for many men must have appeared increasingly harsh. The expansion of population during the thirteenth century had brought a growing scarcity of land, a rise in rents and a decline in wages, leaving many peasants with smaller resources than their twelfth-century ancestors may have had. For this reason climatic conditions, though in general probably no worse than they had been in earlier periods, are likely to have had more sharply-felt effects. Even if there was no gradual decline in the population from *circa* 1300 onwards, [6] natural disasters like the great famine of 1315-17 or the cattle plague of 1318 certainly brought ruin and death to many. [7] When the resources of many peasants were thus much at risk, the

---

[4] *Cal. Pat. Rolls, 1340-3*, pp. 363-4.

[5] As is argued by W. S. Thomson, *A Lincolnshire Assize Roll for 1298* (Lincoln Rec. Soc., xxxvi, 1944), pp. lviii-lix, cxxv.

[6] Cf. B.F. Harvey, "The Population Trend in England between 1300 and 1348", *Trans. Roy. Hist. Soc.*, 5th ser., xvi (1966), pp. 23-42.

[7] For which see I. Kershaw, "The Great Famine and Agrarian Crisis in England 1315-22", *Past and Present*, no. 59 (May 1972). The related effects of dearth and taxation are examined more closely below, pp. 72-3.

king's demands for taxes were bound to strike harder than they had done in more buoyant days and to compound the already difficult circumstances in which numbers of small men were placed. The sale of seed-corn to provide cash for tax payments, the loss of plough-oxen through purveyance, the uprooting of villagers from their holdings to perform military service — all these impositions left men even less well-equipped to face a hostile economic environment.

Matters of this sort have never been given much importance by historians. Because the crown's demands cannot be precisely measured, they have usually been dismissed as a negligible factor in the life of the peasant, or, at most, mentioned *en passant* as merely one among the many exactions which depleted his income. [8] Such a depreciation has other causes. It stems partly from the unhealthy separation which exists between the study of economic and of political history, partly from the consideration of only one form of taxation, the levy on movables, and that not the most important, but more particularly from the silence of the economic historian's usual sources. Manorial documents — court rolls, accounts, rentals, surveys and extents — tell us very little about the effects of the king's taxes, except in so far as they affected the lord for whose use the documents were drawn up. In 1341 ten virgates of land lay uncultivated in the Herefordshire manors of Alansmore and Clehonger because of the poverty of the inhabitants "on account of divers taxes and levies imposed upon them"; yet the court rolls for Clehonger record nothing remarkable in that year or in the previous decade. [9] Even if we possessed accounts to complement the court rolls, it is likely that without the Inquisitions of the Ninth we should be quite ignorant of the effects of taxation here. The regular and systematic demands of manorial lords can be quantified and their impact assessed, but the less regular, more capricious and more arbitrary (and for these reasons sometimes more burdensome) demands of the king do not lend themselves to this kind of treatment. Yet we may suspect that royal government and its agents often posed a more immediate threat to the peasant's livelihood than did the customary and largely predictable levies made by landlords. In 1258 the villein sokemen of Brill in Buckinghamshire complained that the depredations and extortions of the king's bailiffs there had left them so impoverished that they were hardly able to pay the royal

---

[8] E.g., J.Z. Titow, *English Rural Society, 1200-1350* (London, 1969), p.63; M. M. Postan, *Cambridge Economic History of Europe*, i, 2nd edn. (Cambridge, 1966), p. 603.

[9] *Inquisitiones Nonarum* (hereafter cited as *Inq. Non*) (Record Commission, 1807), p. 143; Bodleian Lib., Oxford, MSS. Herefordshire Rolls, 22a-30.

farm.[10] Even before the 1290s the hundred bailiff may have been a more familiar figure on many manors than the non-resident lord, and perhaps a more frightening one than the lord's agents, the steward, the auditors and the reeve. From the 1290s onwards the powers more frequently exercised by him, particularly the power to distrain for non-payment of taxes and to collect prises, meant that he played a still larger part in determining the prosperity of many peasants. [11] Yet if we studied manorial documents alone, this fact too would be concealed from us.

In trying to gauge the effects of royal taxation, then, the standard sources for the economic historian are of comparatively little use, and we have to turn to other evidence — to the findings of royal inquiries into ministerial corruption, like those of 1298 and 1340-2, to parliamentary petitions, to the records of the Exchequer, to political poems and polemical tracts. Such material, upon which most of what follows is founded, may easily mislead; a large part of it consists of grievances against royal ministers and might be thought to reflect not only an increase in the burdens which the crown was laying upon its subjects, but also an increase in the opportunities for complaint and, to some extent, for redress. If taxation was heavy, the more frequent meetings of Parliament which it necessitated provided the occasion for more regular petitioning. If the general eyre, which had facilitated the laying of complaints against royal officials, became from the 1290s merely a spasmodic and archaic survival, the special inquiry partly took its place. Not all was loss. But even when these allowances have been made, the evidence suggests that from this time onwards English government was becoming harsher, more comprehensive and more far-reaching in its impact. These circumstances were not unremitting, and after about 1341 conditions improved. Taxation, though still heavy, was partly counter-balanced by the profits of the French war and, from 1349-50, by the benefits which the Black Death brought to those small men who survived it. But between 1294 and 1341 neither the economic situation nor the crown's military policies offered much compensation to those on whom the weight of taxation fell most heavily.

---

[10] E.F. Jacob, *Studies in the Period of Baronial Reform and Rebellion* (Oxford, 1925), pp. 44-7, 344-9.

[11] For the extortions practised by hundred bailiffs, see H.M. Cam, *The Hundred and the Hundred Rolls* (repr. London, 1963), pp. 145-66.

II

The peasantry was most affected by three sorts of tax: by the levy on movables, by purveyance, and by the costs of military service. In addition, there were from time to time other impositions, like the maltolts on wool, which, although not directly paid by the countryman, might nevertheless strike hard at his financial resources. Each of the three main forms of taxation will now be considered in turn as far as the mid-1330s. Between that time and 1341 the ways by which the crown raised money changed drastically and to the peasant's severe disadvantage, and this short period will therefore be treated separately in the penultimate section of the discussion.

We begin the most obvious of the king's taxes, the levy on movables. From the 1290s the frequency and weight of the tax on movable goods increased markedly, so that it became the crown's most profitable source of extraordinary revenue. The seventy-five years between 1216 and 1290 had seen only seven such levies, while by contrast six were collected during the last fourteen years of Edward I's reign, four of which fell between 1294 and 1297. Edward II took seven in a reign of twenty years and Edward III three from 1327 to 1334. In a period of forty-one years there were thus sixteen levies, almost twice the number collected in the century prior to 1294. The rate of taxation showed a parallel increase. Between 1225 and 1290 the rate had varied between a fortieth (1232) and a fifteenth (1225 and 1275), but after 1294 the shires paid at rates which ranged between a ninth in 1297 and a twenty-fifth in 1309; the average rate from 1307 to 1334 was about an eighteenth. In the 1290s there also began the placing of the proceeds of taxation under the direct control of the Exchequer and the institution of different rates for town and country.[12] One result of more expensive wars was thus to make the levy on movables an accepted part of the government's resources.

From these figures the years between 1294 and 1297 stand out sharply as the period when taxation was at its heaviest. Not only were taxes assessed at particularly high rates during four successive years, but the amount which they actually yielded was very large: the tax of 1294 produced nearly £82,000 and that of 1295 nearly £53,000. Though there had been a remarkable decline from the £116,000 produced by the fifteenth of 1290, each of these two taxes

---

12 J. F. Willard, *Parliamentary Taxes on Personal Property, 1290-1334* (Cambridge, Mass., 1934), pp. 3-4, 9-11; Prestwich, *War, Politics and Finance*, p. 179.

nevertheless yielded more than any other single levy during our period.[13] The total burden imposed by all forms of taxation during the mid-1290s will bear comparison only with that of the opening phase of the Hundred Years' War, when the crown's military and diplomatic commitments were still greater. The burden was less severe under Edward II, although it remained considerable. The period of heaviest taxation came in 1315 and 1316, when, to meet the resurgent Scottish threat after Bannockburn, subsidies were collected in two successive years for the only time during the reign. The coincidence of the great famine with these levies made them especially onerous, but nevertheless they hardly approached in scale and effect those taken during the 1290s and the 1330s.

The subsidy was by its nature an inequitable tax. Its imposition not on income but on movable goods meant that all those whose livelihoods came primarily from rents escaped lightly. Landlords were thus assessed only on the produce of their demesne manors, and it is possible that the change from the direct exploitation of the demesne to its leasing out, which was taking place on many estates about this time, may partly be explained by the lord's wish to avoid the now frequent levy on movables. Tenants, on the other hand, who needed to produce both to maintain themselves and to find the money for the rents and dues demanded by their lords, were bound to be caught within the net of the subsidy.

How seriously did this burden them? Most historians have expressed scepticism about the damaging effects of direct taxation,[14] and indeed if we consider only the "official" evidence, preserved in the Exchequer's instructions to the chief taxers in each county and in the tax assessment lists, there would seem to be good reasons for taking this view. First, the peasant was taxed only on the goods which he had for sale and not on those intended for his own domestic use.[15] Hence the levy might reduce his capacity to accumulate, which might be important in an era of high rents, but it would never drive him to starvation. The tenant paying a money rent for his holding is likely to have been affected more severely than he whose obligations consisted mainly of labour services. Unless the rent-payer relied largely on the profits of wage-labour to meet his lord's demands, he would be driven to sell at least part of his produce, thus making himself liable to taxation. But although the weight of taxation might

[13] Willard, *op. cit.*, pp. 343-5.

[14] E.g., at the Past and Present Conference held in 1961 Professor Hilton "doubted if medieval subsidies much affected the peasantry": *Past and Present*, no. 22 (July 1962), p. 15.

[15] Willard, *op. cit.*, pp. 81-5.

thus vary in practice with the conditions of tenure, none (it might be thought) would have found it intolerably heavy.

Secondly, each man's goods were normally assessed at well below their market price. Livestock was often undervalued by as much as 50 per cent, and so was corn. Hence when the government imposed a tenth or a fifteenth, the true value of the cash raised might be as little as a twentieth or a thirtieth of the real market price of the peasant's produce.[16] The sub-taxers responsible for the assessment and collection of the tax at a local level were drawn from the villagers, and it is usually assumed that under-assessment was one way in which they could lighten the weight of taxation for their own villages, to the approval of their friends and neighbours. Assessment by local men provided a safeguard against whatever burdens the government might choose to impose.

Thirdly, the government itself offered some protection for the poorest. After 1294 there was for each subsidy (with the exception of that taken in 1301) a minimum level for taxation, usually 10s., which was fixed by the Exchequer. Possession of marketable goods worth less than this amount guaranteed exemption from the subsidy, and the fact that in some districts the lowest assessment was rather larger than the stated minimum suggests that the village sub-taxers sometimes drew the line above that decreed by the Exchequer.[17] By these arrangements the cottar or the poor widow might be thought to have been shielded from the impact of direct taxation.

Lastly, a comparison between the sums collected from the peasant in manorial rent and in royal taxation suggests that rent was by far the heavier of the two burdens. Unfortunately such a comparison is rarely possible, because of the difficulty of finding a rental or extent which coincides even approximately in time with a tax assessment. One manor for which this can be done, however, is East Coker in Somerset, where we have both an extent for 1321 and an assessment for the twentieth of 1327.[18] The two documents show a clear and apparently equitable pattern of taxation, with most of the burden falling upon the more prosperous freeholders. Richard Elys, who held a carucate of land by knight service, paid 6s. 7d. in rent, and owed suit to the hundred court, was taxed at 4s. William Neville and his wife had a life tenancy of the mill, for which they paid 30s. a year, half a virgate for 1s. 4d. rent, and an acre of meadow for 6d. In 1327 Neville was taxed at 5s. William Pyllard, who held half a virgate by knight service and paid 6s. 8d. a year, was taxed at 2s. Of the five

16 *Ibid.*, pp. 138-41.
17 *Ibid.*, pp. 87-92.
18 M. Nathan, *The Annals of West Coker* (Cambridge, 1957), pp. 476-71, 479.

villeins common to both extent and tax assessment, each held a half-virgate tenement for a rent of 10s. (or 10s. 2½d. in one case) and for works which, when commuted, were worth about 9d. For the twentieth, one paid 6d., two 1s., and two 1s. 6d. The poorest tenants appear to have escaped the tax altogether. Of the ten smallholders with less than half a virgate, only one has a place in the tax assessment six years later; most of the others presumably fell below the taxable level. All seems to have been as it should have been. Within the manor the well-to-do pay most and poor pay nothing, while for most the burden of rent is some five to ten times as heavy as that of taxation. If we take into account both the seigneurial dues to which the villein was occasionally subject — tallage, merchet, heriot, etc. — but which are obviously omitted in the extent, and also the sporadic nature of taxation as against the annual payments to the lord, the disparity between tax and rent will appear larger still.

The customary sanguine views on the effects of direct taxation have been founded on considerations of this sort. But if we look behind the facade presented by the government's instructions to the tax-collectors and the resulting assessments, and try to discover what actually happened when a tax was levied, we may come to a rather different conclusion. Certainly the levy on movables was rarely a crushing burden, but at the same time it was often more than a mere irritant. Evidence drawn from the periodic inquiries into the behaviour of royal officials, including the chief taxers for the counties and the sub-taxers for the villages, suggests that the sums appearing on the assessment lists may represent only the bare minimum of the peasant's losses through taxation. Though there was undoubtedly much under-assessment, as Willard rightly noted, on many manors much also disappeared into the pockets of the sub-taxers and was never recorded on any assessment list. In 1294-5, for instance, the sub-taxers at Ingoldmells (Lincs.) extorted 20s. from the vill for their expenses, while Burgh-in-the-Marsh lost 15s. in the same way in 1296 and another 5s. 1d. in 1297.[19] The inquiries of 1323-4 disclosed many similar examples. In the North Riding of Yorkshire the sub-taxers of Thornton levied 2s. 6d. more than they paid to the king; those of Pickering, 24s. 5d.; those of Lebberston and Gristhorpe, 19s. 11d.; while at Howden in the East Riding the very large sum of 58s. was taken and concealed.[20] Such cases, which occur repeatedly in all areas and throughout the period, suggest the inadvisability of taking the assessment figures as an accurate statement of the weight of the subsidy.

19 Thomson, *A Lincolnshire Assize Roll for 1298*, nos. 277, 294, 295.
20 Public Record Office (hereafter P.R.O.), J.I.1/1117, mm. 4-4d.

Nor did the Exchequer's orders for the exemption of the poor necessarily offer much protection. The possession of marketable goods to the value of 10s., the level at which a man normally became liable to tax, hardly indicated even moderate prosperity. It represented only about two quarters of wheat or two to three quarters of oats or four to six sheep or one cow. A peasant might have such goods for sale and still be very poor, and it was perhaps in recognition of this fact that the sub-taxers sometimes seem to have set a higher level for exemption than that laid down by the government. They may have been taking a more realistic view of their neighbours' ability to pay what was demanded. But equally often they seem to have taxed those whom even the Exchequer would have exempted. In the Lincolnshire inquiry of 1298 the taxation of "non-taxables" is the commonest charge against the sub-taxers.[21] In one wapentake twenty of those who should have escaped the tenth of 1294 paid over to the sub-taxers sums ranging from 2d. to 1s. 9d., and many of the same persons found themselves similarly subject to the twelfth of 1296.[22] Despite the ostensible dependence of liability to taxation on the possession of a certain minimum of wealth, it is not safe to assume that the poor always, or even regularly, escaped the burden.

These conclusions have some bearing on the interests and activities of the village sub-taxers. They were clearly not habitually concerned to keep their neighbours in easy circumstances. The profiteering and peculation characteristic of local government were not the prerogative only of the "middle-class" sheriffs, coroners and escheators, and some peasants may have regarded temporary office-holding as a means to self-advancement just as did their social superiors. The common interests of the "village community" — that comfortable concept — may not always have extended much beyond matters of open-field husbandry. It is never easy to tell where the sympathies of the village officials, royal or manorial, lay, but they did not invariably lie with the men of the localities. In 1332 Thomas Jordan, sub-taxer on the Ramsey manor of Hemingford Abbots, was said by his fellows to have bribed the chief taxers "to procure the office of tax assessor over his fellow villagers", and then to have revealed to his supervisors "the hidden goods of his neighbours, so that the whole vill was taxed for a greater amount through the efforts of this said Thomas to the sum of 40s.".[23] The opportunities for

21 *Lincs. Assize Roll*, p. 1.
22 *Ibid.*, nos. 256, 258.
23 J. A. Raftis, *Tenure and Mobility: Studies in the Social History of the Medieval English Village* (Toronto, 1964), pp. 97-8, 252.

profit which the taxation system offered to the unscrupulous sub-taxer could be taken only at the expense of his fellows. The sub-taxers were not always wholly to blame, for they themselves were often subject to pressure from their overseers. The chief taxers and collectors, for instance, regularly refused to accept their subordinates' local assessment rolls until a shilling or two had been paid over to them. Although this practice was officially prohibited by the Exchequer for the levy of 1327, it nevertheless survived, as the inquiries of 1340-2 continually demonstrate.[24] Corrupt practices were not necessarily to the villagers' disadvantage, as the evidence for under-assessment makes plain, but the frequent assumption that the balance of corruption was always tilted in the tax-payers' favour is hardly tenable.

The odd pennies and shillings from each village which went to the sub-taxers and their directors partly invalidate the conclusions commonly drawn from surviving tax assessments. But they were probably less burdensome, though more general in their incidence, than the penalties for non-payment of taxation. In times of financial stringency the crown collected the debts owing to it, including debts for unpaid taxes, with unusual vigour. Edward I's ordinance of 1297 appointing justices and clerks to supervise the collection of debts in each county is paralleled by the similar policy put forward in the Waltham Ordinances of 1338.[25] Even in more placid times the levying of the crown's debts was always much resented, largely because of the powers for mischief which it placed in the hands of the hundred bailiffs; the "summons of the green wax" (the procedure by which most debts were called in) had been a subject for interminable popular complaints long before the 1290s.[26] But if the abuses recorded from 1294 onwards were not new, the frequency of taxation and the crown's less lenient attitude towards its debtors may have meant that they were now more common.

The collection of debts could on occasion thoroughly disrupt peasant agriculture. Unlike the initial levying of taxation, which usually began between August and November, when the harvest was gathered, men might be pursued for debts at any time of the year; Edward I's 1297 ordinance was issued in March. Collection in spring and summer, when the arable farmer's cash resources were probably at their lowest, could be very inconvenient, and failure to pay, which was common, might result in the distraint of essential livestock. In

---

[24] Willard, *Parliamentary Taxes*, pp. 212-14; P.R.O., J.I.1/521, *passim* (Lincs.).

[25] *Lincs. Assize Roll*, pp. xl-xliii; D. Hughes. *Social and Constitutional Tendencies in the Early Years of Edward III* (London, 1915), pp. 55-6.

[26] Cam, *Hundred and the Hundred Rolls*, pp. 95-6, 160-3.

May 1293 William Fyngge, servant of the bailiff of Thurgarton wapentake (Notts.), came into the fields at Fledburgh and took two oxen from the plough-team of Robert, son of Ivette Fledburgh, as a distress for his arrears of the previous levy on movables.[27] Four years later, in July 1297, the sheriff of Northamptonshire received a sharp letter from the king because he had taken growing corn and plough-beasts belonging to Simon, son of Robert Daventry, and had then put them up for sale in order to meet the debts which Simon owed to the king.[28] The 1298 inquiries brought to light many similar cases,[29] just as the Hundred Roll inquests had done in 1274-5 and as the investigation of 1323-4 was to do in the next reign.[30] A statute of 1275 had specifically prohibited local officials from distraining on plough-beasts and on sheep as long as other distresses could be found, and this was repeated in a slightly different form in the *Articuli super Cartas* of 1300, perhaps with the evidence of the 1298 inquiries in mind.[31] But, as was also the case with purveyance, legislation unsupported by executive powers was quite ineffective.

The collection of royal debts gave multiple opportunities for bullying and extortion. Often, for example, the hundred bailiff would refuse to give an acquittance when a debt had been paid, with the result that the debtor was subsequently dunned again.[32] In one not untypical case of 1296 from Yorkshire a man who had already paid a debt of 4s. to the crown proffered his tally of acquittance to the sub-bailiff, only to have it torn from his hand and carried off, and to be later forced to pay again.[33] Although not all such abuses sprang from debts for taxation (for judicial penalties were perhaps a more frequent cause of indebtedness), they do suggest that the incidental results of taxation may sometimes have stung more sharply than the sums which went directly to the crown.

The practical effects of both sorts of exaction are shown by the literary evidence. This is, of course, open to some of the same objections as the material drawn from the inquiries of 1298 and later: it gives us only the tax-payer's side of the case, it is difficult to

27 P.R.O., J.I.1/672, m.7.

28 P.R.O., E.159/70, m.104. Cf. m.107d for a similar distress taken from the prior and convent of Lewes.

29 E.g., P.R.O., J.I.1/587, m.3 (Norfolk); J.I.1/673, mm.3, 9, 10d (Notts.); *Lincs. Assize Roll*, nos. 153, 229, 328.

30 E.g., P.R.O., J.I.1/255, m.4 (Essex, 1323).

31 Cam, *op. cit.*, pp. 84-5; *Statutes of the Realm* (hereafter cited as *Stat. Realm*), i (Record Comm., 1810), p. 139.

32 *Lincs. Assize Roll*, nos. 320, 321, 407.

33 P.R.O., J.I.1/1105, m.4.

control, and it may indicate the opportunities as well as the reasons for complaint. But although poems such as the *Song of the Husbandman* cannot always be taken at their face value, they are nevertheless illuminating, and this piece particularly so.[34] It is customarily dated to about 1300,[35] though its two references to very severe weather might suggest a date between 1315 and 1317. It comes at any rate from a period of very heavy taxation, since we are told that "for ever the fourth penny must go to the king". The subject of the poem is a moderately prosperous man (he has cattle and a mare, and he is able to offer the royal bailiff a mark as a bribe) and he complains against his lord and his lord's officials as well as against the ministers of the king. It is this second group, however, which provokes his most specific grievances. The bailiffs have dunned him for the king's debts so frequently that he has paid them more than ten times over. The crown's demands have severely hampered his ability to make a living from his land: to raise money for taxes he has been forced to sell his corn before the proper time and, more seriously, to market his seed-corn, thus allowing his land to waste for lack of seed. His cattle have been taken (perhaps as a distress for debt or as prises), he has had to bribe the chief bailiff, and the "wicked weather" has added to his troubles. Though there may be exaggeration here, the writer's lament, if it was to strike a chord with its intended audience, cannot have been entirely without substance. And the fact that the poem is in the vernacular, and not in Anglo-Norman or Latin, suggests (what is perhaps not always true of fourteenth-century "protest" literature) that both author and audience may have been comparatively humble in their social standing.

One other literary piece refers to the levy on movables — the *Poem on the Times of Edward II*, which dates from the 1320s.[36] This belongs to a common genre, typified both in poems and in sermons, which pours indiscriminate abuse on the rich and on those in authority, and it is hardly surprising that it should have something to say about the king's tax-collectors. What it does say is predictable, though not without interest. Whenever a tax is levied, much goes, so the author implies, to the "many partners" who collect it. The rich man worth £40 is taxed at 12d. and so also is the

[34] Printed by T. Wright, *The Political Songs of England* (Camden Soc., 1839), pp. 149-53, and, most recently, by R. H. Robbins, *Historical Poems of the XIVth and XVth Centuries* (New York, 1959), pp. 7-9.

[35] As, for instance, by Robbins, *op. cit.*, p. 249, and Prestwich, *War, Politics and Finance*, p. 256.

[36] Wright, *Political Songs*, pp. 323-45. A variant version is printed by T. W. Ross in *Anglia*, lxxv (1957), pp. 177-93.

man with a "heap of children" whom "poverty hath brought to ground". The poor are robbed and the rich escape. Half the money raised for the king is stolen before it is accounted for, and if the poor man protests he is "foul affronted". Though the main theme of this plaint is a standard one, it remains valuable evidence, for it supports the facts already cited on the quantities of cash collected and never recorded in the assessment lists, and points to one easily overlooked factor which greatly affected the peasant's prosperity — the size of his family. Child allowances for the tax-payer have been devised since the fourteenth century.

The levy on movables, then, might be a grievous imposition. It was probably not generally or nationally so, and it was certainly less resented and less damaging than purveyance. It is hard to generalize about its effects. Much depended on the honesty of the sub-taxers in each village, on the attitudes of the chief taxers in each county, on the extent to which extortion was balanced by under-assessment, and on other imponderables. In years when one levy followed fast on another, as between 1294 and 1297, or during periods of bad weather, then its impact might be especially heavy and hard to bear. It is significant that the most vigorous and widespread local resistance to the levies came during the famine years between 1315 and 1317.[37] Such taxation could bring confusion to the peasant's agricultural routine. The barons complained in the *Monstraunces* of 1297 that the king's demands (by which they meant prises as well as subsidies) had left many without the means to subsist and to cultivate their lands,[38] and the *Song of the Husbandman*, with its references to the forced sale of unripe corn and seed-corn, shows just how this might happen. Though the subsidy was undoubtedly more burdensome than has commonly been assumed, it was perhaps only the very unlucky who were affected thus severely. And yet the system sometimes worked with a capriciousness which could not be bargained for and which might bring ruin. For the levy of 1334, taken to finance a new Scottish campaign, the men of Ottery St. Mary in Devon found their assessment raised from the £15 10s. 7d. which they had paid in 1332, to £20, merely because (so they said) the chief assessors in Devonshire bore a grudge against the dean and chapter of Rouen, who currently held the manor. So grievous was the

---

37 Willard, *Parliamentary Taxes*, pp. 170-2.

38 "They say that they cannot give an aid on account of their poverty, by reason of the aforesaid taxes and prises; for they have scarcely the means to keep themselves alive, and there are many who have no sustenance and cannot cultivate their lands": *Chronicle of Walter of Guisborough*, ed. H. Rothwell (Camden 3rd ser., lxxxix, 1957), p. 292.

extra imposition that twenty-six out of the 134 tenants took the most desperate step which any peasant could take: they left their holdings and departed.[39] Like many others, they were the indirect victims of the state at war.

III

(i)

The levy on movables was nation-wide in its incidence. Purveyance, by contrast, was geographically more restricted, but also more oppressive in the areas which it most affected.[40] Its essence lay in the king's prerogative right to purchase compulsorily the victuals and means of transport which his household needed for its subsistence as it moved through the countryside. This was not a new right. It had certainly been exercised by the kings of the twelfth century and even under the Angevins it may have been used not only to supply the household, but also for the support of the king's armies.[41] It had, too, been a cause for complaint long before the 1290s, and the main abuses disclosed by early attempts to limit it were those which were equally common later — private profiteering, the seizure of goods without payment or consent, and payments made inadequately or after long delays.[42] But, like other forms of taxation, purveyance was much expanded during the second half of Edward I's reign. The forces which Edward raised for his Scottish campaigns were far larger than those of his predecessors, his financial difficulties were greater, and his military commitments on

[39] P.R.O., C.145/135/13. The figures quoted are roughly confirmed by the assessments, which stood at £15 11s. 10d. in 1332 and £20 in 1334: *The Devonshire Lay Subsidy of 1332*, ed. A. M. Erskine (Devon and Cornwall Rec. Soc., new ser., xiv, 1969), p. 131. Throughout the country the 1334 assessments were higher than those of 1332, but the increase of nearly 33 per cent at Ottery St. Mary was considerably larger than that borne by most of the other Devonshire vills. This offers at least a partial confirmation of the story.

[40] There is no good general survey of purveyance. For Edward I's reign, see Prestwich, *War, Finance and Politics*, pp. 118-36, and Thomson, *Lincs. Assize Roll*, introduction. For Edward II, J. R. Maddicott, *Thomas of Lancaster, 1307-22* (Oxford, 1970), esp. pp. 106-8. And for Edward III, H. J. Hewitt, *The Organization of War under Edward III, 1338-62* (Manchester, 1966), pp. 50-63; E. B. Fryde, "Parliament and the French War, 1336-40", in T. A. Sandquist and M. R. Powicke (eds.), *Essays in Medieval History presented to Bertie Wilkinson* (Toronto, 1969), esp. pp. 258-9; and Hughes, *Early Years of Edward III*, pp. 13-15.

[41] Prestwich, *War, Finance and Politics*, p. 119; *Pipe Roll, 4 John* (Pipe Roll Soc., new ser., xv, 1937), pp. xii, xiv.

[42] W. Stubbs, *Select Charters*, 9th edn., ed. H. W. C. Davis (Oxford, 1913), pp. 296-7, 376; *Stat. Realm*, i, pp. 27-8.

the continent were extensive. In these circumstances purveyance came to be seen as a means by which a hard-pressed government could anticipate and supplement the yield from direct taxation in order to feed its armies and to supply its castle-garrisons. And so it remained until the 1340s and beyond.

The objections to purveyance were part constitutional, part economic, though naturally the two cannot always be nicely separated. Purveyance was an entirely arbitrary exaction, which needed no consent but which might considerably augment royal resources. The crown usually intended to pay for the goods which its servants took, and precise instructions were often issued about payment, as we shall see. But it remained true that much went unpaid for, both because of the government's inability to control its local officials and because those officials frequently did not have the ready cash to pay for what they took. Although the raising of supplies by purveyance was intended primarily to allow the crown to anticipate the levy on movables before a campaign, when no payment was made it became in effect a means by which Parliament could be circumvented and a form of taxation imposed without any corresponding form of consent. That purveyance was an undoubted prerogative right made matters all the more difficult. Precedent and custom justified the taking of goods for the king's use, provided that these were paid for. From the 1290s, however, this limited prerogative was stretched and distorted to an unprecedented degree. Edward I and his successors were using purveyance as King John had used the feudal incidents: just as John had done, the three Edwards exploited the undefined nature of their prerogative in order to make new financial demands on their subjects. But the crown's actions in the late thirteenth and fourteenth centuries were more generally oppressive, for the burden of purveyance, unlike that of the feudal incidents, fell not upon a limited number of tenants-in-chief, but directly upon the peasantry.

A constitutional issue thus became an economic one. As with the levy on movables, the economic effects of the tax were partly determined by its frequency, and this varied with the scale of the crown's military activity. The raising of prises (that is, goods taken by purveyance) preceded most campaigns, and even when no campaigns were pending much was levied, particularly under Edward II and Edward III, for the use of garrisons in the north. Between the mid-1290s and the mid-1330s there were three periods when purveyance was especially oppressive: from 1294 to 1297, when supplies were being raised both for Scotland and for Gascony;[43] from 1314 to 1316, years which saw the Bannockburn campaign, the attempted despatch of a new expedition northwards, and efforts to hold Berwick and Carlisle in the face of increasingly difficult conditions;[44] and from 1333 onwards, when English armies again began to intervene extensively in Scotland.[45] These were periods when, as has been shown, direct taxation on movables was also very heavy. It was the frequent imposition of purveyance in conjunction with the levy on movables (a coincidence explained by the origins of both taxes in the crown's military needs) which made it especially hard to bear.

Not all parts of the country suffered equally. Throughout the period purveyance fell most often upon the counties of the east coast and the east midlands. From 1296 to 1307 Yorkshire was called on for supplies some thirteen times; Lincolnshire, Cambridgeshire and Essex, twelve times; and Huntingdonshire eleven times.[46] Under Edward II the pattern was roughly similar, though the southern and western counties were then more frequently burdened. Lincolnshire and Essex were asked for supplies some nine times; Gloucestershire, Cambridgeshire, Huntingdonshire, Norfolk and Suffolk, eight times; and Somerset, Dorset and Hertfordshire seven times. And in the first ten years of Edward III's reign Norfolk and Huntingdonshire were affected six times, Suffolk and Cambridgeshire five times, and Lincolnshire, Nottinghamshire, Surrey, Sussex, Lancashire, Gloucestershire and Somerset four times.[47] The counties afflicted most regularly and heavily were Lincolnshire, Cambridgeshire and Huntingdonshire, while others more fortunate, particularly those of the western and southern midlands, escaped almost entirely: in a period of just over forty years prises were raised only once in Herefordshire, only twice in Wiltshire, and only three times in Oxfordshire and Buckinghamshire. There were obvious reasons for such a distribution.[48] The eastern counties constituted the chief corn-growing areas in the country, some of them could supply other commodities, like salt, which were difficult to obtain

[43] P.R.O., J.I.1/1314, mm.1-3; E.159/69, mm.76d, 80d; E.159/70, mm.119, 121; E.159/71, m.64; *Cal. Pat. Rolls, 1292-1301*, pp. 224, 314.

[44] *Rotuli Scotiae* (hereafter cited as *Rot. Scot.*), i (Record Comm., 1814), pp. 122-3, 141-2, 150-1, 156-7, 160-1, 169-70, 172, 178-9.

[45] *Ibid.*, pp. 229-30, 278, 297, 316-17, 409, 436-7, 444.

[46] Prestwich, *War, Politics and Finance*, pp. 133-4.

[47] These figures are deduced from the *Rot. Scot.* and from *Cal. Pat. Rolls, 1321-4*, pp. 93-4, 243-4.

[48] Cf. Prestwich, *War, Politics and Finance*, p. 134.

elsewhere,[49] their inland waterways provided cheap transport facilities, and their ports were conveniently situated for the shipment of provisions to armies mustered at Berwick or Newcastle and to garrisons stationed along the Scottish border. The possession of suitably placed ports sometimes led to the raising of similar prises along the south coast for shipment both to Gascony and to Skinburness, the Cumberland harbour normally used as a supply-base for English forces in the north-west.

In geographical terms purveyance thus fell very unevenly. Its disposition has an important bearing on its economic effects, for the counties which it most burdened were characterised (at least in parts) by over-population, acute land shortage and rural poverty. Miss Harvey has suggested that in 1332 only about 35 per cent of the householders in Pinchbeck and 26 per cent of those in Spalding, both in the Lincolnshire wapentake of Elloe, reached the minimum level of wealth necessary for contribution to that year's subsidy,[50] and conditions in Cambridgeshire, Norfolk and in much of the rest of Lincolnshire are not likely to have been very different. At Little Abington (Cambs.), for instance, there were in the 1270s more than thirty free tenants, none of whom held over two acres.[51] It is often assumed that the very high tax assessments in some of these areas demonstrate their prosperity: parts of central Cambridgeshire, of west and north-east Norfolk and of Kesteven were rated at over 50s. per square mile in 1334, among the highest averages in England.[52] But this inference may be fallacious. In districts without large towns to swell their assessments, such figures must point to a massive population, though not necessarily a thriving one. Many (the majority at Pinchbeck and Spalding) may have been exempted from taxation by their poverty, while the tax-payers were still thick enough on the ground to produce the collectively large assessments which we find. Unless we know the population of an area, high tax assessments provide only a very dubious indicator of per capita wealth and of prosperity; they could as well show the reverse.

---

[49] P.R.O., J.I.1/521 provides evidence for the purveyance of large quantities of salt from Lincolnshire in the 1330s.

[50] Harvey, "The Population Trend", p. 28. I accept the interpretation put upon these figures by Titow, *English Rural Society*, p. 91. For the minute size of freemen's holdings in the Fenland, see H. E. Hallam, *Settlement and Society* (Cambridge, 1965), pp. 215-18.

[51] *Victoria County History of Cambridgeshire*, ii, ed. L. F. Salzman (London, 1948), p. 64.

[52] R. E. Glasscock, "The Distribution of Wealth in East Anglia in the Early Fourteenth Century", *Trans. of the Institute of British Geographers*, xxxii (1963), pp. 116, 118-23; "The Lay Subsidy of 1334 for Lincolnshire", *Lincs. Architectural and Archaeological Soc. Reports and Papers*, x, pt. 2 (1964), p. 121.

In some of these regions a partial compensation may have been offered by the weakness of lordship. The most typical countryman was the small freeman, not burdened by the seigneurial dues and services which affected the peasantry in other parts of the country, and to this extent the peasants of eastern England were better off than those who lived elsewhere. But it is doubtful if the comparative lightness of seigneurial exactions could make up for holdings which were often entirely inadequate. Indeed, when prises were levied the absence of the ties of lordship might be a positive disadvantage to the peasant. In other counties it was in the lords' interests to protect their tenants, and they often did so.[53] In eastern England such protection was lacking. Purveyance fell most heavily and regularly on a population which was in all ways least fitted to sustain it.

This conclusion carries with it the tacit assumption that it was the peasantry, rather than the gentry or the nobility, who were the main sufferers. This is what might be expected and it can be precisely demonstrated. Wealth, access to the king's favour and influence on local officials were all advantages possessed by the middle and upper classes which helped to give them *de facto* exemption from purveyance. The bribery of purveyors was frequent, and most manorial accounts from this period contain examples of it. In 1314, for instance, the reeve of the Ramsey manor of Allington (Hunts.) paid 3s. to a royal minister in order to persuade him not to take the abbot's carts for the current Scottish campaign; and the Cuxham records provide other similar instances.[54] Bribery was not, of course, the sole prerogative of the rich, but bribery by the peasantry is likely to have been less effective, partly for the obvious reason that the peasant's financial resources were smaller than those of the large landlord. The point is graphically made by the accusations levelled against Richard le Hostage, a royal clerk commissioned to raise corn in Gloucestershire in 1296. Most of the great religious houses in the county, including Gloucester, Tewkesbury, Winchcombe, Cirencester and St. Augustine's, Bristol, offered him money to be spared the prise, as did some of the lesser houses like Horsley and Stanley. Considerable sums changed hands. At Gloucester Hostage had 60s. and a gold brooch from the abbot, four marks from the almoner, 40s. from the master of the works and 60s. from the chamberlain; and of the other religious houses only Stanley, which gave a mark,

---

53 Below, p. 306.

54 *Elton Manorial Records, 1279-1351*, ed. S. C. Ratcliff (Roxburghe Club, Cambridge, 1946), p. 210; P. D. A. Harvey, *A Medieval Oxfordshire Village: Cuxham, 1240-1400* (Oxford, 1965), pp. 110-11. For other examples, see, e.g., F. M. Page, *Wellingborough Manorial Accounts* (Northants. Rec. Soc., 1936), pp. 99, 109, 112.

offered less than £2. Three villeins of Nympsfield, on the other hand, could raise only the pathetic sum of 9s. between them.[55] When it came to bribing royal officials, villeins could hardly compete with their social superiors. We meet the same abuses in other counties. During the 1298 inquiries in Norfolk Richard de Karkney was accused of taking corn "from the poor and impotent" and of leaving alone "the able and powerful" — "namely Robert de Schelton, knight", said the jurors with precision (and perhaps with malice).[56] Since each county normally had to supply specified quantities of corn and livestock, the ability of the rich largely to escape the levies inevitably made for a greater load on the peasantry. When various men in Kent bribed Richard de Louth, a royal purveyor, to spare them, it was said that those unwilling to offer bribes had been burdened more heavily in consequence.[57]

W.S. Thomson, the editor of the Lincolnshire assize roll for 1298, noted that "with certain exceptions the great ones of the county do not appear in the roll", and he explained their absence by arguing that if they had complaints they could afford to sue by individual writs.[58] But it is more probable that few of them did have complaints. Great men and powerful institutions were often able to deflect the king's demands, to their own advantage and to the loss of others. When Edward II asked Worcester Cathedral Priory to supply goods for his Scottish campaign in June 1310, the prior temporized, pleading the high price of corn and promising to do what he could after the harvest. The general response to other similar requests was so poor that in September the king told the Chancery that almost all the religious houses had failed him and that the sheriffs were to be ordered to levy prises throughout the country.[59] A default by one section of the community thus meant the imposition of its share of the prise burden on to others who were less able to resist the crown's demands and also less able to meet them. Even when the religious houses could not escape their obligations, the load may sometimes have been passed on to their tenants. So expensive was the entertainment of the king and court at Crowland in 1314 that the abbey sought to recoup its losses by imposing a double tallage on its

55 P.R.O., E.159/70, m.42d.
56 P.R.O., J.1.1/587, m.6.
57 P.R.O., E.159/71, m.12.
58 *Lincs. Assize Roll*, p. cii.
59 J. M. Wilson, *The Worcester Liber Albus* (London, 1920), pp. 96-9; *Cal. Chancery Warrants, 1244-1326*, p. 324; P.R.O., E.101/14/19; *Rot. Scot.*, i, pp. 94-5. It is possible that the king's attempt to avoid general purveyance may have been due to pressure from the Ordainers, then in session.

villeins. In such a way prises too may have been transmitted. [60]

The great men in each county did not always have to resort to bribery, hedging or dunning their tenants in order to avoid purveyance. They could do so more formally and legitimately by obtaining royal letters of protection which, *inter alia*, guaranteed the holder against the taking of his goods by shire officials.[61] Protections were normally respected, but they were expensive. Each cost about 2s.,[62] compared with 2d. for a common law writ, and they cannot have been easy to come by. How many peasants would have had the money, time and knowledge to seek protections from the Chancery or to fee an attorney to act for them? That protections exempted the rich from purveyance, while the poor paid, was a common grumble and one which bitterly angered the author of one of our most valuable sources on purveyance, the *De Speculo Regis*, written about 1331. Consider, he says, the poor man who comes to market with an ox, intending to sell it in order to meet a debt, for the repayment of which he has pledged his lands. The ox is taken in the market by the king's ministers, the poor man receives nothing for it, and consequently he loses his holding. The rich man, on the other hand, who comes to market with both sheep and oxen, can show his protection and go free.[63] The sufferers themselves sometimes made similar complaints. In one petition a group calling itself "the poor people of the realm" told the king of their grievances against the "wrongful and outrageous doings" of his ministers (and it was probably the levying of prises which they had in mind). They could obtain exemption, they said, only by procuring writs from the Chancery and the Exchequer, but these cost more than poor men could pay.[64]

The fact that numerous men could afford and did obtain protections meant that a great burden was laid on those who stood outside the king's grace. Members of the royal household,[65] captains and their retinues fighting in Scotland or France, and those

60 F. M. Page, *The Estates of Crowland Abbey* (Cambridge, 1934), pp. 59-60.

61 *Lincs. Assize Roll*, pp. xxxix, liii-liv.

62 P. Chaplais, *English Royal Documents* (Oxford, 1971), p. 22.

63 *De Speculo Regis Edwardi Tertii*, ed. J. Moisant (Paris, 1891), pp. 99-100. For the date and authorship of this work, see J. Tait, "The Date and Authorship of the 'Speculum Regis Edwardi' ", *Eng. Hist. Rev.*, xvi (1901); L. E. Boyle, "The Oculus Sacerdotis and some other Works of William of Pagula", *Trans. Roy. Hist. Soc.*, 5th ser., v (1955), pp. 104, 107-8; and L. E. Boyle, "William of Pagula and the Speculum Regis Edwardi III", *Medieval Studies*, xxxii (1970), pp. 329-36.

64 P.R.O., S.C.8/334/E.1149.

65 As, for instance, Edward II's keeper of the wardrobe, Ingelard de Warley, and Edward's yeoman, Oliver de Bordeaux: *Cal. Chancery Warrants, 1244-1326*, pp. 318, 502.

with friends at court — all these groups could normally secure protections, and to knights and nobles serving in the army they were given almost as a matter of course. Since the mustering of an army invariably coincided with the levying of prises for its maintenance, the heaviest prise impositions must often have come when the number of potential contributors was at its lowest.

While it is broadly true, then, that the gentry and magnates were not greatly harmed by purveyance and that the peasantry was affected much more severely, this conclusion must be qualified. Much depended, as we have seen, on the part of the country where the peasant lived, and much too on the protective power of his lord. In 1297, when cash levies were imposed on the hundreds of Worcestershire in order to buy sheep and oxen for the king's use (a variation on the normal prise system), eleven vills in Pershore hundred escaped, because they were held by the earl of Warwick and Sir Walter Beauchamp, then on service in Scotland.[66] In the same year the bailiff of Thurgarton wapentake in Nottinghamshire took 8s. from Sir Thomas Furnival's villeins in Gristhorpe for the purchase of provisions. Later, during the 1298 inquiries, Furnival charged him with this offence, arguing that at the time he had been with the king in Scotland and that his possessions had therefore been under royal protection.[67] Nor, in other circumstances, did the rich always escape and the poor always pay. When the religious houses excused themselves from meeting the king's demands in 1310, several of them stated in mitigation that they had already provided horses, carts and quantities of corn for the king's use.[68] It is probable that monasteries were more generally subject to prises than secular lords, both because the king had less need for their political support and because they had a slighter influence on local officials than did the lay magnates (though this was not invariably so, as the activities of Le Hostage in Gloucestershire prove). At the other end of the social scale the very poor may normally have been exempt from purveyance. The government provided some safeguards for them, and their goods in any case are not likely to have been substantial enough to attract the attention of the purveyors. As with the levy on movables, it was probably the landless, lacking corn and livestock, who suffered least.

But despite these qualifications and exceptions purveyance in general afflicted the upper and middle classes much less harshly than it did the peasantry. Why, then, when gentry and magnates

66 P.R.O., J.I.1/1314, m.3.
67 P.R.O., J.I.1/672, m.2.
68 P.R.O., E.101/14/19.

came together in Parliament or in extra-parliamentary opposition to the crown, were they so concerned to restrict what the *De Speculo Regis* calls this "diabolical prerogative"? [69] The *Confirmatio Cartarum* in 1297, the *Articuli super Cartas* in 1300, the Statute of Stamford in 1309, the Ordinances in 1311, and a series of statutes in the 1320s and '30s, all made ineffective attempts at its limitation. At the root of these attempts there may have been a constitutional complaint: that the king was in effect imposing taxation without parliamentary consent. But the impression remains that this was not the primary grievance. Only in 1297 and 1339, for instance, did the nobility demand "common consent" to prises, [70] and they were usually more preoccupied with local abuses — purveyance without warrant, under-valuation of goods, the taking of corn by the heaped measure instead of the razed, and so on. Concern with purveyance was probably not so much the product of reflections on the constitution, but rather of the position of gentry and magnates as rentiers and of their possible fear of a peasant rising.

For the first of these suggestions there is some indirect evidence. The extension of the king's protection to cover the goods of the lords' tenants shows the lords' anxiety to safeguard the economic standing of their own men. Purveyance may have made it more difficult for those men to find their rents, and while there is no proof of this, it is only a short step from saying that prises hinder the poor man from paying his debts, as the *De Speculo Regis* states, [71] to saying that they also prevent him from paying his rent. Direct taxation could certainly have this effect: in 1340 the abbot of Malmesbury told the king that the abbey's tenants had been so impoverished by the extortions of the collectors of the tenths and fifteenths that they could no longer render their rents and services. [72] Purveyance, more capricious and harsher in its incidence than the levy on movables, is not likely to have been less damaging to the economic interests of the lords.

As for the fear of rebellion, the evidence is slight but suggestive. We know that there was sometimes violent resistance to the work of the king's purveyors. In 1321-2, for instance, the sheriff of Warwickshire and Leicestershire told the king that when, during the previous reign, he had been commissioned to take horses and carts for the current Scottish campaign, seven men had assaulted him on

[69] *De Speculo Regis*, p. 115.
[70] Stubbs, *Select Charters*, pp. 493-4; *Rotuli Parliamentorum Hactenus Inediti*, ed. H. G. Richardson and G. O. Sayles (Camden Soc., 3rd ser., li, 1935), p. 369. Fryde, "Parliament and the French War", p. 256, n. 34, dates this second petition to 1337.
[71] *De Speculo Regis*, p. 99.
[72] *Cal. Pat. Rolls, 1338-40*, pp. 435-6.

the high road and left him for dead, taking with them the cart which the sheriff had confiscated from one of their number.[73] Again, about 1330 the liberty of Fordwich in Kent, held by St. Augustine's, Canterbury, was taken into the king's hands after the abbey's tenants there had attacked royal purveyors who were carrying off their livestock.[74] These are mere straws in the wind; but other sources leave a more solid impression. The Ordinances of 1311 were quite explicit about the dangers of a general revolt. In their preamble they stated that "the realm of England is upon the point of rising on account of oppressions, prises and destructions", while the clause ordaining the abolition of prises began by declaring that "it is to be feared that the people of the land will rise by reason of the prises and divers oppressions made in these times".[75] Equally blunt was the author of the De Speculo Regis, who told the young Edward III that if the people had a leader they would rise up against him because of his exactions, just as they had done against his father.[76] By the late 1330s many thought that a revolt was imminent.[77]

The justification for the anxieties of nobility and gentry on both scores — the effect of purveyance on rents, and its possible provocation of a revolt — can be understood only if we move to the localities and see how prises were levied and how they may have affected peasant agriculture and income. It is to this subject that we now turn.

(ii)

When purveyance was ordered on a national scale, usually a month or so prior to a campaign, its general supervision in each county was entrusted to the sheriff, working in co-operation with a royal clerk appointed by the government.[78] What happened next seems to have varied very much from county to county and from period to period, and since the government rarely provided detailed instructions for the levying of prises, as it did for the tax on movables, our information is usually of an incidental sort. In some counties during the 1290s the county court divided the quantity of provisions required among the hundreds and wapentakes. This

73 Rotuli Parliamentorum (hereafter cited as Rot. Parl.), i (London, 1783), p. 408.
74 W. A. Pantin, "The Letters of John Mason: A 14th century Formulary from St. Augustine's, Canterbury", Essays . . . to Wilkinson, pp. 204-6.
75 Stat. Realm, i, pp. 157, 159.
76 De Speculo Regis, p. 96.
77 Below, pp. 348-9.
78 E.g., Rot. Scot., i, pp. 94-5 (1310).

happened in Nottinghamshire in 1297, when the court assessed each wapentake at a certain number of sheep and oxen for the king's prise.[79] In the same year the sheriff of Shropshire and Staffordshire was told to provide five hundred quarters of wheat, eighty oxen and two hundred sheep for the king's use. This he did by dividing the total quantity of wheat required between his two counties and then, either by himself or with the help of the county court, assessing each hundred at a certain amount. Next, the burden imposed on the hundred was subdivided among the villages according to the size of each, the assessment being carried out by two knights of the hundred. Within each village two sworn men levied money to pay for the quota of wheat which the village had to supply. The price for a quarter of wheat was set at 4s., and when the stipulated quantity had been bought it was carried to Chester at the villagers' expense. Cash for the purchase of sheep and oxen was raised in the same way.[80]

In the instance of Staffordshire, for which we have the fullest details, the purveyance seems to have been carried through fairly, and the villagers made no complaints (though this may not mean that they had none). The prises were assessed; the assessment was carried out by local men, without the interference of the hated hundred bailiff; and the low figure at which the wheat was priced (the average price per quarter was 5s. 3d. in 1297)[81] helped to ensure that the burden was distributed both among those who paid over their cash and those who sold their wheat. But points could be made against these deductions. We do not know precisely how the assessment was carried out in each village, and such a system did not necessarily lead to an even allotment of taxation, as the evidence from the levy on movables shows.[82] There is no suggestion in the records that the villagers were ever fully repaid or that they expected this; for those who gave money for the purchase of corn, purveyance might thus amount to the imposition of a direct tax. And, in any case, the costs of carriage had to be met by the village. The arrangements were probably as equitable as any that could be devised, but they may nevertheless have been very onerous.

Other communities assessed their members in slightly different ways. In one Lincolnshire wapentake during 1296 or 1297 twelve jurors decided on each man's contribution of grain for the prise, while at Sutton-in-Holland ten years later the whole village assessed

---

[79] P.R.O., J.I.1/672, m.4d.

[80] P.R.O., J.I.1/1314, mm.2-2d, 1-1d.

[81] J. E. Thorold Rogers, *A History of Agriculture and Prices in England*, i (Oxford, 1866), p. 228. Unless otherwise stated, all prices subsequently quoted are derived from this work.

[82] Above, pp. 293-5.

its members.[83] Under Edward II, however, there is little evidence for similar procedures in any area, and it is probable that over the whole period assessement was the exception rather than the rule. Much more frequently the sheriff's subordinate, the hundred or wapentake bailiff, simply descended on a village and took what he wanted, often quite arbitrarily, without payment (or at best with payment deferred through the giving of tallies), and in a way which bore little relation to the owner's ability to sustain the prise. One Nottinghamshire case may stand for very many. In October 1295 the wapentake bailiff of Risley took from Henry Cosin of Bunny fifty quarters of corn, which Cosin was forced to carry to Nottingham at his own cost. In return he received neither money, tallies nor receipts.[84] The giving of tallies was often no more satisfactory, because of the common difficulty of getting them cashed. In 1306 the men of Kirby Misperton (Yorks.) complained that the sheriff had levied thirty-three quarters of oats from them in 1303-4, in exchange for a tally which had still not been cashed. The whole vill had been assessed at only 18s. 5d. for the fifteenth of 1301, yet the market value of the oats taken (just over 74s.) was four times this amount.[85] Attempts to obtain payment were costly, vexatious and usually vain. In 1338 a Nottinghamshire man went twice to York and many times to Nottingham to seek payment for four oxen which the sheriff had taken from him, but he got nothing.[86] It was not surprising that contemporary moralists and versifiers treated the tally system with indignant vituperation. "It would be better", said one articulate critic, "to eat from wooden platters and pay in coin for food than to serve the body with silver and give pledges of wood. It is a sign of vice to pay for food with wood". This voiced the feelings of many silent men, just as, in a more public way, did the similar complaints brought in the *Monstraunces* of 1297. [87]

When payment was made for prises, it was sometimes offered at less than market rates (though royal officials managed to obtain high prices for their produce[88]), or, more frequently, covered only

83 *Lincs. Assize Roll*, no. 419; G. C. Homans, *English Villagers of the Thirteenth Century* (Cambridge, Mass., 1942), pp. 332-3.

84 P.R.O., J.I.1/672, m.3d.

85 *Rot. Parl.*, i, p. 195; *Yorkshire Lay Subsidy 30 Edward I*, ed. W. Brown (Yorks. Arch. Soc., Record Ser., xxi, 1897), p. 113.

86 P.R.O., J.I.1/691, m.1d. For the similar journeys of the reeve of Cuxham in the 1340s, see Harvey, *Cuxham*, p. 111.

87 I. S. T. Aspin, *Anglo-Norman Political Songs* (Anglo-Norman Text Soc., 1953), p. 186; *Chron. Guisborough*, p. 292. The Dominican, John Bromyard, later made the same point: G. R. Owst, *Literature and Pulpit in Medieval England* (Oxford, 1961), p. 338.

88 Prestwich, *War, Politics and Finance*, p. 135.

a part of the goods taken. The men of Somerset and Dorset complained in 1330 that the sheriff had levied from the two counties five hundred quarters of wheat and three hundred bacon pigs for the king's use (or so he had said). For every twenty quarters taken, however, he would allow them only sixteen, and for these he paid at the rate of 10d. a bushel, afterwards selling the wheat for 1s. 3d. a bushel. No-one, they said, had previously dared to complain because of the sheriff's great power.[89] The grievances shown up by this petition — under-payment, private profiteering, and the difficulty of getting redress — were common ones. The author of the *De Speculo Regis*, writing about the same time, had much to say on the corresponding iniquities of those who took goods for the court. If the royal purveyors want hay, he writes, they offer 3d. a bushel for it, although it is worth 5d.; they pay 3d. for a bushel of barley, worth 8d., and 3d. for a bushel of beans, worth 1s. They take the hens which sustain widows, poor women and orphans, for 1d. each, although a hen is worth 2d. "Where is the justice in this? It is not justice, but rapine".[90] What makes these statements the more striking is that the *De Speculo Regis* was written during a period of peace, is entirely concerned with purveyance for the royal household, and deals with abuses which were mainly confined to the Windsor area, where the court stayed most frequently. In war-time, when much wider areas were subject to purveyance and when the goods taken had to supply not only the household, but whole armies, then those abuses are likely to have been far more damaging.

Petitions, the evidence of royal inquiries, and the legislation of the 1320s and '30s, all provide plenty of material for a catalogue of other corrupt practices. Prises were often taken without proper authority or by men who held forged commissions. The *De Speculo Regis* speaks of the "great outcry from the people" resulting from the purveyance of goods by those acting without royal authorization, and from the *Articuli super Cartas* onwards one of the objects of almost all legislation concerning purveyance was to ensure that purveyors should have proper warrants under the great or privy seal for their work.[91] Corn was taken without being valued by the village constables, and it was often measured by the heaped measure rather than the razed, to the purveyor's advantage.[92] When grain or livestock could not be found, money might sometimes be levied

---

[89] *Rot. Parl.*, ii, p. 40.
[90] *De Speculo Regis*, pp. 97, 103.
[91] *Ibid.*, p. 106; *Stat. Realm*, i, pp. 137, 155, 266.
[92] P.R.O., J.1.1/587, m.1; *Cal. Pat. Rolls, 1338-40*, pp. 283-4; *Stat. Realm*, i, p. 262.

instead,[93]while on other occasions men might be distrained by the bailiffs to buy corn as a contribution towards the prise.[94] The system offered manifold opportunities for extortions, swindles and tricks of all kinds.

It is possible to exaggerate the hardship which such abuses brought. Although non-payment was a frequent and justified grievance, much that was taken was paid for; this is shown well enough by the decline of the sheriffs' cash payments to the Exchequer between 1298 and 1307 as a result of their increased expenditure on provisions.[95] Nor were the sheriffs always able to supply the huge quantities of goods demanded by the government. The sheriff of Nottinghamshire and Derbyshire, asked in 1300 to provide 1,100 quarters of grain, produced only 134 quarters.[96] The volume of provisions ordered, recorded on the chancery rolls from 1298 onwards, is thus not necessarily a safe indication of the volume raised. Moreover, in their directions to the sheriffs for the levying of prises the authorities at least showed their good intentions. Under Edward I instructions were issued, sometimes with great particularity, for the protection of the king's subjects. In 1296 the purveyors were told to consult with the assessors of the twelfth on movables in order to find out how much each man could give, and prices were specified for the goods to be purveyed. In 1301 the communities of the counties, not the sheriffs, were made responsible for raising victuals. And in 1303 it was ordered that no corn should be taken from anyone who did not possess at least £10 worth of goods.[97] During the next two reigns it became common practice for the king to charge his officials to take supplies "in places where it can be done most conveniently for us and with the least damage to the men of those parts",[98]while occasionally prices might again be specified, as in 1316 and 1335.[99] Sometimes very drastic measures were authorized against purveyors who misbehaved. In 1331 those who failed to obey the appropriate statutes were made subject to the penalties for larceny and now risked a death sentence. This was "a

---

93 G. H. Tupling, *South Lancashire in the Reign of Edward II* (Chetham Soc., 3rd ser., i, 1949), p. 62.

94 Prestwich, *War, Politics and Finance*, p. 130; *Lincs. Assize Roll*, no. 241; P.R.O., J.1.1/588, m.1.

95 M.H. Mills, " 'Adventus Vicecomitum', 1272-1307", *Eng. Hist. Rev.*, xxxviii (1923), p. 351.

96 Prestwich, *op. cit.*, pp. 122-4; R. Nicholson, *Edward III and the Scots* (Oxford, 1965), pp. 113-15.

97 Prestwich, *op. cit.*, pp. 128, 131-2, 135.

98 E.g., *Rot. Scot.*, i, pp. 122 (1314), 141 (1315), 157 (1316), 184 (1318).

99 *Cal. Pat. Rolls, 1313-17*, p. 543; *Rot. Scot.*, i, p. 319.

remarkable provision", as Plucknett has noted,[100] and it showed by implication the extent of the abuses, the extreme dislike with which they were regarded, and the real concern of Parliament to amend them.

But despite these considerations purveyance undoubtedly struck very hard at many men. There is no sign that the legislation and the penalties with which it was backed had any effect; its frequent repetition suggests the reverse. The crown's concern for its subjects' welfare was rarely translated into practice at a local level, and if some prises were paid for, enough was taken without payment for many livelihoods to be put seriously at risk. The central government had no means of ensuring that its orders were carried out in the shires, and the regular raising of prises merely increased the opportunities always present in medieval local government for the crown's ministers to profit at the expense of its other subjects. The defects of a system which relied upon unpaid local men for the management of the shire were greatly magnified by the levies of these years. Even when local officials were well-intentioned (and not all were dishonest), harsh measures were often forced upon them. Between 1312 and 1316 the sheriff of Norfolk and Suffolk wrote to Edward II in response to the king's request for horse and carts to be sent to Berwick. He told the king that he had already purveyed more than he could pay for from the issues of his bailiwick and from the green wax, and he begged to be excused from this latest imposition.[101] There must have been many other harassed officials who found it more expedient simply to take what the king wanted without payment, rather than risk his displeasure by excusing themselves. Caught between the demands of the king and the interests of the small men in the localities, the overworked sheriff inevitably bore most severely on those who lacked the power and influence to protect themselves.

The government's attempts to ensure that prises were paid for did not always improve matters. The sheriffs were normally directed to make payments from particular sources, first from their own county revenues and then from the proceeds of the current subsidy. (This latter stipulation emphasized the role of purveyance as a means of anticipating the levy on movables, rather than of supplementing it.) But frequently relief could be applied in one direction only by exerting pressure in another. In 1310, as in many other years, the

---

[100] T. F. T. Plucknett, "Parliament", *The English Government at Work, 1327-36,* i, ed. J. F. Willard and W. A. Morris (Cambridge, Mass., 1940), p. 118.

[101] P.R.O., S.C.1/35/197. For the similar plight of the sheriff of Gloucestershire in 1301, see S.C.1/27/109.

sheriffs were told that if they could not pay for prises from the issues of their bailiwicks, then they were to levy the king's debts.[102] We have already seen the consequences which this might entail — the increased scope for bullying and profiteering by the hundred bailiffs, the unseasonable sale of corn to raise money, the possible distraint of plough-beasts. Prise-payers might be satisfied, but only at the expense of the crown's debtors, who were often equally ill-equipped to meet new demands.

There are good grounds, then, for supposing that purveyance affected the peasantry very seriously, at least in certain areas (such as Lincolnshire) and at certain times (as between 1294 and 1297). But it is very difficult to quantify its effects more narrowly, and we can rarely do more than show that the burden fell on the peasantry rather than on gentry or magnates. Only exceptionally do the sources enable us to distinguish between different sorts of peasants, between villeins and freemen, or between the near-landless cottar and the prosperous freeholder farming perhaps two or three virgates — though, as already suggested, there is a fair presumption that the very poor suffered least. (That rye, the main cereal crop of the poor, was very rarely taken, tends to confirm this.) Nor does our knowledge about particular villages and manors often complement the evidence derived from petitions, royal inquiries and purveyors' accounts. We can frequently say how much a particular man lost in prises; we cannot say what proportion of his total produce this constituted. Lastly, it is not always easy to distinguish between the effects of purveyance and of other forms of taxation, partly because the sources (like the *Monstraunces* and the *Song of the Husbandman*) do not always make that distinction and partly because different sorts of taxation might produce the same effects; the loss of plough-oxen, for instance, could as well be the result of purveyance as of distraint for debt. These irksome limitations make it hard to generalize about the effects of purveyance on the peasant economy.

Some deductions can be drawn from the quantities of corn successfully levied by the crown, which were often very large. Lincolnshire, for instance, gave 2.741 quarters of cereals in 1297, and Kent 4,884 quarters in 1296-7.[103] We have seen that the sheriffs did not always raise all that the government ordered, but sometimes (as in 1304) they provided more than was expected of them.[104] These supplies were the fruits of thousands of acres. If we assume, with

102 *Rot. Scot.*, i, p. 95.
103 Prestwich, *op. cit.*, p. 121.
104 *Ibid.*, p. 125.

Titow, that the peasant's average yield per acre for all types of grain was about one quarter,[105] it can be seen that in the above two cases the king was taking the produce of about 2,700 acres in Lincolnshire and about 4,900 acres in Kent. Levies on this scale were often carried through without regard for the resources of the suppliers. In April 1296 the sheriffs of thirteen counties were reprimanded by the king for depriving some men of all their corn, so that nothing was left for their sustenance.[106] While the tax on movables fell only on the peasant's marketable goods, purveyance might cut deeply into his means of subsistence, as this example shows. It might also weaken his agricultural capabilities over a long period, for if the purveyors took the peasant's seed-corn (and the *De Speculo Regis* twice suggests that they did),[107] he would have had nothing to harvest in the following year. We are reminded again of the "Husbandman's" complaint that because of his enforced sale of seed-corn, his land had gone to waste.[108] Both purveyance and the levy on movables might thus bring about a direct reduction in the amount of land under cultivation.

Purveyance of livestock was even more harmful. The peasant's livestock was never prolific at the best of times,[109] and its confiscation for the crown could have consequences which were quite ruinous. This is shown most starkly by evidence from Nottinghamshire produced during the inquiries of 1340-2. In 1338 the sheriff of the county had taken twenty oxen from four men — five from one man, four from another, and eleven from two others. As a result their plough-teams had been broken up, they had been unable to carry out their winter sowing, and, brought to complete poverty, they had had to sell their land.[110] Purveyance might thus strike with crushing severity at the comparatively well-off (for in terms of the livestock which they owned, these men had been quite prosperous) as well as at the poor. Nor was this case unique. At Sutton-in-Holland (Lincs.) thirty-two oxen were taken from the village's plough-teams in the same year, putting sixteen ploughs out of action for six months.[111] Although the seizure of draught animals was carried out on a larger scale during the 1330s, it had not been

105 Titow, *English Rural Society*. p. 81.

106 P.R.O., E.159/69, m.77d.

107 *De Speculo Regis*. pp. 94, 100.

108 Above. p. 297.

109 M. M. Postan, "Village Livestock in the Thirteenth Century", *Econ. Hist. Rev.*, 2nd ser., xv (1962-3), pp. 219-49; R. H. Hilton, *A Medieval Society* (London, 1966), p. 106.

110 P.R.O., J.I.1/691, m.1d.

111 P.R.O., J.I.1/521, m.3.

rare forty years earlier. During the purveyances of the 1290s, one man had refused to let the sheriff of Yorkshire take his horse, since he had no other on his farm and he needed it for the harvest. Purveyance of corn could bring the same results. The parson of Knavering in Norfolk complained in 1298 that the local bailiff had unjustly taken his corn, making it impossible for him to feed his beasts and preventing his sowing for six weeks.[112] Although we cannot at any point estimate the scale of the harm done by prises of this sort, their results for individuals evidently varied from severe inconvenience to complete disaster.

Less damaging but probably more general were the effects of purveyance on marketing and on prices. When a prise was expected great men could sometimes cut their losses by launching their goods on to the market before the purveyors could take them. Thus in 1308 the bishop of Winchester sold oxen at Ivingho (Bucks.) in expectation of the prise.[113] But it is very unlikely that peasants would have the same information as was available to the managers of great ecclesiastical estates and which would enable them to anticipate purveyance in this way. In any case, if the time for marketing was determined by the proximity of a prise, the seller was likely to suffer by having to sell at a time when prices might be unfavourable to him.

The withdrawal of large quantities of corn from the market by purveyance may have raised prices, benefiting the man with corn to sell. The 1,017 quarters of cereals which the two small counties of Cambridgeshire and Huntingdonshire provided for the king in 1304 [114] can hardly have failed to affect local prices. Although the long-term trend in grain prices seems to have been downwards in this period, the sharp short-term fluctuations which appear to have occurred, and the variations in price-levels between different areas,[115] may both have been partly due to purveyance. It is remarkable that in 1316 the counties of Cambridgeshire and Huntingdonshire, which had been jointly ordered to supply 1,200 quarters of grain for the king,[116] showed a level of corn prices considerably higher than that obtaining in other parts of the country — and this despite the fact that these two counties normally formed an area of low grain prices in the later middle ages. In the

112 Prestwich, *op. cit.*, p. 130.

113 D. L. Farmer, "Some Grain Price Movements in Thirteenth-Century England", *Econ. Hist. Rev.*, 2nd ser., x (1957-8), p. 218.

114 Prestwich, *op. cit.*, p. 125.

115 N. S. B. Gras, *The Evolution of the English Corn Market* (Cambridge, Mass., 1915), pp. 55-9.

116 *Rot. Scot.*, i, p. 157.

Cambridgeshire region corn reached 18s. a quarter in this year, while the national average was just over 16s. 6d.[117] It might be argued that little reliance can be placed on these figures, since they may be distorted by the abnormal famine conditions of 1316, but a later piece of evidence needs less qualification and points to the same conclusion. In July 1327 it was reported to the king that merchants bringing corn, meat, fish and other victuals into York and other places in Yorkshire had been frequently raided by purveyors for the royal household and for magnate households. As a result merchants no longer dared to come to York or to other towns and food supplies had consequently become much more expensive.[118] If the high prices which purveyance thus brought profited those with goods to sell, they are, on the other hand, likely to have borne heavily on all those who were dependent on the market for their provisions. In this way the detrimental effects of purveyance may have extended beyond the ranks of those from whom goods were actually taken.

Even when no campaign was imminent, purveyance for the royal household and its subsidiary households continued at all times. In some parts of the country the grievances which have been discussed were much more than merely occasional ones: in districts through which the household travelled frequently, the threat of purveyance was rarely absent. The *De Speculo Regis,* which provides some of our most vivid examples of the damage which purveyance might do, deals entirely with purveyance for the household, and most of the prises which fell upon the manors of Cuxham in Oxfordshire and Cheddington in Buckinghamshire, both belonging to Merton College, seem to have been of this sort.[119] These levies produced a constant undercurrent of grumbling and complaint which was directed at all the institutions and officials concerned with purveyance. It is probable, for instance, that the household court of the steward and marshal owed much of its unpopularity in the fourteenth century to its connection with the provisioning of the household.[120] When "national" prises, levied for campaigns, were superimposed on to the normal demands of the household, complaints became louder still. Of course, purveyance for the household covered only a very limited area, but it was often the area

117 Gras, *op. cit.,* pp. 60, 48-9.

118 *Rot. Scot.,* i, p. 216. Cf. *Cal. Close Rolls, 1318-23,* p. 684, for a similar instance.

119 Harvey, *Cuxham,* pp. 111-12; Merton College Muniments, nos. 5561-5566, 5569-5570.

120 *Select Cases in the Court of King's Bench,* ed. G. O. Sayles, vii (Selden Soc., 1971), p.xlvii.

most severely affected by war-time prises. The counties of southern and south-eastern England, where the court travelled most frequently, were regularly subject to the depredations of the household purveyors, but so also were Huntingdonshire, Lincolnshire, Nottinghamshire and Yorkshire, which had the misfortune to carry the main road to the north. When a Scottish campaign was in the offing, villages along the road might find themselves visited both by the hundred bailiffs seeking corn and livestock for the gathering army and by purveyors engaged on the same work for the royal household.

But the effects of purveyance cannot be judged merely in terms of its economic consequences and the frequency of its imposition. What men disliked about the system was not just the threat which it offered to their livelihoods, though this was often considerable, but the arbitrary and unjust way in which it worked and the opportunities which it gave for corruption and extortion. On most manors prises were levied without warning, without assessment and without regard for the means of the inhabitants, and in the parts of the country most affected they might be taken again and again within the space of a few years. The hundred bailiff — already perhaps the most unpopular figure in the hierarchy of royal and seigneurial officials set over the peasantry — was given new scope for profiteering, and the divisions between rich and poor may have been widened not only by the ability of the rich largely to escape from the levies, but by the jealousy and discontent which this provoked. It is hard to be sure that the author of the *De Speculo Regis* was exaggerating when he wrote that purveyance had brought many to their deaths,[121] or that the possibility of rebellion was not as real as the Ordainers twice stated it to be. Purveyance was rarely a countrywide exaction and only in certain areas was it a recurrent one — yet between 1290 and 1340 it probably did as much as any other single factor to diminish the popular reputation of the crown. It was not only success or failure in warfare which determined the king's standing, but also the fiscal burdens imposed by all wars, whether they ended in victory or in defeat.

IV

As well as direct taxation and purveyance, many villages had also to face the crown's military demands. The increased size of armies and the frequency of campaigns meant that the wars which began in the 1290s made heavier calls for manpower upon the peasantry than

121 *De Speculo Regis.* p. 101.

that class had ever had to meet. The 25,700 infantry present on the Falkirk campaign of 1298 constituted probably the largest army ever raised in England prior to the Hundred Years' War, and the armies of other years, though not as great as this, were still numerically impressive. That assembled for the campaign of 1296, perhaps 25,000 strong, may have been almost as large.[122] Under Edward II it is possible that there were some 15,000 infantry at Bannockburn in 1314[123] and almost certain that about 11,500 infantry served on the Scottish campaign of 1322;[124] while Edward III's army of 1335 comprised some 15,000 men.[125] Long intervals between campaigns were rare. In the forty-seven years from 1294 to 1340 there were some twenty years which saw substantial English armies in Scotland, four years of operations in Gascony, two of campaigns in Wales, and two of expeditions to Flanders. In some years, as in 1297 and 1338, simultaneous campaigns were on hand in Scotland and on the continent, and even the occasional lengthy periods between campaigns (from 1314 to 1319, for instance) were sometimes punctuated by the despatch of "holding" expeditions and by the summoning of armies which were disbanded before they had been tested in the field.

During this period of intense military activity, the nature of military obligations changed, to the disadvantage of the crown's subjects.[126] The bulk of the infantry in Edwardian armies were not professionals, but conscripts, selected for service by the men of their localities or by commissioners of array. During the last ten years of his reign Edward I had set an awkward precedent for the monarchy by generally paying these shire levies from the time when they left their counties, though the local communities still had to meet the costs of equipment for their men. Edward II was unwilling or unable to continue with such a policy and from 1307 onwards we begin to hear much of the grievances which were to recur incessantly until well into the 1340s — that the local communities were forced to supply their representatives with heavier and more expensive armour than was customary ("custom" usually being considered in terms of the obligations defined by the Statute of Winchester); that they were

[122] Prestwich, *War, Politics and Finance*, pp. 94-5, 113.

[123] J. E. Morris, *Bannockburn* (Cambridge, 1914), p. 41. This is a guess, based on the number of those summoned; the pay-roll for the campaign does not survive.

[124] J. E. Morris, "Mounted Infantry in Medieval Warfare", *Trans. Roy. Hist. Soc.*, 3rd ser., viii (1914), p. 89.

[125] A. E. Prince, "The Strength of English Armies in the Reign of Edward III", *Eng. Hist. Rev.*, xlvi (1931), pp. 356-7.

[126] The best guide to the subject is M. R. Powicke, *Military Obligation in Medieval England* (Oxford, 1962), chaps. 7, 8 and 10.

compelled to do unpaid service beyond the county boundaries; and that they were subject to novel and oppressive forms of levy, like the demands made in 1316 and 1322 for one man from every vill. In these ways the burden of the war was being moved away from the Exchequer and on to the localities. The popular discontent which helped to topple Edward's regime in 1326 may have been partly produced by such innovations and by the Despensers' supposed responsibility for them. The *Brut* chronicle blames the Despensers specifically for the 1322 levy of one man from every vill to serve at the cost of the vill, while the *Vita Edwardi Secundi* similarly lays to their charge the non-payment of the levies raised for Gascony in 1325.[127] When the Commons in 1327 asked that henceforth men should not be distrained to arm at their own costs, contrary to the Statute of Winchester, and that they should not be forced to serve outside their counties except at the king's expense,[128] they were acting as the mouthpiece for popular, and peasant, opinion.

The statute which resulted from the Commons' requests did not persuade Edward III to abandon his father's practices. Between 1327 and 1333 there was no large-scale intervention in Scotland, but when the wars resumed, innovations in equipment and technique meant that the putting of an army into the field rapidly became a more burdensome business. The growth in numbers and importance of hobelars and mounted archers[129] brought new expense to the countryside which supported them, for they were paid more than the ordinary foot-soldier and their equipment was more costly: in the 1340s the horse alone of the mounted archer cost about £1,[130] probably over twice as much as all the gear belonging to the foot-soldier. Moreover, it was during the 1330s that the regular wearing of uniforms began,[131] and this also was an expense which had to be met locally. The gain of the home cloth industry was to some extent the loss of those who had to buy its products. Every year between 1334 and 1338 saw campaigning in Scotland an army which these innovations had made more proficient but also more expensive. By this time, too, the army was becoming more distinctively English. The Welsh foot who had been so prominent in

---

127 *The Brut*, ed. F. W. D. Brie, i (Early English Text Soc., 1906), p. 225; *Vita Edwardi Secundi*, ed. N. Denholm-Young (London, 1957), pp. 135-6.

128 *Rot. Parl.*, ii, pp. 8, 11; *Stat. Realm*, i, pp. 255-6.

129 A. E. Prince, "The Army and Navy", *The English Government at Work*, i, p. 338.

130 Morris, "Mounted Infantry", p. 97.

131 Prince, "The Army and Navy", pp. 362-3. Uniform had occasionally been required at an earlier date — see Prestwich, *op. cit.*, p. 101, for one such instance (1295), and *Cal. Pat. Rolls, 1321-4*, p. 93, for another (1322).

the 1290s were less so in the 1330s,[132] and the higher proportion of English troops in the army meant that the burden of supporting them was concentrated more directly upon the English shires. It was no wonder that complaints stemming from the crown's military demands, particularly from the imposition of unpaid service, formed a recurrent theme in the petitions and legislation of the 1330s and '40s.[133]

The raising of troops, like the raising of prises, did not affect the whole country equally.[134] Under Edward I the brunt of the fighting in Scotland was borne by troops drawn from the north and the north midlands, as well as by the Welsh. In the two reigns which followed, devastation by the Scots severely reduced the offensive capacities of the far north, and it was mainly the counties of Yorkshire, Lancashire, Cheshire, Nottinghamshire, Derbyshire and Lincolnshire which supplied troops, though the southern shires were called on for service in Gascony and for coast-guard duty, which could be very onerous.[135] Some counties, like those of the south-west and of the west midlands, were not much affected: Herefordshire, for instance, seems to have escaped military service as successfully at it avoided prises. Only a few areas were heavily burdened both by prises and by recruitment: Nottinghamshire, Yorkshire and Lincolnshire were perhaps the chief sufferers. Here the crown's demands must have been particularly painful to many communities, but elsewhere heavy demands for prises were often balanced by lighter military obligations.

Although the commissioners of array were given general supervision of the raising of troops within each county, the selection and arming of men for service, and the levying of money for their wages and equipment, were normally left to the local communities. How they tackled these tasks is not always clear, and, as with purveyance, local practice seems to have varied widely. The village's troopers were often chosen by their fellows. This was the case at the East Riding village of South Cave in 1300, when a man "was chosen with certain others by the men of South Cave to go off to the Scottish war".[136] The actual selection probably took place in the village

132 Morris, "Mounted Infantry", p. 93.

133 *Rot. Parl.*, ii, pp. 149 (1344), 159 (1346), 200 (1348); *Rot. Parl. Hactenus Inediti*, pp. 269, 271 (1339?); *Stat. Realm.* i, pp. 278 (1336), 301 (1344).

134 Morris, "Mounted Infantry", pp. 95-6; Prestwich, *op. cit.*, pp. 103-4.

135 For coast-guard duty, see Prestwich, *op. cit.*, pp. 139-41; Hewitt, *Organization of War*, pp. 4-21; and below, p. 328. It might affect villages which were far inland: in 1336-7 Cheddington, Bucks., gave 12d to men going to guard the coast (Merton College Muniments, no. 5568).

136 *Select Cases in the Exchequer of Pleas*, ed. H. Jenkinson and B. E. R. Formoy (Selden Soc., 1932), p. 197.

assembly, but occasionally the manorial officials may have had a hand in the business: this, at least, may be the implication of a case of 1325 in which John Beaucosin, hayward at Littleport in Cambridgeshire, took 2s. from a simple-minded villein by telling him that he had been chosen to serve in Scotland, but that he, the hayward, would get him off in exchange for a bribe.[137] Sometimes the villagers might pay others to serve for them, as did the men of four Yorkshire villages who joined together in 1300 to hire twenty men-at-arms.[138] Equally various were the methods used to raise money. At Hemingford Abbots (Hunts.) in 1326 the court rolls tell us that taxers were "elected by the whole community to gather a subsidy for arms *(collectio ad arma)*".[139] In some Somerset villages during the late 1330s the constables of the vill were responsible for levying money, and throughout most of Cambridgeshire in 1316 they had charge of the armour bought for the villages' recruits.[140] In Suffolk during the 1330s the constables of the hundred received money from the villages, paid some of it over to the chief arrayers for the use of the county's hobelars, and spent the rest on arms and equipment for the hobelars.[141] The evidence in general suggests that the local supervision of military arrangements, other than the actual choosing of men for service, was almost always the job of the constables.[142]

But the economic aspects of military levies matter more than their mechanics, although the two cannot always be entirely separated. At the start of our period the burden imposed by military service was lighter than that of the levy on movables. The 187 men whom the Norfolk hundred of Launditch produced for the array of 1295 cost £52 10s. 8½d. in equipment and expenses, while the hundred was assessed at £241 19s. 6d. for the tenth of 1294 and at £97 5s. 7d. for the ninth of 1297.[143] In one or two places we can compare costs more closely. In the case of the four Yorkshire villages which combined together to hire troops in 1300, we have figures both for

137 *The Court Baron*, ed. F. W. Maitland and W. P. Baildon (Selden Soc., 1891), p. 141.

138 *Select Cases in the Exchequer of Pleas*, pp. 194-5.

139 W. O. Ault, *Open-Field Husbandry and the Village Community* (Trans. American Philosophical Soc., new ser., 1v, pt. 7, 1965), p. 53.

140 P.R.O., J.I.1/770, mm.13, 15; W. N. Palmer and H. W. Saunders, "Arms and Monies raised from Cambridgeshire Villages in 1316 for the Scottish War", *Documents relating to Cambridgeshire Villages*, no. 1 (Cambridge, 1925).

141 P.R.O., J.I.1/858, mm.6-7.

142 On village constables, see Cam, *Hundred and the Hundred Rolls*, pp. 189-94, and "Shire Officials: Coroners, Constables and Bailiffs", *The English Government at Work*, iii, 1327-1336, ed. J. F. Willard, W. A. Morris and William H. Dunham, Jr. (Cambridge, Mass., 1950), pp. 169-71.

143 Prestwich, *op. cit.*, p. 101.

military expenses and for assessments to the fifteenth of 1301. The village of Cottingwith paid 5s. 6d. in military expenses and was assessed for taxation at 32s. 3¼d.; Thorganby paid 20s. and was assessed at 32s.2d.; Kelfield paid 14s. and was assessed at 70s. 7d.; and Stillingfleet paid 24s. and was assessed at 79s. 7¾d.[144] If military expenses are expressed as an approximate percentage of the tax assessment, we find considerable variations, ranging from Cottingwith's 14 per cent to Thorganby's 63 per cent, but on average the military expenses of each village amounted to only 36½ per cent of the tax assessment. These calculations can be only very crude ones, since, as already noted, tax assessments are very unreliable guides to the amounts actually paid over to the tax collectors. Nevertheless, they do suggest they by comparison with the levy on movables, the fiscal aspect of military obligation, though burdensome, was not yet unduly so.

This is much less true of the period which followed Edward I's reign. The oppressiveness of the levy on movables may have decreased somewhat between 1294 and the reassessment of 1334; the steady decline in its yield lends itself to this interpretation.[145] The oppressiveness of the crown's military demands, on the other hand, grew considerably, both because of the introduction of heavier equipment and because of the extension of unpaid military service. This can be demonstrated, if only in an approximate fashion. First, reverting once again to our four Yorkshire villages, we find that Nicholas Stillingfleet, the man chosen to provide soldiers on the villagers' behalf, claimed to have received 9s. from Kelfield for the expenses of two footmen and for their arms — a sword, bow and arrows for each. From Stillingfleet he had similarly been given, so he said, 20s. for four footmen. Military costs per man (presumably compounded of wages to the muster as well as of arms) thus amounted to 4s. 6d. or 5s., or perhaps a little more if we accept the villagers' figures, given above, rather than those of Stillingfleet. This agrees very closely with the average of about 5s. 6d. per man which the thirty villages of Launditch hundred spent on their foot-soldiers in 1295.[146]

The figures next available for local military expenses come from Cambridgeshire in 1316, when one man was summoned from each vill to serve for sixty days at the vill's expense on a projected Scottish campaign.[147] Most of the Cambridgeshire villages raised an average

---

[144] *Select Cases in the Exchequer of Pleas,* pp. 194-5; *Yorkshire Lay Subsidy 30 Edward I,* pp. 104-7.
[145] Willard, *Parliamentary Taxes,* pp. 343-6.
[146] P.R.O., E.401/1656.
[147] For this scheme, see Powicke, *Military Obligation,* p. 143.

of 24s. for the expenses of their representatives, of which 7s. to 8s. was generally spent on arms and armour. The amount of armour supplied was quite large: the village trooper was normally provided with an aketon and bacinet, together with a variety of offensive weapons — often a sword, knife or bow and arrows, and occasionally all three together.[148]

The levy of 1316 was subsequently cancelled (though not before most vills had raised money and bought armour), but an almost identical levy was successfully carried through for the Scottish campaign of 1322. For this muster we have two accounts of local expenditure, one from the borough of Leicester and another from the manor of Cheddington (Bucks.). Leicester supplied twelve foot-soldiers for forty days' service at the town's expense. Their equipment (gauntlets, aketons, bacinets and unspecified arms) cost £20 7s. and their wages another £10, giving an average figure of £1 14s. for each man's equipment and 16s. 8d. for his wages. A special tallage produced the necessary money.[149] Leicester may have been more than usually lavish in equipping its men, as might be expected of a wealthy urban community, for the one man sent on the same campaign by Cheddington cost only 23s. in expenses and arms — almost the same amount as each Cambridgeshire vill had raised in 1316. This was the second levy in six months, however, for late in the previous year the manor had sent several men against Thomas of Lancaster, at a cost of 26s. 8d. The total expenditure on the two campaigns, £2 9s. 8d., amounted to more than the £2 0s. 9¼d. at which the village was assessed for the twentieth of 1327 (the nearest tax return available for comparison).[150]

Finally, a Hertfordshire example shows how costs had risen again by the late 1330s. In June 1338 the men of Hatfield chose two men to serve for them as hobelars. They were jointly given two horses with saddles and other equipment, worth altogether 40s., 10s. for their clothing, and 13s. 4d. for other expenses, giving an expenditure per man of £1 11s. 8d.[151] That the horses and their gear formed the largest item in this bill shows clearly enough how the new reliance on hobelars placed heavier burdens on the local communities. It was not surprising that about this time counties began to commute for

[148] Palmer and Saunders, "Arms and Monies".

[149] M. Bateson, *Records of the Borough of Leicester*, i (London, 1899), pp. 340-1, 344-5.

[150] Merton College Muniments, no. 5554; *Early Taxation Returns*, ed. A. C. Chibnall (Bucks. Rec. Soc., 1967), pp. 118-19.

[151] P.R.O., J.I.1/337, m.6d.

cash the levies of hobelars and archers laid upon them.[152] The sums paid in commutation imply even larger expenses than the Hatfield evidence would suggest. In 1335, for instance, Kent paid £200 for relief from 120 hobelars (£1 13s. 4d. per man), Nottinghamshire £40 for twenty hobelars (£2 per man), and Berkshire 200 marks for forty hobelars (£3 6s. 8d. per man).[153] Some of these figures may represent more than the actual expense of supplying troops, but if taken at face value they suggest that one hobelar might cost his village perhaps £2 (the price of four oxen or eleven quarters of wheat) to equip and despatch.

Between the 1290s and the 1330s the cost of military service thus rose considerably. Starting at about 5s. per man under Edward I, it increased to about 23s. under Edward II, and reached £2 for a hobelar in Edward III's early years (though of course many of those who served would still be the less expensive foot-soldiers). Such a rise in costs was due very largely to the increased expense of equipment, to the lengthier periods for which men were expected to serve, and to the higher wages paid to the hobelar, who commonly drew 4d. a day as against the foot-soldier's 2d.[154] The unfavourable comparison between the wages of an ordinary foot-soldier and those of the labourer was perhaps another source of grievance. The foot-soldier's wages of 2d. a day remained constant throughout the period. He was paid slightly more than the unskilled labourer, whose wages on the manors examined by Beveridge fluctuated between 1.49d. and 1.87d. per day. But the wages of skilled and semi-skilled labourers were considerably higher. A tiler earned around 6.19d. per day in the decade 1300-9 and 5.73d. in 1330-9; a thatcher earned 3.19d. in 1300-9 and 3.82d. in 1330-9; while a carpenter received 2.82d. in 1300-9 and 3.18d. in 1330-9.[155] Though we know nothing about the standing of the men whom the villagers chose to serve for them, none can have expected to make much money out of military service and some may have lost by it. The ordinary labourer might gain a little, but the skilled worker, taken from his thatching or tiling to serve in Scotland, might lose a great deal.

Although some of the grievances produced by demands for military service were peculiar to this type of exaction, others

[152] *Cal. Pat. Rolls, 1334-8*, pp.131-2; *Cal. Close Rolls, 1333-7*, p. 525; *Rot. Scot.*, i, p. 348; Prince, "The Army and Navy", pp. 360, 363.

[153] *Cal. Pat. Rolls, 1334-8*, pp. 131-2.

[154] For rates of pay under Edward I, see J. E. Morris, *Welsh Wars of Edward I* (Oxford, 1901), pp. 92-3; and under Edward III, Powicke, *Military Obligation*, pp. 210-12.

[155] W. Beveridge, "Wages in the Winchester Manors", *Econ. Hist. Rev.*, vii (1936-7), pp. 40-1, 43.

stemmed from abuses similar to those which accompanied the levying of prises and of the lay subsidy. The recital of such abuses is a dull business but a necessary one, for their effect, like that of purveyance, was often to increase the load which the village had to bear and to generate dissension and bitter feeling. The two most frequent complaints throughout the period were that the strong or wealthy offered bribes to the commissioners of array to escape their obligations, usually with the result that men poorer in both senses were selected for service, and that the arrayers and those responsible for collecting money in the villages retained for themselves part of what they levied. In 1323-4 inquiries in Kent into the conduct of the array of 1322 disclosed a situation which was not at all abnormal. Several of the county's hundreds had offered bribes, usually of 40s., to the commissioners to choose few men; Dunhamford hundred had offered one such bribe for the reduction of its eighteen-man quota to ten. Many individuals had offered similar bribes, ranging from 12d. to 10s., to be allowed to stay at home. Sir John Savage, an arrayer, had received £8 from Kinghamford hundred for the purchase of armour for three selected men, but he had spent only £5 6s. 6d. on the armour and had kept the rest. When Savage had been choosing troops at Middleton, one John Scopesdone, "a man old and weak", had come before him. Savage had had him arrested and imprisoned for five days until Scopesdone had paid him 20s. for his release. Daniel Burgham, another commissioner, had forced the men of Faversham hundred to collect eight marks for the hundred's sixteen chosen men, but to one of those chosen he had given equipment worth only 3s. 4d. Ralph Borstall, bailiff of St. Augustine's, Canterbury, had levied £3 from Dunhamford hundred for the armour of three of its representatives. He had then gone to London with the money and bought armour which was worn-out and quite useless, and this the three men had refused to take. If the jurors' returns can be relied on, the illicit profits of Sir John Savage, who seems to have been the chief offender, totalled about £28.[156] This was probably as much as the yearly landed income of a middling knight in the early fourteenth century.

Much evidence of this sort can be dismissed as mere grumbling, the product of the backbiting, suspicion and general discontent which any array was bound to provoke and which any official inquiry allowed to surface. Much also points to the ability of many men to avoid their responsibilities; from the point of view of the potential recruit, corruption was not always a bad thing. Nevertheless, the

---

[156] P.R.O., E.101/16/3.

total flow of money from the local communities to the pockets of the commissioners was obviously quite large, while those who escaped from service were often those most able to serve. Such abuses sometimes stimulated and exacerbated the feuds and quarrels which probably characterized village life at all times. Far from acting as a unifying force, as one might suppose, the military exactions of the government might prove to be a divisive one. In 1296, for instance, the men of Puttingdon in County Durham refused to pay their chosen recruits.[157] At other times the whole village might be burdened by individuals who defaulted on their obligations. When those elected to serve for Heptonstall in the West Riding failed to appear at the muster, individual culprits were fined 6d. each and the whole vill was fined 3s. 4d. — a small enough sum, but one which probably appeared a good deal larger in that year of famine, 1316, when the offence took place.[158] And we have already seen how, at Littleport, the crown's military demands provided an opportunity for the hayward there to cheat one of the villeins![159] It cannot have been easy to select foot-soldiers and to devise some means of paying them, while at the same time maintaining intact the bonds (fragile at the best of times) which held the community together.

The effect of recruitment upon the peasant's livelihood is harder to gauge. The cost of wages, arms and clothing which the village had to meet is unlikely to have been as burdensome as purveyance, even during the period of greatest military expense in the 1330s. Purveyance fell very heavily upon particular individuals, while military expenses were spread more evenly. A payment for the community's representatives might be one more imposition to add to an already long list (and for some it may have been the last straw), but by itself it would not bring ruin, as purveyance sometimes did. Failure to pay might do so, though we cannot tell how common this was. There are instances in the 1330s of men being distrained by their plough-beasts for their refusal to contribute to the military expenses of their villages,[160] and such action could be very damaging as we have seen. It is equally difficult to decide how the withdrawal of men from the village affected its economy. Dr. Michael Prestwich has suggested that in 1298 "some five per cent of the adult male population was probably called to arms", though because recruitment severely affected only certain areas, the drain on

[157] *Durham Halmote Rolls,* ed. J. Booth, i (Surtees Soc., 1889), p. 1.

[158] *Wakefield Court Rolls,* ed. J. Lister, iv (Yorks. Arch. Soc., Record Ser., lxxviii, 1930), p. 140.

[159] Above, p. 322.

[160] *Cal. Close Rolls, 1337-9,* pp. 516-17; *ibid., 1339-41,* p. 329.

manpower in those areas must have been much heavier.[161] The thirty villages in the Norfolk hundred of Launditch each supplied an average of six men to the muster of 1295; two of these villages, Swanton Morley and Weasenham, supplied as many as twelve. [162] In the two reigns which followed there is no evidence that local levies on this scale took place. A populous town like Leicester sent a mere twelve men on the 1322 campaign, and the levy of that year, the only one resented enough to attract a chronicler's attention, demanded only one man from each vill.[163] In a country which was over-populated (at least until the beginning of the fourteenth century) and in manors and villages where there was probably much under-employment, the withdrawal of a few men for service in Scotland is not likely to have had much effect on wage-rates or to have made the agricultural work of the community much more difficult.

For those called on to serve the prospects were more gloomy. They could, of course, refuse to appear at the muster or they could desert while on service: Edward I's winter campaigns of 1299-1300 and 1300-1 were crippled by such desertions.[164] But if they performed their duties, their holdings at home might suffer in consequence. When campaigns spanned the harvest period, as did those of 1297, 1310, 1322 and 1335, for instance, they might be unable to gather their crops. Or, equally disastrously, they might be called away at seed-time. In the Hampshire parish of Eling in 1341 much land lay uncultivated because the men of the parish had been frequently summoned to do coast-guard duty at seed-time and in the autumn, "to their great harm and expense".[165] There were small compensations for such losses. The *famulus* or the man who supplemented his income by unskilled labour might find himself earning slightly more than usual in the army: if he served as a hobelar in the 1330s his wages might even be double those which he could expect from the land. The recruit might also gain judicial advantages in the form of an indemnity in the manorial court for any petty crimes which he had committed. In July 1316 Gilbert Lamb, bizarrely described as "a malefactor of vegetables", had his offence pardoned in the court at Ingoldmells (Lincs.) "because he is in Scotland", and another defendant had a plea of debt postponed for the same reason.[166] But

161 Prestwich, *War, Politics and Finance*, p. 286.

162 P.R.O., E.401/1656.

163 Above, p. 320, *Brut*, p. 225.

164 Prestwich, *op. cit.*, pp. 95-7.

165 *Inq. Non.*, p. 126.

166 *Court Rolls of the Manor of Ingoldmells*, ed. W. O. Massingberd (London, 1902), pp. 65, 67. Gilbert's precise offence cannot be determined from this edition, since the original Latin is not given.

the returning village trooper would hardly find that benefits of this sort made up for land unsown or corn unharvested.

While the crown's military demands thus affected the whole village, it was those selected for service who suffered most. The system of array was a financially burdensome one, more so at the end of our period than at the beginning, and although by itself it was probably not disabling, it coincided in time with other and more oppressive exactions. In the worst affected areas, military service, the levy on movables, and purveyance were cumulative in the hardships which they brought, and each was aggravated by the abuses with which it was accompanied. Yet it may be that these aspects of military service were not ultimately the most significant. The movements of large armies sent those who served into a wider world, taking them from their villages, bringing them into the presence of great men and great events, and breeding news, gossip and scandal. When the English were besieging Berwick in 1319, the army was clearly alive with rumours about Thomas of Lancaster's supposed collusion with the Scots, and from the remark of the *Vita Edwardi Secundi* that the Earl's suspected treachery turned the favour of the people into hatred, we may guess that those in the army took their suspicions home with them.[167] The common knowledge of the Ordinances[168] and of Edward II's defects of character, the growth of Lancaster's cult after 1322, the part played by the lower classes in the revolution of 1326 — all these things suggest that the *populus* had some degree of familiarity with the doings of those who ruled them. The more frequent assembling of large armies brought economic burdens, but in the long run it may also have served to widen the political consciousness of the peasantry.

V

The exactions so far described reached their peak of oppressiveness between 1336 and 1341; indeed, in these six years the weight of taxation may have been greater than at any other time in the middle ages, greater even than in the years preceding the revolt of 1381. The rise in military expenses, onerous though it was for some communities, was probably the least important of the impositions which the peasantry had to bear. More burdensome were the levy on movables, which became both more frequent and more comprehensive in its incidence, and prises, now collected in new and harsher ways. These traditional forms of taxation were

---

167 *Vita Edwardi Secundi,* pp. 97-8.
168 Maddicott, *Thomas of Lancaster,* pp. 328-9.

accompanied by novel taxes on wool and in wool, and, in 1340-1, by a levy in kind which had no earlier parallel. In addition, the standing of many men was rendered still more precarious by abnormal economic circumstances, which made it exceptionally hard for the tax-payer to find the money to meet the fiscal demands laid upon him. What is surprising is not that so many succumbed to these conditions, but that they did not produce a more violent and general protest.

This conclusion is suggested even by a mere recital of the taxes imposed by the crown.[169] First, direct taxation was unprecedentedly heavy. The concession of a tenth and a fifteenth in March 1336 was followed by another similar grant in September — the first time that two grants had ever been made in the same year. In September of the next year Parliament conceded three tenths and fifteenths, to be spread over the period from October 1337 to February 1340. This was the first occasion on which taxes had been granted for more than one year, though the practice became common from the 1340s onwards; the next grant of direct taxation in 1344, given for two years, followed the same principle. The levy on movables was thus collected annually between 1336 and 1340. Almost as onerous were the crown's attempts to profit from the wool trade. An embargo had been placed on wool exports in August 1336, and in July 1337 the king granted a monopoly of exports to a syndicate of wool merchants in exchange for the promise of a £200,000 loan from the proceeds of their sales. Meanwhile, the duty on wool was raised in two stages, reaching a total of 40s. per sack for English merchants and 63s. 4d. for aliens in the summer of 1338. Between August 1336 and the autumn of 1337 very little wool was exported, making it impossible for many men to realize much profit from their main cash crop, and when export began again the higher duties and the monopolistic nature of Edward's arrangements meant that the home producer received less for his wool than he would otherwise have done.[170] Even after the collapse of the wool scheme in 1338, not much relief was afforded to the wool grower, for the Parliament of February 1338 granted the crown a loan of 20,000 sacks of wool, each man being

---

[169] Unless otherwise stated, the information in this and the following two paragraphs is drawn from: E. B. Fryde, "Edward III's War-Finance, 1337-41: Transactions in Wool and Credit Operations" (University of Oxford D.Phil. thesis, 1947); E. B. Fryde, "Edward III's Wool Monopoly of 1337", *History*, xxxvii (1952); E. B. Fryde, "Parliament and the French War, 1336-40", *Essays . . . to Wilkinson;* and J. H. Ramsay *A History of the Revenues of the Kings of England,* ii (Oxford, 1925), pp. 169-87. (I am very grateful to Dr. Fryde for allowing me to use his thesis.) No account has been taken of clerical taxation.

[170] Below, p. 344.

obliged to surrender half his wool and to accept repayment at a later date The failure of this scheme too led in July 1338 to the institution of a new tax in wool, to which all contributed according to the sums at which they were assessed for the levy on movables. This was more successful in raising money for the crown. Periodic embargoes continued to disrupt the free export trade, while in July 1340 Parliament granted the crown another loan of 20,000 sacks. Although this was abandoned in the following year, it was not until 1347 that wool levies ceased entirely.

The money produced by the lay subsidies and by the wool taxes was largely spent on the support of Edward's continental allies, to whom he dispensed at least £130,112 between 1337 and 1341,[171] and on the maintenance of English armies in Scotland, Gascony and the Low Countries. The problem of supplies for those armies was met as usual by purveyance. In 1336 and 1337 extensive prises were levied for the army in Scotland, for the garrisons of castles there, and for the provisioning of the south-coast fleet.[172] In the spring of the following year still larger quantities of victuals were ordered, both for Edward's expedition to the Low Countries and for his forces in Scotland. Four counties — Lincolnshire, Nottinghamshire, Derbyshire and Yorkshire — were twice laid under contribution during this year[173] and it was these levies which gave rise to most of the bitter complaints laid before the commissions of inquiry of 1339 and 1340-1. Purveyance for Scotland and the continent continued in 1339,[174] but thereafter it diminished in oppressiveness.

Finally, in April 1340 Parliament granted the king a tax in kind — the ninth sheaf, lamb and fleece of all those who lived on the land (townspeople and merchants were taxed separately). The supplies raised were to be sold and the proceeds taken by the government. Although there were good reasons for these novel arrangements,[175] the scheme in its initial form was not a success. The government tried to insist that produce should not be sold below a minimum price level, but it was not until January 1341, when minimum sale prices were abolished, that the tax began to yield much, and by that time Parliament had already conceded the loan in wool to compensate for the meagre receipts from the ninth. The virtual abandonment, first of the ninth, and then of the wool levy, and the

171 Fryde, "Financial Resources of Edward I in the Netherlands", *Revue Belge*, xl (1962), p. 1,170.

172 *Rot. Scot.*, i, pp. 444-5, 451, 453, 480-1, 496.

173 *Ibid.*, pp. 526, 540-1; T. Rymer, *Foedera*, ed. J. Caley and F. Holbrooke (Record Comm., 1821), II, ii, p. 1,021; Hughes, *Early Years of Edward III*, pp. 14-16.

174 *Rot. Scot.*, i, pp. 555-6, 559-60, 563-4.

175 Fryde, "Edward III's War-Finance", pp. 504-9.

lull in English activity on the continent before the re-opening of the war in Brittany, brought the period to a close.

The effects of such intensely heavy taxation were much aggravated by the peculiar economic conditions which marked these years. From 1337 until about 1342 the country was afflicted by an acute shortage of coin, which depressed the purchasing power of the population and drove down prices. The chronicler Higden says that at London in 1339 a quarter of wheat fetched only 2s. and a fat ox only 6s. 8d. (about half the normal prices), and he is supported by other chroniclers and by the statistics gathered by Thorold Rogers.[176] The reasons for these conditions are not all plain, though one is obvious enough — the extremely good harvests of 1336, 1337 and 1338.[177] But good grain harvests alone will not explain the concurrent fall in livestock prices nor the continuing low prices which followed the very hard winter of 1338-9; such a winter might have been expected to drive corn prices up in the summer of 1339.[178] It is clear that there was in addition a currency crisis, which stemmed partly from the low volume of coin produced at the mint over the previous decade and partly from the effects of taxation in withdrawing coin from circulation. From 1325 to 1336 mint production had been running at a very low level. Between 1316 and 1320 the output of the mint had averaged £7,882 worth of coin per year, but this had dropped to £3,119 in 1321-5, to £346 in 1326-30, and to £539 in 1331-5, rising again to £1,975 in 1336-40. The rise was almost certainly due to the attempt made by statute in 1335 to increase the quantity of coin by prohibiting the export of coin and bullion, the melting down of coin for plate, etc., and to the crown's policy, begun in that year, of debasing the silver standard of halfpence and farthings.[179] It may be, however, that the debased coinage took some years to find its way into general circulation and that in the meantime the deflationary conditions of 1337-42 continued to reflect the period of exiguous minting which had ended in 1335.

[176] *Polychronicon Ranulphi Higden*, ed. J. R. Lumby, viii (Rolls Ser., 1882), p. 334; *Adae Murimuth Continuatio Chronicarum*, ed. E. A. Thompson (Rolls Ser., 1889), p. 89; *Chronicon Abbatie de Parco Lude*, ed. E. A. Venables (Lincs. Rec. Soc., i, 1891), p. 36; *Brut*, ii, p. 292; Rogers, *Agriculture and Prices*, i, pp. 205, 346, ii, p. 108; Fryde, "Parliament and the French War", pp. 264-5.

[177] J. Z. Titow, "Evidence of Weather in the Account Rolls of the Bishopric of Winchester, 1209-1350", *Econ. Hist. Rev.*, 2nd ser., xii (1959-60), pp. 394-6.

[178] *Murimuth Chron.*, p. 89.

[179] J. Craig, *The Mint* (Cambridge, 1953), pp. 61-3, 410-11; *Stat. Realm*, i, pp. 273-4. The trends in mint output are usefully shown by the graph in H. Miskimin, *The Economy of Early Renaissance Europe, 1300-1460* (Englewood Cliffs, New Jersey, 1969), p. 140.

Heavy taxation similarly acted to reduce the supply of coin. A contemporary, writing in 1338 or 1339, implicitly makes the connection: "There is a desperate shortage of cash among the people. At market the buyers are so few that a man can do no business, although he may have cloth or corn, pigs or sheep to sell, because so many are destitute *(multi sunt egentes)*"[180] Such distress must have been due largely to royal taxation; it cannot have been the result of poor harvests, since conditions were precisely the reverse. Holinshed, writing in the sixteenth century but using sources now lost, blames royal taxation still more explicitly for shortage of coin and low prices.[181] And the linkage was noted by at least one manorial official: the reeve of Launton (Oxon.), explaining why the farm of the manor's cows yielded only 50s. in 1339-40, said that it had not been possible to sell butter or cheese as in previous years because of the severity of the winter, the dryness of the summer pasturage and "the taxation of the people".[182] For this situation the crown's interference in the wool trade may have been especially responsible. The monopoly of 1337, the embargoes, the levies on wool and the tax in wool — all these are likely to have impoverished the wool producer and to have made it more difficult for him both to pay the king's other taxes and to purchase any arable produce which he needed.

Royal taxation thus struck at the peasant in two ways. It hit him directly, as a tax-payer, and indirectly by reducing the purchasing power of his potential customers. Since most countrymen were both buyers and sellers, taxation came to have a depressing effect on the whole rural economy, which was reflected also in the inability of some men to pay their rents. When the king approached the Devon county court for a grant in September 1337, the bishop of Exeter, deflecting his request, replied that the district was notoriously infertile and that money was scarce there, with the consequence that the local magnates could levy their rents only with difficulty or not at all and that the people were unable to sell their corn.[183] As in earlier years, parliamentary complaints against taxation were perhaps rooted not in the tax burden immediately borne by the parliamentary classes, but in the indirect effects of taxation on their rent incomes and on the prices for which they could sell their

180 Aspin, *Anglo-Norman Political Songs*, p. 111. For the date of this poem, see Fryde, "Parliament and the French War", p. 263, n. 71.

181 *Holinshed's Chronicles*, ii (London, 1807), p. 605.

182 Westminster Abbey Muniments, no. 15341. I am very grateful to Miss Barbara Harvey for this reference.

183 *The Register of John de Grandisson, Bishop of Exeter, 1327-69*, ed. F. C. Hingeston-Randolph, i (London, 1894), p. 301.

produce. The peculiar form taken by the grant of the ninth may have been partly intended to meet these grievances. The magnates' original offer, made in the Parliament of October 1339, linked the grant of a tax in kind with the prevalent shortage of cash, and its terms offered some protection for the lords' resources by exempting their villeins from the levying of corn.[184] Moreover, it represented an attempt to change the balance of taxation in favour of the towns, for the tenths and fifteenths burdened the towns more heavily than the countryside, while the reverse was true of the ninth.[185] It was a tax designed to leave untouched the peasants' small reserves of cash by taking his produce instead, to secure the livelihoods of the magnates' bond tenants, and to conserve the purchasing power of the towns, the chief customers for corn and livestock, by imposing a tax which was predominantly rural in its incidence. The main tax-payers, however, would not be the peasants who surrendered a part of their goods, but those who voluntarily purchased such goods at the government's prices.

These elements made up the complex economic crisis which affected England between 1337 and 1342. The effects of a low output of coin at the mint and of a run of good harvests combined with taxation on a massive scale to produce a severe shortage of money. It became extremely difficult to pay taxes and probably rents, and these abnormal circumstances led to the unique levy of 1340, which was designed to give the crown its supplies as painlessly as possible. But despite the frequency of taxation such conditions might not have been found so burdensome had not the method of levying the subsidy also changed during the 1330s. In 1334 the sums payable for that year's tenths and fifteenths had been fixed by negotiations between the crown's commissioners and the local communities, who were made responsible for dividing among their members the totals agreed on. This system was perpetuated in the levy of 1336, which called for the same quotas from the villages as had been produced in 1334, and it remained in use for all subsequent levies. It meant that the crown knew in advance how much a tenth and a fifteenth should yield (about £38,000) and that the communities too knew what they were expected to contribute to each tax. The crown had lost interest in the individual tax-payer and was now concerned only with his community. As a result, tax assessment lists no longer give the sums payable by each man, but merely the quota at which each village was charged.[186]

184 *Rot. Parl.*, ii, pp. 103-4.
185 Fryde. "Edward III's War-Finance", pp. 506-7.
186 Willard. *Parliamentary Taxes*. pp. 5-6; Fryde, "Parliament and the French War", p. 255.

These changes worked to the detriment of many men. The quotas fixed in 1334 were larger than the sums yielded by the last levy under the old system, that of 1332, and while they were fixed at a time of relative economic prosperity they had to be maintained in the much more adverse conditions of the late 1330s. Except in rare and special circumstances[187] the quotas were not adjusted to meet the changing fortunes of the communities on which they fell, and between 1337 and 1341 the fortunes of most villages changed only in one direction. The inflexibility of the new system may help to explain its second disadvantage — the increased burden which it laid upon the poor. In 1334 and after, the old rule which had given exemption to all those possessing less than 10s. worth of goods was abandoned. One consequence seems to have been that the very poor were now subjected to taxation. In Kent — the only county for which detailed post-1332 assessments survive — the number of tax-payers rose from about 11,000 in 1334 to 17,000 in 1338, an increase of nearly 55 per cent[188] and it is hard to think that Kent was exceptional. Very occasionally the government ordered the continuance of the 10s. exemption level (as in Northumberland, Cumberland and Westmorland in 1336),[189] but in most villages the frequency and weight of taxation must have created great pressure for the placing of all inhabitants under contribution. Despite the government's instructions, the poor had never been entirely exempt from taxation, as we have seen,[190] and they were perhaps made to subscribe to the first levy under the new system; this at least may be one implication of the increase in the yield of the 1334 subsidy as compared with that of 1332. In the late 1330s the inducement to spread the burden far down the social scale is likely to have been much greater.

Tax evasion, on the other hand, was probably as common as it had ever been, but there was now the difference that it worked to the loss of the village community and not of the king. If the resident gentleman or prosperous freeholder refused to contribute to the subsidy, then the other villagers, encumbered since 1334 with a fixed quota, would have to pay more. (In this respect the levy resembled the third poll-tax of 1380.)[191] There are several complaints on this theme in the record of the 1340-2 inquiries in Lincolnshire. John

---

187 E.g., *Cal. Close Rolls, 1337-9*, p. 293.
188 C. W. Chalklin and H. A. Hanley, "The Kent Lay Subsidy of 1334-5", *Documents Illustrative of Medieval Kentish Society*, ed. F. R. H. Du Boulay (Kent Arch. Soc., Records Branch, xviii, 1964), p. 58; Fryde, "Parliament and the French War", p. 256.
189 *Cal. Fine Rolls, 1327-37*, p. 487.
190 Above, p. 294.
191 M. McKisack, *The Fourteenth Century* (Oxford, 1959), pp. 406-7.

Bolingbroke was said to hold five carucates of land and 1,500 sheep at Hainton in Lindsey, "for which he would never give a tax to the king, charging the rest of the vill". John Trehampton had three carucates of land and three hundred sheep in Blyton "and for six years would not give a tax to the king, charging the community of the vill". Peter Mandevill, taxer of the fifteenth in Bilsby, took nothing from himself nor from his brother Robert, though Robert was the richest man in the village, and as a result the community was burdened with the whole tax.[192] Sometimes a refusal to contribute might go beyond mere words. When the sub-taxers of the fifteenth approached Sir Stephen Bassingbourne of Hertfordshire in 1339, Bassingbourne beat them with his sword and so threatened them that they dared not levy the tax.[193] But in whatever form it was expressed, non-payment by the gentry was now bound to burden more heavily the villages in which they lived. The crown had succeeded, inadvertently perhaps, in passing on the financial consequences of tax evasion to the local communities. Faced only by their inferiors and unsupervised by the central government, all those gentry who were minded to take advantage of the new situation were able to do so. This perhaps helps to explain why the initiative in 1336 for perpetuating the scheme introduced two years earlier should have come from Parliament.[194] As a contemporary noted, "those who make the grant give nothing to the king; it is the poor who pay".[195]

Changes in the population and social composition of the village could have similar effects. If the population fell or if only one or two of the wealthy departed, the fixed burden of taxation had to be shared among a smaller number of villagers. In a petition of 1347 the men of Budleigh in Devon told the king that French raiders had carried off many of the richest merchants and sailors in the vill, who had formerly paid the greater part of its taxes. Those who remained had been forced to pay according to the old assessment (that is, of 1334), with the consequence that some had gone begging and others were about to leave their holdings.[196] The men of Beverley made a similar complaint in 1341: some tax-payers had died, others had migrated because of heavy taxation, and those who remained were

192 P.R.O., J.I.1/521, m.11; Hughes, *Early Years of Edward III*, p. 195. For a similar case in Essex, see J. Bellamy, *Crime and Public Order in England in the Later Middle Ages* (London, 1973), p. 82.
193 P.R.O., J.I.1/337, m.6d.
194 P.R.O., E.159/112, m.140; Fryde, "Parliament and the French War", p. 255.
195 *Anglo-Norman Political Songs*, p. 110.
196 *Rot. Parl.*, ii, p. 213; *Cal. Pat. Rolls, 1345-8*, p. 467.

intolerably burdened.[197] As both these petitions show, and as the Inquisitions of the Ninth make clearer still,[198] men might leave their homes and lands in order to avoid taxation, but their departure merely afflicted more heavily those who were left. To some extent taxation was cumulative in its oppressive effects.

There is no doubt that many communities found the recurrent levy on movables quite insupportable during these years, as they had probably not done (except in isolated instances) in any earlier period. The inquiries of 1340-2 show that all the traditional abuses in the collection of the tax continued, but they were now likely to count for less than the deleterious effects of the changes introduced in 1334, made still more painful by the general shortage of coin. It was not surprising that great difficulty should have been found in collecting the successive subsidies; there were long delays in payments,[199] and the government resorted to threats of imprisonment against those who could not or would not pay. Such threats were particularly numerous in the winter and spring of 1339, when a long period of freezing weather was making rural conditions still harsher,[200] and they marked a sharp advance on the normal penalty of distraint for non-payment. Men were forced into desperate measures to meet these demands. The versifier already quoted wrote that "the fifteenth now runs in England from year to year ... it obliges the common people to sell their cows, their utensils and their clothing"; while in 1341 the men of Sunbury in Middlesex were said to have had to sell the greater part of their sheep "because of excessive taxation *(propter nimiam taxationem)*".[201] The statement of the magnates in the Parliament of November 1380, forty years later, that "the tenths and fifteenths are in many ways very oppressive to the poor commons" was fully borne out by the levies of the late 1330s. [202]

The methods used to raise prises changed in ways which were similarly detrimental to the peasant and which are strikingly revealed in the records of the inquiries of 1339 and 1340-2 into

197 *Cal. Close Rolls, 1341-3*, p. 188; Cf. *Rot. Parl.*, ii, p. 184: the poor tenants of Hardwick, Oxon., are unable to maintain in 1347 the tax quota of 49s. 11d. fixed in 1334. Unless given some relief, they will have to lease out their tenements and leave the village.

198 Below, pp. 346-8.

199 Fryde, "Parliament and the French War", p. 264; Hughes, *Early Years of Edward III*, pp. 22-3. There were similar difficulties in collecting the clerical tenths — see *A Calendar of the Register of Wolstan de Bransford, Bishop of Worcester, 1339-49*, ed. R. M. Haines (Hist. MSS. Comm., 1966), p. 1.

200 *Cal. Pat. Rolls, 1334-8*, p. 496; *ibid., 1338-40*, pp. 76, 187-8, 273, 281, 284, 365, 368; *Murimuth Chron.*, p. 88; Titow, "Evidence of Weather", pp. 396-7.

201 *Anglo-Norman Political Songs*, p. 109; *Inq. Non.*, p.198.

202 *Rot. Parl.*, iii, p. 90.

ministerial misdeeds. As in earlier years, purveyance severely affected only certain counties: Lincolnshire and Nottinghamshire were again among the main sufferers, though the other counties of eastern England were burdened little less heavily.[203] It was not merely the large quantities of victuals ordered which made purveyance especially oppressive during this period, but also the government's almost complete loss of control of its agents. The old system whereby in each county the sheriff and a royal clerk worked together to raise supplies, each acting as a partial (though admittedly ineffective) check on the other, was very largely abandoned. Instead, small groups of men, often merchants or royal clerks, were given a "roving commission" to purvey goods throughout several counties or over an unspecified area. They were normally made superior to the sheriffs and were empowered to appoint deputies and to imprison those resisting. The first such commission seems to have been that granted in February 1336 to William Melcheburn, a Norfolk merchant specializing in the corn trade, who was ordered to purvey with his deputies 1,000 quarters of wheat and 1,000 quarters of oats in Norfolk, Suffolk and Huntingdonshire, for delivery to Berwick. The sheriffs and other royal officials were to aid him, and he was given full authority to arrest and punish those who resisted.[204] Of the many similar commissions which were issued prior to 1340,[205] that which subsequently produced most complaints was given to William Dunstaple, a royal clerk, in 1338. Dunstaple was instructed to provide 3,600 quarters of wheat and quantities of other victuals in seventeen eastern counties, and for this work he was authorized to appoint deputies and to arrest those resisting, handing them over to the sheriffs of their respective counties for imprisonment. Another royal clerk, Stephen le Blount, received a similar commission for the counties of the south and west.[206]

203 For the inquiries of 1339-40, see P.R.O., E.101/21/38 (Hunts., Northants., Notts., Lincs.); E.101/21/39 (Hunts.); E.101/22/4 (Northants., Notts.); E.101/35/4 (Beds.); and C.145/137 (Lincs.). For the 1340-2 inquiries, see J.I.1/521 (Lincs.); J.I.1/691 (Notts.); J.I.1/258 (Essex); J.I.1/74, 75 (Bucks.); J.I.1/770 (Som.); J.I.1/715 (Oxon.); J.I.1/337 (Herts.); J.I.1/858 (Suffolk). Some proceedings are recorded on the memoranda rolls for 1340-2: E.159/116, mm.176 (Hunts.), 189d (Lincs.); E.159/117, mm.143-143d (Hunts.), 149 (Northants.), 156d, 179d (Lincs.), 159, 183d (Beds.). There are no records for Yorkshire, but in 1339 a commission was appointed to inquire into the misdeeds of Dunstaple, one of the two chief purveyors, "on clamorous information of divers men of Yorkshire" (Fryde, "Parliament and the French War", pp. 262-3).

204 Rot. Scot., i, p. 409. For Melcheburn, see Gras, Corn Market, pp. 172-3.

205 Cal. Pat. Rolls, 1334-8, pp. 273, 549; Rot. Scot., i, pp. 438, 480-1, 555, 559.

206 Foedera, ii, p. 1,021.

The object of these measures was to circumvent what had become the traditional methods of raising prises and to hasten the whole procedure. Corn merchants like Melcheburn, it was probably thought, would know where corn could be most readily found and would have the ships to transport it; commissions extending over several counties would obviate the necessity of directing and supervising several different sheriffs; the power to imprison would deal effectively with resistance. But in fact these innovations allowed the levying of supplies to become completely out of hand. The purveyors' powers of imprisonment, which they also conferred on their deputies, were grossly misused, often for the purveyors' own profit. In 1337 three purveyors, after levying nineteen quarters of wheat, malt and peas in Lafford (Lincs.), had taken and imprisoned the vicar and constable of the village and had kept them until the captives had paid over 51s. Another seven such cases are recorded in Lincolnshire.[207] The power to appoint deputies was similarly abused. In Lincolnshire some sixteen men were described as deputies of William Dunstaple (one of the two chief receivers of victuals) or of his brother Thomas, two as deputies of William Wallingford, the other chief receiver, and twelve others merely as purveyors.[208] Wallingford subsequently disowned many of those who claimed to have acted as his deputies in Nottinghamshire, while Dunstaple later asserted that all the blame for profiteering and extortion lay with his subordinates, not with himself.[209] The means formerly used to authorize the work of the purveyors, such as their holding of warrants under the royal seal, were apparently abandoned — not surprisingly, since the powers given to the chief purveyors to appoint deputies meant that the government often had no means of knowing who was acting in its name. Nor could the central authority effectively check the purveyors' accounts. In Lincolnshire and probably in other counties Dunstaple took far more than he accounted for. Typical were his activities at Holbeach, where, the jurors said, he had taken ten quarters of wheat, afterwards answering to the Exchequer for six according to his account, three sides of bacon and three cheeses, for none of which he accounted, and a bribe of 10s. to take no more, which he naturally failed to report.[210]

The main abuses which accompanied purveyance were the usual ones, much magnified in scope and incidence as a consequence of

207 P.R.O., J.I.1/521, mm.3, 12, 3d, 4d.
208 P.R.O., J.I.1/521; E.101/21/38.
209 P.R.O., E.101/21/38; C.81/251/11516.
210 P.R.O., E.101/21/38.

the large number of purveyors who were active, the great quantities of victuals demanded by the government, the new powers given to the purveyors, and the breakdown of central control. The system of assessment for prises, which had been used quite extensively in the 1290s,[211]seems to have disappeared. There is only one instance of assessment in the late 1330s (by the county court of Buckinghamshire), and that, significantly, for a prise raised in the old way through sheriff and hundred bailiffs.[212]The very lengthy records of the inquiries in other counties fail to disclose any evidence of assessment, and often the activities of the purveyors became mere plundering expeditions, on which anything might be taken. In Leverton (Lincs.) two purveyors took from one man two carpets *(tapeta)* and two sheets *(linthiamine)*, which they retained until given a bribe of 3s., and at Boston Thomas Dunstaple and another purveyor took twenty ells of cloth, worth 5s., from one Martin Bakest.[213]Violence was not unusual. At Daventry in Northampton-shire Richard Colingtre, deputy of William Dunstaple, broke down the doors of William Yonge and carried off two sides of bacon, worth 2s; at Weedon he broke down the doors of Richard le Skinner and took a box containing two charters; and at Brackley, Colingtre's groom broke into the house of Isolda Newbotle and carried off her goods.[214] As with almost all our information on purveyance during this period, we have only the jurors' word for these happenings, but the details are circumstantial and the evidence is spread widely enough over several counties to carry conviction.

Incidents of this sort, though they provoked bitter discontent, were perhaps less generally damaging than the purveyance of corn and livestock and the steps taken to avoid such levies. Bribery was commonplace, but not always effective. In 1336 William Merston, William Dunstaple's deputy, came to Lady Butler's manor of Weston Turville (Bucks.) and demanded from the bailiff ten quarters of wheat and ten of oats. He was bought off with a bribe of 6s. 8d., but three days later he was back again and this time he took two and a quarter quarters of wheat and two and a half of malt, giving in exchange a tally for a total of four quarters.[215]Some communities were struck repeatedly. Many vills in Huntingdonshire, for instance, were raided two or three times between 1337 and 1339

211 Above, pp. 308-10.
212 P.R.O., J.I.1/74, m.9d.
213 P.R.O., J.I.1/521, mm.16d, 7d.
214 P.R.O., E.101/22/4.
215 P.R.O.. J.I.1/75, m.3.

and often had to hand over money as well as goods. Abbots Ripton, a Ramsey manor, lost on one occasion six quarters of wheat, five of malt, forty sides of bacon, and 3s. 4d. for the return of other bacon which had been seized; at another time two of Dunstaple's deputies took eight quarters of malt (afterwards accounting for seven), six sides of bacon, and 6s. 8d.; and on a third occasion the village lost six sides of bacon, six and a half quarters of wheat, and 5s. in cash, while from the Ramsey demesnes were taken nearly five quarters of wheat and six of oats. These losses were paralleled in some eighty or ninety other villages.[21b] Some communities made double payments. At Sutton-in-Holland (Lincs.) the purveyors received 26s. 8d. for giving back the victuals which they had taken and 13s. 4d. to take no more.[217]When prises were levied they were almost never paid for directly, prices were often not discussed, and the giving of tallies for the full amount taken was rare. Very many Nottinghamshire villages, for instance, gave supplies "without tallies and without a price."[218]

We can determine with rather more precision than in earlier periods the classes and institutions on which these burdens fell most heavily. As we might expect, the gentry were scarcely affected, although most counties provide the occasional instance of the mistreated knight. Sir Richard Bayouse in Buckinghamshire;[219]Sir Walter Launcelyn in Bedfordshire;[220] Sir Robert Silkeston at Kirton-in-Holland in Lincolnshire;[221]Sir Thomas Newmarket at Whatton in Nottinghamshire;[222]Sir Ralph Weedon in Northamptonshire;[223] Sir Humphrey Walden in Essex;[224] these were the few gentry whose complaints found their way into the records of the inquiries. Monastic estates, on the other hand, were struck severely, probably more so than in earlier years, though they had never enjoyed the near-complete immunity of the secular landlords. The great Fenland abbeys of Ramsey, Peterborough, Thorney and Crowland, all lost a good deal. In Huntingdonshire at least nine Ramsey manors were affected and at least three belonging to Thorney,[225]and in Lincolnshire the manors of seven monastic

[216] P.R.O., E.101/21/38.
[217] *Ibid.*
[218] P.R.O., E.101/22/1,4.
[219] P.R.O., J.I.1/74, m.9d.
[220] P.R.O., E.101/35/4.
[221] P.R.O., E.101/21/38.
[222] P.R.O., J.I.1/691, m.4.
[223] P.R.O., E.101/22/4.
[224] P.R.O., J.I.1/258, m.5d.
[225] P.R.O., E.101/21/38.

houses (including three of the most important, Spalding, Louth Park and Kirkstead) gave up some of their stock or grain to the purveyors.[226] The absence of a powerful man must have made monastic manors particularly vulnerable; in most of those in Huntingdonshire the goods were handed over by the reeve, who was hardly in a position to refuse the purveyors' demands.

Religious institutions could probably afford to give generously. This was less true of the parish clergy, who also suffered considerably and whose stores of tithes may have made them attractive prey. The rector of Long Stowe (Hunts.) gave up nearly forty-five quarters of wheat, twenty-one quarters of malt and just over thirty-two quarters of peas, and the rector of Leighton surrendered thirty-one quarters of wheat and thirty-one of malt.[227] There were similar cases in other counties, notably in Lincolnshire, while at Cropwell Butler (Notts.) a chaplain, Ralph, gave 13s. 4d. to save the village from the purveyance of wheat and fodder.[228]

But although the monastic houses and the lower clergy contributed to prises, it was upon the peasantry that they fell most heavily, as in earlier days. The remark of the jurors of one Nottinghamshire wapentake that in each village the more powerful men had been spared by the purveyors was probably true in most other areas.[229] Unfortunately the evidence does not lend itself to any closer analysis of the standing of those affected. The very poor, with least to give, may have lost least, though it is possible that they were put under contribution when cash had to be raised for bribes. Some men were forced into debt by the need to find money to save their corn or stock. When oxen and sheep were taken from William de la Mare at Sutton-in-Holland in 1337 by John Podenhale, the king's purveyor, de la Mare borrowed money from another villager to save them and in the following year his creditor brought a case in the manorial court for the repayment of the debt.[230] As for the more purely agrarian consequences of these levies, much has already been said which does not need repeating. Only two fresh points need emphasis. First, purveyance of oxen seems to have been more common at this period than in earlier days. Two examples have already been cited to show how the loss of plough-oxen might bring inconvenience or even ruin, and both come from these years.[231] In

226 P.R.O., J.I.1/521, mm.3, 4, 6d, 17d, 7, 8, 9d.
227 P.R.O., E.101/21/38.
228 P.R.O., E.101/22/1.
229 *Ibid.*
230 P.R.O., D.L.30/86/1173, m.5d.
231 Above, p. 315.

one expedition in 1337 or 1338 John Podenhale took 200 oxen and cows in south-east Lincolnshire, once (at Croft-iuxta-Wainfleet) as many as twenty from one village; and on another occasion Wallingford took forty oxen from the village of Sibsey.[232] The object of such prises was probably not merely to provide the king's armies with beef, but to put many peasants into a position where they would be forced to buy back the possession which was most essential for their arable husbandry. And, secondly, the period when purveyance was at its heaviest was also the period of extremely burdensome direct taxation and of levies on and in wool. Each of these impositions made the others more difficult to meet. In the case of purveyance, a village's loss of stock and corn would make it all the harder to pay a tax quota which could not be adjusted to meet changes in communal prosperity.

One other aspect of purveyance deserves a brief mention — the misdeeds of the keepers of the king's horses in their travels around the countryside. Under Edward II this matter had not been a prominent source of discontent, but in the 1330s it began to produce a multitude of complaints. The usual grievance was that keepers, grooms and horses frequently came to a village and stayed there for days or even weeks at the village's expense. So it had been at Fiskerton (Lincs.) in 1338. On 24th March William Otteford, keeper of the king's horses, had arrived there with his companions, who brought with them thirty great horses and ten hackneys. During their stay, which lasted until mid-April, they consumed £10 worth of hay, oats and peas without payment and even forced the villagers to buy oats outside the village for their visitors' use; they took £5 worth of fish from the village ponds; and they were given 40s. in cash.[233] Grievances of this sort were both general and serious enough to provoke legislation in 1336 and 1340.[234] As early as 1331 the *De Speculo Regis* had spoken bitterly of the hardship caused by such enforced hospitality,[235] but it was probably not until the mid-1330s, when the Scottish wars began to take the king and his armies northwards in most years, that the king's horses became an affliction to many villages outside south-east England. It was not by itself a crushing burden, but it was one more to add to an already heavy load.

The distress brought by direct taxation and by purveyance was greatly aggravated by the crown's manipulation of the wool trade.

[232] P.R.O., J.I.1/521, mm.5, 3.
[233] *Ibid.*, m.9d.
[234] *Stat. Realm*, i, pp. 277, 288.
[235] *De Speculo Regis*, pp. 104, 106-7.

There can be little doubt that the maltolt introduced in 1336 and raised in 1338 resulted in the lowering of the prices offered to the home producers by the wool merchants, despite the schedule of minimum prices adopted in 1336 and despite too the claims which have been made on behalf of the foreign buyers of wool as the main sufferers from the extra duties. [236] The earlier maltolt of 1294-7 had certainly led to a decline in wool prices, [237] and Thorold Rogers's figures suggest a similar conclusion for the later period. Between 1337 and 1340 both sheep's wool and lambs' wool reached an average price lower than at any time since 1294-7. [238] This fully bears out the statement of the Meaux chronicler that after the imposition of new duties on exports, wool prices sank lower than ever before and that the duties were paid not by the merchants who had granted them, but by the wool growers. [239] As for conditions broad, the comparatively low sale prices recorded in Flanders in 1339-40 do not suggest that English merchants had yet had much success in passing on the maltolt to the foreign buyer.[240] The burden of this particular method of war financing was carried neither by England's customers nor by her enemies, but by her rural population.

All those with an interest in the land — not merely peasants but great lay and ecclesiastical lords as well — are likely to have suffered from the lowering of wool prices. Can we be any more precise about the effects of the various wool levies on the peasantry? In the case of the first levy, which was linked with the monopolistic export scheme of 1337-8, the exporting merchants were empowered by the government to purvey wool, with the promise of repayment to the grower within a year. In Bedfordshire this wool was collected in very small quantities, which suggests that the contributors there were mainly peasants, and in all counties repayment probably took much longer than a year, since it was dependent on the exporting merchants obtaining their payments from the king — a lengthy business. [241] Some possessors of wool preferred to sell it at a low price for ready cash rather than to wait for repayment at a higher price.[242] But whether the wool was sold on credit or for cash, the grower is likely to have been the loser.

[236] E.g., K. B. McFarlane, "England and the Hundred Years War", *Past and Present*, no. 22 (July 1962), pp. 8-9, 15.

[237] Prestwich, *War, Politics and Finance*, p. 198; Rogers, *Agriculture and Prices*, i, pp. 372, 388.

[238] Rogers, *op. cit.*, pp. 388-90.

[239] *Chronica Monasterii de Melsa*, ed. E. A. Bond, ii (Rolls Ser., 1867), pp. 378-9.

[240] E. B. Fryde, *The Wool Accounts of William de la Pole* (York, 1964), pp. 12, 15.

[241] Fryde, "Edward III's War-Finance", pp. 62, 87-8.

[242] Hughes, *Early Years of Edward III*, p. 35.

The effects of the next levy — the parliamentary grant of 20,000 sacks to the king in 1338 — were mitigated by the evasion and concealment which made the scheme a failure. It may nevertheless have affected some men severely. Although the government had stipulated that wool was to be taken only from those with more than one sack, cases later came to light in which the wool collectors had been bribed not to take all a man's wool or to take only the half to which they were entitled.[243] But most complaints were provoked by the collection of the tax in wool according to the rate of the fifteenth, which superseded the levy of 20,000 sacks in July 1338. By this arrangement the tax quota due from each village for the levy on movables was assessed in terms of wool, ten stones of wool being reckoned equivalent to every 20s. of assessment to the fifteenth.[244]

The great majority of the grievances which sprang from this imposition were directed at the corrupt practices which accompanied its levying. The collectors often weighed wool falsely or reckoned by a stone of sixteen pounds instead of fourteen. They charged the villagers for the delivery of acquittances for wool surrendered, and they took much for their own use. Villages were forced to give up more wool than their tax quotas justified or to bribe the collectors to keep to the quotas. The jurors of Kesteven and Holland reckoned that 500 sacks had been taken by extortion during 1338.[245] It is probable, however, that this tax in wool was found to be most oppressive for the same reasons as was the post-1334 lay subsidy from which it was derived: it may, that is, have burdened the poor unfairly and have placed the consequences of tax evasion by the wealthy on the shoulders of their fellow villagers. But whether this was true or not (and we have no proof, as we have in the case of the subsidy), the wool tax came in a year when the levy on movables was also being collected, and the seizure of what was for many men their main cash crop cannot have failed to make payment of the subsidy much more difficult. When the anonymous versifier of 1338-9 spoke of the collection of wool as having forced men to sell their property, he was probably not exaggerating.[246]

Between 1336 and 1341 taxation thus imposed a cripplingly heavy burden on many men. In 1338, when royal demands were at their peak, the peasant in the worst affected parts of eastern England might find himself facing two successive wool levies, the lay subsidy, prises and a contribution towards his community's expenses for

243 *Murimuth Chron.*, p. 85, n. 9; P.R.O., J.I.1/521, mm.10, 13d.
244 Fryde, "Edward III's War-Finance", pp. 130-1.
245 Hughes, *op. cit.*, pp. 199-201; P.R.O., J.I.1/521, *passim.*
246 *Anglo-Norman Political Songs*, p. 109.

foot-soldiers or hobelars. Even in those localities which escaped more lightly, he would still be subject to direct taxation and probably to the effects of a dislocated wool market. Some idea of the relative priority of his grievances can be gathered from an analysis of the complaints made during the Lincolnshire inquiries of 1340-2. Of the 186 villages appearing in the record, about 124 brought forward complaints against purveyance, fifty-six against the wool levies, thirty-four against the king's horses and their keepers, eighteen against the levy on movables, and eight against military service.[247] These complaints, however, were almost exclusively concerned with corruption and maladministration in the levying of the exactions, not with their oppressiveness as such. If we wish to gauge the more directly burdensome aspects of taxation, we must look at the Inquisitions of the Ninth.

The Inquisitions of the Ninth were drawn up in 1341 in connection with the assessment of that year's levy in kind. They have already been used to chart the abandonment of arable land in England at this time and to indicate the reasons for it,[248] but their reflection of the effects of taxation has not been given proper prominence. They have, of course, the drawback to which many records concerning taxation are subject — that is to say, they seek to explain to the government why the yield of the tax is less than it ought to be and in doing so they advance pleas of poverty and general distress which may be amplifications of the truth. But this is a reason for treating their evidence with caution, not for dismissing it.

The inquisitions show that in many counties much land lay uncultivated — 4,870 acres in Cambridgeshire, for instance, and at least 5,539 acres in Buckinghamshire.[249] It would be absurd to pretend that taxation was the exclusive or even a main cause of such land reverting to waste and of the widespread poverty which the inquisitions disclose: a very large number of explanations was given by the parish juries, ranging from bad weather and sheep murrain to the devastation wrought by the bishop of Chichester's rabbits.[250] Nevertheless, in some counties royal taxation was associated with land abandonment and general indigence, and even when it was not specifically mentioned we may suspect it to have been a contributory cause. Perhaps surprisingly, complaints were most common in Shropshire, where eight parishes linked their uncultivated land with

247 P.R.O., J.I.1/521.

248 A. R. H. Baker, "Evidence in the 'Nonarum Inquisitiones' of Contracting Arable Lands in England during the Early Fourteenth Century", *Econ. Hist. Rev.*, 2nd ser., xix (1966), pp. 518-32.

249 *Ibid.*, pp. 526, 529.

250 At West Wittering, Sussex (*Inq. Non.*, p. 357).

the king's taxes. Typical was Wistanstow, where "twenty virgates lie uncultivated on account of the divers taxes which the tenants there have sustained"; while at Clungunford "much land lies waste because of poverty and the king's many taxes". A striking glimpse of the way in which taxation might lead to land going out of cultivation is given by the inquisition for Cold Weston, where it was stated that only two tenants remained "and the rest have taken to flight for fear of the said ninth, as many others have done in those parts". [251] Further south, in Herefordshire, three parishes spoke of taxation, [252] and in both counties many more said either that their inhabitants were impoverished or that their poverty had caused them to leave their lands, but gave no reason for their distress. At Tugford in Shropshire, for instance, "the tenants do not cultivate their land because of their poverty, and six go begging". [253] In some parishes sheep murrain and destructive storms were blamed. Where taxation is expressly noticed, we cannot tell what sort is meant, but it is most likely to have been the levy on movables; the other main imposition, prises, had been levied only once between 1336 and 1341 in both counties. [254] It is interesting (though it may be nothing more) that the poem, already much quoted, which complains so bitterly against the king's taxes and which speaks of their exaction as having forced men to sell their property, comes from a manuscript which was compiled about 1340 and which has a Herefordshire provenance. [255] Through these verses we may be gaining a closer look at the conditions which lay behind some of the laconic entries in the inquisitions for that county.

On the eastern side of the country, particularly in Bedfordshire and Cambridgeshire, the situation was similar. Here the complaints were sometimes rather more detailed and diverse. At Swaffham Prior "the majority of the tenants are reduced to such poverty by frequent taxes that they cannot sow their lands and much of the land lies waste". [256] At Long Stowe "the land of the village lies almost uncultivated on account of the weakness of the tenants, who are vexed and destroyed by the king's frequent taxes and tallages and by the arrival of the keepers of the king's horses". [257] At Studham (Beds.) "sixty messuages ... are derelict and without inhabitants

---

251 *Ibid.*, pp. 186, 189, 188.
252 *Ibid.*, pp. 143, 150, 152.
253 *Ibid.*, p. 186.
254 *Foedera*, II, ii, p. 1,021 (1338).
255 *Facsimile of British Museum MS. Harley 2253*, with an introduction by N. R. Ker (Early English Text Soc., 1965), pp. xxi–xxiii.
256 *Inq. Non.*, p. 211.
257 *Ibid.*, p. 208.

because of men's poverty and of insupportable burdens and impositions".[258] There is little point in reciting other similar remarks in these counties and elsewhere, but one further entry from Mayfield in Sussex shows more precisely how taxation could bring poverty: "the corn was sold before seed-time in order to hasten the levying of the aforesaid money" (that is, presumably, for the ninth).[259] Unfortunately the inquisitions from Lincolnshire, where there was undoubtedly much distress, have virtually nothing to say either about uncultivated land or taxation, but this is almost certainly due to the "lack of standardization in the conduct of the inquiry" rather than to the county's relative prosperity.[260] Occasionally the inquisitions say nothing of royal taxation in other places where we know it to have been oppressive. In Northamptonshire there is some evidence for land abandonment (for example, at Pitchley) and for lack of seed (for example, at Charwelton), but no mention is made of taxation — yet we are told in another source that by October 1340, before the inquisitions were taken, "many are compelled by necessity in Northamptonshire and other counties to desert their own places and to seek food from others' distribution" because of the levying of the ninth.[261] Though the tax-payers' burdens may have been exaggerated in some counties, the absence of complaints against taxation in others does not necessarily mean that the crown's demands were not responsible for much of the impoverishment which the inquisitions disclose.

This source, then, tells us much about the king's taxes and their effects. In one place or[262] another it shows us men leaving their holdings through fear of imminent taxation, the sale of seed-corn to raise money for taxation, and, more generally, the abandonment of arable land because its cultivators were so depressed by taxation and other disasters that they lacked the resources to work it. Why did men tolerate these conditions, and why was there no rebellion, as there was after the exactions (probably less harsh than those of the 1330s) of the late 1370s? This is a hard question to answer. Certainly the threat of rebellion was never far below the surface. Knighton hints that the purveyances of 1338 might have provoked a rising if timely remedies had not been provided.[262] The *Song against the King's Taxes*, written at the same period, stated that "people are

258 *Ibid.*, p. 11.
259 *Ibid.*, p. 376.
260 Baker, "Evidence . . . of Contracting Arable Lands", p. 521.
261 *Inq. Non.*, pp. 29, 26; *Cal. Close Rolls, 1339-41*, pp. 585-6.
262 "Because of this [purveyance] there arose a mighty outcry among the people, from which a greater evil might have come had not the king taken wiser advice": *Chronicon Henrici Knighton*, ed. J. R. Lumby, ii (Rolls Ser., 1895) p. 3.

reduced to such distress that they can give no more. I fear that if they had a leader they would rise in rebellion".[263] A London chronicler, writing of the situation in 1340, says that Edward's ministers at home told him that they dared not raise more money for fear of war and that rather than give more the people would rise up against them.[264] Their alarm was apparently borne out by resistance in the localities. In 1338-9 there were many refusals to pay the levy on movables[265] and some resistance to the work of the purveyors.[266] Later, in 1340-1, there were sporadic attacks on those purveying wool[267] and much more interference with the levying and selling of the ninth.[268] The new powers given both to tax-collectors and to purveyors to imprison recalcitrants demonstrate the opposition which the government expected and which, in the event, it found.

And yet there was no general rising. Despite clear similarities, many of the elements which went to produce the revolt of 1381 were missing in 1341. The unsettling effects of successive plagues, the "seigneurial reaction" which to some extent followed the Black Death, the restrictions imposed by the labour legislation, the discontent created by a long-drawn-out but unsuccessful war, the position of one politician, John of Gaunt, as a focus for revolt — all these factors (to name only the most manifest) were missing at the earlier date. As the anonymous versifier noted, the people were leaderless in the late 1330s; there was no Wat Tyler or John Ball. To judge from the sermon literature, plenty of priests held views almost as radical and violent as those of Ball at all points in the fourteenth century, but the clerical proletariat from which Ball emerged did not express its grievances through action until attempts had been made to fix its wages after the Black Death. Rural conditions were very different at the time of the first attempt to levy the ninth in 1340 from those which existed when the third poll-tax was imposed in 1380. Of course, in both periods the weight of taxation was extremely onerous: the obvious parallel lies here. But even in this respect circumstances differed. Fryde has pointed out, for instance, that the ninth could be passively resisted as the poll-tax could not be. In 1340 men might refuse to pay the government's prices for the

[263] *Anglo-Norman Political Songs,* p. 110.

[264] *Croniques de London,* ed. G. J. Aungier (Camden Soc., 1844), p. 83.

[265] *Cal. Pat. Rolls, 1338-40,* pp. 76, 187-8, 273, 281, 284, 365, 368; M. M. Taylor, *Some Sessions of the Peace in Cambridgeshire in the Fourteenth Century, 1340, 1380-3* (Cambridge Antiquarian Soc., 1942), p. 17.

[266] *Cal. Pat. Rolls, 1338-40,* p. 72; Taylor, *op. cit.,* p. 14.

[267] *Cal. Pat. Rolls, 1340-3,* pp. 324-5.

[268] *Cal. Close Rolls, 1339-41,* pp. 495, 536, 546, 625-6, 647, 652; *Cal. Pat. Rolls, 1340-3,* pp. 103-4.

produce levied under the terms of the ninth, and they successfully did so, forcing the crown to abandon any attempt to maintain minimum prices in 1341. The levying of the poll-tax did not permit this sort of compromise.[269] And although the poll-tax itself bore heavily on many men, it was only the despatch of special commissions to inquire into the evasion of the tax in each locality which fired the revolt of 1381. In the 1330s the levies on movables were collected in each village by the villagers for delivery to the two chief taxers in each county. Even supposing that communal resistance was contemplated, it would have been much harder to decide against whom it was to be directed. Resistance there certainly was, but it was mainly the resistance of individuals rather than of communities. More frequently men simply took to flight.

But more important than any of these factors was the readiness of the government to make concessions, sometimes perhaps (as Knighton implies) just in the nick of time. The clamour against purveyance bore fruit in July 1338, when the commissions issued to William Dunstaple and Stephen le Blount were revoked, less than five months after their issue.[270] Dunstaple and Wallingford, the two chief offenders, were arrested soon afterwards,[271] and from 1340 onwards large-scale purveyance was abandoned in favour of the making of contracts for supplies with important merchants.[272] It was still a source of grievance in the 1340s, but a much less serious one than in the previous decade. Popular and parliamentary pressure had brought results. The history of the ninth represents a similar concession. The levy of a tax in kind was itself intended to burden the peasant less heavily than the normal levy on movables, and, as we have seen, the scheme was virtually defeated by the refusal of the crown's subjects to co-operate. The crown showed too some tenderness towards public opinion. Commissions to inquire into wrongful purveyances were issued in 1339,[273] and in December 1340 nation-wide inquiries were inaugurated into the misdeeds of the king's ministers.[274] Even though these commissions brought

269 E. B. Fryde, "English Parliament and the Peasants' Revolt of 1381", *Liber Memorialis Georges de Lagarde. Studies Presented to the International Commission for the History of Representative and Parliamentary Institutions,* xxxviii (London, 1968), p. 83. The letter which Dr. Fryde here cites concerning the possibility of rebellion in 1340 (Westminster Abbey Muniments, no. 12195) does not bear out his interpretation.

270 *Cal. Close Rolls, 1337-9,* p. 449; Hughes, *Early Years of Edward III,* p. 15.

271 Fryde, "Parliament and the French War", pp. 263, 266-7.

272 *Ibid.,* p. 269. For two such contracts, both with the Melcheburn brothers, see P.R.O., E.159/117, mm.198, 200.

273 Fryde, "Parliament and the French War", p. 266.

274 *Cal. Pat. Rolls. 1340-3,* pp. 106, 111-13.

expense to many local communities [275] without permanently improving the standard of local administration (and here they resembled the eyres of the previous century), they did at least allow the venting of grievances. As for military service, it continued to provoke discontent during the 1340s, but the county levies were gradually losing place to retinues raised by contract. On the Scottish campaign of 1341-2, which interrrupted the otherwise militarily uneventful period between the truce of Espléchin in September 1340 and the beginning of English intervention in Brittany two years later, levies still outnumbered retinues, though by a smaller margin than on previous expeditions. But by the early 1350s the levies were invariably limited to defensive work.[276]

The continental truce of 1340 and the concessions made about that time may have forestalled a popular rising. In the 1380s concessions — in the form of Parliament's reluctance to grant the levy on movables and its complete refusal to experiment with new forms of taxation — came only after a revolt had shown them to be necessary. Conditions in the 1340s were harsh and taxation remained heavy, but burdens were not heaped one upon the other, as they had been in the late 1330s. In economic history, as in political history, the crisis of 1340-1 marks a turning-point, for the compromises then forced upon Edward III's government gave some relief from the intolerable taxation of the previous six years. They also justify the terminal date of this study.

VI

Between 1294 and 1341 the king's taxes bit deeply into the peasant's resources, at no time more heavily than during the last years of the period. This conclusion may seem contentious to some, and it is true that much of the evidence cited can be given a minimal interpretation rather than a maximal one. "Complaint and evasion", it has been said, "often indicate not so much the oppressiveness of exactions as the opportunities for resistance to them in a society which was for many a very free one".[277] Literary evidence, like the *Song of the Husbandman* of c. 1300 and the *Song against the King's Taxes* of 1338-9, may be taken to demonstrate new abilities to articulate complaints as well as new reasons for complaint. Special

[275] W. N. Bryant, "The Financial Dealings of Edward III with the County Communities", *Eng. Hist. Rev.*, lxxxiii (1968), pp. 762-3.

[276] Powicke, *Military Obligation*, pp. 184-9.

[277] J. Campbell, "England, Scotland and the Hundred Years War", in J. R. Hale, J. R. L. Highfield and B. Smalley (eds.), *Europe in the Late Middle Ages* (London, 1965), p. 195.

inquiries, like those of 1298 and 1340-2, may be viewed as novel methods of redressing grievances rather than as responses to grievances which were themselves new. The recurrent complaints of poverty and distress in the Inquisitions of the Ninth may be written down as the predictable pleas of tax-payers anxious to avoid further burdens. Petitions to Parliament against purveyance and military obligation, and the legislation which often resulted from them, can be treated not as the reflection of peasant grievances, but as the grumbling of a middle class which was by no means over-taxed. Only special pleading, however, can justify a general interpretation along these lines, and such an interpretation would hardly be consonant either with the quantity of the evidence or with its sometimes surprising geographical distribution. Grievances may occasionally have been exaggerated, but they were not imaginary, and their volume throughout the period makes it hard to think that an exposition of them should give priority to the nature of the sources rather than to the nature of the burdens.

The form of our evidence does provide problems, but this is not the chief one. Our primary difficulty lies in measuring the scale and extent of the difficulties which taxation brought. In geographical terms, only the eastern part of England (a large area) was afflicted severely at almost all times; not until the late 1330s were national burdens heavy and frequent enough to spread general and continuous distress to the counties of the west. Such distress cannot be precisely gauged. Our evidence is patchy and the only source which gives us fairly wide coverage of the whole country, the Inquisitions of the Ninth, comes from the end of the period. Most of our material is random and haphazard in its distribution and lacking in the chronological continuity which gives value to so many manorial records. We cannot, for instance, say how many men were ruined by the loss of their plough-oxen; we can only cite examples of some who were. In no village can we build up a picture of the impact of royal taxation over a long period, in the way in which we can sometimes chart seigneurial exactions. Opportunities for complaint were not regular enough, nor the records of purveyance and military service detailed enough, to make this possible.

Secondly, it is hard to tell how different sorts of peasant were affected by taxation. The frequent use of the term "peasant" is itself a confession of weakness, disguising the fact that the precise economic and social status of the tax-payer is usually indeterminable. Tax assessments, purveyors' accounts and the returns of special inquiries often provide us with names, but they can rarely be correlated with the manorial documents which might distinguish the tax-payer more clearly. We can be sure that the peasantry rather than the gentry bore the main burden, and we can indicate the measures taken by the government to protect the very poor and can point to the frequent inadequacy of those measures. But a sharper focus is impossible to achieve.

These caveats and qualifications, however, do not put the subject beyond generalization. It is clear that in years of successive subsidies and when such subsidies were combined with purveyance and other exactions (as, most notably, in 1294-7, 1315-6 and 1336-41), then the peasant's livelihood might be put greatly at risk. He might be forced to sell his seed-corn in order to raise money for the levy on movables; his plough-oxen might be taken as prises or distrained on for non-payment of taxation; he might even flee in anticipation of a new tax. Flight was one response to excessive taxation and it was a common one. Because of an increase in the lay subsidy twenty-five tenants left their holdings at Ottery St. Mary in 1334; twenty Nottinghamshire men gave up their lands in 1338 when the sheriff took their oxen, preventing their autumn sowing; at Beverley in Yorkshire and Budleigh in Devonshire the new quota system introduced in 1334 forced men to leave their homes; and at Cold Weston in Shropshire fear of the new burden of the ninth drove most of the inhabitants from their lands in 1340.[278] What happened to such unfortunates and to their holdings is not always clear. Some, at least, were reduced to begging. The author of the *Song of the Husbandman*, written well before the period of greatest distress in the 1330s, had spoken of the "many bold beggars" bred by the levy on movables and by purveyance,[279] and this was not just a rhetorical flourish. Three widely separated Shropshire parishes reported in 1341 that some of their inhabitants had left their holdings and were wandering as beggars,[280] and at Budleigh in 1346 heavy taxation brought others to mendicancy.[281] Some may have ultimately found work as labourers, others may have taken to crime for a living; we cannot tell. But in conditions of general economic difficulty, such as those of 1340-1, it is likely that many would simply have starved to death on the roads, as had happened during the great famine of 1257-8.[282]

When such damaging taxation occurred sporadically or in isolation, as at Ottery St. Mary, the holdings vacated were probably

---

278 Above, pp. 298-9, 315, 336-7, 347.
279 *Political Songs*, ed. Wright, p. 152.
280 *Inq. Non.*, pp. 185, 186, 192.
281 Above, p. 336.
282 Petition of the Barons (1258), cl. 21 (Stubbs, *Select Charters*, p. 376).

quickly filled up, either by immigrants or by those who remained behind. But when royal exactions burdened the whole countryside over a period of years, then lands might remain untilled and soon revert to waste or pasture. At Hockcliffe (Beds.) in 1341 "forty acres used to be sown and are now pasture", and at Caddington "many houses have fallen down where sheep now graze". The case was the same at Eversholt.[283] If the frontier between corn and grass was moving in favour of grass during this period, as the consistently high figures for wool exports suggest,[284] such a shift may have been related to the desertion of arable land brought about — *inter alia* and at certain times only — by the king's taxes.

These facts and hypotheses have some bearing on the much disputed question of the population trend in England before the Black Death. Professor Postan has for long argued that the early decades of the fourteenth century saw a reversal of the population growth which had characterized the thirteenth century and the inauguration of a period of economic decline. The population had increased beyond the capacity of the land to support it and nature retaliated through the operation of Malthusian checks and of soil exhaustion. Many countrymen were living near subsistence level, and when disaster struck, as it did during the great famine of 1315-17, many died, much land was abandoned, and, in the long term, land values and prices fell and wages rose.[285] This general thesis has been questioned and qualified, most notably and skilfully by Miss Harvey, but not convincingly replaced.

Even if Postan is correct in viewing the early fourteenth century as an era of economic regression, his explanations need not be accepted *in toto*. Several of the phenomena which he brings forward to support his case could be accounted for, not only by the effect of climatic disasters on a "calamity-sensitive" population,[286] but also by the supplementary consequences of royal taxation. Miss Harvey has argued that the controversy turns on "land values and the topography of settlement",[287] and on both these subjects our

283 *Inq. Non.*, pp. 12, 13; Baker, "Evidence . . . of Contracting Arable Lands", p. 524.

284 M. M. Postan, *Cambridge Economic History of Europe*, i, 2nd edn. (Cambridge, 1966), pp. 553-4; E. M. Carus-Wilson and O. Coleman, *England's Export Trade, 1275-1547* (Oxford, 1963), p. 122; Harvey, "The Population Trend", pp. 33, 37.

285 This argument has been elaborated in many of Professor Postan's writings, including, e.g., his *The Medieval Economy and Society* (London, 1972), pp. 35-9. For a list, see Harvey, "The Population Trend", p. 23, n.1. I. Kershaw, "The Great Famine and Agrarian Crisis in England 1315-22", *Past and Present*, no. 59 (May 1973) is the fullest and by far the best examination of the effects of the famine.

286 Postan, *Cambridge Economic History*, i, p. 565.

287 Harvey, *op. cit.*, p. 24.

evidence has something to contribute. Taxation undoubtedly led to the abandonment of land, though just how widespread this was is impossible to tell. The "Husbandman's" plaint in Edward I's reign, "to seek silver for the king I sold my seed, wherefore my land lies fallow and learns to sleep",[288] is as convincing as the much greater amount of evidence in the Inquisitions of the Ninth. As for land values, their movement has not yet been convincingly charted. Professor Postan considers that from about 1300 rents were falling, while Miss Harvey doubts whether they moved much at all.[289] Whichever is the case, in most places rents certainly did not rise as they had done in the thirteenth century. It is worth considering whether such a change may not have been related, at least in some areas, to the increasing share of the peasant's resources taken by the king. We have seen that in 1337, during the middle of a period of intensive taxation, Bishop Grandisson of Exeter had spoken of the difficulty which local landlords were finding in levying their rents, and that in 1340 the abbot of Malmesbury complained that the levy on movables was making it impossible for his tenants to pay their rents; and it has been argued that much of the feeling behind parliamentary complaints against all forms of taxation derived from the fear of landlords for their rents.[290] Again, we cannot estimate how general such difficulties were, but it is incontrovertible that in the early fourteenth century far more of the peasant's surplus cash (and not always his surplus) was finding its way to the king and his officials. With the ebbing of the colonizing movement and a possible decline in grain yields,[291] and in the absence of improvements in the techniques of husbandry, many men are likely to have found it hard to compensate for such losses, and their landlords may have suffered in consequence.

The population trend, like the trend in rents for which it was partly responsible, may have been a falling or stable one, but it was clearly not rising, as it had been in the previous century. Did taxation contribute directly to this change too? Those who died as an immediate result of taxation were probably not numerous, but many more may have been so reduced in resources by it that they became very vulnerable to a harsh winter or a poor harvest; the weather may have finished off the work begun by the seizure of stock

---

288 *Political Songs*, ed. Wright, p. 152; above, p. 297.
289 Postan, *Cambridge Economic History*, i, p. 566; Harvey, *op. cit.*, p. 39.
290 Above, pp. 307, 333.
291 J. Z. Titow, *Winchester Yields: A Study in Medieval Agricultural Productivity* (Cambridge, 1972), pp. 20-9. Titow's conclusions apply, of course, only to demesne yields; yields on peasant holdings may have declined still more sharply.

or the forced sale of grain. The "calamity-sensitive constitution of society" may have derived not only from the shortage of good land, but also from the incidence of the king's taxes.

We can demonstrate this, if only in speculative fashion, by using the work of Postan and Titow concerning heriots and prices on the Winchester estates. In most years the number of heriots levied, and therefore of deaths, reflects the level of grain prices; a poor harvest in one year will produce dearth, high prices and a high death-rate in the next. Now in 1342 the number of deaths (115) was very high, higher in fact than in any year between the great famine of 1316 and the Black Death, and markedly above the average number of deaths per year (about 90) for the period 1290-1347. [292] The main reason for this high death-rate was undoubtedly the bad harvest of 1341, the yield of which had been 14.88 per cent below average. (That this was not reflected in the price of corn in 1342, which remained at the moderate figure of 5.33s. per quarter,[293] was almost certainly due to a factor already discussed — that is, the failure in purchasing power brought about by a shortage of currency.) But although the 1341 harvest was well below average in its yield, it was not, by Titow's criteria, "outstandingly bad",[294] and it is very doubtful if the quality of the harvest alone can account for the large number of deaths. For comparison, a rather worse harvest in 1310 (15.67 per cent below average) produced rather fewer deaths (102).[295] It may well have been the effects of royal taxation which raised the death-rate above the predictable level. 1341 had seen the levying of the ninth and of another loan in wool, the culmination of a long period of exceedingly heavy taxation. The surrender of produce for the ninth, the sale of seed-corn and stock to raise money for the levies on movables, the seizure of wool (particularly important as a cash crop on the Winchester estates) — all these impositions may have reduced the peasant's standard of living to the point at which one poor harvest like that of 1341 would strike him with quite exceptional severity and quickly carry him off.

As this hypothesis is intended tentatively to suggest, the king's taxes were difficult to face not only because different sorts of burden were often imposed together, but also because they sometimes coincided with very intractable economic conditions. Over the whole period of forty-seven years, 1294-1341, there were eight years when

[292] M. M. Postan and J. Z. Titow, "Heriots and Prices on Winchester Manors", *Econ. Hist. Rev.*, 2nd ser., xi (1958-9), p. 399 and Graph 1.

[293] J. Z. Titow, "Evidence of Weather in the Account Rolls of the Bishopric of Winchester, 1209-1350", *Econ. Hist. Rev.*, 2nd ser., xii (1959-60), p. 398.

[294] *Ibid.*, p. 363.

[295] *Ibid.*, p. 383; Postan and Titow, "Heriots and Prices", Graph 1.

corn was exceptionally scarce — 1294, 1295, 1311, 1316, 1317, 1321, 1322 and 1340.[296] In one of these years, 1295, purveyance, the levy on movables and the maltolt on wool exports, all fell together; in 1316 and 1322 prises and levies on movables were collected simultaneously; in 1294 the maltolt coincided with the levy on movables; in 1311 and 1317 prises alone were collected; and 1340 saw the levying of the ninth. Taxation and dearth were thus frequent companions, and we might expect the peasant's livelihood to be threatened most seriously when they ran together, and not necessarily when taxation was heaviest. One or two pieces of evidence suggest that this was so. In 1322, for instance, "the community of the county of Lincoln" told the king that their livestock had been afflicted by murrain, their lands had been flooded, their corn had failed, and they had suffered greatly in the recent war between Thomas of Lancaster and the king. On top of these tribulations had come the demands of the crown. They had been asked to supply 4,000 well-armed footmen for the king's service, whose expenses were to be paid by the county. The total cost of this array, amounting, they said, to £8,000, would ruin them for all time. And in addition to this, great quantities of corn and malt taken by the king's ministers had weakened them still further.[297] There may be some exaggeration here, particularly in the estimate of military costs, but the petition nevertheless shows vividly the hardships which might be brought by a combination of natural and political disasters. It is striking, too, that prior to the late 1330s the levy on movables was resisted most forcefully in the localities during the famine years of 1315-17.[298] In these periods taxation aggravated economic conditions which were already extremely harsh.

If climatic difficulties sometimes added to the tax-payer's troubles, so also did the demands of his lord, particularly in the early

[296] In 1310, 1315, 1316 and 1339 harvest yields were at least 15 per cent below average and "outstandingly bad", according to Titow's classification ("Evidence of Weather", p. 363). As will be seen, however, I have not cited the harvest years in my list, but the years which followed them, since it was then that corn became scarcest. The years 1294, 1295, 1321 and 1322 are not covered by Titow's documents, and I have included them as years of dearth on the basis of the figures provided by D. L. Farmer, "Some Grain Price Movements in Thirteenth Century England", *Econ. Hist. Rev.*, 2nd ser., x (1957-8), p. 212; all were years in which wheat prices reached the famine level of 8s. per quarter or above. In general I have preferred to use yield figures rather than wheat prices as indicators of dearth, since prices do not always offer a true guide to the quantity of corn available; they were, for instance, boosted by inflation between 1305 and 1310 (Farmer, "Some Livestock Price Movements in Thirteenth Century England", *Econ. Hist. Rev.*, 2nd ser., xxii [1969], p.14) and depressed by a shortage of coin between 1337 and 1342.

[297] *Rot. Parl.*, i, p. 400.

[298] Above, p. 298.

years of our period. On many estates seigneurial exploitation reached its height around 1300. On the Glastonbury and Winchester manors in Somerset entry fines were at their highest about this time;[299]on some other estates, as at Chalgrave in Bedfordshire, lords were attempting a stricter control of their villeins' land transactions in the 1290s;[300]and in general labour services were at their maximum extent, though temporary commutation for money was widespread[301] Refusals to perform services and appeals to ancient demesne privileges marked a common reaction.[302]

It is against this background that we should set the demands of the crown, which, for many men, may have been coming to matter more than the demands of individual lords. Despite their weight, the lord's exactions were mainly recurrent and predictable, and they were tempered by the restraining force of custom, exercised in the manorial court. By contrast, royal taxes (particularly purveyance) were often collected in a quite arbitrary manner and their irregularity meant that they could not be bargained for. The activities of those who levied them were usually beyond appeal. Although special inquiries and petitions to Parliament might offer occasional possibilities for redress, there were no familiar and accepted procedures for checking the behaviour of avaricious officials. The community which could make its voice heard in Parliament was probably lucky rather than typical. At the end of the thirteenth century the burden of taxation had increased too sharply and in too short a space of time to allow the development of the restrictions which custom and legal process might ultimately have imposed upon a more gradually evolving tax system.

For much of the later middle ages war formed the dominant influence in the shaping of English society, and the history of the crown's demands upon the peasantry is only a part of this wider story. The expansion of the state's resources, marked by heavier taxation, the use of larger armies, and the growth of the centralized tax-granting assembly which was Parliament, affected many men besides the producers of the country's basic agrarian wealth. Yet it was upon them that these developments weighed most heavily, both

299 Postan, *Cambridge Economic History*, i, p. 553; Titow, *English Rural Society*, pp. 77-8.

300 M. M. Postan and C. N. L. Brooke, *Carte Nativorum* (Northants. Rec. Soc., xx, 1960), pp. xlv-xlviii.

301 R. H. Hilton, *The Decline of Serfdom in Medieval England* (London, 1969), p. 24.

302 R. H. Hilton, "Peasant Movements in England before 1381", *Econ. Hist. Rev.*, 2nd ser., ii (1949), reprinted in E. M. Carus-Wilson (ed.), *Essays in Economic History* (London, 1962), ii, pp. 80-5. For a caveat see Titow, *English Rural Society*, pp. 58-9.

because their means could not easily be extended to meet new impositions and because most of them already had pre-existing obligations towards their lords. Each set of demands, royal and seigneurial, is likely to have made the other harder to meet. We should not forget that the oppressed narrator of the *Song of the Husbandman* represents himself as being the victim not only of hundred bailiffs, tax-collectors and purveyors, but also of the lord and his officials, bailiff, hayward and woodward. As this suggests, the peasant probably did not distinguish as sharply as we do between the exactions of lord and king. Prises and subsidies, labour services and money rent, may all have seemed to him conjoined parts of the bleak and inequitable world in which he moved.

Taxation thus made its mark not in isolation from the peasant's other afflictions, but in association with them. If the population was checked during this period and if the area under cultivation shrank, it was not solely because a countryside full of land-starved smallholders had become especially vulnerable to the impact of poor harvests and grain shortages, but rather because dearth, seigneurial exploitation and the king's taxes all worked together to place the peasant's resources in a new and more precarious position. It is hard to assess the relative contribution of each of these burdens, since all interacted. Heavy taxation reduced a man's chances of surviving a particularly bad harvest, just as the commutation for cash of labour services due to his lord may have made it more difficult for the villein to meet the demands of his other and more distant master, the king. But we cannot assume that the Malthusian checks imposed by sporadic bouts of bad weather necessarily did most to determine the economic fortunes of the peasantry at this time. Equally significant, though less direct in its impact, was the inauguration of wars which were more continuous, more extensive and more costly than those of earlier days. Turning-points and watersheds are part of the historian's stock-in-trade; but it may be that in the history of rural England such terms are used less justly of the famine of 1315-17 than of the wars with France and Scotland which had begun twenty years before.

11. *Family, land and the village community in later medieval England**

ZVI RAZI

IT HAS BEEN ARGUED THAT IN THE PERIOD AFTER THE BLACK DEATH rural society underwent a number of structural changes as a result of the demographic decline and stagnation, the greater mobility of the population, the abundance of land and the high level of real wages. In her study of the inheritance customs in medieval England, Dr. Faith has observed that "the family claims to land were disregarded, or seldom pressed, and in place of the strict and elaborate arrangements which had previously governed the descent of land there came to be no laws but those of supply and demand".[1] Similarly, Miss Harvey has noted that the family sense of inseparable association with a particular holding, which had been so marked a feature of rural society in the early middle ages, weakened, indeed in some places it more or less disappeared.[2] Some historians, notably Professor Raftis and Dr. Dewindt, have claimed that the loosening of the ties between peasant families and their holdings after the Black Death coincided with the weakening of communal bonds;[3] "the old cohesive and deeply interpersonal and interdependent aspect of village life was fading, as private and independent interests and activities took precedence over those of groups".[4] All these and similar observations have recently been mobilized by Dr. Macfarlane to support his original thesis that rural England in the middle ages was not populated by peasants but by individualistic farmers who, free from any familial and communal restraints, were able to pursue a quasi-capitalistic system of production.[5] In this paper I will try to test the above-mentioned observations against the data available in the Halesowen court rolls. However, in order to find out the nature of the bonds between the peasant family and its land, between the villager and his neighbour, and how ties changed after the Black Death, it is useful to look first at these bonds during the pre-plague period.

* The comments and suggestions of Professors M. M. Postan and R. H. Hilton and Drs. R. Smith and R. J. Faith have been of great assistance in the preparation of this article.
[1] R. J. Faith, "Peasant Families and Inheritance Customs in Medieval England", *Agric. Hist. Rev.*, xiv (1966), pp. 86-7.
[2] B. Harvey, *Westminster Abbey and its Estates in the Middle Ages* (Oxford, 1977), pp. 318-19.
[3] J. A. Raftis, *Warboys* (Toronto, 1974), pp. 216-23; E. B. Dewindt, *Land and People in Holywell-cum-Needleworth* (Toronto, 1972), pp. 263-75.
[4] Dewindt, *Land and People*, p. 274.
[5] A. Macfarlane, *The Origins of English Individualism* (New York, 1979), pp. 131-64.

The manor of Hales, or Halesowen as it was later called, is located west of Birmingham, upon which it now borders. The parish of Halesowen was coterminous with the manor, which was eight miles long and about two and a half at its greatest width: its area amounted to some 10,000 acres. The manor is situated in a broken hilly terrain of mixed heavy and light clays. The hilly terrain of the parish shaped the structure of the local settlement which was not concentrated in large nucleated villages but scattered in small hamlets. In addition to the small market town of Halesowen there were twelve rural settlements or townships in the manor: Oldbury, Langley-Walloxhall, Warley, Cakemoor, Hill, Ridgeacre, Lapal, Hawne, Hasbury, Hunnington, Illey and Romsley. Oldbury in the north and Romsley in the south were the largest settlements in the parish; each had about 30 to 35 families in *circa* 1300. The other hamlets had only between 10 and 20 families each, and Illey no more than six.

The villagers of Halesowen practised, as in many other contemporary places, mixed agriculture. They sowed in the open fields of the parish cereals and leguminous crops: wheat, rye, barley, oats, beans, peas and vetches. The peasants also reared cattle, horses, pigs, sheep and poultry. As in other rural settlements there were in Halesowen villagers who engaged in non-agricultural activities: manufacture of textiles, metal-working, leather-working, wood-working, building, food production and ale-brewing. These activities played an important role in the economy of Halesowen. However, the court rolls clearly indicate that agriculture was the major economic activity during the period under study.

Although legally land in Halesowen, as in other contemporary villages, was not held by family groups but by individuals who could alienate it, between 1270 and 1348 the bulk of the land in the parish was transmitted through blood and marriage. During this period 1,125 transfers of land were recorded in the court rolls; 713 (63 per cent) were intra-familial and 412 (37 per cent) were extra-familial. These figures do not give a true measure of the amount of land transferred among family members, since the inter-tenant land market in pre-plague Halesowen, as in many other contemporary manors, was concerned primarily with small plots, a few selions and odd acres. It is quite difficult to find out the exact size of the plots transferred *inter vivos*, as well as the size of some holdings bequeathed *post mortem* or granted by the lord. However, I estimated that 6,916 acres (80 per cent) were transferred intra-familially while 1,383 acres (20 per cent) were transferred outside the family. Although my estimate is quite crude it indicates that only a small part of the land transferred in pre-plague Halesowen was taken outside the family.

In such circumstances it is not surprising to find that in Halesowen, probably as in many other rural areas, large numbers of landholdings remained in the hands of the same families over several generations. In the court rolls between 1270 and 1282, 174 landholding families are identified; 124 (71 per cent) of them still kept their holdings on the eve of the Black Death. Fifty families failed to maintain their hold on their land, not because they had a different attitude to the land or to their own family members, but because they were pushed out of landholding as a result of the unfavourable economic conditions which existed in pre-plague Halesowen. Among the 174 families identified in the records between 1270 and 1282, 40 (23 per cent) families were rich, 64 (37 per cent) were middling, and 70 (40 per cent) were poor. While 40 (100 per cent) of the rich families and 58 (90 per cent) of the middling families kept their farms continuously until the Black Death, only 25 (35 per cent) of the poor families were able to do so. The court records show clearly that many of the families who lost their holdings sold them piecemeal to their wealthier neighbours, while other families were entirely wiped out in the subsistence crises which hit the parish in the first quarter of the fourteenth century. Some lost their holdings probably because their descendants were too poor to pay entry fines and had to emigrate.

The history of these unfortunate families is well documented in the court rolls and would fill many pages. Therefore, only one case will be discussed here. Thomas Collin, a bond tenant from Hawne, appears in the records for the first time in 1270.[6] The size of his holding was about half a virgate. In addition to arable land he had livestock and geese, and he also engaged in ale-brewing. As a solid member of the community Thomas frequently acted as a pledge and was elected a few times as a juryman.[7] As the court records between 1282 and 1292 are missing, we do not know what went wrong with Thomas Collin, but it is clear that in the early 1290s he was heavily in debt. In 1294 he recognized in the court that he owed 5s. to Walter, a rich villager from Oldbury. Thomas failed to fulfil his commitment and therefore, in October, his pledges were given three weeks to induce him to pay his debts. In the same court the abbot prosecuted him for failure to render his dues.[8] It seems that he had other creditors as well, since all his crops were mortgaged. Thomas was pressed so hard that he had no choice but to sell some land. In February 1295 he sold a plot of land and thirteen strips to Master Richard of Hawne, and two months later he sold to the abbot for £2 all his land in Hawne with the exception of his house and a curtilage.[9] Only his land in Lapal, which his wife brought as a dower, remained in his hands. In 1297 his economic situation improved considerably as his wife inher-

[6] *Court Rolls of the Manor of Hales, 1270-1307*, ed. J. Amphlett, S. G. Hamilton and R. A. Wilson, 3 vols. (Worcs. Hist. Soc., Worcester, 1910-33), i, p. 13.
[7] *Ibid.*, pp. 48-112.
[8] *Ibid.*, pp. 292, 301.
[9] *Ibid.*, p. 330.

ited more land in Lapal after the death of her sister. Thomas exchanged this land with the abbot for thirty-two strips in two fields and two crofts.[10] In 1306 he was even able to reclaim and enclose a piece of wasteland.[11] However, in his last years, between 1308 and 1312, he fell again on hard times. As before, he was frequently sued in the court for debts, and bit by bit he sold the bulk of his land.[12]

Thomas Collin was blessed with seven daughters but he was able to marry off only two of them. In 1308 he surrendered to Christine, his eldest daughter, and her husband, John, "a room at the far end of his house and a quarter of a curtilage".[13] His second daughter, Juliana, was married in 1311 to a villager by the name of Henry Plais, but he either left her or died soon afterwards as she appears in the court records under her maiden name.[14] Agnes, Isabella, Margaret, Alice and Matilda Collin remained single. They are noted in the records several times, along with their married sister, for brewing ale, but more frequently for gleaning, or for using their neighbours' fences as firewood.

Thomas Collin died at the end of 1312 and his seven daughters, according to the local inheritance custom, shared between them the remainder of his holding. However, since they had difficulty in raising the money to pay entry fine and heriot, the holding remained in the lord's hands for a few months. When they entered the holding in February 1313, it included a house, a curtilage, a garden, seven ridges in a croft and a plot of enclosed moorland.[15] Collin's daughters found it very difficult to make ends meet; they had not only to glean but also to sell their land in the above-mentioned croft. All Thomas Collin's daughters probably died during the great famine of 1316-17, or emigrated, since their names disappear from the court records after 1318. In that year their tiny holding in Hawne was given by the abbot to a new tenant, Thomas ate Mersch.[16]

The experience of families like the Collins who were pushed out of landholding stands in sharp contrast to that of the majority of the pre-plague Halesowen families who managed to keep their holdings continuously over several generations. This can hardly be explained unless one assumes that, despite the legal situation which allowed landholders to alienate their farms, they had a strong moral obligation to their families which prevented them from doing so. Moreover there is further evidence in the court rolls which suggests that the villagers regarded their farms as belonging to the family as a whole in the sense

[10] *Ibid.*, p. 351.
[11] *Ibid.*, p. 540.
[12] Birmingham Reference Library (hereafter *BRL*), 346357.
[13] *BRL*, 346355.
[14] *BRL*, 346232 3.11.1311.
[15] *BRL*, 346233 21.2.1313.
[16] *BRL*, 346237 25.10.1318.

that every member of the conjugal family had a claim to be supported by it.

In Halesowen, as in other contemporary villages where impartible inheritance was practised, parents usually endowed non-inheriting children with land. The commitment to do so was so strong that parents did not hesitate, if they failed to acquire additional land during their lifetime, to reduce the size of the original landholding given to the heir, in order to provide the non-inheriting siblings with land. Despite the acute land shortage in pre-plague Halesowen among the two hundred families reconstituted from the court rolls who had more than one son over the age of twelve, 140 (48 per cent) families succeeded in settling more than one son in the village. The moral obligation to use the family land to provide for all its members was manifested not only by parents, but also by brothers and sisters. Although very few of the villagers in Halesowen were as generous as Richard Schirlet, who gave his brother Thomas in 1280 half of his holding, many of them provided their younger brothers and sisters with some land, which enabled them to settle in the village and to marry.[17] In the court rolls between 1301 and 1320, for example, are the names of sixty-three young landholders who had brothers or sisters; thirty-eight of them (60 per cent) provided their brothers or sisters with land. Landholders not only helped their brothers and sisters, but also usually cared and provided for their parents in old age. It is true that some of them maltreated and neglected their aged parents, but there is evidence which suggests that such persons were in a small minority. A villager who wished to retire, and who had reason to believe that he would be maltreated by his heir, could go to the manor court to make a formal maintenance agreement with the person to whom he handed over his holding. For example, in 1280 William of Langley surrendered all his holding to his son Nicholas. It was stipulated that if Nicholas would not sustain his father as he should, his father would immediately reoccupy the whole house and half the holding.[18] On the other hand, one finds in the court records many cases in which retiring parents gave their sons all their holdings without any maintenance agreement. For example, in 1313 William of Townhall, a yardlander from Ridgeacre, gave all his land to his son Henry without any formal conditions concerning his maintenance.[19] Between 1270 and 1348, forty-one retiring villagers handed their holdings over to their sons. Nevertheless, only eight (20 per cent) of them found it necessary to make maintenance agreements with their sons. If it was common, as Dr. Macfarlane argues, that children in medieval English villages had no obligation to provide for their aged parents once they

---

[17] *Court Rolls of the Manor of Hales*, i, p. 148.
[18] *Ibid.*, p. 179.
[19] *BRL*, 346235 18.10.1313.

had obtained the legal title to the holding, the retiring landholders of Halesowen must have been really stupid.

Despite the scarcity of land in pre-plague Halesowen, local families managed to provide non-inheriting siblings with land, enabling them to start their own households in the village, which must have promoted a high degree of intra-familial solidarity and co-operation. In order to test this hypothesis a representative sample of a hundred tenants who had relatives in the village who were also landholders was obtained from the court records between 1310 and 1325. Twenty-three of the tenants belonged to the upper stratum of the village, thirty-five to the middling and forty-two to the lower stratum. Then, two of the closest neighbours of each of the hundred tenants were identified, namely those who not only lived and held land near these tenants, but also had the most intensive pledging relationships with them. Lastly the degree of the interaction between these tenants and their relatives and neighbours was compared in cases indicating both conflict and mutual help. Table 1 shows that there was a high degree of interaction between the villagers and their relatives and closest neighbours, as they were responsible for 46·6 per cent of the total number of interactions observed. We can also see that, although a villager's closest neighbours and relatives quarrelled with him from time to time and caused him damages, they also helped him when he needed financial guarantees, and that relatives did this more often than close neighbours who were not related to him.

TABLE 1
INTERACTIONS BETWEEN FAMILY MEMBERS AND NEIGHBOURS OBSERVED IN HALESOWEN COURT ROLLS 1310-1325

	Total no. of interactions	Interactions with relatives	Interactions with two close neighbours
Trespass	987	191 (20·3%)	182 (18·4%)
Assault and bloodshed	60	17 (28·3%)	15 (25·0%)
Hue and cry	83	22 (26·8%)	25 (30·1%)
Pledges in land transaction	268	90 (33·6%)	61 (22·8%)
Pledges for debt	260	82 (31·5%)	52 (20·0%)
Pledges for entry fine	210	73 (34·7%)	60 (27·6%)
Totals	1,868	475 (25·4%)	395 (21·2%)

Although the evidence given so far suggests that there was a strong link between the conjugal family and its land in pre-plague Halesowen, it tells us very little about the nature of this link. Professor Homans and Dr. Faith, however, have interpreted the regularity with which land was transmitted in the same family from generation to generation before the Black Death as an indication that the villagers had a very strong emotional attachment to their patrimonial land.[20]

[20] Faith, "Peasant Families and Inheritance Customs", p. 86; G. C. Homans, *English Villagers of the Thirteenth Century* (New York, 1968), pp. 121-32.

Although such a feeling could have existed, its intensity and significance should not be exaggerated. After all, the records in which such an emotion has been detected come to us from the period between 1250 and 1350 when, as Professor Postan has shown, there was a land shortage almost everywhere. In a situation like this the only land available to very many peasants was the land to which they had a natural right, namely the patrimonial land. But from this it does not necessarily follow that "keeping the name on the land" was regarded by the villagers as an end in itself. As peasants exchanged patrimonial land with the lord or their neighbours, or sold land in one field in order to buy land in another, it is reasonable to assume that what was really important to them was to have land, preferably of good quality. It is hard to believe that, given the choice, a medieval husbandman would have preferred an inferior piece of land to a better one just because the former was tilled by his forefathers.

The strong familial commitments of the villagers in pre-plague Halesowen as far as land was concerned had far-reaching socio-economic consequences. The economic conditions which existed in the parish, as in other contemporary rural areas, namely land shortage, rising prices and falling wages, coupled with a number of very bad harvests, should have enabled the kulaks to accumulate land and to increase the size of their farms from generation to generation. Indeed, the court records show clearly that the kulaks usually accumulated land by taking vacant holdings and by buying land from their unfortunate neighbours. Yet over the period of eighty years from 1270 to 1349, the size of their holdings remained remarkably stable. This happened because the rich villagers who had usually more than one adult child to provide for used the additional land they had acquired to endow their non-inheriting siblings. Willam ate Pyrie (1293-d.1322), for example, inherited from his father half a yardland in Romsley.[21] William, who, as the court records indicate, was a very successful husbandman, succeeded in enlarging his holding by reclaiming land from the waste in 1297 and by buying in 1317 the quarter-virgate holding of John le Couper.[22] But when he died in 1322 his eldest son William (1313-d.1350) inherited only half a virgate because his father used the extra land he had acquired to give a dowry to his daughter Alice (1312) and a small holding to his younger son Simon (1315-55).[23] The constant redistribution of the land accumulated by the kulaks among their non-inheriting siblings prevented the village society from polarizing into a small minority of substantial farmers and a majority of smallholders and landless labourers. This explains why, despite the unequal distribution of wealth in pre-plague

[21] *Court Rolls of the Manor of Hales*, i, p. 297.
[22] *Ibid.*, p. 254; BRL, 346236 5.10.1317.
[23] BRL, 346796 15.12.1322. See also 346793-802.

Halesowen, the village community was able to maintain its cohesion and solidarity, as will presently be shown.

In the court held on Wednesday 16 April 1281 all the tenants of the manor of Halesowen were ordered to shut all the fences around the common fields (*rura communia*) by the following Sunday.[24] Similar orders and other references to common fields indicate that the villagers of Halesowen practised open-field husbandry. Admittedly there were also parcels of enclosed land called crofts and closes. However, it would seem that the bulk of the arable land in the twelve settlements in the parish lay in open rather than in enclosed fields. As a common-field husbandry was practised in medieval Halesowen, there must have been a considerable element of economic co-operation between the villagers. However, the economic relationships between the peasants were not confined to the mutual adjustment, consideration and co-operation required in an open-field system. The court records indicate that there were other intensive and varied inter-personal economic relationships in the parish. The evidence obtained from the records between 1270 and 1349 is presented in Table 2. The figures there do not provide us with an accurate measure

TABLE 2
ECONOMIC ACTIVITIES OF HALESOWEN VILLAGERS RECORDED IN THE COURT ROLLS 1270-1349

	No. of cases
Brewing and selling ale against the assize	5,476
Debts	301
Land sales (extra-familial)	244
Leases (extra-familial)	185
Sales of grains and hay	51
Sales of sheep, pigs and cattle	42
Sales of wood and timber	23
Sales of cloth	12
Sales of commodities made of iron	8
Hiring of cows for milk	35
Hiring of oxen	15
Hiring of horses	9
Hiring of various facilities like ploughs, harrows and carts	32
Short-term leases of pasture and herbage	18
Agreements on pasturing and keeping of animals	67
Failure to pay wages	52
Agreements to do jobs on contract like ploughing, harrowing, marling, fencing and carrying	57
Crop-sharing agreements	21
Failures to pay rents by sub-tenants	11
Total	6,639

of the inter-village economic activities; transactions in free land and leases for periods of less than two years are not recorded in the court rolls at all. Moreover, with the exception of ale-brewing, the cases recorded in the court rolls probably represent only a small minority

[24] *Court Rolls of the Manor of Hales*, ii, p. 92.

of the inter-village transactions made by the peasants during the period under study. Nevertheless, it suggests that village economy was highly monetized and competitive. There is no doubt that the well-to-do villagers were exploiting the needs of their less well-off neighbours in order to maximize their profits. They appear in the records as creditors, buyers and lessees of land, sellers of grains and livestock, and as employers, much more than their poorer neighbours. Even the village ale industry in Halesowen was largely dominated by the kulaks. Although middling and small villagers appear among the brewers who sold ale in the village, members of the rich families, who constituted only 23 per cent of the families, were responsible for 62 per cent of all the breaches of the assize of ale recorded in the court rolls between 1270 and 1349. Yet monetization and profit-seeking do not necessarily mean, as some historians have recently argued, that medieval village economy was a capitalistic one.[25] Postan, Hilton, Titow, Dyer, Miller and Hatcher have demonstrated that village economy in the later middle ages remained largely a subsistence economy.[26] Moreover, it is important to remember, as Professor Hilton has noted, that there was an element of the transfer of use values from household to household in the village. But since our evidence is drawn mainly from litigation in the manor court, the element of cash nexus will be exaggerated rather than minimized.[27] It is also a mistake to assume that all the inter-personal economic relationships in the village were motivated by the praiseworthy desire for profit. There is ample evidence in the court rolls that the peasants were lending to their needy neighbours grain, animals, tools, household utensils and clothing, and were helping them in various agricultural jobs. Admittedly in the court records between 1270 and 1349 only sixty-three clear cases of neighbourliness are recorded. But this does not mean that mutual help was rarer in the village, because acts of neighbourliness are less likely to end in litigation. It is interesting and perhaps surprising that cases indicating neighbourliness and generosity were much more prevalent among the middling and small peasants than among the kulaks.

Another way of assessing the significance of mutual help and support in pre-plague Halesowen is provided by the institution of the personal pledge. The procedure of the manorial court required that suitors should usually bring suitable persons as sureties. Pledges had

[25] Macfarlane, *Origins of English Individualism*, pp. 131-64.
[26] M. M. Postan, *The Medieval Economy and Society* (London, 1927), pp. 121-42; R. H. Hilton, *A Medieval Society* (London, 1967), pp. 88-123; R. H. Hilton, *The English Peasantry in the Later Middle Ages* (Oxford, 1975), pp. 37-53; J. Z. Titow, *English Rural Society, 1200-1350* (London, 1969), pp. 64-96; C. Dyer, *Lords and Peasants in a Changing Society: The Estates of the Bishopric of Worcester, 680-1540* (Past and Present Pubns., Cambridge, 1980), pp. 316-54; E. Miller and J. Hatcher, *Medieval England: Rural Society and Economic Change* (London, 1978), pp. 161-4.
[27] Hilton, *English Peasantry*, p. 44.

also to be brought to ensure payments of fines, debts and compensations for broken agreements and damages. Sometimes pledges were provided by the court itself from its officials and from a small group of semi-professional pledges. However, it would seem that in the great majority of cases the choice of pledge, as well as the agreement to act as a pledge, was the result of a personal agreement between the villagers. There was an element of risk in serving as a surety.[28] Pledges were amerced between 2d. and 4d. when their men failed to appear in the court, but when contracts, land transactions and undertakings to pay amends, fines or debts were involved, pledges were required not only to induce their men to honour their obligations, but also, if they failed, to pay the costs themselves.[29] It is very unlikely that pledges were normally paid for their service. The great majority of the villagers in the pre-plague period needed sureties so frequently that it is reasonable to assume that they were prepared to take a risk and to pledge their neighbours free of charge because they knew that there was a very high chance that they themselves would need their neighbours to stand surety for them. In the court rolls between 1270 and 1349, 25,314 pledges are recorded, which means that on average each of the 1,533 males identified in these records acted 16·3 times as a pledge. There was a direct relationship between the socio-economic status of a villager and the number of times he served as a surety; the wealthier he was the more he served as a pledge. Landless villagers never acted as pledges, and smallholders only a few times, but many of the kulaks often acted as pledges hundreds of times. Nevertheless, 80 per cent of the peasants both pledged their neighbours and were pledged by them at least a few times during their adult lives in the manor, which suggests that a significant degree of inter-personal support and mutual help prevailed in pre-plague Halesowen.

The life of the individual in the parish was greatly affected not only by the high incidence of reciprocity in social and economic intercourse, but also by the existence of a strong village community. The word "community" is used in the court records to describe both the people of the manor (*tota communitas manerii*) and the inhabitants of each of the twelve townships of the manor (*tota communitas villatae*).[30] The best way to tackle the controversial problem of the village community and to assess its significance is to examine its functions, which are well reflected in the court rolls since the manor included all the rural settlements in the parish.

[28] J. A. Raftis, *Tenure and Mobility* (Toronto, 1964), pp. 101-3.
[29] John Oniot was amerced 2s. for pledging Douce de la Grene. Thomas de Nottewik was in mercy, 2d., for pledging Agnes Dunnes who did not pay her fine for not doing ploughing services. See *Court Rolls of the Manor of Hales*, i, p. 288, ii, p. 75. In 1310 Thomas and Henry Oniot had to pay to Philip atte Broke 5s. since Richard de Nottewik whom they pledged failed to pay the debt: *BRL*, 346456 12.7.1310.
[30] *Court Rolls of the Manor of Hales*, ii, p. 92; *BRL*, 346351 8.5.1308.

As each of the settlements in Halesowen had its own open fields, common wasteland and woodland, the vill saw that the common-field arrangements and discipline were kept by its members, and also regulated the use of the common rights like grazing and the collection of wood for firewood and fencing. In 1309, for example, the whole community of Oldbury ordered a number of individuals to repair their hedges in order to prevent damages to the crops growing in the common fields. In May 1315 the vill of Hasbury presented in the court that some of its members "have ploughed where it was forbidden to do so", and that two of the villagers did not contribute their share to the pooling of draught animals or ploughs (*carucae*) for ploughing.[31] In a court held in 1281 the township of Romseley defended its refusal to allow a villager to use the common pasture on the grounds that he was neither a member of their community nor a landholder.[32] Numerous presentments were made by the townships of the manor between 1270 and 1349 against individuals who encroached on the common waste, over-used the commons, over-gleaned during the harvests and neglected their obligations to maintain roads, ditches, hedges and gates in good condition. However, the responsibility for the maintenance of certain public facilities like bridges and main roads lay on the whole community rather than on the individual landholders. In Halesowen, as on other contemporary manors, the vill sometimes acted as a collective tenant. In June 1302, for example, the abbot of Halesowen "granted to the whole vill of Oldbury a plot of wasteland in Oldbury so that the aforesaid land should ever remain waste and never be enclosed, *for the common benefit of all the men of Oldbury*".[33]

Another important function of the vill was the keeping of public order in the village. Breaches of the peace were countered immediately by the hue and cry to which all villagers present had to react. In the leet court, which was held twice a year, the township representatives as well as the jurors of the peace presented assaults, petty thefts, trespasses and the arrival of undesirable aliens. When a vill failed to take the necessary steps to prevent breaches of the peace or to report such acts it was collectively amerced between 2d. and half a mark. Moreover, the village community as a whole was often required by the court not only to provide information about the claims of suitors, and about their rights and status, but also to take the responsibility for bringing a dispute to an end outside the court. This was usually done by various bodies of jurymen elected by the township itself. As a third of all the disputes brought before Halesowen manorial court between 1270 and 1349 were eventually resolved out-

---

[31] *BRL*, 346359 13.5.1315.
[32] *Court Rolls of the Manor of Hales*, i, p. 162.
[33] *Ibid.*, p. 457.

side the court, the vill must have had an indispensable role in resolving the conflicts among its members.

In addition to collective amercements and fines, certain seigneurial exactions like tallages and state taxes were also levied on the townships. In April 1297, for example, the abbot of Halesowen ordered that five marks should be paid to him "by the whole community of the manor".[34] In 1293 Thomas Hill was summoned to answer about 3s. 8d. imposed on the township of Romsley for its share of six marks debt to the king in the exchequer.[35] The townships were also used by the central government for military purposes. In the last quarter of the thirteenth century, during the wars in Wales, the vills of Halesowen were required to recruit and to supply a number of foot soldiers. The money to fund collective undertakings as well as to pay seigneurial exactions and state taxes was collected by the townships themselves from their members. In May 1340 the township of Oldbury gave the lord 18d. to hold an inquiry by the whole court as to whether John Ordrich held his tenement in Oldbury or in the neighbouring township of Langley. The judgement of the court was that Ordrich's holding lay in Oldbury and that "he has always been tallaged with that vill".[36]

In order to perform its various functions the vill must have had not only regular assemblies but also a well-organized internal governing machinery. Unfortunately, by their very nature, the manorial records give very little information about these matters. However, it seems that each township was officially represented in the manorial court by two villagers elected by its members. These people were probably also responsible for collecting the money for the community fund, as they appear in the court records of 1306 both as *collectores* and *jurati* presenting the members of their township who did not contribute their share.[37] It is possible that they, like the capital pledges in those parts of the country where the traditional frankpledge system operated, had other functions and acted as a kind of elected headman of the township.[38]

In Halesowen, as in other contemporary manors, all the tenants elected various officials who played an important role both in village and manorial affairs. The customary tenants elected every year two reeves, a forester or woodward, and four ale-tasters. The election was done through the internal organization of the vill as sometimes townships were amerced for electing unsuitable persons to one of these offices. In addition, both the free and the customary tenants elected every year four assessors who assessed the damages injured parties

[34] *Ibid.*, p. 361.
[35] *Ibid.*, ii, p. 169.
[36] BRL, 346293 10.5.1340.
[37] *Court Rolls of the Manor of Hales*, i, pp. 539-40.
[38] Raftis, *Tenure and Mobility*, pp. 98-101.

were entitled to claim as compensation, and twelve *jurati pacis*. The jurors of the peace were called upon to present offenders against the lord and the public peace, to provide information which decided the court's final verdict, and to declare and to interpret the customs of the manor which determined almost every aspect of village life.

It is well known that local organizations played an important role in the lives of Englishmen far beyond the middle ages. But as far as the individual was concerned the medieval village community was far more important than any local organization in later periods, because in no other period of English history were so many disputes concerning property and rights, as well as inter-personal conflicts, resolved locally by the villagers themselves through the mechanism of the manorial courts. Although the effectiveness of the manorial courts depended upon the landlord's jurisdiction and coercive power, without the co-operation of a strong and well-organized village community these courts could not possibly have successfully performed their comprehensive duties.

It is true that the village community was largely dominated and run by the rich peasants who usually fulfilled the majority of the village and manorial offices. It is also likely that they took these offices not so much as a result of a deep sense of duty, as one historian has recently suggested, but because it gave them power to further their own ends and strengthened their economic dominance.[39] However, they must have been restrained both by the authority of the lord and the power of the middling peasants constituting a third of the village population. Moreover, they had to strike some balance between their own interests and those of the village community as a whole because they needed the support and the backing of their fellow villagers in the constant struggle against the seigneurial regime. As in many other contemporary manors this resistance turned sometimes into a bitter and fierce conflict, and even into open rebellion. In 1276 "all the men of the manor of Hales" were amerced ten pounds for refusing to elect a reeve "for the abbot's use (*ad opus abbatis*)" and for many despites and disputes against the local abbot and the convent.[40] In December 1279 Roger Ketel, a wealthy serf from the township of Illey, was fined five pounds "because he impleaded the abbot unjustly in the court of the lord king and was in aid and council with his other neighbours impleading the abbot".[41] The bitter struggle between the peasants and the abbey, however, which had started in 1243 and ended in 1286, is mainly told in the royal and ecclesiastical records. The peasants reacted to the abbot's attempts to exact heavier services, higher fines, rents and tallages by pleading their case in the court of

[39] Dewindt, *Land and People*, pp. 240-1.
[40] *Court Rolls of the Manor of Hales*, ii, p.5.
[41] *Ibid.*, i, p. 119.

King's Bench at Westminster. During the course of almost fifty years the villagers and the abbot not only appealed several times to the royal courts, but also resorted to violence. Eventually, the royal court rejected the tenants' claims that the manor was an ancient demesne and declared that they were villeins for ever. The peasants' reaction to the court verdict was an assault on the abbot and his men on their way to the abbey in 1278, and to continue in their resistance.[42] Only in the late 1280s or the early 1290s did they give in, after the murder of Roger Ketel by thugs employed by the abbey.[43] It is hardly possible that the peasants of Halesowen could have waged such a long and expensive struggle without a well-organized and strong village community.

To sum up, despite the unequal distribution of wealth and a monetized and competitive economic system, village society in the pre-plague period maintained a high degree of cohesiveness, co-operation and solidarity as a result of the requirements of an open-field husbandry, a highly developed corporate organization, and a sustained and active resistance to the seigneurial regime. The activities of the most acquisitive, aggressive and best-documented individuals, namely the rich villagers, indicate clearly that they were restrained by strong familial and communal commitments. In order to succeed in life the villager needed not only wealth, health, intelligence and ruthlessness, but also the goodwill and co-operation of his relatives and neighbours. Even the most acquisitive and self-centred villager had to restrain himself in order to keep those things which existed for "the common benefit of all" because such things were conducive to a strong community which was essential to the rich as well as to the poor.

There is no doubt that the economic and demographic conditions in Halesowen were very different in the post-plague period, but the question to be examined here is to what extent these new conditions weakened the familial and the communal bonds which prevailed in Halesowen before the plague.

It has been argued that family claims to land were disregarded or seldom pressed, and in place of the strict and elaborate arrangement which had previously governed the descent of land, there came to be no laws but those of supply and demand.[44] In order to test this hypothesis I examined all the transfers of land, *post mortem* as well as

---

[42] Homans, *English Villagers*, pp. 276-82.
[43] *BRL*, 383853.
[44] Faith, "Peasant Families and Inheritance Customs", pp. 86-7; Harvey, *Westminster Abbey*, pp. 318-19. Dr. Howell also finds "a sharp decline in hereditary continuity between 1350 and 1412": see C. Howell, "Peasant Inheritance Customs in the Midlands, 1280-1700", in J. Goody, J. Thirsk and E. P. Thompson (eds.), *Family and Inheritance: Rural Society in Western Europe, 1200-1800* (Past and Present Pubns., Cambridge, 1976), p. 127.

inter vivos, and grants from the lord recorded in the court rolls between 1350 and 1430 in order to see how many of them remained in
the family and how many went to non-family members. Transfers
from husband to wife were regarded as non-kin transfers. The results
are presented in Table 3. We can see that 57 per cent of all the

TABLE 3
LAND TRANSACTIONS RECORDED IN HALESOWEN
COURT ROLLS 1351-1430*

	Post mortem		Inter vivos		Grants by the lord		Total trans-actions	Total kin	Total non-kin
	Kin	Non-kin	Kin	Non-kin	Kin	Non-kin			
1351-60	14	1	3	10	—	11	39	17 (43·6%)	22
1361-70	35	2	4	18	—	10	69	39 (56·5%)	30
1371-80	17	1	10	13	—	9	50	27 (54·0%)	23
1381-90	15	—	5	6	1	9	36	21 (58·3%)	15
1391-1400	24	2	9	12	1	10	58	34 (58·6%)	24
1401-10	27	1	14	15	—	17	74	41 (55·4%)	33
1411-20	28	1	7	8	—	3	47	35 (74·4%)	12
1421-30	14	1	9	6	1	13	44	24 (54·5%)	20
Totals	174	9	61	88	3	82	417	238 (57·0%)	179

* Note: Grants from husband to wife or wife to husband have been regarded as
non-kin transactions.

transactions were between family members. This is clearly an underestimate of intra-familial transfers, because the genealogical information available in the court rolls is not complete. Moreover, the
mere number of land transfers does not give us a true idea about the
extent of the land transferred within the family, because while family
members usually bequeathed or transferred whole or half holdings,
some 40 per cent of the land sold by the peasants and granted by the
lord consisted of parts of holdings. Taking into consideration the
amount of land transferred in each transaction it was found that,
although only 57 per cent of all the land transactions were intra-
familial, the land transmitted within the family amounted to 71·3 per
cent of the total. There is a decline of some 10 per cent in the amount
of land transferred to kin in the eighty years after the plague. But the
difference is neither great nor anything like that found by other historians who studied the problem. Dr. Faith, for example, has found
that on many manors family transactions dropped from 56 per cent
of the total in 1300 to around 35 per cent throughout most of the
fourteenth century, and fell sharply to 13 per cent after 1400.[45] Other
historians have also found that intra-familial transactions in the late
fourteenth and the beginning of the fifteenth centuries were much

[45] Faith, "Peasant Families and Inheritance Customs", pp. 89-91.

lower than in Halesowen. Such transactions constituted 26 per cent of all the transactions recorded in Holywell court rolls between 1397 and 1457.[46] In the midland manors of the bishop of Worcester, Dr. Dyer has estimated that transfers within the family constituted only between 18 per cent and 39 per cent of all transfers.[47]

It is possible, of course, that the difference between Halesowen and other places for which figures are available was perhaps a result of a more stable family structure in the former parish. But it is more probable that the difference is due both to the methods used in this study and to the quality of the records. All the historians who have attempted to measure the extent of kin land transfers in the post-plague period have grossly underestimated such transactions because they have used surnames as their sole guide and have not undertaken comprehensive family reconstitution. Everybody knows that two people with different surnames can nevertheless be related and yet we always immediately assume that they were not. This leads to un-believable underestimation of familial relationships in the present as well as in the past. For example, in January 1403 Roger Webb came to the court and took a customary holding in Cakemoor which was previously held by Richard Jurdan.[48] Judging by the different sur-names, we have here an extra-familial land transfer. However, when I checked the file of Richard Jurdan I found that twenty-one years earlier in 1382 he transferred this half-yardland holding in Cakemoor to a newcomer to the manor, a fellow by the name of William Scot.[49] Again one would assume that this is also an extra-familial transfer and that the holding changed hands three times in twenty-one years between villagers who were not related. However, the sad truth of the matter is that Richard Jurdan, William Scot and Roger Webb were related, as Richard was the father-in-law of William and Roger. I know this because in the record of the land transfer of 1382 it is stipulated that if William Scot and his wife should die childless the half-virgate holding in Cakemoor will revert to Roger Webb.[50] In 1401 when the wife of William Scot died, a court inquiry decided that Roger Webb had a right to share her chattels with her surviving husband, William.[51] In June 1403 when Roger Webb sold the holding he took from the lord six months earlier it is stated that he was holding the half yardland in Cakemoor in his wife Agnes's right, and she declared in the court that she voluntarily agreed to the transaction.[52]

[46] Dewindt, *Land and People*, p. 134.
[47] Dyer, *Lords and Peasants in a Changing Society*, p. 302.
[48] BRL, 346380 17.1.1403.
[49] BRL, 346359 13.1.1382.
[50] *Ibid.*
[51] BRL, 346379 10.12.1401.
[52] BRL, 346379 25.7.1403.

A half-yardland holding in Romsley was held between 1357 and 1402 by five villagers with different surnames who were nevertheless related. In 1357 Roger Spring took the holding which was the dowry of his wife, Alice atte Lych. Since they had no children they transferred the holding in 1377 to her brother John atte Lych, and got it back from him for life. In 1380 Roger Spring died and his brother-in-law John took a part of the holding. However, John atte Lych organized a rebellion against the abbot for which he was put in the Shropshire gaol, where he died in 1386. Thus the land reverted to Roger atte Lowe, who was the second husband of Alice atte Lych. In 1392 they transferred the half-yardland holding to John Sadler, who was married to Agnes atte Lych, Alice's niece. In 1402 Agnes and John Sadler transferred the same half-yardland holding to Richard Squier, the cousin of Agnes.[53] Stephan de Baresfen, who lived in the township of Langley in the parish of Halesowen at the beginning of the fifteenth century, had a brother, Edmund Stevens, who lived in Stanton (either in Worcestershire or Staffordshire), and both of them had another relative in Halesowen by the name of Thomas Turhill.[54] It is possible to gain a much more realistic estimate of intra-familial land transactions in Halesowen in the post-plague period not only because a comprehensive family reconstitution from 1270 to 1430 is available, but also because for these 162 years the records of only fourteen years are missing, eleven of them between 1282 and 1292. Moreover the court records survive *in extenso* without any editing so that it is possible to reconstruct an almost complete and very detailed land register for the parish.

In order to measure the extent of the underestimation of familial relationships if only surnames are used, I re-counted the 417 land transfers recorded between 1351 and 1430 and found that only 132 (31 per cent) of them are identified as intra-familial. This suggests that by using surnames only we underestimate intra-familial transfers by at least 80 per cent. Moreover the use of surnames as the sole criterion to estimate the role of kinship in the transmission of land is bound to lead to the current view that, unlike the pre-plague period, in the post-plague years kinship became less important, even if such a change never occurred, simply because the population was rising in the first period and declining in the second. Professor Wrigley has found that theoretically in a stationary population 20 per cent of the married men will have no children to succeed them when they die, 20 per cent will have only daughters, and 60 per cent will have at least one daughter and one son. When the population is rising the percentage of married men who die childless or only with daughters is falling, while the percentage of fathers who have sons to succeed them

[53] *BRL*, 346340/357/359/822/823.
[54] *BRL*, 346377-397.

is rising. On the other hand when the population is declining the proportion of married men who have no children or only daughters to succeed them is rising, while the proportion of fathers who have sons to succeed them is falling.[55] Consequently, even if kin relationships were as important in the transmission of land in a period of population decline as they were in a period of population growth, by using only surnames as a criterion one is bound to find that kinship became much less significant in a period of decline. This is because in such a population the proportion of landholders who were succeeded by people with the same surname is likely to be much lower than it would be in a period of growth. The distorted results obtained by the use of surnames as the only criterion to estimate the role of kinship in the transmission of land becomes even greater if the extent of migration intensifies during the period of population decline, because often peasants changed their surnames when they emigrated. Since the population of England was rising during the hundred years which preceded the Black Death, and was declining during the hundred years which followed it, and since it is very probable that the rural population became more mobile, the usual evidence brought by historians to substantiate the hypothesis that kinship became less important in the transmission of land in later medieval England does not prove anything. Because familial relationships are more difficult to detect in the post-plague sources, in order to find out what really happened it is necessary to use only those records which enable us to study a locality over a long period and to complete family reconstitution. Moreover, even if an excellent series of fifteenth-century court rolls is available, it is impossible to find out the true extent of kin relationship in that locality if at the very least the records of the period from 1350 to 1400 are missing.

We have found that in Halesowen during the period 1350 to 1430 kinship was almost as important in the transmission of land as it had been during the period 1270 to 1349. This becomes even clearer when one reads the exceptionally detailed and informative court roll entries which deal with land. For example, in November 1385 it was recorded on the court rolls that Agnes, who was the wife of Philip Hypkys who held from the lord a toft and certain lands and a holding in Lapal, died. After death duties of two oxen valued at 16s. were taken by the lord "came John le Warde the closest heir to the above-mentioned Agnes, namely the son of her sister by blood, and claimed to succeed to the above-mentioned holding with all its appurtenances which Philip Hypkys held in his wife Agnes's right in the manor of Hales, to be held by the above-mentioned John and his descendants for services and customs".[56] In 1404 Thomas Adams succeeded by hereditary

[55] E. A. Wrigley, "Fertility Strategy for the Individual and the Group", in C. Tilly (ed.), *Historical Studies of Changing Fertility* (Princeton, 1978), pp. 135-54.
[56] *BRL*, 346365 28.12.1385.

right to half of the half-yardland holding of Roger Ketel in Illey, after the death of his niece Alice. It is stated that, if Thomas died childless, his younger brother William would inherit the land.[57] The court rolls for 1382 show that Thomas's father, William, arranged a marriage between his sister, Felicity, and one Roger Ketel.[58] In 1420 Felicity gave the rest of the Ketel place to her nephew Thomas Adams, but nine years later, out of the blue, a certain Henry Putter came to Halesowen manorial court and claimed to have rights in the Ketel holding. After an inquiry conducted by twelve villagers it was decided that he had a claim to the holding since he was the closest blood relative to Roger Ketel.[59] In 1404 John Baker and his wife Margaret transferred to their son John the customary tenements which were previously held by Robert Sweyn and John Watterhurst, both of whom were cousins of Margaret. The rolls state that if John died childless his brother Thomas would inherit from him, and if Thomas died childless his brother William would inherit the land, but if William also died childless he would be succeeded by one of the descendants of Robert Sweyn.[60] These, and many other examples in the Halesowen court rolls, not less than the overall proportion of intra-familial land transactions, cast serious doubts upon the validity of the view that the importance of inheritance as a mode of transmitting land was fading, and that familial claims to land were disregarded or seldom pressed in the post-plague period. Not only inheritance by near and more distant relatives, but also marriage, played a very important role in the transmission of land in Halesowen. It would seem that many kulaks accumulated more or as much land by good marriages as they acquired via the land market. For example, Thomas Collin, the son of John Collin of Oldbury, was amerced 2s. for seducing young Isabel Lovecok.[61] Isabel, however, was not only attractive, but also well endowed with land, as she had inherited her uncle John Lovecok's half-yardland holding in Hasbury in 1382, and therefore Thomas subsequently married her. Sixteen years later Thomas obtained another half yardland in Oldbury which his wife inherited after the death of her mother Agnes.[62] Richard Moulowe of Hill, by far the wealthiest villager in Halesowen, came from an affluent background, but his family did not rank among the most prominent in the village during the first half of the century. Richard's meteoric rise was due to a successful marriage and to the Black Death. Just before the outbreak of plague Richard married one of the daughters of Philip Hill. Philip, who had four daughters and four sons, was

[57] BRL, 346381 30.4.1404.
[58] BRL, 346359 10.2.1382.
[59] BRL, 346399 5.10.1329.
[60] BRL, 346382 26.11.1404.
[61] BRL, 346363 9.10.1383.
[62] BRL, 346360 26.11.1382, 346376 19.3.1399.

one of the five richest peasants in the manor. Philip himself, and many others of his family, fell victim to the plague, and only three of his daughters survived to share the fortune he left. Richard Moulowe acquired a third of the Hill lands through his wife Juliana, and another third he obtained through Juliana's elder widowed sister Agnes, whom he took into his household. The third part of Philip Hill's land and property went to his daughter Milicentia and her husband Robert Cutler.[63] Thus, through his marriage, young Richard acquired within four years some 60 acres of land and probably a lot of cash, many livestock and other property, which enabled him to build a substantial fortune in the second half of the fourteenth century. There is no power in the world which can prevent a tough, cunning and ruthless peasant who has made a good marriage and a pact with the Angel of Death from becoming a village "millionaire".

The main difference between the post- and pre-plague period, as far as the relationship between family and land is concerned, was that before 1349 the majority of the holdings in Halesowen were transferred to local villagers who were closely related, usually through the male line. After the Black Death, as a result of the demographic crisis and recession (see Graph), a higher proportion of the holdings were transferred to villagers, many of them immigrants, who were more distantly related to the deceased tenants and often through the female line. Therefore one finds so often in the court rolls of the pre-plague period that a certain holding is associated with the same surname over a long period of time, whereas in the post-plague court rolls it becomes much rarer.

It is reasonable to assume that the shortage of tenants, the scarcity of labour and the opportunity to regain freedom from serfdom encouraged migration in the post-plague period. However, there is some evidence which suggests that the peasants during this period did not wander all over the place to snatch the first opportunity which came their way, as it might appear. It would seem from the evidence, at least for the west midlands, a villager usually left his native village either because he had inherited land or to marry a bride with land in another village. In the court rolls between 1349 and 1430 there are 137 cases (30 per cent) of all the recorded land transfers in which outsiders came to Halesowen either to claim hereditary rights in land or to quitclaim such rights. For example, in 1424 the three daughters of John Bate came to Halesowen to surrender their rights in their father's holding in the township of Warley to Thomas Haket of the same vill, and probably the husband of the fourth daughter. One daughter came with her husband from Cradley, the second came with her husband from Northfield, and the third, who was a widow, came

[63] *BRL*, 346317-347.

GRAPH

THE POPULATION OF HALESOWEN 1271-1435

(Adult males identified in the court rolls 1270-1435)

500

400

300

200

100

1270 1280 1290 1300 1310 1320 1330 1340 1350 1360 1370 1380 1390 1400 1410 1420 1430

from Thickbroom in Staffordshire.[64] In 1414 Alice and Juliana, the daughters of Joanna Sweyn, succeeded to the family half yardland in Oldbury. A year later Alice, who was married to William de Feleford and who lived in Yardeley, quitclaimed her rights in the holding to her sister Juliana and her husband Gerald Wower.[65] In 1423 John Perkys of Frankley and Lucy his wife surrendered her rights in the Haneford half yardland in Romsley to her nephew, Roger Stampis.[66] In 1409 John Stevens, who lived in Harborne, succeeded his brother Nicholas to the Palmer holding, which he transferred to John Kembersley and his wife Juliana in 1419.[67] There are also many cases of outsiders who settled in Halesowen when their titles were recognized by the court. In 1414, for example, William, son of the late Henry Atkys of Ludlow, took the yardland holding of Philip Whyteley from Hasbury, and since he was under age he paid the lord a mark for his ward and marriage.[68] In 1407 John Taylor left Stourbridge and took the holding of his father, John Smyth of Oldbury.[69] Several members of the large Turnhill family of Rowley Regis moved to Halesowen in the second half of the fourteenth century and the beginning of the fifteenth century because they inherited land there.[70] The majority of the outsiders who had relatives in Halesowen or who married local girls came from the neighbouring parishes around Halesowen, but others immigrated from more distant parishes in Warwickshire, Shropshire, Worcestershire and Staffordshire, and even from Herefordshire and Derbyshire.

The marriage of Halesowen bondgirls in neighbouring parishes and, after the Black Death, the subsequent appearance of their offspring claiming inheritance rights in the manor, created an unpleasant problem for the lord. According to the custom which prevailed in the parish, as was the case in many other places in England, the legal personal status of a peasant was determined by his father rather than by his mother. Therefore, bastards were not allowed to inherit customary land since according to the rule a bastard born to a bondwoman was, *ipso facto*, a freeman, because the legal status of his father could not be ascertained. If a bondwoman emigrated from the village and married a freeman in the neighbouring village, any offspring of that marriage would also become free. In the pre-plague period the lord was only interested in securing a licence fine from the bondgirl who married elsewhere, and this was the end of the matter as far as he was concerned. In the great majority of cases there were always

[64] *BRL*, 351345-347.
[65] *BRL*, 346390 4.7.1414, 346391 31.7.1415.
[66] *BRL*, 346826 6.10.1423.
[67] *BRL*, 346386 22.5.1409, 346389 22.6.1412.
[68] *BRL*, 346391 10.10.1414.
[69] *BRL*, 346384 20.7.1407.
[70] *BRL*, 346331-337.

members of the bond-family of such a girl who inherited the holding. But in the post-plague period, and especially from the 1370s onward, more and more descendants of local bondwomen who had emigrated came back to the manor and took the customary holdings which had probably been held by the bond tenants from the beginning of the twelfth century. Since the revenues of the abbey were diminishing as a result of the fall of rents, entry fines, tallages, recognitions, amercements and rising labour costs, the abbot, like many other contemporary lords, tried to make up for this loss by exploiting the financial side of his seigneurial rights. He stood to lose when a vacant customary holding was taken by the free son of a former Halesowen bondwoman, instead of by the sons of local bondmen. Sons or daughters of emigrant bond tenants came back to claim land and to settle in Halesowen when they had a claim through the female line, but rarely through the male line. This was because if the son of an emigrant bondman came back to take, say, his uncle's land, he lost the freedom which he had enjoyed in the village in which he was born. In the 1370s and early 1380s, therefore, the abbot of Halesowen demanded that bondwomen who wished to marry out should quitclaim all their rights in their family land as a prior condition for granting a licence. In 1380, for example, Juliana, the daughter of a kulak by the name of Richard atte Green, "came into the court as a pure virgin and surrendered to the lord's hands all the rights and claims that she has or will have in future in all the lands and holdings in the manor and in those which will descend to her by hereditary succession. Then the lord conceded to the above-mentioned Juliana permission to marry outside the manor where she chose and she paid 5s. licence fee".[71] It would seem that the villagers saw in the abbot's demand from bondwomen, a demand which had never been made before the plague, another manifestation of seigneurial exploitation which prejudiced their deep-rooted belief in the bond between blood and land. It is probable that this demand was one of the more serious grievances which led the peasants of Halesowen to rebel against the abbey in 1386. After the peasants' show of force the lord never raised this demand again. When Agnes, daughter of William Holy of Lapal, decided to marry out in 1392, she paid only a marriage fine, and this is also true of Alice, the daughter of John Hill of Honinton, who went in 1423 to marry in Frankley, and of Felicity Adams who, in 1426, went to marry in Levendale, Staffordshire.[72]

There were three reasons why the peasants manifested high preference for family lands when they emigrated in a period of a shortage of tenants and abundance of vacant holdings. First, although land became cheaper after the plague, and especially in the period 1375-

[71] *BRL*, 346357 7.2.1380.
[72] *BRL*, 346395 15.11.1423, 346396 6.10.1426.

1430, good-quality holdings were very much sought after, and some of them were very expensive indeed. While one finds in the court records between 1349 and 1430 that the entry fines for 18 per cent of the holdings were waived altogether, for 25 per cent half the pre-plague rate was demanded, for 42 per cent of the holdings the same entry fines as before the plague were taken, and for 15 per cent of the holdings much higher entry fines were required by the lord. For example, in 1382 a tenant paid 10s. instead of 20d. as an entry fine for a customary croft of 3·75 acres.[73] In 1390 £1 instead of the customary fine of 40d. was paid for a quarter virgate.[74] In 1397, for half a yardland, a tenant had to pay £3. 15s. 4d. instead of 6s. 8d. and in 1427 a similar holding was taken for £3.[75] When I checked all the cases in which unusually high entry fines were paid, I found that the holdings concerned were not only of a good quality but also that the incoming tenant had no familial relationships with the previous one. On the other hand I discovered that when a tenant entered a good holding to which he had blood right, he always paid the customary entry fine.

Secondly, as a result of the demographic crisis, when a tenant took a vacant holding from the lord to which he had no blood right, there was always the danger that when he died someone would appear from outside the manor with a good claim to the holding, which might prevent the tenant's heir from occupying the holding. Therefore one finds instances in the court records of new tenants and their wives surrendering their holdings to the lord only to receive them back again for life, together with an undertaking by the lord that, on the tenants' death, the holding would descend to their heir. Often, since the villagers were all aware of the unusually high mortality among children at that period, the names of all their children were given in the court entry. Take, for example, the case of Richard Pachet, who obtained in 1382 a messuage and a half-yardland holding in Honinton, which had previously belonged to Richard Schirlet. Neither Richard nor his wife, as far as I could ascertain, had any familial link with the Schirlets. Richard and his wife Alice surrendered the holding to the lord and received it back for life. It was also stated that after their death the land would revert to Thomas, their son, for life, if he died before them, to John, and if the same happened to John, the land would revert first to Isabel, then to Christine, and eventually to baby Alice. Further, that when Richard Pachet and his wife Alice died either Thomas, John, Isabel, Christine or Alice would pay the cus-

---

tomary heriot.[76] Such arrangements often cost a lot of money and were not always safe. Hereditary rights to land were determined by the village community, not by the lord, and the villagers, at least until 1430, always gave the first priority not to those who held a recent legal title to land, but to those who had blood right, which sometimes went as far back as the fourth generation. Thirdly, a newcomer who inherited land in the village or married a local girl was not regarded by the villagers as an alien. This is shown by the fact that a significant number of immigrants were elected by the villagers to positions of authority and responsibility as jurymen, reeves, constables and assessors shortly after their arrival in the village.[77] A peasant who settled in a village in which he obtained land through inheritance or marriage probably found it much easier to be absorbed into the local community.

To sum up, family land was much more attractive than non-family land because it was cheaper, it gave a better title, and it facilitated the absorption of the immigrant into the local community.

The evidence so far suggests that in the eighty years which followed the Black Death, the strong bond between family and land was neither severed nor weakened; it simply became less visible in our records. In the pre-plague period as the population was growing and the supply of land was diminishing, the deep-rooted principle that land, whenever possible, should remain in the family brought about a situation in which land was passed from generation to generation to members of the conjugal family. During the period 1350-1430, however, when the population was diminishing at such a high rate, as a result of the same principle family land was often shared by wider kinship groups than the conjugal family. Therefore, as far as land was concerned, distant relatives were more important to a villager living in 1400 than to one living in 1300. The extension of the effective family ties beyond the nuclear group after the plague coincided with a spatial extension of the family. Between 1270 and 1349 the territory and the centre of gravity for landed families in Halesowen was the parish. A certain number of their younger sons and probably a higher number of their daughters always emigrated. But unlike the cottagers and peasants with very small holdings, the majority of the members of landed families remained in the parish. In the period between 1350 and 1430 the territory of a significant number of old landed Halesowen families ceased to be the parish and was widened to include the neighbouring parishes.

For the individual living in post-plague Halesowen, family ties

---

[76] BRL, 346359 6.8.1382.
[77] Z. Razi, *Life, Marriage and Death in a Medieval Parish: Economy, Society and Demography in Halesowen, 1270-1400* (Past and Present Pubns., Cambridge, 1980), pp. 122-4.

were very important, not only as a means to obtain land but also for support and help. For example, in the records of the court of April 1381 it is written, "Thomas son of William Warde came into the court with Richard his brother, Henry his uncle and William Perkys his kinsman (*cognatus*) to make his law against Thomas atte Lych in a plea of trespass".[78] In 1387 Juliana Wheler of Hagley brought a suit through her attorney against Philip Boury for broken agreement, namely he promised to pay her 3 marks on the feast of the Nativity of John the Baptist (24th June), and as he paid only one mark she sued his pledges, William Townhall and Henry atte Grene, for 2 marks and 6s. 8d. for damages.[79] I found that Philip, William and Henry were brothers-in-law. John Squier borrowed money from Thomas Kelmestowe and mortgaged his holding for the loan. In 1365 Thomas Kelmestowe came to the court and made a claim to seize John Squier's holding, since the old man could not pay his debts. Then the large Squier family came to John's help. His nephew, young Richard Squier, paid his debts, and then John transferred the land to Richard. Richard, in his turn, then transferred the holding back to John, and undertook to serve him faithfully all his life.[80] In 1371 Richard Squier, his brother Thomas, their uncle John, and their cousin John atte Lych leased from the abbot the demesne land in the three common fields in Romsley for twelve years for a yearly rent of £2. They also obtained half the harvest labour of the serfs of Romsley and the right to use freely the abbey wood for fencing.[81] Similarly in 1376 Philip Thedrich and Richard Jurdan, who were both relatives and neighbours, leased from the abbot his demesne land in the township of Cakemoor.[82]

It is more difficult to estimate the extent of the intra- and extra-familial interaction in the court records between 1350 and 1430 since, as a result of a procedural change, suitors were not required as before to bring a pledge except in cases of debts, contracts, some land transactions and delayed payments of entry fines. However, a representative sample of fifty tenants who were resident in Halesowen between 1370 and 1390, and who had relatives in the parish who were also landholders, was obtained from the court rolls. Then two of the closest neighbours of each of these tenants were identified. Lastly, the degree of interaction of these tenants with relatives and neighbours was measured using cases indicating both conflict and co-operation. The results are presented in Table 4. We can see in the Table that while the villager quarrelled more often with his relatives than with

[78] *BRL*, 346358 10.4.1381.
[79] *BRL*, 346366 20.2.1387.
[80] *BRL*, 346815 14.2.1365.
[81] *BRL*, 346816 27.6.1371.
[82] *BRL*, 346354 5.11.1376.

his neighbours, when he needed financial help and support he appealed to his relatives more often than to his neighbours. If we compare this Table with Table 1 we can see that there was a rise in the degree of interaction between the villager and his neighbours and relatives after the plague, both in cases indicating co-operation and conflict. But in order to assess the significance of this development we have to look closely at the village community during the period 1350-1430.

TABLE 4

INTERACTIONS BETWEEN FIFTY TENANTS AND THEIR NEIGHBOURS AND RELATIVES OBSERVED IN HALESOWEN COURT ROLLS 1371-1390

	Total no. of interactions	Interactions with relatives	Interactions with close neighbours
Trespass	215	75 (34·9%)	64 (22·8%)
Assault and bloodshed	90	38 (42·2%)	31 (34·4%)
Hue and cry	127	57 (44·9%)	41 (32·3%)
Pledges for debts, agreements and entry fines	119	59 (49·6%)	36 (30·2%)
Totals	551	229 (41·6%)	172 (32·2%)

It has recently been claimed by Dr. Macfarlane that the village community as a real and significant social entity never existed in medieval England.[83] Professor Raftis and his school, however, have argued that the village community did exist, but only in the pre-plague period.[84] The plague not only killed many of the villagers but also imbued the survivors with a spirit of rampant individualism which destroyed the village community. Unfortunately Dr. Macfarlane has not tackled the problem of the village community as seriously as he dealt with the relationship between family and land in medieval England. Therefore there is no point in taking issue with him on this matter. As far as Professor Raftis and his school are concerned, their claim about the breakdown of the village community is based entirely on a misinterpretation of the court rolls.[85] So let us get back immediately to the records.

On reading the court rolls between 1350 and 1430 one can immediately see that the village community continued to fulfil its manifold functions. Jurymen, court assessors, reeves, constables and other officials were elected by the villagers as regularly as before. The vill continued to maintain the common-field discipline, to supervise the use of the commons and the maintenance of public facilities. It continued to keep the public peace and helped its members to resolve their conflicts peacefully, and collected money to pay taxes, fines and

[83] Macfarlane, *Origins of English Individualism*, pp. 162-3.
[84] Raftis, *Warboys*, pp. 216-22; Dewindt, *Land and People*, pp. 263-75.
[85] Z. Razi, "The Toronto School's Reconstitution of Medieval Peasant Society: A Critical View", *Past and Present*, no. 85 (Nov. 1979), pp. 149-57.

other expenses. In 1377 the vill of Hunnington was amerced 6d. for preventing two villagers from Romsley pasturing their beasts when the fields were opened.[86] In 1396 it was ordered by the agreement of the lord and the four vills of Cakemoor, Ridgeacre, Lapal and Hill that if a member of these townships kept his beasts in the common fields and as a result the crops of their neighbours were destroyed, a view of all the neighbours would decide who was to blame and the culprit would pay as a punishment 20d. to his neighbours and 4d. to the lord.[87] In April 1429 the township of Oldbury was amerced 40d. because it failed to keep the "ancient road in a good condition". In the same court the jurymen rejected Thomas Haris's claim that he was falsely presented by his township.[88] Thomas, who was one of the bigwigs in the village, and who often served as a juryman himself, was furious. At the next meeting of the court three weeks later he gave the lord 6d. to hold an inquiry about the various transgressions and wrongs done to him by the vill of Hunnington. The bailiff chose twelve free and legal men to conduct the inquiry.[89] Unfortunately, we are not told how the dispute ended but it is possible that, as in many other similar cases, the presentment of the vill was upheld in the manorial court. In 1387 the jury presented that Juliana Moulowe sold foodstuffs with unfair profit to the injury of the lord and her neighbours. She had to cease to do this under a penalty of half a mark.[90] There are other entries which suggest that the individual was bound by the informal decisions of the community of the vill. In the court held in October 1397, for example, John ate Yate, a half yard-lander from Ridgeacre, was amerced half a shilling because "he broke (*fregit*) the counsel (*consilium*) of the neighbours of Ridgeacre".[91]

In the post-plague period, as in the one preceding, collective agreements were concluded between the lord and the tenants. In December 1363, for example, "it has been ordered and agreed between the lord and his tenants of the whole manor" that no tenant who had grains or other foodstuffs would sell them out of the manor before first bringing them to the weekly market held at the borough of Hales.[92] In 1401 all the tenants of Romsley quitclaimed to the abbot and the convent of Halesowen "all common pasture" over the cemetery of Kelmestowe provided that they had a right of way through the cemetery for their carts and wagons. They promised not to cause any damage to the cemetery when passing through its gates.[93] The fact

[86] *BRL*, 346355 14.10.1377.
[87] *BRL*, 346375 17.10.1396.
[88] *BRL*, 346398 6.4.1329.
[89] *BRL*, 346398 27.4.1429.
[90] *BRL*, 346367 16.10.1387.
[91] *BRL*, 346375 2.10.1397.
[92] *BRL*, 346345 6.12.1363.
[93] *BRL*, 346823 30.9.1401.

that the old communal institutions in Halesowen continued to function is important. But we have to ask ourselves whether or not the old cohesion and solidarity also survived the post-plague economic and demographic changes.

Admittedly, the gap between the small and the big men in Halesowen was widened during the period 1350-1430. Although the average holding size, and probably also the income *per capita* rose after the plague, the rise in the size of the farms and the incomes of the kulaks increased proportionally much more than those of the less well-off peasants. They inherited and acquired much more land through marriages, the land market and the lord than other villagers and, as they had on average less offspring to provide for than in the pre-plague period, they were able to accumulate land from generation to generation. Ralf Walloxhal, who inherited from his father a yard-land holding in 1357, bequeathed to his son, William, in 1411, in addition to the old family holding, 2 messuages, 7 curtilages, 7 crofts, 4 cottages, and freehold lands whose size is not specified. Two-thirds of the land which he farmed was obtained by him through marriage and inheritance from relatives.[94] Thomas Williams from Hill (1364-d.1412) paid for all his land an annual rent of £3. 10s. while his grandfather and father had paid only 13s. 4d.[95]

Despite the growing polarization of village society its cohesion and solidarity were maintained as a result of a rise in the economic interdependence and co-operation in the village after the plague and the intensification of the struggle against the seigneurial regime.

When one compares the court records in the fifty years before the Black Death and in the fifty years afterwards, as far as the problem of labour is concerned, one finds two striking differences. Whereas before the plague at least 43 per cent of all the families employed servants for some time, after the plague only 20 per cent of the families identified in the records employed servants. On the other hand the number of cases in which it appears that yardlanders, half yardlanders and, to a lesser degree, quarter yardlanders were using each other to perform various agrarian jobs under contract rose dramatically after the plague. In the court records between 1300 and 1349 there are 49 such cases, whereas in the records between 1350 and 1400 there are 163 such cases, 106 of them (65 per cent) during the period 1375-1400. The rise is even greater than is seen at first glance, since the population of the parish shrunk by some 40 per cent after the Black Death. Before analysing the significance of these figures let us look at a few examples. In 1381 William Wayte sued Henry atte Grene for a debt of 12d. for tilling 8 acres.[96] In 1379 Daniel the Walshman sued

[94] *BRL*, 346340 4.10.1357, 346388 21.1.1411.
[95] *BRL*, 346354-389.
[96] *BRL*, 346359 4.11.1381.

Henry atte Grene for breach of agreement whereby he undertook to fence his land.[97] In 1387 John Holt sued Thomas Schirlet for a breach of agreement whereby he undertook to carry fuel for him. Thomas admitted his failure and accepted the payment of damages. At the same time he claimed that John owed him 3s. 3d. for four and a half days of ploughing.[98] In 1387 Richard Moulowe sued Philip Boury for breaking his promise to sow for him 5 bushels of oats in a certain field.[99] In 1385 John Parler sued William Wayte for not taking his cows to the pasture.[100] In 1381 Richard Fokeram sued John Baker for not feeding well five bullocks which had been put under his care for the winter.[101] These, and many other similar entries, show clearly that as a result of the scarcity of labour after the plague and the rise in wages, the villagers of Halesowen were using their labour resources more efficiently by mutual agreements regarding ploughing, mowing, harrowing, reaping, livestock-rearing and other jobs. Many of the entries are presented as claims and counter-claims. A sued B for a failure to do a certain job for him and claimed damages, and then B sued A for not doing some other job for him, and claimed damages. Therefore, it is possible that, although such claims were presented in the court in monetary terms, in reality a villager often undertook to do a certain job for his neighbour and in return the neighbour undertook to do some other job for him. Such arrangements, also found by Professor Hilton in other west midland villages in the post-plague period, led to a blurring of the distinction between separate household economies.[102] In any case as far as Halesowen is concerned there is no doubt that the degree of economic interdependence of peasant households increased considerably after the plague and especially in the last quarter of the fourteenth century.

It would seem that a more efficient and intensive use of the labour resources of the whole village community enabled the rich peasants to tackle the problem of labour shortage more successfully than the landlords. The kulaks, as we have already seen, formed much larger holdings after the plague than before. Moreover the bulk of the demesne lands were also farmed by these rich peasants. The court rolls show clearly that these tenants employed living-in servants and labourers, but they employed also many other big, middling and small tenants to do piece-work for them. Richard Moulowe, the Halesowen "Rothschild", whose file contains hundreds of entries, employed in this way almost everybody in the parish. He also used to let various plots of land under a share-cropping agreement. For example, in 1375

[97] *BRL*, 346357 30.1.1379.
[98] *BRL*, 346366 8.5.1387.
[99] *BRL*, 346366 3.4.1387.
[100] *BRL*, 346365 8.11.1385.
[101] *BRL*, 346359 16.10.1381.
[102] Hilton, *English Peasantry*, pp. 37-53.

he sued Henry Townhall, another kulak to whom he leased various plots of land, for half the crops for taking to himself the whole lot. Then in the next court one finds that they were suing each other for various debts, breach of agreement and trespass, which indicates that they had many mutual arrangements with each other.[103] Richard employed a number of living-in servants, who are mentioned many times in the records. For example, he was sued by John Parler for not paying his son 3s. 2d. wages.[104] In 1385 he and his servants trespassed the lord and in 1383 he and a number of his servants made an illegal path in Lapal.[105] Richard Moulowe was sued eighty-seven times for debt but he sued others for debt only thirty-eight times. The same thing was found in the files of other kulaks in the post-plague period, while in the pre-plague period kulaks appear more frequently as creditors than as debtors. The reason for this is not that in the post-plague period rich villagers borrowed more money than before, but that many pleas of debt did not arise from straightforward credit transactions, but from broken piece-work contracts. Therefore, as the rich villagers after 1350 used this method to a much larger extent than their predecessors, they appear in the court records more often as debtors than as creditors.

Although the degree of economic interdependence in post-plague Halesowen increased considerably, it would seem that the large farmers who produced grains and livestock for the market must have been dependent to a much higher extent on the piece-work system than the smaller tenants who produced mainly for subsistence. If they had to use only full-time hired labour they would have encountered the same problems as the abbot of Halesowen, who had already started in the 1360s to lease out his demesne because of high labour costs. Therefore, although the economic gap between the kulaks and the rest of the villagers widened, they had a vested interest in the survival of the tightly knit village community which was based on co-operation and reciprocity. The people whose labour resources they were using in order to make a profit in a difficult situation, when the prices of grains and livestock were falling and wages were rising, were not cottagers and migrant labourers, but independent and proud husbandmen who could not easily be pushed around. There is even some evidence which suggests that the kulaks in the post-plague period were physically restraining themselves more than in the pre-plague period. In the pre-plague period a kulak was presented in the court on average once every three years for assault or bloodshed, or for forcefully breaking and entering his neighbour's house. Although in the post-plague court rolls there are proportionally more present-

[103] *BRL*, 346353 7.2.1375 and 28.2.1375.
[104] *BRL*, 346359 5.2.1382.
[105] *BRL*, 346364 26.7.1385, 346363 28.10.1383.

ments for such offences, on average a rich peasant was presented for committing an act of violence against his neighbour 0·45 times every three years. However, as far as their wives, sons, daughters, brothers and uncles were concerned, they continued to assault them with sticks, knives, fists, legs and teeth with the same frequency and pleasure as they did before the plague. As far as the middling and small villagers are concerned, there was a rise in their involvement in acts of violence in the post-plague period. It can be argued, though, that as the village rich presented offences against the peace in the view of the frankpledge, and as they strengthened their hold over village government, they could get away with under-representing offences committed by their own group. However, if one compares the number of trespasses committed by kulaks against their less well-off neighbours, one finds that such offences usually caused by straying animals increased after the plague. Moreover, while in the pre-plague period the damaged party usually brought the case before the court, in the post-plague period in Halesowen, as in many other places in England, such trespasses were brought to the court by the presentments of the jurymen and the capital pledges. The fine for breaking the peace was usually 6d. but the fine paid to the lord plus the damages which a trespassing peasant had to pay his neighbour usually amounted to 12d. or more. Therefore it is reasonable to assume that the decrease in the number of assaults committed by the rich villagers reflects a higher degree of self-imposed physical restraint on the part of these people as a result of their greediness which forced them to obtain the co-operation of their neighbours by peaceful means.

Another factor which counteracted the divisive effects of the economic competition and growing inequality was the struggle which the villagers waged against their landlords in the second half of the fourteenth century. The relationships between the abbot of Halesowen and his tenants were always strained and deteriorated even further after the Black Death. Like many contemporary lords the abbot of Halesowen attempted to make good his diminishing income by exploiting the financial side of his seigneurial rights.[106] He collected more assiduously than ever before from his customary tenants who did not grind their corn in his mills, sold livestock outside the manor, or failed to attend the three-weekly courts. The abbot raised marriage fines and lerwytes from 12d. or 2s. to 5s. and 6s. 8d., and tenants who took customary land to which they had no hereditary claim were made to pay through the nose. The following example illustrates the so-called seigneurial reaction. In the court records of April 1362 it is written, "the lord gave Juliana the daughter of Thomas Squier permission to marry where she wishes in or outside the manor and she

[106] Hilton, *English Peasantry*, pp. 60-73.

gave the lord for the licence 2s. and no more because the above-
mentioned Thomas her father is a friend of the lord abbot of
Hales".[107] In addition, although the labour services of the tenants
were commuted in 1323 they were required to do boon-works during
the peak periods which became for them almost an unbearable obligation as a result of the severe shortage of labour. The villagers of
Halesowen who became, as other contemporary villagers, more as-
sertive, reacted initially to the lord's seigneurial pressures by individual or group acts of insubordination and defiance. The abbey's servants and officials were assaulted and abused, and there was an orgy
of plundering of the abbey property by almost all the peasants cease-
lessly and shamelessly day and night. Never in the recorded history
of the manor had so many peasants trespassed so openly on the poor
monks' crops, pastures, fish ponds and warrens. In the 1380s the
tenants undertook more collective and organized action. We do not
know exactly what they did, but in the court held in September 1380
all the tenants in the manor, free as well as bond, were declared to be
in mercy except a small number of villagers who bought their
peace.[108] Late in 1385 Thomas Harboury, a bond tenant from Hasbury, sneaked into the abbey courtyard under the cover of darkness
and released all the doves from their dovecots. "Maliciously", it says,
"with an intent of causing the lord a damage".[109] Two months later,
at the beginning of 1386, the bondmen of the largest and most populous village in the parish, Romsley, which had also proportionally the
highest number of bondmen, rebelled against the abbot. When he
demanded that they do fealty and recognize their services to him,
they answered that they neither wished to remain his bondmen nor
to do any more service for him. I cannot deal here in detail with the
rebellion. However, the bondmen, led by Thomas Puttway, John
atte Lych and his sister Agnes Sadler, ended victorious.[110] After 1386
the lord considerably relaxed the seigneurial pressure on his tenants.
However, this was only one battle in a long and bitter struggle between the peasants and the abbey. In the last quarter of the fourteenth
and in the fifteenth century the abbot still had a significant measure
of coercive power exercised through his courts over both free and
bondmen. He continued to try to exact higher rents and other payments which they, for obvious reasons, resented, and although the
number of serfs in Halesowen in 1430 was perhaps lower by 20 per
cent than in 1350, serfdom was still a significant source of conflict
between the peasants and their landlord.[111] In 1423, for example,

[107] BRL, 346814 28.4.1362.
[108] BRL, 346357 5.9.1380.
[109] BRL, 346365 18.10.1385.
[110] BRL, 347156; Calendar of Patent Rolls, 1385-98, p. 317.
[111] Among the 178 adults identified in the court rolls between 1431 and 1435, 86
(48·3 per cent) were customary tenants.

judging by the quality of the handwriting and the faultless Latin, it is clear that the proceedings of the court were recorded by the abbot himself or by one of the more educated monks. Two merchet entries are recorded in this year, but unlike similar entries in other more usual court rolls in which only the licence fee is noted, in the entries of 1423 after the record of the licence fee is written, in a beautiful hand, "by custom, for merchet *pro redemptione sanguinis*".[112] This indicates that, unlike many modern historians and especially for those who do not consider serfdom to be an important issue, the monks of Halesowen were well aware of the importance of being the lords of a significant number of bondmen. The struggle against the lord of Halesowen was carried well into the fifteenth century, both by individuals and by the village community which, according to Dr. Macfarlane, never existed even in thirteenth-century England, and which fell victim to the plague according to Professor Raftis and his Toronto school.

Although there were many rural parishes like Halesowen in the west midlands and in other regions, what has been found in this study does not necessarily apply to England as a whole in the late middle ages. However, it suggests that the sweeping generalizations made recently about familial and communal bonds in medieval England have been somewhat premature.

[112] *BRL*, 346359 I.II.1423.

12. *Historians and peasants: Studies of medieval English society in a Russian context**

PETER GATRELL

IT HAS NOT GONE UNNOTICED THAT RUSSIAN WORK ON PEASANT SOCIETY
has been prolific and has profoundly influenced rural studies elsewhere.[1] Two aspects of this influence deserve consideration. Firstly,
during the half century between 1880 and 1930 a wealth of new data
was accumulated about the Russian peasantry, giving rise to differing
interpretations of social structure, social mobility and peasant economic behaviour.[2] These debates have provided a substantial body of
theory upon which social scientists in other countries have subsequently been able to draw. This is most clearly true of Lenin's famous
book on *The Development of Capitalism in Russia*, though an alternative vision of peasant society associated with A. V. Chayanov has
enjoyed increasing currency in the last fifteen years.[3] Secondly, in
the final quarter of the nineteenth century Tsarist intellectuals turned
their attention to the historical study of western European society.
The fruits of their labour, which was stimulated in part by a search

* I should like to thank members of the History Department at the University of
Manchester for their comments on an earlier version of this article, and the third-year
students who contributed to the course from which it derives. The detailed comments
and advice of Dr. Michael Bush, Dr. Ian Kershaw and Dr. Steve Rigby have been
particularly helpful, but they are not responsible for any shortcomings the article may
have.

[1] D. Thorner, "Peasant Economy as a Category in Economic History", in T. Shanin
(ed.), *Peasants and Peasant Societies* (Harmondsworth, 1971), pp. 208-9; A. Macfarlane, *The Origins of English Individualism: The Family, Property and Social Transition*
(Oxford, 1978), pp. 17-18, and ch. 1, *passim*; N. Charlesworth, "The Russian Stratification Debate and India", *Mod. Asian Studies*, xiii (1979), pp. 61-95; P. Worsley,
"Village Economies", in R. Samuel (ed.), *People's History and Socialist Theory* (London, 1981), pp. 80-5.
[2] For general background, see T. Shanin, *The Awkward Class: Political Sociology
of Peasantry in a Developing Society* (Oxford, 1972), pt. 2; S. G. Solomon, *The Soviet
Agrarian Debate: A Controversy in Social Science, 1923-1929* (Boulder, Colo., 1977);
T. M. Cox, *Rural Sociology in the Soviet Union* (London, 1979), ch. 2.
[3] Chayanov's major theoretical work only became accessible to English-speaking
readers following the translation that appeared as A. V. Chayanov, *The Theory of
Peasant Economy*, ed. D. Thorner *et al.* (Homewood, Ill., 1966). Translations of this
work had appeared in German and Japanese in the 1920s. One might also note that
some of Chayanov's writings were available in English at the time. See, for instance,
A. V. Chayanov, "Agricultural Economics in Russia", *Jl. Farm Economics*, x (1928),
pp. 543-9; A. V. Chayanov, "The Socio-Economic Nature of Peasant Farm Economy",
in P. A. Sorokin *et al.* (eds.), *A Systematic Source Book in Rural Sociology*, 3 vols.
(Minneapolis, 1931), ii. A good idea of Chayanov's importance can be obtained from
past issues of the *Journal of Peasant Studies* and *Peasant Studies* (previously *Peasant
Studies Newsletter*). For a guide to the accumulating theoretical literature, see E. P.
Durrenberger and N. Tannenbaum, "A Reassessment of Chayanov and his Critics",
Peasant Studies, viii (1979), pp. 48-63.

for clues as to the possibility in Russia of a transition from feudalism to capitalism along "western" lines, have similarly provided an important literature for non-Russian historians to consult.[4]

The most obvious instance of the impact of Russian scholarship in both respects is the investigation of medieval English peasant society.[5] The work of historians such as Paul Vinogradoff and E. A. Kosminsky occupies a central place in the historiography.[6] Russian research in problems of medieval English society reflected issues that emerged from a specifically Russian background. Their work cannot be located solely in the context of a developing British and continental historiography, any more than it could be considered *in vacuo*. As Vinogradoff himself said, "Questions that are entirely surrendered to antiquarian research in the West of Europe are still topics of contemporary interest with us".[7] Alexander Savine, one of Vinogradoff's best-known pupils, posed some of the key questions thus:

> What have been the causes and results of the rural revolution in the West? How far has it been of a universal character, and how far can it be avoided or modified in a society living in different circumstances? What has been the balance of good and evil during and after the change?[8]

How this interrogation of the English medieval material has been handled is the subject of part of this article. It is not intended to suggest that the study of English rural society has been determined by Russian historical scholarship, the precise contribution of which may be left for medievalists to judge.

The continuing relevance of the Russian social science tradition to contemporary scholars of medieval England is demonstrated by references in the work of such historians as Postan, Hilton, Dyer and Razi.[9] These ought not to be dismissed as casual asides. Russian social

---

[4] Richard Cobb informs us, for instance, of the influence on the young Georges Lefebvre of two books in particular: N. Kareiew, *Les paysans et la question paysanne en France dans le dernier quart du XVIIIe siècle* (Paris, 1899); J. Loutchisky, *L'état des classes agricoles en France à la veille de la Révolution* (Paris, 1911); R. C. Cobb, "Georges Lefebvre", *Past and Present*, no. 18 (Nov. 1960), pp. 52-67.

[5] This verdict might be challenged soon on the grounds that Indian social scientists are turning to Russian rural sociology in the course of interpreting social change on the subcontinent. See Utsa Patnaik, "Neo-Populism and Marxism: The Chayanovian View of the Agrarian Question and Its Fundamental Fallacy", *Jl. Peasant Studies*, vi (1979), pp. 375-420.

[6] Some recognition of this point may be found in E. A. Kosminsky, "Russian Work on English Economic History", *Econ. Hist. Rev.*, 1st ser., i (1928), pp. 208-33; F. Polyansky, "O russkikh burzhuaznykh istorikakh angliiskoi derevni" [Concerning Russian Bourgeois Historians of the English Countryside], *Voprosy istorii* (1949), no. 3, pp. 93-107. For the importance of Kosminsky himself, see the introduction by Rodney Hilton to E. A. Kosminsky, *Studies in the Agrarian History of England in the Thirteenth Century* (Oxford, 1956), pp. xv-xxii.

[7] P. G. Vinogradoff, *Villainage in England: Essays in English Medieval History* (Oxford, 1892), p. v.

[8] A. Savine, "English Customary Tenure in the Tudor Period", *Quart. Jl. Econ.*, xix (1904), pp. 33-80.

[9] M. M. Postan, *The Medieval Economy and Society* (Harmondsworth, 1975), ch. 8, *passim*; R. H. Hilton, *The English Peasantry in the Later Middle Ages* (Oxford, 1975),

science has provided hypotheses about stratification and class formation to test against available evidence. In some instances historical work has been informed by a sense of the direct and immediate relevance of Russian developments, often on the assumption (to misquote Marx) that the less developed country shows to the more developed an image of the latter's past. Again, there is no chauvinistic suggestion that this alone has influenced the course of the historiography. Readers of *Past and Present* are well aware of the variety of methodologies operated implicitly or explicitly in the analysis of agrarian societies.[10] Here the intention is to explore the circumstances under which an influential body of ideas has been shaped and the ways in which they have been applied. As we shall see, their application has sometimes been quite crude.

The latent interest of Russian intellectuals in peasant society received a boost in the 1840s, with the publication of August von Haxthausen's *Studies in the Internal Conditions . . . of Russia*.[11] Haxthausen, a Prussian nobleman, advanced the thesis that the Russian peasant commune (*mir*) represented a specifically Russian form of social organization that would allow her to avoid the trauma of proletarianization by encouraging the peasantry to retain a claim on communal land which was periodically redistributed among peasant families. Those who accepted this argument might contemplate one of two options: either the *mir* operated in such a way as to stabilize existing social relations, as Haxthausen believed, or it would allow the peasantry to find their way from feudalism to socialism without having to experience capitalist industrialization. This was the view taken by Alexander Herzen. The imminent emancipation of the Russian peasantry in the second half of the 1850s gave a considerable edge to these arguments. Among both conservative and radical thinkers there were those who assumed that peasant society operated on broad principles of equality and harmony, but this assumption was not universally accepted. So it was that on the eve of 1861 the claims

(n. 9 cont.)
pp. 5-8; C. Dyer, *Lords and Peasants in a Changing Society: The Estates of the Bishopric of Worcester, 680-1540* (Past and Present Pubns., Cambridge, 1980), esp. ch. 14; Z. Razi, *Life, Marriage and Death in a Medieval Parish: Economy, Society and Demography in Halesowen, 1270-1400* (Past and Present Pubns., Cambridge, 1980), pp. 88-9.

[10] R. Brenner, "Agrarian Class Structure and Economic Development in Pre-Industrial Europe", *Past and Present*, no. 70 (Feb. 1976), pp. 30-75; Z. Razi, "The Toronto School's Reconstitution of Medieval Peasant Society: A Critical View", *Past and Present*, no. 85 (Nov. 1979), pp. 141-57.

[11] August von Haxthausen, *Studien über die inneren Zustände, das Volksleben, und insbesondere die ländlichen Einrichtungen Russlands*, 3 vols. (Hanover and Berlin, 1847-52). There is an abridged version in English: *Studies on the Interior of Russia*, ed. S. F. Starr (Chicago, 1972). For the context of Haxthausen's work, see N. M. Druzhinin, "A. Haxthausen i russkie revolyutsionnye demokraty" [A. Haxthausen and Russian Revolutionary Democrats], *Istoriya S.S.S.R.* (1967), no. 3, pp. 69-80; S. F. Starr, "August von Haxthausen and Russia", *Slavonic and E. European Rev.*, xlvi (1968), pp. 462-78.

that Russia was unique in her communal institutions, that she could avoid western European economic and social upheavals and, finally, that peasant society was fundamentally egalitarian were hotly debated among the intelligentsia.[12]

These issues assumed even more importance with the emancipation of serf peasants in 1861. Serfdom had been abolished, but existing peasant institutions were left intact and actually consolidated.[13] Although, as Isaiah Berlin points out, the Slavophil notion of Russia's uniqueness ceased to arouse passions in the 1870s and 1880s in the way it had done a generation earlier, this was not to say that echoes of the claim did not provoke fruitful historical enquiry into the origin and function of the community in the Russian and European past.[14] As will be seen, this led Russian scholars to enter discussions taking place in England, Germany and elsewhere about the evolution of village communities. But from the point of view of contemporary debate in Russia more attention centred upon the internal organization of peasant society and social relations. Some elaboration of this debate is called for.

According to those Russian intellectuals who have come to be called populists, the traditional commune was a viable, healthy and egalitarian institution. This belief derived from the observation that a prime purpose of the *mir* was to ensure an equal distribution of communal land according to the number of mouths each household had to feed. Periodic reallocation of land according to this criterion made it impossible for any one household in the *mir* to acquire land at the expense of another household of similar size. In addition, because the commune encouraged family labour to remain on the land and prevented the progressive concentration of peasant land, it was a bulwark against capitalism.[15]

---

[12] For an elaboration of the condensed argument in this paragraph, see F. Venturi, *Roots of Revolution: A History of the Populist and Socialist Movements in Nineteenth-Century Russia* (London, 1960), chs. 1, 3; E. Lampert, *Studies in Rebellion* (London, 1957), pp. 242-3, 246-7; J. Blum, *Lord and Peasant in Russia from the Ninth to the Nineteenth Century* (Princeton, 1971), pp. 508-9; Alexander Gerschenkron, "Agrarian Policies and Industrialization: Russia, 1861-1917", in *Cambridge Economic History of Europe*, vi pt. 2, ed. H. J. Habakkuk and M. M. Postan, p. 750; P. F. Laptin, *Obshchina v russkoi istoriografii poslednei tretei XIX-nachala XX veka* [The Commune in Russian Historiography in the Last Third of the Nineteenth Century and the Beginning of the Twentieth] (Kiev, 1971), pp. 126-7.

[13] For details, see G. T. Robinson, *Rural Russia under the Old Regime* (Berkeley, 1972), pp. 68-71; Gerschenkron, "Agrarian Policies and Industrialization", pp. 745-56.

[14] Isaiah Berlin, *Russian Thinkers* (London, 1978), p. 213.

[15] The clearest and most intelligent discussion of the operation of the Russian *mir* is contained in G. Pavlovsky, *Agricultural Russia on the Eve of the Revolution* (London, 1930), pp. 81-4. See, in addition, Robinson, *Rural Russia under the Old Regime*, ch. 7; Blum, *Lord and Peasant in Russia*, ch. 24, *passim*. The argument about the character of the commune is set out in A. Walicki, *The Controversy over Capitalism: Studies in the Social Philosophy of the Russian Populists* (Oxford, 1969). On the attitude of populists towards capitalist industrialization, see A. Gerschenkron, *Economic Backwardness in*

Populist thought was not, however, a rigorously formulated set of principles and never amounted to more than the sum of the writings of individuals who adopted, or did not reject, the label.[16] So the picture is inevitably more complex than the above characterization suggests. Several populist writers in the 1870s, for instance, began to detect a strong impulse of economic individualism among Russian peasants who, hitherto, had been regarded as instinctively egalitarian. Closer investigation revealed, in the words of the exiled landowner A. N. Engelhardt, that "the ideals of the kulak reign among the peasantry; every peasant is proud to be the pike who gobbles up the carp. Every peasant will, if circumstances permit, . . . exploit every other".[17] Since economic differences disclosed themselves to observers, it followed that the notion of a uniform and homogeneous peasant society had to be modified. To some, such as N. N. Zlatovratsky, the possibility remained that peasants might form a "free communal union" by pooling factors of production along co-operative lines.[18] And L. Tikhomirov, writing in 1885, argued that while inequalities in peasant landholding had developed after 1861, the traditional redistribution of communal land had started up again after an interval of some twenty years.[19] In these ways, populist writers tried to come to terms with new observations of reality. The argument that peasant society was fundamentally egalitarian had not entirely vanished, while it was by no means certain that peasant society would polarize into capitalist farmers and landless proletarians.[20]

Internal differences of status and power in the peasant community had been placed on the agenda for discussion. So, too, had the need to consider the *mir* in relation to the evolution and function of the village community elsewhere. If, increasingly, intellectuals came to accept the argument of N. G. Chernyshevsky that the commune was not unique to Russia, did it follow that Russia would proceed along the lines of western European capitalist development?[21] On this point, Russian socialists sought the advice of Karl Marx. In a famous

---

(n. 15 cont.)
Historical Perspective (Cambridge, Mass., 1962), ch. 7; A. P. Mendel, *Dilemmas of Progress in Tsarist Russia: Legal Marxism and Legal Populism* (Cambridge, Mass., 1961).

[16] Isaiah Berlin, "Russian Populism", in his *Russian Thinkers*, pp. 210-37.

[17] Quoted in R. Wortman, *The Crisis of Russian Populism* (Cambridge, 1967), p. 58.

[18] *Ibid.*, ch. 4.

[19] L. Tikhomirov, *Russia, Political and Social* (London, 1888; repr. Westport, Conn., 1978), pp. 124-9. His point was that peasants had delayed redistribution of land in the expectation that a new census would fix tax obligations for each commune and define the burden to be borne by each household. Since more than twenty years had elapsed since the previous census, members of each *mir* renewed land reallocation to redress inequalities that had emerged. His observation was subsequently confirmed by a non-populist economist: A. A. Chuprov, "The Break-Up of the Village Community in Russia", *Economic Jl.*, xxii (1912), p. 177.

[20] Wortman, *Crisis of Russian Populism*, *passim*.

[21] Laptin, *Obshchina v russkoi istoriografii*, pp. 128 ff.

reply to an enquiry by Vera Zasulich in 1881 (which was not published until 1924), Marx indicated that the *mir* could survive and flourish, providing an alternative road to socialism: "the commune is a point of support for the socialist regeneration of Russia". However, "in order that it may function as such it would be necessary to remove the harmful influences to which it is exposed . . . and guarantee to it normal conditions of free development".[22] In a more lengthy draft letter Marx acknowledged the importance of the context in which the commune was located; there was no inherent and absolute tendency for the community to disintegrate. In Russia, the *mir* was oppressed by the state's fiscal exactions and by the opportunities these impositions gave to village usurers. It followed that a "rural revolution" would free the commune and allow Russia to develop without becoming "enslaved by the capitalist system".[23] Marx thus came close to the position adopted earlier by Herzen, who had suggested to a west European audience that Russia "need not pass through those swamps which you have crossed".[24]

Engels had taken a rather different view, which made the *mir* a basis for socialism only "in the event of the victorious proletarian revolution breaking out in western Europe before the final collapse of this common property". European workers would then be in a position to offer material aid to Russia.[25] This line was adopted in the revised Russian version of the introduction to the Communist Manifesto, published in 1882.[26] Engels apparently encouraged Russian socialists after Marx's death to engage in independent research into agrarian society in their country, so that they could confirm or deny the validity of Marx's views. But of his doubts about the universality of capitalism they had no means of knowing. All they had to work with were the vague remarks in the Communist Manifesto; even the bald statement contained in the reply to Zasulich was unavailable to them, since she and G. V. Plekhanov suppressed its contents and hence Marx's uncertainties. Engels himself was convinced by the Russian economist N. S. Daniel'son that capitalism had triumphed in Russia and that the issue was closed. This anticipated the conclusions reached by Lenin. In other words, the ground had been laid for a rigid analysis of Russian social and economic devel-

[22] The text of the letter, dated 8 March 1881, is printed in *K. Marx, F. Engels i revolyutsionnaya Rossiya* [K. Marx, F. Engels and Revolutionary Russia] (Moscow, 1967), pp. 443-4.
[23] For the draft letters, see K. Marx and F. Engels, *Werke*, 39 vols. (Berlin, 1961-8), xix, pp. 384-406. There is a composite letter, put together from Marx's drafts, in *The Russian Menace to Europe by Karl Marx and Friedrich Engels*, ed. P. W. Blackstock and B. F. Hoselitz (Glencoe, Ill., 1952), pp. 218-26.
[24] Quoted in Gerschenkron, *Economic Backwardness in Historical Perspective*, p. 168.
[25] *Marx, Engels i revolyutsionnaya Rossiya*, p. 70; *Russian Menace to Europe*, ed. Blackstock and Hoselitz, p. 213.
[26] *Marx, Engels i revolyutsionnaya Rossiya*, pp. 88-9.

opment. This hardly squared with the more flexible and open-ended interpretation being framed by Marx on the eve of his death.[27]

The study of peasant institutions was not confined to Russia, as Marx's own interests show. Peasant emancipation in early nineteenth-century German states had provoked an interest in the status and economic conditions of peasants, not just in Germany but elsewhere and at other times.[28] Another stimulus derived from the comparative study of peasant communities undertaken by Maine, who believed that "the primitive condition of the progressive societies is best ascertained from the observable condition of those which are non-progressive".[29] For Maine, it was India that represented "the great repository of verifiable phenomena of ancient usage and ancient judicial thought".[30] To his preoccupation with the progress of society from barbarism and serfdom to civilization and contractual obligation, Russian intellectuals injected a new urgency and sense of purpose. Here the question of rural social organization, peasant status and the future of the peasantry as a social group assumed, in Vinogradoff's words, "contemporary interest". It was natural for them to turn to English material for illumination of institutional practices and peasant fortunes in the European past. Not surprisingly, then, two young Russian scholars, Maxim Kovalevsky and Paul Vinogradoff, were the first to bring archival material to bear on the systematic study of the English peasantry.

Where Vinogradoff, after initial research in French and Italian archives, steeped himself in the history of medieval England, Kovalevsky drew upon the experience of a variety of countries in whose development he was interested. He ransacked the libraries and archives of Europe and produced a massive amount of published work, albeit of uneven quality.[31] Throughout his career he was, as an ad-

[27] There is some discussion of these issues in E. H. Carr, *The Bolshevik Revolution, 1917-1923*, 3 vols. (Harmondsworth, 1972), ii, pp. 381-91; Walicki, *Controversy over Capitalism*, p. 184; H. Wada, "Marx and Revolutionary Russia", in T. Shanin (ed.), *Late Marx and the Russian Road* (London, 1983), pp. 40-76.

[28] The emancipation of the Russian serfs was marked by a summary of emancipation elsewhere: S. Sugenheim, *Geschichte der Aufhebung der Leibeigenschaft und Hörigkeit in Europa bis zum die Mitte des neunzehnten Jahrhunderts* (St. Petersburg, 1861). Knapp's monumental work on German emancipation appeared a generation later: G. F. Knapp, *Die Bauernbefreiung und der Ursprung der Landarbeiter in den älteren Theilen Preussens*, 2 vols. (Leipzig, 1887).

[29] Cited in J. Burrow, *Evolution and Society: A Study in Victorian Social Theory* (Cambridge, 1966), p. 171.

[30] *Ibid.*, p. 159. Further discussion may be found in J. W. Burrow, " 'The Village Community' and the Uses of History in Late Nineteenth-Century England", in N. McKendrick (ed.), *Historical Perspectives* (London, 1975), pp. 255-84; C. Dewey, "Images of the Village Community: A Study in Anglo-Indian Ideology", *Mod. Asian Studies*, vi (1972), pp. 291-328. Dewey's remark (p. 293) that "advocates of the village community remained conservative" would not, of course, apply to Russia.

[31] For biographical information, together with a bibliography of Kovalevsky's works, see *Materialy dlya biograficheskogo slovarya deistvitel'nykh chlenov Akademii nauk* [Materials for a Biographical Dictionary of Members of the Academy of Sciences], 3

mirer later put it, driven by the "animated arguments and hypotheses about the past and future of the Russian village system".[32] How these impinged upon his scholarly work was not, unfortunately, made clear by Kosminsky, who brought Kovalevsky's name to the attention of English economic historians. What seems certain, however, is that his ideas underwent some modification during his career. It is conceivable that the evolution of Kovalevsky's thought can be attributed to his association and familiarity with Marx.[33]

In his early writings Kovalevsky, following earlier "westernizers", argued that communal institutions were universally subject to eventual decay. This applied with equal force to the Russian *mir*. The collective form of property identified in the commune would ultimately give way to private property under the challenge mounted by ambitious and progressive members and the constraints imposed by the commune on economic development (such as rural-urban migration).[34] The general point, that comparative study revealed the universal substitution of private for communal land tenure, tallied both with Maine's enquiries and with those of the early Marx. However, in his later years Kovalevsky came to believe that the *mir* should be maintained and that it answered the needs of peasant families. He follows Marx in accepting the possibility and even desirability of entrusting to the *mir* the future development of Russia. Kovalevsky defended the commune against the attempt by P. A. Stolypin to undermine it after 1905, arguing that the new reforms would lead to mass pauperization, social discontent and economic crisis.[35]

The view that established social relations in the Russian village need not be disrupted by internal divisions or external assault appears to have led to a modification of Kovalevsky's earlier interpretation of

(n. 31 cont.)
vols. (Petrograd, 1914-17), iii, pt. 2. The judgement about the quality of his work was shared by contemporaries and by Kosminsky, in his "Russian Work on English Economic History", pp. 213-15.

[32] Kosminsky, "Russian Work on English Economic History", p. 213. The comment, by Savine, is quoted more fully in E. A. Kosminsky, "Issledovaniya A. N. Savina po istorii Anglii" [The Researches of A. N. Savine on the History of England], in *Sbornik statei pamyati A. N. Savina* [Collection of Articles in Memory of A. N. Savine] (Moscow, 1926), p. 22.

[33] Some of the correspondence between the two men is reprinted in *Marx, Engels i revolyutsionnaya Rossiya*. The relationship between the two men is also discussed briefly in I. L. Andreev, "K. Marx o zakonomernosti razvitii obshchiny" [K. Marx on the Law of Development of the Commune], *Voprosy istorii* (1979), no. 12, pp. 3-17.

[34] M. M. Kovalevsky, *Obshchinnoe zemlevladenie: prichiny, khod i posledstviya ego razlozheniya* [Communal Landholding: Causes, Course and Consequences of its Decay] (Moscow, 1879). See, in addition, Laptin, *Obshchina v russkoi istoriografii*, pp. 254-5.

[35] M. M. Kovalevsky, *Die ökonomische Entwicklung Europas bis zum Beginn der kapitalistischen Wirtschaftsreform*, 7 vols. (Berlin, 1901-4), vi, ch. 8 (see the remarks on p. 481). His attitude to the Stolypin reforms is also mentioned in the entry on Kovalevsky in *Sovetskaya istoricheskaya entsiklopediya* [Soviet Historical Encyclopaedia], 16 vols. (Moscow, 1961-76), vii, cols. 452-6. For the reforms, see Gerschenkron, "Agrarian Policies and Industrialization", pp. 783-98; Robinson, *Rural Russia under the Old Regime*, ch. 11; Pavlovsky, *Agricultural Russia on the Eve of the Revolution*, ch. 5.

medieval English society. This may be gauged from remarks he made in an article on Wat Tyler's revolt and in chapters on England in his work on the economic development of Europe, where he implicitly distances himself from previously held beliefs.[36] In these later pieces Kovalevsky rejects an explanation couched in terms of the crisis in social relations caused by the intensification of feudal obligations, an explanation he appears to regard as too narrow. Instead, he offers a characterization of the uprising that stresses the dissemination of Lollard ideology and propaganda, the oppressive labour legislation of Edward III and the socio-economic consequences of the Black Death. For such eclecticism he was roundly condemned by the young historian Dimitri Petrushevsky, whose own work on the rising of 1381 appeared shortly afterwards.[37]

Kovalevsky's thought and historical understanding cannot, therefore, be regarded as static. It may be suggested that the change in his approach, from a straightforward insistence on a common global path of development to a more complex belief in the viability of the Russian commune resulted partly from his awareness of Marx's views and, perhaps more, from his observation of the persistence of the *mir* as an institution and its refusal to wither away.[38] It would not be surprising if Kovalevsky was also prepared to concede that the English village community had a greater resilience than he first believed and that the crisis caused by the rising of 1381 originated in a more complex set of circumstances than changes in rural social relations. Thus his adoption of a quasi-populist position is reflected in a changing perception of the English past.

Kovalevsky had been the first to indicate to Russian scholars the potential of material available in English archives. This potential was subsequently exploited in a more thorough and profound way by Paul Vinogradoff.[39] To appreciate Vinogradoff's intellectual development

[36] Kovalevsky, *Die ökonomische Entwicklung Europas*, iv, ch. 6; "Angliiskaya pugachevshchina" [The English "Pugachevshchina"], *Russkaya mysl'* (1895), nos. 5, 7-9.

[37] Kovalevsky, *Die ökonomische Entwicklung Europas*, iii, ch. 3, and iv, ch. 6. The criticisms made by Petrushevsky are to be found in D. P. Petrushevsky, *Vosstanie Uota Tailora* [Wat Tyler's Rebellion], 2 vols. (St. Petersburg and Moscow, 1897-1901), i, pp. 37-75. They were excised in later editions. Kovalevsky replied to them in *Russkaya mysl'* (1897), no. 5.

[38] In fact the *mir* enjoyed considerable vitality until collectivization. See D. J. Male, *Russian Peasant Organization before Collectivisation: A Study of Commune and Gathering, 1925-1930* (Cambridge, 1971); Shanin, *Awkward Class*, pp. 37-8, and chs. 8-9.

[39] For biographical and other information, see the "Memoir" by H. A. L. Fisher in *The Collected Papers of Paul Vinogradoff*, 2 vols. (Oxford, 1928), i, pp. 3-74. Additional material and a comprehensive bibliography of his writings before 1914 are to be found in *Materialy dlya biograficheskogo slovarya*. Two valuable discussions of Vinogradoff are D. P. Petrushevsky, *P. G. Vinogradoff kak sotsial'nyi istorik* [P. G. Vinogradoff as a Social Historian] (Leningrad, 1930), and B. G. Mogil'nitsky, *Politicheskie i metodologicheskie idei russkoi liberal'noi medievistiki serediny 70-kh godov XIX v.-nachala 900-kh godov* [Political and Methodological Ideas of Russian Medieval Studies from the Mid-1870s to the Early Twentieth Century] (Tomsk, 1969).

it is essential to recall that he grew up at a time of rapid political and social change which his family and teachers encouraged him to regard positively. When he was seven, Alexander II promulgated the decree that emancipated the serfs. During his later boyhood and adolescence a wealth of other reforms followed, giving a measure of representative self-government to municipal and rural authorities, modernizing the legal system and liberalizing education.[40] To many intellectuals these changes signalled the beginning of a new era in Russia, taking her into the community of European democracies typified by England. England seemed literally exemplary to Vinogradoff, in the sense that she "anticipates the development of other parts of Europe by several generations".[41] Yet there was sufficient contrast between England, which had progressed gradually from barbarism to democracy, and Russia, which was being dragged to modernity through government intervention, to make Vinogradoff's fascination with England all the more understandable.

These remarks indicate that it is not sufficient to place Vinogradoff solely in a German legal tradition.[42] He belongs as much to a Russian tradition in which he found himself exploring both the relevance of populist idealization of the village community and the work of liberals such as T. N. Granovsky and B. N. Chicherin who had no sympathy with populism. While the opposition of these men to serfdom inspired Vinogradoff and others in moral terms, a more immediate impression was made by Chicherin's famous and controversial assertion that the *mir* had been imposed quite recently upon an already enserfed peasantry for fiscal purposes.[43] The insistence that the community was not deeply rooted in peasant custom stimulated Russian historians to study the origins of village communities in Russia and elsewhere. In so doing they joined a long line of scholars in western Europe who were interested in early land tenure and the origins and character of feudalism. But when Vinogradoff read the work of Frederic Seebohm and Fustel de Coulanges he cannot but have been struck, as a Russian intellectual, by the similarity of their arguments about the growth of the peasant community within a feudal frame-

[40] The reforms are discussed in H. Seton-Watson, *The Decline of Imperial Russia, 1855-1914* (New York, 1961), ch. 2.

[41] P. G. Vinogradoff, *Issledovaniya po sotsial'noi istorii Anglii v srednie veka* [Studies in the Social History of England in the Middle Ages] (St. Petersburg, 1887), Preface.

[42] See M. M. Postan, "Medieval Agrarian Society in its Prime: England", in *Cambridge Economic History of Europe*, i, ed. M. M. Postan, 2nd edn. (Cambridge, 1966), pp. 604-5. Cf. Petrushevsky, *P. G. Vinogradoff kak sotsial'nyi istorik*, pp. 11-12.

[43] Vinogradoff's appraisal of Granovsky is contained in P. G. Vinogradoff, *Self-Government in Russia* (London, 1915), pp. 18-19. See also J. H. Billington, *The Icon and the Axe: An Interpretive History of Russian Culture* (New York, 1970), pp. 450-1; R. Pipes, *Russia under the Old Regime* (Harmondsworth, 1977), pp. 17-18; A. Walicki, *The Slavophile Controversy: History of a Conservative Utopia in Nineteenth-Century Russian Thought* (Oxford, 1975), pp. 422-6, 462-3; Blum, *Lord and Peasant in Russia*, pp. 509-10.

work to the argument of Chicherin a generation earlier.[44] The results of Vinogradoff's researches, as is well known, diverged sharply from those of Seebohm. Vinogradoff found that the English community antedated manorial jurisdiction, which was imposed upon a free peasantry. Whatever the merits of Chicherin's version of Russian history, therefore, Vinogradoff rejected its equivalent for medieval English history.[45]

Villainage in England, as Vinogradoff's dissertation appeared in print in English, contains a wealth of ideas that strike a chord in anyone familiar with Russian conditions at the time he was writing. This is true of his examination of the progressive substitution of quitrent for labour service on the demesne, an argument that echoes the contemporary debate in Russia about the relative importance of *obrok* (quitrent) and *barshchina* (labour service) on the eve of 1861.[46] It is also true of his discussion of such fundamental questions as the organization of agricultural production and peasant social relations.

The most striking aspect of medieval English rural society, which Vinogradoff repeatedly emphasized, was the existence of indivisible units of arable land which constituted a family holding. The units were not divided, because they would otherwise cease to be viable as parcels of land to be ploughed by a team of oxen. Vinogradoff also detected arrangements whereby the total number of units worked by a family (that is, the holding) was normally kept intact. He returned to this point on several occasions. "There is no shifting of strips, no change in the quantity allotted to each family. Everything goes by heredity and settled rules of family property".[47] The holding was not divided in accordance with changes in relative family size, as it was in Russia: "there is nothing to ensure that the differences in growth and requirements arising between different families will keep square with the relations of the holdings".[48] In other words, a growing family would not be compensated for a decline in mean arable per person. Other strategies would have to be pursued, such as non-agricultural employment, marriage or migration.[49] The general point recurs in *The Growth of the Manor*. Land might on occasion be redistributed,

---

[44] M. Kovalevsky, "Early English Land Tenures: Mr. Vinogradoff's Work", *Law Quart. Rev.*, iv (1888), pp. 266-75. Having cited Frederic Seebohm, *The English Village Community*, 2nd edn. (London, 1883), Kovalevsky went on to say that "Russian historians and lawyers felt bound to convince themselves how far these views were in accordance with documentary information".

[45] Vinogradoff, *Issledovaniya po sotsial'noi istorii Anglii*, p. 29; P. G. Vinogradoff, "Ocherki zapadnoevropeiskoi istoriografii" [Studies in West European Historiography], *Zhurnal Ministerstva narodnogo prosveshcheniya* (1883), no. 4, pp. 176-98.

[46] See Pipes, *Russia under the Old Regime*, p. 162.

[47] Vinogradoff, *Villainage in England*, p. 403.

[48] *Ibid.*, pp. 401-2.

[49] *Ibid.*, p. 403.

but "the strips of arable held and cultivated by the different households were usually handed over from generation to generation".[50]
Vinogradoff, it appears, implicitly contrasted the emergence of a
sense of family property in medieval England with its absence in
Tsarist Russia, where the *mir* reapportioned peasant allotment land
according to changes in family size. He also suggested that the integrity of family holdings accorded with an entrepreneurial willingness
to improve productivity rather than enforce any sense of distributive
justice.[51]

At the same time, the contrast between medieval England and
Tsarist Russia was not absolute. Vinogradoff detected in the scattering of strips of arable a similarity in tenurial arrangements. The village
community decided to equalize the use of land of varying quality and
accessibility. The alternative, to make holdings compact and to adjust
for differences in the quality of land, was difficult to implement: "you
will have to make a very complicated reckoning of all the very many
circumstances which influence husbandry, will have to find some
numerical expression for fertility, accessibility and the like . . .".[52]
The existing system met the needs of a community of peasant farmers
who took joint decisions about cropping and grazing and who did not
wish to discriminate against each other. Whether this explanation is
sufficient to account for the persistence of open-field agriculture is
once more the subject of debate.[53] What is certain is that Vinogradoff's view reflected a feeling for rural "economic solidarity" that was
common currency among many non-Marxist Russian intellectuals in
the late nineteenth century, underpinning their analyses of agrarian
society.[54]

It is not necessary to go as far as Maitland, who said that "Vinogradoff's first-hand acquaintance of Russian agrarian communism
enabled him to see many things in our English medieval documents
which had remained obscure to a people who had long lost any contact
with the working of communal village life", to acknowledge that his
familiarity with contemporary Russian social thought allowed him

[50] P. G. Vinogradoff, *The Growth of the Manor*, 2nd edn. (London, 1911), pp. 179,
207; see also *Villainage in England*, pp. 236-7.
[51] P. G. Vinogradoff, *English Society in the Eleventh Century: Essays in English Medieval Society* (Oxford, 1908), pp. 459-60, 477.
[52] Vinogradoff, *Villainage in England*, p. 235.
[53] Recent surveys are undertaken by R. Dodgshon, *The Origin of British Field Systems: An Interpretation* (London, 1980), ch. 1; Carl Dahlman, *The Open Field System
and Beyond: A Property Rights Analysis of an Economic Institution* (Cambridge, 1980),
ch. 2. Donald McCloskey has introduced the idea of "insurance against risk" to account
for the continuation of open-field agriculture, which may be implicit in Vinogradoff's
argument: D. N. McCloskey, "The Persistence of English Common Fields", in W.
N. Parker and E. L. Jones (eds.), *European Peasants and Their Markets: Essays in
Agrarian Economic History* (Princeton, 1975), pp. 73-119.
[54] Vinogradoff, *Issledovaniya po sotsial'noi istorii Anglii*, pp. 25-6.

insights into the nature of communal activities.[55] Indeed, it might be argued that his demonstration that "underneath this (manorial) system ancient principles of communal action and responsibility were still fully alive, being more deeply laid than the manorial order", owed at least as much to his observation of the vitality of the *mir* after 1861 as it did to his immersion in Germanic theories of the community.[56]

Vinogradoff remained throughout his life preoccupied with the contrast between England, his adopted home, which had progressed organically from feudalism to democratic freedom, and Russia, where new social relations were determined by government intervention and where the prospects for liberal democracy seemed alternately poor and (as in 1861 and 1905) encouraging. His views on Tsarist Russia were set out in a series of lectures he gave in 1914 and 1915, when he confronted the possibility of development in Russia along west European lines.[57] The pressing need, as he saw it, was for more constitutional and political reform, substituting "the rule of law and freedom for the reign of arbitrary discretion" and building upon the reforms that had been undertaken by the "glorious generation of the 1860s".[58] The government should tap the democratic instincts of the mass of the peasantry as well as the intelligentsia. Its economic policy created the prospect of social upheaval, in that "the mobilization of landed property is bound to occasion an immense amount of distress in spite of certain beneficial effects", but local and central government could together help lessen the distress. The price had to be paid for what was a progressive development in society and the economy. In short, Vinogradoff argued that Russia could join the community of west European democracies, albeit in a distinctive manner that owed much to enlightened reform from the state, in conjunction with the progressive intelligentsia.[59] The alternative was too awful to contemplate: "what we want in Russia is not gambling with revolution with its fantastic prospects and terrible realities. We want thorough organic reforms, something like the movement of the sixties on a larger scale".[60] With such an attitude, it is understandable that Vinogradoff was shattered by the October Revolution, ushering in what he called

[55] Fisher, "Memoir", p. 21.
[56] Vinogradoff, *Growth of the Manor*, p. 365.
[57] P. G. Vinogradoff, *The Russian Problem* (London and New York, 1914); P. G. Vinogradoff, *Self-Government in Russia* (London, 1915).
[58] Vinogradoff, *Russian Problem*, pp. 6, 8. There is a fuller discussion in P. G. Vinogradoff, "The Reforming Work of Tsar Alexander II", in F. A. Kirkpatrick (ed.), *Lectures on the History of the Nineteenth Century* (Cambridge, 1902), pp. 237-56. The emphasis here is on the failure of Tsar Alexander's successors to maintain the momentum of reform.
[59] Vinogradoff, *Russian Problem*, pp. 12-13, 17-26; P. G. Vinogradoff, "The Meaning of Present Russian Development", in Kirkpatrick (ed.), *Lectures on the History of the Nineteenth Century*, pp. 257-76.
[60] Vinogradoff, *Russian Problem*, p. 40.

a "maniacal tyranny".[61] Events in Russia stifled his creativity.[62] In this most dramatic form we see the importance for his philosophical outlook and historical awareness of the Russian background.

Before he finally left Russia for England in 1901, following an unresolved dispute with the Ministry of Education over university freedom, Vinogradoff had encouraged a number of scholars in their initial archival research in medieval and early modern social history. Two of these to achieve prominence in the late Tsarist and early Soviet periods were Alexander Savine and Dimitri Petrushevsky. Savine, whose research was curtailed by the world war, the revolution and finally by his death in 1923, is the better known to English historians, although only a small proportion of his work has appeared in English.[63] As noted earlier, Savine broached a series of questions about the transformation of rural society, including the social and economic gains and losses. His historical research, organized around such questions, centred on the process whereby English copyholders were increasingly dispossessed in the sixteenth century, to the advantage of large landlords.[64] In Tsarist Russia Savine detected a similar transformation, with the decline in the number of "middle-sized peasant households". But here the determining factor was the rapid growth of rural population. In Tudor England it appeared to be the opportunistic claims of self-assertive rural capitalists.[65]

Petrushevsky concentrated his attention on the later medieval period, and wrote a lengthy study of the rising of 1381. This work went through four editions between 1897 and 1937 and thus affords an opportunity to gauge the impact of changes in Russian political life on interpretations of medieval English society.[66]

In the first edition of *Wat Tyler's Rebellion*, Petrushevsky concentrated on the emergence of new social relations in fourteenth-century England, which pitted wage labourers against entrepreneurs and peasants against feudal lords. These relations he attributed to the

[61] P. G. Vinogradoff, "The Situation in Russia", in P. G. Vinogradoff (ed.), *The Reconstruction of Russia* (Oxford, 1919), p. 17.

[62] Fisher, "Memoir", pp. 59-60.

[63] A full bibliography of his writings can be found in *Sbornik statei pamyati A. N. Savina*, pp. 45-8. This list suggests that Savine must have been well known to a Russian audience for the articles he wrote on contemporary British political life before 1914. For a discussion of his work as an historian, see Kosminsky, "Russian Work on English Economic History".

[64] Savine, "English Customary Tenure"; A. Savine, *Angliiskaya derevnya v epokhu Tyudorov* [The English Village in the Tudor Era] (Moscow, 1903). Subsequently, Savine turned to the economic and social impact of the dissolution of the monasteries; part of this work appeared as *English Monasteries on the Eve of their Dissolution* (Oxford, 1906). On the eve of his death he was engaged on problems of seventeenth-century agrarian history.

[65] Savine, "English Customary Tenure", pp. 39-40.

[66] For Petrushevsky, see Kosminsky, "Russian Work on English Economic History", pp. 216-18, and the entry in *Sovetskaya istoricheskaya entsiklopediya*, xi, cols. 120-1.

progressive substitution of a money economy for a natural economy: the expansion of the internal market and the emergence of profit-seeking landlords undermined traditional ways of life. Petrushevsky found a new pool of hired labour in the second half of the fourteenth century and, as a corollary, arbitrary land seizures and the conversion of common land by those who wished to farm commercially. Agriculture in its classic early medieval form of integral peasant holdings was transformed. "The lord cared not a whit whether the villein paid his dues out of an independent holding, or by leasing his property, or selling part or all of it".[67]

In order to characterize more fully the classic manorial economy that was being thus undermined, Petrushevsky had recourse to a quasi-populist stance, and it was this that was likely to cause difficulties after the Bolshevik Revolution. The villein, to begin with, was not an economic agent responding to market forces, but a producer whose family labour and capital alone imparted value to the land. Without the labour and implements supplied by the villein, the demesne land was useless. In this sense, according to Petrushevsky, the villein exercised leverage over the lord, and not the other way round. Furthermore, Petrushevsky found no indication of socio-economic differentiation among medieval English peasants at this time: "Factors of production are still naturally combined, and all members of the peasant society engage in one and the same task. We find ourselves in a natural economy with its purely subsistence requirements".[68]

In the second edition of the book the conflict generated in the later fourteenth century is contrasted even more sharply with the harmony of peasant society and the stability of peasant-lord relations, based upon the supply of peasant labour to the manor and the access granted in return to the lord's forests and rivers. This idyll is disturbed by the encroaching monetization of the economy which, in Petrushevsky's words, "created the conditions for the development of a class of rural petty bourgeois village kulaks".[69] Thus Petrushevsky offers the reader a curious blend of quasi-populist idealization of the village community under feudalism and a Marxist representation of its disintegration. Both of these were to expose him to criticism after 1917.

Petrushevsky's response to new circumstances was to eliminate his references to a natural and harmonious rural order before 1350. In this respect, the third edition marks a real shift in interpretation. Instead, he pushes the emergence of class relations further back in time, for which he is now roundly condemned in the *Soviet Historical Encyclopaedia*.[70] More trouble at the time, however, was occasioned

[67] Petrushevsky, *Vosstanie Uota Tailera*, ii, p. 218, and ch. 3, *passim*.
[68] *Ibid.*, pp. 229, 231.
[69] D. P. Petrushevsky, *Vosstanie Uota Tailera*, 2nd edn. (Moscow, 1914), pp. 553-69.
[70] *Sovetskaya istoricheskaya entsiklopediya*, xi, cols. 120-1.

by his new insistence that feudalism could not be interpreted as a set of social relations. Rather, it was a political institution, constructed by and for the state. For adopting this stance Petrushevsky was taken to task by officialdom in the shape of a "publisher's preface" to the fourth edition, issued in 1937; this stated that the analysis of feudalism presented in the book was not acceptable. Unfortunately, the acceptable interpretation was not specified. Nonetheless, the book was published more or less as it stood, and the author's career was not ruined. Younger historians who failed to adopt the new stereotypes could hardly expect such relatively benevolent treatment.[71]

Petrushevsky owed much to Vinogradoff's example, even if his conclusions did not always tally with those of his mentor. He occupies a position both chronologically and philosophically between Vinogradoff and Petrushevsky's own pupil, Kosminsky. In order to see the change in approach and method within Russian scholarship it is necessary to consider next the genesis of a Russian Marxist interpretation of agrarian change and social relations. This interpretation also marks a turning-point in the tradition of Russian rural sociology.

It has already been demonstrated that the early populist image of an egalitarian peasant society had been attacked from within. The extent of stratification among Russian peasants and the degree to which differentiation intensified continued to dominate contemporary discussion. The most important new stimulus to this debate was provided by the penetration of Marxism, in the form of its two most famous Russian interpreters, G. V. Plekhanov and Lenin. Its culmination was the publication of Lenin's *The Development of Capitalism in Russia*.

Conventional populist beliefs in the homogeneity of peasant society were strongly attacked by Plekhanov, whose ruthless prosecution of populism may perhaps be explained by his wish to distance himself from his previous colleagues. In a long article written in 1885, entitled "Our Differences", he set out to undermine the basic tenets of populism and establish the grounds for an interpretation of progressive capitalist dominance in Tsarist Russia. The commune, he argued, did not preserve egalitarianism, but was an agency of exploitation; some peasants had succeeded in carving out for themselves a position of economic superiority which rested on the ownership of capital. The commune was already dissolving itself, because rich peasants wanted to rid themselves of its fetters in order to enclose land and poor peasants wanted to be free of communal taxes and other obli-

[71] The third edition of *Vosstanie Uota Tailera* appeared in 1926. The second and subsequent editions were all in one volume. For some of the difficulties experienced by historians in the early Stalinist period, see John Barber, "The Establishment of Intellectual Orthodoxy in the U.S.S.R., 1928-1934", *Past and Present*, no. 83 (May 1979), pp. 141-64.

gations.[72] Unlike Marx, his mentor, Plekhanov had obviously become convinced of the withering away of the commune. Lenin simply continued where Plekhanov left off. The first part of *The Development of Capitalism in Russia* largely restates Plekhanov's argument and that of another Russian Marxist, Isaac Hourwich.[73] These chapters are devoted to an analysis of stratification in peasant society, based upon statistics of sown area and livestock which were collected and processed by *zemstva* (rural local government) officials. The data revealed, as was already clear to Zlatovratsky (a populist) and Plekhanov (a Marxist) that peasant society was composed of rich and poor, defined according to land held and capital equipment owned. Following Plekhanov, Lenin also made the point that rural society was polarizing into a small number of rich and a large number of poor peasants. The middle peasant, whose plot was normally sufficient to satisfy subsistence requirements, was being squeezed out.[74]

Lenin had a simple concept of peasant mobility. To understand it, it is convenient to imagine a "snapshot" of peasant households in a given area at a given time. These are grouped according to land held per household. In a hypothetical example, where the number of households does not change, a second snapshot is taken several years later.[75] According to Lenin's interpretation, the original group of poor peasant families or households had been swollen over time through the addition of large numbers from the middle stratum. A small proportion of middle peasant households experienced upward mobility to the rich or kulak stratum. Since poor peasants had to sell

---

[72] G. V. Plekhanov, "Our Differences", in his *Selected Philosophical Works*, 5 vols. (London, 1961-81), i, pp. 122-399. See, in addition, the discussion in S. H. Baron, "Plekhanov on Russian Capitalism and the Peasant Commune", *Amer. Slavic and E. European Rev.*, xii (1953), pp. 468-73.

[73] The reference is to I. A. Hourwich, *The Economics of the Russian Village* (New York, 1892; repr. New York, 1970). There is no reference to Hourwich or Plekhanov in V. I. Lenin, *Podgotovitel'nye materialy k knige: Razvitie kapitalizma v Rossii* [Preparatory Materials for the Book *Development of Capitalism in Russia*] (Moscow, 1970). Instead, Lenin devotes some space to the work of Postnikov, whose empirical investigation and analysis of the *zemstva* data served as his starting-point. On this, see N. Valentinov, *The Early Years of Lenin*, ed. R. H. W. Theen (Ann Arbor, Mich., 1969), pp. 159-69.

[74] V. I. Lenin, *The Development of Capitalism in Russia* (Moscow, 1977), ch. 2. This is an English translation of the second Russian edition of 1907. The first edition appeared in 1899.

[75] A table of hypothetical mobility among peasant households may help to clarify what Lenin had in mind:

Peasant households by category	1890	1900	Net change
Poor	300	650	+ 350
Middling	600	200	− 400
Rich	100	150	+ 50

Note: The figures refer to the number of households in a hypothetical village. It is assumed in this instance that none of the original households disappears from the population during the decade.

their labour to kulaks or to non-villagers, one could no longer talk of peasants but only of proletarians and capitalist farmers in the Russian village.

The main evidence for this dynamic process, used by Lenin and by Plekhanov before him, was provided by statistics of peasant horse ownership. By juxtaposing army horse census data in the late 1880s and late 1890s Lenin discovered that the number of households without horses had increased.[76] This is the only empirical evidence offered in support of the hypothesis about polarization. This evidence was hardly sufficient to warrant the conclusion Lenin drew from it, the more so as he could detect only marginal shifts in horse ownership which might be explained entirely in terms of deficiencies in the collection of data.[77] It is not surprising that later Marxist sociologists should have attempted a more sophisticated quantitative analysis.

By the early twentieth century it was clear both to Marxists and to neo-classical economists that Russian peasant society had stratified along class lines and that traditional social relations were falling apart. It became a commonplace that the growth of a more integrated internal market had condemned the peasantry as a distinct social group to imminent extinction.[78] Lenin's analysis, in particular, attracted the attention of Russian Marxists after the Bolshevik Revolution, which accorded it an authoritative status that it could hardly otherwise have attained. More than this, the revolution imparted to his argument a universal applicability, making it inevitable that Soviet and non-Soviet scholars would turn to *The Development of Capitalism in Russia* for inspiration and guidance. That there were other ways of interpreting the evidence gradually ceased to concern Soviet intellectuals, while elsewhere a consensus emerged that "the facts . . . decided the issue in favour of the Marxists".[79] This revelation was bound to influence the study of medieval English peasant society.

The most distinguished post-Revolutionary historian to draw upon Marxist-Leninist thought in order to explore the nature of medieval English society was E. A. Kosminsky.[80] He was, at the same time,

[76] Lenin, *Development of Capitalism in Russia*, pp. 148-9.

[77] This is not entirely fair, since Lenin does go on to say that "to view intelligently the differentiation of the peasantry, one must take the picture as a whole": *ibid.*, p. 150. However, as far as the horse census material is concerned, their very nature made it unlikely that peasants would vouchsafe perfect information. Whether or not that information was then accurately transcribed and recorded is another problem. This seems an obvious illustration of the problems discussed in Oscar Morgenstern, *On the Accuracy of Economic Observations*, 2nd edn. (Princeton, 1963).

[78] See, for example, Chuprov, "Break-up of the Village Community", pp. 173-97. A. H. Johnson concluded his Ford Lectures on *The Disappearance of the Small Landowner* (Oxford, 1909; repr. Oxford, 1963) with the observation that "even in Russia, the small peasant proprietor is declining" (p. 164).

[79] Carr, *Bolshevik Revolution*, ii, p. 19. For the contrary argument, see Sorokin *et al.* (eds.), *Systematic Source Book in Rural Sociology*, i, pp. 375-7. Further discussion of the context in which Lenin wrote may be found in Shanin, *Awkward Class*, ch. 3.

[80] For biographical information, see Kosminsky, *Studies in the Agrarian History of England*, pp. xv-xxii.

keenly aware of the tradition of Russian historical scholarship that went back to the middle of the nineteenth century.[81] He shared with his predecessors a central concern with the nature of feudalism, and from this followed his research in manorial structure and organization. Kosminsky added to this a particular interest in the problem of social stratification, which had been underplayed in the literature. As a Marxist-Leninist, Kosminsky saw that this had a direct bearing on the disintegration of feudalism. Economic changes taking place under the feudal system created "the germs of new relations of production" which signified an emerging capitalist society.[82]

The appearance of Kosminsky's book on the English village during the thirteenth century constituted something of a landmark.[83] This was due both to the freshness of the insights into the diversity of manorial organization and to the use of the Hundred Rolls, hitherto neglected as an empirical basis for medievalists to consult. The book drew upon Leninist analysis to suggest that there were clear signs of stratification in peasant society, revealed in the differential access of households to arable land and in the growth of hired labour. The monetization of the economy to which this process was linked, primarily through the increased proportion of money dues that flowed out of peasant agriculture, led to a gradual polarization in the English village. This affected all peasants, whether free or unfree.[84] According to Kosminsky, almost half the holdings of free peasants in the thirteenth century were below five acres, while one-third of villein land fell into this category. Such poor families were compelled to work on the holdings of their more prosperous neighbours, who had acquired land in a piecemeal but progressive fashion.

This was no mechanical application of Leninist argument to medieval England on Kosminsky's part. He was conscious of the difficulties raised by any suggestion that stratification in village society before the thirteenth century had an economic foundation in commodity production: "The deep-seated causes of peasant differentiation probably lie as far back as the disintegration of the pre-feudal lands into the ownership of separate families".[85] His point was rather that commodity production had by 1300 begun to accelerate the creation of a permanent core of poor peasants and a wealthy stratum. In this way

[81] Kosminsky, "Russian Work on English Economic History", *passim*.
[82] Kosminsky, *Studies in the Agrarian History of England*, p. vii.
[83] E. A. Kosminsky, *Angliiskaya derevnya v 13-om veke* [The English Village in the Thirteenth Century] (Moscow, 1935). Much of the material contained in this book was reissued in E. A. Kosminsky, *Issledovaniya po agrarnoi istorii Anglii 13-ogo veka* [Studies in the Agrarian History of England in the Thirteenth Century] (Moscow and Leningrad, 1947). It was this book that appeared in translation a decade later; see n. 6 above.
[84] Kosminsky, *Studies in the Agrarian History of England*, pp. 211, 227, 250-5.
[85] *Ibid.*, p. 207.

"capitalist relations are gradually generated within the feudal mode of production".[86]

These ideas received further elaboration in the early work of Rodney Hilton who, with M. M. Postan, did most to bring Kosminsky's researches to the attention of English-speaking readers. This is particularly true of his widely cited monograph on Leicestershire estates.[87] Here, Hilton drew attention to an active land market which created a stratified peasantry: "the rich peasant and the day labourer became separate agricultural classess of a new type". In comparing the distribution of land on the Abbey estates in 1341 and 1477 he found evidence of embryonic "capitalist farmers", while the poll-tax returns of 1380 and estate accounts revealed a "significant percentage" of landless labourers, referred to as the nascent "agricultural proletariat". This polarization of peasant society is regarded as progressive and uninterrupted.[88]

Elsewhere, Hilton and Fagan argued that "petty commodity production in agriculture as in industry constantly throws up small capitalists, and at the other end of the scale depresses the unfortunate into propertyless wage-earners".[89] All the same, market relations in the early fourteenth century were still insufficiently developed for this process to have ripped the peasantry asunder as a distinct social group.[90] The authors still speak of peasants as members of an identifiable estate, subject *en masse* to the power of feudal landowners. Most peasants were barely able to eke out an existence and all were pawns used by the superior estate.[91]

The emphasis on the economic determinants of progressive differentiation in peasant society is also found in Maurice Dobb's *Studies in the Development of Capitalism*. Drawing upon the research of Kosminsky and Hilton, he suggested that between the early thirteenth and early fifteenth centuries the economic differences between rich and poor peasants "must have increased quite considerably".[92] The scope afforded an "ambitious stratum" of peasants by the "growth

[86] *Ibid.*, p. xiii; see also pp. 206-7, 227-8. A similar point is made in E. A. Kosminsky, "Izuchenie istorii krest'yanstva i agrarnykh otnoshenii v Anglii" [The Study of the Peasantry and Agrarian Relations in England], in his *Problemy angliiskogo feodalizma i istoriografii srednykh vekov: sbornik statei* [Problems of English Feudalism and Historiography in the Middle Ages: A Collection of Articles] (Moscow, 1963), pp. 131-2. This essay was first published in 1947. For a more rigid Leninist formulation, see M. A. Barg, *Issledovaniya po istorii angliiskogo feodalizma v XI-XIII vv.* [Studies in the History of English Feudalism in the Eleventh to Thirteenth Centuries] (Moscow, 1962), chs. 3, 5.

[87] R. H. Hilton, *The Economic Development of Some Leicestershire Estates in the Fourteenth and Fifteenth Centuries* (Oxford, 1947).

[88] *Ibid.*, pp. 95, 100, 105, 148.

[89] R. H. Hilton and H. Fagan, *The English Rising of 1381* (London, 1950), p. 190.

[90] This point is made even more unambiguously in R. H. Hilton, *A Medieval Society: The West Midlands at the End of the Thirteenth Century* (London, 1966), pp. 268-9.

[91] Hilton and Fagan, *English Rising of 1381*, pp. 190-2.

[92] M. Dobb, *Studies in the Development of Capitalism* (London, 1946), pp. 61-2.

of local trade and local markets" allowed them to "accumulate a small amount of capital" and lease additional land. While he conceded that other factors, such as variations in soil type and random occurrences, may have played some part, Dobb stressed the same processes of accumulation, exploitation and expropriation in medieval England that Lenin had identified in Tsarist Russia. In this way, Dobb remarked, the rich English peasant "may have much in common with his counterpart in the history of the Russian village in the nineteenth century".[93]

Such an interpretation can be challenged on the grounds that stratification in present society existed long before it was possible to speak of the emergence of local or regional markets and the monetization of the economy on the scale implied by Dobb. This point was conceded by Kosminsky, as we have seen.[94] Furthermore, the hypothesis that medieval peasant society exhibited a progressive tendency to polarize was also questioned, most strongly by Postan.[95] While he accepted as useful the division of peasant society into rich, middling and poor, Postan rejected any suggestion that the middle category disappeared in the later medieval period. In fact, "there were always large numbers of smallholders, a small group of village kulaks and an intermediate mass of middling peasants".[96] Any changes in the magnitude of these groups followed from changes in the ratio of peasant households to available land. Thus, middling peasants grew in number in the fourteenth century as a result of the declining rate of population increase, which emptied holdings and raised their mean size.[97] A broadly similar conclusion is reached by other scholars, although some of them suggest that the gains during the fourteenth century were not evenly distributed; that is, the number of landless households declined, but rich households consolidated their position at the same time.[98]

---

[93] Ibid., pp. 60-1.

[94] See n. 86 above.

[95] Most recently in Postan, Medieval Economy and Society, ch. 8. For some more general remarks about the danger of interpolation in the absence of empirical evidence, see M. M. Postan, "Function and Dialectic in Economic History", Econ. Hist. Rev., 2nd ser., xiv (1962), pp. 397-407.

[96] Postan, Medieval Economy and Society, p. 154. Middling peasants are defined as being in possession of between one-quarter and three-quarters of a virgate.

[97] Ibid., ch. 8. See also R. H. Hilton, "Reasons for Inequality among Medieval Peasants", Jl. Peasant Studies, v (1978), p. 279.

[98] For a recent discussion in support of Postan's argument, see E. Miller and J. Hatcher, Medieval England: Rural Society and Economic Change, 1086-1348 (London, 1978), pp. 48-9, 145. DeWindt details the decline in landless households in the east midlands, but argues that the "particularly industrious and opportunistic peasant" gained most: E. DeWindt, Land and People in Holywell-cum-Needingworth: Structure of Tenure and Patterns of Social Organization in an East Midlands Village, 1252-1457 (Toronto, 1972), pp. 111-16, 124-5, 161. See, in addition, G. Duby, Rural Economy and Country Life in the Medieval West (London, 1968), pp. 336-41; Razi, Life, Marriage and Death in a Medieval Parish, p. 147.

It became increasingly apparent after Stalinist collectivization that Soviet Marxism was unable to generate new hypotheses and research methods.[99] This was reflected in the often mechanistic application of Leninist orthodoxy to rural society. At the same time, Stalinism crushed an alternative non-Marxist theory of peasant society. In assembling a critique of the orthodox economic determinism of the sort indicated above, historians have resurrected this other work, which had hitherto received scant attention in the west and which still remains unacknowledged in the Soviet Union.

It has already been established that Russian populists maintained a belief in the virtues of the commune and the inherent loyalty of peasants towards it, but that the simplistic notion of an egalitarian society was undermined by evidence of social stratification. To resolve the difficulty presented by the evidence and by Marxist-Leninist analysis, populism could respond in two possible ways. One was to argue that divisions were artificial, unjustifiable and in need of revolutionary action to promote a more egalitarian social order. V. M. Chernov, the most well-known exponent of this view, which was enshrined in the political programme of the Socialist-Revolutionary Party, proposed a redistribution of the means of production so that they would remain only in the hands of those who could work the land directly, "the working peasantry". This was a programme designed to rid Russia of large landed proprietors, but it also represented an attack on the kulak and a restoration of communal land to the dispossessed.[100] Another response, which emerged in the years 1910-25, was to maintain that stratification was not susceptible to class analysis and that in the long run inequalities tended to be redressed through the automatic levelling process at work in the *mir*. In order to justify this diagnosis, its adherents formulated the proposition that peasant behaviour and aspirations were specific to that social group; the laws of capitalist development did not apply. Chayanov gave this view its classic expression in his *Organization of the Peasant Economy*.[101]

Like Chernov, Chayanov suggested that the actions of Russian peasants were not determined by entrepreneurial instincts. Unlike

[99] Cox, *Rural Sociology in the Soviet Union*, pp. 13-14.
[100] See O. H. Radkey, "Chernov and Agrarian Socialism", in E. J. Simmons (ed.), *Continuity and Change in Russian and Soviet Thought* (Cambridge, Mass., 1955), pp. 63-80; Maureen Perrie, *The Agrarian Policy of the Russian Socialist-Revolutionary Party from its Origins through the Revolution of 1905-1907* (Cambridge, 1976).
[101] See Chayanov, *Theory of Peasant Economy*, for the translation of this work. It must be emphasized that Chayanov was not alone in adopting a theoretical stance *vis-à-vis* the Russian peasantry which contradicted Lenin. Nor should it be supposed that Chayanov's views always commanded unanimous support among his colleagues. Finally, he continuously refined his ideas over the course of two decades of research; it is as well to remember this when speaking of Chayanov's "theory". These points are discussed in Mark Harrison, "Chayanov and the Economics of the Russian Peasantry", *Jl. Peasant Studies*, ii (1975), pp. 389-417.

Chernov, however, he considered this to be a characteristic feature of peasant society at large. Although there were circumstances in which peasants acquired property, they did not accumulate it for its own sake. In the long term, according to Chayanov, the peasant was motivated by the desire to maintain a family holding until such time as the claims of young adults to create their own households had to be met. In the short term the peasant did not seek to maximize profits, but to adjust economic activity to the changing balance of workers and consumers in the household, a higher dependency ratio requiring more intensive work patterns. It followed that peasants preferred to work only in so far as was necessary to ensure the subsistence of family members and sought leisure thereafter. Peasants did not respond to market forces, such as the changing price of crops, but to internal family needs. Overall, the peasant family farm proved more resilient than a capitalist enterprise.[102]

These arguments were not unknown to scholars before Chayanov's main work appeared in English, but they have circulated more widely since the mid-1960s.[103] Thus, the centrality of the non-capitalist family farm to any definition of "peasantry" is espoused by medievalists such as Postan and, to a lesser extent, Hilton.[104] According to Postan, ouput and the acquisition of the means of production were geared towards the survival of the peasant family. Land was not something "to be acquired or got rid of in obedience to calculations of profitability", but a source of status that in turn rested upon the ability to sustain the peasant family.[105] It is, however, worth emphasizing that neither Postan nor Hilton lose sight of the reality of medieval society as a whole, with given relations between peasants and feudal lords and a given agricultural technology, both of which imposed constraints on the decisions taken by peasant producers.[106]

The definition of peasantry recently employed by Alan Macfarlane also bears some resemblance to the ideas of Chayanov, albeit in a

---

[102] See Chayanov, *Theory of Peasant Economy*, pp. 57-61, 78-82, *passim*; Mark Harrison, "The Peasant Mode of Production in the Work of A. V. Chayanov", *Jl. Peasant Studies*, iv (1977), pp. 323-36.

[103] See n. 3 above. Chayanov's writings were known to *émigré* sociologists (Sorokin), economists (S. N. Prokopovich) and economic historians (Gerschenkron, Postan). In their German translation they are referred to by J. H. Boeke, *Economics and Economic Policy of Dual Societies, as Exemplified by Indonesia* (London and New York, 1953). For a well-known application of Chayanov's work to hunting and gathering societies, see M. Sahlins, *Stone Age Economics* (London, 1974).

[104] M. M. Postan, "Legal Status and Economic Condition in Medieval Villages", in his *Essays on Medieval Agriculture and General Problems of the Medieval Economy* (Cambridge, 1973), pp. 278-89; Hilton, *English Peasantry in the Later Middle Ages*, p. 13.

[105] Postan, "Legal Status and Economic Condition", pp. 279-80.

[106] *Ibid.*, pp. 278-9; Hilton, *English Peasantry in the Later Middle Ages*, ch. 1.

pre-packaged form.[107] The peasantry is defined by a reliance on family labour, by production for family consumption, by a lack of participation in markets (especially for land) and by the absence of extremes of wealth and poverty. Macfarlane proceeds to exclude English society from this definition, on the grounds that English "peasants" do not conform, do not even exist. The difficulty with such an approach is that it rests upon a sclerotic model whose conditions could not even be satisfied by the Russian peasantry who, as Chayanov himself acknowledged, engaged in transactions in land, labour, capital and agricultural produce.[108] Chayanov was simply making the point that such transactions were conducted in accordance with family requirements, which changed over time. He also conceded that peasants might act "individualistically", although the opportunities for such action rarely presented themselves: "No peasant would refuse either good roast beef or a gramophone or even a block of Shell Oil Company shares, if chance occurred".[109] Worsley has shown that Macfarlane's argument rests on the definition of peasant society "à la Chayanov";[110] but the model is not even Chayanovian, nor is it rooted in Russian peasant society, which it is supposed to fit best of all.

It is in the context of social stratification that Chayanov's theoretical work has evoked most response from medievalists. In order to understand the issues raised by Chayanov, it is necessary to recall the difficulties raised by the data used by Lenin. This material was limited in the information it imparted, primarily because it was not designed to reveal change over time. However, in the course of accumulating data on peasant income and wealth, *zemstva* statisticians found a means of expressing dynamic trends by tracing the fortunes of all households in a specified area over several years. This procedure, which was developed before 1914 and refined after the revolution, constituted a major methodological advance.[111]

All households were classified according to land sown in a given year. Over the course of, say, a decade some households underwent what were termed "substantive changes". That is to say the family holding ceased to have an independent existence, either because it was partitioned among its members, or was amalgamated with

[107] Macfarlane, *Origins of English Individualism*, ch. 1. There is no reference to Chayanov in the bibliography; his ideas are instead embodied in the work of Shanin and Galeski, which is cited.

[108] For confirmation of this, see I. D. Koval'chenko and L. V. Milov, *Vserossiiskii agrarnyi rynok XVIII - nachalo XX veka* [The All-Russian Agrarian Market from the Eighteenth to the Early Twentieth Centuries] (Moscow, 1974).

[109] Chayanov, *Theory of Peasant Economy*, p. 48.

[110] Worsley, "Village Economies", pp. 80-5.

[111] Shanin, *Awkward Class*, pp. 71-6. For a fuller discussion, see N. A. Svavitskii, *Zemskie podvornye perepisi: obzor metodologii* [Zemstvo Household Censuses: A Survey of Methodology] (Moscow, 1961).

another holding, or because its members died or migrated. Wealthy households, having more arable at their disposal, were especially prone to partition, since they also had more members who at some stage had to be satisfied in their desire for independent status.[112] By definition, these households evolved into less wealthy households in terms of land worked. This appeared to conflict with Leninist analysis, which anticipated the cumulation and preservation of economic advantage and disadvantage.[113]

Other households experienced no substantive changes and remained intact. But the fortunes of these households varied, and this proved crucial to the "neo-populist" interpretation of Russian peasant society.[114] Within the initial group of middling peasant households, for example, different individual experiences were reported. While at the end of the chosen decade some households remained in the original category, others had experienced either upward or downward mobility.[115] This phenomenon has been termed "multidirectional mobility", and there was no place for it in Lenin's framework.[116] Chayanov saw this primarily as a function of the changing requirements of households, determined by changes in family composition and size. A growing family added to factors of production, especially land, in order to satisfy new consumers and workers, while a family that was shedding adults (through death, the marriage of females, or the loss of adults to urban employment) required less land. Such households either chose to relinquish part of their holding or were required by communal pressure from the *mir* to do so. It should be noted that this feature of the Russian village was not es-

[112] For the well-attested correlation between family size and arable, see Shanin, *Awkward Class*, pp. 63-6; Harrison, "Chayanov and the Economics of the Russian Peasantry", p. 400.

[113] Some of the difficulties with this alternative analysis are discussed below. Statistically, the "levelling" process is also reflected in the tendency for poor households to disappear from the population; the reasons for their disappearance could include economic failure and differential rates of mortality, which hardly squares with the expectations aroused by Chayanov's theory. For illustration of differential mortality among medieval peasant households, see Razi, *Life, Marriage and Death in a Medieval Parish*, pp. 87-8; Hilton, "Reasons for Inequality among Medieval Peasants", pp. 279-80.

[114] The term "neo-populism" was first coined by L. N. Litoshenko in 1923; see Solomon, *Soviet Agrarian Debate*, p. 244.

[115] Another table may help to illustrate the hypothetical mobility of peasant households not undergoing substantive changes:

Peasant households in 1900 by category		1910		
		Poor	Middling	Rich
Poor	650	300	250	100
Middling	200	50	100	50
Rich	150	50	50	50

Source: Based upon Shanin, *Awkward Class*, p. 72.

[116] The term "multidirectional mobility" was coined by Shanin in *Awkward Class*, p. 74.

sential to Chayanov's argument; a land market could serve the same function of reallocating land according to family needs. A land market was still consistent with his concept of a peasant economy. All the same, Chayanov conceded that "in another agrarian regime less flexible than that of the repartitional commune the influence of the biological factor of family development on the size of land for use would not stand out so prominently and be so evident as in our material".[117] Whether the "biological factor" can be identified at all in medieval England is something that has recently exercised economic and social historians.

As far as substantive changes are concerned, Cicely Howell has suggested that households tended to fragment upon the death or retirement of the head, despite the formal existence of impartible inheritance. Without such a mechanism, she argues, it would be impossible to ensure the continued livelihood and status sought by all offspring. By the sixteenth century, however, wealthy families settled cash portions on the younger children: the capital acquired at a time of increased profits from farming enabled the family to meet the claims of children without having to alter the size of the farm. The growing diversification of the economy brought forth non-agricultural employment opportunities for younger sons. Population growth no longer exerted pressure to subdivide the original holding.[118] In the late fourteenth and early fifteenth centuries, of course, demographic pressures were altogether less intense. Dyer and Razi have shown that this allowed children to be satisfied with a viable holding.[119] The problem must have been more acute before *circa* 1350. As Razi demonstrates, the situation is complex. Parents wished to pass on the holding intact; if they were sufficiently wealthy they sought to acquire additional land in order to provide for younger children. But there are cases in which the eldest son provided for brothers and sisters by ceding part of the holding to them.[120] There

---

[117] Chayanov, *Theory of Peasant Economy*, p. 68. He made the same point on pp. 111-12. One must note in turn that the repartitional commune did not operate in all parts of the Russian empire: Robinson, *Rural Russia under the Old Regime*, ch. 5.

[118] Cicely Howell, "Stability and Change, 1300-1700: The Socio-Economic Context of the Self-Perpetuating Family Farm in England", *Jl. Peasant Studies*, ii (1975), pp. 468-82; Cicely Howell, "Peasant Inheritance Customs in the Midlands, 1280-1700", in J. Goody, J. Thirsk and E. P. Thompson (eds.), *Family and Inheritance: Rural Society in Western Europe, 1200-1800* (Past and Present Pubns., Cambridge, 1976), pp. 112-55.

[119] Razi, *Life, Marriage and Death in a Medieval Parish*, p. 149; Dyer, *Lords and Peasants in a Changing Society*, pp. 303-4, 309-11; cf. p. 107, where Dyer argues that in the thirteenth century free tenants partitioned holdings, whereas customary tenants were discouraged by the lord from so doing. For the need to recognize the constraints imposed by the feudal system, see W. Kula, "The Seigneury and the Peasant Family in Eighteenth-Century Poland", in R. Forster and O. Ranum (eds.), *Family and Society: Selections from the Annales* (Baltimore, 1976), pp. 192-203.

[120] Razi, *Life, Marriage and Death in a Medieval Parish*, pp. 50-6; Hilton, "Reasons for Inequality among Medieval Peasants", p. 278.

is thus no unambiguous demonstration either of the inviolability of wealthy households or of an inherent propensity for wealthy households to fragment. Even if they did fragment, the implications for socio-economic mobility would have to be examined very carefully. As has been shown with regard to Russian peasant households, a reduction in arable need not necessarily coincide with a loss of status and downward mobility in terms of wealth per capita.[121]

The neo-populist assumption that demographic factors determined the socio-economic position of households that remained intact has also attracted the attention of medieval historians.[122] It will be recalled that Vinogradoff stated that changes in family size in medieval England did not result in automatic adjustments in arable. The village community did not redistribute land in accordance with family size.[123] But this leaves open the possibility, as Chayanov recognized, that a peasant family could find other means of satisfying requirements that arose from additions to family size. In this respect, Postan suggested that the land market in thirteenth-century England was instrumental in rectifying inequalities which arose from differences in family size. In his view, a land market came into being because of "certain abiding features of peasant life".[124] Although Postan's analysis of some actual transactions has been questioned,[125] his suggestion highlights the possibility of a link between land reallocation and family size.

The main criticism to be directed at this interpretation is that peasants required capital to engage in such transactions. A growing family that lacked the means could not necessarily enter the market, and the purchase of land would consequently be confined to wealthy asset-holders.[126] Given this constraint, differentiation remains a function of economic power rather than of demographic shifts. This criticism does not take into account the possibility that peasants could lease land or borrow the money to finance land purchases.[127] Yet the fact

---

[121] Mark Harrison, "Resource Allocation and Agrarian Class Formation: The Problem of Social Mobility among Russian Peasant Households, 1880-1930", *Jl. Peasant Studies*, iv (1977), pp. 127-61.

[122] See, in addition, W. Kula, *An Economic Theory of the Feudal System: Towards a Model of the Polish Economy, 1500-1800* (London, 1976).

[123] See n. 48 above.

[124] M. M. Postan, "The Charters of the Villeins", in *Carte Nativorum: A Peterborough Abbey Cartulary of the Fourteenth Century*, ed. C. N. L. Brooke and M. M. Postan (Northants. Rec. Soc., xx, Oxford, 1960), pp. xxxiv-xxxv, repr. in Postan, *Essays on Medieval Agriculture*, pp. 107-49. See also Hilton, *English Peasantry in the Later Middle Ages*, pp. 6-7.

[125] Razi, *Life, Marriage and Death in a Medieval Parish*, pp. 89-92.

[126] P. R. Hyams, "The Origins of a Peasant Land Market in England", *Econ. Hist. Rev.*, 2nd ser., xxiii (1970), pp. 18-31; E. King, *Peterborough Abbey, 1086-1310: A Study in the Land Market* (Cambridge, 1973), ch. 6; R. H. Hilton, review of *Carte Nativorum*, ed. Brooke and Postan, in *Eng. Hist. Rev.*, lxxvii (1962), p. 326. See also the remarks of Dyer, *Lords and Peasants in a Changing Society*, ch. 14.

[127] The possibility of short-term leases is mentioned in Hyams, "Origins of a Peasant Land Market", p. 28, but he regards the thirteenth-century evidence as insufficient.

remains that they would be burdened with interest payments or rent payments at a stage in the family life cycle when other claims on income were acute. Furthermore, it is not clear that such households, assuming they did acquire land in accordance with increases in family size, were also able to acquire complementary factors, such as livestock.[128] This problem is not resolved by a recent study which argues that peasant families acquired and shed land according to changes in household size. No evidence is offered in support of this proposition.[129] The onus would appear to be on its adherents to demonstrate how the problems raised by the neo-populist hypothesis might be resolved. They could address themselves to two questions. If there is a correlation between wealth and family size, are households wealthy because they are large or large because they are wealthy? How were difficulties of acquiring land and the other means of production overcome?

Stalinist collectivization dealt a double blow to the spirit and purpose of enquiry which this article has traced. The "great turn" of 1929-30 finally settled the question of the future development of rural society and foreclosed the options open to Russia. Historians ceased to look to the western European past with the partial aim of uncovering processes that might be reproduced in Russia.[130] Collectivization also put paid to the open debates within Russian rural sociology that had generated hypotheses, research methods and data for around half a century. Even now, Soviet scholars make few published references to non-Leninist interpretations of rural change.[131]

It is evident, all the same, that this body of theoretical and empirical material has not lost its force for medievalists. This is testimony to the enduring quality of work produced by Russian historians such as Vinogradoff and Kosminsky (and the intermittent translation of Russian work). It also reflects the continued stimulus of Russian social science, as moulded before 1930. It would, then, be unfortunate if this tradition were seen to constitute an enclosed system of thought, either Marxist-Leninist or neo-populist. The alternative is to recognize it as dynamic and engaged in uncovering social processes which operated in the real world. It should not be regarded as static and a

[128] Harrison, "Peasant Mode of Production"; Harrison, "Chayanov and the Economics of the Russian Peasantry", pp. 401-3.
[129] A. DeWindt, "A Peasant Land Market and its Participants: King's Ripton, 1280-1400", *Midland Hist.*, iv (1978), pp. 142-59.
[130] There is no suggestion that Soviet historians have ceased to be interested in medieval England; but the passion and commitment, evident in the 1920s for example, have been spent.
[131] For a discussion of differentiation that entirely ignores the contribution of neo-populist scholarship, see, for instance, I. D. Koval'chenko and L. V. Razumov, "Istochniki o khozyaistve i polozhenii krest'yan" [Sources for the Peasant Economy and Social Position], in *Massovye istochniki po sotsial'no-ekonomicheskoi istorii Rossii perioda kapitalizma* [Mass Sources for the Social and Economic History of Russia during the Period of Capitalism] (Moscow, 1979), pp. 276-317.

source of neat and unassailable propositions about peasant society. Hence the need to appreciate the context in which this Russian tradition arose and evolved; hence the need to continue to refine and qualify the insights generated by contributors to the social science tradition. To fail in these tasks is to preside over its fossilization.

Index

Past and Present Publications

General Editor: PAUL SLACK, *Exeter College, Oxford*

*Published also as a paperback
**Published only as a paperback
†Co-published with the Maison des Sciences de l'Homme, Paris